The Marvelous Adventures of
Pierre Baptiste
Father and Mother
First and Last

NEW YORK UNIVERSITY PRESS
GRATEFULLY ACKNOWLEDGES THE SUPPORT OF
MADELINE AND KEVIN BRINE
IN MAKING THESE AWARDS POSSIBLE.

NEW YORK UNIVERSITY PRESS
New York and London

PATRICIA EAKINS

The Marvelous Adventures of
Pierre Baptiste
Father and Mother
First and Last

Including:

The Tribulations of Bondage in the Sugar Isles
Pierre's Escape from Certain Harm to His Person
How He Was Marooned
His Friends & Religion
His True Wife & Fishy Consorts
His Children, Born from His Mouth Like Words

✦

Physics and Metaphysics
Cyclopedish Histoire
Flora, Fauna, & Mysteriosi
Revenge and Devotion
Divinations
Commonplace Book

✦

Being a True Account of the Life and Times of an African Man of Letters,

a Son of Guinée Born into Bondage,
Whose Ambitions Were Realized in STRANGE AND UNEXPECTED WAYS,
Yet Who Made His PEACE with Several Gods
and Established A REALM of Equality & Freedom & Bounty,

✦

in Which No Creature Lives from Another's Labor.

NEW YORK UNIVERSITY PRESS
New York and London

Library of Congress Cataloging-in-Publication Data
Eakins, Patricia.
Patricia Eakins's novel The marvelous adventures of Pierre Baptiste :
father and mother, first and last, including: the tribulations of
bondage in the Sugar Isles, Pierre's escape from certain harm to his
person, how he was marooned, his friends & religion, his true wife
& fishy consorts, his children, born from his mouth like words,
physics and metaphysics, cyclopedish histoire, flora, fauna, & mysteriosi, revenge and devotion, divinations, commonplace book.
p. cm.
"Being a true account of the life and times of an African man of
letters, a Son of Guinée born into bondage, whose ambitions were
realized in STRANGE AND UNEXPECTED WAYS, yet who made
his PEACE with several gods and established a REALM of Equality &
Freedom & Bounty, in which no creature lives from another's labor."
ISBN 0-8147-2209-1 (alk. paper)
I. Title. II. Title: Marvelous adventures of Pierre Baptiste
PS3555.A424 M37 1999
813'.54—dc21   98-58147
CIP

New York University Press books are printed on acid-free paper,
and their binding materials are chosen for strength and durability.

Manufactured in the United States of America

10 9 8 7 6 5 4 3 2 1

FOR GEORGE CHAMBERS
WHO MORE THAN ANY OTHER SHOWED THE WAY

Acknowledgments

Excerpts from *The Marvelous Adventures* have appeared in the following publications: *Asylum; Attaboy!; Black Warrior Review; Caprice; Fiction 86; Open; Open Places; Parnassus;* the *Iowa Review; Sources: Revue d'études anglophones;* and the *Word Thursdays Anthology, II*. In addition, several parts of the novel were included in earlier versions in the collection *The Hungry Girls and Other Stories* (San Francisco: Cadmus Editions, 1988).

The editors of the *Paris Review* have honored an excerpt from "The Garden of Fishes" with the 1996 Aga Khan Prize for Fiction.

The work was supported in part by a Fiction Fellowship from the New York Foundation for the Arts (1991), in part by a residency in the literature program of The Woodstock Guild, Woodstock, New York, under the program directorship of Michael Perkins (1992).

The citation on p. 46 is taken from *Buffon: A Life in Natural History*, by Jacques Roger, translated by Sarah Lucille Bonnefoi (Ithaca: Cornell University Press, 1997).

For details of sugar production Eakins is indebted to *Sugar and Slaves* by Richard S. Dunn (New York: W. W. Norton, 1973). The divinations are adapted from *Rituals and Spells of Santeria*, by Migene Gonzalez-Wippler (New York: Original Publications, 1984). The story of Fait-Tout in chapter 3 was adapted from "The Do-All Ax," in *World Folktales*, by Atelia Clarkson and Gilbert B. Cross (New York: Scribner's, 1980). The call-and-response song was adapted from one in *Singing the Master*, by Roger D. Abrahams (New York: Pantheon, 1992). "The Children of the Two Doors" was adapted from "Demane and Demazana," in *African Folktales*, by Roger D. Abrahams (New York: Pantheon, 1983).

ACKNOWLEDGMENTS

The Marvelous Adventures is a better book for the deft and sensitive interventions of editor Barbara Epler. Also, Despina Papazoglou Gimbel, Elyse Strongin, Andrew Katz, and Andy Fotopoulos at NYU Press took unusual pains with the production of the book despite the constraints of a very tight schedule.

Contents

Overture

→

WHO FINDS and reads this testament, GREETINGS: It is I, Pierre, who have scribed with sharpened gull's-wing feather dipped in ink of squid and ash. I, PIERRE BAPTISTE, FATHER AND MOTHER, FIRST AND LAST, have scratched on paper woven and pounded by my offspring. With stone mauls have we flaked the arks of rock in which the several books repose. With levers and pulleys and our own strong backs have we raised the cairns of sweat-rolled rock that loft my screeds' sarcophagi, raising them above the tides that in hurricane season roll across our isle. And so the arks are skulls of stone in which the words of my tongue are enbalmed, for I refuse to yield to Death.

You who read my words have raised with your own hands, or hands of your servants, the tight-fitting covers of the arks. And so corresponding labors, patiences, & wills marry us for the covenant, your reading of my testament. Would your discovery resurrect my person, yet I doubt you shall find me quick. Shall you find my offspring? Their offspring? My consorts and their ilk? *"La plus grande merveille,"* said the great Buffon, *"c'est dans la succession."* All the greater the marvel when the succession were

1

untoward. Like any dramatic voyage, mine must commence *in medias res,* yet I cast off in a swift-stopping lyric mode, limning my consorts in portrait fit as I can muster, being a man whose hours of light are much taken up.

THEY SING from both sides of their mouths, this I can vouchsafe. On calm, cloudless nights, when the dome of heaven is bright with stars, they lie in the breaking moonlit waves, combing them to ribbons, silver rushing through their teeth. Yet, while they live, they are never truly in repose. Their gold-and-pink-flecked bodies quiver in foam, their green-white tresses writhe like eels among strands of sea-weed, while fishes fin in the shifting tangles.

The consorts themselves I would name *fish,* from the wound-red gill slits puckering behind their ears, the pointed teeth in their lipless mouths; I would name them *frogs* from their round gold eyes. Yet frogs do not have the hands of women, lovely as lace but without nails. And could fish construct the "cities," the minuscule towers spiraling from reefs? Beneath the glimmer and shift of waves, the towers appear solid, adamantine edifices. Yet I have dived to grasp at their spires, only to squeeze a crumbling, then to peer at craters in the reefs. Around me, hidden in clouds of sediment, specks of tower turned among bubbles. Were they bubbles of my own breath or bubbles of the consorts' laughter? Did the faithless consorts crouch behind the reef, snorting in cupped hands?

Oh, sometimes, did I bathe at night, they have chased me, moonlit bodies glittering in foam. Oh, then have I seen their locky tendrils trailing the spines of breakers, their fingers long on the waves. Then have I heard their singing, their chorale without returns. Once I was caught, in embrace near-fatal; it was my shadow the sea shade caressed, my shadow vanishing under the breakers.

2

I DID COAST IN atop these amorous, delusome waves, a-bobble in a rum keg, a chattel-servant escaped of a sugar-cane planter of Saint-Michel, of the French Anduves. My plan were to float into a shipping lane to be taken aboard some packet as errant specimen cargo, viz., the salted-down carcasses of birds for Buffon's cabinet. I would be transported to France to the eminent natural historian, for I had marked the keg "*M. de Buffon, Intendant, Jardin du Roi, Paris.*" Once arrived, I would be esteemed a savant, to stroll among the flowers & fountains of the garden and to study the stuffed & mounted animals and the mineral curiosities of the cabinet, and to enjoy the duties and perquisites of philosophy, for according to law I would be free on touching the soil of France. And a free man can rise to his worth.

Had not Graman QUASSI escaped from Suriname and made his way to Holland and so become free? Had he not brought with him a tea of bitter wood, useful in treating fevers and worms? Had he not found favor in the eyes of Linnaeus, who named the bitter tree for him? Were not BUFFON a more magnanimous genius than Linnaeus with his carping taxonomy of life?

But alas! My cask having drifted from the lanes, I was sucked into a serpent's gut and vomited on this wild shore, near or far from the isle I had fled. I feared I would be caught, and returned to my master, and whipped with the stinger, and caged in the sun without food or water, and sold to a master worse than Auguste Henri Lemoyne Dufay, the very same so celebrated for his portraits of creatures, who governed the movements of pencils and brushes lamentably better than the twists and turns of his own affairs. Now read the account, in its several parts, of my escape and my life as a free man. I will tell in time what I know of the fates of my several connections, including my beloved WIFE.

The Garden of Fishes

→

MY MASTER'S TEMPER were by spasms choleric, the spasms exacerbated by trespass, real or fancied, of his slaves, all of whom had had occasion to beg their fellows daub their backs with salve of rum and lard. Yet Dufay had raised up drivers to lash the hands to work, drivers on whom he palmed off most of the stewardship, that he might dedicate himself to advancement of universal knowledge. Far from the carries where his hands labored, he tramped in sun and rain, peering under leaves, down burrows, and up into nests to discover and name what creatures inhabited the wilderness parts of his domain.

An excellent draftsman, he delighted in sketching particulars of feather, fur, and scale; the curve of claws, of teeth and beaks; the depths of eyes; the stretch and shove of limbs. On sketching expeditions to the rockiest, most surf-pounded tips of Saint-Michel, he spied from blinds he had had constructed on narrow ledges, to watch the sea birds fighting and fishing and rutting. (Some said he spied on the slaves, yes, on his own wife and children, in like manner, but I never saw him loiter in the shadows of human habitation.)

From the age of five, I, whom the whites called Goody, had been laboring in the carries, coughing from the fire that burned off the leaves, stepping and stooping to chop the canes and singing between my gritted teeth to keep the bone-grinding pace. One day, M'sieu was riding his mare past the gang, his cockaded hat abob on Yolande's trot as he passed on his way to more tangled parts of our isle to sketch. His old servant trotted behind, one Christophe, called Long-Shanks, carrying the tools of his master's art. Alas, this worn-out soul, Christophe, keeled over; without further adieu, he gave up the ghost and died.

"Hop! Hop! Hop! Do not leave Long-Shanks asprawl to be chewed by dogs," said M'sieu to his driver. "Yet pick out a sturdy young boy to wait on me at once! Not again a scrawny dotard too worn-out to lift." And, rueful-ironic, he doffed his hat to Christophe.

Pierre was called from the gang then, to lay down his bill and serve the master as porter. Wriggling joyful I was, who had no notion what a world of fetching made a BODY SERVANT'S WORK! Though I was then a strapping youth of ten, they had not yet given me a pair of pants. So, on the first day I turned my eyes from cane to follow Yolande's tail, I did not look around me much, but only mulled over the question: Would I get a pair of drawers? And when I did, that very eve, and not coarse Osnaberg, but silk, however faded, I strutted like a cock, and capered to the piping of the cane flute, the first capers I had cut in a very long time, for my smock had ceased to cover my privates, and I had learnt to shrink over Johnny Fish.

Yet the drawers they had given me were pantaloons from years before, very baggy and covered with tufted ribbon loops. And these stale fancies gave great merriment to Pamphile, the master's son, and his stepmother, who swore they would grow my frizz to a full-bottom—"he would need no curling iron, and nits would lose

5

themselves in the maze"—and send me over the seas to court, to wait on the jades that yawned around the King. And they conceived a plot, to give me a name from antiquity, like a hero's in a tragedy, but M'sieu stamped his foot and swore, "I'll be damned if I learn a new name I must cry in the bush when I call for a snare set."

At night, in the dark, I lay with the fancy pants in my hammock. With my fingers I tugged at the falls, so they tore, and, when I donned the pantaloons, revealed Johnny Fish to the company.

"The stuff be so old it has rotted," I allowed.

So they gave me some drawers more plain and recent.

Once decently covered, I straightened my back and willingly shouldered THE MASTER'S EASEL. I looked about me smartly, as he enjoined me over Yolande's withers: "Observe the curious cunning with which Nature has devised the creatures."

Dutifully at first I gaped at the mole, all fur and snout, with shovelly hands, that blindly hunches and wriggles a path like an endless pant leg to inhabit. How came he to Saint-Michel? Did he tunnel under the sea? Or was he pushing like a hungry root at Creation?

The island had not the variety of creatures, allowed M'sieu, that are known on the continents; yet creatures there were sufficient to preoccupy an inquiring philosopher, most particularly the varieties of lizard and bird. And soon enough Pierre began to observe for the pleasure of the scrutiny. There very greatly charmed him the red-and-green throat of one small lizard, puffed like a lady's coyly dropped handkerchief as the creature took the sun. All languor he lolled till he cast his tongue to snag a fly! Servant no less than master marveled at the parakeets, their feathers brighter than flowers, cleaning themselves with their toes and hooking with their beaks the mites, smaller than lice, that inhabited their feathers' underbrush.

And the white egret, and in season, the blue heron.

Then there were fishes, more multivarious than birds, a garden of flesh in the waters, impossible to catch and hold, their form their movement, their movement one with the water they had their being in, the salty tear-drenched garden of the dead my godmothers had told me of, where I did not want to linger, though I ate any fish my elders caught, for I knew they took the fish with gratitude, and were forgiven.

The master did not trust the waters any more than I, though his dead slept beneath the earth, patient as seeds, waiting their time. Yet Dufay would not take off his shoes to wet his feet in the sea, let alone remove his clothes to wet his person. He did not like it, that was all; he did not care for it, so he said. 'Twas a slimy, endless chaos; he did not want it to impinge on his person.

Still, he must have fish to sketch and paint if his natural history were to be complete. So it fell to me to catch these fish, yet without spoiling their form. So I must into the sea. If I would not do it, he would send me back to the fields. Yet I knew not how to comport myself in the sea, nor did my master. Yet he would teach me by hypothesis, trying one expedient then another.

First, he had me dangled as bait on a rope he tied to a pole held by two big men. And he lowered me choking and bellowing into the sea, till I learned to hold my breath. And he bade me agitate my arms and legs, like a human mill, and thus make myself an engine for motion in the sea. And when he saw my terrors had eased, he bade the two men throw me in, without the rope or the pole, so I must save myself with the motions I had learned. And in this manner I was trained to be nimble in the sea, to capture the fishes Dufay would sketch.

As I must paddle about with a spear in one hand, so I must keep the other, and both my legs, in motion, as an ox on a treadmill, to churn myself afloat. Yet—could I quiet my heart that pounded loud in my ears as depths rose to claim me, could I bring myself to open my eyes—then I saw, not the flesh-shrouded bones of the dead, but a paradise shimmering in veils of light. Surely the dead must be at peace in their garden of fish. I prayed I would be forgiven for plucking blossoms of flesh, not to eat, but for M'sieu to paint. Yet the longer I spent in the garden of the dead, the less fearsome seemed the prospect of death. Was I not floating in a bliss that laved me, luxuriant and enjoyable? So Pierre splashed among his ancestors' souls, visible only as movement in water. He celebrated their sweet repose, free of the whites who feared to set foot in their domain. Seeing how Pierre smiled when he rose for breath, the master clapped his hands and patted his slaveman's head.

"Good Goody," he said. "Good boy. Do you fetch me the fish, one by one, I will capture their likenesses."

Alas! Though I popped to the surface with a spear-dead fish for him to sketch, or even a live one, squirming to escape and smothering in air, there was no way to capture the gracile essence save by immersion. So much the worse for M'sieu, his knowledge and his art. He did not revere the fish, and his stiff fillets, dull eyes already rotting, were not his truest portraits. He never even saw the hermaphrodite plants, with thick stalks and bright-petaled flowers, yet with roots emerging from the calyx, squirming and grasping at tiny fish, which they did feed into the calyx as hands would stuff a mouth. For M'sieu did not believe Pierre when Pierre spoke of them, and offered to bring one up, though it might be a pet of the dead. M'sieu did not believe a slaveman could discover creatures a master had not. "Tut tut!" he said.

'Twere not merely underwater creatures M'sieu so blindly eschewed. For he took apoplectic fits at the sight of certain vermin, viz., the legions of rats that encamped in his fields to commandeer cane. M'sieu refused to limn them, though most assuredly they be "principal fauna." And I do suspect they are as dear to their Creator as any other creature. Some other planters would eat the rats—oh, not when friends came to dine, but for a family dinner. Why not? The creatures have fed on sugar; their flesh is sweet. And as they eat so much of our crop, to eat them in turn is a sensible economy. Yet our M'sieu forbore this dainty for himself and his; the old mistress— the first one, the haughty and pious—sent the slave-children into the fields, to hunt and catch the rats, that at very little cost to the whites we slaves might daily dine on flesh, and so keep up our strength, without our sweat smelling fishy, or any expense for pork or beef. At the same time, we would help to save the crop.

This scheme fermented among us great bubbles of resentment—we to eat what the whites refuse as unfit? Our people left the vermin corpses for pigs, preferring to feed our strength with fish leaping fresh to the net, the gift of death to life, and so much the better if our sweat stank. Come Mardi Gras we hung that mistress in effigy, her figure sewed of sacking stuff, a block of wood for a missal in her paw. This straw mistress we roasted above our bonfire. When she burned, she gave out a satisfying, piteous plaint, for we had filled her body with rats and mice.

No more than PILFERING VERMIN or INVADING INSECTS were we slaves to be discovered in M'sieu's chaste pencil-and-chalks or his fastidious ink-washes, unless we be those dim, tiny, bent figures seen from afar in rippling fields of cane. Front and center the feathered creatures, most especially those of a gaudy and brilliant plumage and distinguished profile, with warrior's crest and aquiline beak. Dearer to Pierre the drab pelican, its beak a belly of fish, and after the pelican, among featherless creatures, the crab that skulked in the brush, till, spying an enshelled slime shuck off his outgrown house, Sergeant Crab nipped in to occupy. How quaint to see patrolling crabs reconnoiter tunnelish paths through the brush, a rag-tag army in purloined uniforms. Were these the army of maroons, the runaway slaves, my godmothers spoke of in whispers?

In time the habits of pirate crabs seemed no less strange than the CHARACTER OF M'SIEU himself. For though he deemed himself a well-bred man, he observed no niceties of deportment or dress. Indeed, by the time he threw me his breeches, they were out at the knee, his coat tattered streamers; I would rather get my clothes, of lesser stuff, from the captain of the drivers, Master Squint, of whom more later. But as for M'sieu, he forgot to close up his falls when he pissed. When his servant was slow, and he took a fit of pique and dressed himself, he rolled one stocking over his breeches, buckled his cuff over the other. He consistently forgot to wind the watch he carried on a chain, and he ignored the beating of the dinner gong.

Once, when his brother's agents came from France, he bade me shave his head, though I had not the knack of the razor and nicked him more than once. He would not pay a barber, you see. Yet over his wounds, his full-bottom snugged his head most accommodating, so he might have cut a good figure had he not dragged from his fraying cuff a huge nasty rag to wipe his nose after pinching snuff. Those come from France remarked, he had lost the habit of bowing, though surely he had had it once.

He never took a man's hand nor kissed a lady's, but only nodded absently when presented—did I say "kiss a lady"? When sober, he fondled neither maids nor men and eschewed intrigues, though when he had drunk himself sodden amidst a crush of planters he indulged in the jovial pinch. And now and then took a woman without ceremony, as a dog smelling rut, and so had fathered a brat or two in the yard.

His visitors returned to France, his wig gathered dust on a stand, the hair of his head pushed in tufts around his bald pate, like the tonsure of a depraved monk, so devilish wild he must wear a nightcap so as not to fright the maids. Yet there were worse.

Had he kept his counsel, he might have been a tolerable master, save he exacted from those he lorded it over punctilios he himself forswore. Madame, his second young wife—the first had died in a fluxy sweat—he bade dress and speak as a queen, though she minced through the pantry fearful of scorpions. Badgering the maids to scrape the mold off hanging meat, she must wear three sleeve flounces, & a sack, & a useless apron of lace, & a pinner with trailing lappets. She must be rouged and powdered, and patched and plucked, and teeter on high heels, her head dressed out with false curls. She must embroider perfect lilies on the household linens and read the scriptures every day as befitted a lady who, though born in these islands, had been schooled in a convent in France. M'sieu flew into fits of pique did he catch her with her sleeves rolled, calling her "Rogue" and lambasting her as a slavey.

POOR MADAME! She struck false notes on the pianoforte, the keys of which the air's moistness had swollen from tune. Her thread often tangled as she passed and repassed her needle. M'sieu then pined for a wife who knew what to do with the keys at her waist. Indeed children tittered in their sleeves as she passed with her nose in the air. And though she would crack those keys on a servant's skull, the smell of meat that had hung too long could not be masked with spice and wine. Yet again the bread was not too stale for willful jaw to crack! It is true the stuffing poked from the chairs, but M'sieu himself had scored the silk with the rowels of his spurs, neglecting to call for his boots taken off.

If M'sieu's wife were buffeted by his fits of discontent, consider: his slaves were entirely at his mercy. Pierre who had been trained to catch a bird unharmed with his hands did marvel at his master's alternation between three states: the first, a profound, faithful, & innocent regard for the animals he observed; the second, an absent-minded, brisk accord with his fellow human beings, including myself; the third, a sudden & violent animosity toward all Creation, which consumed his bandy-legged, potbellied person and laid waste roundabout. Was the tyrant who snapped his quills and tore his paper the same who stood so still to lure a lizard the tomtits lit on his head? In his rages he caned me and whipped me, yet still I pitied him. For, though a slave, I did live within myself a free man, master; M'sieu the converse.

Yet HIS DRAWINGS were all control, more exact than Nature herself had been, so scrupulously did he render the shape of each lineament, each color shade or tint, each hillock and valley of musculature and quirk of physiognomy, so exactly did he capture the needle-prick stare of the hawk and the desperate trembling gaze of the mouse, for whose delicate and whiskery deliberations he forgave its resemblance to the loathed rat.

Yes, and the thorny brush, the bent of which reveals the wind; the smoke tree's haze of ground twigs; the monstrous hairy soursap fruit; the manchineel with its blistering milk, its horrible charmy apples—ah, First Woman!—the amaranth, center stalks a fountain of blood; the rocks and the stones, earth with its packings and crumblings—yes, so truly did M'sieu draw all these, so meticulously paint, with such accurately mixt colors, one might have thought him a devil, tempting poor sinners, take one hesitant, fateful step into the world of his creation, a world seeming purer than our own, in which each creature, nay each rock, turns always for inspection, if not its best side, then at least that side most expressing its essence.

The purity came from this effect: though M'sieu did limn the animals precisely in all proportions and attributes, he refused to draw the shadows that, contrasting with the dapple of light, revealed and covered them. Were I to judge from the plates in books, the rendering of shadow, velvet and dense or hazy and dim, does give to the painted world its appearance of movement, suggesting alternation of day and night, and hence the round of seasons, the progress through shift and transformation to death, and thence to life again, from which no man can escape. Yet in the works of M'sieu, Creation is suffused in a pure, bright, even light, as if all creatures were caught in the terrible stillness before the palsy strikes, the storm breaks, the lava flows, caught in this moment as in Eternity, not the eternity of Paradise, earned by the good, but a terrible stasis, the paralysis of Sun's merciless glare. Ah, what be any man but damned who casts no shadow? Shadow, shadow, the dark blot of being, stain of the blood waters, deep and heavy and old, mark of suffering, God's fiery tears, trail of ashes drenching our bones. He who casts no shadow, is he not unquiet in quiet forever, dead in life and live in death?

In one other more mundane particular the art of M'sieu lacks verisimilitude: in the vine-swagged jungles that climb the mountain sides; in the groves of mango and orange trees, flaunting their gauds of fruit; among the tidy coffee trees; the cutlass-leaved bananas; the feathery palms; deep in the cane carries' green and land-locked sea, the island of Saint-Michel, like this, where abides Pierre, be festooned with a florid plant called *orchid,* which displays itself in sun and shade, windward and leeward, high and low. M'sieu would not draw the brown-bagged blossoms, and cursed and stamped if he found but a grain of the pollen on his sleeve, calling for me to brush from him the devil-take-the-stinking-fish-hole crumbs. AH! If Buffon had come out from France, he would have seen in what respects his *histoire* of these islands be incomplete. Yet many an artful work was sent to France for engraving, and Pierre vaunted himself he served a worthwhile master, though sorely the master tried his servant.

Those of HIS FINISHED WORKS M'sieu cherished too greatly to send forth, he locked in his old campaign chest with several

THE GARDEN OF FISHES

tattered standards and a sword he had worn in battles with Protestants before he came out to the Anduves. There in his chest he supposed his *oeuvre* would be safe from theft or spite or the depredations of rats or of armies. Alas! The chest was not close-fitted. In the leathern interior damp took hold and bred up slimes to soften the paper, spoil the colors, and blur the exact outlines of the images. This I discovered one evening in a damp season when the company sat till midnight smoking pipes and drinking toasts from a bowl of fired brandy. Forsooth, I was ashamed to see M'sieu debauch himself among idlers. To cool the rebellious heat that rose in my head with the fumes of the burnt brandy the dissipates imbibed, I ventured into the keeping room, to pick the lock of the campaign chest, as oft I did, for the sole purpose of examining, however furtively and briefly, the pictures and notes stored within, to renew my sense of my master's worth.

What a PUTREFACTION did I spy and smell! From the pigments on his pages there bloomed a terrible colony of proliferating, stunted monsters, regiments of blue & green & white spoilers, obliterating the limpid symmetries of M'sieu's vision, as if creatures of shadow and orchid-dust mites, obscure, hot vermin and hermaphrodite flora-fauna he had refused to draw, had vengefully mingled their juices and their rage and given birth to generations of vileness so wicked their stench was worse than death. All was rotting, beyond rotting, and would soon be lost altogether, as I pray my own pages, in their careful confinement, will not. Indeed, I did not like to think what life might fly from his trunk into the world, a greater plague than Pandora set free (though of course I did not yet know of her), without any mitigating hope.

To stifle the slimy creatures, I hastily doused the *oeuvre* in a dusty particulate reserved for the wigs, which did whiten those heads and smother nits and might, the Gods be willing, sweeten the moldering pages in the chest. This good powder did possess a most pleasing scent, mixed of many magical essences of the several flowers of France, compounded with musk and orris root. It did indeed seem to stifle the odor like rancid cheese and stale piss that soured the chest. Yet before the slimes could flee the carnage, Pierre relocked the chest. He sat by it then, guarding against any seepage from under the lid. And he listened for the master's call.

As he sat, he composed on his breath a secret anonymous missive to the very esteemed and revered Monsieur de Buffon. And later, when opportunity presented itself, Pierre copied out his letter, accusing his master of indolence & sloth & wasting his talents & spoiling the pictures destined for the *Natural History* in preparation across the sea, moreover accusing him of capricious and scandalous disregard of fishes & orchids, vermin & shadows & slaves, aspects of the world and its history to which a disinterested philosopher ought to pay attention. I slipped the wily Squint my hordings of coin, comprising three quarter bits, to see my letter safely on a ship to Buffon.

When no letter from France came for M'sieu by the next packet, I most cynically supposed myself abused. *Would I be caught and whipped with Stinger?* A boat came over, and again, and again. *Stretched till I pull apart?* Yet in time, the redoubtable Sage wrote my master an elegant reproof, entreating him to "take measures, Dear Sir!" Whether this ploy succeeded in saving the pictures, you may discover yourself. I am ignorant of their powdered fate, for I am here and they are where they are. Yet in time I will relate what I have heard. But e'en so much of my tale as I have told I pull ahead of myself in telling, as you have yet to hear of my schooling, the font of my learning, and thus, of my TESTAMENT.

The A, the B, the C of My Education

→

Pierre Baptiste his master observed with the self-same scrutiny trained on the creatures. It did not escape M'sieu that his servant possessed CAPABILITIES BEYOND HIS STATION. Pierre was not constrained to speak the patois but spoke the master's language as well as he, and remembered as well the names of fauna and flora. I disguised my facility by affecting a blithe ignorance, for fear the master would suppose I had forgotten my place, yet his suspicion dogged me.

"Goody," he once inquired, "how came you to speak so learned a tongue?"

"I am a simple fellow with a pattern to follow," I avowed.

"And what habits of mine may he imitate next?" mused M'sieu, who brooded on the question of my abilities. He had directed a servant teach a hound to gigue on its hind legs. In like spirit had M'sieu seized the notion of having me taught to read and cipher. I began taking lessons with his son and heir, Pamphile, and the mixed-blood whelps M'sieu had got when drunk, whom he hoped to help to a useful place in his service.

THE A, THE B, THE C OF MY EDUCATION

Now I did not at first take to EDUCATION, for it meant leaving the protection of my master's presence. This I was reluctant to do. Though he be demanding and terrible-tempered, his body servant did not have to break his back with field-work. I preened myself on the variety of my chores: finding the master in picturesque vantage; mixing his colors; snaring specimens then strangling them with silken thread so as not to bruise or muss them; arranging the corpses to appear undisturbed, in their accustomed settings; running back to the kitchen to fetch my master's dinner upon hearing the midday gong; trotting after his horse like a pack horse myself, sacks & cases & easels slung about my person. Now, a slave is not reared to look forward. Indeed, Pierre were wont to look back, in fear his pants would be taken, he must gangle in a smock again. Above all other considerations I did not wish to be returned to my childhood duty, the chasing and killing of rats, though once I had relished it. For each rat a child brought before Old Mistress—the first one, haughty, stern, and pious—he was awarded a credit. She measured the creature, nose to tail, then entered the credit in a book she kept in her pocket. When the child had brought her so many rats, she would give him a marble, a crystalline sphere with a colored tissue suspended in it, like a wounded eye. While I had earned bloody points toward marbles, choking rats with a forked stick, Pamphile and the farrago of light-skinned brats had been squirming in hard chairs, blabbing their lessons from their hornbooks. The priest—not Père Gouy, who came out later, but the first I knew, a thin, frail man—taught an alphabetic catechism, fluting the names of marks he drew in charcoal on a board. (This was before his complexion turned yellow, and he died of flux.) The murmur of children naming their letters floated out the window. I peeked through the louvers of the shutters only to flee the boards and blab, for on the whole, in those salad days, I preferred killing rats.

Yet I waxed keenly curious about the HOUSE, which I had never been inside. The whitewashed stone building floated in the conjure-mist of fitful sleep. In reveries I wandered through in flower-broidered breeches, like a white boy, though in the conjure house the whites slept in hammocks as we did. In the world of natural light I had seen through open doors the wooden floors of the whites' house, yet I had not stood on them; my conjure planks were soft to the foot as soil. I could not conjure curtains, nor candlesticks, nor plate. Some of us slaves had stools in our kennels, even chairs, though without arms. None of us had tables, nor even tabourets; I did not yet know these furnishings existed. Alas, though I was to be educated, I was not allowed to indulge my curiosity in the matter of the house, viz., to sit with the others inside; I was directed to a seat on the ground outside the windows of the blue room. From there I crept forward and peered between the louvers, craning my neck to see the paradisickal ceiling, the gardens on the walls, the bright wood table at which Pamphile did his lessons, the elbow chair with flowered satin cushions in which the scion sat, and the looking glass on the wall, that made another world beyond the apparent one, and gave me back my round amazed eye, which I did not at first recognize between two louver slats.

At first, I was puzzled by lessons that bored Pamphile and his mixed-blood brethren, squirming on benches brought in from the yard. The wan, fussy governor Modeste Devere, who had taken the place of the priest, did not address me, nor hear my lessons, nor furnish me a hornbook, yet still I learned, for I wrote my letters and sums in the dust and corrected myself.

I did grasp the elements of instruction very much quicker than the privileged youths with their hornbooks, and a very good thing this was for me. Though I had been picked out to learn, my parsimonious master did not look to waste my training as a body servant, so, even while I absorbed instruction, I waited on my master's one legitimate son. I must leave my seat to fetch him a drink; I must carry his books. When the hours of instruction were complete, I must polish his boots and his buttons and take his linen to the washerwoman, then clean his musket. Pamphile would elaborate my duties, viz., he would lie on his back while I dropped some dainty foodstuffs in his maw. But when his father heard of this from his new young wife, who thought it droll, M'sieu wore out his son himself.

"We will have no epicene Nero here," said M'sieu.

The son resented this comeuppance for as long as he remembered it. He had been accustomed to have his way and was petulant when he could not. His mother, Old Mistress, she of the rats, had doted on him above any other creature or thing, including her rosary, which she had carried always in her hands, praying to leave "this dreadful isle" and return to La Belle France.

Now when Pamphile's father whipped him, the boy evoked his pious mother's memory, saying his father's new young wife had turned M'sieu's head with mixed-blood ways, M'sieu had forgotten he was white, and sided with the blacks, whereupon M'sieu beat his son the harder, though he did not break the skin, nor even raise a welt, but only made a lot of noise, to advertise the punishment and humiliate the brazen boy.

I indulged no fancy Second Madame be in league with us full-bloods. Since her arrival, rheumy old chattel-folk minded rat traps to earn their keep; we children languished in the kitchen waving flies from the pots; alas, the custom of doling out marbles had abated with the custom of measuring rats, and who to blame but Second Madame?

Yet though Pamphile cried out against his stepmother, he bore me no grudge. He was an impulsive boy, an impetuous, moody, willful one, but his rages were less fearsome than those of his father, his calculations less exigent. In uncharitable moments, I judged the boy weak, & self-indulgent, & irresponsible, & indeed, useless, yet I must own he helped me. When he saw I meant to learn, though I started with the youngest brats, he commenced a sulky supervision, drilling me to improve my knowledge of the numerals and letters, commanding me to write each one in the dust with my stick. To indulge his humor, I feigned ignorance of what I already knew.

"Goody, you fool! The mount, the mount! Cross—no! *Up* then *down* then *cross*—oh, I will make it for you once again; you will learn, damn creature!" he said, cracking me in the head with the hornbook, "or I shall never sail for France."

Oh, there a glimpse into the coils! Yet I dare not demonstrate too facile an apprehension, so I continued to feign intractable stupidity, suffering my vexed tutor beat the letters and numbers into my head, one by one, in the miserable chinks of his very short attention. By a judicious display of loutish amazement, I drew him out on the subject of his own great learning, and heard what books he had studied to acquire his scant proficiencies in Latin, in geometry, in history, Greek, in geography and in all manner of philosophy, both physical and metaphysical. In this way I formed a clear notion what curriculum the great whites studied to master the world, though I did not see that Latin played much part in the elaborate conquest that preoccupied Pamphile, viz., to wink and leer at the serving wenches, seducing them from their duties.

The number and intricacy of my own ruses could not completely disguise my aptitudes; I was unmasked altogether when Pamphile came out to teach me the letter *Y* and found me engrossed in a treatise I was composing in the dust, an inquiry into a moral question that had arisen whilst I drowsed through the droning lessons Modeste Devere was conducting inside.

From my vantage point outside the house I had observed a diligent swarm of bees and noticed within it the CURIOUS PARASITE, which I call CHANGELING. Now as the morning sun climbed the hill of heaven, pale green eggs in the tufts of grass did burst in the gathering heat, and from these eggs there crawled some yellow-and-black-striped wormlets, with sacklike bodies and many hundreds of paws. Hunching and squirming, the creatures contrived to lug themselves over ground, up stalk or vine, to lurk in the cavities of orchids, to feign the appearance of bees drinking nectar. And the purpose of this ruse, though obscure at first, soon enough became manifest. Soon enough my sidelong watch disclosed some changelings, clinging with grains of pollen to bees' hindmost legs, the bees thus freighted but straining progress.

The hive toward which the bees labored had been constructed against the louvers of a shutter in the green room. Upon remarking this, M'sieu instructed the schoolmaster repair thereto with his charges, to watch through the slats the bees that grumbled and drudged in the hive. As the squeamy bright brats balked at exposing their tender hides to the assaults of aroused bees, I was urged to be bold with my tough dark hide. So, holding my fingers in front of my eyes, to make a palisade with a sighting slit, I sacrificed hands and forearms for the sake of vision.

Between a number of stings, I was able to remark not only the diligent labors of the bees, but a number of changelings attentively succored with the bees' queens and grubs. So drawn was my attention to the changelings cradled in the nurseries of the comb, I did not remark the maps and books that complemented the furnishings of M'sieu's best room. 'Twas my first visit, indeed, inside the house, that had loomed so large in my dreams, but I was intent on calming myself, lest I reveal my QUICKNESS IN DISCOVERING, as I believed I had, A CREATURE NOT PREVIOUSLY KNOWN, the one M'sieu was to submit to Buffon in the name *Metamorphosa dufayensis*, Pierre having contrived to credit the master's vanity, that the servant's discovery might in this guise survive in the archive of learning. (True, I was never acknowledged a collaborator of the noble Intendant of the King's Garden, Count of Buffon and Sage of Montbard, yet neither was Dufay. Buffon does not always acknowledge.)

Weeks after taking the indoor louver, or sectional, view, peering as was my wont at the papery hive from my seat of outdoor learning, I was given to remark, on the verge of the rainy season, a number of needle-ish creatures drawing themselves through ruinous holes in the hive, shuddering and unrolling the hair-thin organs that trembled on their heads as the halos of angels in desperate prayer, their quivering wings yet folded. The creatures did scrub these wings with their legs, then pass their legs through their mouths repeatedly, thus, amidst their travail, enjoying a fine honey dinner.

Some were taken by birds before their wings, all clean, had flared, but others embarked on a dainty debauch of dipping and soaring. All summer long, they fluttered across the parterres and dallied along the allées. Then, pirouetting on gusts, they beat their flimsy wings more ardently as the rainy season approached, which would shred their wings and drown the creatures in downpour. Ah, the needles were born but to couple and perish, a lamentable short ballet, alas!

Now I had wheedled into complicity the lass we called Marie-Jeanne, that the white men called Full-Bags (though not in front of their wives), a serving girl charged with making tidy, a task which must bring her smack up against the hivey shutter, though not for long. She was wary of the bees, yet she was feisty and game, for she thought me a very nice boy and was impressed with my learning. So she would aid me by some assiduous observations if my duties took me on an errand for Pamphile or if I must take for my dinner when offered the crumbs he dropped.

I fitted her hands with raggy bandages and taught her to peer through a finger-slit. Between us we ascertained the bees' comb was wracked with needle-bore. The rain-soaked hungry bees would die in droves! Thus was the needles' double nature disclosed, their cover thrown off! Thus were the pillaging brigands indicted, nay, convicted! Thus did I contemplate the delicate imbalance, the disorder of the order of the world, even as I learned my sums and letters.

It did not escape me, the analogy borne by this paradox to our plantation worked by servants and slaves. Many masters of whom I had heard might, with a less-than-flattering reversal of gender, be compared to the bees' queens, in their continuous and cosseted begetting; our M'sieu were a proper changeling. His principal employment swung between intemperate devastation of others' useful lives and the pursuit, through his art, of universal knowledge. Yet though his laurels were earned at slave expense, I could not whole-heartedly wish him ill.

Did I not possess some traits of a changeling myself? Though I be full-blood, hence black, and not mulatto, not quarteron, nor marabou, nor sacatra, nor even sang-melé, as had been rumored Young Mistress were, concealing the one black part in the one-hundred-and-twenty-seven white parts, yet I had already begun to hope I might make myself so useful, in my diligence on Master's behalf, I might one day be manumitted, with some small property, to live a free man, with a garden and cow and a mortgage for my person I could pay with my time. In this modest desire I plotted to infiltrate the "hive" of those whom I resembled in certain traits—if not in hue, then in learning—to ignore, mayhap wrack, the many compartments into which their society had been divided. So be it! Some unfortunate souls, like the laboring bees, are doomed their entire lives to toil, while others, queens or drones, are free to indulge some whims! And changelings burrow to the heart of lord-and-lady-over-all! Who would not choose to be fortunate? So I thought in those gone days.

I was but twelve years old, my conjectures half-formed; yet the very act of meditation on the notion of justice would have got me flogged, had Pamphile, upon discovering my writing, been curious enough to read what I had written. It did not occur to him a poor black slave, who took so long to learn his *A*, his *B*, his *C*, might write a treatise in dust from which a white might learn, even the depth of insubordination with which he must contend. I moved to rub out what I had written directly I remarked my young master's spread shadow legs, swaggering back on their heels, fell across my periods. So he read aloud but a phrase, "useful lives and creation of beauty," and the pretension to homily amused him. He did not beat me for deceiving him, but whooped in boyish joy. He slapped me on the back and vowed I would have a fine supper that night. So instead of buttermilk and cornbread, he gave me meat of a bird he had shot. Yet I was not pleased, but fearful, for I did not know what would become of me.

The enterprise of my education M'sieu had undertaken in defiance of the planters roundabout, who swore into their rum he would instill in me tastes at odds with my station. They said he should hire a small white or train a very high yellow, lest the laboring blacks, from the conjunction of my color & my privilege, suppose their own merits deserved elevation. His neighbors reminded him of certain laws. M'sieu persevered with me partly in spite of these friends, for he did not care for their condescension; partly in spite of the law, which he said had no doubt been promulgated by brothers of those who farmed the taxes; partly to satisfy at once his curiosity & his vanity, to see if a full-blood would learn, and he could have me taught; partly to win respite from his stewardship without incurring the expense of hiring or purchasing a clerk. He loathed the small whites, and with them mulattos, including his offspring, who gave themselves airs. All his intentions floated as congealing fat to the surface of broth when Pamphile reported my schooling be complete: I could read, write, and cipher full as well as half the whites in the islands.

THE A, THE B, THE C OF MY EDUCATION

Then directly Pamphile took ship for France, while I was charged to sit at a slant-topped desk in the office & waiting room to make fair copies of letters, orders, & bills and to keep the journal & ledger of the plantation, recording its profit & loss, having been led, stumbling and gawking, past the turkey rugs & gilded hangings, the cabinet inlaid with ivory and the peacocks & pagodas on the green-room walls. At the desk, in tempting proximity to piles of books and half-rolled maps of the world with its vasty seas, I was dipped at once, pen in ink-pot, into the BUSINESS OF THE PLANTATION.

So much to the factor and so to the dealer in slaves, so much for salted meat, so for salt herring (yet though the sea be full of fish). So much for damask, so for books, for linen, for nails, for corks & tinware & cordage, for rosin & glasses, pitch & tar & guns. All that spending and then the losses! Losses to rats and losses to blight! Losses to fire & storm! Losses to pilfering! Losses of shipping, foundering at sea! And losses of slaves, when a careless one was scalded in the trying works or a desperate one threw himself in the boiling 'lasses vat. Here in ciphers our hanging ourselves and poisoning ourselves to end our misery! And when the times were bad, M'sieu would cut the dole of grub, though the work could not slack. We were sickening and dying, then, punished with a vengeance for our mortality. Yet however a slave died, the investment must be written off.

If in so much loss a profit be turned, it were at dear cost, from a slavish perspective, but our perspective weighed naught in the balance with rum; molasses; and sugar, refined and raw. The receipts coming in served to stave off creditors, and from them rich white men lived well, both here and in France. All the rest were but inky numbers, black numbers, yes, black numbers crossing the page, loss to profit and profit to loss, lives disappearing while numbers like ants crossed back and forth across the page, number-slaves at a master's bidding—ah, a master? The lord of the hand that guided mine, was he but in name my master? M'sieu came to seem but the occasion for little black numbers, moving about, making a pattern in the shape of which could be divined all the lofty purpose of fermenting yeast.

So it seemed to this poor slave, who did see in the growth of a tree from a sapling a movement toward light. Yet he did see in the growth of his master's enterprise but a stale accumulation, more land, more slaves, more horses, more debt, the latter piling up as a heap of midden outside a kitchen door. These scraps are all that remains of dinner, but what are they worth in themselves? For in them what is foul and noxious is bred, flies spring forth to buzz and plague us long after tasty morsels have been devoured.

Ah, but what of M'sieu's artistry? Did his drawings & paintings transcend the ferment of numbers? Or did he make them in default? For, distracted as he was, did not his drivers take advantage, and the factor in Saint-Domingue, and the captains of the ships? And the merchants in France? Did not their letters grow angrier? And ours to them? In these lights, the drawings must be entered on the debit side with the other losses which threatened to swamp the plantation enterprise. Yet midden is in the reckoning; sure to the flies the midden be the sacred ground of birth; each man— even a man in bondage—possesses his own perspective and sees what he sees. What Pierre Baptiste saw he kept to himself in those days.

M'sieu's father, who had long since died, had stipulated in his will the Anduves plantation be run by his sons, in a joint partnership, on a partable account, with the elder son, Alexandre Hippolyte, acting as agent with the merchants in Europe, the younger, Auguste Henri, going out to manage the plantations, for which he received one-third of all the net profits. Now the father meant to ensure the prosperity of the younger, for he had left the bulk of the estate to the elder, yet he wished the younger might have a respectable living that would sustain him in the manner of a gentleman, that he might not fall into ruinous poverty & dependency, like the children's governor, Modeste Devere, that poor fifth son of negligent improvidence.

M'sieu did not mind his third of the profits, but he wished his brother might allow him to hire a steward, that M'sieu might retire to France, to live on his income in a comfortable manner, and put aside forever the noisome business of supervising blacks. Yet the plantation was profitable enough, and, inasmuch as Lord Alexandre Hippolyte got a thousand per annum clear, he would not agree to a change of the stewardship.

In desperation, M'sieu had commenced to set aside his third from the gross, rather than the net, that he might eventually buy his own plantation and hire a steward and live in France, on income that did not depend on his brother's good will. Because there were diversions to conceal, then, M'sieu had excellent reasons for encouraging frugality, though he could not easily persuade his wives or his children to stint on food or drink or clothing. He more easily imposed economies on his slaves, and was very exact in calculating rations & yardage. He avoided hiring men or women, free-black or yellow or white, but raised up his slaves despite the risks. Thus, Pierre Baptiste owed his perquisites to his master's concealments. And Pierre was never a fool! He did not hesitate to elevate certain prices and charges, at his master's bidding, and to stipulate phantom salaries, including his own, to conceal how much cream be skimmed off the milk. When Pierre was charged to draft a letter detailing how matters stood here in the islands, in the management of the plantation, he subtly and dexterously emphasized economy & vigilance & the difficulty of all the undertaking, so that M'sieu's—shall we say his independence?—was covered with a thick layer of prevarication, a gloss of glittering, reflective mendacity. In this way Pierre earned his master's gratitude.

Did Pierre have a CONSCIENCE? Ah, it was not a white man's conscience—that Pierre could not afford. What hope had he but to augment his master's opportunities? For we slaves strangled cattle to eat, and said they had died of mosquitoes clogging their windpipes—as some did die—and sure we did not call it "theft," nor drawing down from the rum vat, "pilfering." A slave is a possession, as what he takes. How can chattel steal from itself? If I eat my master's beef, do I not improve his property in the flesh of my person?

In like manner, I will say my master but moved around the property that belonged in his family, as a man may move his family's furniture from room to room of the house. What difference to Pierre? This master, though frugal, were tolerable. Who would look to see him disgraced and recalled? No slave could relish the prospect of a slovenly steward augmenting his draw with one sottish paw, fondling wenches with the other. We bondsmen looked not to see the mill-house knee-deep in cattle dung, the coppers burned and filthy, the curing-house pots overflowed and crusted, the cane fields choked with weeds. For an overseer little inclined to preserve his master's property would stint as well on planting corn; the mules and the stock would starve, the slaves languish. A greedy, short-sighted steward would confiscate our hogs and fowl, give us no new clothes nor salt for what food we got. We had heard of it happening, and some of us had seen it. Oh, when an interested master left his place to indifferent oversight, the plantation could founder, the slaves still alive be sold to a brute or a pauper.

Why should Pierre, or any bonded man in these islands, care about lining a master's pocket in France? Alexandre Hippolyte sent dirty linen for our women to wash, so we knew his smell, but we had never seen his person. Why would we tattle if the younger brother, our master in more than small clothes, drank some wine that Duke Fine-Linen-Over-the-Sea had sent round-trip in the belly of a ship to age? Pierre would not tell, but wrote to elder brother for M'sieu, "The culprit like be some disgruntled hand we look to catch and whip."

Pierre Baptiste, a prudent man, inspected each notion from every angle; he feared the success of his master's plan to hire an overseer; he feared its ignominious failure; yet Pierre contented himself with dropping a word in the ears of the hands. They would be well advised to sabotage the profits, though not too greatly, by a leisurely disregard of rats in the stores, by setting the odd fire, or by spoiling with piss a vat or two of rum. Pierre all the while curried favor with his pen.

In making himself more and more useful, Pierre Baptiste was entrusted to ever more DELICATE DUTIES. He was permitted to draft in M'sieu's name the correspondence with Buffon in which observations and speculations were transmitted, with the very best drawings for engraving. This correspondence he did very much embellish, to M'sieu's great glory, and thus Dufay and Buffon were both unbeknown to themselves in Pierre Baptiste's debt. That one did delight in the elegant, revealing phrase! If you chance to have subscribed for the *Histoire Naturelle*, and have been privileged to read of the "red-and-green throat of the small lizard, puffing like a dropped lady's handkerchief," or of "fishes a garden of flesh in our waters," you will know these locutions first danced from the pen of Pierre Baptiste, though not, to be sure, on his own authority.

To assert authority—this is precisely what a bondsman never may do, for he be deemed a pissant number, a cipher moved from column to column on the great white page with never a qualm for the wish of the number. Pierre Baptiste knew what risks he could take. Describing the flora and the fauna from the slant-topped desk, he was content to savor the pleasure of composition without the renown of authority, for this in itself was more glory than he had yet dreamed—he who had supposed, before he served in the big house, the whites slept in their fine brocades in the same hammocks as we!

For his part, M'sieu undertook longer and longer excursions to more and more remote parts of our isle, and was even rowed in boats, though he could not swim and had not ceased to hate the sea with its monotonous tides and dank & perilous depths. Pierre at the ledger was now frequently alone in the office for hours, yet he finished his work with ever greater alacrity. Once he might have whiled away the idle time in jumping out windows to distract boys on errands for a stealthy game of marbles. He might have gossiped with footmen blacking boots or chatted up the wenches shelling peas. He might have gazed out at the busy work of the estate, imagining a sovereignty he would never possess. Yet, though he be young, he had learned much more than he wanted of the business he surveyed. Having written so many LOSSES in the books, he did not care to gaze at bare-backed field hands hoeing and picking, cutting and stripping and bundling cane beneath the lash, singing their all-too-regular song, the hounds licking sweat from the backs of their legs. Pierre saw his brothers already bones, strung on handles to be rattled for a dance. Yes, Pierre saw skeletons grubbing in the carries, though these were men who ate well enough.

He particularly loathed the slow, wet months of the year, while the cane is growing to its full height, ripening from a grass-green color to deepest popinjay, for then the hands must battle the blood-red earth itself, working the fallow resting fields. Then the terrible rise and fall of picks, of hoes, in time, did seem to turn the very ground that reeled and shook in the heat, as the cattle turned the mill that crushed the cane when harvest began in drier months. Pierre had seen a mill-feeder catch'd by a finger between the turning mills he fed, his whole body drawn in after, to be squeezed to pulp. And all the while the oxen plodded round and round, round and round, wearing a path in the earth, the juice dripped, drop by bloody drop, into the cistern. The crushed feeder's body fat was skimmed off the tops of the boiling juices in the coppers, with bits of his bone & skin & guts, as dross. Another feeder had already stepped into the crushed one's place. Is it any wonder Pierre loathed the languorous, fiery substance that dripped from the still? Is it any wonder he choked when the whites spoke of "anthropophagi" in Africa, claiming we had eaten the flesh of our brothers and deserved for our baseness to suffer as slaves? Pierre had puked when he smelled the fires, the burning sugar, puked again at the sight of the muscovado, the golden brown sugar knocked in loaves from curing pots, like boiled brains from a human skull, puked again at the sight of the clay-cured white stuff, phantom of cane. *Sweets are Death,* he said to himself, *Give me salt,* the sweat of life, though he did not yearn to be sweating once again in the carries. Yet, though a life be living death, still it is all a man may have. It is itself and no other thing till it is burned to what it is not, to death, white death, and oh, even then, the motto floated in Pierre's nose like the smell of burning sugar, *Death to whites.*

On the occasional amble to the waterfront to survey the dockside bustle, I did count in a state of fascinated fear the hogsheads of sugar, molasses, & rum, rolled from the warehouse into the boats to be rowed under guard to the port of Saint-Domingue, there to be loaded in ships and sent to Europe. I knew why M'sieu imported barrels of dried salt fish. The hands were too exhausted from work in the fields to catch their dinner. The irony of calico & bluecloth imported to cover our nakedness, that our master might boast he treated us as men, not beasts! Oh, there were much that a man who had finished the counting might brood on, much he might worry between his lengthening teeth, be he given to rumination. Yet I would be assigned more work, mayhap less to my liking, were it reported I be idle; so in slack hours Pierre feigned diligence at his desk. The ledger open, his ear pricked to footfall, a page of fool's cap ready to cover his reading, Pierre embarked on the curriculum for mastering the world that he had heard as he scratched his *A*, his *B*, his *C* in the dust. Yes, once Pierre had found his place in the world on maps, losing himself in the vast sea-stretch separating SAINT-MICHEL from GUINÉE, he began to read his master's books. So he became a man of letters; all on his own, he came to the end of his alphabet.

Shadow Histoire

→

PIERRE READ Latin and Greek, languages he had learned from Pamphile's errors, though not to perfection. Walking, then trotting, then roughly cantering, Pierre rode bareback through Caesar's commentaries on the Gallic wars; through Pericles; through Plato; Aristotle, Sophides, Virgil, Cicero, Horace, Tacitus, Veratius Aurelius. Then, reading in the latter-day tongue, Pascal and Nerf, Montaigne, La Mettrie, Pintal, Descartes; the Englishman, Newton, in the translation of Buffon; Fénélon, La Rochefoucauld, La Bruyère, and various compendia, viz., of Bossuet, Diderot, and, of course, Buffon. Through DILIGENT APPLICATION Pierre became conversant with scriptures as with satires; with comedies, tragedies, sermons & axioms; anatomies & essays; commentaries, letters & fables; chronicles & epics & herbals & the frail fancy-tales of Madame de Larme and her ilk. And much of what he read he did not understand; and much he did. And his head became so stuffed with notions, he found they were spilling into oblivion; he must needs write them down, to keep and hold, but he had no commonplace book.

Soon, then, I inveigled the kitchen help to steam tea packets over the stew pots so I could have the labels. The grumbling boss-grudge, Vérité, who had come to queen the kitchen, scowled me out the door, did she catch me coaxing wenches. Yet I prevailed through dogged persistence, for I would have the obverse of the labels on which to copy certain sentiments from the books I read—words I wished to secure, for remembrance or effect, in a talisman pouch I carried in my bosom, with relicts of my lineage.

So the noble heart cracks in vain, men choose for honor when they cannot choose for love.

—Egregon in Tontine's *Polyphon*

The path of faith is a thread strung over a chasm of doubt.

—Nerf

The Father and Creator, All-Powerful, All-Understanding, Eternal, Infinite, Wonderful and Glorious—the eye of an angel is not bright enough to contemplate Him, nor the tongue of an angel golden enough to name Him. And yet He Cares for the least of His creatures as the tenderest mother her babes, sending Death to quiet suffering. And our suffering? If we did not suffer, would we know we lived?

—Aiguillard Rostant

I pant, I rage, I quiver, I sweat—in short, I desire, and my desire has reduced me to a beast, nay, elevated me to an angel, for I cannot believe my passion is base.

—La Duchesse d'Espoir
in Madame de Larme's *Romance of Desire*

The Word is a fire and its keeper is not the mouth but the heart.

—Pintal

Of all these tidbits none seemed nobler, nor more inspiring, nor more sublimely elegant, than passages of our exalted correspondent, M. de Buffon:

> Though the works of the Creator are all in themselves equally perfect, the animal is, according to our perception, the most complete work of Nature, and man is Nature's masterwork.
>
> —*A Comparison of Animals and Vegetables*
>
> Man alone constitutes a class apart, from which one must descend through an unimaginably vast expanse of space, to reach the animals.
>
> —*On the Sense of Sight*

How these words pierced the heart of a slave, whose every impulse and perception told him he was as quick and as virtuous, as complete a work of intricate cunning, as his master, yet who knew himself counted on the estate books as chattel, enrolled with horses, chicken, and pigs! At best, as real property!

To avenge my degradation, I must confess, I defiled the chastity of many a volume, the pages of which had not been cut, but I did ravage with pains, for I prided myself on civility. Dear Reader, you may allow I was taking seigneurial rights in defiling these books, stealing perquisites from the master. I confess it was so. Shamelessly I quaffed the liquor from the phials, his books, the quintessence of his people's genius! Yet what I took were little enough of all my master had, and, like the bread and wine of Baucis and Philemon, remained for him to take again. Indeed, the general stock of learning were not depleted by my taking, but rose! Consider too the son, Pamphile, whom his father's economies scarcely touched, this silver-gilt scion with three pair of breeches, & shoes that fit, & his own handkerchief, nicely worked, & a pony with a braided tail, & a little chest of leaden soldiers—

35

had not this boy tried to steal what little I had, the one small memento of the very great genius of my kind? I mean my talisman pouch.

MY TALISMAN was a curiously wrought bag, nicely woven of tough and prickly fibers not of these islands, very likely from a vine or a pod or the hull of a nut or seed of the forest from which my mother was taken. In it were relics of mysterious provenance: some teeth of a very small creature, not so large as a mouse, but mouselike; the beaks & claws & tiny bones of several birds, contained in the case of a sizable beetle, from which the creature had drilled an exit, as I have seen these creatures do, this exit stoppered with a sliver of cork. And also, within that same beetle's case, what I took for a lizard's tongue; and in the pouch, though not in the case, a white feather of a hen or pigeon; some very small, very smooth red and black stones, as from a river bed; a stick of cinnamon, broken in two, and seven cloves. Petals of a white flower, dried brown; skin of a snake, rolled and tied; five kernels of maize; a pumpkin seed; a fish hook carved of bone; garlic skins; cumin seed; pepper corns; a rag doll smaller than my smallest finger; a dead palmetto bug; a very small, light, white cylinder of paper, wrapped round and nearly covered with black thread; bits of crumbling earthlike matter with a pungent odor; a shard of glass, such as I have seen others use, holding it to water to see the homeland in Guinée.

It needs no water-glass return-gaze to see the girl, MY MOTHER, hanging back in dappled shade, a younger daughter of scant importance in an uncle's household, possessing little beyond her body save the pouch which her mother had hung around her neck on the eve of her departure for her uncle's house with a basket of cola nuts balanced on her head. She had rarely been given anything anyone else wanted, yet she had what she needed. She followed the ox that pulled the plow, followed the cattle her uncle kept, followed the lion and the dog-cat, picking up bits of their dung to keep about her the acrid smells for protection. It needs no water-glass to see her, pounding yam harder than her sisters. Did I but close my eyes, I conjured them on the day of the night they were captured, heard the gales of hearty laughter that broke the rhythm of the pounding song, the thumping of strong young girls at their mortars. One breaks into dance; another leaves her pestle to fetch back a toddler who crawls into underbrush at the edge of a forest where anyone might be lurking, counting on his fingers the number of houses, and, from the number of mortars, the number of people who eat there, guessing how many are men, who might resist the raid on the pounder-girls' village, the return of the lurker by night with his fellows to fire the thatch.

Clutching her talisman pouch she was traded and traded again, bought and sold and bought and sold, until sold to the whites who brought her over the sea to sell her and buy and sell her again, men as white as the clay of the masks the men of the Fombé wear when they dance to honor the ancestors, running back from the river into the forest, tossing food to uncles' uncles who have been furnished with too few provisions for the journey to the other world, so loiter and dawdle in this one, making mischief until they are fed. Bought and sold and bought and sold— should anyone, least of all Pierre Baptiste, doubt that men's greed smells more pungent than the excrement of beasts?

Now my mother's name was MARIE MANDILÉ-BA—Little Girl, the whites made so familiar to call her, yet though they had given her a grand name, Ernani, of a tragical heroine, that they might smirk at the irony thereof. And Dufay took her, my mother, Marie Mandilé-Ba, took her, nay, dragged her to auction. And why? Because she, who had served him well, no longer earned her keep.

They had given her old shoes; her feet slid back and forth; she slipped on a banana peel; her arm broke and was improperly set by Captain Squint, to save the expense of a surgeon. Her driver, Fanfaron, called Catiline, covered her lagging in the fields, but there was no hiding her bent clumsiness when the gang fell behind, inviting the scrutiny of Captain Squint, who petitioned to move her to the house, where First Mistress deemed her crooked arm too unsightly to live with.

"Sell her," she muttered, clicking her rosary, *France! France! Return to France!*

The master refused then relented, on grounds my mother was costing too much. So my father, Jolicoeur, called Juba, who lived abroad, on another plantation, stole in by night in his hollow-log canoe to find his Marie Mandilé-Ba gone. Some say Jolicoeur hung himself, others he simply stopped coming by, still others he was sold himself. Why was I, a nursing babe, not sold with Ernani? Ah! M'sieu was too parsimonious to give up the stock.

My mother wept most piteously as I was pulled from her palm-oiled breast. It needs no water-glass to see her tears! Already planters who could afford no better peered nervously into her mouth, anxiously testing her remaining good joints. I have often prayed she was sold to one who could feed her all the year.

The TALISMAN BAG played a part in the service of the several gods of my mother's people, whose names and powers Marie Mandilé-Ba was saving to tell me (along with my true name, her mother's brother's name) when my voice had changed. Alas! She was not to hear me speak as a man. I know little of the kin who may be calling from across vast stretches of sea. Fombé. I am of the Fombé. My people were different from those of the other bondsmen on the place, many of them Oro. Ernani was unable to talk to these Oro until she had learned the patois. She had no one to talk to in her own tongue, for Jolicoeur did not speak it, but had wooed her with smiles and gifts. Nor was she able to teach it to me, for she was sold before I had been weaned. Yet the reward she had most looked for was the name-gift she would make upon my coming of age.

Had she known she would be sold so soon, she would not have let old Rose choose my first name, when I had lived but a day past the peril of ninth-day fits. 'Twas Rose who named me Pierre Baptiste, after a white babe who had died, so the mistress would look on me kindly, yet Rose believed my mother would name me my true name later. Nobody thought I would grow to a man with the white boy's name; old mistress had said, it were touching and loyal, I had been given her son's name, yet I could only keep it till another white boy be born, he be given it; then I should be called Cato or Lucius. Yet she died before she could give her husband this new boy. And the young mistress would not name her children any names the old one had fancied; even so, her womb proved barren. I kept the name of the dead white boy, though the whites called me Goody, believing me docile and subservient. I was entered on the books as Lucius and never learned the name my mother had been saving to give me.

"Go among the trees," said Rose. "Sit on the ground in the dark and listen to merrywings. From within the buzz a path will open; from between the isle-lapping waves will walk your mother. She will sit behind you. She will speak for your ears, and only for yours. She will tell you all she could not while she was here."

"Is she dead then? I do not believe you. How came you by my mother's secrets? If she visits, then why has she not come to me?"

"Go among the trees," said Rose. "I will show you where, but you must never look around. You must never try to see her face, or reach to hold her, for if you do, she will vanish. She will not return."

A voice spoke in the dark from among the trees. I did not look around. "Rose, it is you," I said, when the voice at my ear said my name, but the voice did not acknowledge. "Rose? Rose?" If Rose made MY MOTHER'S HISTOIRE, then it be an Oro story, or Rose's story, or Rose's mother's. Yet if it is, then so be it. The story I heard from among the trees is what I have of my mother, which I shall presently relate, how she was stolen from her uncle's house by raiders attired as ghosts, with clay cracking on their faces.

"We knew they were Gon. The Fombé ghosts are blue," said my mother, who was only a voice, smoke in my ear. "Blue," she said, "with faces of smoke. For sure these were men wearing smoke-masks, and wreathed in smoke. I had not yet bled; I am not even sure I had my second teeth. But I knew those men were Gon. I knew from the long red baskets dangling between their thighs. They were men of the Gon, looking for women to work in their fields.

"Fire woke us. Coughing and crying, we stumbled from the house. The Gon killed my uncle and took his wife and my sister and me, and my two brothers who had not yet been given names, and three very young cousins, two boys and a girl, who had not yet gone to my aunt's eldest brother. My aunt's younger brothers were visiting us, but they had gone hunting; they could not help to fight off the raiders who had found a weak spot in the wall of saplings around the yard.

"So they caught us as we stumbled out from under our burning roof. At first my aunt thought the ghosts were her younger brothers, killed on the trail, and she shook her fists at them. 'You big boys had to sally forth by yourselves. You never liked my husband; you couldn't wait for him. In so great a hurry to try out your arrows, you would not stop to place the stones for the hearth where I wanted them, further from the wall. Now what disaster!'

"But the ghosts were Gon. They fired all the buildings in our yard, then bound our wrists and marched us away in a line, with our household goods and the grain we had threshed. When my aunt's brothers returned from the hunt, did they find but ashes? The sour smell of smoke drifting on the wind? A cold trail of broken twigs leading across two rivers toward the Gon country . . . ?

"I never saw any member of my uncle's household again, nor did I ever again see my mother and father, who lived a day's walk away on the other side of the camp where all my people lived together when there was more than enough to eat. I dwelt among the Gon through clearing season, through planting season, through harvest season, sleeping curled against a silo where they stored the dung of their cattle to work into the soil of their gardens. The warm dung heated the mud of the silo wall, and I curled around the silo like a wife around her husband's back when he has had all he wants of her. Though I was not yet old enough to marry, the men of the place bothered me, and bothered me, and used me, and the boys too. I hugged the silo wall and cried myself to sleep at night. By day the women watched for my blood, for whatever the men did, I was still a virgin till it came. But the Gon women did not prepare a bleeding house for me, as my aunt would have. No, they meant to sell me as a virgin when I ripened.

"I vowed to conceal my blood when it came. I would bear a child of the Gon and marry among them, so they would not sell me to people stranger than they who lived further away. When the blood came, I was in the garden, bending and bending to harvest yams. A Gon girl saw blood on my legs and cried out, and the Gon sold me for salt.

"They tied my arms behind my back, and they tied a rope around my neck, and they led me like a calf along the river—I counted four bends—then they turned away from the river, and followed an ancient track through the forest, chopping at vines as they passed. They could not continue on the river path, they

41

explained but poorly in the Fombé tongue. They feared I would cry out when the caravan went by the camps of the N'H'ou-la, and beg them to save me, though N'H'ou-la stink of fish. So I knew they had not gone far past the river; still I hoped to return to my people, who trade with the N'H'ou-la.

"But when the caravan came out of the forest, after five days' march, it was to another river. And the N'H'ou-la to whom the Gon sold me spoke with an accent I could not understand, though they scarred their bodies in the N'H'ou-la way. They were fatter and more arrogant than the N'H'ou-la I had known. The fish were different; I liked not the taste, but it mattered not. They did not keep me long but traded me to men in odd flat boats that were carried downstream on a strong, fast current. Then the boat-men poled them up another, narrower, yellower river. And I was traded, again for salt, which 'twas said the N'H'ou-la would trade for more slaves to buy more salt!

"All this trading, back and forth, back and forth—like the crazy old man of my mother's village who made a trough in the earth from walking back and forth, back and forth.

"The boat men traded me to the Perg, for nine strings of beads and a bolt of cloth, and the Perg hoisted me onto a monstrous humpback beast where I hung with jars of palm-oil and wine. And I was carried from waterhole to waterhole across an expanse of parched earth, ghosts shimmering before me in the sun. They had not covered me, so the sun burned me, and my skin blistered, and I wept as I tossed in the feverish heat, wrapped in a thick blanket so I would live long enough to sell.

"Though I was weary, I did not shut my eyes, for everything around me was strange, the boys with feathers in their hair, like girls, the humpy beasts that stamped their great round hooves and swished their skinny tails at flies. The women who dressed in tents. The blue stripes on the faces of people and the hours they spent in the early evening outlining each other's eyes with a murky substance so black that it made the whites of their eyes burn from their faces like sudden torches in a moonless night.

"Though I might never see my family again or hear the language of my people, I thought I could live among these blue-faced ones. I would learn to milk the she-hump-beasts. I would let the Perg pierce my nose and ears. I would learn to walk in a tent without stepping on its edges. I would learn Perg dances, and outline my eyes, and pick out men, rather than waiting to be picked. Indeed, I had smiled on one, who had smiled at me as I gathered dung for a fire. Perhaps if I bore him, or another man, a child, a son, the man would keep me. The Perg would not sell me further from home, to people stranger than they.

"The Perg carried me into a walled town, with tall towers of mud, where I was displayed in the marketplace with hump-beast-hide bags the Perg had made to sell in the great open square, among people who dressed like the blue ones, but were paler and did not paint themselves. Beneath the sun's relentless glare, I was jammed into a wooden pen with other captives, and fattened on millet, and bowed down with many pounds-weight of stone, swinging on a yoke from my neck. So many of us, crowded together, rubbed raw against our fellows and against the boards, fainting and dying and reviving back again! At last I was traded for guns to men paler still, some of whose bodies were covered in silvery scales, like fishes'. They smelled like their own dung, for they did not wash themselves after they shat; they ate with both hands, and so thought nothing of confining us with our own excrement.

"The one who bought me—for bars of copper and for brandy—was fat and greasy white, blinking and squinting in the sun like a termite queen. He wore monstrous pantaloons that billowed over his living human stool, a servant who crouched on all fours so the master's silken fancies would not touch soil. More slaveys swung broad-leaved branches over his head to keep off the

flies. And he smirked from under his beetle's shiny skull at cara-
vans of skeletons, tied together by a cord through their ears,
stumbling beneath a lash, falling against one another as they
cried out for water. So many dead had been thrown into the bush
that the sated dog-cats ignored the feast. While a slavey swung a
pomander, the termite "king" pinched his nose and chewed on a
leaf that darkens the teeth, as if blood had dried on them. And
the gang of skeletons who still walked and breathed moaned in
terror on the shore, as I did, upon seeing for the first time the
vast-stretching sea. They clutched each other's shoulders, and
some tried to run away, tearing their own ears and the ears of others. Then they were all flogged, for mutilating themselves and
lowering the prices they would fetch. Not long after, I, too,
crossed the sea, trembling and sweating, with a rope through my
ankles and another through my ears, so it hurt me too much to
eat. M'sieu bought me, for rum and a bill of credit, in the market
of Saint-Domingue. And the rest of my life until Dufay again sold
me you can see all around you, my son. Alas, you bear it in your
bones."

Some time after Dufay sold my mother, when I was but a kid in
the yard, the lordling Pamphile put out his hand and wagged his
fingers, as at a dog, to make me give him the pouch. He had observed the birds come closer when I was about; he had divined my
"powers" resided in the crumbling collection of relicts sequestered in the bag. He wished to examine my jujus, but I hung
back, and sidled behind a tree, and regarded him warily. So I have
been told.

He stamped his foot. "Come, Boy! Do not cross me."

Then Rose bore down, who cared for all the children, white &
yellow & black, and taught them to be good. Shaking her head,
she shamed me for malingering. She snatched up the bag and she
handed it to Young M'sieu, quoting from a homily of the priest

some words about Caesar and his own, though with the gloss that all was Caesar's in that yard.

Did Rose know the bag would prick Young Master's skin through the cloth of his pocket? For the pouch was not meant for him. Yet he did not return my talisman to me. Rather, he commanded the butler, Jean-François, called Sénégal, bury the bag near the kitchen shed, not far from the cooks' garden, whence a runty pup dug it up and retrieved it to me. Grown to a man, I felt no shame to raid the young master's father's books, indeed to violate their chastity, those virgin volumes which, were they to escape heat and damp, would be Pamphile's.

Like many another slave, I pilfered from resentment and yearned for my freedom. Yet I was not dissatisfied with scrivener's work. Indeed I counted myself FORTUNATE, for I had seen my lot improve in all particulars. I ate not only the lard-fried yams of the field hands, but scraps from M'sieu's own table, thrown at his behest by the grudging slampoke Vérité, whom he had recently bought from Ravenal. (She was a secretive, muttering cripple whose fierce aspect frightened all, yet whose kid *aigredouce* with sesame seeds did ravish the palates of high and low.) I had been issued a bowl & a jar of my own to daily wash, and two sets of linen, nicely mended, if short in the sleeves, and the lace torn off. As my work involved ink, and bending of the elbow, I wore no footman's livery, but M'sieu's old breeches and a sleeved waistcoat, though with no cravat for my shirt. Had my shoes kept their buckles, I would have passed for a schoolmaster, or even, so I fancied, a factor's clerk. I sat on the stool with my book poised above my ledger sheet, my quill close at hand, watching lest the knob turn in the door. And when I slit folios, I did it with panache—a grand gentleman poring over maps of a huge domain.

Yet along a secret byway of my soul's back country, I had sequestered A PLOT. My intrigue were to shadow M'sieu in the

philosophic project he had undertaken with the Sage of Montbard. I would compile a prodigious compendium of natural &
moral histories, setting forth in orderly fashion the commemora-
tive particulars of Guinée, fauna & flora & diverse terrains along
with accounts of industries & customs & beliefs, not neglecting
the maxims & fables by which we bondsmen have been guided
since captivity and transportation.

You may say, Kind Reader, our history had been set forth in the
copious works of M. de Buffon. Yet I tell you plain, he has not observed us close enough. Oh, never could I bring myself to inscribe
on tea labels any part of the passage I am about to set down,
which cut and soothed me, at the same time, like the ministrations
of a clumsy surgeon. From the moment of my first reading, these
words have been inscribed on my heart, in all their sympathetic
treachery:

> Even though Negroes have little intelligence, they do not fail
> to have a great deal of feeling; they are gay or melancholy,
> hard working or idle, friends or enemies according to the way
> they are treated; when they are well fed and they are not mis-
> treated, they are happy, joyful, ready to do anything, and the
> satisfaction of their spirit is written on their faces; but when
> they are mistreated, they take the sorrow straight to heart and
> sometimes perish from sorrow; they are therefore very sensitive
> to kindnesses and insults, and they carry a mortal hatred
> against those who have mistreated them; when, on the con-
> trary, they have a liking for a master, there is nothing they are
> not capable of doing to show him their zeal and devotion.
> They are naturally compassionate and even tender with their
> children, their friends, their compatriots; they willingly share
> the little they have with those they see as needy, without even
> knowing them except by their poverty. They have, therefore, as
> can be seen, an excellent heart. They have the seed of all

virtues, and I cannot write their history without being moved by their state. Are they not unhappy enough at being reduced to servitude, at being obligated always to work without ever being able to acquire anything? Is it also necessary to exhaust them, strike them, and treat them like animals? Humanity revolts against these hateful treatments that a greed for profits has created. . . .

—"Variétés," *Histoire Naturelle, III*

In asserting we be men of "little intelligence," possessing but the "seed of all virtues," did Buffon himself not fortify the prejudice he sought to counter? And *gay*? Gay, as we are worked to death? Even as this great but sometimes careless philosopher had told of the creatures & customs of the world from the point of view of a white man, I would write from the point of view of a black one. For it must be proclaimed to our captors that we are not only acted upon, as animals or plants or minerals, according to our masters' whims and lights, but are actors ourselves, fully capable of living as our own masters.

In so doing, I would open for inspection THE GENIUS OF MY PEOPLE, proving we who had been stolen from Guinée THE EQUALS IN EVERY RESPECT OF OUR MASTERS, and DESERVING OF LIBERTY. In this tenet lay the disobedience of my plan, though I did not wish a living soul any ill, but sought to reveal our true & noble nature. I was emboldened to undertake this perilous and grand task because I believed I had the capability. And I was so inclined.

Thus, even as M'sieu had tramped about the isle collecting in his own manner, I commenced to reap a harvest of my fellow bondsmen's knowings, like a faithful bee storing up honey. My collection were accomplished in bits & pieces, for I must glean from the talk of my fellows, whose colloquies unfolded around the cooking fires in the short evening between work & sleep. And we were oft interrupted by the drivers, yellow bosses coercing the hands to early retirement to certify the prospect of early rising. Yet from the swift exchange our wits drew sustenance, each sensibility feeding off the ardor of the others. We had little to share but our OWN CREATIONS, nothing to gain but mutual succor. So our words flew from our hearts into air as a chorus of birds that fills the air with music.

> Damzillah's child, he
> *Jumped in the fire.*
> Fire too hot,
> *Jumped in the pot.*
> Pot too black,
> *Jumped in a crack.*
> Crack too high,
> *jumped in the sky.*
> Sky too blue,
> *jumped in a canoe.*
> Canoe got a hole,
> *Jumped in a bowl,*
> bowl too deep,
> *jumped in the creek.*
> Creek too shallow,
> *jumped in the tallow,*
> Tallow too soft,
> *Jumped in the loft,*
> Loft leaked rain,
> *Jumped in the cane,*
> Cane moon-bright
> *Stayed up all night.*

"Was this a man of special powers," asked a hand. "Come into his own by moonlight?"

Some said he was, some said he wasn't.

"Night or day," said old Rose. "Too much mind is given to rumors of magic. No spells cooking around this place, though I have heard of flying slaves. 'Tis said there were one or two field hands on Le Faneau's place whose driver would not let them rest. They raised and lowered their arms, raised and lowered them, fingers spread like vultures' wing-tips, and sailed aloft. Those men sailed all the way over the water, home to Guinée. Some say Juba was one of them.

"Then there was Fait-Tout, the do-all kettle, that could turn into an ax, a bill, a pick, a hoe, would do whatever work needed to be done. Long ago, before any of you were born or brought here, Petit-Jean had Fait-Tout. When it was time to hoe for planting, he'd take his stool and the kettle and go out and sit in the shade. He'd sing:

Ma-wa-loo-si, ko-da-ba-si
Ground need hoeing, get off my knee.

"Fait-Tout would jump off his knee, make itself into a hoe, turn over all the earth in the fields, do the work of a whole gang, everyone just sitting in the shade, no-one even holding the hoe-handle. Then Fait-Tout made itself a shovel, dug the trenches and laid the cane cuttings very nicely end to end, covered them just so, with a light, even layer of soil.

"By this time Petit-Jean was fanning himself with a leaf, laughing with a woman who had come out with a bucket of water. Before their eyes—even before the sun went down—little sprouts grew from the cuttings Fait-Tout had set.

"Petit-Jean sang another song:

Loo-wa sa-si, ki-ta-bay
Time for supper, quit this play.

"Fait-Tout turned itself back into a kettle, went home and cooked Petit-Jean some pork and some greens.

49

"About three days later, the cane was tall and ripe. Petit-Jean went out with his kettle, and it turned into a bill. It went up and down the rows by itself, cutting cane until the whole field was done. Again the gang was resting in the shade, fanning themselves with leaves, even the driver. They only got up and looked busy when the captain rode by.

"That Fait-Tout even fed those stalks into the mill, though truly I can't imagine how it did that. All the while everyone was resting, fanning themselves with leaves, all except Marius, a hand in that gang, who was squinting out of one eye, scheming how he might get that kettle. He thought it was wasted doing everyone's work, giving all the hands a rest. Marius would use it to show what he could do by himself, and get himself hired out, and earn money toward his freedom. When he was free, he would buy a piece of land, and Fait-Tout would work it for him, and Marius would become very rich, and buy a great house, and lord it over all the souls around there.

"He wanted that kettle so much, he could taste the bitter juice of wanting in his mouth. Marius thought he would die if he did not get that kettle. So, one night when Petit-Jean was visiting Li-Lu, the woman who came to the fields with the bucket of water, Marius crept into Petit-Jean's house and stole the kettle.

"The next day Marius went to the captain. He said he was sick and tired of the slow, lazy workers he found himself among. He wanted his own field to turn over, his own cane to plant. If the master were satisfied with the crop, he could hire Marius out, bring in ready cash.

"Marius ran home and got his stool and went out into the field the captain gave him to work. He set the kettle in his lap, and he sang as Petit-Jean had:

Ma-wa-loo-si, ko-da-ba-si
Ground need hoeing, get off my knee.

"Fait-Tout went to work. The kettle turned over all the earth, dug trenches, and set cane cuttings, laying them end-to-end just so. Fait-Tout did that whole field, cleared some ground next to it that had never been cleared before, turned that ground over, dug more trenches, laid more cuttings end to end, and covered them just so. By sunset, the cane shoots were already poking through the ground. Meanwhile, Petit-Jean's gang was back out in the sun, everybody breaking his back. Petit-Jean was too busy to wonder where Fait-Tout had gone, and nobody missed Marius much. At the end of the day, the people were glad to go home, and Li-Lu made Petit-Jean's supper for him, because he no longer had a kettle.

"Marius was hungry too. He said to Fait-Tout, 'You have put in one fine day's work! Now it's time we went home.'

"Fait-Tout paid no attention, but started jumping up and down at the edge of the fields, as if he could hardly wait for that cane to grow up, so he could cut it.

"'Did you hear me?' Marius asked. 'Enough is enough. I tell you, it is time we made our way home.'

"The worse for him, Marius did not know the song for day's end. He should have said:

Loo-wa sa-si, ki-ta-bay
Time for supper, quit this play.

"Alas, he didn't know the words. He continued to scold Fait-Tout, and to urge him home, but Fait-Tout went one by one into all the fields the gangs had left. He took up where they left off, doing whatever needed to be done, hoeing and trenching and setting out cuttings. Then, without so much as a pause, Fait-Tout turned itself into a bill. The cane wasn't tall enough to be chopped, but Fait-Tout chopped it anyway, chopped the young sprouts into tiny pieces no good to anyone, then turned back into a hoe, dug up all the cane cuttings laid in the trenches, turned

51

into an ax, chopped those cuttings to bits. Then Fait-Tout went after the corn, planted to feed just about every living creature on that place, save the ones in the big house, which is where Fait-Tout was headed. With his ax-blade self he had chopped down all us bondsmen's houses; now he was going after the master's. Marius had long since fled. They say the militia got him in the swamp over on Sainte-Marie-la-Belle. That kettle worked all night, while everyone hid with his hands over his head, thinking a powerful storm-wind was blowing.

"By morning, the island was devastated. Everyone had to start all over again, but without Fait-Tout. The kettle had tired itself out—lost all its magic powers. It was just a kettle again. Petit-Jean gave it to Li-Lu for a wedding present. Everyone else went back to work.

"Since that time, there hasn't been a kettle like Fait-Tout anywhere around here. We have to do our work the hard way. That is about all the good we have had from magic here."

So Rose had the tale from those who told her, though its shape has changed in seasons of telling. Or its edges have been nibbled by winged oblivion bearers, as it lay for years in the conjure chest in the house called Remember.

Dearer to Pierre than the tale itself, THE MEMORY OF ROSE, who by day presided over prattling infants, white and black, by night told stories in the moonlight, tapping her bare, misshapen feet, her knobby hands folded on her stick. The whites kept her for her uncanny way of spying through dim old eyes the wandering of children and, indeed, of cows, so that, upon her crying out, they could be saved from falling into pit or pot. She let the whites think that spying and saving were her only gifts.

She waited till the cows were penned for the night, the eminent heir had been herded to bed. Then, in firelight and moonlight,

Rose and other godmothers told the stories, so we would learn who we were and whence we had come.

One bright evening, the moonlit children at her feet, Rose looked out through her cloudy eyes and did abjure me thus:

"Good Pierre Baptiste, my godson, you must inscribe our stories in books, so they will not be lost when old Rose goes, for my hands tremble, and my voice quavers. Pierre, you must keep the stories."

Indeed, too few storytellers lived beyond body-pounding labor and coarse, scanty food to wisdom years—yet I was afraid to commit to the physical plane my collection of tellings, my CYCLOPE-DISH HISTOIRE OF GUINÉE AND BEYOND. I hid it in the metaphysical realm, though I wrote on tea labels certain epigrammatical keys, viz., for the kettle tale, "The good we have had of magic here." In the memory house of seraphic crystal with chests of light and dark in all the rooms, each key unlocked a drawer that held an account of many words. In this way I kept my histoire in memory, against the day when I had more and better paper than those scrappy relicts, the tea labels. For I dared not steal my master's fool's cap, as he counted every sheet. Thus did I sequester my cyclopedish histoire in my conjure-house fortress, behind stockade the masters could not breach.

"I am not a coward," I swore it to old Rose. "I am not—"

When I had paid the bond of my freedom, on that day I would scribble from dawn to dusk on very good paper at a very fine desk, with a fine supply of fresh-sharpened quills to hand. My brow fanned by a silent and loyal amanuensis, I would write the ENCYCLOPEDIA OF THE CUSTOMS AND INDUSTRIES AND TRUE RELIGION OF SLAVES TRANSPORTED FROM GUINÉE, WITH FABLES AND MAXIMS, THE COLLECTED ENTIRETY PROVING US WORTHY OF THE STATUS OF FREE MEN.

"I see," said old Rose. "And who would this amanuensis be?"

"Oh," I said, "there will be a great turn in the fortunes of Men. I have it from Squint, who is Protestant and talks to God. The bottom log will be on top, but the day has yet to come."

"You say so," said old Rose. "And who will be driver then?"

Rose did not give much credence to the prognostications of Squint, who made so great a show of sympathy with those he drove. When he whipped a hand, he would draw blood, having laid on stripes, so the master might see he had not shirked his charge; yet he might then lay the last two strokes on the fence or the side of the barn, to gain the gratitude of his victim. 'Twere a stubborn quashee did refuse to bellow on behalf of the plank.

Two-faced, crooked-hearted, worm-tongued: Squint would take a woman for his trouble, were the use of one proffered. But his kindnesses, he said, were not kindness at all. Did not the Bible prophesy a Judgment Day would descend upon Earth in a rain of fire, the dead rise from the deep? Much that was hidden would be known; the last would be first, the poor inherit the earth.

Against that day, Squint would save us, and so himself. He had a Bible, which he could read, along with the signs in the heavens. He would shake the cake from his long Dutch pipe and give a man a complicitous wink, "When the bottom is top, then do remember Tom, who kept you from trouble and gave you the leg up. Do remember Tom when the bottom rail be top."

The captain was proof of the oddity at world's heart. Though TOM SQUINT had no doubt been conceived in the womb of a woman, he was an inconceivable queer-freckled lanky-bones with squinty, side-gazing, light blue eyes, tolerably bright, though very yellow still. His mother had been a fancy girl kept by the son of a planter of Virginie, in the English domains due North of Saint-Michel. By his blood relation to whites, and his skill in diverse trades, viz., the carpenter's, cooper's, smith's, & mason's, he ingratiated himself with his master & father, who let him hire his time around. And he prospered, though his father would not sell him his freedom.

The women in Virginie were given to merriment at the expense of his squintiness; they did dimple and blush when he demanded consolation for their smirking and simpering. And they allowed him to paddle the backs of their necks and fiddle their plackets. And these attentions to a certain girl's person did land him in a right mess of trouble with his father, a huge pink lout who caned him till the blood ran from his head, and he was left for dead. For it seems Tom had been caught squinting into the placket of his mother's successor.

So Tom fled with the clothes on his back, and, having been pressed as an ordinary seaman, saw many exotic ports. He was promoted to bosun before he tired of bloody-crunch biscuit, short-ration rum, & wormy beef. He jumped ship in New Portugal, ran up debts at cards, re-indentured himself to pay them, was lost at cards to a Frenchman, and branded over, and finally bought by Dufay, who saw he would get an overseer he would not have to keep in the style a white man required. Dufay raised him to driver at once, and, by dint of cash bonuses, a snug cot with stone walls, a mule with a saddle, and generous rations of rum, prevailed on him to make peace with his indentures. He could keep his surname, *Blount,* and wear soft shoes fit to his feet and stride with a whip to chastise at whim. He could have what women the whites disdained. Yet, not those points, but ague in his joints & fevers in his blood & fluxes in his bowels—all manner of enervating malady—encouraged him to settle into his lot. He lived no worse than M. Devere, the governor of the master's children, who, though conversant in Greek and Latin, occupied a house no larger than Thomas's and possessed fewer clothes, though he did have a slave to wait on him who slept in his yard.

Squint's fingers might itch for placket, yet he strove to keep the peace and earn a quiet dotage. He taught us to avoid flogging.

And, did he get a goat or a sheep, he gave it to the people to cook. He would give away the last thing he had, but he would take the last thing you had. That was the way he was. Yet, if I am telling of him, I should further digress, and relate what part he played in my bringing up.

When my MOTHER, Marie Mandilé-Ba, had been sold away, Cap'n Tom, 'pon the very night of the AUCTION, regretted the part he had been forced to play, in clapping Ernani in irons, to prevent her running away. He wrapped her legs in rags so the irons would not chafe them. Though she wailed, he said, "like a mourner at her own funeral," he did not stuff her mouth with rags, but smoothed her hair with his hand. After a time she was not as stiff as she had been, so he gave her water, which he could see she but held in her mouth.

"Ernani," he said, "do not revile your jailer. I will not be spit on. Be good enough to swallow, Little Girl."

"Marie Mandilé-Ba!" she choked, with such vehemence he supposed at first she were cursing him, so he made the sign of the cross, to protect himself, though he had forsworn Papist witchery.

"Not 'Ernani,'" she said. "Not 'Little Girl.'"

And he called her Marie Mandilé-Ba until her lot was knocked down and she was taken by people from up in the hills, decent people, though not prosperous, and no longer young, so he feared the work would be hard. This was the last I heard of my mother.

Now he would not have heard her chosen name before, said Rose. For Marie Mandilé-Ba had hoped to please her master by acquiescing to the name *he* had chosen, waiting on him pretty, working without complaint in his fields, caring dainty for his children, and, indeed, bearing his children. Oh, I was Jolicoeur's child, you could see from my eyes. But some of the children Rose watched might have had two fathers. Their eyes did not match.

It would have been better for me to have another father, for Jolicoeur was no protector. Even as Marie was being sold, he was stockaded for impudence in his own master's yard; he tried to run away, but he was turned in to the militia for reward. "Marie!" they said he called from the pen where he was kept. "Marie Mandilé-Ba, you." But she was far away, and they stopped his mouth with rags. Some said he succeeded in running away and reached the maroons. And some said he hung himself with a rope he had made by tearing his smock into strips.

Did Mandilé-Ba pray for deliverance? If she did, the Gods must have hidden in the clouds that day. Only Squint was there, familiar, devious, not unkind. She begged him to WATCH FOR HER SON, to sustain him and help him, even as a FATHER would. Her tears fell on his hands, which she brought to her mouth and kissed, and wept some more. Oh, it were truly a piteous spectacle, he allowed. She should not have been sold without her babe. Squint should have spoken up. Alas! What was done was done. He would do what he could for me.

Sooth, it served Pierre well to be watched by a man who was close to the whites, so said Squint. My favor in the eyes of the Lord be manifest in my election to the company of the saved, viz., himself. But if Judgment were delayed beyond his life in his body, Squint would have me be useful to those who had privilege to dispense in this world. In my boyhood he surreptitiously taught me to lay bricks and hoop barrels, to shoe horses and sharpen knives and distill brandy & cetera, that I might be raised from the gang to a comfortable life, hiring out my time, earning coppers toward my freedom while lining my master's purse. And when old Christophe died in his tracks, it was Tom Squint who touted me for PREFERMENT.

I was taken up to the house from the carries and taught to mix paints and color backgrounds. I was brought on errands to the big island where I saw a barber as black as I who wore a velvet coat and kept four slaves.

Yet Tom warned my master 'gainst my schooling; he said I knew too much already and would not keep my place, to which M'sieu responded, he would not suffer dictation of an o'erreaching driver. He would school me; I would keep my place; Tom must look to his.

When I could read quite well, I came to Tom, and said we should read together, from his Bible, but when I looked at the words, I could not read them, for they were in English. Now I most earnestly sought to learn this language, for there were books in that tongue on my master's shelves. Yet Tom would not teach me.

And how would he stand at The Judgment if he had refused his fellow the Word of the Lord? Ah well, he said, Jesus had made His disciples fishers of men, not fishers of words from books. Yet I could read the scriptures in Latin well enough to know, Tom's readings were unorthodox. His scriptures were Protestant, he said, whereas mine were Catholic. I suppose he read half the words, and invented the rest; perhaps he read not at all, but opened the book at random and improvised, thus fortifying the argument of Père Gouy, that the Bible were best expounded by those upon whom God had laid His Hands.

Yet I did a fair trade with those of my fellows who would learn to read and write in dust, as I had. They traded me necessaries, viz., a bowl of milk, for teaching. And on the Sabbath, except at harvest, I taught in secret in the bush, though only after setting watch. And I earned the disapprobation of that Tom who was not so thorough a Protestant he wished every person born with two legs could read. He threatened me with the cunning whip called Stinger, that had hooked nails driven through the thongs, yet he did not betray our school to Dufay.

Though he imparted a gospel of his own devising and made me a heretic to any creed but his own, still I must allow: Captain

58

Tom Blount, known as Squint, were a USEFUL FRIEND to men below him in the hierarchy of conditions. He had been charged with warning us into our dwellings at night, yet he cut short our suppers only when cane must be harvested. If work were light, he came himself to sit at our fires, a whistle on his lips, pulling fish still flopping from his pockets, and sometimes he brought rum. Though we were constrained in his presence, we did not discourage him with silence, for we knew he did not carry tales.

In all our fireside gatherings, he took a lively part, having learned the patois smart enough, though he knew less of his lineage than I, nor did he care for old stories. He be a man in motion, he said. Removing his shoes and lighting his odd curved pipe, he gave us in tales the ports he had seen when his ship touched shore, in the time when he lived as a seaman. Thus I got the scent and hand of the stuff called *Freedom*, from one who had been freer than any of us were.

My earliest conception were never to wrap so bright a yellow's reminiscences & rumors in the same 'cyclopedic bundle with the wisdom of Guinée. But he, queer, speckled yellow, stood at near as great a distance as we from the masters; no more like than the rudest hands to have his accounts incorporated into any histoire but my own. Was not Squint a bondsman too? I expanded my CY-CLOPEDISH CONCEPTION to accommodate all the men—even the smaller whites—who are not great, or patronized by the great, but are simply MEN.

Yet time and again I raised the question of his place in the shadow histoire, for he was our driver, who whipped us. I shall not fatigue you with the full account of my backings and fillings on the sticking point, whether Tom Squint, Captain of Drivers, were meet for a slavish histoire. I have greatly digressed from dilating on the subject of my own ambition: to use my COMMON SENSE to observe and record the history of my people, transported into bondage from Guinée, discovering to the world OUR GENIUS, proving us THE EQUAL OF OUR MASTERS, as deserving of LIBERTY as they. No more than to my master could I reveal to jealous Squint the full extent of my reading, and, more dangerous than reading, writing. Let it suffice to have set forth my manner of preserving in memory, by means of epigrammatic keys, that would not greatly compromise me if discovered, the design & substance of a very compendious histoire.

Having recorded, then, my GRAVE MISGIVING, whether tales of crook-face Squint, the driver, do belong in the histoire, I shall embark on the relation of my own ADVENTURE. For soon enough, I, who had settled into a quiet, bookish life, was tarred with a brush that Providence had surely reserved for the leering Tom, bumping his belly against the buttocks of women bending to cut the cane—Squint, that salty, salty cock.

The Trouble I Took to Wife

➤

I have allowed we bonded men were cajoled to BREED; one day Squint, having taken me aside, mysteriously circumlocuted some nonsensical matters whilst stroking the slant of his sharp-angle jaw, then drove more direct to his point: "Now, as our master has treated you with very great favor, and fostered your excellence in letters and ciphers, he has asked me to beg you consider, would it not be virtuous to answer his magnanimity with a modest loyalty?"

I hoped I had acceded to my master's wishes in the smallest particulars; I would know on what grounds I had given offense. Ah!

Tapping 'gainst his boot the whip that he used on the hands' recalcitrant hides, though never till now on my own, Captain Tom allowed that I had disappointed with a too fastidious CHASTITY. For though I had weathered a score of years, I had not cast my eye on a wife, so did not sufficiently increase my master's estate, and did him as great a harm as did I pilfer rum.

Now I enjoyed my repute as a handsome, fine-talking fellow. Why, Pierre Baptiste no more than the next red-blood forswore to tip a skirt above a head! And prided himself his good John Fish were esteemed a fair-sized catch! Many a placket weir had baited him in, though, yes, 'twere true he swerved back out again, so as not to slight the others who wished to lure his fish. No, I did not care to boast, yet I was certain offspring of mine were inscribed on my master's rolls, and if pressed 'gainst my modesty, would point to a most respectable roster. Yet Squint on the master's behalf would settle not for a furtive tumble but did press me still to a plighted breeder's sober life. And now indeed I were sorely vexed.

For I was an orphan, pulled mewling from his mother's breast. And, though my several godmothers had generously nourished me, I had been sensible from earliest youth of a solitude dispelled by no bright company; I had never looked to be consoled by a mate. Moreover, Reason told me, I could guarantee no prospects to my young beyond the care I took to school the pupils of several ages in my secret school. Pierre's own rise to a protected position had been but a partial good fortune; still he was wholly owned, and subject to the whim of whites. Had not his mother been sold when the first old mistress flinched at her crooked arm? What thoughtful man would visit on the head of a child an inherited affliction?

"Goody, my bucko, I tip you now a wink," said Master Squint, the captain of the drivers. "I bid you prudently take it. Consider a match from amongst the fillies around our place, who carry themselves so dainty, and who eye your position in the house with favor. There goes Mimette, tall, well-grown, fine-boned, with those high breasts, standing straight out. Mimette would make a man a handsome wife."

Indeed, already she was eyed by those above my station. Driver Tom had leering glanced, and Pamphile had handed Mimette an orchid for her hair. I would not marry a woman who sported a white man's favor, though she had no choice, so I would not choose Mimette, nor the full-fleshed Quasheba, with her ready laugh, nor clever Dido, nor any of the girls who quick-stepped work to song in kitchen and yard and field. Nor would I choose among the ladies' maids, who held their chins so high.

"'Tis true she will droop when the young come, year after year, to suck the pertness from the once-fine bags. So it is with women all. Now if she were white, and you, my buck, there'd be no end of trouble to rid yourself of her when she passed her prime. 'Tis as well to be a slave in this; for your choice of a woman have no weight in law. Dufay will sell her if she irk you with reproaches, for these bitches are nothing to him when they are old and please not the eye and no longer earn their keep."

Ah Squint! How low and vile you deemed me, who would plot before the nuptials to sell the mother of his children when she sagged with years and work! Yet I plotted right enough, indeed I did: my work in the big house had bred in me the aspiration to be master of my condition. Oh, I did not scheme as some did, to purchase freedom only to set up my own plantation, with my own slaves, my own hard drivers. No, I did not look to govern others, or enrich myself from their stooping, but, as the ancient stoics commend us, to govern myself, to take of life what could not be taken, or at least, was not like to be.

The curvet and leap of Master Fish 'round the winsome notwithstanding, I resolved to court for a WIFE a plain, industrious, skilled woman, who might be useful, yet was not likely to attract the amorous sighs of whites, of quadroons, of octoroons, of full-bloods, or even of tawnies. And better suited to my intents than plain, I resolved to woo a homely wench. And better suited than homely, ugly. And than ugly, hideous, viz., the fearsome queen of kettle and spit. Yes, unbeknownst to her as yet, my nesting choice had come to settle on the finger-wagging slampoke Pélérine Vérité—Pilgrim Truth—who was called "Sweet Snarl" (*Douce Farouche*) by the whites. She would not bind me in embrace to what I stood to lose! For though one side of her face be smooth and beauteous shapely, and incite to languorous longing, the other be stiff and crooked, its several parts melted together, as a candle mold that has been thrown in a fire, her winsome smile twisted with scars to a leer. Upon any who came up on her good side with covetous supplications, she flashed at once her bad side, and glared at him through her bad eye, muttering and raving 'till the cold hand of her affliction squeeze his heart, and he back away.

The master suffered her snarls for her mousse and paté, her bisque and fricassee, that were the envy of the planters all about, though Master compelled her beneath his gaze to taste each dish, so great his fear of poison.

PÉLÉRINE VÉRITÉ had but one good leg beneath her skirt, the other being stiff and wizened, yet in the light of the full moon some had seen her climbing for coconuts with both legs wrapped supple 'round the tree trunk. 'Twas said the fowl were affrighted by her halting daytime gait, so the bolder wags set up a spirited clucking when she passed, darting malevolent looks from the glittering, slitty eye on her scarred side, the eye of a woman living dead. 'Twas claimed her former master had poured boiling water into that eye—then wide and bright as its mate—when he caught her digging into his wife's grave a length of cloth Vérité had been given for a dress, so the bondswoman could dig it up later to make herself a witchy dress. Yet the boiling water had not blinded the eye, so how could she be human? Fie now! She had been sold from a far-away plantation; how could a soul in the yard be privy to stories she had not told? Yet rumors abounded.

The master himself credited gossip touching on the wisdom of keeping from her hands his cut hair and nail parings and any bodily excretions, with which, it was said, did Vérité brew potions, she could conjure ill upon a body. Dufay did burn his nail parings himself, and those of his wife, and of Pamphile, though not of his yard brats, commending their smoky souls to God. Oh, Vérité

64

scoffed! To see chamber pots steaming secret through daybreak dew in the trusted hands of old Nurse Rose, who dumped 'em in the distillery vat, to keep the hands from drinking the brew.

When Vérité's evening work was done, she sat with her raggedy-eared cat, Scratch, before her fire, smoking a pipe, like a man, while she hooked an exquisite lace of seed-pod floss. Yes, while Scratch licked between his toes, she crocheted with a tiny crook of bone said to be of a human child, muttering her contempt for the whites, from whom she hid her webs of lace, hanging them from the twiggy roof of her house like the nets of a spider.

"Piss in my fingers, they would still be gold. I embroider Old Uncle the air, the clouds, this thread that draws the eye to what it desires, raises the shining flowers, brightest stars, flights to feather birds. Brighter still! He will have lace at His throat that is webbed from fancy, the movement of women beneath men's hands, the reach of the heart to the name of the sky. And all needs blessed with neither back-break nor trouble. For what pleasures fools will kill! No mercy the offal world confers! Blood will not honor bloody Old Uncle. Dress Him in brocade of what you pray against, the dead in their clattery bodies rising. White ladies douse their hands to bleach them whiter. What can Old Uncle want with their piss? Bones stripped of flesh do bleach in sun! Old Uncle cares nothing for whiteness. For Him a woman walks on sand, her bleeding embroiders the cloak that will dress the dead, raise them star-eyed, mango-handed. Uncle is no soul-snatching ghoul, no Baron Skull. He whips no lather from unseen horses to fright the virtuous souls from their beds."

Every morning as the piss walked by, Vérité sprinkled new white sand on the floor of her house and squeezed a lime, then an orange. And around her rose a great pure, sweet, fresh coolness. She bathed herself in three waters, scented with jasmine, ginger, and basil, and wrapped her head in a bark-dyed cloth, bright red, then went to the kitchen of Dufay, to see that the pastry flaked sweet on tooth and tongue, the bird was boned close and pretty. The whites believed her onion patties concocted for them, but Vérité served the will of Uncle, and kept back always a portion for Him, with a bit for Scratch.

Do you hear in your dreams the beating of the drum? Do you hear the tinkle of the clavichord? Sound webbing sound devours the world and spins it to food for spider Soul. Old Uncle! Only to Him would Vérité submit, and she spat on the man that would trifle with her vows. 'Twas said her spittle 'graved marks that burned, and she had oft been blamed for the pox.

"Who would be flayed by her god-boss tongue?" so joked the hands. "A man stand no more chance with her than a rat with her cat."

Yet what had I to fear—I in whose talisman pouch rested broken shells of the eggs of birds that could speak as men; sea shells resembling a woman's pudenda that cried when the wind blew fresh; and labels of tea packets, written over with sayings & epigrams, my commonplace book. In the web of my own intent, I schemed. If I must marry, I would marry, but breed I would not. The kettle-grudge suited my obstinate though apparently obliging purpose, she who was rumored to have sewn up what remained of her burned womb, further paying with her flesh the pillage she had endured. So I made bold to woo her. Though she spat on my first most complimentary approach, viz., "Hail, bright beauty!" I bowed like a prince, and did not from proximity get any pox, and soon events contrived to buoy up my suit.

One fine eve M'sieu entertained an ASSEMBLY of guests. Safe from the night vapors in the great house, the company did sip from the rum bowls, looking out with much merriment 'pon a curious SPECTACLE M'sieu had contrived to mount, emulating a practice of the taxonomical Swede, M. von Linné, the most esteemed LINNAEUS, the rival to my master's own M. de Buffon. Dufay, claiming *he* were no ass-heart, to forswear for spite an ingenious invention, had caused to be fastened to the carapaces of ponderous TORTOISES some candles which, when lit, and the tortoises permitted to take their meandersome way, did bobble in the dark in a glimmering sarabande, flickering but stately, to delight the ladies, who swore they were frightened and made pretense of swooning into sundry gentlemen's laps as the turtles roamed the mazy parterre amidst the plantings of boxwood and lavender that but feebly withstood the onslaught of orchid and the general broad-leafed tropical confusion into which the turtles would soon disappear, though not before the gentlemen had had occasion to relish a game of tickle-and-slap-the-ladies.

Upon spying the flickering LIGHTS in the maze, many women of the yard did fall to their knees on the swept, packed dirt, and clasp their hands in fervent prayer, as did many of our men, for mundane explanations would not overturn our conviction that the lights that beckoned in the dark were the souls of departed TAWNIES who had once inhabited these Anduvean isles, viz., the souls of those Xuacomac enslaved before us.

The tawnies who did not flee altogether had died in a grievous short time of a very great multitude of causes, viz., overwork, & diseases of love, & paucity of nourishment, & a loathing of cultivation and of settled life. The lights on the backs of the tortoises roaming the night, many swore were the souls of these wretched tawnies, whose corpses had not been dispatched upon rafts with the customary rites of kind and kin, but had been rolled into shallow graves at the whites' command, and praised but a hasty farewell under stern surveillance, inasmuch as the whites did not care for their bondsmen to assemble in the honor that death commands.

Now the UNCLE of the place, whose claim was old on these islands, older than the claims of our Guinée Gods, or any claim of the Christian God, had demanded we adopt the tawny practice of pushing the dead out to sea on rafts. Yet the whites did not like us to emulate the tawnies, supposing we plotted a rising. They forbade our gathering. If one of us died, they called up their scurvy militia of landless little whites to roll the dead one into a grave in the dust that dogs and pigs defiled.

When first the whites had thwarted the ancient way of these Anduves, the desecration so cast down the spirits of us, many died of checked mourning, their dammed-up sorrow wreaking in their hearts a great devastation, so they sickened, and lay on their sides to stare at their walls of twigs, and could not or would not stir, though they be whipped to death. Many took their own lives by poison or the rope.

In the time when I, Pierre Baptiste, WOOED Pélérine Vérité, the funeral rites had again been permitted, our masters having overcome their fear of our assembly in greater fear of losing to pandemic grief the capital invested in our persons. Thus we did assemble on memorial occasions to make a seaward procession, singing the candlelit raft into starry night, praising the dead, and the dead before them, and the dead to come, that they might reach their protecting hands from the world beyond, to comfort us in our affliction.

Yet the lapsed rites of the earlier time, when custom had not yet conferred on us the liberty to mourn in the way of the islands, pulsed like one great fearful heart of wrong among us still. And the sight of the bobbing turtle-borne lights, that thrilled the furbelowed, white-wigged guests in the gilded chairs, devastated us ragged servants who knelt bareheaded in the dirt of the yard. For even I, who could read and write, had drunk with my godmothers' milk the stories of the INJURED DEAD, and my heart beat large in my breast in fear of the guttering, wind-buffeted flames. Though I had seen with my own eyes the candles affixed to the backs of the turtles, I feared the tawnies denied their rites, rolling over in their shallow graves, still raw bones and hungry light, waiting for their chance to dispossess us of our bodies, daring not to touch the whites. We hapless blacks would be suffered to wander as lights ourselves, barefoot and naked, desperate in wind, ever fearful of Baron Skull, lest he ride us down and force us to undertake for eternity, at unbearable pace, the meanest bodybreaking labors, viz., chopping, hoeing, & cutting, in the hottest sun, with the poorest food, with no chance of respite, all the while plagued by the itching and scabbing diseases, and hosts of insects and worms, worse than any yet known to living bodies, and all without the blessing of Sabbath or rum.

And 'gainst this dire eventuality, our people set out their suppers of callaloo and cassava bread for the turtle-borne lights, to feed them. And we occupied ourselves in getting up a procession of mourners as best we could without notice, arraying ourselves in our finest clothes despite the fatigue of our accustomed travail. And gently Farouche unhooked from her twiggy walls her lengths of lace and wrapped the men's necks with stocks and draped the women's shoulders with fichus and shawls, and puffed up delicate caps for the women, too. And we squandered our precious stores of candle stubs (which we were wont to pocket when we could), and, lighting them, floated them into the wave on palm leaves, so the restless dead might see how enthusiastically we organized their obsequies. And we went so far as to float our pipes of burning tobacco on the wave. And the solemn dance with which we honored the sacrificial gleaming on the water— the very path to the beyond—was received with shrieks and titters of merriment in the great house, as the cap to the evening's entertainment.

"Suck on a teat of night-chill. Why will you drink from a broken cup? Fie, blood, burn, burn, burn. Oh, this body, who can say it is my own, oh, why will you have me? Pipe ash and rat dung. They have left me an empty pod for a heart, a sweetmeat roasted in sugar, a whore's dainty. Oh, see Him eat it, the rot setting in, how He belches and farts. Pfaugh! Pfaugh! Vapors of pestilence. No heart beats in a plucked, hung fowl. See the stilled and staring eye? Why would you ask a husk to be a horse, to rise and drown them in rum?"

And with no warning at all, a STORM broke sudden, with cracks of light that tore the sky apart, dismembering it and shattering as glass the pale laughter of the powdered specters that crowded the French doors. Then whipped-up waters rose in heights of demon glee and rolled across our island. The whites crawled under the tables and whinnied for the barring of the shutters, but they had to do it themselves, for we bondsmen cowered terrified. Yet in the downpour the lights on the backs of the turtles were dowsed, and we took heart; we threw ourselves on the ground to offer thanks, all but Sweet Snarl, she whom Uncle was already mounting as a horse, Great Uncle Thunder, spirit of the place that had been defiled.

SHE AND SHE shuddered in her drenched fripperies and clapped her hands, and the very earth we lay on shook with the pounding dance of her and her good foot, whilst the huge-eyed Scratch circled yowling in chase of himself. Orchids falling apart in her and her hair, she and she alone with Scratch stood the fury of the storm, nay seemed to rise taller at its center, to become its very eye, the calm at the heart of the anger of wind. Vérité, maimed and reviled, twisting resentment's tighter coil, winding it around her stiff-pin leg, arms raised to the sky. She and she grew taller, till she and she were taller than the tallest palmettos, and Scratch Cat too, tall as a storm head. Her and her best clothes fell away in rags with her wispy mantle of pod-spun lace. As the slicked ebon fur of Scratch, her and her body gleamed in the rain, the scars of her previous master's torture glistening in light-cracks thrown bright across the sky.

70

She and she did chant with caterwauling Scratch, their voices riding the wailing wind as a praise-song none of us knew, nor could we fathom her deep-throated tongue-babble, which yet rumbled with Scratch's purr to quiet our spirits, even as the winds and the waters were calmed. So the Uncle opened the waters to receive into the shadowy realm beneath the sea, where Baron Skull cannot ride, the souls of tawnies honored by lights borne on the backs of turtles. There beneath the waters all souls inhabit a single great HOUSE, the richness of which is not in possession of any worldly goods but in possession of the wisdom of all the world's people, which is shared by the dead and multiplied beyond mortal imagining. And she and she beat her breast and raised a cry for all the souls everywhere who were not already at peace. And fell as one dead into sleep.

Before the SUN had fully risen on the devastation of the cane fields, which even the privileged amanuensis, viz., myself, would sweat to clear, I, Pierre Baptiste, crept from my hut to discover Vérité asleep near the high-water line, sprawled upon the flotsam and jetsam with Scratch curled on her calm and naked breast. Around her had been raised several cairns of pebbles and garlic, and 'pon one of these had been erected a cross of sticks bound with vine. But no God would claim her yet!

I took my priest of a bride in my arms and carried her back to her house. There I deposited her on her mat and lay down beside her with Scratch, praying her fatigue would diminish any ire that she had been touched without granting leave. She opened, first her good eye, then the fearsome slit; it flashed wary, and her lips curled back. I must own I was truly afraid, for I had seen her powers. Moreover John Fish was counseling change of heart, as he were loathe to swim in chill and choppy waters; he prayed I would woo a more serene and warm-hearted wench. Yet I was unwilling as ever to expose myself to exploitation as breeder or cuckold, however impolitic I deemed it to thwart my master's will. So I hissed in the juju woman's ear my plan. We would live together as brother and sister, feigning a union that would protect and shelter us both. I enjoined her give me some sign when she had considered my offer, and I passed from her presence into dawn, even as Captain Tom was sounding on his conch-shell horn the call to work.

Not long after, Vérité approached me: "Fools," she muttered, "can know their minds. If the fly love the spider, it be not the spider's fault. I say 'Shoo!' Will you buzz still?"

Taking this for her consent, I bundled my small possessions in my blanket, so to repair to her house, that I might from thence look up through chinks in *her* daubed roof at her lace-hung sky. In short, I would take up my new ESTATE forthwith. But there came then Jean-François, whom the priest had sold eight baptisms, eight sprinklings of holy water. The upright fellow had taken each more to heart than the last!

"I beg you accept this protection. Put this orchid's root in your pouch and she cannot conjure against it. For I have paid Père Gouy good money to dip it in the sainted water three times, once for Gentle Jesus, once for Marie-Vierge-Belle-et-Jeune, once for Saint Michel. With this root you will have the triune blessing on the nuptials—yea, the full triune!"

In truth I owned I might need the testicular root. I hid it in the bundle I carried to her doorway. I foppled outside her hut, sheepish, indeed, for she came to meet me in a gala red dress, her head wrapped bright and festooned with lace, whilst I languished in my ordinary patched brown clothes.

"Crawl in like a worm, then, man? I will claim a true husband, or live in peace with Scratch as before."

Jean-François whispered, "Though you work in the big house, you are not too grand to dirty your hands. Now you must burn some limestone rock in a very hot fire of grape-vine wood. You must wash her dwelling inside and out with three waters mixed with ash, not forgetting the threshold itself, which you must paint, to make an ash-white lintel between the dirt floor of her house and the dirt of the yard. If you do not do this, you will not have a home."

"What? I labor in the yard?"

"Who are you," declaimed Jean-François, "to set yourself above the estate of a married man? If you will not turn your hand to the wedding work, no one will have you."

I knew the custom well enough. But I had proposed a charade to this spell-cooking termagant. Why did the witch insist on the ceremony? There were more treacheries in the world than I had known. Yet I stood with my bundle by her door. The women of the yard were huddling, conspiratorial, in bunches, covering their faces with their hands to shutter and reveal their laughter. And the driver Tom was there with a drink of rum for all the hands— three fingers all around. So the crafty Pélérine Vérité had bound me in the ropes of custom and expectation. Even the cat smirked, a condescending grimace at my expense. So I rolled up my sleeves and sweated to make some lime while Pélérine swept and swept again her yard with her broom of twigs, tracing cryptic signs in the dust. And when I had painted her house and her threshold, I dressed myself in my Sabbath suit, that mostly I wore to funerals. I made a garland of the brown-throated orchids, dripping pollen. I bowed to the woman I had chosen to wed and I gathered her twisted body in my arms. I lifted her with her wretched broom across the whitewashed threshold.

Yet I did not trust her, but greased my ears with pig fat and stuffed rags in my nostrils and up my arse. I lay awake through several nights, watching her carefully whilst Scratch wreaked havoc amongst the mice, to see if she crawled up into her nets on eight legs, or consorted with raw-bone lights, or sneaked out to catch and eat a black dog, or received any tusky, toothy visitor no human would dare to bed. Yet I found her sleep to be sound. She did not snore but breathed as mild and rhythmical as the meekest maid, as calm as Marie-Vierge Herself, her exhalations fruity and sweet. And so I permitted myself to slumber in the knobbly warmth of her body and did warm her with my own body's store of heat. And as night followed night and she fed me well, reserving my tidbits with those of Uncle and Scratch from the family plates, I came to count myself a canny fellow, who had a mind like a knife that cut two ways.

As for JOHN FISH, he learned pity where most of his kind grow complaisant in lust. For comeuppance had I chosen my wife, to foil Dufay's design that I be bred, for she had been burned inside with a poker, and hollowed out. In her belly naught but scar and grief. Yet she had not sewed herself up. John Fish could wriggle in, snubbing gentle against the scars, which he felt as a blind man feels a woman's face to know the lineaments of her passion. Ah! My wife's passion were one with her woe and mine, the sorrow of enslavement. I took her and wept, running the tips of my fingers over the scars on her face, mingling my tears with her own. Thus was tempered the arrogance of my position in the great house. And Pierre Baptiste became in his own eyes the more a man, covertly and perilously, as ever in the yard, though he got along for quite a while as FORTUNE'S GROOM. Ah, but the complaisant amanuensis who had clapped to his bosom a woman reviled as a twisted termagant, incapable of breeding, harbored still in his heart a SECRET VANITY that poisoned his tranquillity with yearning.

The Sage and the Meemie Worm

➜

You have seen for yourself, Kind Reader, Pierre was an educated man, already a CORRESPONDENT, though by proxy, of the great BUFFON. By craft and subterfuge, the slave's safest means to any end, I fancied I worked my way closer to Montbard, where I would make myself so useful and agreeable, Buffon would wonder how he had ever supposed we slaves possessed, not the full flower, but merely the seed of virtue. Yet, save for excursions to the factor in Saint-Domingue, I had never been away from the master's estate. Though I had seen white men in bag wigs with embroidered waistcoats, I had never seen the likes of the prodigal who now returned from France, viz., PAMPHILE, whose foretop was pomaded so high he must carry his hat beneath his arm, whilst on his other arm he wore a ribboned muff such as I had only seen a woman wear, and seen but a woman walk with an umbrella for a stick or wear red shoes, and patches on the face. His effeminacy might have excited rumors he were a sodomite, had not a doctor of physic, a reliable person who had come on the packet with him, given the lie to the rumor Pamphile loved boys, though without putting it completely to rest.

"Now I would not credit rumors touching on the master's son were they bandied in the jakes by perruquinado'd profligates straining over brandy-bloodied stools. Yet I have it from a learned man of sober deportment—a Bible-reading tea-imbiber, whose hair is dressed in a simple queue—*(Squint pats his neck-nape then puffs to light his pipe from a coal)*—our scion has sailed on the breeze of charges—considerable charges! For it seems he seduced a sweet-eyed seamstress, one Toinette, with promises she would be mistress of a great plantation *(a vasty gesture mapping the round-abouts)* which would come to him when his sickly old sire wheezed his last *(Squint, horribly wheezing),* which Pamphile looked to hear off the very next packet *(hand over heart, Squint gazes heaven-ward).*

"When the eminent heir gets his sugar-puss to a shabby room in the moldy inn where he be hiding from his tailor *(Squint cowers),* he bribes the drunken solicitor who greases with him the bed. *(Squint waves off a pest, then pulls at his shoes, leering all around.)* Pamphile locks the door and falls on the girl *(wiggles his toe through a hole in his stocking),* skewing her nose with his knuckles, opening cuts around the eyes which had not yet healed, as you see sirs, though <u>she rubbed them with ash to keep them open.</u> *(Squint digs knuckles into an eye-socket.)* Ha!

"The heir had ripped her petticoat—'very new, of very good stuff, and the crewel work from my own hands' *(Squint squeaking)*—ripped her bodice, ripped her chemise to tiny bits. Tsk! Tsk! Tsk! How could she 'scape, him? Was she to go naked in a poor, rough street of cut-purse lurkers and randy oglers? He had already let down his falls and stood with the ram aimed at the citadel door and the priest-hole behind. *(Squint threatens toward his falls.)* 'Nay, the warcraft is antique, yet so he said, sirs, "citadel door and priest-hole behind."' And what could she, poor citadel, do? He tied her to the bed, then stuffed his cheesy stocking in her mouth. *(Squint swives the air with his foot.)* He would remove the gag but to ply her with sugared rum, doctored with poppy and mandrigore, which so addled her wits and sapped her will, she scarce knew what she said or did, good sirs.*(Squint with hand on brow feigns a swoon.)* She had not the strength of a feather blown in the air *(fwoooo! Squint blows)* above a night-night pillow when the candle be puffed out.

"She had not been given dinner, only marzipan jumballs in the shape of numbers, which he forced down her throat so she would drop sugar, which he would eat so he could make numbers from the music of the spheres, as Pythagoras had *(Squint, squeaking the while).* 'Nay, his very words, sirs: "Pythagoras," though he said so with his eyebrow raised.'

"He wanted her to hear the music, too, and pulled out the gag to feed her her own sweet turds with his sticky hands. 'None of your foolish dungy-mups, sir.' No drug would make her so forget herself she would eat her own turds. If she would not, said Pamphile, she was a bad girl; he must beat her with his riding whip.

"'And God in Heaven knows, I never expected he would,' yet he did, she said, until she passed out from pain. 'And my back is all scars, and who wants to look on me now? Who will marry me?'

"Not the eminent heir! The linen was nasty now *(Squint petulant).* He had no unsullied spot to take his ease. So he shrugged his shoulders—so she swore—and left her tied for the inn-keep to find, or the drunken solicitor, or his tailor come knocking with a bill.

"'Mayhap he supposed she were dead,' said the doctor. 'An account of most appalling depravity'—his very words. Tom retails it for the moral, my buckos, the moral."

In the yard we had our own tales of the EMINENT HEIR. 'Twas rumored his fish would not swim had it not first supped on the spectacle of a woman's bloody back. 'Twas further rumored he fasted on cow- and pig-shaped jumballs all the days of Lent then dropped marzipan into the mouths of his father's house girls, whom he had dressed as nuns, which they had never seen (though Pierre had seen them in engravings in books), so they thought, poor girls, he had dressed them as vultures. And these pleasures Pamphile could enjoy without fear of reprisal in the shadow of the sword of Michel, patron saint of our plantation isle. His father had whipped his heir when he was young; now the elder had no recourse but to Reason, for Pamphile was larger than he, and stronger. And M'sieu could not permit his heir be disciplined by his slaves, nor suffer his being handed to the militia. So M'sieu drank more rum than before, and smiled in his cups—*all's well, all's well*. And Pamphile mollified his father with a first-hand account of the great BUFFON.

'Twere well-nigh impossible to credit the notion the rogue Pamphile had been invited to visit at his country estate the philosophe who had translated Newton into French. Then again, two watches bulged the fob pocket of Pamphile's breeches, which watches kept the time in the physical and metaphysical realms, of numbers and music, respectively, which watches, moreover, Pamphile consulted with an ostentatious frequency, pursing his lips so knowingly that even his father, who had read so many books, credited him with having learned, in France, something of the new philosophy, though he be too great a dolt to learn it well. Yet if Pamphile could make no credible pretense to learning, he could make a great one to posturing. For this capacity, mayhap, to present himself as an ornament, a human ormolu, or exotic plume, Pierre had inveigled himself, by preening and flattering, into the graces of the Sage of Montbard.

BUFFON, Pamphile recounted, was of less than average height, though erect and muscular, pompous and deliberate in manner, with bright white hair daily set in the crimpety, old-fashioned style by an all-too-confiding dresser, who retailed most

scandalous accounts of lust & vanity & diverse medleys of wickedness, whilst Buffon laughed in a hearty yet supercilious manner,
his eyes popping like the eyes of a glutton who has spied an enormous roast.

"Do not picture him hunched as a scrivener over embryonic
conceptions while the sun is climbing the sky"—here Pierre Baptiste cringes—"for he carries his notions in his head till he has got
them fully fleshed"—here Pierre of the conjure house puffs himself up—"taking endless solitary turns along the fragrant paths of
his garden, attired in a sumptuous dressing gown of yellow-and-
white-striped stuff sprigged with the most exquisite blue flowers.
(I have tried to have the work copied but 'twas too complex for
the blind old whores who would trust me to pay.) Swaggering with
his walking stick, our bold philosophe treads the mazy paths
'twixt his manicured beds, his hand on his hip, like so, regarding
from the superb vantage of eighty thousand a year the shabby,
sprawling jungle of flora and fauna that writhes and struggles outside his hedge. And daintily adjusting his sleeve ruffles, he com-
poses his variations, dictating at intervals in perfect periods to his
ever-patient secretary.

"He will not suffer anyone to beard him, in the musing, preoccupied hours of strolling and dictating, strolling and dictating,
but waits 'til dinner to enjoy the company of his guests, who are
dying of ennui, you may be sure. His horses are tame; no one he
invites plays dice or cards or wagers even in jest. What a yawn!
Précieuses and sycophantes mincing from chair to chair, trying
their wit whilst sucking their snuff—he is the great cock among
these hens, I swear.

"Into the room of gold and blue where his guests are sitting on
the edges of their chairs, he makes a slow, grand entrance, a glid-
ing sarabande. And lo, wasting not the time to call a servant, turns
to close the door himself with discreet and delicate flourish, then
turns to greet the assembly of twits.

"To those who attend his every word as grain-starved fowl some kernels of corn in the dust, he most graciously avows, 'Today have I composed some passages of the most sublime elegance,' winding his side curls around his little finger.

"Then does he read his draft to his guests, now squinting close to the page, now declaiming from memory, taking scrupulous note of the angle at which the meanest serving wench holds her ear to listen"—here Pierre winces at Pamphile's tone of cynical badinage—"even once asking the opinion of a dog, thereby much putting out the tail-wagging *abbé* who dogs him." (Here Pamphile snickers in his green-gold sleeve.)

Pierre would have wagged his tail as Buffon's dog, his dogged anonymous secretary, eyeing from the shadows the long-waisted pink and yellow dowagers primly packing their cheeks with snuff as the great man paces, a noble actor turning and turning to display his best-made side.

"It is well known," Buffon declares, "that in the matter of testimony by witnesses the assertion of two possible witnesses to the effect that they have seen something constitutes completely acceptable proof, whereas the testimony of a thousand or ten thousand negative witnesses, who merely assert that they have not seen something, suffices only to produce a slight doubt."

Pierre yearns to be present, to cry "Astonishing! Wonderful! Quintessentially marvelous!" He might dare suggest the great one refine a point, invert a phrase, to more vivid effect. In this way he would assert his superiority to his station, while flattering the sage.

My hopes were of a mythy ASCENT, like a god in a chair in a tragedy, such a divinity as one sees in the frontispiece of "Chloëthon," rising to a heaven occupied by Buffon and his correspondents, where conversation be an engaging and dramatic alternation of repartée and tirades, such as might have been written for ideal nobles of noble ideals, illustri unmoved by rude considerations, viz., lust & greed & gluttony, who desire only to increase the stock of knowledge and beauty in the world.

Would I not make a more elegant sycophant than the bald, lame Abbé Bexon, hobbling behind the great one, bobbing his fat round head, whining and begging "to be the one allowed to assert, before all others, my conviction before almighty God the present Author were a greater master of rhetoric and substance than any man who had ever lived, unless the King should turn his hand," & cetera? Fie on such fooforal unctions! Consider with what dignified courtesy I would have removed the great one's napkin from his neck, looking for the moment to mention my own shadow histoire, the people's accounts of Guinée, of transportation, & of bondage, the acounts stored in the conjure chest in the memory house, so all that was lost in field and yard be preserved. For my contribution to the completeness of knowledge, might I not look to be promoted, from napkin-tucker, to scribe, to secretary, to under-savant, to savant, to philosophe, to auteur, with no duties to perform but to think? So I was wont to lose myself in reverie, standing behind my master's chair with his napkin over my arm.

And so my Vérité found herself saddled with a useless SAVANT, who did not maintain the thatch or hoe yams or set snare for finch, except as badgered by Jean-François and by Squint, yet who ate from her bowls and beseeched her to drape around his neck, before he supped, the scrap of sacking that was his napkin, to stand behind him as he ate and wait on him, so his manners would gentle.

"Bare. Bare. Look down his nose at lice in our hair. With so much puff in him, how can he walk on the ground? Brass-buttons! Lace cravats! Will fancy-mince roll me in flour? Off to the tailor's, he says. Stand when I enter the room, he says. I sweat eau de mille fleurs; never step out of my chamber unless in my periwig; in the privy, drop roses of sugar."

Yet when Pélérine discovered an itch in her savant's side, an infection of the hideous MEEMIE-WORM, which afflicted the green boys from the tanks, she patiently dug out its head with a knife, having pacified Pierre with rum steeped in a bitterwood cup—Quassi's tea, that did poison the worm. She nailed its cursed head to a twig and twisted the twig a number of times each day, for several days, wrapping the worm around it, until the nasty creature was pulled from its suppurating burrow under my skin. She spat tobacco juice on the wound to purify it, then dropped the worm in boiling water, to murder it body and soul. She unrolled its corpse to a grim, ghastly length of four feet, dried it, chopped it, and pounded it to dust. She wrapped a pinch of this dust in a shred of cloth from an old satin coat of M'sieu's, with lime, & lye, & a vulture's eye, & a worm made of sugar, that looked as my meemish persecutor had looked, and placed this packet in my talisman pouch, to protect me from the meemie worms, the revenge of Guinée for SWOLLEN PRIDE.

Later she dug up a paddle, carved in the shape of a turtle with the face of a man, she had buried under her bed, so no one would find it who searched her house for juju tricks. Rubbing the belly of the turtle with a small, flat stone, she sang in a low, sweet voice a song I had not heard before:

N'go-la-la ha-i-né
B'wa pa-d'ma ha-i-né
N'go la n'd'ha-i-né

This was a song in his tongue she had learn't from a frail old man on Ravenal's place, who had not enough words in the common speech to translate. Yet the strength of the words were an amulet that exerted its power from mystery. Always, if a person who sang this song rubbed the stone against the belly of the man-headed turtle, in the way the rubbing had always been done, lights appeared in the branches of the trees. Just so, the peaceful dead emerged from the sea, the shadow the past would cast on the future. When she saw these lights—and truly they came, for I saw them myself—she shook a gourd she kept hidden under her skirts. Squatting in the light of the cooking fire, she slowly tilted the gourd. From a hole near its top there rolled onto the ground the cowries with which she divined, and falling silent among them, the fragile dry body of a horned beetle, yet without his horns.

When she saw the precise manner in which that headless, hornless bug had fallen amongst the shells, she started, and shivered, and gazed at me sideways, and shook her head.

"Visitor up from the region of forgetting. Don't ask! Among open mouths he shakes down darkness. You suck an orange, fool of wrong wind. Tragedy is high game. How many nipples and how many toes? Sugar fire burn his clothes off, invisible his bones. Visitor. No mouth knows his name. Visitor! Shhhhh!"

One by one she dropped the cowries back into the gourd, but the beetle she left on the ground, only drawing a circle around it. She would not say what she had seen, but busied herself hiding the wooden turtle, which was the paddle we used to start the rafts of the dead out to sea. Then she took some yams we had been saving to break our fast and laid them before the hungry lights in the trees. Ever after, did I mention Buffon or my shadow histoire, she shook her head. Did I look to the day when my fidelity had earned my freedom, or muse on the house in an orange grove I would dwell in then, she chuckled grimly.

For my part, I took the lights in the trees for the torches of maroons, whom chance had brought from some other isle to see what they could steal, yet I was discomfited by my wife's prophetic intimations, which had hatched in my innards a brood of doubts which did consume me under my skin.

Yet I often woke at night to find she watched me as I slept; she would stroke my brow and rub my shoulders, soothing me to slumber, as if I had been a child. Did I but pass my hand across my brow, she hastened to brew me Quassi's tea. And I saw she meant me very well. Her twisted body spoke a word of my godmothers' alphabet, spelling "tenderness" in their tongue. In time she unfolded HER TALE.

When she had been a gay, quick girl, her old master, Ravenal, of Saint-Hildebert, had taken her across the sea to be schooled as a cook, both ordinary and fine, and moreover as a sugar baker, to construct subtleties of almond paste mixed with rice, & scented waters, & various gums. And in the tangible closeness of travel he had taken her into his bed, hedging the expense of finding her. Once in Paris she had a cap with kissing strings and patched her face and went arm-in-arm with her master. She had an apron of lace as finely made as the greatest lady's, and rosettes on her shoes as large. She talked freely with all and soon surmised that under the laws she could not be held in bondage inside France. Yet rather than fleeing she told Ravenal she would fain take leave to seek her fortune. Whereupon he fell to his knees and wrung his hands in her apron and wet her petticoat with his tears, begging her not to desert him, rolling his eyes most piteously. He was accustomed to her presence, he allowed, weeping copiously, besotted with passion, said he, pawing the muff she wore on her sleeve, moreover most bitterly mindful he had spent a fortune in training her to bake gilt sugar pies filled with live frogs that he might shew our islands as refined in the use of our own products and their subsequent manufactures, as any capital of Europe. She owed him a successor, that she must train from among her fellows; when she had indulged him thus, he would release her with perfervid gladness. And this most sweet and reasonable entreaty did sway her. Moreover she pitied his pock-marked face, which the white girls mocked behind their fans.

Vérité returned with Ravenal to Saint-Hildebert. There she taught the people, not only spectacle, viz., a sugar stag that bleeds claret when its side is pierced, though she had never seen a stag, but delectations to tease Ravenal's palate. She confided the rule for peppercorn paté, for tarragon sauce & for duck's-foot pudding, and later gave herself over to please a certain sugary little wife, who had very black teeth, and coughed up blood, and was rumored to have been sent on the packet boat, in the hold with some hounds. And Vérité taught that drab the use of sesame seeds & red pepper, that she might please her husband. Yet despite all Vérité's most pleasant compliance, when she went to her master to remind him of his promise to free her, averring she had fulfilled her part of the bargain most richly, he chuckled in his sleeve ruffle. "Now," he said, "we are home."

"Toad eye in his stew! And droppings of birds in the bread dough! His I spoil and his and spoil! And the little blue shoes of his little blue wife!"

Still faithless Ravenal bade Vérité come to his bed. Though she cursed and reviled him, he did but chortle and slap her, the heat of his temper increasing the heat of his passion. He tied her and took her like an animal, from the rear. He tore her gowns from spite and gave her uncouth smocks of coarse stuff that barely covered her knees. She fled into a swamp to be chased by plashing, barking hounds; shivering in the water, she betrayed herself with a sneeze and was driven home on a lead like an unruly horse he would break to his will. She began lifting her smock above her head in every corner, giving herself freely to the newest hands, desperate, sad men who did not speak a language she knew and gnashed their teeth in their sleep.

"Suffer them—on me. Let them crawl from the holds and jump for meat. Alas! Too high! Hung too long and covered with flies born from what crawls in the flesh. And who will have the bones, the bones, who will have the bones?"

When she gave birth, she smothered the babe as soon as she had bitten through the cord. She trussed its arms and legs tight and snug, and she stuffed it with sausage and leek, with plenty of lardons under the skin and a bitter manchineel apple in its mouth. And she entrusted it to no-one but turned it on the spit herself, in the middle of the night, when all the household were in bed. And when the skin was crackling and crisp, she set the roast on the bottom crust of a sugar pie-shell, with roasted finches all around. And when the top crust was nearly baked, she released under its dome forty-eight live finches, and baked them in. And she showed it herself before her master's company table, raising the platter high above her head and smiling when the guests praised the flight of singing birds that soared above their silent brothers. Then she cut the pie to nice bits and set the platter down in front of her master and his ringleted wife with a sauce of saffron and clove.

"So, Mistress, eat! I have already tasted."

But the lady saw a little hand, and she began to moan and pray. And the master heaved upon the table, though the provenance of the roasted meat was obscured in the brown of its crispy coat. Were it her master's brat the cook would not say, yet though Ravenal seized the whip from his overseer and flogged her himself till her flesh hung in strips from her back. *She would not say whose the babe,* though with his own hands he rubbed her with salt till she fainted. *Would not say whose babe* though he rolled her in molasses and dusted her with golden pollen he had bidden the people, under pain of lashing, shake on her from those cursed orchids. *Would not say* though he tied her arms around a rail and hung her in the sun, sticky and wounded and gleaming, to be tortured by the feet and mouths of ants.

She was guarded by several half-shamed ragged little whites of the militia and some zealous house yellows hissing and taunting her for the privileges she had previously claimed. Ravenal gave orders to leave her hanging while the sun crossed the sky and slipped into the ocean. Unless she say whose the babe, she would be given no food or drink.

And her guards knew she never would say and did not like these duties, for they feared the smell of her blood would bring rats and dogs and pigs and vultures, and they would have to fight them off. For the master had fancied the girl; though he be angry he would not want her body gnawed. Oh, he should have paid them more, for what they had to do. They sent one of their number to petition for rum and said they would leave their posts if they did not get all they wanted. They swore they drank to keep themselves awake, then passed out one by one; soon they were all asleep.

When clouds veiled the moon, some Xuacomac crept past the dozing guards to fill Vérité's mouth with sweet, fresh water and to press healing leaves on her wounds. And these solicitous friends cut the ropes that held her body and lowered her to the ground, where they made a ring of white pebbles around her, to keep the insects away. They prodded her awake to show her their sign, a peg driven into the ground, its upper end wedged into a split twig to form a tall triangle. She must make this sign wherever she was and so solicit their protection. Yet though she begged them, they did not take her away. They could not, for they were dead; her time had not yet come. And this began her instruction in the ways of those who serve Uncle God.

When her master found her on the ground in the morning, he whipped her guards, even the white ones.

He pulled her out of the ring of pebbles to draw his smoking iron down one side of her face.

"Now men who see the fine profile will yearn to cosset you as I did, but they will flee from the side that is ugly. You will know what it is to be mocked and scorned."

He forced his sullen servants to tie her arms and legs to pegs. While his iron heated once again to red, he jumped on her arms and legs, driving down hard with the heels of his boots, though— 'midst so many curses a meager blessing—but one of her legs were broke. Then he drove his hot iron up inside her.

"Now are you branded above and below," he said. "Now I will sell you, not for a cook, but for a hand, to some impoverished planter whose kitchen is one rude pot he throws some birds in. Like as not he will work you to death in his rocky fields, for your face is frightful and your limbs are crack-broke. And I will have it cried from the block your womb is spoiled, have it cried right out, though it lower your price."

But when she came on the block, Ravenal's coachman slipped a word to a postilion of our M'sieu, allowing this twisted, barren creature were a trained cook and a baker of subtleties in sugar, worth a very high price, save for Ravenal's wish for revenge. And she could be kept in the kitchen, so her disfigurement would not repulse the guests . . . and think of her gratitude, not to be sold to a pauper . . . and the savings to your M'sieu, the prestige of his table. "Yet I do not wish to deceive; he must have the dishes tasted."

Our M'sieu did suffer a poor client bid her low for him, to flout Ravenal, and bought Vérité for his estate, to boss his kitchen, and bake him jumballs in the shapes of fauna & flora, and kiss his buckled feet.

"The press-down kettle weight the fly-stuck eye the skull they think cover all is grass, is grass, and smoke groan over the paving stones they have vaunted up—HA! I am patience, circle-hawk the coop, the chickens egg-cracked. So be. So. World spider come to us with tongue-twisted gut rope, smoke-red eyes—I will not be daunted down, will not be flaunted round. You cannot come without say-so. Who say so? Me. In my place, chink-spying all the sky say cry, cry, cry that ember in the stubble. Cinder and ash have whited him, but blow a little past his heart, he catch, he catch, and glow red and black. My talk falls one word dropping after another, rain blurring light. *Iroson.* Still all is rain."

Head patted, tears sopped, nose and arse wiped: my entire life I had known but the kindness of women. So many nursing mothers suckling me with their own babes, warmed my marrow with their own bones' warmth, their voices flowing like molasses:

> Ba-wal loo-mah ba-ha-wa loo-a-to
> Ba-wal loo-mah ba-ha-wa ba-lu-ba wa!

Slung by day on the backs of cane-cutting women, by night passed among their huts, a cosseted child had grown to a cosseted man, a Goody who thrived on the careful ministrations of the female sex. Oh la la! So heartily did I believe in the KINDNESS OF WOMEN, I could not be convinced my wife be wicked, even when she told me she had murdered her child, for she had pulled the meemie from my side.

Yet her sleep were troubled with a haunting visitant, viz., the specter of the roasted infant, its flesh falling in hideous cutlets from its ribs. From the mouth of this piteous haunt there issued a whinny, a wail, a bleat, as if it cried out its suffering and laid it at her feet. When she woke up moaning, stuffing her fists in her mouth to stop her groans, I rocked her stiff and sob-wracked body in my arms as an affrighted child, singing her to sleep with her own lullaby:

> Ba-wal loo-mah ba-ha-wa loo-a-to.

Pélérine Vérité—didn't she name herself, then? Before she was mutilated and came to Dufay's, she was called Beauty, a name Ravenal had given as well to one of his cows, so that, to distinguish between the woman and the cow, they called her Beauty-Girl or even Beauty-Strumpet. Yet she was not distinguished from the cow in all respects, for, like cattle, we slaves were branded on the shoulder, and this were true even on Dufay's estate. But only Beauty-Girl Ravenal branded all over her body, as to say it belonged all to him, cow and cow again, though she would not be cowed. Like a baptized sinner, she stepped reborn from her bath in her babe's blood and her own. She would answer only to "Pélérine Vérité." And she crocheted for herself a tucker and neckerchief from cobweb strands, so she covered the neck of her chemise. And she crocheted a pinner with lappets that sat pert and pretty on her head. So they could not prevent her dressing herself dainty and carrying herself with grace, like a lady.

Her murder of her helpless babe I charge to the wretched institution, SLAVERY, which has hideously deformed the natural goodness of so many sons and daughters of Guinée, even as the iron had scarred to a twisted, close-eyed leer one whole side of my Pélérine's face, one whole side of the organ of expression, in which the volatile lips would otherwise curve a full arc and straighten a full line; the full forehead wrinkle; two delicate nostrils expand and contract; and two eyes, the soul's lanterns, flicker and flare, sparkle and again be shuttered. One whole side, full half her expressiveness, seared and ruined! Was my wife to blame for these afflictions? To rape her with a hot iron had been a cruel revenge for the child's death, that had been revenge in turn. Yet though the iron had scarred her pudenda, a sweetness did well up from within her that belied her MISERABLE HISTORY, WHICH, the more I contemplated, the more I distrusted my own good fortune, to work in the big house, so close to the whites.

Though M'sieu had rescued Pélérine, I blamed him for Ravenal's cruelty. M'sieu, too, owned and used a silver iron. To M'sieu's benefit there turned a mill that had crushed whole men, and, yes, our M'sieu had sold their pulp with the rum, and refused to sieve them out, so their grieving widows had no shred to send into the wave. Oh, this same M'sieu, guileless at his easel, filling an outline with chalk or wash, come nightfall joined his friends in revelry, planter among planters, white among whites. Oh then I saw Baron Skull!

His eyes glittered through the master's chiding slits as he gave me for my wedding gift (on the grounds my wife would feed me from the kitchen) not the garden that was customary, but a cast-off hat, only a little frayed at the edges, & breeches, & a coat, which would have lent more dignity to my new estate had they been furnished with buttons or laces.

Yet I disguised my resentment as a servant must. I bore myself with the stolid mien that was meet for my station. As I could stand so quiet with my back to a wall for so many hours, waiting to change the plates or trim the wicks, M'sieu did frequently charge me to attend him when his friends assembled. And though I loathed that porcine company of sots, I feigned impassivity, not only to avoid punishment, but to hear of the world, retailed in gossip over cards. And my curiosity regarding the great Buffon, whose prose had so ravished my heart, was richly fed by prodigal Pamphile, who warmed to his father's urging and fleshed out his relation.

Pamphile recounted the various IRON BALLS which BUFFON was rumored to have roasted in his oven, till they were red-hot, to be fondled by a number of blushing girls, with soft hands, who must describe the diverse sensations, of burning and pain, they felt upon handling balls of a number of sizes and compositions, their cries and their exclamations recorded by Bexon, and all so

Buffon might extrapolate from these small iron globes to determine the epoch of the formation of the planets and calculate the cooling time of the terrestrial globe, whether there be truth in Newton's revision of Archbishop Ussher's determination, that Creation had occurred on twenty-sixth October, in the year 4004, before the Christian era, at nine o'clock in the morning. These IRON BALLS put the company in mind of diverse LEWD JESTS, which M'sieu insisted they forebear repeating in the house with a lady present, for his wife had not yet gone to bed.

"Oh, we will not be heard above the pianoforte," Pamphile insisted.

A minuet rushed and mangled did score his point, yet M'sieu demurred, for there had been slurs on the character of a well-born, honest gentleman, namely, Buffon: while it were well known that the balls had been forged and tested, to determine the time they took to cool, it were scurrilous to claim that the test had been made on the hands of girls.

"And were the truth established on their buttocks, then?" cried a fellow.

And M'sieu threw up his hands, and left it to Pamphile to repeat a number of hoary canards, having to do with the character, & behavior, & predilections for diverse spheroid phenomena, of women of various sizes, & shapes, & ages, & degrees of comeliness. To hear this dilation the guests leaned in close, so that Pierre, against the wall, heard but a murmur, punctuated by an occasional guffaw or expostulation, viz.:

"Breasts so large?"

"What did she think was between her legs?"

"How did he train them to bring their daughters? Did they fail to sell 'im their wives?"

"Ten years old? Oh fie! A woman's worth nothing under twelve."

To which last a member of the company rejoined that a woman improved with age, like cheese, but not indefinitely. And another allowed that a seasoned widow, with domestic experience and ten thousand a year, might make an excellent wife, for though the face might wrinkle and the teeth rot, that part of an honorable woman which only a husband sees, remains quite ripe.

"And besides, the bitch is grateful."

M'sieu looked up and raised his eyebrows, looking with his odd round eyes past my countenance to the wall, as was the custom of the whites. Ever the philosophe, he said not a word, but sat with the fingertips of one hand leaning against the fingertips of the other, musing on a point.

Then Pamphile plucked my sleeve.

"And tell me, Goody, are the private parts of the black bitch as durable as those of a white?"

I was very little accustomed to address by a white in any particular that did not command my service. Only from my current vantage is it apparent there had been no reply to his question that preserved me from appearance of trespass. Yet the presumption I must reveal my passions as a dog will lick his testicles, in the presence of those who mock him, enraged me. Between gritted teeth, then, I replied I had not his basis to make the comparison.

"Ooh la, la, la," the company breathed.

Pamphile reddened and raised his hand to strike me, but M'sieu held him.

"My son—" the master chuckled—"you have gone too far with our Goody, to goad him to pert speech, for he is patient and mild, though he will try me—! Will try me—!" He waggled his finger and shook his head, as if reproaching a willful child. "Will marry a wench the world knows be barren—naughty, naughty Goody! Oh, well he knows the parts of a woman be fragile! Yet though he stubbornly flout my wish in the matter of breeding, withal he is docile, and very patient and accurate in his work, for which it cost me to train him, my son—a point to bear in mind when you flare up. I have had this Goody since he was a boy. In all that time, his eye has never flashed rebellion. I would not put down a good dog that bit but once. No more will I see my loyal and useful servant put down, which he must be if you goad him to fight, my son—must be. So for the peace and prosperity of our plantations, I pray you, desist. For even these niggers have feelings."

Cut again by sympathy, though saved from a beating, Pierre gritted his teeth. Moreover, he had been moved to ponder the estate of WOMEN, and particularly of BONDED WOMEN TRANSPORTED FROM GUINÉE. Mind you, he would not inhabit an amazon realm where men waited on women, yet he could not walk by a godmother straining to haul a bucket up from a well. Had the masters no pity for these chattel creatures, their daughters, sisters, nurses, & toss-wenches? Must they be worked as animals and taken as animals, their chastity and modesty of no more account than a cow's?

For all his impudent queries, Pamphile had been nursed at the same breasts as I; he had drunk with his nurses' milk the stories of Guinée, stories as old as the beginning, when the world was a denseness of trees—no fields or pastures or fences or barns or human works of any kind—and from these stories he might have learned a better measure of the sorrows of the world.

NOW IN WILDERNESS DAYS, there were no gardens, for every tree bore sweet-tasting fruit, and the leaves of the plants were tender yet piquant. The very first man was invited for a while to sojourn in those forests that had no paths. He slung his hammock wherever he wished, for the trees were so close together he needed no roof to keep out rain. Day and night, he made up riddles and stories and danced dizzy circles around himself. He sauntered and strolled, all the while chewing, with leaves hanging from his mouth. And the cheeks of the very first woman beside him bulged with fruit. They reached and stooped to eat and napped whenever they liked, and their laughing shook in the leaves of the trees.

Yet not long before they had known only mud, for their mother was the goddess Damzillah, Water-She-Earth-She, lissome and sly, Damzillah, Whom Her brother, the God Uncle, tore apart, smashing Her ribs and ripping them out, then cutting off Her head. He threw Her consort Chenwiyi down into the endless waters that surround the world, where He drowned and was lost.

Oh, that Damzillah was tricky! She was hotter than a rat! She lay with Chenwiyi, Her own son, and from this union—this squalid coupling—children were born in mud, First Man and First Woman, brother and sister. Born in mud, they wallowed in mud, and from their muddy passions descended a taint, their weakness and ours, yet they knew no shame. Indeed, they sported and frolicked and blissfully lolled in the mud, though there was little to eat but bits of root they dug with sticks. Still, they crowned each other with hats of dried, sunbaked mud. They painted each other's bodies with mud. They wallowed and nuzzled and snorted and rutted, yet they did not forget the blood and grief of their mother's death.

As the sun went down each day, First Man and First Woman rained tears into puddles around their feet. With sticks they drew in the mud the outline of their mother's torn, ribless body. They twirled their sticks and made a fire by Her, to keep Her warm, and took turns feeding it until the sun came up. And their piety shamed the God Uncle. He beat His breast and wept.

"Pray, what is a little incest?" He cried. "When I Myself was the father of Her son and indeed, there was no-one but Him for Her to marry? As for these muddy children—orphans, alas! Orphans!"

The God Uncle vowed He would make restitution. He would lead Damzillah's children from the mud to His wilderness realm, where they would enjoy an abundance of food that fell into their hands. He would anoint their foreheads with drops of His holy blood-red semen. Their lives would never end if only they humored Him in one small matter dear to His heart. They were not to pick the red-and-yellow fruit of the en-na-a-na tree, which was the Uncle God's food.

First Man said he would obey, and the woman said she would too, but only the man was telling the truth, for the woman was distracted. A little worm, like a meemie worm, had crawled in her ear from the en-na-a-na tree, where it lived, and oh, it nibbled, nibbled, nibbled! A little curling, insinuating worm, ash-white, like the bones of skeletons bleaching in sunlight. The nibblety gnawing of the worm's tiny teeth made First Woman restless; restlessness made her covetous. She walked about and walked about, eyeing the en-na-a-na tree that was the God Uncle's, yet First Man did not have the wit to worry. The woman was growing bigger, swelling up like a kinkwi melon. The man could see she was discomfited, her body changing her every day, her shoulders carried further back as her belly advanced. He wanted to help her, so he asked what he could do.

"Pray, pick me some of that en-na-a-na fruit," she said.

"Uncle says 'No,'" he said.

She cried so hard then! Oh, didn't she cry! She stamped her feet and screwed up her eyes and wept and screamed and allowed that First Man must be calling on another woman, though there were not other women in the world yet. She sulked so, and bawled so, and pouted so, First Man felt most brought down. He would have done anything to calm that woman. He ran to the en-na-a-na tree and tore off some fruit. He even peeled it for her, digging his fingernails into the smooth red-and-yellow skin. They ate the sweet pink flesh together, then they hid the tattle-tale peels beneath a mound of earth. They brushed leaves over the mound so it was hidden from view.

But Uncle had been sending wind to blow around the man and the woman, to skirl up their secrets. And the wind blew the leaves up from the mound of earth that covered the pile of peels, just lifted the leaves for a moment, but Uncle saw that fresh mound of earth. He sent a stronger wind to blast the mound, and the wind bared a few bright peels—only a few. But the Uncle saw. Oh! Wasn't He a whirlwind of fury! He was in a passion!

He whirled around the woman, twirled and spun around and around her.

"You broke your promise, and you lured the man to break his. Now I'm going to punish you. I'm kicking you out of this wilderness where the trees so kindly furnish your food. You will live in the mud forever now, but without the innocence of children. No more lolling and wallowing! Both of you will know what it is to work hard. You will dig in fields and hunt for food from dawn to dusk. You will crouch for shelter from rain in houses with roofs that leak. You will no longer bear on your foreheads the mark of my holy blood-red semen, so you will no longer live forever, but sicken and die. And you, woman—that baby of yours will hurt you coming out, and all your other babies too. Your life will be one long trail of cries and blood. You will walk behind the man you betrayed, and wait on him, and serve him, and do whatever he wants. You will fall asleep still working, while the man at the end of the day will rest, and smoke his pipe, and sing a song while he taps his fingers on his drum. And this will be true forever."

Then the Uncle went away. Only a small chameleon quivered in the sun where He had been, its color changing from green to the brown of dust. And afterwards, everything was just as the Uncle had said, for First Man and Woman, and for their children. They dug in the mud for roots and looked and looked to find fruit. When they found it, it was not the juicy, fragrant, sweet en-na-a-na, but the small, hard, tart siki-siki, the grief plum. And the siki-siki were all too often wormy. First Man and First Woman sighed and ate around the worms, but so little fruit had been left unspoiled! They were hungry all the time. Their son Ba-Wa was born so hungry he swallowed the fruit worms whole, ugly, squirming, slimy and white—tempter worms, like meemie worms. And Ba-Wa's sister-wife ate them too. And from eating those worms, the brother and sister turned white, like sun-bleached bone, and their hearts turned to bone. And when the two had eaten their fill, Ba-Wa killed more worms, and tied them together, and made a whip, and drove his darker brothers and sisters to work, so his bone-white wife could sit with him, feet up, and smoke a pipe and sing songs and tap her fingers on a drum, as men do.

And ever since Ba-Wa made his worm-whip, the white woman does no work, not even for her man. And the dark woman hoes and seeds the mud and pounds the yams for everyone. And when we are all sleeping under our palm-leaf roofs, and it rains, and the roof leaks, the white woman calls to the dark one, "Come and repair my roof. The fronds are not laid properly, one against another. The rain is trickling in."

The dark woman moves through the rain in the night into the white woman's house. She raises her arms to repair the roof, and the sweet fragrance of her body washes over the hard white bone man lying in his hammock. Memory stirs in him, memory of the days and the nights beneath the en-na-a-na tree. And he groans and reaches for her, and he takes her while his hard, white bone wife listens with her hands over her ears. Hard as she is, she is not hard enough for this. She cannot stand it. She feels in the dark for the worm-whip, and she lashes the dark woman out of her house, out into the mud and the rain and the night. Then the bone woman ties her husband into his hammock with the worm-whip. She rides him, her pelvis clattering against his bone-bone thing, *clacketa, clacketa, clacketa.* She must ride him a long time before he squirts his seed, which does not want to grow in her body. That is why the white children grow harder and harder hearts, each generation harder than the last. Someday soon a stone generation will lie still-born in the cradles. Then the people will be free of BA-WA'S CURSE. And there is the proof, some say, the God Uncle has not forgotten us, Damzillah's children, the children of mud and anger and tears, His own. But meanwhile, the white man is calling the black woman, calling her, calling her, whenever the white woman turns her back. And M'sieu, not so very bad a man, not so very at all, gave birth to a son like Pamphile, who would spit on any story with a god in it.

PAMPHILE mocked all Gods, not only ours. He were no disinterested atheist, but styled himself GOD'S SUPERIOR though he would not write pamphlets or give sermons or make any public cause. He had determined to do what he pleased, on the grounds that religion be a bore, conscience be a plague, morality & duty be torture. If there be any God, opined the eminent heir, this Deity be a workman tinkering with the mechanism that drives the engine; an ingenious hurdy-gurdy man building then winding up a music box, letting it play down while humans, poor enchained apes, caper and jig. Belike this God pays no attention to the peccadilloes of Pamphile, opined the eminent heir. So let him have one girl squat on his rod while he chewed the beard of another, the more girls the better, and boys, as long as the frolic-jades were sweet and clean.

And why, Pamphile asked, did his father fear God? Precious de Buffon's philosophy showed the world had formed, not all at once, but over time, expatiated the eminent heir, ever cooling and degenerating. And Buffon might have taken back all his degenerative heresy when pressed by bullies in well-powdered wigs, hinting. He was a hypocrite, as they all were, all the careful old men frightened—still!—by the fates of Galileo and Bacon. The old men wrote letters and debated truth and published CONSID-ERED VIEWS and VAST COLLATIONS OF ALL THAT BE KNOWN but only within bounds of prudence, with pusillanimous prefaces, so as not to affront the priests, that the careful old philosophers might keep their estates and their fortunes and not be burned at the stake or broken on the wheel or confined to prison, where their teeth would rot and their bones be mildewed.

But let us not, Kind Reader, dignify any further the drunken slanders of Pamphile. Let us anatomize his religion, if we can call it such.

Pamphile's Pythagorean Deity had been degraded to the status of ITINERANT MUSICIAN, the music of the spheres to mechanical plinking of pins on a drum, whose timbres the ever more cynical Son of Land and Negroes reveled in, as a curiosity, yet for which he owed no more gratitude or reverence than had God thrown on the ground before Pamphile some pence he might pick up or leave, coins representing weights and numbers he would turn to music, music he would turn to coins, music refined in the manufacture, as sugar is refined, shat out the arse of a world-devise, a world-organ, mayhap shot out the arse of the Hurdy-Gurdy God Himself—*what time is it? In the physical and the metaphysical realms, what time?*

Yet who could offer proof Pamphile's God be less true than the God of M'sieu, viz., the Christian God served by Père Gouy, or even than Uncle God, whom so many acknowledge to be a God of the Tawnies, a God who came from them to us?

In the yard 'twere whispered Rose had had a Tawny father, and maybe others had had Tawny progenitors. 'Twere whispered that the Uncle God were born from a Worm that did impregnate Itself, then bore through the sky, wiggling and wiggling, till It got to the Moon, where It built Itself a sugar house, "like the Chinese temple on the tea caddy in the pantry." Some said God be a huge woman Whose eyes light the world in the dark and Whose voice rumbles thunder. Some others, God be a blue-black man taller than the tallest tree, Who would redeem us when He walked across the sea from Guinée, though they could not say when that would be. If He were coming from Guinée, He would have come with us, said the skeptics. In these Anduves, God must be a white man, a very big, very hairy one, with a very long beard that curls into clouds just above the earth. When He is angry, His beard darkens. He gavottes in old-style galligaskins, yes, pulls His breeches very high and farts crows out their flapping bottoms. Then storms roll over us, the winds blow down the houses, lightning strikes thieves and liars and shirkers. And God does not sit down again till someone runs for Père Gouy, who sprinkles holy water into the billows. Then God unfastens His falls; He pulls out His huge wormy cock and He pours His seed on the ground, and cane grows.

Pierre Baptiste reserved his judgment upon the ultimate NATURE OF DEITY. Savant that he was, he pondered such questions, his scrap of sacking tucked into the frayed neck of his shirt, while his wife served him dainties snatched from the master's pots. And the tenderness of her care for him undid his toughest, most stoic intentions. For despite the sober calculation of his marriage Pierre had come to CARE FOR HIS WIFE. Breathing in nights sweeter than mangos, he wept as the sun came up, glad he had lived another day. Black or white or tawny, a man is not given a long time to live; the sweetness slips between his fingers as water, he cannot hold it. Sweet life, cruel death! Pierre would never have coveted Master's wife though that one had her bodice laced and unlaced in his presence, while Pierre looked carefully to the ground directly in front of his toes that poked from his wrong-sized hand-me-down shoes. "Remember your human dignity," he murmured under his breath, reproaching her, to no avail, with those immortal words of Voltaire, *"Souviens-toi de ta dignité d'homme."*

I do not deny that I pitied MADAME, nor do I deny I would have helped her, more than she had asked, by breaking her of reading fancy-tales, which habit so addled her wits and so exacerbated her husband's temper. Alas! HER FIERY PASSION FOR FANCY was not to be quenched by any damp advice of mine. Kind Reader, you will recall, I durst not reveal the extent of my own passion for reading. Pierre must stand in the stiff silence of stifled disapprobation upon discovering that Madame had sneaked to the library shelves once again in search of Arcadian idylls. For the dalliance of furbelowed pastoral swains, she neglected her stewardship of house and yard, while she read through and through again the few fanciful tales in our collection. She had exhausted the shepherds and shepherdesses, and all the fairy royalty, and indeed, she had read "Beauty and the Beast" a hundred times. Moreover, she had swapped philosophy from the master's shelves for yearnings and sighs from the shelves of the neighbors, hiding the swaps in her sleeves. Thus, she could sigh for perfect-mannered princes in day's nooks and evening's crannies, leaving M'sieu to mourn lost ethics and vanished cosmogonies, gnashing his teeth and tearing what hair remained on his head, threatening to flog Pierre for thieving or negligence. Indeed, Madame knew little more of any serious subject than the ten-year-old child Pamphile's whispers had linked with Buffon. (How that great man, who bandied sallies with wasp-waisted précieuses, could choose for his consort a stripling child, who lisped her catechism—ah, the best of the whites were goosey, indeed.)

Young Madame did read for gowns and *soirées* and oft dressed up pennywoodens in the costumes of fancy, playing at dolls with the children of the yard; though her teeth were already rotting, she had been but fourteen when wed. She cherished as a gallant brother her stepson Pamphile and wept for joy when he returned from France. Alas, the more beguiled she was by the rake Pamphile, the more she must look with chagrin on whom she had wed.

Madame began to conjure an airy husband more to her liking. She charged the housemaids, gather her bouquets of orchids and announce them delivered at M'sieu's request. Ah well! Who would not be moved by the orchids, with their birdlike shape, "wings" spread to fly, & golden pollen? Alas! The bold appearance of passion was deceptive, for though orchids sprouted everywhere on that isle, they were constrained to cling to trees, to fallen logs, to fence posts and roofs and walls. True, their tangled roots sucked air, but no fluting ballad emerged from the twisted pipes. The blossoms but guzzled dust, bark bits, twiggy motes, seed husks, & insect shells, the nutrition of the slovenly flora.

Madame bade the wenches pull the orchids from their greedy roots, wrap their short stems in ribbon, and throw the bouquets in at the windows, whilst she tittered behind her hand at an airy gallant. Without their roots, the flowers drooped, then wilted fast, their faint sweet fragrance of ginger turned to a putrefescent smell of long-standing water.

Pierre in his library passions had perused enough fancy-tales to fathom her tippety-toed tripping to greet her imagined lover with outstretched hand. In a braver moment, she stretched that hand to Pamphile, though she would not be indulgently used by a rogue accustomed to wenches he could roger with no elaborate cozen. Despite his hauteur, he brooked no ceremony in amours. He stared at Madame most coldly, then very slightly bowed.

"And be you so fond of my person, Madame, you would oblige me in furthering with your husband a certain project I have conceived for bettering my fortune, of tickling the fancy of Parisians with highly bred varieties of orchids, so as to create a feverish market, as for tulips among the Dutch, and indeed all Europe, in my grandfather's day."

And he kissed the back of her hand then, and turned it over, and nuzzled the palm with his lips, and the wrist, and, indeed, the tender inner elbow.

"Dufay does not care for these gaudy blossoms," squealed Madame. "It is I who pin one in my bosom. Oh, my good dear friend, I will be your confidante and hear with joy of your unfolding schemes. Oh, I will take your ambition so to heart you will say you have found a veritable muse of orchids."

"Muse?" Pamphile dropped her arm. "What needs me a muse? Damn me, Woman, I look for allotments and letters of credit; you offer no word in his ear on my behalf but only your hand on mine. It will not do, Mistress Stepmother."

"Pray, find me not 'mother' in any degree, but 'sister,' nay, not sister, but friend of your heart, not friend but—"

"Good day, Good Lady. I am pleased to see you are well," said her gallant, and he bowed again, very slightly and stiffly, and turned on his high red heel.

Then her countenance crumbled, like the surface of water broken by the fall of a leaf. Tears fell and her hands shook and she dropped the pocket she had been working. And the dutiful servant Pierre picked it up. And bowing his head held it out to her. And she snatched it petulantly and retired, with no kind word for Pierre, nor any reward. And flouncing in her chair she stroked the long silken hairs of a small white dog brought with the China trade.

I had been young master's body servant. I was accustomed to order the chaos his carelessness spread in its wake. When he had neglected to latch the gate of the poultry yard, and the fowl trooped into the mansion begging for corn, it was I who had shooed them and quieted the maids. So I bowed to the foolish, miserable woman, and fell on one knee and intoned, "Most Reverend Mistress, your devoted servant attends your smallest wish." And in this as in most other servile remedies, ever I tried on the gullible whites, I was pleased to be effective.

She twirled her ringlets on her finger and left off wiping her eyes on her sleeves; seeing her so gladdened I persevered over time in the custom of kneeling & intoning—never, I hope, lapsing into familiarity, nay, I would never have woo'd a woman so lacking in wit.

Yet my appearance pleased. Reflected in the glasses, I cut a better figure than Pamphile, for mine was not the sag-eyed, red-nosed, tobacco-fogged countenance of a dissipated rummy. My manners were more courteous than the young master's, my temper tighter checked. I do not boast of my virtue in this regard. A slave needs a check on his temper, lest in anger he bite his tongue. This fey young Madame could snap her fingers at a house man as at her dog, and madden him with charges he hold his hands as a reel while she wound her silks on them. Oh, it were best not to frequent her paths, and mostly I did not.

Pierre had never looked to a day when Madame might sidle into his library, tucker spilling from her bodice as stuffing from a torn cushion, her hair wired with orchids, as a nymph's in a pageant. Casting glances over her shoulder, she withdrew from her pocket a folded piece of paper to press into my hand.

"You will know the name of my cavalier," she whispered.

And tittering behind her fan, she squeezed up her hoops to sidle through the door. Behind her the nails of her small white dog clicked and skittered across the polished floor.

Not to attend Madame were surely to offend her. Yet to submit to her wishes, encouraging her distraction, were to invite the wrath of M'sieu, for no man likes to be a CUCKOLD, and certainly not to his BREEDING STOCK. What contempt might I invite from my wife if I submit, what anxiety provoke if I refuse? What divine wrath my wife's might echo I could not divine but feared. Many a time Père Gouy had looked out over his randy goats to warn us slaves, the wages of sin be death, we forget at our peril, the terrible Fathergod ruled in the Anduves.

Ah, what is sin?

The sins are gluttony, pride, avarice, sloth, vanity, envy, & LUST.

Could they all be forgiven for a hundred "mea culpas?"

Oh, and "Hail Marys." For the Mother of God is kinder than God, and God will do all for His Mother, yet She too has Her hand out, boys. Now see what pudding you can snatch for Her from your master's kitchen.

Père Gouy would marry us slaves for a fee, and marry again, even as he baptized. He would have closed the eyes of the dead with coins and married the corpse on the morrow had he been paid. He slept with three fat widows in a sagging bed of string and did not marry one. He prayed for his own soul, he said, and lit many candles.

Hail Mary, full of grace. Were the heat and stench of hell worse than those of a boiling house? The devil could be no crueler than an overseer forcing a boiler dip his thumb and forefinger into a bubbling gravy to test if the sugar that stuck 'tween his digits would spin to crystalling thread—thinner than a hair. And narrower than the finest sugar thread the bridge to paradise, said the priest. All those sinners who fall into the chasm it spans must burn forever. *Hail Mary, Hail Mary, Hail Mary.*

The boiler who suffered the bridge of sugar was a man much taken into confidence, a man with extra rations of bacon & rum & cloth for an extra suit of clothes. For these perquisites he toiled in sweat-stained shifts, ladling the scalding juice from copper to smaller, hotter copper, tempering with lime to make the crystals come, yet not too fast. For bacon & rum & cloth, his eyes were fogged with steam and burned, his faculties stewed with heat. Did sugar splatter him, it stuck like birdlime. For bacon & rum & cotton cloth, he cried out in agony begging to be saved, yes, he begged to be taken across the bridge to paradise, to the table under the tree of life where all sit down to eat, without distinction, nor order of precedence. But he was not saved. He only writhed and begged where he was, and did the shimmy-shake, and his masters got a pound of muscovado, cured.

Never mind, said Squint. There would be Judgment, said Squint. Though he it may have been who forced the boiler dip his hand in the gravy, he claimed he but fulfilled the terms of his indenture, and profited not. So he looked up to night's starry vault whence he descried four horsemen bearing down on earth from the cardinal points. With confidence he descried the great glittering horn held up to the glittering lips of the Lord and heard the horn winding the call to Judgment. For what had a righteous man to fear who did his work with his hands but kept for his God his soul? So said Squint. Yet he slept on a strong-roped bed well off the ground where scorpions lurked and roamed. And he had whipped Jean-François for claiming a revelation of Apocalypse in which all who carried out the wishes of the whites were damned along with their masters. Nay, then, Squint would not be smeared with the amorous treason of his erstwhile client PIERRE, the same who had refused to beget children for whom Squint could extract a percentage at the block. Even my godmothers would look on me askance, for courting a demented twit and betraying my wife—indeed, I knew not where to turn for help. Flight was my safest and only course. Yet how was I to devise MY ESCAPE?

On the eve of the fateful tryst, while the moon climbed in the sky, I dallied. I had feigned sickness, and so had not gone to the ledger desk, but lay in my hammock, tossing and turning, considering my prospects. When the moon sailed full overhead, I must repair to the little-used ballroom where Second Madame's missive had enjoined me await her, there to pace beneath sconces furred with mold until she sallied forth in her riding clothes, her face a well-powdered mask in the moonlight, her wig white snakes, stuck high on her cheekbone a patch like a spider.

I threw myself at her feet to entreat her mercy. Yet I could not refuse her favors, nor would it be meet to remind her, she did herself a great wrong, in pitching herself to one so beneath her in station.

"There has been perplexion, Mistress Madame; I have not been able to learn the name of your cavalier, so I have been unable to deliver your letter to the honored recipient for whom it was intended."

"Can you not read?"

"But poorly," I insisted. "And only the estate books. Nor did I wish to trespass by reading the correspondence of my betters."

"Why do you suppose the letter was unsealed?"

She snatched the missive from me and brought it close to her face in the luminous dimness and made as if to read aloud:

"My gallant prince, disguised as a beast, covered with a dusky pelt, who though his lips curl above long, sharp teeth and his eyes, the soul's windows, are glazed with an animal luster, yet does there shine from them, as a candle that lights up a vast, dark room, a soul as noble as the soul of the greatest lord that ever trod on earth. From his graceful, restrained deportment, the pretty speeches he bestows upon a lady, and his glances that mingle passion & modesty, a great cavalier goes under a spell disguised as a toad."

She would never let the adverse opinion of persons of merit stand in her way, but looked to make a noble & generous gift of herself to the worthiest suitor any lady had ever been privileged to be courted by, & cetera, & cetera, & cetera, with many fine expressions of sentiment cribbed from various florid scribblers.

Now whatever responsibility I bore for glances mixt with passion, I accepted none for disguise as a toad, nor did I care for such locutions as "animal luster." Yet circumstances did not permit the bandying of points.

"Mistress Madame, I am unworthy of the privilege you bestow in reading this lyric aloud in my presence. I most humbly beg your indulgence. Not knowing the name of your cavalier, I have not been able to deliver your missive, for I could not inquire of the gentlemen around without compromising your honor, Mistress Madame. Oh, I entreat you—whip me or mete out any harsh punishment I have deserved, for I am a bumbler. I am a dolt."

"Oh, gentle, gentle woolly-head, My Goody," she crooned. "Great-hearted ebon soul! Oh, noble prince in the homely hide of an orangutan lout, oh, I shall kiss you and—"

"Is your cavalier then your stepson Pamphile? That winsome courtier—"

"Kiss you again so that—"

"Mayhap the captain, the eloquent Squint, whose prophecies and tales—"

"—and draw back a little, so you may doff the disfiguring disguise—"

"—Modeste Devere, oh truly a worthy and virtuous soul, or Père Gouy, whose power to absolve—"

"Oh, why are you so stubborn! You must step out of your pelt now and be revealed! There is no time for niceness, Goody. Do as I say!"

"Alas, Madame Mistress, I am incapable of obliging you. Even were my skin like week-old small clothes—"

"Do as I say, Beast. You are Cupid. You cannot fool me!"

"Madame, you mistake yourself. I am poor black Goody, bondsman and scrivener."

"You will not oblige?"

"Madame, I cannot."

"I will tell my husband you have forced yourself on me, and exhibited your member, and tried to club my modesty with it—"

"Oh, Madame, do indeed, apprise your husband of my most egregious derelictions. I deserve both opprobrium and punishment, but only for my loutish ignorance in the matter of your cavalier's identity. Yet say not so, lest you dishonor yourself. Say I disobey and willingly I shall be flogged."

"My husband will indeed have you flogged. The militia will tie your arms and legs to four posts, and winding ropes around the posts, drag them behind four great oxen—"

"Oh, it is only what I have deserved; I will own my stupidity before them all, Mistress Madame! I will mumble my penance from the stocks till I rot in the excrement heaped on me. I only regret that I cannot conjure the name of your cavalier."

"You have killed the god within, Beast. You have smothered him in your wool. You will regret your perfidy. The militiamen will pour red pepper on the instrument you persecute me—"

All this time I had not lifted myself from the ground where I prostrated myself before her, though I caught her booted foot in my hand when she aimed some blows at my head. "I will have you boiled in sugar," she shrieked. "I will have you dunked till you drown. I will have you flogged and flogged again. Oh, Stinger is too good for you! And Four-Post—too good! I will have your sweetmeats pincered from your loins! I will have powder burned in your arse! Boom & splot & splot & boom! Naught but splinter and ingrate shred!"

"All these trials I will gladly and with whole heart endure, for I am callow & stupid & ignorant, not worthy of the trust you have placed in me. There is no punishment too great for an unruly servant who has trespassed as I have. Oh, sell me to the worst master known in this world, to be flogged until my blood runs into my ears and worked, without holiday or sabbath, till I drop with my bill, my worthless flesh nibbled to the bone by rats while I live. Yet I would ask your mercy in one small respect, oh beautiful, saintly princess of Saint-Michel—"

"There is no mercy for a worthless devil who presumes by violence to conquer the modesty—"

"I do not care what you whites with your whips and your chains will do, for I know I deserve to suffer. Yet, before I die I ask that my wife be not made privy—"

"Your wife?"

"Oh, please, do not disclose my worthlessness to her. But if she must know, then do not leave me with her, for her tongue will drive a spear through my heart that is sharper than the heathen one that pierced the side of the Blessed Lord."

"You speak of Him in the same breath as the twisted witch of the kitchen? You call that miserable relict your wife? That slatternly mutterer? Oh, you are a perversion, an abomination. There is no punishment too great for you, not even your wife's tongue-lashing."

And she pointed her bony finger toward the quarter where we slaves dwelt.

"Crawl, Beast!"

Forsooth I crawled through the night till I came to the threshold of the house I had painted for my wife, which gleamed in the moonlight like a marble slab in the graveyard of the masters.

"Here is your worthless dog," cried Second Madame. "Here is the cowardly chameleon who lives in greater fear of your curses than of flogging. Let him soil his breeches till your potions end his worthless life in a wrenching and fluxy ague."

And she kicked me in the reins and walked away, forbearing in her rage to collect from me her missive, which still I held in my hand. I now spelled out its elaborate periods of foofaral prose, for my wife could read but receipts. Yet do not suppose my Pélérine discomfited by what she heard. Kind Reader, I had apprised Pélérine of the mistress's blandishments and the accusations I now anticipated. And Vérité recalled a CURIOUS SUBTLETY that Madame had ordered for a family dinner—a concoction far too elaborate for a private meal—a marzipan bear (though Vérité had never seen a bear) that opened to reveal a prince.

"Oh, let it be a very brown bear," Madame had implored, "and a very fair prince, a gold-haired god with roseate wings sprouting from shapely, creamy shoulders."

Even so! When her mistress kicked me over her threshold, Vérité were in no wise bamboozled. Indeed, she credited not a tittle Second Madame's prevarication, but wept for my peril. I clung to her weeping as my mother must have clung to me when she knew she would be sold, and Vérité stroked my cheeks with her fingers, muttering toward the house:

"Powder your face, you dressmaker's doll, and wait for him plucking your tucker. Will you ply Baron Skull with rum? A dried fish? Will you grant him his papers? Now honey your tongue, Lady Coney. Ask your master to free this slave who has done him devoted service. Give him a brocade waistcoat, a sleek wig. A gun or a dog? Ah, rum! You have the keys, Doll. If the rum should loose your sweetheart's tongue? Skewer it with a needle. Bustle in his face the frame of your hoops. There is the stuff! Ask him to hold your bodkin. Skewer! Skewer! Now you are stitched. 'Husband, he casts his eye on me!' And suspicion hotter than fire burns. The slaveman flees his own roasting. Where can he go? Dog is the world on his track. See, he pants and hides. What is this cooking, cooking smell? Molten sugar, molten money sweats the palms of his hands. Thief! they cry. Then go by the sea where no dog smells the treason of your body. *Iroson*. Go!"

But as she urged on me my flight, I wept the harder, to see in her customarily stoical eyes, both the full and the squint, so many tears. She mopped at the flow with her apron. Then she tied into

her neckerchief my few necessaries, a carved wood comb & a purloined kitchen knife, provisions of biscuit, manioc wrapped in
palm leaf, a shoat's bladder of sweet spring water, & a calabash.
She carefully folded the quilt from our bed, that she had sewed of
slyly pocketed scraps. Most precious of all she gave me, wrapped
in the head cloth she had worn when we married, her divination
shells.

The missive which named an "orchidée brune" Madame's cavalier, Pélérine snatched from my fingers and threw on the coals. As
it caught, the flames were reflected in her good eye, which shone
now with a righteous gaiety. From her pocket she pulled her
sugar-baked poppet dressed in palm frond and cane stalk, feathers pulled through a hole in its chest where its heart would have
been. I knew at once what I had never seen before: it was the
image of M'sieu. Then scraping from the embers the ash of his
wife's letter, she rubbed the face of the doll in them. "Now go!"
she breathed, sprinkling ash into the mouth of my talisman
pouch, ash on the beetle's case, ash on the white feather, ash on
the pumpkin seed, the five maize kernels. Ash on the fish hook,
the garlic skins, the sayings of godmothers and savants. "Go
whilst he cannot see."

With speedy stealth, we repaired to the river's-mouth warehouse from which hogsheads of 'lasses, rum, and sugar were
shipped. With newfound strength in my clerk's hands, I forced the
lock of the cooper's shop. From there we rolled out a tight-
caulked BARREL, not as large as a hogshead, which I painted
with de Buffon's name, having taken for my use in exile, as for
ballast, several sturdy iron tools, viz., a hammer, a chisel, a saw
and an ax. The barrel we upended in a boat, which I rowed out to
sea.

When I had lost sight of land, I clambered into the barrel, perilously swaying in the wave-tossed boat, and, leaning gingerly
over the sea with calabash shell in hand, I bailed the seawater

backward into the boat until I floated free in the bobbling barrel and the boat had sunk beneath me, a laborious & tedious business made the more difficult by the gyring barrel, though fortunately the sea was calm. With the oars he had taken into the barrel, Pierre did his wobbly best to pull away from the trail of bubbles rising from the boat as it sank, as if some creature breathed its last there. And when he had gone quite a way and thought himself quit of the sinking boat, he hacked through his oar handles one by one, with his ax, so he might keep them with him in the barrel when the lid was down. He longed to sleep, yet he feared he would be caught, so he rowed with his stubs of oars all night, only pulling them into his barrel, and his lid down over his head, when the sun poked up from the sea where he had been sleeping in a far better bed than Pierre.

Only one person would fit in a barrel that would rest level in a rowboat; two barrels in two boats might drift apart; and so I left my wife on shore, for I did not wish to risk her life with my own. We believed we would meet soon enough, perhaps at the Jardin du Roi, where I had addressed the barrel and where I trusted—didn't I? Oh, surely I would send for her! Pierre were a man of his word and of words. He would persuade Buffon to hire on the strength of succulent and enticing descriptions, not only of various dishes—her peppercorn paté—oh la!—but of certain mythological SUBTLETIES Pierre had devised, of which Vérité would master the execution. These would scratch the great one's itch for stripling placket. Now in these conceptions, a great God of old, viz., Jupiter or Apollo, has chased with the intent to violate a maiden not above twelve years. The latter has been mercifully transformed to a cow or a tree, and so the God embraces bark or hide to no avail. The fingers of the company at table would accomplish what the God's could not, revealing in laureal or bovine sanctuary the marzipan girl, helpless in the ravagers' hands. And these pandering subtleties we believed to be entirely novel, of an art that none but Vérité possessed. And we prayed that Buffon would covet them—wouldn't he? Covet them for the exclusive prestige of his table, or better yet, keep them on a sideboard, covered with a clean white cloth, until the guests had taken their leave.

Kind Reader, you may wonder, a man of honor, ambitious to make his way, would pander so basely to a base craving. Yet Pierre stood outside the great, bright room where the philosophers remade the world. If the tall doors were latched against the entry of his full-fleshed honor, he would starve it small enough to slide beneath the door, like a hungry mouse, the flexible bones of which give way. The mouse will retake its roundness inside, where it will feast on cake! And beneath the locked doors of the festive chamber, Buffon's salon, two fugitives who were more than hungry, who were terrified of predators, predators even then gaining ground, two fugitives with their stomachs in their mouths wished to slide, and be regaled with cake!

No doubt we were mad with the grief of our parting, and thus we hatched these lunatic SCHEMES that skittered about in our innards, chittering and squeaking. We were desperate to throw ourselves at the feet of a faraway stranger, whom our own M'sieu so revered. Oh, such was our frenzy! Though we knew we must part, our hands did not want to separate. Yet part we must! And so, having professed our mutual devotion to each other, and to our scheme, my wife and I parted, with enough sighs and embraces, despite our haste, to satisfy the reader of any fancy tale, and many satisfying professions of mutual devotion. And these promissory notes alone might have convinced M'sieu, had he been present, my troth be plighted to Vérité, and for my marriage I had deserved a garden, like any other bridegroom in the yard I must vacate for FREEDOM.

Voyage of an Apprentice Savant

→

While the philandering Fire God Whom ancients called Apollo did glister in His knife-wheeled chariot, blood on teeth & cock, I, Pierre, settled into my barrel and pulled the cap down tight above my head, so tight I could lift it but with difficulty from within, where I sat packed in darkness as a magnum in sawdust, praying to be taken for CARGO. I hoped for a tide that would sweep me into the lanes that bore shipping to France, from whence a passing packet's captain, supposing my barrel had rolled off a deck, might salvage me for reward. And if the captain bid his men prize out the cap? I would not dwell on the perils should I be returned; even if caught, I hoped to be sold in a British port to spite the French.

Woe to me if my barrel wash up in the Canaries, I be taken for the sugar plantings there. Better to be pressed for the gang of a ship—no slaver, I prayed. Better, did I touch some populous region of Hispania, work for bread an indentured laborer, nearly free. I did not suppose I might drift to Guinée, for I had examined the maps, finger-hopping estimate. With luck I might float to some stronghold of maroons, thence swoop down to steal Pélérine, both of us live free. Ah, but maroons were ragged scroungers, flee-ing musket balls, I, estate-bred, with a free man's learning and habits. Although I stood charged as a reprobate, I vaunted myself on authorial prospects, so I had staked my hopes on TRANSPORT TO FRANCE AND BUFFON. So great was that worthy's renown, privateers oft honored the labels of crates addressed to him, so I had been told. But set foot on French soil, I should by law be free, if free, make my fortune, and, if fortunate, offer for my wife a price improvident M'sieu could not refuse, most particularly if the offer were conjoined to threats of disclosure.

Upon my arrival in France, then, I proposed to commence my rise forthwith, demonstrating my usefulness as an AMANUEN-SIS. I looked to be articled an apprentice savant, yet though I had arrived in a barrel like a shipment of molasses. Granted, a savant must present a dignified appearance; after a long, crampity sea voyage, my linen would be soiled. Directly upon disembarkation, therefore, I must set up as a scrivener quayside. I did purpose a business on my barrel's very head, where I might scribble bills of lading or copy deeds or wills, bartering for clothes less used than those in which I had arrived. A point in my favor: I wore breeches, however soiled by the master's dribbled snuff, and not merely drawers. If I hid my brand and affected a haughty, cavalier man-ner, I might pass as a very dark creole, a soldier, mayhap, who had preserved the King's claims across the water. Yet my lineaments were the soft ones of a clerk. Moreover I could be undone by an honest response to inquiries after my name, for no free man has but one name; the single appellation is meet for cow or dog. 'Tis true a king is known by his Christian name, but a disheveled voy-ager stepping out of a barrel will not be confused with the King of France. I must get me a SECOND NAME, that followed the first, and not "Dufay's Pierre," if I would rise in the world of savants.

Now some slaves of my acquaintance had taken second names from nostalgia for Guinée. Alas, to contemplate Guinée were to contemplate the past and loss; I looked to future and to gain. Though he had sold my mother, had not Dufay been kind? *Pierre Dufay.* Yes, to compensate his investment in my education, with which I had absconded, I owed him the honor of taking his name. Yet might a zealous bounty hunter kidnap me, taking that name as an address, return me to him from whom I had stolen my person and could now look for punishment. Moreover, the name *Dufay* had been soiled by Master's peculations! Though I had not revealed them, indeed, had concealed them, the blot on his escutcheon had spoiled his coinage to my tooth. Besides, the man had sold my mother! Yet he had saved my wife. Then again: Dufay were revered—by none other than Monsieur de Buffon—for reliably painting avia, flora, & fauna. This glory might reflect on mine. I did not wish to be taken for a quashee pet, but for a worthy man, a man of weight, deserving patronage, promotion, and, indeed, esteem. Holloa! I would proclaim a new allegiance! I would take for my own the name of the sage of Montbard: *BUF-FON. PIERRE BAPTISTE DE BUFFON.* The name had a fine, lofty ring that gave the lie to the cognomen *Goody. Bon-Bon is dead, vive Buffon, Pierre Baptiste de Buffon.*

Would I thrive with the nomen of the grand savant? Or drown in the white man's shadow? I unwrapped my wife's headcloth, which I carried in my bosom. I spilled her shells onto the tiny patches of quilt that covered what there was of barrel bottom between my tools and my feet. I felt with my fingers to see which shells had landed mouth-up: <u>O mouth of mouths, speak!</u> Yet how could they? I had never known the names of the patterns, nor their several services; now they lay silent amongst the tools. I did despair of successful DIVINATION, quite, quite despair.

Then a noisome tickle-foot strolled through the forest of hairs on my face. A louse? A fly? A scorpion? By diameter and circumference of the moving ring of feet, I knew the creature for a spider, familiar of Scratch Cat, familiar of my wife. Oh Spider,

I did importune her silk-speck touchiness, my hands caressing the shells at my feet, I pray you be no poisonous foe in the guise of friend. I pray you disclose my fate as the bearer of my new name. And there whispered in my ear a hissing sound, like the voice of the sea from a cowrie's mouth. *Iroson,* said the voice. It was Pélérine! Speaking from whence I knew not. *Mark you! No one knows,* she murmured, *what lies at the bottom. Your name,* she murmured, *your name you have never known and do not know now,* she murmured. *Your name,* she murmured, *has not yet chosen you.*

"What shall I call myself?"

What you will, she hissed in the voice of the sea that caresses a shore.

"Bon-Bon is dead," I cried. "Here is Pierre Baptiste de Buffon."

No one knows, she hissed. *Iroson: No one knows what lies at the bottom of the sea. Lost at the bottom. No one.*

I saw before me as if present in my keg my Pélérine, embracing the rain barrel in the yard, her cheek laid on the surface of the water, where floated an ashy cork. She sang to the cork, "Ba-wal-loo-mah." She blew on the cork, softly, patiently, entreating it to the harbor of her hand.

Ah Pélérine! Though her speech was broken, yet her spirit was whole. Having once been twisted to the murder of her child, she had learnt how a soul must be true to the good or die more times than lash or fire can impose. How I rued the distinction 'twixt her deep and hard-won knowledge and the frivolous, untried ignorance of Second Madame. How blithely Madame had betrayed the servant who had pitied her, with one careless stroke negating my prospects, destroying my reputation, robbing me of my hearth, my wife, & my friends, exposing me to the direst hazards, mayhap depriving me of life itself. Yet how could I blame her? (I wrapped my cowries in the cloth again.)

I had been betrayed, less by Madame's folly than by my own simplicity. Yes! Attention might have warned me, the simplest acts of kindness, intended but to save the scatterbrained Second Madame from scandal & degradation, were rampant, arrogant presumption in a slave, who must never, never act at his own volition. Now it were fitting for me to be thrown on the mercy of the sea with its capricious tides, hoping to gain some charity through luck. I beat my breast with the palm of my hand, bewailing my foolishness.

In the rumpus of lamentation, the spider jumped off my face. I did not know if she lurked in a cranny or crouched on a stave, yet her presence was everywhere in the stifling barrel, like the hot breath of a deity tickling my neck and knees. I begged her tell me how I might survive, for surely my luck depended on her blessing. "Speak to me," I cried.

There was silence, but the spider walked down my neck and rested in the bosom of my shirt where I kept my cowries.

And then I saw I must throw them again, for the mouths of the shells were the spider's mouth. So again I spilled the cowries onto the quilt beneath my feet, and with my fingers felt to hear the pattern I had cast.

Again I heard the hiss and rush of Vérité's whisper. *From the lie the truth is born. What is known should not be asked. Look forward and backward. Extend your hand as far as it reaches. What is known should not be asked. What you dropped, do not again retrieve.*

"What else?" I cried.

A sloshing spoke, for the caulking had not yet swollen up in the barrel's joints; water was leaking in. Soon the spirits that spoke through the mouths of the shells would drown in sump. So I retrieved them, one by one, till I balanced them all on my thigh. Having dried them on my breeches, I wrapped them once again in the head-cloth and stowed them in my bosom. I must needs take up my calabash, and raise my lid, and bail, now, in the proper direction, viz., from the vessel into the sea.

As I bailed in a rhythm, dip and splash, dip and splash, as regular as a heart-beat, I listened for my name, choosing me, chanting me, yet I heard between the dip and the splash but the expostulations of the finger-wagging butler, Jean-François, hinting about the peril of ogling above his station, thus:

"Did you hear of Guy Montal, the captain at Boucicault's place, who for peeping at his mistress's paps, as she pushed them up in her bodice, was hung by his wrists with tinder lit between his fingers? Guy Montal could have passed for white. And you, fool Goody, you be no captain who manages the labor of an estate, but a tinkering master's experiment, an indulgence who is suffered the appearance of perquisites."

"Pierre looked only at the ground!" I cried. "Oh, speak in my wife's voice, Spider, not in the reproachful tones of a sententious house-man."

But the spider had retreated and nothing replied. The shells were silent in my bosom. Naught did I hear but the dip and splash of bailing. Back and forth went my arm, dip and splash, dip and splash; cutting the time the slap! slap! of waters against my barrel. Back and forth, slap and slap, dip and splash and slap and slap. Still the spider and the cowries were silent. What could I do? I gave myself to bailing with my whole heart and left off seeking to converse with the silence beneath the noise of water and work.

By the time I had dumped the best part of the bilge, I had become dizzy in the glare of Apollo, the glint of Whose golden hair did burn my eyes and stew my wits. I nestled down into my barrel under my soothing lid, and, clutching my dear truncated oars, I closed my eyes, hoping to sleep, yet the waters continued to slap against the sides of my barrel. My mind knew no rest; the engine of ratiocination continued to churn as an infernal mill, run by a wheel, that grinds without cease. And it milled a stream of bitter, bitter retrospections of a highly conditional nature, viz., I wished Second Madame had clamped the jaws of her attention on the horny Squint, so much closer to her station! Alas! He had learnt his lesson in Virginia; he were caution itself with Madame Dufay. Though he might revolve his eyes in his head, to stare at her bosoms, he spoke to her more laconic than her husband. And randy Pamphile? Did not wish to be bothered courting his father's wife. And the hands? Knew enough to keep their eyes on the ground, their mouths shut. Only Goody—alack!—made free, though Pierre will ever swear, 'twere with pity, to assuage Madame's pouts with complaisances. *Talk, talk, talk!*

Was I to be granted no rest, but bludgeoned with blame and reproach when most I needed merciful forgiveness? Now I began to suppose the REMONSTRANCES that tortured me a more terrible visitation. Mayhap the tickle-touch spider were no emissary of my wife nor yet of Jean-François, nor even of Squint, but prowled with malice in every hair of its feet from the realm of GORMILAH, the greedy-guts god-lady commanding the allegiance of the Obangadwon people, like the boiler Beloo, who had taught us to honor Her Fearsomeness & Powerful Strength.

Now Gormilah lives in a very round body, with sixty-four navels and one hundred and eight hands that She walks on as feet when the fancy takes Her, though Her greatest fancy is to sit very still, waiting for the white Gods to doze. If you had met Her, you would not soon forget Her twenty-four tongues in Her twenty-four mouths in Her twenty-four heads, which tongues She rolls out to full length, lures for flies or dogs or men—white men, yes, for She protects the black, but black men too, if they hurt women. Do you know Her? With hands of hair She beckons her prey. *Attention!*

Yet then I heard a more comforting voice, perhaps a ruse to tempt me, yet reassuring all the same, though, as ever, she did scold. 'Twas the old nurse, ROSE, who spoke, saying, "You torment yourself with palaver, heart's son. Alack! Your head is a dry empty gourd with your tongue rattling round as a pebble. Prattle, prattle! You have yourself to blame, for muttering under your breath when you could occupy your days with useful work. Like that poor fellow Granny Nancy conjured, Granny Nancy, worn out from work, who sat before her house, a spindle in one hand, the other out for food, retailing husks of stories for keep—now Granny Nancy knew whereof she spoke."

A long time ago, Nancy told Rose, who told Pierre, who spun the tale in his barrel as now he spins it for you, Kind Reader, a long time ago, then, there lived a HUNTER-MAN named KWAFESI, an ordinary man with but one wife, a man who sat on the ground far from the King when the men met in council. Now one day Kwafesi was walking along a very narrow track through the forest, not far from his garden where he had been digging yams. He was in good spirits; he had a little sling fashioned from some twisted vines, and with his sling he had already shot two finches, killed them with one dart apiece. He was carrying home the birds for stew. He was preening himself as he strutted along his path, which no-one knew about but he, and vaunting himself on the good hunting he always had along it, and singing an expectful stew-song, chuckling and chuckling, his mouth already watering. Oh, he could smell that stew! He could see his wife, SiKwasi, stirring ue-ue berries into it. He could see her slicing in nalima root. He closed his eyes and he breathed in the smell of the stew and FWANG! He stumbled.

"Treacherous, lazy tree root," he grumbled. "Lying across the path." He was all set to kick it. Yet in truth it was no tree root that had tripped him; it was a skull, right in the middle of a bend in the path, with no other bones around it. A human skull!

"Pray, good sir, what business brings you to this bend on my proprietary path?" inquired Kwafesi.

"Good sir, I wish I knew," nattered the skull, clacking its meatless jaws. "La-la-la! One moment, dear sir, I was talking, the next, dear sir, I am here."

Oh, la-la-la indeed! What a tale to preoccupy PIERRE IN HIS BARREL. There he floats, homunculus cogiteur, Seigneur Cogito-Sum, a talking skull! He prattles as one whose wits have lost him, therefore he his wits; so by definition he is witless, and must be acknowledged, by corollary, worthless. Yet all the same, a talking skull is a curiosity, and therefore, a find! There is hope for Pierre. And KWAFESI?

Kwafesi tried to lift the skull from the path, that he might carry it back to its village, but the skull was aghast.

"Please, kind sir! This is my true and right abode. Now would you care to be snatched from your dwelling place, without so much as a by-your-leave? Would you care to be transported as an unwilling object for who knows what purpose? Leave me, sir, I pray! I say leave me! Pray! Put me down at once, sir! At once!"

Kwafesi backed away from the skull, murmuring apologies. It would not do to have the skull cry through the village, like a war-trophy bride, how cruel Kwafesi had abducted the sulky, wretched thing against its will. There was no point taking into his household a talking skull if the skull would not tell entertaining stories and improving proverbs. Besides, Kwafesi did not want to incur the wrath of the undead dead. Who knew how many of those lost souls were skulking roundabout, ready to avenge the honor of this carping skull? Best to humor it, leave it where it was. Yet all the same, it be a find, and he, Kwafesi, be the finder.

Kwafesi mulled and fretted as he walked with his neatly gutted spice finches back to his village; he had lost all interest in stew. A talking skull! Everyone would want to see it. And Kwafesi would not deny them their wish, though he would swear each one to secrecy. From each one he brought to his find, he could ask some favor in return. Oh, he was going to lead one comfortable life from now on!

Yalangawi—now that one had shot a very handsome sipuwaleri bird and was hoarding its long orange tail feathers for a hat. "Like the rays of the sun, my hat will fulgurate, fulgurate," boasted Yalangawi, preening a feather between his thumb and his forefinger. Well now! If Yalangawi wanted to be taken along the secret path to the talking skull, he would have to pay a few orange feathers in toll. His sun would "fulgurate, fulgurate" with skimpier rays.

And Filurawari—her! No more flirting, edging toward the ue-ue bush, then dragging her feet. If she wanted to go along the secret path to the talking skull, she would have to go with Kwafesi under the ue-ue bush. And weren't there ue-ue all along the path to the skull? She would bear his child, he would take her into his household, she would pound yams and help SiKwasi with the roof. He had dreamed of being one of those powerful men who kept two wives—perhaps three, four, ten, twenty, four times twenty. And all of their children. A man with a talking skull could feed a lot of mouths!

A talking skull! Kwafesi told everyone he met! Over and over he told the story. As he told it, the size of the skull grew larger, and its voice louder, until the ordinary prattling skull he had tripped on was as big as his house, its voice as loud as his own when he reproved his wife. Then, as the people Kwafesi told about the skull told their friends, the skull grew larger, still, its voice even louder. First the skull was as big as the olaka-doctor's house, then as big as the King's. Oh it was big! With a voice as loud as a volcano's!

When the King had heard about the skull larger than his house, with a voice as loud as five volcanoes, he was impressed. 'As big as my kingdom!' he said. 'And you say it roars!' he said. 'Oh, most entertaining prospect!'

Now a man was fortunate who could entertain the King. That man would be allowed to sit on a stool when the men gathered in council. He could look down at all those who still sat on the ground. Kwafesi smiled and touched his fingers to his chest.

The King gave the nod to the stool-bearers, and some of them clustered around Kwafesi. And they gently lowered him onto a stool, then picked up the stool and carried Kwafesi, nicely shaded with palm fronds, footing it for him, first along the broad path that everyone took to the gardens, later along the narrow path that only Kwafesi had known. Men with blades went ahead of the King's viewing party, widening the path at Kwafesi's direction. Now everyone would know his path. The hunting would not be as good, to be sure. Yet from now on Kwafesi would be an important man, a finder, a man who directed other men. How sweet his elevation!

As the party proceeded along the path to the bend of the trail where the skull did its talking, the path-clearers and stool-lifters and frond-shaders and professional flatterers were chatting and laughing, boasting and telling stories. And so the time passed quickly; the journey was short. Quite soon they saw the skull, right in the middle of the bend in the path, not quite as large as anyone had hoped, but gleaming and smooth, as if ants had worked all night to clean it for a special occasion. And the stool-men set Kwafesi and the King down with barely a bump apiece, and the King rose from his stool and walked the three steps to the skull with his arm across the shoulder of his fresh-discovered favorite, Kwafesi, so as to hear for himself the torrentially loud and copious clack-talk of the bony jaws.

"I ask you now," said Kwafesi to the skull, "on behalf of this truly great king, tell me, my good, good sir, what are you doing at the bend in my path?"

Several skitter-tits flew chittering up from their branches and settled down again. The flies buzzed and circled and dove. The skull said nothing.

"I most earnestly beg your pardon," said Kwafesi, standing on one foot then the other. "I have failed to make matters clear. As you must needs see, good skull-sir, our King has honored you with a visit. And he would like to hear from your very own mouth exactly and precisely how you came to be talking in the middle of the bend in my proprietary path not far from where this morning I dropped two finches with darts from my sling."

A skink lizard scurried over the skull's face. A glimmeranda butterfly lit on its nose-holes. One of the King's frond-shaders coughed. And the skull?

Silence.

Already Kwafesi suspected betrayal, but he knew not what had occasioned the silence of the skull.

Pierre in his barrel knew, or did he? Homunculus had seen the world contradict itself, turning of a sudden on its axis, invisible but to Cogito-Sum, who apprehended that he had ceased to be at the center, though his apprehension would do him no good. Seigneur Cogito-Sum wished no ill befall Seigneur Kwafesi. He could not and cannot separate the strand of Kwafesi's tale from the strand of his own in the unraveling yarn. Pierre at sea was a man who watched himself in a mirror and found all reversed. He was floating in a sea of reflections that mirrored one another in an endless glimmer of PARADOX, yet, what hurt his heart was not this relentless glimmer; it was the betrayal at the center, where the Gods live, beyond or beneath or inside the play of light. And of this betrayal, Seigneur Cogito-Sum was too choked to speak.

Alas! Poor Kwafesi! They were already murmuring, the path-clearers and stool-bearers and frond-shaders and professional flatterers.

The King was frowning. The butterfly on the nose holes fluttered its wings.

"Please," said Kwafesi, wringing his hands. "I entreat you, good Sir Skull. Let us not shilly-shally, no, nor dilly-dally." He stamped his foot. "Answer at once, as you did before: how came you here to my path."

But the skull remained silent.

With his hand above his heart, fingers fluttering rapidly, Kwafesi bowed his head to the King. "This is how it is with skulls. What can one do? Their eyes have been pecked out, and their wits have rotted away. Your Highness, you are right to glare and stamp your foot. I hold with you: most irritating—Now see here, Skull! Being dead is no excuse for sloth. . . . Great King, wise King, you see what I must endure with Sir Skull—sly—disobedient—deceitful—lazy—cannot be relied upon—"

The frowning King had raised his hand very high, and he brought it down very fast. Two of the strong-armed stool-bearers grabbed Kwafesi's shoulders and pulled him down to the ground, a third one stretched out Kwafesi's neck, and a path-clearer chopped off Kwafesi's head. Then the King was lowered onto his stool. His stool-boys lifted. His frond-men made once again a canopy above the King's most esteemed and, indeed, venerated person. And the King and his follow-boys departed, bobbing and crunching as they walked with Kwafesi's empty stool down the path toward the village where the blood congealed in the fly-blown eyes of Kwafesi's finches, their gutted bellies digesting air. Soon his wife would paint her face with mud and wail.

In the silence at the bend in the path, sun shone on stone and soil. The skull opened its mouth and yawned, then at last in the lazy fullness of warm silence, addressed itself to Kwafesi, asking, "Pray, what business brings you here, good sir?" And the head of Kwafesi replied, "Oh, la-la-la! I wish I knew. One moment talking, the next, dear sir, dear sir, the next I was here."

And this on his own proprietary path! The people called it Kwafesi's Trail, and the hunting was not too bad there, though it was not at all good near the blathering skulls, which everyone walked well around. So it was told, even far across the sea and many years away.

Pierre in his barrel clutched his oars. He leaned his head on them, his eyes closed, his mouth watering. He saw Kwafesi's finches, hanging uneaten. Pierre's stomach cramped and his gorge heaved. How he would have liked to be hiding in the underbrush near Kwafesi's village! He would have waited till nightfall, then he would have sneaked into Kwafesi's house; he would have cut down those finches, grateful that others feared to enter the abode of a man so recently dead, and dead in so unlucky a manner. But Pierre would not have escaped Kwafesi's hungry ghost, hanging around there. It would have entered his body with the flesh of the bird he was roasting over a little fire as far away as he could run. Oh, Pierre might have thought he could escape Kwafesi's fate, but it would have followed him, as men follow their noses to the smell of cooking meat. Oh, indeed, his fate had followed him.

Yes, for talk, mere talk, Pierre floated in the barrel, Cogito-Sum in the wooden head of a dunce who had lost his body, HOMUNCULUS MAROONED on the murderous sea. Yet it might have been worse. He might have had his nose slit, his ears cut off. He might have been flogged to stripes then slipped into an iron yoke fitted with hooks to discourage the rash, swift move; frog-marched and thrown on the ground, his hands and feet cleaved with stakes, his torso impaled on them, a torch held to his feet to burn him up by degrees, with only his head saved to be hoist on a pike through the charred bloody neck lest his fellows think his soul had 'scaped back to Africa, and kill themselves to gain like passage. And what did Cogito-Sum say of that? He says: the pain of cunning appliances can never be the worst; the worst will always be betrayal. For the pike through the neck the driver Squint, who called himself friend, would have rammed himself.

"Oh Goody," Squint whispered in my embarreled ear, "Like a quashee from the tanks you are one great dunce, and greater a dunce than any quashee for they have no privileges, whilst you—fool Goody!—have squandered your perks!"

"Will you lift no finger to save me?"

"What? And ruin myself?"

"Jolicoeur gone, I have no father but you, no protector."

"You betrayed a generous protector," hissed the voice of the master.

"M'sieu! Have you followed? With a patrol?"

"Unto Caesar," Père Gouy sighed, put upon, put upon. "Your body unto Caesar, your soul unto God. Obey and be saved. That is all the religion a slave need know. You, Master Fool's Cap, you ignored the precepts I laid before you, simple as a dish of peas. And nourishing. Yet you waited for pork!" He sighed again.

"Hush now!" scolded old Rose. "You are going to freedom, Goody! Never mind those bright malicious men. You listen to your old Nurse Rose."

Anchor up, mark the bells and say farewell to harbor lights. The circling wings, scavenger beaks. Same water running beneath the slave boat, the free boat. Coils of the sugar still. Rum drips, rain drips, blood drips. The baby is dead.

"No!" cried Pierre, though he saw his wife blowing the cork to the harbor of her hand, and, oh, he would survive and live free. On the lonely wave Pierre rode with a populous company, talking in the barrel of his skull. Finger-wagging chiders abounded; soothing comforters, one or two. And how was Pierre to still the babble and hear his own name speak itself, as his cowry spider urged? And where was his spider? Pierre lifted his barrel-head, and admitted light to his cell, and examined every inch of it. No spider. Perhaps there was none. If no spider, then he had to guide him but his own dead reckoning, though his mute cowries might yet speak through their own mouths—he patted the bundle that lay in his shirt—moreover he had his talisman pouch, though it had never had a voice. He fingered the bag most fondly. Then, alas, to his consternation and distress, he felt on his fingers the tickle-foot, and looked down to see her poking from his very pouch her hairy head, then two hairy legs, though she popped back into the pouch upon hearing the intake of Pierre's breath.

And now Pierre in his great discomfiture dropped his barrel-head overboard and must needs fish it back, with perilous leanings and bendings in his wobbly rudderless craft, an undertaking that so occupied him, he did not look up till he heard a voice cry loud and near, "Aloft lad! Salvage alee!"

And in terror yet in longing, Pierre with trembling hands snapped down above him the soggy barrel-head retrieved in the nick of time. From the bunghole he spied the STURDY BARK that bore down. He heard the luffing of the sails, the snap of the sheets. He heard the muffled chant and curse of the men who hauled up the mainsail, men pressed from gutters and jails, but freer than Pierre. He saw the barefoot ragamuffin swaying in the rigging. And he heard him cry, "'Tis yawing, sir. 'Tis very light, belike. 'Tis very near empty, sir. Belike 'twas tossed when the beef was eat, to clear the deck."

And did Pierre weigh so little, compared to a side of salted beef, a boy whose voice has not yet changed might judge his keg unworthy of salvage? Oh, see the name of the sage writ on the side of the keg, Pierre cried, but he gave no voice to his words, for he dared not court his own discovery. Already the ship were coming about, creaking and flapping and rushing away. And Pierre at the bunghole read her name carved into her taffrail amidst winged women blowing on horns—was it the Resurrection then, the Judgment of Quick and Dead? Would I see my mother and mother's mother?—oh, did these winged seraphs blow for me, these sisters of the angels on the marble houses of the white dead? *Santa Clara*, a Spanee or Portogee ship, her bright sails shining. And behind her, gulls circling and circling, further and further from Pierre. Yet his barrel was not as light as the boy said, for the hammer & the ax & the chisel rested under his feet, and Pierre carried man-weight, so the boy had lied to save him.

"Oh dear spider," cried Pierre. "It is the wrong salvation!" Spider said nothing from within the charmy legacy bag. "Oh messenger of whomever!" pleaded Pierre. "Speak to me! Tell me what I am to make of this dreadful fate, to have been ignored for the kindest of motives."

She would not tell him. Though she spoke from a hundred mouths, she would not or could not advance his knowledge of the fate that had passed him by. Any more than she could or would discover to him the history & customs of his Fombé people. She could or would tell him no more than scores of new hands had, whom he had asked when they came from the tanks to Dufay's. Each one he had asked about the people who had woven the bag, pointing to the bands of darker weaving that were its principle decoration. Yet none among the bondsmen had seen its like. Was Pierre destined to live in ignorance of his lineage?

Yet, when his barrel had been taken to France, and Pierre dwelt among enlightened savants, in the reflected glory of the Sun at the center, what need would he have of the name his mother had been saving for him? What need for tidings of his homeland? What for a stubborn spider who might well be poisonous? Mayhap he had been well advised by Père Gouy, who implored him, wear a cross round his neck, with which, if he were good, and obedient to his master, he would be saved. Overboard with spider and bag!

Nay, Pierre would not jettison spider or bag. His spider could rest as long as she liked among the relicts of Mandilé-Ba's sad journey through unsympathetic hands. It augured well to keep the tickle-foot in the bag! Turn again: if the spider would not tell him of his lineage, then how could she be speaking through the mouths of godmothers, or in the sterner voices of godfathers? Turn yet again: was the spider the emissary of Gormilah, dread companion & intimate of Baron Skull? Why was the spider silent when she was silent, why did she speak when she spake?

UNCERTAINTY chafed at Pierre as he floated upon the brine in his keg, miserably folded in a stifling drift of days, a dank shiver of oceanic nights, yearning to be saved yet leery of discovery. He dare not crack the barrel's top, while the sun shone, to refresh the air, but must close himself in, opening but to bail, or piss or shit, or catch the raindrops in his calabash. Sometimes he feared he would be swamped in the stale wash of RECRIMINATION AND REGRET. Yet each time he slept and woke in the barrel, he pinched his arm and winced with joy that yet he lived. No patrol had come in a boat with nets & clubs & bills. Still he was afloat 'twixt old fate and new.

By night he stood and shook out his legs. He took heart. He had his calabash, his spoon, & his oars; his cowries, his talisman, his tools, his spider. Surely he was a fortunate man! Who might yet breathe deep of land, cheerfully swinging his arms, striding to a desk in a library that stretched from horizon to horizon. He might yet fix eyes on the myriad wonders & terrors abiding in the regions & domains of the world, and hearken to the myriad sounds that give bubble and squeak to the squashed skins of continents floating on puddles in maps.

Yet what was WORLD to Pierre but that bobble-slosh barrel in which he curled? How monotonous the slop beneath and around him! How short his rations, how indeterminate his float! How sodden the quilt beneath his feet! Slosh and more slosh! Sorrowful the lapping sound of the waves, like an infant who sucks from the breast of a mother who has no milk. And Pierre had been brought to this pass by the crackbrained indulgence of a lunatic maggot-mouth whom he had looked to soothe—ah me!

In the despairing and solitary state I was in, I considered, as a man aggrieved by a woman will, the NATURE OF WOMEN. I balanced in one pan the breast-milk tales my godmothers had given me to suck, the meemie-worm cure of the wife whose gift of cowry shells I coddled in my hands; in the other pan I balanced my same dear Vérité's murder of her child; the first Madame's rat-trapping guiles; but heaviest and most baneful, the heartless, arbitrary whim of Second Madame, that had led to my present banishment. And when the benignant pan was down, I heard the sorrowful quivering trill of Marie-Vierge in Père Gouy's church, Her paint all peeled, Whose wooden eyes cried amber tears. Oh angel heart! And when the malignant pan was down, I heard a rending, gnashing sound, the terrible supper of the dam of THE 'RAGO, an omnivorous vermin, that might, said Squint, be running down the ropes of any provisioner that docked, said Squint, looking to sink his teeth into slumbering Quashee.

"She smelled you when you were pulling at the oars of the slaver," Squint might say to a new hand. "Lucky for you, you did not sleep then, but waked all night, gnashing your teeth and plotting revenge. Now you eat your fill of porridge, you do not mind the work so much. You drink your rum and snore. Beware!"

"I sleep in a hammock, like the rest," said the hand.

"Best you sleep alone," hissed Squint.

He bared his yellow stumps of teeth in the flickering firelight, and laid his long Dutch pipe in the ash:

"Now in the darkest and narrowest alleys of Porto Affraia," commenced the shifty-eyed bard, "alleys too dark and narrow even for stand-up whores and small-time thieves, there thrive these small ratty creatures with greasy, ashen coats and greedy big eyes. Now the teeth of these *fragaos* are sharper than scimitars. *(And here he carves the air, as with a curvetted Muslimer sword.)* And with these teeth the 'ragos nibble in the manner of an army, that has not been provisioned or paid, chomp, chomp, chomping its way through some meatlike ranks, carving row after row of crescent-shaped marks, so 'tis said by the poets the 'ragos eat in field of moons. And the people throw in the 'ragos' lairs all the midden of Affraia, rags of flax & muslin & very fine wool *(he pinches the air stingy-like);* worn-out shoes with flopping curled-up toes like those, your prides, M'sieu Pierre *(he bows to me);* cracked ewers; punctured cooking pots; worn-out harnesses; stems & hulls of grain; warped, sea-abraded oars; springy rotten planks. Why I have seen them throw in the stinking carcass of a camel dead for a week! *(Here he digresses to describe the creature, "camel," to men and women, many of whom had been transported by Camel-Packers.)*

"By eating without surcease, and sleeping with their big eyes open, their jaws moving, the 'ragos consume many times their weight each day. They never stop spying out meals; they gobble without a scruple, from earliest infancy. Indeed the young are born with teeth and grab their mothers' paps and chew. While still in the spasm of siblings' breach, she is trying to save herself, dancing and rolling and charging and shaking, her teeth tearing at her young. Sometimes an old mother has but scars for teats!"

Ah me! He did not address an audience inclined to disbelieve a gruesome relation of cruelty! There was the wide-eyed silence of memory and apprehension, broken only by the snap of twigs in the fire.

"Mark you well *(Squint leans in toward the flames, so his bony face shadows and gleams, and he fixes us with a basilisk glare)*, her condition and experience have failed to fan in her miserable bosom the smallest spark of pity for others. Most 'specially she has none for the male of the species—alas! Oh, alas! Smaller than she—who approaches intrepidly his enormous love all eyes and teeth, drawn by the glamorous musk, a heady brew—I tell you it smells like rancid cheese and new-mown hay, like the insides of Prince Goody's shoes and the freshest milk, like a four-day-old fish and a whole field of roses—this musk she sweats to lure him. Mark you, she attends him demurely, as if she did not know she oozed a powerful, gamy enticement, her little wide-eyed face half-masked between her fore-paws *(he holds his hands as a veil to cover his face)*, her steaming buttocks coyly raised *(he hoists his rawbone arse)*, the machine of her jaws moving still *(he chews and chews and chews)*.

"Watch Little Fellow! Watch! Do not run from hiding till her eyes have closed!

"There is his chance, see; her eyes do close for a while *(he brings down his lids, most peaceful-like)*.

"Not much later the blighter concludes he has taken his pleasure in a pinchy spot, for his member has swole up to stick him fast. Hoo! He tugs now more fervently than ever pushee-pullee, but tug as he will, he cannot withdraw, though her eyes are opening *(he rolls up his lids)*, her head is turning.

"Full days after she has eaten him tail and ear, his shrunken member falls from her *(he hunches his shoulders and wiggles in an excess of vulgar delight)*.

"And she SNAPS it up *(here Squint slaps his thigh with startle-awful vigor)*. You shake your heads; you allow she is evil, do you not? Do you not? For indeed she is, she is remorseless wicked, yes? Ah! Yet even she—yes, even she enlarges the stock of blessing in this world. You shake your heads, but wait, now, I implore you. Consider the beggar boys, raggedy spivs who whine and steal and cozen, orphan lads, with nary a settled prospect for bread: They leave off cutting purses to trap the 'rago dams in jars. I know what of I speak, for who do you suppose had got a good fee for devising the jars? No, no, you say, but 'tis true, in Virginia I sequestered one of the jars and perhaps some day I will have it here. But I digress; I digress. Now: when the bait is consumed—the finger of an old glove, a toe-nail paring, a strand of hair will do—the damsels' teeth find no purchase *(he claws at air and affects a pathetic mien, hideous to behold).* Quite soon they are starved stone dead, their little corpses sold to druggists for a very good price *(again he rubs a finger and thumb together).* Now! When the musk is squeezed from the vicious rumps, an exquisite perfume is refined. Ah! It smells like the look of the moonlight falling across the water, yes, a deceptive path a man might drown in, were he fool enough to yield to its beckoning. Ah! I do not recommend it myself. No, I do not recommend it at all. Yet *(he leans in so far his greasy locks are singed in the fire)* 'tis said a seaman mounting a frail whose earlobes have been daubed with this essence will die consumed by the teeth of bliss, and never once think of his home *(he looks back over his shoulder).* 'Tis said a convicted murderer in Porto Affraia was put to death at his own request by a whore wearing *fragao* musk. No, no, you say, but 'tis true, 'twas common report in Virginia *(he throws up his hands).* Come now, come; who would not prefer it to rope or knife?"

No, Quashee said. And yes! And did the white men know this aphrodisiac? And did the maroons know it, and use it to put their traitors to death, and did Squint know it by more than reputation?

"I have told you," he said, knocking the ash from his pipe. "I do not recommend it."

"You have tried it?" asked Quashee, a green hand, oh yes, a new, new boy, who thought he had a liberal driver, the driver, a liberal master.

Tom Squint winked. And some days later did reveal some ancient-looking bottles of foul-smelling stuff he allowed would distract the master from his sketches, did a nubile girl with pointy breasts but smear it over her thighs and under her arms. She might swish her haunches before M'sieu, who might shower her with gold coins, or at least glaze a window for her house, which she would enjoy if the embottled stuff did not kill her first. Despite this threat, girls were set to take the tender, yes, courting death to win release from toil. Squint made sport of them, mocking them with their presumed fate did harm come to their master. "You will be cursed with the stewardship of the swaggering jackanapes, Pamphile. He will hire an agent and flee overseas. Then so much for your coins and your windows."

"We will serve the son and his agent the same as we had the father, and anyone else he sets over us," cried pert Dido.

But Vérité could not abide this rude talk. She bore Dufay no special love, yet she remembered Ravenal. She strode forth boldly and bumped Squint, hard, with her hip, so the bottles flew from his hands, and broke, releasing a smell of rotten eggs & cow's dung & rum that did not charm any men to lascivious thoughts, but made them pinch their noses shut.

And Squint shook his head most sorrowfully. "She has wasted the benefit, buckos, squandered your bliss. Here is one bottle, not broke. If a wench would have it, I will sell for a price she can pay. She need only come with me beneath that tree; when I have done with her, I will close my eyes, so she can snatch the vial, which I would not stoop to give or sell."

But the wenches insisted the stuff was too foul to be good.

Squint said, shrugging, "Maybe it has not fared well in crossing the sea."

Penned in the keg made foul by his own stench, Pierre in his crossing fared ill as a fly adrown in Squint's concoction. His gut cramped when he recalled the bright flames of the fire he had abandoned; his gorge rose into his throat and nose to spoil the taste of his mouth, so he heaved and retched, though he had eaten no food to bring up, only a liverish spittle. He dreamed a cube of pork, a mess of greens, a pungent brew to boil 'em in. Yet NOWHERE WAS DINNER. He surveyed the path of the moonlight falling across the water, and, alas, it conjured no aphrodisiacal bliss, but the ecstasy of buttermilk & bread.

And I fell into a SWOON. I saw Marie Mandilé-Ba cantering toward me, riding side-saddle on a horse with the tail of a fish. And with her Marie-Vierge, Baby Jesuson in Her arms, astride another steed with a billow mane and a tail of foam, galloping, galloping. And riding with them Damzillah the Sea-One that Rose had shown me when I was a babe, holding me aloft in her arms as she walked with me on the shore to quiet my crying, pointing to the waters beyond the breakers, rising and falling, the bosom of a woman dressed in blue who sleeps with a babe at her breast. The babe sucks milk as the mother murmurs of her home in Guinée. Over and over, murmurs of home, till the sucking infant sleeps.

And Rose pushed out on the receding tide for Damzillah's delectation a number of leaf-covered rafts piled with melon quarters and the breast meat of hens she had taken in her apron from the master's table. There were pork rinds, nicely fried, & fried plantains, & coco balls in sugar-cane syrup. And from the sewing room, scraps of velvet and silk to show the Sea-One how we would dress Her if we could.

Rising and falling in my barrel, I rose and fell on the Breast of the Mother of Waters, lulled between Her swelling paps. And She was one with sweet Mandilé-Ba, one with the Mary of amber tears. Was I not a Son of Man? In the arms of the Sea-One I rose and fell; around us Her children who are fish danced and capered, gallimaufry of gambols on the light-struck sea. My eyes were as pearls, that see the world in a haze of gleam, but I formed with my lips the names of the foods on the rafts, manna of memory, melon meat, hen's flesh, pork rind & coco ball. Yet I conjured no true sustenance, but only raised my foul-tasting bile to my mouth.

Pierre might have been the first, the very first old soul. That one lived in the dark alone, said Rose, till one day his belly ached; he puked the world. Indeed, that old soul might have puked Pierre's body, which smelled as foul as a corpse. For all he knew, he was a corpse. When the pitiless noonday sun made the covered keg a fetid prison, Pierre foundered in BLOATED REVERIE; the cap cracked, his eye blinded by ripple glints, he thought his barrel surrounded by grinning skulls, with empty glittering eyes, a vast expanse of death and light, flashing taunts in noon. Hunching back down under the barrel cap for relief, Pierre could barely breathe, the air was so close. Laughter rattled with his heart in his chest. When he had drunk all his fresh WATER, his tongue swole foul in his mouth, as if bumfodder had been stuffed between his teeth. His own breath smelled foul to him, his brain-meat a dainty for Doctor Vulture. His thoughts were bitter, foul, & rank, as he considered what his courtesies, the effulgence of his reasoning, had cost him. To float all stinking & parched & cramped were the cost of the reason that Reason unreasonably dotes on. So much for the white savants, who so reasonably, on such sound economical grounds, have taken the black man in bondage, and worked him to early death, and laid the cruelty off on their stewards! And

the stewards lay the blame on the overseers, overseers dr
and drivers, on Quashee himself.

"White men are ghosts," old Rose said. "That is the secr‹
their dominion."

"Pah! They look like the part of the wound the barber must
bride," said Jean-François, whom the whites called Sénégal.

"The part the maggots eat out," said Vérité-Farouche.

"Whites—death!" swore Quashee, who had not yet learn‹
much language anyone knew, except the language of the Came
Packers who had stolen him from his village.

"Let us waste no words on what is too unspeakable to exist,
murmured pretty Mimette. No one replied. Mimette could bath‹
all she liked. When she crept to our fire, the white men's sweat
glistened on her body like worms, no matter how much she
washed. No one would look her in the eye.

"And what of you, Tom Squint, who are part black yourself?"
cried Dido, who was clever, and lashed for it many a time, though
this time Squint but winked.

"Set a dog to catch a dog," he said.

All these souls might have been punished for Pierre's escape,
their bodies and spirits broken, even Squint's.

Floating in his barrel, oblivious now to the prospect of catchers, Pierre would have traded his own freedom, and all of his
friends', for a drop of water, blessed, sweet water, on his tongue,
which had swollen up so, he could not eat the flesh of the gull he
had caught and torn apart with his hands. Distracted by the
prospect of food, Pierre had let the cap of his barrel float away
while he riveted his gaze on the mangled bird. He clumsily sucked
its blood through his swollen lips and prayed to Steward God, and
only Steward God. What other Deity could be holding sway but a
Deity deaf to supplication, Who created the world, then took His
ease and lay back to watch it heat to fire as it ran, ingenious ingenio, infernal mill? Let the people kill each other with muskets or

staves, let them starve for want of grain, let them pull out each others' tongues with pincers, then again, let them fatten their bodies and their purses, building stout, commodious cities; cultivating orchards & farms; and pursuing every useful art, viz., music & medicine, physics & metaphysics. It is all one to this indifferent God, whom Pierre designates Steward, for He peels a banana and eats it, leaning back on the rear two legs of His chair while the ingenio world, overworked, flares then burns in an awful bright fire like the sun. Or a man drifts on the undrinkable sea to his death, his water all run out, no rain in sight.

"Save me," cried Pierre, and his hand went to his pouch. He stroked it, urging the spider crouched inside come forth and speak. "Save me," croaked Pierre, but only a clicking sound emerged from his throat.

When the SPIDER crawled out, she did so lethargically, as if dazed & hungry & thirsty herself. Pierre made no objection when she dragged her belly to the gull's carcass drying on the edge of the barrel. With her front legs she picked at the leathery flesh to see what dainty remained for her to raise to her tiny, invisible mouth. She was his only companion; he gave thanks for the blessing of her presence. He would not die alone in the watery wilderness spreading around him, clamoring vastness that no voice echoed in, save his own in his head.

Too weak now to rig any shelter against the sun from which his lost barrel head had previously sheltered him, Pierre watched his spider fall from the barrel's rim on a thread she spun from her belly, to land on his breeches' leg. (What vanity now seemed a gentleman's pants!) She crawled to the vicinity of a stave, and hopped thereto, and then to an oar, all the while trailing her line, and making it fast, weaving back and forth, up and down, hither and yon, fashioning a web which had no design that Pierre could see. Mayhap Madame Spider, dazed by the sun, had lost

the pattern. Yet when she had woven a while, Pierre saw she had made herself a ragged silken shelter. She could drag bits of flesh from the gull's carcass under the fragile canopy and eat in as shady and pleasant a circumstance as a village King shaded by his palm-frond-bearers. A great laugh cracked Pierre's stiff, parched body: against impossible odds she had made herself a home in a cozy and ingenious manner, whilst he, fool savant, lolled fading in sunwrack.

Moreover, he, that so-called savant, who puffed and strutted his refusal to grind others to meal, or be ground himself, in the heartless mills of profit & commerce, must soon for his benefit destroy the spider's hard-won comfort, for soon he would stand in gathering dusk to unknot his crampety muscles and refresh himself in a small breeze that was sure to come up, that must come up, or he would perish.

And so minute was his scrutiny of the spider's shelter, and of her dinner therein, and of his gathering moral dilemma, he did not see a BOAT bearing down on him, till he looked out into the dark that had fallen and saw shining there the whites of a number of eyes. And then he saw in the light of the moon that fell across the waters the bright stripes on some men's chests and thought, at first, the men were all riddled with meemie worms, or bore the scars of repeated lashing, though wrapped in peculiar fashion round their ribs. Then he saw the brightnesses were indeed, their ribs, that did seem to protrude from dark flesh, giving them the appearance of skeletons, who rowed their boat to the other world.

And by dint of exertions Pierre could not have made in his weakened condition, they pulled at the oars, two poor souls on each one. When they had come alongside him, they raised the oars, as if they meant to murder Pierre with four-handed cudgels in terrible unison. Were these the anthropophagi, come to carve up his flesh and drink his blood as he had drunk the gull's?

"Hold!" he cried. "It is true I worked in the house and ate from the master's table. I wore his hand-me-downs and brushed my hair into a queue. But I never patched my face, or wore red shoes, or tattled on a shirker or a thief. I never plotted to buy my own slaves or prevailed on a woman with perquisites. I educated my brothers and sisters in a secret school. And in my cyclopedish histoire I inscribed an account of the world reflecting the TRUE condition and experience of ALL its denizens, in the heretofore despised animal kingdoms and the neglected human realms, among persons of diverse & varying parts, to instruct and delight ALL MANKIND."

The men with the upraised oars but stared at Pierre, and those nearest him reached over the gunwales of their boat to lay hold of the rim of his barrel, thus threatening to tip his high-bobbing, small-bottomed craft. If capsized would he be able to clamber back aboard without swamping his vessel and sinking it? When he grew too tired to flail and swim, he would drown. To defend the integrity of his eccentric craft, then, Pierre placed an oar in the water and backpaddled. And destroyed in his first paddle stroke his spider's web. It hurt his heart to do it, for he had not forgotten how patiently she had worked. Yet he picked up one of his oars and struck at a grasping hand, fearfully rocking his vessel, pitching his spider, he feared, into the sea, as he very nearly pitched himself. Yet still the persistent skeletons reached for him.

"Brothers!" he cried. "If you lay hold of my craft, you will tip it. If I capsize I will drown. Why do you wish to board? There is nothing here of value, no room for any man but myself. You have a sturdy boat of your own."

Pierre held his oar before him, as a club, so he could smash the fingers of the rower who was reaching for his barrel. He saw then that the man held a calabash shell in his teeth, and drank from it by throwing back his head.

There was a murmuring among the oarsmen. The man with the calabash dropped it from his teeth; it floated like a little boat on top of the water. With the tips of their oars, the man and his bench-mate pushed the calabash toward Pierre, who remained fearful and suspicious. The oarsmen lowered their oars then and sat with them poised above the water, waiting. Pierre saw that the men at the oars were chained to each other and could not leap out to hurt him.

Watching them carefully, Pierre reached into the water and took up the calabash shell and drank sweet water. Oh, sweet, sweet water! Having emptied the last drop onto the rim of the barrel near the spider's wrecked lair, in the event she were somewhere about, he placed the empty shell on the blade of an oar and pushed it back to the men in the boat, so they would see that he was a courteous, well-meaning fellow. Then he lay upon the blade of his oar the carcass of the gull, keeping only a part of the breast for himself and the spider. And the nearest rower took it from his oar blade with his teeth. And mouth to mouth shared it with his fellows, so that each received a morsel to eat. And they all nodded their heads to him, most courteously, and he to them. Yet for all their courtesy to him and tenderness to each other, Pierre was leery, for they were fugitives in desperate circumstances, and he had struck at their hands. Who knew what they might do?

The men were but late from the tank, that Pierre could ascertain; for they spoke not the patois. Pierre could not understand their several languages until he made out some words of the Oro tongue, and haltingly conversed in that tongue with them, though Pierre and these others did not ask or tell names or origins, lest one be caught and, to gain relief from torture, reveal what should be concealed.

"Where you going?"

"We go home. Then you?"

"France."

"That Europe place?"

"Anyone be free there."

"Who say?"

"I hear it."

"You ply your trade there?"

"I am savant."

"Better you go home. Come, please."

"Too far."

"You know?"

"Too far. Too far."

Pierre shook his head; the men in the boat gaped at his treachery, mouth and eyes round in disbelief. *Too far? The homeland too far?*

How could Pierre instruct in the calculation of latitudes with sextants and triangles and compasses, in a language neither he nor the men in the boat spoke well? He saw they conferred with each other and argued, with frequent nods in his direction. Prudently he began to row his bobbing craft away from them, though they cried out to him, "Wait! Take water!" Their kindly aspect had vanished; now they showed him sly side-gazing faces. Yet who could blame them for wishing to return to their home? If only wishing could gobble the vastness of the waters separating them from Guinée. He feared they would force him into their boat to be their navigator; his heart sank at the prospect of losing his life in an enterprise he knew to be hopeless. Nor did he wish to deceive these poor brothers, and make for the Canaries whilst proclaiming he bore on Guinée. His heart yearning toward his brothers all the while, he rowed away from them, rowed away in the direction of solitude and uncertainty, though his progress were somewhat gyrational, his chances uncertain. A lone man rowing a barrel with shortened oars were no match at all for a dozen men at the proper oars of a proper boat, no matter how he bent his back.

Indeed, he would not have escaped, had not a school of DOL-PHINS leapt suddenly from the water, whereupon the men in the boat began to occupy themselves with the leaping fish, attempting to slash and bludgeon them with their oars, and enjoy the flesh. Though he fainted for food, Pierre kept rowing, for the men were doomed. Despite the blessing of dolphin flesh, they could not get as far as Guinée in an open boat, when they had already suffered so from exposure. Nor did Pierre want to float with men in irons near the shipping lanes. If they did not die, they would likely be caught, and no one in their company would pass for free. Yet Pierre did pray these brothers would drift to a fortress of maroons and thrive. For his part, he would remain in his barrel, and put what distance he could twixt himself and them. Yet without his lid, he would not be salvaged as cargo. Oh, what would become of Pierre? He beat his head with his fists in despair.

Then he espied to his great delight his spider; far from having been tumbled into the sea, she had sojourned in a crack in a shadow. Now she labored to build another nest, a simpler and cruder affair that snugged into the curve of the barrel. Oh good and faithful creature! Pierre would not let himself be shamed by the PERSISTENCE AND INGENIOUSNESS OF AN INSECT. With several determined strokes of his ax, he chopped one of his oars to slats and tied the rude sticks together with strips of his wife's head cloth, having spilled the cowries onto the quilty floor of his barrel among his tools, where he could jostle them fondly with his toes. The lashed-together slatsticks furnished a makeshift lid for his keg; with what was left of his cloth he braided a leash to keep the lid from straying into the sea again.

When he had finished his work, the sun having risen, Pierre settled down in his good-dark barrel, stifling but shaded; he fumbled his cowries about. He waited for the mouth of mouths to hiss from between his toes the divination; he waited and waited some more, but he heard only laughter.

147

Methought the spider mocked me for tearing up my wife's cloth, but the cackling laughter came from outside the barrel. Oh, then did I shrink into myself in the grimmest, most cringing despair! I feared the boat of fugitives had returned to avenge themselves on my traitorous self, or worse, renegade patrols, cannibal catchers who lived on the sea, sustaining themselves with the flesh and blood of fools who had run from benevolent masters.

"If you 'scape, see you 'scape well," Squint had been wont to gloat. "See you make yourself strong, for a man with no place of his own is meat in the mouth of the world, yes? Shreds of meat on its long pink tongue, between its eyeteeth and its stubborn molars."

And the laughter of SQUINT cackled all around the barrel; Pierre must be surrounded by rowboats of predatious anthropophagi. By the vigor of the cackle and the hoot, these abominations were well watered and well fed, patrolling Squinturns who would chuckle as they chained my hands to my ankles; belly-laughing, they would force me to drink salt water till I died of convulsion, blood-guts streaming out my arse while those anthropophagous patrollers stropped their flensing knives, humming between their teeth a hideous tune.

Yet from the bunghole Pierre saw but MIRRORS, dancing and glinting in the water like fragments of broken mirror he and his fellows had been wont to steal from the midden to sew into carnival costumes. These shards the whites would have set in the bricks of garden walls and window ledges, to cut out a man's knees if he clamber over to steal. The shards were forbidden to us, though by vigilance and stealth we found ways to filch them. We sewed them into our clothes, that our stamp-and-pat might scintillate in torch-bright night, glintering to mimic the dance of lights that attends the dead as they ride out to sea.

We danced as if we were Skull himself, infernal and triumphant, cutting the world with glass knives into pieces so small they could not be joined as they had been, the world would become another place if not a better. And the blacks and the small whites wore masks, and danced together, for no one saw who anyone was; distinctions did not prevail. Yet M'sieu and the other grands watched from the porch with their drivers, and the militia kept their muskets strapped to their chests as they danced. Up and down, round and round, the fingers of rum turned to hands, all hands on each other's bodies, John Fish swimming where he would, where he would. Even the master left the porch and danced with Queen Quasheba, whose mask did not disguise her breasts, whilst Madame sulked behind her fan, for she was not allowed to dance—what? Lower herself? Risk innocence & honor? When rude hands mocked their betters, mincing and prancing in scurrilous tableaux? When blasphemers dressed as priests squealed as pigs a burlesque of Mass? When boys from the tanks pulled down their drawers and jiggled their buttocks? Oh, a most convivial and leveling laughter echoed off the mirror-fractured sea-night in which bobbed embarreled Pierre!

Then the laughter died down. The carnival costumes lay across the waters, mirrors glistening and winking. Among the rags of festive garments, boys from the tanks in brightly painted boats, shaded by palm-bearers, sat atop prostrate whites, playing Trey and Whist, wagering the souls of the masters they sat on. There watched from the back of a richly caparisoned sea horse Baron Skull, shrouded in domino, his mirrored waistcoat gleaming, a white plume floating above his head as a cloud. Yet these APPARI-TIONS, too, were as airy as phantom clouds! And soon they were gone.

"Come back! I will put you in my histoire!" begged Pierre. But where would he fit these revelers in? This was a calming question. Pierre considered it, musing, recollecting, taking up several likelihoods in a dainty and meditative manner. You see, Kind Reader, Pierre numbered books in the oeuvre of his mind, and in the books numbered articles, in the articles, numbered propositions. Oh, indeed, all was tidy in his mind! *I, X, L, C*—he walked among the stores preserved and numbered in his conjure house, pulling the riches one by one from the mirror-bright chests where he stored his precious pages. Let the sun glint on Skull's spangles how it would, Pierre walked in the cool of his conjure house, peruked, in a fresh bright coat, shuttlecocking distinguos, considering how his cyclopedish histoire would surpass all other histoires on the library shelves, for his would include much matter not considered by those grand whites who surveyed so much of the world outside themselves yet saw not themselves. No one but Pierre had both learning and perspective to do the work he had laid out for himself. Pierre would illuminate the corners the whites had left in the dark. He would prove that pasty devils be as meet an object of learned inquiry as any darker men, nay more meet.

In my very presence M'sieu had allowed, as a rationale for his judgment I could be taught and learn as a human, not as a chained ape that claps and gavottes to a pipe: the MOVEMENT OF THE BLOOD, attested in Europe but two hundred years before, and still no article of faith among the smaller whites, were known to the MUSLIMERS at the time the Cross-Carriers sacked Constantinople, a noble Christian city, and those Muslimers were dark. Yet there be more.

For as the Muslimer perfected terrible and mighty engines of war, viz., the infidel harrow and the manifold wrist-slicer, so the Muslimers routed those cross-bearing brigands, though they did not deign to kill them, for they did not consider them worthy of swift and merciful death. And for this insulting refusal, and subsequent mutilations, and enslavement from which an honest hard worker could buy his liberty, an animosity was established that persisted. Yet amongst the Muslimers, munificence sprang from victory. The puffed-up rodomontade that is the banner of a heartless army with neither courage nor honor did not enter the Muslimers' songs or talk, yet the Cross-Carriers, those pastry-puff torturers, cowards in victory and defeat, did not forebear to slander nobler, darker men. Only in captivity, beaten and bruised to hatred, did we dark ones stoop to contemn their worth.

Now the DEROGATIONS by means of which the whites belittle the honor and dignity of blacks are very well known, among them as among us, viz., dog lips, shuffle-grin, worm-ass, louse-ring. Less well known to them the derogations by means of which we darker fellows contemn their loathsome pretensions, viz., whey-guts, cotton-snatch, stink-pits, porridge-arse, rule-shitter, clod-squawk, pig-fart, gout-bag, flux-face, bone-nose, bubo-cheeks, widower.

Now we do name them widowers, yet though they have a hundred women, one legal in the house, ninety-nine unacknowledged in the yard. Now the women in the yard but use the white man's rut-lust to prize concessions from him. They throw him out of their minds when they have got what they want, and the thought of him dries up in the sun. *Widower* be the name these white men share with the dog's scats, when the dog has left them in the yard to whiten in the sun.

And for the yellow twixt-tweens: bile-spitter, pollen-face, piss-dipper, wobble-guts. Camel-Packers: sneak-snatch, cozen-purse, pinch-arse, bum-swipe, but these names belong in another part of the histoire.

O Disinterested Philosophe Reader, is it not a strange phenomenon, how the whites do vaunt themselves of the layers of precious stuff that cover and recover their persons, said stuff all channeled, and stuffed, and slit, and lined, and broidered, and otherwise worked, with seed pearls sewn on, and florets woven in, and ribands and lace ruffled and tucked, which grand costume they strut in till it rot, their bodies beneath stinking and bloating? Yet they will sneer at us for the scars decorating our flesh and the plugs in ears, though these prevent us not from cleaning ourselves, cannot be taken from us in any reversal of fortune, and do not wear out.

Further CATEGORIES OF QUESTION Pierre did look to INVESTIGATE, upon his establishment amongst the French:

Category the First: why they collect their excrement in a pot with their dreams at night, and keep it close by them in their shuttered house. Nor do they dispose of the pot when the excrement has been dumped, but use it over and over, as they might a souptureen, thus accumulating all the bad spirits their bodies dispel, a very pernicious reserve of the vile. And often these pots are precious stuff, viz., porcelain of Meissen or Dresden, the very same from which they eat their food. Moreover, they fancy they are very refined if they do not piss and shit in the open, but repair to a little house set over a great trench, into which they drop their stuff, collecting it and allowing it to fester as a great stinking wound they inflict on the earth, to punish it. Yet they could spread their dung on the fields, to replenish them. And whey-guts eat meat with the same hand with which they have wiped their arses, save for the greatest ones, who have their servants perform this office. Yet to watch a great one on his pierced chair is a mark of honor all the little ones solicit.

Category the Second: the big clod-squawks collect their snot in cloths, which they carry in their sleeves and guard most jealously, only to foist these cloths upon their serving persons who must wash away the loathsome snots. Yet those who have blown them will peer into the cloths as if they discerned there deposits of rubies or pearls.

Category the Third: how they swing some refined scent before them in pomanders or censers, even as dogs swing their testicles, dispersing precious fragrance over the landscape, rather than reserving it to sweeten their persons in a bath.

Category the Fourth: how they attach foul leeches to their bodies, to draw out their blood, or cut themselves open, to let the blood flow into a basin, and assert their well-being is established by this sapping of their natural strength. And then they will go to their Church, where their poor gentle Jesus drips Blood down the tree He is nailed to. At the foot of this tree they drink wine, which they allege to be the Blood of this God, and they eat of a very flat bread, which they allege is His Body. Yet they will rant against the anthropophagi, whom they claim we be.

Category the Fifth: how they will take to cosset a small pet dog or a parrot or a monkey; they will feed this creature all manner of gilded sweetmeats, with their own fingers, from their own plates, yet they will feed their slaves old bread soaked in sour milk, which they will pour in a trough set on the ground, so the slave has a very hard time eating dainty, this though the slave be a skilled and ingenious artisan, worth more in the marketplace than a thousand of the dog.

The most esteemed philosopher ROUSSEAU did speak in his *Eloise* of distinguishing, oh yes, distinguishing, now what were the words he wrote? Pierre in his barrel closed his eyes and clasped his remaining oar to his chest, and tried to remember. Distinguishing what? He must slide his tea labels from his talisman pouch and hold them one by one to the bunghole light, that he might read, *distinguish between the variety in human nature and that which is essential to it.* Yes, yes! Bounds! Bounds! Nature herself must be prescribed within bounds lest "monsters, giants, pygmies and chimeras of all kinds" be admitted. Yes, lest—oh the irony! Pierre shuddered. "Every object would be disfigured, we should have no common model of ourselves."

Oh, Pierre laughed. An awful sound emerged from his parched, swollen throat! And a shaking moved his barrel. And he shuffled his labels as a pack of cards, laughing all the while, till he found a certain saying of Diderot, "The devil take the best of all possible worlds if I am not part of it."

Again Pierre shook his barrel with painful laughter, oblivious of the impression a frenetic quaking of the barrel had made on a number of TAWNIES in palm-leaf hats who were sitting with their spoonlike paddles across their laps in their dug-out canoes, watching most warily, silent as phantoms.

How had he failed to spy them through the bunghole, sleek craft sliding through the sun-glint sea? Oh, consider the nature of a barrel, with a man all miserably folded inside. Even if the man should pop off the barrel head, to stand erect, dancing for balance in his ill-poised craft, he sees but water, a mirror of winks, the light-struck spectacle of which, without apparent end, throws him back into himself. The compass of his world is the compass of his skull, then; all other persons, and his own past and future, are as mythy to him, as, on land, the dawning light on a spider's web to the spider. Only the spider is real to herself, hunched in the middle of the spun web, spinning what and as long as she can to live. So Pierre spun accounts and tales to amuse and succor himself, and peopled the waters with the phantoms of his shadow histoire. He spun for his life, yet he did not see the force outside that had overtaken him to damn him or save him.

Were these that surrounded me in their canoes the same tawnies who had pressed healing herbs on Vérité's wounds when she hung from a rail at Ravenal's place? XUACOMAC, they had called themselves. Directly I raised my head above my barrel's rim, they raised up feathered shields and shook their feathered cuffs, whereupon small, hollow gourds, dangling among other decorations, did jangle most sweetly a welcome. Then I luxuriated in the pleasing prospect of imminent discovery; I would float no more on the fearsome empty sea. Yet the tawnies frowned and tipped each other winks; they seemed to be moving toward me. They raised their paddles, as if to strike.

Like a turtle, I withdrew my head into my shell—my trusty barrel. Whereupon the tawnies, after a moment's brief conclave, put paddle to water and departed, their paddles striking the wave most sedately on the accent, though no one set the time with a tune.

"I pray you, rest a while," I remonstrated, popping up again, "let us make each other's acquaintance." I did so wish to be rescued, to sleep on land, and to live amongst humans, but alas! The tawnies had taken leave.

Now day followed weary day. Pierre no longer bothered to scratch and count. He grew ever more perplexed by refractory, light-struck ripples on the waters that broke the world to shards. In his splintered isolation he took to blabbing to himself, that he might hear one word follow another in an orderly temporal manner. Though the sunlight bleach and empty him as a dead mollusk in its shell, he said aloud his cyclopedish histoire, as a schoolboy learning his letters, that he might keep and hold the learnings and the observations he had organized into propositions and articles and books.

More questions Concerning the CUSTOMS OF WHEY-GUTS:

Category the Sixth: how they pack their cheeks with snuff and spit on the floor around the gaming table, then, having filled their handkerchiefs with phlegm, do wipe their stink-herb lips on the sleeves of their coats, the stuff for which they import at hideous expense, and for the cutting and sewing of which they are in debt to a tailor of Saint-Domingue.

Category the Seventh: how they cause the fly-struck meat to rot, hanging it till it turn blue, whereupon they burn it till it is charred, and eat it in ember.

Category the Eighth: how they curtsey to their women and kiss their hands when company is about, but give them the back of their hands as soon as the door is closed on the visitors' carriage. How they waste on cards and drink the leisure they have stolen from others, which would permit them to rest a sweet long while with their women, who have made themselves so pretty.

Category the Ninth: how they bind their infants in swaddling clothes, restraining their natural movements and confining them with their excrements, which wet them, and chill them, and irritate their fine and delicate skin. How they leave their children in the care of a woman whom they kennel as a dog. Oh Rose! Oh Rose!

So Pierre drifted with his observations and his memories, all thought of navigation abandoned. Then one numberless evening, when the Fire God was taking ease on His verandah before He slipped to His bed beneath the sea, the TAWNIES RETURNED. Again they ringed Pierre in their carved wood canoes, save now there were more of them. Surely this time they would welcome him with ceremony, as a distinguished visitor, who keeps in his conjure house the precious volumes of a shadow histoire! There would be bed and food and drink, song and dance and the tender ministrations of women. The men would commune and converse—however halting in each other's tongue—around a blessed fire. Pierre stood on his shaky legs and tugged at his clothes and patted and brushed himself to a semblance of propriety, then waved his arms and curved his swollen lips as best he could, displaying his teeth to advertise his delighted gladness to see these saviors.

Yet they did not come nigh him, but made odd gestures with their shields and bobbed their heads, which were now dressed with feather bonnets in which they resembled shuttlecocks, the sturdy-looking palm hats of the previous visit having been discarded. Several tawnies with more elaborate headdresses and capes of bright soft stuff that appeared to be parrot feathers stood with burning brands in the prows of the canoes. These dignitaries now brusquely commanded the paddlers, who laid flat on the water the blades of their paddles. And on these turtle-shaped paddles were plump bundles wrapped in coarse, pale, thick leaves, as well as smaller, thinner bundles, twisted knots of darker, more delicate leaves, which latter the dignitaries in the prows did fire with their torches. And the paddlers then dipped their paddles beneath the surface of the water, so the bundles floated free on chips of wood. To a most unpleasant, monotonous chant of the prow-worthies, the paddlers flailed at the sea with their paddles, which flailing did stir up the waters, even beyond the natural action of the waves, and thus move the bundles on their chips toward Pierre. And the mien of the tawnies was as solemn and forbidding as their chant.

Yet the plump bundles were carefully tied with vines and decorated with feathers. Surely the bundles were gifts! Pierre unwrapped one to discover flat yam cakes, the food the living share with the dead. Pierre's belly twisted and his hands trembled. His hunger was so great he would have drooled onto the sacred food had there been juice in his mouth. He did not long hesitate to bite into a luscious cake, which had been prepared with a rich, sweet sauce of the dildun berry known to be favored by those who have passed. Pierre bowed in all directions, to show any dead who were about that he would gladly share with them this holy food. And he bowed to the tawnies all around him, to show he meant no dishonor to their dead by eating this food. If those in the canoes were themselves dead, he prayed they would not reproach him for eating their food, and raise their hands against him. But indeed, they were already turning their canoes, the prow-men making the "rise not" sign with their hands, as if they supposed that Pierre were dead.

And so they fled and left him alone with the sadness of his abandonment. Yet they had saved his life with their gifts of food and ameliorated his discomfort with the burning knots of leaves, which were of hemp and tobacco. And of all these gifts, Pierre took but half, leaving the true dead a portion that would honor them. He satisfied his hunger and thirst, then with his oars he pushed the wood-chip rafts, freighted with the portions of the dead, toward the house of the Fire God, Who had fallen into bed like a glowing stone a cook drops into a pot of milk and sorrel soup.

Of his portion of tobacco and hempen torches, he extinguished all but one. He then sucked the smoke of each in succession as it burned, lighting one from the last, puffing and blowing to keep the fire burning, which miraculously did not further parch his already parched throat, but refreshed him and soothed him. He sucked so much soothing and savorous smoke that he fell asleep, his head rolled back on the rim of the barrel, gazing at the heavens to discern what constellations were in view, vainly hoping he might ascertain his whereabouts and propel himself again into the shipping lanes, for still he hoped to pass for cargo.

The tawnies had believed him DEAD. He? Dead? He pinched himself, and felt it sore. He breathed a deep, rich breath of smoke and air and felt it expand in his mouth and mingle with his being, which now moved in him fresh and quick. *Cogito Sum!* Cogito-Sum triumphant in his barrel, Cogito-Sum ascendant in his breast, his skull, his crampety fingers and toes. Oh surely he lived, and would yet take his place in the world as savant. And this be the glory of Creation, that whilst a man lives he hopes for amelioration of his lot.

Yet even as Pierre lit the blessed leaves, and breathed their pungent smoke, and drowsed, he saw through the smoke of another fire the dour evangelist driver Squint, drawing on his long clay pipe in the yard.

"Believe how you will in the glory that is the world," said Squint. "The dead are dead unless Jesus come to quicken them, which He will not do lest you repent in your inmost heart. 'Tis not about the holy water, nor about the rosaries, nor about Confession nor the words of creeds and prayers *(Squint smites his chest).*

"If there be no Jesus, we are as Parsees, that fear life itself and well they should. For they live far from the Spirit and the Light; the serpent that tempted Eve, and through Eve, Cuckold Adam, do make its dwelling even within the Parsees' living bodies, using them as a bird will use a tree, without consideration."

"Is it a story of lovers?" This, Quasheba, hunching closer to the fire.

"'Tis another tale of a rat he had shot that hopped from the stew pot when the water boiled," jibed Dido.

"There is a hook in it somewhere, will catch more than rats," said a disgruntled hand.

"Likely this tale is of people far away, which no one here has had occasion to see nor is like to see."

"Oh, that it is," said Squint, laying his pipe in the ash to keep it warm. "For I have sojourned in many climes and tasted much of the world. If this be ash on your tongue, you may ask that I stay mine. But if you would hear an adventure, and know what I have seen and heard, then bid me say on."

He was the boss. He would say on. And we would see the world through freedom's eye, though he who displayed it were no longer free and showed it but to spite us. We were hungry for the world; we would not ask him to stop his mouth. A TALE OF SQUINT, then, as if he has laid his pipe in the ash to keep it warm.

159

"In the Parsee city of Galub, there streak and glide in the ditches snaky creatures known as JITSEYS, which twine in the legs of the camels and donkeys, and in the wheels of handcarts, and slither up the peoples' robes *(he wriggles here, then leans in complicitous).* The young of this serpent are hatched from a mother's mouth like so many words, to shed her quick upon entering the world *(he shakes his body, as a wet dog that would dry itself),* a habit they continue in shedding their own skins, at every turn, streaking out of their past lives faster than you can pull your foot from your stocking *(here the slippered Squint was wont to kick off his shoes and strip off his week-ripe stockings).*

"This is the snake the mothers warn their daughters of *(and here he wiggles his crooked yellow toes and gives a little dig with his foot, to show how it crawls up the pantaloons the girls wear there),* THIS SNAKE! insinuates itself into the purse between the legs, thus! to count the coin, mind you *(digs with his foot in the air again),* to count the coin, yes? Count coin *(here he pauses to permit a salacious contemplation)* . . .

"Then that horriblacious snake does most luxuriously slither through the ravine in the buttocks fastness to reconnoiter the ridge of the spine *(here spies beneath his hand),* taking a turn around the ears beneath the tent that hides the women's faces *(here he draws a veil with his hand across his visage)* before nipping back down and out the pantaloons *(shakes a bony leg)* faster than a frog snaps a fly *(tweaks a nose)*—ALL in the innocent *(tweaks still another nose)*—insolent *(another)*—manner *(Quashee ducks before Squint can tweak and Squint stands up to stretch his legs)*—innocent, insolent MANNER of your sauntering priva-teeeeer's man on shore leave *(scratches his underarms and leans in).* And it is not just the privacy of laaaay-dies' persons the jitseys invade *(leans in closer, so we are sickened by his goatish breath, thick and foul in our faces).* For the rammish men it is worse than being taken like a ewe of which the hind legs have been discomfortably stuff'd in some horny conscript's

BOOTS *(And rears back, hands on hips).* IT is a violating species of invasion—as your invasions go. Now!

"Once a comfortable Galubi merchant, Salah Dey Oum, a dealer in carpets, reclined on his cushions in his private rooms at midday, having been served a ragout of beef and pomegranate—them's reddy fruits all jeweled and seedy—at the soft, fair hands of Fatima, his wife *(he holds his hands in front of his chest as one supporting melony breasts).* Digging between his teeth—like so—with an ivory pick to skewer pomegranate seeds, he found—ahh!—jitsey skins. Though he jettisoned the skins at once, he could not shake off the specter of his violated mouth *(shakes again like a wet dog, and covers his mouth),* the which wriiiiii-thed in his dream like a fresh-butchered liver cut from the carcass to quiver in his face. Pfew! He spat to his right and pfew! to his left and turned pfew! to spit behind himself pfew! pfew! muttering curses. Pfew! Pfew! Alas! He called for a looking glass that he might examine his tongue and his gums. And he looked pfew! and looked pfew! not once, but many times. Weeks pfew! months later pfew! pfew! he was muttering and staring at the image of his tongue in the looking glass *(Squint pulls a noisome rag from a pocket and wipes some spittle from his chin).*

"Now. Seeing him so afflicted with PECULIAR habits and DE-BILITATING fears, his customers lost confidence in his judgment and began to take their trade elsewhere *(hunches servile and lewd).* The servants whispered, he refused to take off his shoes at night, for fear jitseys would curl where his feet had been *(pokes a toe back into one of his shoes, hunches more lewdly).* Everyone saw how he cowered before the rolled carpets stacked in his shop, and his helpers tittered behind their hands. *(Squint, obligingly.)*

"Yet even as his 'prentices openly jeered him, Fatima stood with her hands modestly crossed upon her breasts—like so—betraying no hint of contempt or even reproach *(rolls his eyes to heaven, showing their whites).* Now when Salah had given away the household furnishings, railing and pointing his finger at their jitsey-bearing crevices—like so—he shuddered at the folds of his wife's clothing—yes, even so—tapped her shoulder gingerly—ta-ta-ta! Ta-ta-ta! Out the door! *(Squint wipes his brow, as a man relieved of an onerous obligation, clasps his hands pious-like.)*

"Fatima's parents had long since died. Though she had brothers, they would not have her, nor would her brothers-in-law. Her married children advised her she was too old to dower for a second marriage. They enjoined her return to her husband *(wags his finger, bossy-bossy)*. Meekly she shuffled back to his shuttered house, putting one foot before the other—e'en so. *(Knocks with his knuckles on the end of a log poking out of the fire. Silence. Knocks again. Silence.)*

"No one answered her knock on the door *(knock)* though she waited a long time *(knock)*. Finally the servants of the neighbors poked their heads over the wall to whisper *(does whisper)* 'Salah had left the place, wandered away, no one knew where.' *(Speaks hoarse and soft, like a little wind, barely rising to disappear.)* The house was about to be taken by someone else, who had already brought in some moveables. . . .

"Once again, Fatima put one foot down in front of the other, not daring to raise her eyes. And in this cautious, mincing way she came soon enough to a quarter of the city where she was unknown. She was tired by then, and sat down, like so, and held out her hand, palm up, e'en so. And thus she became a beggar, sleeping in doorways and gutters. *(Lies down and curls about himself like a dog.)* She who had been a modest, closeted wife, whose plump, cosseted body had known cushions and silks *(mournful and nostalgic gaze)* now felt her hipbones grind on the paving stones and cradled her head 'gainst a hitching post. Even among the beggars her life was accounted hard, for she had no bowl for coins and was much too timid to jostle passers-by. *(Wipes the corner of his eye, then sits up straight, gazing around at each of his interlocutors.)*

"Yet, though she had neither cloak nor blanket, the night wind's soughing did not alarm her. No, no, no. For she was warmed by jitseys streaking in and out of her clothing *(here looks up his sleeves and down his breeches),* covering her person with cast-off skins. *(Oh, all confidence again.)* 'Tis said the paths the serpents traveled did clean and brighten behind them, yes! Washing her sooty person, they did heal her mendicant's sores and chase away her fleas and lice *(brushes and picks the pests from his sleeve).* Over her ribs her chaaaaastened flesh was soon as fresh as a child's, her fragrance—ahhhhhhhhh!—a maiden's. Snakeskins wreathed her brow to CELEBRATE her cast-off miserable condition. And her life *(shakes his head amazed)* was wondrous long *(portentous silence).*

"When one morning she did not wake up, yet though the sun burned bright on her eyelids, the beggars who moved in to strip her of her rags to sell saw all her clothes were jitsey skins, that crumbled—e'en so—to the touch. Her corpse was ablush and silken, though the bottoms of her feet were crusted and yellow *(picks up each of his feet; gazes at their fissured bottoms).*

"And the beggars bowed their heads before her sleek and lustrous hair and washed her body themselves *(lewd caress of air),* having gone without bread to buy the lemon-scented water. *(Hoists a giant burden the which he groans beneath.)* They carried her on their shoulders to the tower where the carrion birds come to pillage the bones of the dead *(flaps most shameless).* Yet the birds would not drive their beaks into her flesh, but only hovered around her *(flap flap),* their handlike wingtips spread, e'en so, their caw, caw, caw refined to a song as melodious, oh, and mournful, yes, as the dirge of high-paid mourners *(and shows again the whites of his eyes).*

"And a rich man had carved above the door a motto which read: 'Life a service, death a prayer.' *(Nods, as, oh! the veracity!)* The Galubis sealed the tower door and boarded up the windows. *(Nods, nods, nods.)* And for all I know she is up there still—the fair, fair bride of an unknown groom. *(Lays his finger sage by his nose.)*

"Thus began the cult of Fatima's Redemption *(now pragmatic and pedagogical),* a sect whose most faithful members make beds in the street near the shrine. *(Now has the gall to lie down on his back and turn to us smarmy and confidential.)* They claim the divinest love of the Lord is in His messengers, the jitseys, that saw a woman more naked than any paramour and flinched not nor faltered at flaws! Or age! Or disease! *(Pause!)* But healed what was wounded! Cured what was ill!"

"Amen," said a godmother.

"Amen."

"Amen!"

"Amen!"

"Putting aside their clothes, the faithful lie very still to attract the snakes *(Squint stiffens),* gritting their teeth as the jitseys wriggle blithe in their chinks *(wiggles most luxuriant and exuberant).* Some men send their wives to wait salvation for 'em, plotting substitution when the jitseys commence . . . . the RAPTUROUS . . . . GLEAMING *(now sits up, eyes all wide).*

"At the Gleaming . . . . . . it is claimed . . . . . jitseys will dive down through the open pores of the faithful to swim the inner seas of each body . . . . . . perusing and blessing what it has been given no living person to fathom! His own innards . . . . . . floating jellyfish!"

"No jellyfish in me!" cries old Rose.

"Amen!" cries a godmother.

"Amen!"

"And! Wait! In their circum . . . circum . . . circumnavigation! The jitseys will discover the seat of the soul!—yea truly!—whether it be near the Heart *(shamelessly thumps his chest)*—"

"A hollow sound," mutters Jean-François.

"Squint have no heart," says Quashee.

Squint glares innocent and reproachful. "Whether it be near the Heart! Or the Mind *(taps his bony head)!*"

"Squint have no mind," says Quashee. "Ask this green-boy: Squint have the master mind."

"What?" Squint glares at him.

Quashee waves off the driver. "On. On. On."

Squint do squint then, very suspicious. A pause. He continues. "The Kiss of the Jitsey (*smack!*) will bless the soul in its naked neediness! Bless, I say, Bless! Then, like a sailor (*eyes his falls*) shucking his pants in a brothel—"

"Don't you do it," says old Rose. "Not before children and decent folks."

"Man will shed generations of death! And the sun will shine a gleaming path across the salt lagoon of his body! And he will travel it to glory . . . I say glory . . . ! I say glory, glory, GLORY . . . ! Forever!"

"Amen!"

"Yet—I'm not finished! Yet never! Since the redemption! Of Fatima's bread-begging flesh! Has the love of the snakes! Again cheated Death's messengers. (*Shakes his head as one whose hairs be snakes.*) Patient Fatima sleeps, breathless, in the tower, her memory taunting the seekers from whose fathers' fathers she begged! (*His hand cupped like a begging bowl.*) And the birds circle the tower, singing and spreading their handlike wings—yes, e'en so—you have it now—sometimes they swoop! Yea, swoop! To eat the skins the jitseys shed in the street! (*Retrieves from the ash where it has kept warm his long Dutch pipe.*) I say, swoop! To eat the skins! The jitseys shed! In the street (*he sucks on his pipe*)!

"Yet a saved man, a man of his faith who talks to God, need not wait for the Gleaming, no, need not, my children, need not wait. He is saved as soon as he confesses; the rest is dross, friends, offal. (*Bangs his pipe on the ground to loosen up the cake, for he must fill and fire anew to draw.*) SKINS (*mutters fierce now*)! SKINS OF THE SERPENT. Mark you well, sons of Adam, mark how the skins of the very same serpent did seduce Eve, who ate the forbidden fruit, thus angering the Lord, who cast her with her husband from the garden, booted them into the mire of sin, from which we must elect to be saved. *(Glares all around to see his weary audience nods, heads fallen on breasts, so fatiguing be work in the fields.)*"

A most piteous exemplum, the snakeskin tale, yet some of those still awake around the fire be digging each other in the ribs, at the missing rib's very location, for this yellow did perpetuate certain GRIEVOUS ERRORS we yearned to correct, though we dare not gainsay the driver.

Error the First, that First woman be born of First Man. Oh, no, no, no. At our mothers' breasts we had nourished ourselves on the milk of truth. Every child amongst us knew how First Man and First Woman were born of Damzillah, Whom Her angry father had torn apart. Error the Second, that a serpent, or snake, had come from a crack in the earth to speak to First Woman. Oh, no, no, no, no, no! Indeed, no serpent came, but a tiny small worm, smaller than the meemie worm. Error the Third, that those jitseys are a kin of the serpent of their holy books, for Pierre had read in the accounts of Baron von Salmis, how jitseys came as a plague that afflicted people in those Galub regions with fear & false hope & accidie. And the jitseys came within the memory of a living man, and not at the dawn of time.

Pierre could prove by syllogism, and direct evidence, the jitsey was not the same as (a) the meemie worm or (b) the serpent, and (c) it had not abided in the wilderness—for it had been a wilderness, not a garden—with First Man and First Woman. And these PROOFS be one more EXEMPLUM of the fruitful and important KNOWLEDGES which Pierre had stored in the chests of his conjure house and which he would fain DISPLAY in France, first for savants, then for the wider world of curious, discerning men who would provide him with PENSIONS & PERQUISITES. As he lay in his barrel, his ambitions eddying with smoke in his brain, the taste of dildun berry sweet on his tongue, his soul once again found repose in his conjure house, where he wandered as Buffon in his garden, composing his CYCLOPEDISH HISTOIRE.

And from this delicious slumber, the splash of the sea on my smoke-cured face awoke me. Alas, the OCEAN had commenced to run in long, swooping swells that tossed my barrel, even as a feather which leaps and dances in steam from a kitchen kettle—a trick we boys had been wont to try on a kitchen wench who peeled onions and grimaced and wept. Whilst her apron covered her eyes, we leapt from the ground where we had been plucking chickens near the bloody block. We dropped handfuls of feathers into the torrent of steam that rose from the kettle's spout, to see them whirl and dance as demons.

"You boys are bewitched," cried the godmother who stirred the pot. In the lowering fog, I saw her.

"You see those stewing legs? Those are the legs of devil boys; buckra butchers them whilst they live."

As the sea washed over my circumferential gunwale, I pulled up my homemade hatch, which had been trailing on its leash in the sea, clacking against my barrel to give the alarm as a clapper outside its bell. Yet I was not snug inside my hold, for the sea still rose. To plug the bunghole, I wadded up the umbilical cord that attached my lid to Mother Barrel, yet though the air in the barrel grow stale.

As the barrel rose on the swellings and sunk into the troughs, it did not stay upright when the wind whipped up the waves, but somersaulted to toss and batter me while my guts scrambled to keep up with its tumbling. Yet I did not curse my barrel. Better be damp than drenched, though I be powerfully crimped and bruised. Alas, now I must piss in my calabash and dribble the piss out the bunghole with my spoon, only to have the sea spit the piss back on me. All the while the barrel were turning and turning, round and round, slosh and turn, to addle and befuddle me in a heartless, infernal mill, the maw of the insatiable.

Gormilah had swallowed the sea and the sea had swallowed me, as so many others, numbers crossing a page, skeletons crossing the sea with their ankles pierced, boats and barrels of dizzy bondsmen, pickled. Two three a hundred a thousand, myriad kegs, pickled meat of innocent men, barrels of arms and legs and heads and bellies, churning bellies. Pickled! Can't climb out of the barrel. Got to stay in. Stay in your bed, brother. Old Raw-Head be prowling, trailing bloody bones. That one grab you by your tongue and strip your flesh from your bones, will Raw-Head. Then Baron Skull flaunts your crow-picked bones in the mirror of his waistcoat. If he catch you, you wish you had stayed in your bed, had shut your mouth, had done as you were told and never pitied the patch on your mistress's sullen little paps the color of rot.

In a lull, I fumbled for my cowries between my legs, but before I could count half the shells, to determine which mouths spake, the barrel somersaulted, I must grab my lid's leash, to hold it fast, the wadding was pulled from the bunghole, which I must cover with a hand. And then the shells were dancing and clacking around me, I myself was a shell among others in a gourd, tumbling.

"Oh Spider!" I cried. "Bless me how you can! Speak some last word. Let me hear the voices of those who have cared for me in my life!"

And though the cowries fell around me, and fell again, even as the rain drove down to plash up against the barrel as it tumbled in the roiling waves, I heard—was it the voice of the spider? Or the voice of Jean-François, or Gormilah's voice, or Damzillah's, or Uncle God's, or the voices of the tawny dead, whose food I had eaten, or the voices of the maroons I had shrunk from guiding to

Guinée, who had died of exposure in their open boat, or was it my Vérité's voice hissing REPROACHES in my ear? *You are defeated through your own fault. A noble soul does not tell lies. The head carries the body. Arguments and tragedy are caused by misunderstanding. No one knows what lies at the bottom of the sea. He who aims at too much gets very little. If you don't know how to live here, you'll learn how to live there. Extend your hand as far as it reaches. No one knows what lies at the bottom of the sea. No one knows what lies at the bottom of the sea. No one knows what lies at the bottom of the sea.*

I closed my eyes and repeated these PROPHETICAL MAXIMS to myself, blabbing as a schoolboy to commit them to memory. And the moving of my lips was a comfort, a consolation, indeed a prayer. And so I repeated this cowry litany to myself, again and again, even when the hissing could no longer be heard, so loud the screaming of the winds around my barrel, & the terrifying roar of thunders, & the hideous crackle of lightening, as if the world were torn apart, whacked in two as a melon under Vérité's hatchet. After an Armageddon blast had wafted a hellish odor through the wadding at my bunghole and under my barrel's tight-pulled lid, I drew the plug but a little back from the bunghole, to ascertain if aught remained of the watery world outside.

Methought I had been blasted to a VOID, an emptiness inhabited only by the peaceful dead whom neither God's care nor His indifference can move. Yet there met my eye, not the dead sitting up on their rafts, chagrined that their sleep had been disturbed, but a SERPENT OR FISH with the crested head of a bird and a spiny mane on its back, the armored coils of which lay across the swell and curl of the water as far as the eye could see. And its eyes were enormous, as if the beast had emerged from a very deep, dark lair where it was at pains to see. The writhing slapping coils did whip the waves to a frenzy of foam as the mouth of the creature opened.

I saw teeth like the rows of glass the whites embedded in their window ledges, but larger, and pointier. And there dangled betwixt two of the teeth what appeared to be a rope. And, further within the creature's opening mouth, a large tortoise, flipped over onto its back with its legs feebly waving, peering dumbly and meekly and helplessly around from its upside-down eyes. And what did the tortoise make of the splintered planks and the keg of nails, breached, with the nails spilling out the top, and, banked up against a further tooth, what appeared to be a man's leathern boot, and with it a plank carved with women blowing horns around the words "Santa Clara"?

And then a sudden darkness, and fetid stillness. Now the rushing and beating of the storm sounded muffled, as if at some distance; then a powerful putrefescent odor, as of week-old fish, mixt with stable-straw that has not been changed for a month; a convulsive shudder; a tumbling movement of the barrel; Pierre was being SWALLOWED.

"Who knows what lies at the bottom of the sea," he cried, clutching handfuls of cowries and kissing them most fervently, stroking the sodden quilt beneath his feet. And the spider's hissing now was the murmur in a child's ear who holds up to it a conch's shell. Pierre heard old Rose chuckling; she was waving her apron at some boys who had snatched feathers from the floor near the butcher's block. They were stroking them across her arms and tickling her legs beneath her chemise; she was laughing as she flapped her apron. Pierre opened his talisman pouch, fumbled for the white feather and pushed the feather out through the bunghole to tickle the serpent's long, long throat, through which the barrel seemed to be shuddering a kind of progress, no doubt toward the belly.

Pierre had seen a snake swallow a mouse—the woeful passage of the lump through the glove-finger body; frantically he wiggled and woggled his feather. <u>Oh Spider, oh Steward God, oh Gormilah, Damzillah, Jesuson, Fathergod, oh Chenwiyi, Ogun, God Uncle, save me!</u> Spiggle wiggle tiggle smiggle. Pierre jiggled his feather and jiggled some more. His barrel continued a shuddering progress toward the certain doom of digestion. Jiggle jiggle nothing . . . nothing . . . nothing . . . then, of a sudden, of an infinitesimal, tiny sudden, a shift, a jerk, a rumbling gurgling, a barking, a cough or a hiccough. The feather was sucked out the bunghole; Pierre's hand was empty; he cried out. Blessed holy miracle, his barrel was now moving in the opposite direction to digestion's progress, and rapidly, and was soon ejected from the creature's mouth with a shudder, followed by a bouncing plash. And a little spot of sunlight came through his bunghole and quivered on his wrecked stocking, as if to say, "The world be intact. Ergo, you live." And a wondrous fresh smell permeated the barrel. And Pierre was emboldened to crack the lid, and so was privileged to see the creature's scaly back arching and diving, as a heaven-spanning rainbow, descending to the lower depths, yet barely ruffling the now-calm waters. A few bubbles came up, but the creature did not return. It had vanished with his mother Marie Mandilé-Ba's feather in its belly, which loss, though of talisman, Pierre regretted but slightly. He heaved a sigh of relief. For he had been SAVED from a WATERY DOOM in the stinking belly of a monstrous fish.

He wept, and thanked his mother, his feather, his shells and his spider, and recalled a story Rose had told.

ONCE LONG AGO lived a clever, fortunate boy and girl, very merry and lithe, but with fussing, worrisome parents. These saucy children ran away from home to see the world and to do as they pleased, laughing at their own boldness. They went to live far from their parents in a cave with two doors, one small enough for birds to fly in, which the slender children could crawl through, the other tall enough and wide enough for the huge bully who, unbeknownst to the children, had been following them, sidling from shadow to tree, watching.

The bully saw how the boy went out hunting, having told his sister to stay in the cave, with both the doors barred. When the boy returned with a goatsucker bird he had shot, he sang a little song so the girl would know he had come:

Sister, Open, Sister, Open
The one small door.
Oh what a fine-marbled godwit flies in.
Oh what a lip-smacking treat.

And the girl licked her lips, for her brother had forbidden her to roast while he was out, lest the smell draw those hungry ones who skulk everywhere and will not hesitate to eat anyone. But the sister was a pert girl, and willful. One day while the boy was out with his sling, she made a very small fire of twigs and leaves in the cave, and she roasted a breast of spice finch left over from the day before. And then a heavy thick breathing shook the cave; the bully was at the big door, snuffling around its edges.

When the girl would not open to his knocking, the bully drew back a little, for he was sly. He sang a song very like her brother's song, but, unfortunately for him, in a growly, rumbling voice:

Sister, Open, Sister, Open
The one big door.
Let me in with my bag so huge
With meat of the black-throat priest-wit I've killed.
Oh what a lip-smacking treat!

The girl was hungry, yet she was not fooled. She sat in the corner and sucked on the bones of yesterday's finch. Oh, but her sucking sound brought the juice up into the bully's mouth. And he drooled and licked his lips and stroked his enormous belly. And his hunger made him even more cunning than before.

Now he sang again, in a high, sweet voice:

Sister, Open, Sister, Open
The one big door.
Let me in with my bag so full:
A flock of gull-billed terns I've killed.
Oh what a lip-smacking treat!

Now the foolish girl unbarred the door. In one gulp he ate her and her finch breast, then he hid behind a stone, waiting for the brother.

The boy had killed no bird that day but had found a honey tree. "Wing to wing," he said to himself. "All that is sweet is not flesh." And he stole the comb after stunning the bees with smoke from a fire he had made by rubbing together sticks. And so bees slumbered in their comb in the bag on the boy's back as he skipped home to the cave, humming to himself, looking forward to the sweet treat he and his sister would enjoy. And the bees woke up and hummed with him. And soon enough he came to the cave, where he sang:

Open, Sister, Open, Sister!
Open now the big door—
Let me enter with my bag so huge.
I bear greater sweetness than mango-birds' flesh.
Oh, what a lip-smacking treat!

And the bully reached out with one big toe and unbarred the door, and the boy walked in and snicker-snap!

Inside the bully's dark belly, the boy embraced his sister, then he opened his sack. "Wing to wing," he murmured. The bees flew out. Wide awake now, they stung and stung the bully from within. The bully rolled on the floor, clutching his belly. Hiding behind

173

the bully's rocklike heart, the boy squeezed his sister's shoulder, and she squeezed his back. The two children crawled on their hands and knees up the bully's throat, just ahead of a wave of muck the bully was vomiting. And the bees flew before the children, after them, and all around them, but did not sting them.

The bully did not stop hurting even when the bees had flown from his mouth. He ran from the cave until he came to a wallow where cows rolled. He swallowed cooling mud and rolled and rolled, but the bees followed him, stinging from the outside now. He could not shake them off, for whichever part of his hide was up as he rolled, that part did they sting. So many stings did he receive that he fell on his back and died like an animal, with his arms and legs sticking straight up in the air. And his teeth, which he had been gnashing and gritting, opened. He belched, an awful stinking belch. Then he farted, an awful stinking fart. And then the bees flew back inside him through both doors, for now he was quiet and clean. And they made their home in his belly. And when he had dwindled to a skeleton, naught but bones, anyone could reach in to get all the honey he wanted. And so the boy and the girl lived quite content, with sweets every day of their lives.

And the sweets they ate improved their temper, said old Rose. They were not as stubborn or as willful as before. They brought their parents to the cave with the two doors, and they all lived together, in harmony and joy, until it was time for the children to go to their mother's brother, as children did then in that place. But that was another story, and it did not end completely well.

Long ago IN ROSE'S LAP Pierre had popped his thumb in his mouth and had wept, for he could not return to his mother, Marie Mandilé-Ba, who had been sold, he knew not where, nor was there reason to suppose he would ever find his father, Jolicoeur, called Juba, who was dead or gone and came no longer to see him. And during all the time that Rose was telling the story, Pierre did not once look up at her face or look into the fire or look out at those others crouching into the warmth and light, but only cradled his head between the old nurse's two soft paps and nestled into her big soft belly and listened, contented, as a satiated spider in the middle of a web.

The sea became very calm when the serpent had spit out Pierre and dived back down to the bottom whence it must have come. The barrel had come to a shivering halt, with the water lapping gently against its sides. Night was falling once again. Far away the carnival of the dead lit up the sky; on the waters they danced in mirrored clothes while Pierre rested in the bosom of the Sea-One, nursing his hunger and thirst like two little babes. He was alive! He prayed he was not becalmed beneath the gaud-fest of stars in the doldrums, yet, though he was thirsty, he slept contented, as one who has returned from death. Soon enough, as he rocked between waking and sleep, there wafted into his nostrils a fresh, rich, green exuberant fragrance. And before he had moved from the dreamless doldrum he had floated into, yes, before he had opened his eyes, a fearsome jolt shook his barrel, and it crunched on LAND.

The Motherhood of Man

→

Yet I did not leap forth, but crouched still, Homunculus Soul in my skull of wood, ears pricked to the slapping, murmuring waves. I braced myself to the cask's shift, assaying the grunt of sand beneath, delirious, desiccated, sitting still as a man whose leg irons chafe at his smallest move, my mind rubbed sore by the press of PARADOX. Surely it were meet to rejoice, for I were REDEEMED FROM SLAVERY, SERPENT AND SEA. Yet how numbly I mourned my likely loss, the loss of all I had known: children running through the dusty yard, the women's voices floating after them, the smell of yam and manioc porridge bubbling in the pots. And after supper, before sweet sleep, the stories of wives who changed to doves to please their husbands, and husbands who changed to snakes to spy on their wives, of naughty children changed to grain and eaten by their parents' hens and jealous gods who stole the rich men's cows.

Grounded in the sand of an unknown shore, I feared I would not hear again the firelight testaments, and feared I would; not to hear I was derelict in freedom, to hear, returned to M'sieu. Oh, I did not want to be caught, to be spitefully rented to cruel, harsh slave-breakers, to drudge in their carries, grinding bones and tearing muscles, hoeing and cutting, hoeing and cutting, dreaming of the book-filled room where I had read the words of savants. I feared the suspended whippings—the ladder, the hammock, the Four-Post. I feared I would be sold to a poor planter who could neither clothe nor feed me. When Baron Skull came for my corpse, he would find but broken bones in a bag of scars, all that made me a man having long since died within and been eaten by rage and grief. Oh better a barren solitude, relieved by what comfort I could contrive!

Yet still I saw before me Vérité, her cheek to the rim of the rain barrel, blowing an ashy cork across the water to her hand, spelling me to safety, as she had promised. <u>Courage, Vérité! You will not yet see my features written on the surface of the water! It is not yet my time. I have been redeemed from the sea and now my hopes reside in land!</u>

But what land? Despite my dilemma, I was curious. I shook off my fear to spy out the bunghole; my eye told me I had washed ashore on an island resembling Saint-Michel, even to the proliferation of orchids. This coincidence did not encourage me, yet though the isle appeared little if any inhabited. And so I stayed in my barrel while thirst increased; the sky darkened a second time before I screwed up courage to explore. Then I peered out one last time, to ascertain my safety in emerging.

Through the bunghole my eye met a round yellow one with a black center—the eye, methought, of a FRIGHTFUL LARGE FISH, the terrible serpent risen from the deep to claim me!

In thoughtless panic, I popped the cover of the cask and saw in the dusk no greedy monster come to sup on my flesh, but a homelier haunt—the first old rat-counting madame, wrapped in rosaries, clouded crystal marbles and boys' round eyes, necklaces of rats strung tail to mouth, squeaking vengeance. Her undressed hair did appear to billow about a sea-wrinkled face, illumined from within by pale phosphorescence that shone with a fey green light. Her feet had been changed to frogs' feet! Oh, what restlessness had floated her out of her grave to loom before me, petulant and terrible?

"Mistress!" I cried. "I have only arrived and have not yet had time to kill any rats. I am too old for marbles. I wear drawers now; nay, I have been raised from drawers to breeches."

Her mouth opened and closed; she fixed my eye with her fishy stare.

"Pierre did not manufacture the effigy that foretold your fate, nor stuff it with rats, nor set it on fire. I pray you, show mercy!"

I threw myself at her froggy feet to plead for my life. She squeaked in an odd inhuman voice and hopped back on those amphibolous feet, her wary eyes inscrutable. She had no nose! How could she live and have her being? I gaped at her as she gaped at me.

After we had eyed each other some wary time, she turned on her flippered feet and dove beneath the waves. I ran behind some brush, and nestled into my haunches, and watched a while, but soon I took heart from the wave-slapped silence. For, if she were old Madame, changed by the sea, or if she were not, what boot it? She had not summoned boatloads of men with muskets and whips to break me body and soul to their will. I had best put aside my terror and see to my immediate circumstances, for my throat was painfully woody, my tongue swollen monstrous in my mouth.

Soon enough I had drunk my fill at sweetwater pools among rocks 'pon which I was lucky not to have foundered. I cautiously circumambulated my island, peering about me 'til I knew its parts, and knew them uninhabited save by palm rats, run-go to-fro mice, the lady-puff lizards and flocks of red butterfly birds. I tore off the bottom of my shirt, and tied it on a stick, and planted this banner so as to CLAIM THE PLACE for my own. The amphibolous-footed lady I had pegged for a hapless shade, a phantasm with no body, a refugee from Skull. So I banished my terror, devoting myself to comfortable, necessary tasks, viz., I constructed a hut of stones chinked with sea-weed—which the wood lice abhorred, mayhap on account of the salt—an abode larger and roomier than my plantation kennel, with a roof of reeds and a porch that furnished a view of the setting sun.

I had discovered betimes an erratic freshet, moreover, varieties of juicy fruit to suck, viz., guava, and sweet and sour sops, and mambins and mombees, and dildun berries. My dwelling erected, I dug and gingerly tasted of roots; I nibbled the spiny pear or artichoke fruit called *cactus*; I washed my sodden quilt in the sea and hung it to dry, whereupon I settled in to battle insects, like any land-holder. If I had been able to send my linen out, and get in some books, I might have accounted myself in paradise, though I did want company.

Where was my spider? And where the boats of men I had floated past on the sea? Mayhap, in my circumambulations of the isle, I had missed them. I called down the crevices of rocks and up into trees: "Holloa! Pierre comes as friend. You need not fear him. He is hale; moreover he is possessed of many useful, ingenious skills."

Silence but for the slapping waves, the rippling crickus of the butterfly birds and the buzzing racket of insects.

"I am writing a compendious histoire," I cried, "in which are chronicled the habits and attributes of beasts and the customs and events of men who are scanted in Europid accounts."

If anyone were biding his time to speak, he kept his counsel. If I wanted conversation, I must PRATTLE TO MYSELF, bidding myself good morrow and good evening, asking and answering questions.

"Where am I?" I did ask me.

"An island very like Saint-Michel," me did respond. "At a meridian on a parallel I could not ascertain."

"And climate and vegetation?"

"Familiar . . . familiar."

"And does this place have a name?"

"Not one known to me, but it is mine to name by shirt tail's claim."

"So you must ponder the question of suitable names, their provenance and power."

All the places I knew had the names of white men, and were under the dominion of white men's Gods, viz., Saint Michel. Now that Saint with His sword were a brave Christian martyr, His likeness a powerful charm to protect who would implore Him to intercede with Son and Father to bless the inhabitants of His name-place. So I had been told by Père Gouy, and could believe, for these celestial hierarchies were very like mundane etiquettes I had known, wherein a slave-man must entreat the driver or the overseer, to gain from his master some favor, viz., extra salt or cloth or a holiday. Yet on my new island, no hierarchy, indeed, no society at all. It made no sense, then, to NAME THIS PLACE for a celestial go-between. Indeed why name it for any God of the whites?

The whey-guts had not found my present island, or if they had, they had deemed it too trifling in size, or too far removed from other settlement, or too rocky for large-scale planting. If they had o'erlooked this isle, then no doubt their Gods had.

Might I not give the place some name from Guinée, to honor the Gods Who walked on invisible legs? One of those Great Ones might protect me! Yet I was the only African domiciled in this, my freehold. I had explored it over and over again and found no bandit maroons, nor any other derelicts or fugitives. Were the Gods of Africk more needfully employed where more Africkans sojourned? Could these Gods see PIERRE, so alone and far away

180

from his kind? Though I knew the name of my mother's people, I did not know the name of my father's, nor any of my ancestors' lineages, so how could I prove my dignity and worth to the Gods Who watch the Fombé? Though yet I hoped my name would claim me from my pouch, the bag had been silent lo! these years.

Did I await the Black Redeemer, taller than any tree, walking across the sea from Guinée? Had He already saved me? Did He make my acquaintance closer, would He cast me out of His presence, who had tucked a napkin into my collar and read the books of savants and set myself above others, even in creating my 'cyclopedia from accounts and relations of my fellows? Dare I approach Him?

"Spider," I called. "Dear and only friend of my voyage, where, oh where, have you gone?"

Ah me! Without my spider to speak for my cowries, I must fall back on what good sense an erstwhile napkin-tucker possessed, without his wife on hand.

Yet where was good sense in the tight circle of dancing Speculation? My thoughts whirled as my wife had whirled when the Uncle rode her, dancing in a circle drawn in dust, her useless leg nailed to the spot where Uncle had clapped her between His thunder arms, filling her with light.

Yet my wife were not here, my spider not here, indeed very little were here in this wilderness place. If a God be resident in my newfound home, He must live as a God of men with nothing, a God of bare-scratched gardens Who follows the seasons' food, without the faith of persons settled in numbers to sustain Him. He must live on the transpiration of tiny, humble creatures, viz., jutias and mango hummers, or even vegetables, that gently raise and lower their leaves, creating a wind that is a humble breath, like the ah! of faith.

Had not Uncle already reached from the tawny past, to speak in the tongues of red men to Africans miserably captive, who could offer Him little but the steam of fish and yams aboil? Had not Uncle guided with my wife my own escape? There were no tawnies on my isle, yet perhaps they came here to hunt or pray. I whittled a driftwood peg and drove it into the ground, its upper end wedged in a split palm-frond to form a tall, leafy triangle. I resolved to name for Uncle the island of my freedom. And I wrote *Isle de l'Oncle* in the sand, and spelled out in pebbles by the door of my house, *Pierre Baptiste de l'Isle de l'Oncle,* and asked myself, did I know now, where I was?

Here, Kind Reader, I beg you consider the LONELY DISCOMFI-TURE of a derelict, who has hitherto marked the vicissitudes of his existence but in relation to others. Thus he has made the map by which he knows himself. The peril I had escaped notwithstand-ing, I longed for company. I longed to taste once again the man-ioc stew of my godmothers. I longed to hear the people throwing stories back and forth round the fires. I did even long for the company of the master, Dufay, for though he had sold my mother, yet we shared the passion for learning. Still I fancied I heard his footfall, a damp entrance from the dew with sketch in hand, "My Goody, I have finally got that blue parrot, which is like no other we have seen. Now do you write Buffon for me to sign, and Dr. Hamel in Saint-Hildebert, and inquire if another has seen the bird and drawn it."

Yet more than any other of my connections I missed my wife, the spicy scent of whose melon-ripe person rolled with mine I could but faintly sniff in the quilt I had brought in the bottom of my barrel. In truth, the whiff of home so sickened me with yearn-ing, I flung the quilt from me, preferring to shiver in the evening damp. I sometimes dreamed of jumping back into my barrel and trying to row it home, where they would be so glad to see me I might escape punishment. Idle fancies! I had no idea which way was home.

I feared I would live out my days in isolation more complete than First Man's. No one like me was with me. First Man enjoyed the company of sister and wife, his own First Woman, born with him of Damzillah, Water-She-Silver-She, who had lain with Her son, Chenwiyi, in the mud. Didn't Uncle cut off Her head with a swing of His hammer, while Chenwiyi was still inside Her? Didn't Uncle stomp on Her body, smashing Her ribs with His horny feet, forgetting that Chenwiyi squatted between the roots of the en-na-a-na tree, diving to catch the ribs that Uncle was throwing away? Didn't Chenwiyi bury half those broken ribs in earth, so they would grow into Gormilah and Gormilah and Gormilah, Who sprouted all the other Gods, each separate, each born from Gormilah, hairy, monstrous, many-hearted, Gormilah? Then the Uncle threw Chenwiyi down into waters that surround the world, down into Chaos, and He was lost. So were they all to me, or I to them, far, far away. Lost the Gods immortal, brothers and sisters, all far, far away. But for birds & ghosts & insects, I was alone. Oh, the *insectae*!

Fanning myself with a palmetto frond one afternoon, I contemplated my banishment amidst the contumely of buzzing and whining. Quite idly I drew open my pouch, to see what comfort its tea-label commonplaces might afford; though I sought a soothing proverb of my godmothers, my groping fingers fastened 'pon an epigram of Pintal: "At the heart of solitude is sorrow, at the heart of sorrow, bliss, to know thyself."

Then my hands on the tea label trembled. I spoke angrily to the philosopher who had dared to utter the sentiments I had formerly thought pretty enough to copy.

"What cosseted individual," cried Pierre, "living peaceful in a social state, isolated but momentarily in a book-filled room, can deign to preach to one whose singularity is so bleak and all-encompassing?"

And a ghostly Pintal did speak in my ear, saying, "There is no choice but to embrace one's fate, and in so doing, transcend."

Spider? Be you there? And speaking as Pintal?

Pierre Baptiste: "If you are to preach so brazen a homily, filled with wisdom yet without sympathy, then I dissolve you back into air, you and all other savants so insensible of my condition."

As I said these words there stole into my breast and limbs a power not my own. I am but Man, and can but as A HEAVENLY SIGN account for the fire that sprang up in my hand to consume the tea label, charring it to ash, yet without burning my hand. Amazed, I sprinkled these ashes back into the pouch from which the label had come, though not without first attempting to catch and save the elusive fire, that I might use it to ward off the mosquitoes and merrymen that plagued me. Yet the fire extinguished itself quickly.

Looking up from its ashes in the palm of my hand, my eye fastened once again upon the words "Pierre Baptiste de l'Isle de l'Oncle" I had spelled out in pebbles by my door. And looking further around I saw that all the geographical features of the place did now spell out *l'Isle de l'Oncle* and *Pierre Baptiste de l'Isle de l'Oncle*. Yea, the very leaves of trees and ground plants, the twigs and motes of debris that littered the island floor, the flock of parrots whose flight darkened the sky, all spelled out these words in changing and shifting patterns, a whirling and shifting dance that lifted me out of myself. I raised my arms above my head and shouted "Uncle!" "Uncle!" The floor of the world rocked beneath me.

Though the island were but wind-bent growth, sand and rock, lizard and bird, with no prominent features that might send my voice back as an echo, yet did my call softly reverberate, as if every leaf did catch and magnify His Name, every mote cry "Uncle!" "Uncle!"

184

Then I found my feet moving, my body swaying. Yet who chanted, who drummed? My bare feet marked the time with a resonant slap, but a greater heart than mine beat "Uncle! Uncle!" in my breast. I and I turned and swayed in a pattern I did not know I knew, twisting my and my body to shape the letters of an airy alphabet, and in that alphabet, to spell *Uncle God*. Then the world hissed and turned blue, as if swallowed by the sea: I and I picked up the pebbles with which I had not long previous formed in mortal language the words "Pierre Baptiste de l'Isle de l'Oncle"; I placed them in my and my mouth, and the sea spit back the world. I and I made a broom of silver-thatch, and swept-wrote His name in the letters of enigma in the garden of sand, and knew then and then my place.

Yet even as a Chosen of Uncle my ERSTWHILE AMBITIONS claimed me. I lay on my back in the porch of my house, regarding the sky through a crack that had opened in the thatch. And the clouds rolled upward as a glory in the frontispiece of a tragedy. And clothed but in draperies, with laurel circling his brow, Pierre ascended to a world of ink, constructed all of word and line, the shadow erased. Pierre sat on a chair, of which the left leg were a Doric column, the right an Ionic. Between his legs in both his hands Pierre held the staff of Aesculapius, snakes curling around it, the wings of Mercury fluttering and live at its top. As to Pierre's deportment, every gesture were revelatory, frontal, and symmetric with some other gesture. If he raised his right hand, then the left foot must twitch. So he was arranged for himself as a spectacle for a single omnipotent observer. He listened with the indifference of one all-powerful upon overhearing a learned dispute among a number of men in very bright wigs, some kneeling or standing to his right, some to his left. They shook their heads, and the powder of their wigs dispersed as dust motes in the light. A steaming volcano of ink rose behind Pierre, coughing but not coughing, as he coughed without coughing, as if he had been created only to listen in stifled silence to voices of those who speak. He was King, yet specimen in cage of light.

"To asseverate that the ordinary world around us, viz., God's Creation, of the Great Year 4666 before Our Lord, were other than perfect, were blasphemy," argued a gentleman in a full-bottom. M'sieu in his father's wig? "Though I cannot deny that men and beasts and vegetables and perhaps the winds and water do suffer from uneven distribution of benefits on Earth, mayhap in HEAVEN."

"Still the presumption must be honored," cried another, "our divine Creator were as skilled, at least, as a watchmaker; the Creator did know what parts were needed for the working of the whole. This, were He verily of loathsome character!"

Yet another, haughtier eminence asserted that "perfection is dependent on the onlooker's perspective; moreover, perfection itself has its lights and shades. It is not always revealed in the world with clarity. It has not always the *apparency* it possesses in M'sieu's paintings, or in the chopping, static categories of too-rigorous taxonomy."

And who were this punctilious worthy wagging his finger at M'sieu? Could he have been—? The great Buffon? Had Pierre arrived in Montbard a homunculus trapped in a drawing that exists but for engraving, to be contemplated as a copy of itself? Was Pierre trapped in this perpetual noon among pedant-savants who dispute and dispute? Oh marooned! Marooned in pendulum perpetuity, ticking inside a clock of crystal through which light is bent into colors arrayed in a hierarchic band—a band, a bond, a band for a bondsman, abandoned. Yet not abandoned, for here he were, as he had hoped and wished and feared, PIERRE NOVELLANIS, who creates himself. Who or what created Pierre to create the conception, Pierre could not have said, and cannot now. For even as M'sieu, to take a known *exemplum,* were temperamental, eccentric, and absent-minded, despite the clarity and purity of his rendering, so the nature of the Supreme Artist be unfathomable in paradox beyond "Omnipotent," "Eternal," "Omnipresent," and other grandiloquent honorifics. Indeed the Supreme Artist may be One who has no glass to see His world, even as His world has no glass to see Him.

Yet this is a cold conception. A man who suffers cannot afford it. Pierre would live in a universe he could charm, yea, influence, to act on his behalf. "My behalf! My behalf!" Pierre in his Doric-Ionic chair smote the ground with the staff of Aesculapius. He heard then a faint, astonished, dismayed cry, and the tearing of paper. A volcano erupted. Hot ink flowed around, and all the learned men were burned as the clouds melted. The sun was extinguished. The world darkened, and Pierre was submerged in oblivious sleep, though still the brightness of noon were hot on his lids.

I opened my eyes on my volcanoless isle to find I had slept through a night into day. I remained in the imperfect world, my rock-bound sea-girt shirt-tail kingdom stinking with orchids. The noon of perfect light? The noon of awful heat! I thought to dip my sleeve in a puddle to cool my temples, but I felt parched from within, as if the shadow that spilled on the ground behind my heels had been my spirit flowing out of me, leaving me with a thirst like a hungry tide, pulling me out of myself. And I called not Uncle, but the name of Pélérine, who served Uncle. And I lay with the sun burning my eyes, wailing without tears, clutching the ragged quilt she had given me.

"Woe!" I moaned, hugging the quilt. "Woe again! And Woe, and Woe, and Woe!" At last, the sun began dropping in the sky;

my shadow returned and opened around me like a mother's lap. Rain fell into my mouth, the sky's tears. Though I would learn my place anew, I would never be content alone.

"Oh Uncle, if you love me, barrel my WIFE and deliver her into my hands like a hog's-head of bacon; let her cradle in her arms a pile of books from M'sieu's shelves, it scarcely matters which. If you cannot bring Pélérine, then deliver me, at least, from the endless hum of merrywings, the louder buzz of mosquitoes. For these noises do rouse me to a frenzy of distraction. My body is covered with pea-sized knobs that itch. I need my wife to daub them with vinegar. I need her help to devise a bed. For any hammock I string of vines to raise me above the jaws of ants, they devour the very next day! Let her come with tar to smear on the cords!

"If I cannot have my wife, then let me have fire to make smoke; let me have a burning mirror, like Buffon's, yea, let me have a tinder box; for how can I make fire without one? Yet fire you brought, Uncle, to burn my label. Bring it again, in a captive manner, a blaze to drive off winged furies. And pity, I pray, my poor feet, for chiggers have burrowed under my toenails and ulcerated all the tender parts. My knife is rusting; when it is dull, how will I dig the chiggers out? How will I cut reeds for thatch when my roof is devoured by wood lice? Yea, I cannot even do women's work!"

Only the drones of insects answered my ravings.

"A hoe!" I called as an afterthought. "If not my wife, or a fire, or a whetstone, give me a hoe to clear some ground, to mound up cones of earth around the roots of plantings."

Now I missed the master's estate because the land was cultivated! Oh, such is the lot of the derelict civic in his expectations!

Two dainty pickamon lizards, their tongues darting rapidly, precise and fussy in their movements as well-trained gentlemen soldiers, did bring with them from nowhere a cooling breeze. I fanned myself in it, and thanked Uncle, for surely He had brought the breeze. I would yet achieve my destiny through His intervention, HIS KIND BROWN HAND tearing through the paper world to snatch me up and set me down among savants. To bind my ambitions in Uncle's web I wrapped the tea-label sayings of philosophes with those of my godmothers, pairing them in threads unraveled from my ragged shirt, till the paper weddings were invisible inside the cocoons. I put the cocoons in my pouch with that other paper wrapped in thread, the secret bound to Who-Knew-What-God my mother had given me to protect.

And half of each meal I ate I gave to Uncle, arranging it carefully on leaves before His name in stones at my door. And always when I killed a nacarette or a bongon bird, the blood and feathers I gave to Uncle, smeared on His stones, mixed with what had been in the bird's gut and with some of the flesh, which I must eat raw, for I had no fire. And half the salt I dried was His, and half the water I collected His. And around the trunk of each tree on the isle I tied a cord braided of silver-thatch. I renewed each day my vow never to cut the trees, though I might take a few leaves or a frond at a time, for the bodies of the living trees were Uncle's body, His sanctuary.

Yet Pierre was not the fool to suppose the God Uncle worked in the world unaided. No, Pierre must assist. If he wished to be reunited with his wife, and commence his apprentice savantship, he must HELP HIMSELF. And so Pierre, who had saved his barrel outside his house, to collect the rain, planned a SECOND OCEANIC JOURNEY, this one prepared as an expedition, with provisions & gear & wherewithal to navigate.

Pierre could have no charts, but, as ancient mariners, would ascertain his mundane position from the fixed constellations, in relation to the horizon. He could establish the time of year from the sun's position at its zenith. So, if he but studied the heavens and noted the positions of stars on days recorded in the calendar he had made of notched driftwood, he might navigate.

Yet unfortunately, though its joints had swollen at sea, the outside of his barrel was cracking in the hot sun, while the inside rotted, from the rainwater it held. And that barrel had never been easy to steer, for she lacked any semblance of rudder or tiller. Moreover, she moved entirely with and upon the tide, having no sail to catch the wind. She was all hold and no deck, no prow, no keel, though she could be weighted, as on his previous journey, with his tools, and for a second journey he could add in stones to keep her from skidding adrift on the wave.

Yet ballast would not suffice to hold direction. He must dismantle his barrel to build a BETTER VESSEL, that he could steer, or he would never reach the realm of savants, where he could publish his histoire and show his people worthy of liberty. He could not pass for cargo in the open boat he proposed to build, yet he must give up safety in hiding for a truer boat, one which could hold his wife, if he could contrive to purloin her. He would saw his barrel into halves, two pods. Pierre and his wife would each be a pea in one pod. When he had the boat, he would find a way to snatch her.

He began to devote a part of each day to hacking through his keg with his rusted saw, halving her through her crosswise circumference at her most swollen middle, preserving intact the hoops that held her staves together. Though the work were arduous, it yielded in time two sound pods, which he joined circumference to circumference with ropes of twisted & braided fiber of the silverthatch. Yet, even in the calmest of waters, the lashing gave way. Moreover, striding a swell, the down pod shipped water. So Pierre plotted to elevate the two pods on a driftwood raft, which he might have constructed of sawn-up trees, had not Uncle forbidden him to cut trees. More than once Pierre stood at the base of a well-grown tree, rusty ax in hand, only to hear the voice of Uncle rumbling a thunderous reproof. He had not the heart to swing the ax. So, alas, he must wait for driftwood, wait and wait.

Yet he continued to make improvements in his craft. He tied his oar aft of his aft pod, and thus ruddered the whole. He devised a balance frame, of drift sticks lashed with vine, that floated on hollow coco shells, plugged up and tied at intervals along the frame, to buoy his still-clumsy vessel and prevent her o'erturning. And now he was ready for a sail, and on this point he stuck again.

Yet it came to him he might weave mats of silver thatch, which, if woven very fine and tight, might catch and hold wind. He commenced to try proofs of his hypothesis, weaving first small patches of the stuff, then larger, which he lashed to his arms, and held to the wind, to see if he rose above the ground, a human kite. When he rose a little off his heels, he tried larger squares and found he rose as high above himself as a bird above a tree, though his heart be left on the ground and his body plash in the sea like the carcass of Icarus. Yet now he had reason to believe his stuff might hold, he commenced to weave still larger squares, and added for strength a diagonal crossing of his warp and weft, and then a cross-diagonal. This most tedious and intricate business his fingers came to effect on their own, while the thread of his musing wove itself an intricate, seditious plot whereby he would take a tree or two yet fool the Uncle into supposing His timber intact. Mayhap a lumber raft were too greedy a conception, for it would take all the trees. Mayhap a smaller conception, for which one small tree would suffice, a tree so small Uncle would feel the loss no more than Pierre the burrowing of a chigger. Yet of this one tree, Pierre could make a prow and a taffrail and an armature to stabilize his boat in its balance frame. Still too greedy a conception? Pierre would settle for a prow, made of a tree so small the Uncle would feel its loss no more than Pierre the bite of a merrywing. Too greedy still? Pierre passed his shuttle of a hand through his warp threads, filling, filling, filling. So occupied was he weaving sails and plots, he did not trouble to eat for a day and a night. But now a hunger gnawed at his belly like a rat chewing its way from an effigy into which some boys have sewed it.

Methought I would quiet my belly with turtle meat. So, after paring a spear from a drifted branch, I took me to the rock outcropping at the westward side of my domain where turtles fed. Were I to frequent these unsheltered rocks by day, the sun made me dizzy. I had fallen into the custom of standing upon them by night, to hear the boom of the surf pound in time with my heart, when my longings overwhelmed me as they did if I stayed on my pallet of thatch, pining for my wife in the dark.

Imagine my chagrin, this mild adventitious evening, to perceive wriggling on my spear point THE SEA SHADE that I had mistaken, first for a serpent, then for First Madame! I had speared it just beneath the shoulder blade, where the "arm"—that long fin with fingers—joined the body. If it had been Madame I might have relished the vengeance of puncture. Yet, though blood gushed from a hole in pink-specked skin, gill slits heaved most piteously—gills! The specter was corporeal, but she was a fish!

I lay the head in the water, so she could respire, and stanched with the rags of my shirt the flow of her blood. Still she lay in a swoon. When the sun came up, I saw she would be burned if I did not arch over her a roof of fronds and sticks, cadged from the debris at the tideline. This I did, and she lay calmly, her gills palpitating in the brine, her eyes gaping.

As the tide went out, I saw that she would no longer be able to respire, so I moved her body, lifting it in my arms to follow the receding waters. At first she struggled in my embrace, but after I had lifted her several times, she lay still, her shanky legs draped over my arm and her head with its coarse-crimped curls lolling on my breast. Only once did she bare her teeth, and then for the first time I saw the double row of needles. I took from my talisman pouch my mother's bone hook, which I fastened to a line I had braided with threads from my shirt. I caught with this tackle the smallest, tenderest fishlings that flashed and turned in tide pools. I offered them to her, flopping still, in a seawater gravy contained in a clam's shell, pushing said shell between her jaws lest she sink her teeth into my hand. But, seeing she took the fish very dainty from the shell, I vouchsafed to feed her with my fingers, and found she nibbled nicely. So we got on well, and her wound mended.

I wondered I had ever confounded her with Rat-Ma'am, even granting the proposition that First Old Mistress be a species other than human; even so, this creature I now entertained were more foreign a species still, even as a snake is less penetrable in nature than a dog or a goat. I do not know why I thought of her as "She." She bore no mark of the female sex, unless one count her long tarnished locks—not in truth hair, but some bony substance like coral—and elegant, long-fingered hands, that called to mind the filigree of lace.

In time, I got to know her ways, a fillip of her feet, fast, as a cat will fillip its tail when plagued by a nuisance; or a gaze following my hands when I had a fish. I came to know many a place on her scaly skin, most particularly on her forehead, she did shiver to have touched, moving closer to my hand.

Upbraiding myself the while for foolishness, I commenced to call her "ma bonne amie" and finally "Amie." I directed all my prattle to her and wept tears of joy and distress when, her wound having healed, she dove beneath the billows, returning only for brief nocturnal visits, to be petted on the forehead, provided the shadow of spear or hook fall not across her path.

In this independence as in her former helplessness she gawked at me as if mesmerized by my babble, but it were the talisman, hanging from my neck, she did eye in its swinging. This I discovered when she snatched it and dragged it beneath the sea, consigning it to the oblivious depths with all its charms save the fish hook, which I had accustomed myself to daily use, and so had hung with its looped line from a stick poked into a chink in a wall of my house.

She surfaced without the bag the next time she came to be cosseted; though I did scold her and wag my finger, she would not bring the talisman back. Perhaps she had snatched it to repay the wound I had inflicted, but justice at my expense were small comfort. I had clung to the talisman as an orchid with its phallical roots clutching air. Yet I kept more than my fishing hook. For I stored in my cranial conjure house my 'cyclopedic histoire of mystical, natural & diverse knowings; I had fashioned a rustic domesticity in my physical abode; my boat was abuilding. Bereft of my cherished talisman, I did not wither or fade, but continued to weave my sails and plot my future course, which now I could do without thought of food.

Though AMIE did not breathe through a nose, she compensated the theft of the talisman and indeed made good the debt of her life according to her custom, repaying my solicitude with fish, which she chewed into mush and regurgitated at my feet. Thus, I could leave my mother's hook hanging in my house as a charm and did not have to risk it atrawl. Nor did I need to use my spear. I would have preferred that the fish be brought me whole, yet she could not fathom my revulsion: at last I bade her vomit the stew into the calabash I had of my wife, and drank while holding my nose. I found the stew most sweet and mild, like a medley of fish and yam.

Without my rain barrel I must search for shallow pools of sweet water in the rocks, and risk desiccation if there be drought, yet I made some assurance of supply, by hammering at a number of very large boulders, till I found one that would flake if I beat it. So by my labors I made a cistern, and in time made others, and my days fell into a pleasing pattern. I wove my sails, and Amie brought my dinner, and I gazed at the sky reflected in my cisterns and saw my Vérité, reflected in the barrel of rain in Dufay's yard. Through the open door of the kitchen, I saw she, too, built boats, though hers were of sugar. With a long-handled spoon of charred wood she spun crystal threads from a pot, and with those threads rigged ships that would sail, not on water, but on light that shimmers atop the waves, joining sea to land and air. I prayed we might finish our vessels at the same time; we might meet in the middle of the sea.

One evening Amie spewed into the calabash a strange seashell, a SMALL ROSY CONE which crumbled upon my inspection. Thereupon she emitted a yawp, the first noise I had heard of her, and slapped her feet on the water. She brought no more food for several evenings.

When she returned I was hungry, for I had been reluctant to leave off weaving to fish. I lay on my back then and bade her spit the mush directly into my mouth. She did so willingly, spitting into my maw as well several sharp objects I surmised at once were the cones, which crumbled on my tongue. Though I did spit out shell bits, and pick them from my lips and from between my teeth, my tongue burned as if stung. I dared not swallow for fear the shells be poisonous.

After a while the burning subsided, so I judged it but the consequence of a fish-frog prank! I constricted my gullet to swallow, and my tongue, though swollen, did waggle in my mouth as before. Thus, when it became too dark to weave, I passed the evening prattling, according to my custom. I called for Amie, who came not again, then called for the spider that had abandoned me. I would ask the mouth of mouths what boot it wait for driftwood, the esoteric price of cutting a tree, my prospect of finishing a seaworthy boat, the likelihood of reaching France, the imminence of reunion with my wife. I asked and answered myself, and asked and answered again, as was my wont. Having talked myself to sleep, then, consider my great surprise, 'pon waking, to find myself unable to bid myself good morrow.

In vain the fingers of one hand then the other did walk past my lips, sortie between my jaws, and explore the salty cave behind my teeth. Where my tongue had rooted, there poked a stump which by wagging I could cajole to an idiot's speech, being now unable to voice half the words in my lexicon. In my disappointment I failed to remark the lumpiness swelling my cheeks, but lay all day in a damp hollow in the sand, shedding tears, too mournful and weak to weave.

I woke to discover Amie squatting above me, butting me with her forehead to be petted. Her puffed-out cheeks told me she intended to dribble gruel between my lips; though the gruel carry more shellfish to undo me, I was too weary and hungry to protest; I parted my lips. There came from my mouth then a faint squalling sound. When I stretched a finger gingerly into a cheek pouch, it warmed to the gentle clutch of one minuscule pair of arms, then another. By careful feints with the finger, I counted four—dare I call them infants? Two in each cheek pouch.

I surmised that I was in a condition I had never looked to be in—a condition in which I believe no member of my sex has been before. If MY PREGNANCY had not, my astonishment unmanned me. Of all men to be so enmarvelled, I, Pierre, who had not wished to breed—now, unnatural, quick! Yet I owed a duty to these young. Thus, I parted my lips and permitted Amie to flood my mouth with gruel, forbearing to swallow until by a manner of reckoning I had not known I possessed, I surmised my young had drunk their fill.

I did not sleep in my hut that night, nor any night of my gravidness, but lay curled in my dank hole by the sea, burning in the sun by day and shivering in the night's chill breeze. Yet I could not move, for the infants squealed most piteously did I but turn my head. At the end of my confinement I scarce opened my eyes and relied entirely on Amie to feed me, the tide to clean out my nest. I no longer worked on the half-woven sails, which later I found had dried and crumbled in the sun. My boat remained unfinished, two weathering pods by the side of my abandoned house. Nor did I dream of glory among savants or scheme much, now, to snatch Pélérine. I was suffused with tender thoughts for the young in my cheeks and thought of little else, but lay very still, crooning as best I could with a shortened tongue in a gravid mouth:

Ba-wal loo-mah ba-ha-wa loo-a-to
Ba-wal loo-mah ba-ha-wa ba-lu-ba wa!

Methought Marie Mandilé-Ba had crooned this refrain; she had learned the song from the sufferers beside her, when she was brought from Guinée. So I had been told by my godmothers, whose stories I were at greater and greater pains to recall—did the king whose wife turned into a coorucu bird lure her with barley grains or millet seeds?—even as now I had trouble recalling the names of animals and plants in patois, Latin, or French. I no longer knew the difference between Pintal's idea of faith and Nerf's. I had forgotten the names of Squint's ports of call. Alas! The prism conjure house were falling to ruin with my roof of thatch. Yet sometimes I saw it, whole and radiant in the sky, at the close of day, when the clouds are layered with colors, the colors with story.

To prompt my memory, I talked to myself in my head as my own blab school, mingling part-passages of authors with bits of moonlit story, but the effort was fatiguing. Soon enough I returned to crooning "Ba-wal loo-mah," which I could pronounce but as "ah-ah ah-ah," for I could not work my lips or move my tongue or jaws for fear of discommoding the young in my cheeks.

From the corner of an eye, I looked down at the curve of a distended cheek, stretched taut across the squirm and kick of life within. Did I resemble the crack-cheeked cherub winds who blew above the roses, directing sailors to the world's four corners?

Alas! The erstwhile sailor was confined to his hold, prey to whatever vicissitudes of fortune befell him, most especially to caprice of tropical weather—to merciless sun and sudden storm. I dare not bestir myself to build another roof but must lie in my seaside hole like a shelly fish. Yet I did not crave a dry bed as greatly as I craved companionship. For alas! Vérité no longer appeared to me in sky or water. My consort disappeared beneath the sea each evening. I feared the young in my mouth would follow at the breeching, be lost to me as talisman and memories. So I lived in moist apprehension, waiting.

Then push! Pull! Push! Pull! *Honor the Gods, though They cannot be seen.* Pull! Push! *Shining Great Ones, help with the breech. Stay here with me; do not fail!* Push! Pull! Push! *I beseech You, take care.* Push! Push! Pull! *I bear the honor of this birth with joy. Shining Great Ones!* Push! Pull! Push! *Though the storm in my cheeks undo me, I submit to the will that consumes.*

And when the inner storm subsided, FOUR OFFSPRING fell from between my teeth and tumbled into the sand before my face, squirming and squalling in the manner of human infants.

They were as helpless as any human babes, and indeed they bore the impress of my features, and had the lidded eyes of men, and toes on their feet, and skin, not scales, though mostly of mottled coloration. They had gills behind their ears, but noses as well; as they matured, the gill slits narrowed. They were fine, lusty fry, of a velvety, very dark green, though very much smaller than human young; all four could lie on their backs in the palm of my hand.

Curiously, they lacked those external organs by which we ascertain gender, having between their legs neither the stamen of the male nor the female's sepals and calyx. They had been reproduced; their presence in my hand proved progenitors. Yet, if they bore no organs of reproduction, how would they generate themselves? Here was a question for a philosopher, most especially one with a microscope. Be the offspring not hybrids, like mules, but without genitalia, 'twere likely their organs of reproduction were minuscule, as in certain plants that lack flowers. When he visited Montbard, Pierre would show his offspring to Buffon, for the great man had studied in his youth with a microscope the organs of animal reproduction.

The disciple of Buffon must here confess the disloyalty of framing a most Linnaean question—with what other creatures did his progeny fit in the great panoply of speciation? Yet Pierre had given birth to these offspring, so unlike himself. Did not their existence call into question the very notion *species*? Mayhap his offspring would give birth to creatures as unlike themselves as they were unlike Pierre. Mayhap a NEW FORM OF LIFE had sprung from Pierre's mouth as heroes had sprung from the forehead of Zeus-God in days of old. As Gods to men, so Pierre to his offspring, and his offspring to theirs.

Yet, since First Man and First Woman had been born of Damzillah, Gods had been Gods, men, men; were Pierre's offspring truly his offspring? If a man put a piece of food in another man's mouth, would young be born? Or if he put food in a woman's? Or a woman food in a man's mouth? Or a fishsprite in a man's? Could Pierre's young have been generated spontaneously, as flies, not from rotten meat or greasy rags, but from his tongue? And if Pierre's tongue were rotten or greasy, what had made it so? If Pierre had not gangrene, had not the pox, nor any buboes, he must be rotten in a manner of speaking; he must be rotten-wicked, his offspring a punishment. Now as he had been a slave, his wickedness must have been the wickedness of a slave, viz., disobedience. Yet why had this punishment fallen only on him, and not, that he knew, on slaves who pilfered rum or wrecked the works or set fire to the cane? And what of the wickedness of masters, who drank rum in which their servants' bodies were dissolved? These questions, for which even now I have not the answers, much occupied me, even as I peered at the offspring waving their legs in the palm of my hand.

Now I cannot say these offspring altogether pleased me. Their very strangeness made me homesick for my godmothers' accounts of strangenesses haunting the world, viz., dog-faced demons who left point-eared babes in women's cradles, having spirited away the round-eared ones. Yet what parent warms not at the clasp of tiny fingers on his finger, the miracle the more apparent if the fingers of the babe do but grasp a hair on the parent's knuckle? Be these offspring sterile as mules, yet they would provide me companionship. Yea, if they could not, would not, gratify as children, then they would do as pets, to caper and fetch, to sit and roll 'pon my command, to slumber at the foot of my bedplace, if I did not kick 'em in my sleep.

The fry grew rapidly and soon toddled. *Jérome Marie, Léo Charlotte, François Martine, Emile Hélène:* these were the names I gave them when they had lived past the ninth day and were no longer like to take fits. Having honored Uncle in the naming of the isle, I would gratify other Gods in the BAPTISM, the blessing by water, which honored in the bargain the cone-bearing parent. Indeed, in the water blessing, I did pay homage to Chenwiyi, banished bone-lord under the sea; yet first and foremost, inasmuch as I purposed a journey to France, I took a decision to baptize with Christian names and so honor the French (the deistic Not-God of certain aristocrats being necessarily indifferent to supplication, hence without servitors or names). So I proceeded in the manner of Père Gouy, though I could remember no scriptural texts, nor any suitable aphorisms of priests or philosophers, but only a comic line of de Vereau, spoken by Amouradet:

And so with firm resolve to be brave, and hopeful heart, we embark on our noble adventure.

I willingly acknowledge that these words are less than eminently suitable, and do not come from an author of consequence; I was forced to eke out the dignity of the occasion with scraps. Ah well! I commended my offspring to live as sensibly, and kindly, and joyfully as they could, injuring no creatures except the need arise to kill for food, and, even as haltingly shaped by my nub of tongue, these seemed precepts enough for young whose apprehension be but suck and slurp.

In time, I taught my offspring, in accordance with their names, not only Hail Marys and Pater Nosters, Credos and Confiteors, but the service of Uncle, the sacrifices required, the respect of trees, the manner of sending forth the dead. I taught them Chenwiyi, Damzillah, Ogun, Steward God, the Hurdy-Gurdy God and various other Deities I had known, or heard of, not neglecting Gormilah. In this manner I sought to furnish my young with full benefit of HEAVEN'S GOOD WILL.

And, since the spider had vanished, my dear cowries had ceased to speak, I would teach my offspring to divine by a new system, not requiring the spider to interpret. Now Pierre was wont to divine by clouds, through staring into the air. Much he had seen in stones and water, much in shadow. Vérité saw in water, in fire, & in smoke. Pierre had known others who read the entrails of beasts or the skin or the bones; those who made much of names or numbers or the rumble of bellies, the shape of hands or of feet, of navels or of nails. He had known those who read the stars or the lees of wine, those who cast lots or threw dice.

Yet he thought he would teach his offspring to divine with coco shells, for these be abundantly present on the isle and are as clear in their outlines as engravings, so suitable for the young to read. Thus, Pierre devised a system of COCO-DIVINATION RULES.

Now, THE FIRST RULE IS, the coco shell be broken with a stone, to which one bows as to the name of Uncle in pebbles. Broken with a stone! The cocos are not to be thrown on the ground as Jéro once did. Alas, poor Jéro! Punished when the Sea-One took his arm, which had been broken in a fall from a coco tree, and hung by a shred from his shoulder. And this She may have done as a courtesy to Uncle, though Jéro keened for his arm! So the Gods conspire if but one of their number take offense at the breach of custom, yea, even those customs tricked up to dazzle the young. So the Gods hold us to the portion we promise and jealously guard the rites we contrive.

And THE SECOND RULE IS, when the coco shells are broken for divining, the meat is divided into four parts, and these parts are thrown; the pattern of dark and light, up and down, speaks. And if all the shells come to land dark-up but one, we must pull our earlobes and open our eyes very wide, to show Uncle we are not afraid. Whereas, if all land dark-up, we must leave some food at the tideline, for the dead in the water are circling, and the ocean is calling someone's name, & so forth & so on.

Now proper observance keeps the dead from glassing over the waters; fish in the burble frolic and are easily caught. Thus the divinations and rites I had devised were well received. Let it not be supposed, however, that Pierre enjoyed an equal success in his attempts to teach his young the manners of civilized persons, such as they would meet in Montbard, viz., to wait for your betters to eat before you; to sip from a cup, rather than to lap from the water, sucking in greedy and ceaseless as a fish; to piss and shit in a privy place; to blow not the nose onto the common table; to make no untoward noise with mouth or arse. Nor let it be supposed that his offspring were quick to master the rudiments of reading and ciphering he sought to teach.

Did the pupils of Modeste Devere look longingly to sea and the prospect of sport? The more my progeny yearned from lessons, who could disappear beneath the waves for days, to return only when they supposed I had forgotten my wish to examine their knowledge of the Latin subjunctive or the Sermon on the Mount, a godmother's maxim or one of La Rochefoucauld. Erudition was not to be my offspring's forte.

Yet Jéro, Léo, Framo, and Émlo were versatile, tender sprites, now undines aflimmer in the watery element, now sylphs, leaping and turning in air, now gnomes digging into holes in land. And were their powers limited to these three of the four elements recognized by the ancients? Could my progeny, like salamanders, thrive in flame? Yet I had no flame, only a curious affinity for the paradox of flame. *Nutrisco et extinguo nul.* So be it. Though I live as an alchemist of old, secret and inventive, devising transformation, I need not take up my time with proofs in the cumbersome, inadequate categories of antique fools. Pierre be a man of the new ideas. *Sunt, ergo sunt.* Charmed or damned, chimeras, gorgons, cockatrice mongrels, my little crossters lived and breathed and had their being, and, from the wily inventiveness with which they avoided their lessons, it were apparent they thought. *Cogitent, ergo sunt.* Thinking, but slippery thinking, of lissome bodies sliding into sea. Yet, in their fishlike way, they grew to be as elegant, indeed, fully as elegant as the comely youth I had preened to discover in M'sieu's pier glasses, half as large, it is true, but every bit as game.

Now had my offspring been bondsmen, they would have prospered in learning a servile obedience mixed with a shifty resourcefulness, a swiftness to master any useful task, combined with a wily apprehension of the posture suited to any situation, to serve, to dissemble, to fawn, to grovel, to rebel but in secret. Yet this EDUCATION would not suit free beings, slipping in and out of the sea. As theirs was a freedom less of privilege or rank than of ease and grace, they need not learn dominion or a masterful manner. Yet if they were to mingle in the world on terms, they must learn a forthcoming confidence. They must judge the usefulness of others, and inspire loyalty beyond their kind. So I must urge them to brighten their moist, even temper, yes, cultivate in them a radiance of manner. Were my offspring boys, with wombs in their mouths? Girls, who had no breasts? If my young bore no gender at all—then how should I train them for their places in the world? I must abandon all precept and watch. Whatever I teach them, I must preserve them and extricate them from harm, viz., a foot trapped in a crevice.

I sought to teach by example, prattling to myself with my stub of a tongue. Lest it has not been made evident: my young have all been born with tongues, and taught, however slurred and indistinct, an excellent SPEECH, first by me, and later, as my tongue did diminish even further, by siblings. 'Tis true, the faculty of speech dwindles with the loss of the tongue during progressive confinements, but sing we can into old age, through shaking the cords in our throats, a song very like the chirping of birds. And indeed, my offspring do most copiously chirp, spouting maxims, flaunting commonplace, yet I have never been assured they sing for the meaning. Rather, they may sing but pattern and rhythm. Yet beauties they spout and seem to know.

Émlo was first to write in sand, where the tide would wash it out, enigma, viz., "the sea-starved sea." Be the like an exhortation to understanding? The expression of a sentiment? There is no response but to write in turn "O milk of light" or "Slippery glass of the past," conning my own enigmas no more fully than my offspring's. So we have proceeded, obliquely, by contraries, trusting our fingers.

Tireless water rompers, merry souls with ready laughs, by day my offspring frolic in the shallows or dive beneath the sea. In the evening they wait with me for their mother—or is she, or he, their father?—to come with food. In time other sea shades have joined Amie, to spit fish and cones in our mouths and have their foreheads rubbed. So we live a most congenial household, half in, half out of the sea.

Yes, but Pierre has not always been satisfied with this watery and domestic idyll. Consider the OBSERVATION OF PARTICULARS that were the very foundation of Pierre's cyclopedish oeuvre. By means of CLOSE OBSERVATION, he had discovered as a youth the true and marvelous nature of the changeling. 'Twas OBSERVATION enabled him to school himself beyond mere reading and ciphering. (Observation and mayhap diligence.) Through OBSERVATION he discerned the multivarious virtues of his wife. 'Twas OBSERVATION furnished Pierre with confidence to saw his boat-pod-holds from keg halves and patience to weave his sails from silver-thatch. If he would OBSERVE his young, he must note the particularity of each, yet they frustrated him in their slippery comings and goings, for in truth they looked as much alike as the pupils in a school of fish. Yet was I firm in my scrutiny; I applied my powers of observation most vigorously and so learned to distinguish them. Émlo was smaller than the others, and most resembled me, for his flesh was tinted a pleasing earthy black, with a fine texture of skin not much marked by bronzy spots. Léo had been born with a twisted leg and with different-sized ears. Through a large one, he heard nothing at all; yet through a tiny one he could hear the landing of a bird on a ledge across the isle.

This Léo, alas, had been cut with the adze I had chipped from volcanic obsidian and fastened with thatch rope into a split handle, only to see the binding break, the adze fly out of the split. The blade cut to the bone my Léo's already twisted leg, causing him to bleed profusely—bright red blood, had I doubted it. I could but stanch the flow by wrapping more of the rope around his leg, and twisting it tight with the handle of the adze to make a tourniquet, which I implored Jéro and Framo hold, praying they would not be distracted by the prospect of dinner flashing in the nearby sea-water, as so often they had been when I donned my pedagogue's hat. I prayed harder still, I must confess, my young would not prove to be incarnations of Squint's anthropophagi, frenzied by the smell of a brother's blood. Yet I need not have worried, for Jéro and Framo held the splint as tight against Léo's wounded leg as any well-trained surgeon's apprentices; I stitched the wound shut with a fishbone needle and thread unraveled from my shreds of a shirt. And we laid our Léo in a nest that the tide cleansed of blood even as the blood seeped from the wound, and after a while the bleeding abated.

I enjoined Émlo, then, hasten with me to collect tree moss so as to cover the wound, and keep filth out of it till it heal. Émlo sat on his haunches looking out to sea, then put his lips to the water and emitted a barking, rattling, shrieking whistle, a gurgling yelp that stirred the waters to roil and bubble like some infernal concoction brewed in Gormilah's kettle. Had his grief robbed him of his wits, my feckless child?

Upon my return with a bundle of moss to dress Léo's wound, I saw that Émlo's agitation of the sea kept circling sharks at bay. For though they were drawn to the blood that reddened the water, spreading from the nest where Léo lay, they feared the foam and noise that spread from Émlo's lips, and they cruised at a distance. Thus, we had time to move Léo to a nest beyond the tide line.

My offspring's useful art of repelling shark-attack I thought to practice myself, that I might navigate beneath the surface of the sea without fear of predation. Then I could search for the underwater aeries of the fish-sprite consorts, my undine paramours, to penetrate some little into the mystery of my offspring's hybrid parturition. But my mouth parts were unsuited to the agitation of any sufficient amount of water to discomfit sharks; nor could I reproduce the timbre and pitch of shrieks and whistles that discomfited the enemy fish; nor indeed (though I had long ago learned to propel myself through the water with gusto and efficiency) did my body flatten beneath water's weight, to round again as I rose to the top; nor could I hold my breath long enough to follow offspring and consorts down to the bottom of the encircling reef that surrounded our island as a halo the head of Marie-Vierge. A great horror stifled me when I could not breathe. This horror, the greater the further down, my offspring knew not.

DOWN they went and down still, whilst my lungs throbbed with desperate need to be filled again with air. So I flailed in panic for top, though I had glimpsed the consorts' sapphire and amethyst dwellings, always just below me, and floating before them, their pearly paladins caparisoned in glimmering streamers. Or were the streamers linelike arms that trawled for specks of dusty light suspended in the columnate sea, which the spine-coifed consorts ate? Gold I saw, coins and plate, and ship-wrecked sailors, floating, transparent, without a will of their own, turning when the schools of rainbow fish did turn, and turn again, searching as one for food. Among these wraithy, wracked phantoms turned others of a more uniformly dusky hue, like air that is colored with smoke. Slaves who had died on the passage, thrown overboard, their legs still chained, swayed among the fish that kiss the bottom where the rays whip their tails and luff their edges in the blurry gloom. The irons of these damned ones would not fall off till their kelp-draped bones rot. And did such a specter hold in bony hands a driver caught by the throat?

Deeper still, sitting cross-legged on the bottom, His long hair floating out from His head to tangle Him as in weeds, the banished bone-lord Chenwiyi, Who ravished His mother even while the God Uncle tore Her apart with awful hands of wind and stone. And Chenwiyi collected Her bones from the chaos over the edge of the world where Uncle God had thrown them. And some of them Chenwiyi buried in the earth, and the rest He collected and clutched to His breast. And He dove into the sea to escape Uncle God, to whom Chenwiyi still holds out His bone-filled hands, imploring—or was He holding out to me my talisman pouch?

Or did I see, not Chenwiyi, but a sea-shade consort, embracing another, who resembled him or her? Yet the consorts had no pudenda, so they could not copulate, and indeed, my mouth be the womb. Were the consorts then sodomites? Mayhap these were no consorts, but the dead, tipped off their rafts, who embrace, not to engender, but to celebrate the wisdom they have stored up since Creation, lo, in the thousands of years since unfolding.

No matter how deep I dove, wonders shimmered out of reach, as ephemeral as the mirages in desert air said to haunt thirsty Camel-Packers with evanescent watery shine. What had I seen? What could I know? What was true? Alas, my sojourns in the watery depths had corroded and spoiled my confidence. I wondered; I wondered. Oh, I wondered.

And this shifty, watery wondering began to wear away Pierre's good sense as the persistent coy waves will wear away a rock exposed to their ceaseless entreaty. A tormenting SUSPICION lodged in Pierre's heart as a grain of sand in a shoe. I came to wonder if the offspring who returned to me night after night were those I had borne at expense of my tongue, and they had borne at expense of theirs. Even Émlo, dear little Émlo, I came to doubt I knew, and Léo with his scarry, twisted leg. Framo who cocked his head and winked an eye, one-armed Jéro who wrinkled his brow like a troubled bookkeeper—mayhap there were more than one of each. They were not my progeny at all, but had been hatched in my mouth as the changeling is hatched in the bee-hive, to feed himself in wreaking devastation. And my naming of these creatures be no more than a sentimental conceit, for others like them were born wherever the shells could batten on flesh in a moist, dark hole.

Yet one of them bore an indisputable sign. The shiny scar on Léo's leg recalled those other cicatrices, the master's mark written on our skins with the silver iron. With this iron the branding crew—the same that in another season marked the cattle—did sear each new boy or girl from the tanks, or baptize in fire a newborn, or run over another planter's burn, or mark as Cain a reprobate. To mark was to know, to know to own. And so Pierre—having caught beneath the sea a sickness cured neither by gulping draughts of air nor by hugging the land while he drained—was seized by a sinful and covetous wish to BRAND HIS YOUNG.

Yet he could not brand without burning, or burn without fire, and fire he did not possess. Words had brought flame to his hand, words on a tea label. But Amie had stolen his labels; he had no papers to attract fire; he must bring it some other way, for Uncle did not spark in his naked hand. Glass he coveted, glass to focus the rays of the sun. Lying on his back in a pod of his boat, looking up at the sky, he saw in the clouds a wondrous engine, a bow on a spindle, the rapid revolution of which spun fire. Yet though this be an ingenious engine—as good as Buffon's mirror—for one in a civil country to patent, here the patent must be shift. Pierre settled on the homely expedient of the boy who brought honey home to his sister, who had stunned the bees with smoke from a fire made by frotting sticks. Pierre hunched over a shabby pile of wispy, chippy debris, frotting, frotting, frotting, huffing and puffing on the spark that fell at last on specks of crumbled frond and desiccated sea-weed, blowing till a flame sprang up.

Yet he did not cherish that flame for its heart of blue; all his effort were bent to A SCHEME. In a frenzy of will, he pillaged his weathering boat for a hoop, which he pounded with stones to flatten and lengthen, and filed against rocks to point. He pillaged his boat again for staves to devise a tongs of wood with which to lift the hot iron. And now he fed his hungry fire the driftwood he had collected for his balance frame and raft. More and more of his cache he fed his greedy flame, for his iron must be red-hot each time he dropped it on a child's shoulder. He must get the children the first time he tried, and get them from the back, so they knew not what hurt them, else they would shun him. Now if they shun him, what boot it he had marked them? Ah well, he must win back their trust; he would carve them tops and dancing Jacks. He would teach them Blind Man's Bluff and Tag and Catch. There would be Treasure Hunts. The young would each endure but a moment's pain, to be marked and subsequently known. Framo, the largest and sturdiest—Pierre would start with him.

So Pierre lured Framo to his fire on the pretext of a game of N'importe-Quoi-Donc, having made of well-matched, well-rounded pebbles a pair of dice. But even as the brand was glowing above the shoulder of the trusting fish-sprite enraptured by the roll of dice, a spider walked across a hearth stone. Vérité's visage shone in the calabash of water that Pierre had brought to cool the iron. The spider voice hissed in his ear, *Mouth of Mouths. Know what you know.* And Pierre's heart stayed his hand. He could not burn his offspring's flesh. He pulled what was left of his shirt off his shoulder, and saw there the *D,* and cried aloud. Though he had been burned as an infant, he remembered the pain. So he extinguished his fire. He did not keep it burning to ward off merry-wings, but ate of the ashes each day until they were gone, as a gesture of ATONEMENT, and drove the point of his mother's hook through the lobe of his ear, as a penance, and wears this ear-hook still, as he writes.

How could Pierre have doubted the offspring's singularities? Who but Framo had that deep, croaking voice, those long arms, and that large, square head? Who but Jéro that smaller, narrower head with one protruding eye in the middle of his wrinkled forehead, one arm and a breathy voice?

How could Pierre, son of suffering, husband of injustice, who bore on his own body the cruel mark of proprietorship, have so forgotten who he was that he sought to brand his young as chattel beasts? O Master Pierre! 'Twere vile and 'twere futile. His off-spring can no more be owned than the sea. Nor do they seek to own, or to master, nor even to set themselves apart from their fellows with trifling, portentous distinctions, viz., the difference between breeches and drawers.

Like the consorts, my offspring are neither exclusive nor proprietary, though they are faithful as tides. They remember and forget and remember again, attaching neither importance nor sentiment nor any anxious apprehension to what can neither be kept nor lost. For them, COMMONALITY is complete, all attributes glimmering & changeable, like light on the surface of the sea.

They play all their games in a group, Troll-Madame & Lasquenet & Papillon, & games of their own devising, with rules I cannot fathom, for they never take their turns in the same order. All they do, they do all together, frolicking and rollicking, sharing their gruel among themselves and with me. An observer might say they are not individuals of a mongrel species, but one manifold orchidaceous organism. What boot their singularities to them? How could I have presumed to own what grows for itself and for whatever Gods there be? How could I have doubted the solid ties of an affection beyond affection, a communality beyond loyalty or kin? How indeed! I vowed to stay out from under the water that had addled my wits and confounded my morals.

For even if Pierre's young be parasites, who exist but to be preyed on by other parasites, for ends that will be forever hidden under the sea, still he could never abandon them now. For by his very-near cruelty he had joined his fate to theirs, and lost his independence. Moreover, in his zeal, he had burnt all the wood collected for his raft; now he must start again. And now he must have a very large raft, like the ARK OF NOAH, for if he sail to France, he must take as many of his young as wished to go, and could not presume they were good for so long a swim. No, they might tire, and must be able to climb aboard a solid craft. There must be room as well for Vérité; he must steal her as other maroons steal beef or rum. (Nor would it hurt their cause to purloin these commodities.) And what of his godmothers, and Jean-François? Sure Squint he could leave behind, for Squint could take care of himself. Besides, he was yellow enough to pass for white, if he live among whites too poor to escape being browned by sun.

Now often Pierre looked into his cistern, and in the mirror of the water he saw Vérité, building ever-larger subtlety ships for Dufay's banquets, and indeed, forcing Dufay to ever-larger displays of hospitality, to accommodate the ever-more elaborate subtleties he would flaunt. Hers be no mere rafts, but true ships with twelve tall masts, and twelve times twelve sails, and rigging like the webs of a hundred spiders. Does Dufay inquire why all the subtleties now are nautical? Does he know she will one day launch? Does he shrug, supposing sugar will not hold against water? He might be amazed to discover, she has baked in a cyclopedish ark, so large it must be fired in a volcano's fiery throat, two of every bird M'sieu has drawn for Buffon.

So Vérité would come to Pierre. Meanwhile he must do his part. He must educate his fishy offspring, not only to charm, but to perform useful work. Thus would Pierre ensure, they would not be perceived among the savants of France or among Pierre's kinsmen in Guinée, as abominations. He must train his offspring to present far beyond expectation, so they impress, not as talking fish that amuse little more than a dog walking on its hind legs, but as PERSONS.

Yet if they were PERSONS, their PERSONHOOD lay partly in their fishiness. Were there some respect in which HUMANNESS might be married to FISHINESS, beyond what Pierre had hitherto conceived? Pierre much occupied himself in like rumination. Often he bailed the rainwater from a pod of his boat, and lay back in it, and looked up at the sky, and saw floating there in the reef of clouds, not only birds, but fishes. And he recalled then M'sieu's aversion to the finny creatures and their element. Indeed, Pierre recalled the stiff-fillet portraits M'sieu had sent for Buffon's *histoire*. And Pierre vowed to teach his offspring to be FISHY PHILOSOPHERS. Their HISTOIRE would relate the annals of FISH, that M'sieu had so egregiously neglected.

Commencing with the *exempli* of birds, then, that Pierre himself knew well, he would teach to fishy end the methodology of Buffon, viz., OBSERVATION, AND PHILOSOPHIZING UPON OBSERVATION, yet with a magnanimous spirit; for to grasp the nature of any creature, one must be able to see before one the whole history of the beast, "their procreation, gestation period, the time of birth, number of offspring, the care given by the mother and father, their education, their instincts, their habitats, their diet, the manner in which they procure food, their habits, their wiles, their hunting methods," & so forth & so on.

And so Pierre's young, having observed with him the common thrasher and the oven thrush and the spackled beater-wing, did then plunge into the element of their greatest affinity, the sea, and commence to record the habits and proclivities of ladyfish and puffers; grunts, wrasses, and tallywags; surgeonfish and triggerfish; parrotfish and snappers. And not only these fish, well known to the denizens of Saint-Michel, even to sea-anxious Dufay, but other fish, quite unknown, that lived far down. And among these the whipperlux and needlenose, the whiskered grumpkin and rainbow skate—for so we have named them.

And not only fin-fish, my offspring observed, but shellfish, pearl-oysters, limpets, slippersnails, murexes; and scuttling hardskins, viz., the crab. Of the latter my offspring discovered several varieties that lived very far down, which shattered when brought to the top, which we called the glass-skins, viz., the glass-skin blue, the glass-skin double-claw, the glass-skin mottle. And further down than the glass-skinned crabs, peculiar creatures, very tall columnar jellies with rootlike toes grasping the rocks on the floor of the sea. They have no arms nor any discernible motility, yet though they take in water and release it again, their bodies swelling and sagging. And with these columnates on the ocean floor, shellfish as large as houses, which very rarely close their doors, but constantly expose their meat to the watery element, for they have no enemies there at the fundament.

And a serpent worm, mayhap of the species that had swallowed me, lying quiet beside another, the two copulating in manner hermaphroditic, each with its male organ quivering in the other's female, the great scaly bodies trembling among the quiet, invisible legions of dead, yet with shimmers of iridescence sparkling along their spinal fins, what seemed to be the full length of the beasts. For my offspring (though their gaze well penetrate the murk at the bottom) could see neither head nor tail. Nor did my offspring possess—even they!—the stamina and strength to paddle to the distant tails or heads of the beasts, but must extrapolate from the evidence of the middles, shaking and finning. (I did inquire whether my offspring had seen the bone-lord Chenwiyi, sitting on the bottom of the sea with His mother's ribs in His arms. "Perhaps worm food," Framo surmised.)

Yet my offspring's most NOTABLE DISCOVERIES were not on the bottom of the sea, nor even on top, but on the very Isle of the Uncle, which I believed I had so thoroughly perused. Still I had not observed the pinket tiny tiny, that minuscule blossom that flourishes in the narrow dark depths of certain crannies. Nor observed the scrubby stink-fruit bush, which grows on the rocky ledges where gulls roost, near the promontory where I had speared Amie.

And these botanical discoveries revealed the breadth of the powers for observation my offspring possessed. Truly, Pierre had bred up a lineage of PHILOSO-FISH SAVANTS! These knowings must not be lost!

Because we had not ink to write—having found no medium to fix squid's pigment—and no paper—inasmuch as my palm-weavings were too coarse for sharpened plume to inscribe—I taught my off-spring to build their own conjure house. Yet when I had told them what I could of how I had constructed mine, I was amazed to dis-cover they already had their own, though they had not hitherto stored in it provision Pierre would call Philosophic. It is different from human conjure houses, in that it is shared; they wander in it together, as if they had no minds of their own, but furnished out the rooms of a common one. And this be not so different from the common ground between the memory houses of humans, who speak to one another by whatever means. Yet my offspring need not such artifacts as books, or any conversation, but know each other's thought through a sensitive affinity that we humans do not possess. Though I had classified my offspring as less than myself, indeed, as parasites, they had powers a human had not. They speak and write to humor their progenitor!

And by such shifts as these, Pierre came to a separate view from Buffon of the gulf the great man had charted between humans and other creatures. For if the offspring be *exemplum,* this gulf were no deep chasm, that is impossible to cross, but a sea, in which all creaturely conception floats. Among animals, humans alone float upon it entirely ignorant, some more than others. For when the Gods speak to us, through shadows or water or stones, we are being furnished with provision from a great COMMON STORE at which the coco shells but hint.

I who had observed the web of life in its aggrandizement, nay, had wandered across it a blind spider—I yearned more than ever to present my findings to other savants, along with those of my philosophish young. So Vérité would recover in honor a husband who had fled in disgrace, however ill-deserved. Yet more than the unfinished state of my ship, more than my obligation to my fishy progeny, who did not all crave a journey to France, I was held to my island by MY OWN SPECULATION. For never did I cease to inquire why the sea shades chose to grace me, as later my off-spring, with cones. Where do the sea shades come from? Are they born, or created in some other manner?

Chenwiyi fell as a stone to the bottom of all that is, holding the bones of sorrow. From these bones, were the consorts born? How else can Pierre explain the attraction of the consorts to the tongue of one who knows the story of Chenwiyi? Sea ribs and earth ribs, joined at last.

Pierre sometimes lay on his back in a pod of his ruined boat, the iron rusted, the wood weathered silver. He looked up at the clouds and saw them, fading, dissolving, rotting—rotting and fruiting, rotting and fruiting. Rotting and fruiting and CHANGING. And all the past since Creation might have been for him one single de-sign of Providence, that had brought Pierre to this place. He lay on his back in his foundered boat, watching the clouds give birth to themselves, celestial aether, fruit to fruit, a tree of life that branches in death, the sacred tree that sailor-man shepherd-man Jason saw. At the close of day, the sun-gilt twigs finer than threads of the thinnest-spun sugar; the tree hung with gold-illumated sugar leaves that looked to that shepherd-man sailor like fleeces of golden perfect wool, golden fleece between a golden woman's legs, the legs of the Sea-One, stretched gold and purple at close of day, Her labia opening, closing, opening, closing. In the gloam-ing, huge and seraphic, cloud-water vulva, opal and pearl, the Sea-One passionate in gathering storm, passionate yet perfect, immaculate and perfect as all conception. Now there would be a subtlety to ravish!

The Old Temptation

→

That the Deities move on the face of earth and water in a manner most mysterious, has been revealed to me, not only in the inwardness of my reverie and the outward grace of my progeny, but in one other most purely miraculous gift that Providence has bestowed upon me since our fish-sprite dynasty was established. This generous gift did consist in my being granted, once again, to look on the features of a purely HUMAN COUNTENANCE and hear the syllables of purely HUMAN SPEECH.

Strolling in the weedy-smelling wrack-trace of a storm, to see how the shape of my isle had shifted in the tide, Pierre discovered rolling and slapping in sea wash a slime-white form which he took at first for that of a moribund fish sprite. Yet upon circumambulating the putrid, puffy creature, he discerned the veiny feet were not flippered ones, with membrane between the toes, but twitching digits of a pallid, sea-wrinkled, lepriferous-looking person, in gender male, one no longer young, who feebly groaned at my approach. I knew him, I swore, as I turned him over, knew his dissipated, water-logged, scapegrace face. He were—Pamphile! Had he come to claim me? Trembling and leery, I started and stopped, guarding my liberty, fearful still of rack, of dog, of Four-Post and Stinger. Yet here on this isle the master lo! these many years be I! *Master thyself, then,* I muttered. *Be master in more than name! And if master, be worthy of thine elevation, for thou knowest full well the piteous condition of a derelict.*

However much my erstwhile tormentor, who had stolen my talisman from my neck, Pamphile had been my benefactor, who had passed to me with toes-out shoes the barely used A-B-C's that had been my refuge and consolation. I would not abandon him helpless.

So I did approach him, and pour fresh water between his lips. I lugged him to a shady nook and nursed him as tenderly as I had nursed Amie, when I had speared and hurt her. And dappled by a tender palm-leaf light, fanned by solicitous Zephyr, he breathed more easily. Yet soon he was afflicted with a terrible fever that shook his frame with shivering. I sprinkled water on his lips, and he opened his eyes. He sat up on his frondy pallet; though he stared ahead as one who has waked from death, he knew me. "Goody!" he cried, "You maroon Devil! Have you come for me from Hell?"

I could scarce explain with the scanty grunts my stub-tongue— oh, my fish-sprite concubines! I wished once again I had never indulged in unnatural affection that unvoiced me. I patted Pamphile's hand and nodded and smiled. He pulled on the hook I wore in my ear, and pointed to his own mouth, then to my mouth and his ear. How was I, with my stubble-dumb tongue, to speak? I shook my head. Again he pointed to ears and mouths. He would not be gainsaid! I must reveal how well I wrote. Inscribing on a broadleaf platter of wet sand the particulars of my condition, I did entreat him to tell me his needs; for though I spoke with great trouble, I could hear quite well. Thus did he commence to speak.

If I but close my eyes, I am a bonded boy in his first set of drawers, who stumbles beneath a heavy load, while his master, unburdened, pontificates from his horse. Flora & fauna & fauna & flora. If I but keep my eyes closed, the boy becomes a proud youth in a passed-along coat, dreaming over accounts. Already he hears in his head the voices of savants, authors whose ruminations free him from bondage long before he escapes.

Would there pour from Pamphile's lips the liquefaction of patois, lilt of comfort and callaloos? To him, ours were but a nursery language he would not deign to speak. Even so, I had been granted a boon I could not sniff or peck at, though the individual the sea had vomited at my feet were never a philosopher with wit to banter, but ever an impulsive and petulant rake, weaker in wit than in will. This Pamphile now were much inclined to relate his history; he would not husband his strength.

To tell me how he came here would shake his frame with hellish laughter, so he said, which he feared would jelly his bones, yet he would go on. He had launched himself on a funeral raft of the servants, to escape the wanton conflagration engulfing his father's plantation, a fiendish REBELLION—he checked himself, yet he would go on.

"Had I not been carousing with a fancy girl," he rasped, "I might have saved our fortunes from ruin. I might have roused my tranced father, called the militia before the hands whom we had clothed and fed burned the house, the fields, the boiling shed, warehouses, stables—all! Yet I have paid for my folly, having watched my hapless father, the inveterate loather of water and fishes, swamped in the storm from which you have salvaged the wreck of my life."

So he spoke, the débauché, no less the fool for his white hairs. Had my fellows razed and pillaged all they had labored to build?

"Pray, what occasion?" These words I tried to shape with my mutilated tongue, then shrugged and wrote in the sand.

"His wife, my stepmother, had died before," whispered Pamphile. "I cannot say I lament her passing, the scheming vixen, yet who could be indifferent to the manner of it? For she died of some suppurating sores on her breasts, from which such hideous worms did emerge upon her expiration, my father shrank from touching her. On pain of the lash, he ordered the cowering housemaids dress her body.

"'M'sieu! M'Sieu! Have mercy!' they cried. They would rather have risked the whip or the block than touch their mistress's wormy corpse.

"The field hands then declared they would dress the body themselves, so as not to see the women suffer for refusing. The hands of those bucks on my stepmother's person my father never would stomach, nor the mutinous negotiation of his slaves, and so he bid his driver—Tom, you recall—Tom Squint—my father bade Tom whip 'em all, which the driver refused to do, declaring it monstrous unjust to make the people pay for their terrors. So astonished was my father at this cool rebellion on the part of his driver, his temper vaporized into amazement. He subsided to an inner room, where he occupied himself in sketching. He forbade all intercourse with the corpse that had been his spouse; she lay 'neath a blue-green blanket of flies for a very great number of days.

"Finally Squint sneaked into her room through a balcony window, even as a lover, to beat off the flies. He discovered not only worms in her breasts, but maggots along her spine—the once-fair flesh, now most vile. Yet her grim-jawed suitor persevered. Snuffing up some dried rose petals the wench had spread in a pretty dish, Squint bundled her sleeping form, that oozed and crawled with life, and tossed her over his shoulder. And despite the protests of Sénégal, who had poked his head through the cracked door, Squint carried her over the balcony rail, like one eloping, to rendezvous in a pit of clay. Though if he buried her, sneezing rose petals in the ditch, or sequestered her body in a vault he carved in the reef, no one saw him.

"Hastening to tell my father she had been taken, Sénégal left ajar the door of the room where she had lain. A peeping maid discovered she was gone, and the wretch cried aloud in fright, 'Baron has come. The Baron has come and taken her. Woe! Driving his silent horses, Mist and Dread, Baron has stolen her body. Now poor mistress wakes in a strange place. She dashes with startled heart through Baron's foggy fields, pursued by his bodiless dogs, their bark so awful silent. Oh why were there no rites?' And so on and so on, nefarious mewling and puling, contagion that spread through the yard, for Sénégal but shrugged and refused to gainsay the rumors. My father, gone slack, would not have the babbling housemaid flogged, or his recalcitrant butler, but protested he would have buried his wife himself, by filling with dirt the room where she lay. Already the slaves were muttering against him. He was a marked man, they said, a marked man.

"That very night the house burned down. And Squint could not be found for the bucket brigades, nor could Sénégal, nor the boiler Beloo (whom we continued to feed though his carelessness had burned his fingers to useless stubs), while the field hands—who had given them rum?

"My father swung no buckets but stared at his burning house as if it were another's property. He called for his inks. Most carefully, precisely, and minutely, he drew the house, not as it glowed before him in flames, but as it had been, white-washed, dignified, four-square above the bay. . . ."

Pamphile paused to draw his breath. I chafed his hands and chuckled to ponder the unwonted calm of choleric Dufay as he viewed the lurid scene, his fields all charred, his house an inferno, his drunk hands brandishing bits of his clothes and his plate, capering to the suck of the harp, the racket of the drum, laughing and showing for once their teeth. Serenely he paints the house in the shadowless calm of an ultimate noon. And the hands who loom with picks and bills fall back into smoky gloom, fearful what subtle devil has evicted his wits and camped in their erstwhile precinct.

"The girl had roused me from a sound sleep," wheezed Pamphile, "yet I saw at once there must be no delay. I pleaded with my father, who stared round-eyed at my protestation we must fly or lose lives with fortunes. On my knees I implored him, and gave the girl my purse for her help. With but one half-shuttered lantern to light our way along a rocky path, we trundled my father's person, not to our quay, for they had already burned all our boats, but to a landing on the shore, where the hands beached an ancient tub we had given them for fishing. Even if two men bailed, it shipped so much water, it would never carry them far away. Yet this tub too had been set alight and was a glowing ghost of itself, a crimson ember boat that fell to ashes as we watched.

"But one craft remained seaworthy, the narrow raft on which lay the bloated corpse of a field hand, I knew not which one, who had died, I knew not how, yet which the slaves had covered with orchids and odd little bundles of leaves. I did not doubt this body, rubbed with oil to a dark shine, had been prepared for a funeral, then forgotten in the mêlée. I crossed myself, yet we must make use of the means to hand. As the girl cried out angrily, I tipped the body into the wash.

"Under the garlanded negro lay curled as a babe the naked worm-eaten corpse of my father's wife. Someone had closed her eyes and weighed down the lids with stones, but no-one had bound up her jaw. Her mouth opened blue and terrible between her teeth; she screamed a scream as loud as the end of the world. My father, who never had paid her mind in her life, fell to his knees before her corpse and clutched her stiff little feet. He sobbed and moaned, oblivious to his own fate. This corpse too, I tipped into the sea. He threw himself on it, blubbering in the wash.

"I shook him and shook him, to no avail, then slapped him, God forgive me. Then he was still. I bade him lie on his belly on the raft, which he did. Now he was docile as a child. I lay on top of him and bade the girl, who was already counting the coin in my purse, shove us off. With the now unshuttered lantern 'twixt my legs, to light us through the shoals to open sea, I paddled with frantic hands, helped by the tide's running out. Yet before I could fix what way might take us to the Spaniards, the wind rose. A fierce storm vented its blast upon us, to smite us with pounding strength. As the raft rocked perilously back and forth, the lantern slid into the sea. That we might keep our balance, I entreated my father paddle with me, yet he answered not. I jabbed at his calves with my toes, yet still he answered not. I pummeled his ribs and head with my fists, yet still, silence. Then rose a wave larger than all the others, which swept us up to the heavens and suspended us over the void, then dashed us to chaos. The raft was o'erturned. My distracted father sank from sight."

Tears rolled down Pamphile's cheeks. He was mourning the irascible master who had educated me to spite his fellows, and raised me to save the hire of a keeper of accounts, and granted me the freedom of the library. He was mourning the master who had saved my wife but sold my mother. Sold her! And ground up my brothers in his sugar mill! And now he spoke of the whites in the big house as if they alone possessed their fates, as if they had not lived on the backs of so many slaves like myself, who also had the effrontery to possess their fates! Oh, what of my godmothers? My wife? Did all my connexion perish in the rising?

"*Vérité?*" I wrote in my sand-slate. "*Marie-Jeanne* and *Jean-François?*"

Pamphile screwed up his face. The demands of a new courtesy addled wits that were already addled by water, yet I must grant him gameness.

"Marie-Jeanne . . . Marie-Jeanne . . . ah, Full-Bags!" he cried. "Jean-François! By 'Jean-François' you mean *Sénégal*! And Vérité, Vérité, you must mean the cook! Yes, Douce Farouche, that witch. Well now, Goody, I forgot you married that barren cripple. Yes, and in that, and to tell truly, that only, disappointed Papa—before you fled, that is—for you are a comely fellow, who might have been bred for excellent foals—excellent!"

This rude fool were never master of his tongue. I wished he were well and strong, so I might slap him, to call him out to duel, as heroes do in tragedies.

"I would know what became of my wife," I muttered through my clenched teeth. Of course he could not make out my words; I must draw the letters on my slate.

"Ah! If you must know, the wench was freed."

"Freed when she was old and too crippled to work?"

His soaked conscience was not entirely ruined, for he squirmed as he lay on my lap.

"Ah, Goody, do not lay on me that charge. Mayhap she was old and hunched till the boat set her down on the little neighbor isle, Saint-Jean-de-Mer—you must remember, where they go for herbs. To the maroons, she went, the crooked shrew. Yet her manumission had an effect so rejuvenating, I wish it might revive my own drenched flesh. Yes, Her Slyness straightened fast when she was freed! Imagine! A surly hunch transformed to a snarling amazon! La Terreur! Mayhap it was she, your sorceress wife, who sneaked back onto our place to call up the rising that burned it. But the fleeing planters of Saint-Domingue, where the rising had commenced, would swear they had descried in the vanguard of the bilious army foaming over the land 'Your cook,' so they threw it up in our faces when their boats landed them amongst us, 'Your cook!'

"Though lame she strode like Joan before her army of raggy ruffians. Her Slippery Slyness now stood firm, her lame foot holding her fast as a root to earth, her chest swelled up. She sailed as on a wind before her men, flying for her flag, 'twas said, a lady's gown of very fine stuff, yet splashed with blood. Even so she called up the rising, she!"

I had no doubt it was Vérité.

"But what—?" I wrote on my platter of sand, "What be the nature of this rising?"

Pamphile stared at me, as he might at a man who said he had seen his own ghost. He shook his head.

"Am I delirious," he murmured, "to rave of these fearsome events to a treacherous maroon, who has me at mercy? Ah well, 'tis no time to mince nice. You are as far from these events as I; the world goes on without us both. I will tell you, Goody, the topsy-turvy, some say it is general, and may soon o'ertake the entire world. The throwing down of all enlightened good, the rising of a dark, chaotic evil—everywhere! And of course, on Saint-Domingue, and on our Saint-Michel, the hands rose up, and snatched their miserable freedom, even as the drudges of France had taken theirs, by force of numbers, and, yes, by a kind of right, one sees, if one puts aside one's own interest. . . . yet they were inflamed, inflamed by the words of heedless prophets, men like that English incendiary, Locke, and Paine—"

"Snatched their freedom?" I wrote on my sand-slate.

"That fool Lafayette—"

"And were not caught and whipped?"

"Well, Citizen, I see you know nothing. So much the worse for you! You rely for this news on one good as dead, a chill creeping up from his feet. Well, I join a good frolic, death topping death topping death. And rogue Napoleon—I see you frown—you do not know of the King who lost his head—and the carnival of corpses—the litter of bones and death in the streets—then that King of Fools, that parvenu Corsican general tricked up as angel of justice, climbed on the wheel and rode it. On and on the madness rolled. Now the world has struggled with itself like a rabid dog with two heads. From many who had much, much has been taken; many who had little, something they have taken—what they say was their own. Oh fiddle! Have you never heard how the Englishmen north of here threw off their King's taxes? Hardly any taxes those petty imposts were, yet those ingrates would have their independence. Oh, before you fled, but of course we never told you, nor any other dependent—of course!

"Yet the war of those English 'gainst their King, this was a war, for he hired good troops and sent them overseas, bright-buttons insulted by their opponents, ragged, dull militias mustered from the poor. Ah, but the rebels' general had fought the sneaking tawnies, and now he sneaked in turn. He hid his shabby paupers behind rocks and trees; they lurked without regard to rules of war. The king's bright chessmen were tumbled in their ranks. Yet still, this sordid rebellion was a *war*.

"But in France no war; naught but carnage and vengeance, lust and rage. They cut off the heads of their betters, then they killed the leaders they themselves had raised from the ranks, snarling and biting, turning on their own, again and again. This was the bitch wheel, turning and turning—with every turn, more heads rolling, the spokes of that wheel knives. The Corsican mounted the wheel of knives and rolled it all over Europe, cutting. And the rumbling wheel of slashing knives was heard across the sea, and your own people then heard they would be free despite their masters' ruin, as if our lives and prosperity counted for naught. Yet Napoleon sent no soldiers to free you! No, indeed, he sent soldiers to clap more irons on your legs, for the revenues of our plantations were precious to France. Now she regrets the damned proclamations in the damned assemblies! She regrets the insanity of leveling gone too far! The Corsican were never fool enough to free the sugar hands, whatever the assemblies said—though you would free yourselves, fools, to starve. I suppose I must call you *Citizen*, now, if you have stolen your freedom with the others. I like it not. Yet your general, your Toussaint—I must say, I like him better than spit-curled Bonaparte, whose incompetent soldiers lost our plantation."

"Bo-na-parte . . . !" I mouthed the name and poked my stubby tongue in it, but knew not its shape. Nor did I know the shape of *Tous-saint,* yet these were the names of men with ideas—men and ideas, the powder and spark that made the gun of revolution fire—men and ideas, the noblest combination that ever were, that I had never known were a weapon but had thought were a kind of light.

"'*Man,*'" I wrote on my slate, "'*Man is Nature's masterwork. Man alone constitutes a class apart,' though one does not descend through an 'unimaginably vast expanse of space to reach the animals.'*"

"Oh, what nonsense you write," cried the sick man, testily turning his head from side to side. "What nonsense! What nonsense!"

"*I cite the philosopher, Monsieur de Buffon, with embellishment of my own,*" I wrote in my plate of sand.

"Buffon? Ah!" he cried, "The late Intendant of the King's Garden. Count of the Labyrinth, Duke of the Gazebo, Chevalier of Water Plants, Marquis of Glass Houses, the author of the *Histoire Naturelle,* who died without granting my father right of signature. Fourteen horses and nineteen servants, Citizen, all in livery. Thirty-six choir boys and sixty clerics in lace collars and cuffs. And right behind the funeral procession, the carts rolling down the streets toward the knife. Buffon died in his bed, of stones, but his son, Buffonet, walked up the wooden stairs. Now he had been as profligate as I, Goody, yet on the scaffold he was very brave.

'Citizens,' he said, 'my name is Buffon,' and made no excuses. He stuck his neck beneath the blade and did not soil his breeches. So he died in a manner he had not lived. So I too die as I have not lived. Oh, I have wasted myself, wasted, but still I am my father's son. . . .

"Goody, you may repay my father's trust. I pray you will shrive me before I die, and attend me with the unction, for you—a faithless runaway—you are the meetest priest in these parts! Keep both my watches"—he patted his empty fobpocket. "Grant what I ask for the sake of our ancient friendship. Grant it in homage to the Master who claims all loyalty. In the name of our Lord and God, the Father, the Son, and the Holy Ghost, I pray you not leave me expire alone, Citizen, croaking as Our Lord for water."

He did not call me *Citizen* with the degree of conviction he called me *Goody*. Yet more earnest than the conversion to an egalitarian courtesy seemed the conversion of the erstwhile cynic to PIETY. And who is so sinless he would not be afraid to die? I stroked his sparse white hair back from his wrinkled brow. I bathed his forehead and fed him from rinds filled with gruel, which my offspring were bringing from the sea, which surely were the best food in all the world to sustain him, though its fishy smell did make him cough.

"Seeing you take all so calm, and subordinate your advantage to your kindness, I will tell you more of this revolution, which even now is spreading like plague across the world."

"Do not agitate yourself, Good Sir," I insisted, though memories did smolder in my breast as the hazy glow on embers that have all but died.

In the clouds that covered and uncovered the moon, I saw Vérité stealing into the smoldering ruins of M'sieu's library, kneeling in the warm ashes by a bucket she had lugged. She was about to bury

228

a doll with feathers through a hole in its heart. Though she had often pricked it with pins, she had snuggled it in the hammock of her pocket, for she knew how much worse a master than Dufay the world could harbor. Now she ignored the triumph all around. She dug a grave, scratching the ash and then the soil, clawing with an unburnt chair leg and shoveling with a half-burnt book. Then she laid the doll to rest in this hole, where no one would find it, and sprinkled on it the ashes of books, and emptied on it her bucket of sea water. Now was the fire extinguished. Now was the spell broken.

"The horror is general," rasped Pamphile. "I do not know what good this revolution has turned up. For I tell you in France the poor are still the poor, though more and more merchants live as landed rich. And still the wretched toil. I tell you, little has changed in the proportionate distribution of privilege. Blood has been shed, that is all."

"And the Anduves?"

"I pray these isles will choke on ash," he gasped. "Do not ask after those who have ruined my father and me. Damn their freedom! Damn 'em, I say, damn 'em."

I resented his MALEDICTION, oh most heartily. Yet now his breath rattled most horribly, so I stifled the heat that rose from my belly. I banked in dried sea-weed the trembling body of Pamphile Maxime Célestin Aubignole Dufay. I covered the weed with sand, the sand with fronds, and did all to keep him warm. Despite my ministrations, his lips were turning blue, his hands a deeper blue. I called my offspring and bade them lie with me on the mound, to warm Pamphile with our bodies' warmth. As if he had been a faltering newborn, we patted his sand-covered feet and crooned encouragement. He did smile as if to bless us; my offspring stroked his face.

"Ah, Goody . . . ," he breathed.

Why did we labor to save him? We creatures treasure life as fire. We cannot bear the losing of a spark, so precious is it. And this were true, be the dying one a worthless profligate, still we cup the flame of his life in our hands, 'gainst the cold wind of death.

Were not Pamphile my enemy? Were not all whites my enemies? They had pressed me and hounded me and kindled my hopes but to douse them again. They had punished and degraded and tortured and wounded my mother and my wife. Yet I held to my bosom this hapless, insolent man, presumptuous and foolish and dying, and listened to his faltering heart, and roused myself to console him.

"Courage, Citizen," I murmured, chafing his cold blue wrists. "Fear not for your soul. But die in peace, you will dwell beneath the sea in the house where wisdom is shared. Knowledge and joy bring bliss, and all souls bask in eternal contemplation of the Gods."

"Night. . . ." whimpered Pamphile, "Night—a candle—look you. . . . 'Tis early but . . . nightfall—I say—I say—you, boy!—a light. . . . Why? . . . Turn down my bed—I say!—'Tis—look you—look you, now, wash . . . . . . wash my small-clothes—press 'em—you there! A light, damn you—have you . . . . . . ? Black my boots! What? . . . . . . the morrow? Tonight, whilst—both wigs—powder and curl my . . . . . . look! A candle for't—fallen, already . . . . . . and stockings there—mend . . . . . . mend—"

I soothed his forehead and sang him my godmothers' lullaby, "Ba-wal loo-mah ba-ha-wa loo-a-to."

"'Tis as before. . . ." he murmured.

Leaning so my looming shadow did cut off the sunlight that had suffused and warmed him, I intoned in most sea-like, tide-pulling tones, "Even so. You are returning . . . returning . . . returning. . . ."

And I rocked like the sea, covering and uncovering his light, so he flickered in his own fading, the world spoke to him, and he came a little back to life.

"Are there—are there women on the other—?"

Struggling up from the cocoon of sand we had banked on him, he raised himself onto his elbows with a difficulty that rattled his breath in his chest.

"Fancy women?" he rasped. "Full-bloods?"

Oh, then gorge rose. Then my heart cried out for the memory of my poor Pélérine, my Vérité, whose thin, broken fingers had lain so sweetly in mine—*terreur, terreur,* my own.

"And what would you do with a full-blooded woman?" I whispered cold as the bottom of the sea in his ear.

"Oh, be she very black—very hot—revive me . . . ," he gasped.

His round, wild eyes looked straight through mine, as if he saw past my heart. There counted for naught the man who cradled in careful hands the tiny flame of his wretched life. Was I no more than a beast, that felt not slights? And my sisters? Were they beasts? Raw and dumb? Created for the service of Pamphile? All the seas that had washed him had not softened his heart. A stone is more subject to the action of waves than the flint in the breast of Pamphile to the action of pity. I gritted my teeth. Again I brushed the sand from his face and sang again the dear old song, "Ba-wal loo-mah ba-ha-wa loo-a-to." Even as a hawk falls on a mouse, shadow first, I lowered my palm on his face to stop his talk for good. Yes, I MURDERED him. I killed him for Uncle, in the name of all I had missed. I killed him for Vérité, for *La Terreur.* I killed him for Juba. I killed him. And my fishy progeny, though they knew him not, gave up a wailing of grief, an unceasing ululation, a frightful whistling and piscine howling.

Now there is an intimacy in water, which moves so palpably on the skin, ferocity be lissome under-sea. The ruthless shark; the vicious, flapping skate; the monstrous, fountainy whale; the fire-breathing worm that eats all these others, yet barely ruffles the tides with hundreds of paws—even at the prospect of these ruthless beasts, my sons but shrug. For water is ever in motion, there are many oysters clutched in the fingers of the reef, and every creature kills to eat. Yet only to eat!

When I said, "I murdered Pamphile because he was white, and looked past my heart," my offspring eyed me as one who has lost his wits.

"He slandered my wife," I explained, "and defamed my sisters with vile insinuations." They but howled until they were distracted by a run of fishlets, which they dove to catch.

I saw them not for a full procession of the moon's faces. My offspring shunned me as a reprobate who had taken life in vain and left it to the consorts to bring my food. Yet I did not regret what I had done. I claimed my deed. Mine and mine again! Mine the grief, mine the transgression, and mine the sweet revenge. Pamphile was not smooth in the groin as a pennywooden doll, his sex in his mouth and that a female's generative organ—no, Pamphile had been a human male, born from a belly, who poured his seed from the spout where he pissed. Of all the creatures in my purview, only the man whose end I had hastened had come into being as I had come and was shaped like me. I ignored my fishy progeny, who did not know passion. I cradled Pamphile in my arms, singing in his cold, stiff ear, "Ba-wal loo-mah ba-ha-wa loo-a-to," which I have always known means "Death to whites."

Now I was part of the REBELLION, though I had killed with my hand. The insurgents in France had fought, said Pamphile, with knives—strong blades, like those of the bills that cut the cane. Sugar knives to cut sugar lords who wore sugar shirts and pickled themselves in sugar-fire drink. Had their chopped-off sugar heads been baked in sugar pies? How many heads? How many pies? The wheel of knives had not stopped rolling and cutting, rolling and cutting, so Pamphile had sworn. The blades cut then turned to cut those who had cut before. Did they never stop?

Pamphile had spoken of black generals, viz., some men placed higher in the rebellious ranks than others. And did lowlier men roll out the wheel to cut down those? Did brothers shove each other from the high bed and the long table?

Piffle of whey-guts! We who had suffered together so much grief would not cut each other down for profit or gain. No humans were ever as communal as my fishy offspring, who know not rivalry or lust, yet we bondsmen have lived as helpmeets, in reverence of Deities and with respect for living and dead. Yet if crops and stores, docks and boats had been burned, mill-house and curing-house and kitchen-house, if all by which men gain a livelihood were ash, then how could men continue to thrive in the Anduves? Would help come from far-off Guinée? Oh, Pierre must go to the people, offering his strong hands and back and his mind of a savant, to help them rebuild all, better than before, but for our own benefit. If we succeed not? If the citizens of the new polity founder, yea, if we starve, as Pamphile predicted, then we would starve together.

All men must die. I would die free, among friends, near their fires. I would not die like the wretched Pamphile, stifled by his only mourner, who loathes him. Now my offspring had abandoned me, who would arrange my body in posture of sleep on its raft, who place the stones on my eye-lids and sprinkle them with dust? Who would intone a dirge as the bark is shoved out to sea? Who weep? What circling mourners sing songs of lamentation, standing waist-high in the sea, their wet smocks billowing around them? Let me die among mourners cooking skillet pie with the grief around the fires, let me die among mourners who mount a night-long vigil, with chants and processions, oh let me not die alone as Pamphile! I pitied him now. I would grant him decent rites in the manner of his people, lest, when my time come, I be punished by Baron Skull for a transgression worse than murder.

Before I bury him I would relate the tale of Pamphile's most un-looked-for ILLUMINATION. In saving his tale from oblivion I weave my thread into the same cloth as his, yet though I murdered him. I trust his tale to the same prospect for redemption to which I trust my own, to you, Kind Reader. So we are all tipped off our rafts into the maw beneath the tides of Time.

Now the raft the girl pushed into the outgoing tide, the raft on which the escaping father and son lay stretched—this raft floated who knows how long, Pamphile lying atop his father and gripping his ribs. Awake and asleep, they floated together, as flies copulating, toward they knew not what destiny, only to be separated by the waves of a storm that suddenly rose. The father slid off the o'erturned raft and under the waves; Pamphile righted the raft and climbed back aboard with the grimmest determination, he who had not known a fixed ambition in his life. When the storm subsided, still he clung to his raft with a desperation that bleached his knuckles, the sun pummeling his wits, his thirst-numbed tongue swelling in his mouth. The winking mirrors of the waters mocked his thirst, the witless flashes of waves burning spots on his eyelids when he had closed his eyes.

Yet, upon opening his eyes in the velvet dark, he discovered himself surrounded by gentler lights, further away. He feared the rebels had come for him. He feared the tawnies & maroons. Then he thought the turtles his father had loosed in his garden, with candles on their backs, had come to light his way through the maze of the sea. There were no turtles. The lights, he saw, were not the flames of candles but were themselves creatures, each a single, silvery orb, like the eye of a fish, yet translucent, opalescent, like the fish's scales, each orb reflecting in its depth the encompassing, starry vault above.

The solitary eyes were drawn to one another, to mingle some underwater dangling parts. They pulled each other beneath the water's skin, where a force, peradventure the weight of darkness, shattered them. Thereupon each shard rose an exact miniature of its parent, a smaller eye already reflecting in its roundness the heavens' starry vault. And when Pamphile covered one of the eyes, floating near him, with his own cupped hand, then withdrew his hand, he saw written on the eye, "as veins on the membrane of a moth wing," the lines of his own palm that he had often scrutinized, for a parlor game, to see his destiny. His reflected fate in the creature's eye was now superimposed on the reflected heavens.

Curiously, he splashed the water to propel an eye creature as yet unimpressed with his fate toward one that had been marked with his palm print, "like a specter, or memory." Brought thus together, the two did shudder and shatter. Each of the young bursting up from the wreck of fragmented parents now bore the impression of Pamphile's hand superimposed upon the heavens. And he told himself he was a fine fellow, to have left his mark on the heavens as a brand on kine!

He branded all he could reach. For a while the creatures drifted around him, an illusion of omnipotence. Yet they exuded a powerful odor of fish. Pamphile's hunger and thirst become very great, he picked up several of the eyes he had marked as his and ate them, dangling roots and all. Thereupon his field of vision exploded in splinters of light, as if he himself had been a shattering eye.

He saw in that state much that he could not have known: the smoke rising from the fresh-snuffed candle by his parents' bed; the lace his mother had crocheted on the pillow slip, his father's spectacles, earpieces crossed, on the table. Through his parents' eyes, he saw the dull-gloss pewter of a basin and a ewer, saw an etching of a stag and a virgin and others of the city of Paris and the village of Montbard. There were excellent engravings of his father's father's time, principally of tulips, the variety named

Viceroy; another not named, black as the swan of Juvenal; and the Semper Augustus, that a sailor filched and ate off the counter of a trader, supposing it an onion, out of place among the cut velvets and the water silks. There were proofs of plates for Buffon's *Histoire,* engravings from M'sieu's drawings of bright-eyed fauna, perfect-feathered birds. Pamphile read some words of galleys his father proofed, Buffon's description of desert, terrifying and complete, barren amplitude. Then darkness.

He felt his mother's breast, a cool rose-painted cup beneath his hand. Petals opened, pollen spread down her belly, a mouth between her legs gaped and puckered like a jellyfish sucking in food. A finger moved between his legs, feeding the mouth like a tongue, moving in the dark throat as if to speak, and she cried out or he did.

Pamphile walked from his mother's bed and read with his father Buffon's account of THE SEVEN EPOCHS OF NATURE, seeing all as if he had been present: In The First Epoch, a comet strikes the sun. Fiery molten matter is spun off to become the planets. In The Second, the liquid fire spins and spins and spins and cools into spheres, which wrinkle and hollow and blister as they further cool. The Third Epoch: steam cooling in drops, the drops falling on earth as rain, the rain flooding the planet with a very hot and steamy sea. The giant shellfish congeal in the deep. It is The Fourth Epoch now—quakes and shakes beneath the weight of the waters. The shellfish are shedding their shells to form the calcareous rocks. By The Fifth Epoch, the terrestrial beasts are born from the cooling folds of the wrinkling earth as words are born from the alphabet. They form in the north, where the evaporation of heat is greatest. Elephants, hippopotami, rhinoceroses, leopards, horses, bison and, yes, men. In The Sixth Epoch, they walk toward the equator, following the warmth, for the planet chills from the poles. And the further the beasts walk from their birthplace, the smaller and more degenerate they become, viz., the elephant loses his hair and his tusks grow shorter—

"Damnation!" cried Pamphile in my arms. "Eyes or no eyes, I cannot sort these epochs out. The earth is cooling off. Some day all will be dark and cold. We are now in The Seventh Epoch, the epoch of man's dominion over the other animals, whom we so vastly excel. We must use our talents, not only to further our own ambitions, but to prolong the duration of life on earth. We must dwell in considerable numbers and burn the cold, gloomy forests. We must keep our stables and barns full of horses & cows & other manner of domesticated creatures that take cold air into their bodies and blow out hot, like great bellows blowing up the fire of a forge. Thus we will slow down the cooling of the earth. Cold! I am cold. Rose?" cried Pamphile in my arms. "Mama? Rose?"

Pamphile afloat among the eyes awoke to sun, the light-wrinkled water, the taste of fish in his mouth. Still he looked at the world as through a veil, thin and spectral, impressed with the image of the star-studded vault, impressed with the lines of his palm. Still his fate was written large as all Creation in the stars. By the time I held him and heard him, his vision, he said, had cleared. Yet not long after, his eyes had clouded with the final knowledge, the shadow of my hand descending ahead of his future.

Holding his stiffening body in my arms, I crooned his name, "Pamphile, Pamphile." Then I threw his body from me. I thought I had heard a silky voice in my ear, Pierre Baptiste! A sweet voice, a sugar voice, dripping poison: Eat the eyes! Eat the eyes! said the voice. Scoop out and swallow Pamphile's eyes. While still they are firm in his face, enjoy sweet knowledge. Eat the eyes!

So stroll with Pamphile through the yard on Dufay's estate, espy poor Beloo, staring at his fingerless hands, as if they were starfish that had scuttled from the sea to batten onto his wrists. Drawn by the fragrance of boiling chicken, peek into the kitchen. My wife with her skirt tucked above her apron mixes a posset of wine with cinnamon to restore to M'sieu his vigor.

"Vérité! Some posset for Pierre growing old without you."

She does not hear.

Pierre, if you would be heard, eat the eyes!

Jean-François has brought into the yard the boots he has collected. He sets them on the ground and looks around for the boys he would set to blacking them. They are hiding. Only a little white girl pulling the pigtails of two dark girls careful not to retaliate, lest they be beaten. She has a sickly look, very blue. She will not live, but will join her siblings in the line of little graves. And one of the dark girls too will die young and be sent out to sea on a little raft, the candles blinking in the wind. Who is watching the girls? Why Quasheba! Is Rose then dead? Yes, Rose is dead, and Granny Nancy. And Jean-François walks stooped over and has very white hair. Quasheba and Dido and a new man named Vergil pull their stools to the fire. Vergil is boiler now, the favorite of Squint, yet righteous and bold, a captain the hands would choose for themselves. What stories will he tell? Vergil, before you were taken from Guinée, did you meet the Fombé people who wear on their breasts certain pouches woven in a pattern of dark and light bands? Alas, Pierre, you must eat the eyes if you would have him speak. Eat the eyes if you would have his tale for the shadow histoire. Eat the eyes!

Walk with Pamphile in Buffon's gardens, following along the allées the savant who paces, mumbling, mumbling. Now he pauses to dictate to the scribbling secretary who breaks the points of his pens, splashing ink on the pages. The wind rises; the pages drift across the parterres from the campaign table set in a pergola.

Buffon declaims with such force the words strike petals from the roses.

Buffon pauses, wipes his brow, and claps on his head the hat he has carried under his arm, though it will not settle, so great is the frizzed-up volume of his wig. He holds the hat to his head with one hand, to keep the sun from his eyes with its brim. With his other hand he waves the air tenderly. He mutters and shakes his head. His hat falls to the ground. <u>Now, Pierre. Pick up the hat. Speak.</u>

Pierre will hand Buffon his hat. When Buffon's eyes, as blue and as cloudy as marbles, settle on Pierre—Pierre will look straight into those eyes. He will speak of his shadow histoire. <u>Alas, he cannot hear. To be heard, you must eat the eyes. Pamphile's eyes. Buffon's eyes. Eat the eyes!</u> Then hear Buffon dilate on The Seven Epochs of Nature. You will astonish him with your discovery of an Eighth. You will walk with him, talking all the while, along the allées, <u>if only you eat the eyes. Eat the eyes. Buffon's eyes, Pamphile's eyes. Why not?</u>

Were it not meet I should pluck my truth from a white man's skull, even as, long ago, Pamphile had plucked my bag from Rose's hand, stealing what little I had from my mother? What had a murderer to lose and what to gain in scrupling niceties? Why not eat the eyes before they rotted to slime or were pecked to pulp by birds?

Yet rocking in my arms the corpse of feckless Pamphile, sensing his soul depart his body with his warmth, I could not defile his flesh. What? To hear ever after the silent hooves of the Baron Skull's horses, Mist and Dread? Cursed by my own lights and Heaven's, which I could see well enough without devouring eyes? No, I could not disfigure the face of my brother, my enemy, the man I had killed whom I held in my arms. I was not the AN-THROPOPHAGUS! I was a man of resolve. I buried him whole in the manner of his people.

239

Digging with clam shells, I excavated a pit and rolled him in. I was covering him with loam, up to the height of the surrounding terrain, as was the custom of whites, and sweating to do it. While I was working, there fell on me a shadow. Alarmed, I looked up into the face of my smallest child, twisted Léo. With his tiny ear my Léo had heard, he said, the spider, who had not spoken since she delivered my offspring from the branding iron. Now she demanded, he said, other obsequies for Pamphile than I had commenced.

"What?" I did most bitterly protest. My labor for naught? The corpse was covered with dirt.

"Throw rinds," said Léo. "The spider said Uncle would speak."

"The matter is between me and this dead man. It is not for sprites and deities. Get on with your fishing."

"You have said it yourself. Bad men weight down with earth the dead, or immure them in vaults of rock, confining to torture, preventing return to sea. Why do you wish to be bad?"

I threw up my hands.

"Throw rinds, Papamam. Very most please consider."

What could I do?

The rinds fell *shaggy, smooth, smooth, shaggy.* Spider whispered in Léo's ear. Léo picked up a clam shell. Together we tossed clam's-shellfuls of dirt back off the fly-blown corpse. Then we must hack at the vines that o'ergrew the two-tub boat. *Shaggy, smooth, smooth, shaggy.* So swore the rinds. So Uncle directed me to employ as a funeral barge my cherished boat. Yet I did not immediately acquiesce.

"This vile scapegrace?" I cried. "This abomination & perversion? In Pierre's boat? Which was built to take the cyclopedish histoire to the seat of the savants? This boat, now the only means of return to the Anduves, my home? Where not only the instruments of the masters' cruelty, viz., Four-Post and Stinger, have been burned, but the houses and crops and sheds, the cooper's and carpenter's shops, the kitchen? Now in the new republic of free men there be need to design manufactories and found schools. Surely, there be need for ingenious savants, with knowledge of ledgers and accounts, who know shipbuilding and navigation and can draft letters to eminent men, in a fair hand, to further the conduct of diplomacy! How can we journey to the isle of need but in this very boat which you propose to waste on this damn-dead bloat-bag!"

"Many good place for fish-catch, different year-time," said Léo.

"Damn me!" did I hotly cry. "You fish can sustain your living anywhere in the sea. Whereas men—civil men—have fixed abodes. They must make their fortunes where they live, or be made by them. Now that I will not be caught and hurt, I must return to my wife!"

"Uncle claim," said Léo, pointing to the tiny ear that heard the spider. He gave a spritely shrug. "Uncle want Pamphile rest in boat."

What could I do? I had given myself to Uncle, long, long ago. I had dedicated my life to His rites and His service; He had not forsaken this otherwise God-forsaken isle. I could not refuse Him. Though I did not believe there remained to me sufficient lifetime to gather drift for another boat, I picked up my hack-piece. I commenced to uncover the boat. In it, Pamphile might arrive in France, to have his high-born head chopped off. Was this justice? Water is ironic; she changes her mind.

"We must send him off to sea with gifts," said Léo. "We must pray the sea be kind."

Though I rued the day I had taught my young to divine with coco rinds, I was glad to have Léo back! I would have undertaken all that Uncle required, yet I was prevented by the condition of the boat, which proved to have rotted from beneath. When we lifted it from its resting place, it fell to pieces.

Spider then spoke again in Léo's tiny ear. She bade him clamber to the top of a very large rock, the highest point on our isle.

There he threw the rinds again. *Shaggy, smooth, shaggy, smooth.* Spider spoke long into Léo's ear. He was advised we must burn the body in the boat remains, though the damp, rotten wood make difficulties in kindling and sustaining fire. We dragged what driftwood I had collected since My Temptation. With dried fronds and beach grass we built a PYRE, having cleared a ring of earth around it so the fire would not spread and drive us into the sea. And once again Pierre frotted sticks.

We laid the bloaty blue Pamphile across the crumbling tubs, and we covered him with brush, filling the tubs beneath him as well. Before we fired him, I again sprinkled sand on the stones that weighed down his lids. I murmured again the words that I had heard from the mouth of Père Gouy. "Dust to dust!"

Yet the honor I owed his body I did not owe his clothes. That sprinkle of dust were his funeral suit! Before I burned him, I stripped off his rags, that I might dry them, and lay them as patterns against palm-fiber stuff I wove, as of old my sails; so he gave me, in death as never in life, a new suit of clothes. *The savants are dead! Long live the savants!* I wove a suit for Léo too. As my other progeny forgave me one by one, I wove each a suit.

Then I commenced making PAPER of palm fibers, rotted in solution of stink-fruit and fish-gruel. Later my offspring devised a method of separating the fibers with their teeth—very fine & excellent for paper. We make thin, strong, exquisite stuff, which we pound to a smooth surface, meet for writing.

My shadow grows shorter with each new day now. Drawing to a close my chronicle, I desire to append a brief account of the return of my TALISMAN, which did wash up on shore one day, unexpected and unbidden, the pouch much rotted by the sea, its contents entirely vanished, but the tattered bag still possessed of a power to quiet my heart.

Never had I known the true significance or provenance of the lizard's tongue & cumin seed, cinnamon sticks & flower petals my mother had collected. And my godmothers' proverbs, and the shapely phrases I culled from books—could these have represented Wisdom, scrawled on the obverse of tea labels? It were fitting the pouch be empty, yet no less painful a grief.

In the cisterns where I had been wont to see Vérité, I did sometimes see the faces of children—human children—strangers to me, bright and black, plump and hale, with sparks of quickness in their eyes. Even as Pierre's fishy offspring are the children of his mouth, these cistern-young are the CHILDREN OF THE ANDUVES, born in freedom. I pray they will be schooled in letters and ciphers, but if the library were burned, I fear they will not. Alas, I cannot see in the cistern whether they have learned some useful trade, and cowries and coco shells tell not.

Surely the Anduvean children will live more prosperous and peaceful if each among them have a patent to trade on in the world. Would it not be the highest calling for a savant, to furnish them with the wherewithal to bring the world in trade to their door? With what patent would I furnish the Anduves?

The manufacture of paper from fibers of palm, rotted in stink-fruit and fish gruel, cannot be exported, for the stink fruit grow but on this isle and the gruel be fermented in the mouths of fish sprites without propensity to settled industry. Pierre would impart the secret of ORCHID-POLLEN SALVE, how it may be rubbed on the skin to ward off insects, moreover how the rubbing imparts to the rubbed parts a golden glow. This would be pleasing on the flesh of men and women, and most especially might be pleasing if smeared in rings around the eyes of the latter. Pierre would demonstrate the mixing of the pollen with jelly of pounded uglimousse fish, to make a paste, which can be packed into coco shells, and sold or traded for all manner of necessities, corn & barreled beef & ax-heads & cloth. <u>What do you say, oh cistern children?</u>

The children respond not, but pensively gaze from the water of the cistern, as if they would study and learn the world. Oh, these children would not have burned M'sieu's books! Perhaps there were saved out a few, and the paintings of M'sieu—kept in a safe trunk in a safe place. It is the dominion of masters, not their art or philosophy, bonded men find their freedom against.

Daily I circumambulate our isle, spying what drift I can pull ashore. Yet I believe that all I will leave the sons of the Anduves, and their sons, yea, and daughters too (strong, comely girls, surely) be the CYCLOPEDISH HISTOIRE in the writing down of which the fishy progeny now assist. I leave the histoire for the Anduveans, then, and for whoever find it.

Sometimes reflected in the cisterns, I see my own withering countenance and ask myself how my derelict's life has gone. I answer me thus: by my own cleverness have I transported myself to a station higher than that to which I was born. None other than I, methinks, has undergone my transformation. In the realm of philosophy, the children of my mouth have gone beyond me; in the realm of discovery their accomplishments are greater than Quassi's (and his were great enough), greater even than Buffon's. Yet it is I and I alone who have discovered THE EIGHTH EPOCH, for Buffon did not see beyond The Seventh. He did not foresee an epoch when man must acknowledge the end of his dominion over other creatures, even as, come the Revolution, some men have had to give up their dominion over others.

Now, if Pamphile were a credible witness, M. de Buffon came to believe that the cooling of the earth can only be slowed by the industry of men, settled in numbers. Small wonder a man who operated forges did believe such manufactories could prolong the duration of life on the cooling cinder of Earth. Do we also increase the longevity of the planet by boiling sugar in vats that men fall in to drown? If this be true, then let the planet slowly die, while the men on it live happily, with neither sugar nor slavery.

Yet if, in The Eighth Epoch, men learn to dwell as one family with all other creatures, then we shall have a new histoire to write together, more compendious than any conceived before. From the honest labor of this conception will be born forms of language and thought, and thus of life, that were not present in the rock and fire of Creation. This Pierre believes. For, after much reflection, he does not hold with the Christians, that all that may be, already is. Rather he submits, all that may be is not yet born. Thus, there can be no death of the planet, for it continues to give birth. If a man dies, and his children live, and their children, can the lineage of the man be dead? And this is true, even if his children's children are living far from the land of their origin. And it is true, even if a man's children are philoso-fish.

Yet I do divagate, wandering far from my course. No one has asserted that the death of all life on the planet be imminent. I, who have seen my wizened countenance reflected in the cistern, will sooner see the end of my own life approach. So I have begun to consider my contribution to the sum of knowledge in the world, whether it be small or great. One question does remain in my mind: will I be granted, before my time runs out, reunion with my wife? Much the spider will whisper in Léo's tiny ear, but nothing of Pierre's voyage home. For comfort I have the remains of her quilt; I sleep with the rags in my nest.

Like other men, I must be as content with what I do not know and cannot have as with what I know and have. Truly, a power lies in having NOT and knowing NOT, by which I intend no willful, base, and indulgent ignorance, but a tranquil reverence that enters the heart as a murmur from a departed mollusk's shell. What we cannot know reaches out of the dark to eat our tongues and bring forth life.

I tell you, the power of NOT has risen in me to help o'erthrow the habit of being catered for—preposterous grub queen! After the death of Pamphile, I no longer wished to be fed the vomited gruel, like a bird-babe in its nest. Marie Mandilé-Ba had given me, not gruel, but a hook carved of bone; once again I would pierce the mouths of fin-meat.

I will set down the manner of my FISHING. First, I tease a number of hairs from my plaits, which long-armed Framo has braided. I twist these hairs to twine, knot the hook to them, impale on the hook a palmetto bug, and troll from the promontory whence so long ago I impaled Amie on my turtling spear.

In the swath the consorts cut around my hook, I lower and raise the bug in the sun-shafted waters until dinner rises to the bait. I cut the gill-luffing head from the flopping body. I bow to Uncle before I grill, and leave Him half the fish, and eat all my part but the head and bones, so my offspring will see this were no gratuitous murder.

Oh, the fragrance of flotsam fire, upon which I have thrown diverse & fragrant herbs! Oh the succulence of stick-grilled fish flesh, eaten from the skin! After my meal, I burn the hairs that had served as my line and throw the bones and the head to the sea. The hook I return to my ear, for my relict pouch cannot contain it. So I feed myself.

Émlo, the first to compose a trope, has asked that I say more of my hairs, which are useful not only for fishing. For when Framo plaits them, he strings on them the cowrie shells where spiders dwell so tiny no eye can see them nor even the tiny ear of Léo hear. And these shells speak through their mouths, which speak through my hairs to my heart. Thus am I able to scribe the words you read, my powers sufficient to the task if a number of the cowries be mounded at the end of each of my plaits, to hold my soul to earth awhile. For I am very old. My hairs are very white. My soul yearns to fly to Chenwiyi's lap.

Émlo begs me to stay awhile, to bear witness to the customs and beliefs of this isle.

"If we are The Eighth Epoch," he says, "you must write us down."

"After me—you, my Émlo."

"You know founding. Very much please, say what no other know, so we dream who we."

"And what of the Sea-Ones? Who will tell Their story?"

"Dark," he says. "Very dark way down."

"I would shed light."

"Waste not powers, Papamam. Lest Eighth Epoch be tissue scar, very much please consider."

Having ground to a powder the gritty ash that had been Pamphile, having mixed the powder with squid's ink, yea, verily, I, Pierre, commenced to write these pages, calling on the shards of memory, unite and be whole. From burned bones, shadow histoire. And so I too give the wheel another turn.

Though I hastened Pamphile's end, his arrival inspired in me the hope our island might one day be discovered by other men, yea, and women. In The Eighth Epoch, human souls will profit by my reflections even as my fish-sprite progeny do. And our reflections will continue, light on light in the dark. I have given each of my offspring the bone-fire ink. We have copied onto our coats the pattern of light & dark bands that was woven into the relict pouch. The pattern will be preserved when the talisman crumbles to dust.

After I have gone, my offspring will fend for themselves. And what have I given them? The simple righteousness I learned from Rose in the yard? Savantish subtlety? What profit these by immersion in sea water? Still, I count my offspring, and their off-spring, as civil as any other creatures, notwithstanding MAN, who presumes himself the nonpareil. To the Anduves I would say: learn from the philoso-fish. To savants who still have their heads: Man is separated from other creatures but by a crack. In The Eighth Epoch, the crack will be mended, the universe Man has broken be made whole. If this be blasphemy, may the Gods & Their Parents & Their Parents, all the way back to Grandmother Emptiness, forgive me my trespass.

Through the clouds reflected in the cistern, I see my Pélérine, who comes in her ship of sugar threads, gossamer on the light. It is manned by hundreds of spiders, golden-bellied, crimson-legged, opal-eyed, amethyst-tongued. Yes . . . through gold and purple light glides the *PÉLÉRINE,* a ship that needs but one great sail, that spreads so high the top is lost in clouds. Through a porthole that looks like a silver eye I see in the belly of the ship the prism conjure house, with all its crystal rooms & chests intact, its facets reflecting dreams of the denizens of air & land & sea— the true, universal cyclopedish histoire.

And this ship with its payload of conjure histoire is stopping at all the isles of the Anduves. Pierre takes on board all his friends, whether they be in high place or low. The *Pélérine* sails again, this time for Guinée, stopping always at each island where sugar is grown, or any other commodity, and men & women are slaves to Toil, even if they are called Free. In the rigging, the spider sailors, neat and pretty in their footing, keep their eyes alert for cast-aways. If they spy one, they pull him up, on a hawser of sugar. And there is room in the hold for all his conjure. All the sufferers sail with Pierre in his ship to Guinée, and each is united with his own lineage, and marries well, and prospers in his garden beneath his orange tree, and achieves full measure of honor and wisdom, and has two changes of linen a week and all the books he can read, and learns the true name that his mother has placed in his talis-man pouch. The girl Vérité waits in Guinée for Pierre, her eyes bright and gay, her cheeks round. Her step is lively and even. Her arms are held out to Pierre; a tender, joyous smile curves her per-fect lips. I go now. Iroson. It is time.

The humble servant
of my children, may
they thrive and increase,

Pierre, Mère et Père,
Premier, Dernière, yes,

AMEN

ABOUT THE AUTHOR

PATRICIA EAKINS is the author of *The Hungry Girls and Other Stories*, which was hailed by the *New York Times Book Review* as a "work of imaginative brilliance" and by *Hungry Mind Review* as "an astonishingly ambitious and accomplished book." Eakins's prose has been published in *Transgressions: The Iowa Anthology of Innovative Fiction, Parnassus, Fiction International, Conjunctions, Storia, Hotwired,* and *Race Traitor: The Journal of the New Abolitionists.* She has received two literature fellowships from the National Endowment for the Arts and was awarded the 1996 Aga Khan Prize for Fiction from the *Paris Review.* Her web site is http://www.fabulara.com.

CHEERS

COMPLETE BOOK OF
THE OLYMPICS

"An indispensable addition to the shelves of both sportswriters and serious fans . . . an extremely meticulous—one may even say Olympian—piece of scholarship. . . . This is a volume that will be of service for many Olympiads to come."
—Erich Segal, New York Times Book Review

"If ever a book was properly titled, this is the one. . . . The ultimate Olympic source book . . . humanity in all its pride and wonder."
—Los Angeles Times

"A staggering compendium of results, highlights and oddments dating from the first modern games in 1896. . . . Stuffed with fascinating tidbits about the contestants. . . . You'll enjoy this book even if you're not keen on the Games."
—Wall Street Journal

"The perfect source for someone who wants to know everything about the Summer and Winter Games"
—USA Today

"Invaluable"—The New Republic

"Superb"—Providence, R.I., Bulletin

"The encyclopedia of modern Olympiana"
—Baltimore Sun

"The most-plundered of all the books available to the nation's sporting scribblers. . . . A guy can look real smart after reading Wallechinsky's treasure trove of Olympic good stuff."—Houston Post

"Author David Wallechinsky has amassed mind-boggling information. He stirs an aura of excitement into his superb writing . . . . Not a dull passage mars this book."
—Wichita Falls, Tex., Times

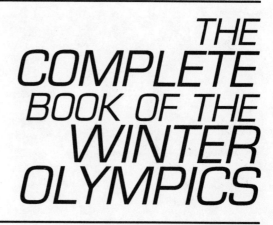

THE
COMPLETE
BOOK OF THE
WINTER
OLYMPICS

1998 Edition

THE
COMPLETE
BOOK OF THE
WINTER
OLYMPICS

DAVID WALLECHINSKY

THE OVERLOOK PRESS

WOODSTOCK & NEW YORK

TO ELIJAH AND AARON

First published in the United States in 1998 by
The Overlook Press, Peter Mayer Publishers, Inc.
Lewis Hollow Road
Woodstock, New York 12498

PICTURE CREDITS: *ADN, p. 254; Allsport, pp. 23, 174; AP, p. 192; AP/Wide World Photos, p. 251;
AP/Wide World Photos/Al Behrman, p. 49; AP/Wide World Photos/Michel Euler, p. 218;
AP/Wide World Photos/Merline Summers, p. 85; City of Calgary Archives, p. 69; Frederick Fliegner,
p. 220; Minto Skating Club, Ottawa/Bill Newton, p. 75; New York Times/Barton Silverman, p. 42;
NTB-Photo, p. 203; Pressen Bild, pp. 77, 210; Scan-Foto/Colin Samuels, p. 199; Scan-Foto/Johnny
Syversen, p. 117; Klaus Schlage, p. 80; Sportverlag Berlin, p. 217; U.S.O.C., pp. 19, 73, 95, 147.*

Library of Congress Cataloging-in-Publication Data

Wallechinsky, David.
The complete book of the Winter Olympics / David Wallechinsky.—1998 ed.
p. cm.
1. Winter Olympics—History. 2. Winter Olympics—Records. I. Title.
GV841.5.W26 1998 796.98—dc21 97-28942

Manufactured in the United States of America
ISBN 0-87951-818-9 (pbk)
ISBN 0-87951-849-9 (hc)

First Edition
9 8 7 6 5 4 3 2 1

CONTENTS

Permabind

THE WINTER GAMES

THE WINTER OLYMPIC GAMES

				EVENTS	COMPETITORS Men	COMPETITORS Women	NATIONS REPRESENTED
I	1924	CHAMONIX, FRANCE	January 25–February 4	14	281	13	16
II	1928	ST. MORITZ, SWITZERLAND	February 11–19	13	468	27	25
III	1932	LAKE PLACID, U.S.A.	February 4–15	14	274	32	17
IV	1936	GARMISCH-PARTENKIRCHEN, GERMANY	February 6–16	17	675	80	28
—	1940	SAPPORO, JAPAN; ST. MORITZ, SWITZERLAND; GARMISCH-PARTENKIRCHEN, GERMANY	Cancelled because of war	—	—	—	—
—	1944	CORTINA D'AMPEZZO, ITALY	Cancelled because of war	—	—	—	—
V	1948	ST. MORITZ, SWITZERLAND	January 30–February 8	22	636	77	28
VI	1952	OSLO, NORWAY	February 14–25	22	623	109	30
VII	1956	CORTINA D'AMPEZZO, ITALY	January 26–February 5	24	686	132	32
VIII	1960	SQUAW VALLEY, U.S.A.	February 18–28	27	521	144	30
IX	1964	INNSBRUCK, AUSTRIA	January 29–February 9	34	986	200	36
X	1968	GRENOBLE, FRANCE	February 6–18	35	1081	212	37
XI	1972	SAPPORO, JAPAN	February 3–13	35	1015	217	35
XII	1976	INNSBRUCK, AUSTRIA	February 4–15	37	900	228	37
XIII	1980	LAKE PLACID, U.S.A.	February 14–23	38	837	234	37
XIV	1984	SARAJEVO, YUGOSLAVIA	February 7–19	39	1000	277	49
XV	1988	CALGARY, CANADA	February 13–28	46	1113	315	57
XVI	1992	ALBERTVILLE, FRANCE	February 8–23	57	1318	490	64
XVII	1994	LILLEHAMMER, NORWAY	February 12–27	61	1313	488	67
XVIII	1998	NAGANO, JAPAN	February 7-22	68			
XIX	2002	SALT LAKE CITY, U.S.A.	February 9–24				

NATIONAL MEDAL TOTALS IN EACH OLYMPICS

1924 Chamonix

	G	S	B*
NOR	4	7	6
FIN	4	3	3
AUT	2	1	0
USA	1	2	1
SWI	1	0	1
CAN	1	0	0
SWE	1	0	0
GBR	0	1	2
BEL	0	0	1
FRA	0	0	1

1928 St. Moritz

	G	S	B
NOR	6	4	5
USA	2	2	2
SWE	2	2	1
FIN	2	1	1
CAN	1	0	0
FRA	1	0	0
AUT	0	3	1
BEL	0	0	1
CZE	0	0	1
GBR	0	0	1
GER	0	0	1

1932 Lake Placid

	G	S	B
USA	6	4	2
NOR	3	4	3
SWE	1	2	0
CAN	1	1	5
FIN	1	1	1
AUT	1	1	0
FRA	1	0	0
SWI	0	1	0
GER	0	0	2
HUN	0	0	1

1936 Garmisch-Partenkirchen

	G	S	B
NOR	7	5	3
GER	3	3	0
SWE	2	2	3
FIN	1	2	3
SWI	1	2	0
AUT	1	1	2
GBR	1	1	1
USA	1	0	3
CAN	0	1	0
FRA	0	0	1
HUN	0	0	1

1948 St. Moritz

	G	S	B
NOR	4	3	3
SWE	4	3	3
SWI	3	4	3
USA	3	4	2
FRA	2	1	2
CAN	2	0	1
AUT	1	3	4
FIN	1	3	2
BEL	1	1	0
ITA	1	0	0
CZE	0	1	0
HUN	0	1	0
GBR	0	0	2

1952 Oslo

	G	S	B
NOR	7	3	6
USA	4	6	1
FIN	3	4	2
GER	3	2	2
AUT	2	4	2
CAN	1	0	1
ITA	1	0	1
GBR	1	0	0
HOL	0	3	0
SWE	0	0	4
SWI	0	0	2
FRA	0	0	1
HUN	0	0	1

*G = gold, S = silver, B = bronze.

1956 Cortina d'Ampezzo

	G	S	B
SOV	7	3	6
AUT	4	3	4
FIN	3	3	1
SWI	3	2	1
SWE	2	4	4
USA	2	3	2
NOR	2	1	1
ITA	1	2	0
GER	1	0	0
CAN	0	1	2
JPN	0	1	0
GDR	0	0	1
HUN	0	0	1
POL	0	0	1

1960 Squaw Valley

	G	S	B
SOV	7	5	9
USA	3	4	3
NOR	3	3	0
SWE	3	2	2
FIN	2	3	3
GER	2	2	1
CAN	2	1	1
GDR	2	1	0
SWI	2	0	0
AUT	1	2	3
FRA	1	0	2
HOL	0	1	1
POL	0	1	1
CZE	0	1	0

1964 Innsbruck

	G	S	B
SOV	11	8	6
AUT	4	5	3
NOR	3	6	6
FIN	3	4	3
FRA	3	4	0
SWE	3	3	1
GDR	2	2	0
USA	1	2	3
GER	1	1	3
HOL	1	1	0
CAN	1	0	2
GBR	1	0	0
ITA	0	1	3
PRK	0	1	0
CZE	0	0	1

1968 Grenoble

	G	S	B
NOR	6	6	2
SOV	5	5	3
FRA	4	3	2
ITA	4	0	0
AUT	3	4	4
HOL	3	3	3
SWE	3	2	3
GER	2	2	3
USA	1	5	1
FIN	1	2	2
GDR	1	2	2
CZE	1	2	1
CAN	1	1	1
SWI	0	2	4
ROM	0	0	1

1972 Sapporo

	G	S	B
SOV	8	5	3
GDR	4	3	7
SWI	4	3	3
HOL	4	3	2
USA	3	2	3
GER	3	1	1
NOR	2	5	5
ITA	2	2	1
AUT	1	2	2
SWE	1	1	2
JPN	1	1	1
CZE	1	0	2
POL	1	0	0
SPA	1	0	0
FIN	0	4	1
FRA	0	1	2
CAN	0	1	0

1976 Innsbruck

	G	S	B
SOV	13	6	8
GDR	7	5	7
USA	3	3	4
NOR	3	3	1
GER	2	5	3
FIN	2	4	1
AUT	2	2	2
SWI	1	3	1
HOL	1	2	3
ITA	1	2	1
CAN	1	1	1
GBR	1	0	0
CZE	0	1	0

	G	S	B
LIE	0	0	2
SWE	0	0	2
FRA	0	0	1

1980 Lake Placid

	G	S	B
SOV	10	6	6
GDR	9	7	7
USA	6	4	2
AUT	3	2	2
SWE	3	0	1
LIE	2	2	0
FIN	1	5	3
NOR	1	3	6
HOL	1	2	1
SWI	1	1	3
GBR	1	0	0
GER	0	2	3
ITA	0	2	0
CAN	0	1	1
HUN	0	1	0
JPN	0	1	0
BUL	0	0	1
CZE	0	0	1
FRA	0	0	1

1984 Sarajevo

	G	S	B
GDR	9	9	6
SOV	6	10	9
USA	4	4	0
FIN	4	3	6
SWE	4	2	2
NOR	3	2	4
SWI	2	2	1
CAN	2	1	1
GER	2	1	1
ITA	2	0	0
GBR	1	0	0
CZE	0	2	4
FRA	0	1	2
JPN	0	1	0
YUG	0	1	0
LIE	0	0	2
AUT	0	0	1

1988 Calgary

	G	S	B
SOV	11	9	9
GDR	9	10	6
SWI	5	5	5
FIN	4	1	2
SWE	4	0	2

	G	S	B
AUT	3	5	2
HOL	3	2	2
GER	2	4	2
USA	2	1	3
ITA	2	1	2
FRA	1	0	1
NOR	0	3	2
CAN	0	2	3
YUG	0	2	1
CZE	0	1	2
JPN	0	0	1
LIE	0	0	1

1992 Albertville

	G	S	B
GER	10	10	6
SOV	9	6	8
NOR	9	6	5
AUT	6	7	8
USA	5	4	2
ITA	4	6	4

	G	S	B
FRA	3	5	1
FIN	3	1	3
CAN	2	3	2
KOR	2	1	1
JPN	1	2	4
HOL	1	1	2
SWE	1	0	3
SWI	1	0	2
CHN	0	3	0
LUX	0	2	0
NZE	0	1	0
CZE	0	0	3
PRK	0	0	1
SPA	0	0	1

1994 Lillehammer

	G	S	B
RUS	11	8	4
NOR	10	11	5
GER	9	7	8

	G	S	B
ITA	7	5	8
USA	6	5	2
KOR	4	1	1
CAN	3	6	4
SWI	3	4	2
AUT	2	3	4
SWE	2	1	0
JPN	1	2	2
KAZ	1	2	0
UKR	1	0	1
UZB	1	0	0
BLR	0	2	0
FIN	0	1	5
FRA	0	1	4
HOL	0	1	3
CHN	0	1	2
SLO	0	0	3
GBR	0	0	2
AUS	0	0	1

A BRIEF HISTORY OF THE OLYMPIC WINTER GAMES

Figure skating was included in the original program of the 1900 Summer Olympics, but the competitions never took place. In **1908,** however, four figure skating events were held at the Prince's Skating Rink in London. Three years later, I.O.C. member Count Brunetta d'Ussaux of Italy proposed that the Swedish Organizing Committee in charge of the 1912 Games include winter sports in the Stockholm Olympics or else stage a separate Olympic gathering for winter events. The Swedes flatly rejected the suggestion on the grounds that it would threaten their own Nordic Games, which had been held every four years since 1901. The German organizers of the **1916** Games planned a separate Skiing Olympia to be held in February in the Black Forest. The Swedes opposed the idea, but discussions became irrelevant when World War I broke out and the Olympics were canceled.

When the Summer Olympics resumed in Antwerp in **1920,** figure skating and ice hockey were included. The following year the proposal for separate Winter Olympics was again discussed by the I.O.C. In 1922, over the objections of Olympics founder Baron Pierre de Coubertin, a motion was passed to stage "International Sports Week **1924**" in Chamonix, France. This event was a complete success and was retroactively named the First Olympic Winter Games. Even the Scandinavians, pleased by the fact that their athletes won 28 of the 43 medals presented, dropped their objections and enthusiastically supported a proposal to continue the Winter Olympics every four years.

The **1928** Winter Games were the first to be held in a different nation than the Summer Games of the same year. They also marked the beginning of the endless battle between the Winter Olympics and the weather. Warm temperatures forced the cancellation of the 10,000-meter speed skating contest. Then, 18 hours of rain led to the postponement of an entire day's events.

The third Winter Olympics, in **1932,** was held in Lake Placid, New York, a town of fewer than 4000 people. Faced with major obstacles raising money in the midst of a depression, the president of the organizing committee, Dr. Godfrey Dewey, donated land owned by his family to be used for construction of a bobsled run. Governor Franklin D. Roosevelt opened the Games, and his wife, future first lady Eleanor Roosevelt, took a run down the bobsled course. Leftover rain on the outrun of the ski jump caused some athletes to end up in a pool of water. The first example of ugliness in the Winter Olympics occurred when European speed skaters discovered that the local organizers had decided to impose a completely different set of rules than those with which they were familiar. Ignoring the outrage of the foreigners, the North Americans cheerfully won 10 of 12 speed skating medals, nine more than they won in either the preceding or following Olympics.

The **1936** Games were held in the twin Bavarian towns of Garmisch and Partenkirchen and were viewed by the Nazis as a tune-up for the Berlin Summer Games. Efficient bus service allowed 500,000 people to attend the final day's events. Alpine skiing events were included for the first time, and this led to a major controversy. The I.O.C., overruling the International Ski Federation (F.I.S.), declared that ski instructors could not take part in the Olympics because they were professionals. Incensed, the Austrian and Swiss skiers boycotted the events.

This dispute carried on after the Games and became so heated that it was decided that skiing would not be included in the **1940** Games, which were scheduled for Sapporo, Japan, on the island of Hokkaido. War with China forced the Japanese to admit, in July 1938, that they would be unable to host the Games. St. Moritz was chosen as an alternative site, but the continuing dispute about ski instructors led the Swiss to withdraw as well. The Germans volunteered Garmisch-Partenkirchen in July 1939, but four months later the reality of World War II forced the cancellation of the Olympics.

The first postwar Games were held in St. Moritz in **1948.** Germany and Japan were barred from competing, but everyone else took part eagerly, and it was clear that the Winter Olympics had successfully survived the 12-year hiatus.

In **1952,** the Olympics were finally held in Norway, the birthplace of modern skiing. The Olympic flame was lit in the hearth of the home of Sondre Nordheim (1825-1897), the first famous skier, and relayed by 94 skiers to Oslo. The **1956** Winter Olympics were most notable for the first appearance by a team from the Soviet Union. The Soviets immediately won more medals than any other nation. The Cortina Games were also the first to be televised and the last at which the figure skating competitions were held outdoors.

The year **1960** saw the return of the Games to the United States, which led to another controversy when the organizing committee refused to build a bobsled run because only nine nations had indicated an intention to take part. This was the only time that bobsledding was not included in the Olympic program. On the other hand, in the interest of international friendship, U.S. Secretary of State John Foster Dulles magnanimously announced that the requirement that all foreign visitors be fingerprinted would be waived in the case of Olympic athletes and officials. As the Games were held in California, it seemed fitting that the chairman of the Pageantry Committee in charge of the Opening and Closing Ceremonies was none other than Walt Disney.

The **1964** Winter Olympics were threatened by a terrible lack of snow. In a panic, the organizing committee pleaded for help. The Austrian army rushed to the rescue, carving out 20,000 ice bricks from a mountaintop and transporting them to the bobsled and luge runs. They also carried 40,000 cubic meters of snow to the alpine skiing courses and laid in a reserve supply of another 20,000 cubic meters. When rain caused further havoc 10 days before the Opening Ceremony, the army packed down the slopes by hand and foot. Politically, the Games were notable because East and West Germany entered a combined team. On a sad note, two competitors, a British lugist and an Australian downhill skier, were killed in practice.

In **1968,** sex tests for women were introduced, and the greatest of Winter Olympic controversies took place: the mysterious man in black who appeared out of the fog during Karl Schranz's slalom run (see page 126). Schranz was also involved in the biggest incident of the **1972** Sapporo Games, the first to be held outside Europe or the United States. This time he was banned from the Olympics by I.O.C. President Avery Brundage, who accused him of being a professional.

The **1976** Winter Olympics were awarded to Denver, but the people of Colorado wanted nothing to do with it. In a move without precedent, the state's voters ignored appeals and threats from their government, business leaders, and the media and voted overwhelmingly (59.4 percent to 40.6 percent) to prohibit public funds from being used to support the Games. Innsbruck stepped in and hosted the Games only 12 years after its last Olympics.

The **1980** Winter Olympics *were* held in the United States, but turned out to be an organizational disaster. Poor transportation planning left many spectators stranded for hours in freezing weather, and many tickets were left unsold even though people wanted to buy them. This happened because tickets were available at the venues, but only people who already had tickets could enter the area. The Lake Placid Games also saw the only national boycott in the history of the Winter Olympics. The I.O.C., seeking to lure China into the Olympic movement, ordered the team from Taiwan to use the name Taiwan instead of the name it had previously used— The Republic of China. The Taiwan Chinese chose to boycott instead.

In **1984,** the Winter Games took place in a Socialist country for the first and only time. The people of Sarajevo gained high marks for their hospitality, and there was no indication of the tragic war that would engulf the city only a few years later. By 1992, in fact, the Olympic bobsled run had been transformed into an artillery position for Serbian guerrillas. The site of the slalom races was a Serb military installation and the Zetra Figure Skating Center had been reduced to rubble.

The **1988** Calgary Games were equally popular with athletes and spectators, although there was some grumbling about the choice of competition sites and the condition of the venues. The celebration was also marred by the gruesome death on the slopes of the Austrian team doctor. For the first time, the alpine events were held on artificial snow.

Only 18 of the 57 official events included in the Albertville Olympics of **1992** were actually held in Albertville. In an attempt to satisfy the various competing resorts of the Savoy Alps, seven other towns hosted medal competitions and still others were used for the main Olympic Village, demonstration events, and the press and broadcasting centers. This may have satisfied the locals, but the athletes complained bitterly about the lack of Olympic atmosphere because they were unable to mingle with athletes from other sports. The day before the Closing Ceremony a Swiss speed skier, Nicolas Bochatay, was killed in a noncompetition-related accident.

In 1986 the I.O.C. voted to change the schedule of the Olympics so that the Summer and Winter Games would be held in different years. In order to adjust to this new schedule, the Lillehammer Olympics were slated for **1994,** the only time that two Games have been staged just two years apart. The 1994 Winter Games were extremely successful. Not only were they well-organized, but the Norwegian hosts' natural love of winter sports added a refreshing purity of spirit.

ACKNOWLEDGMENTS

In the course of my research I have encountered numerous people who have graciously helped me on my way, starting with C. Robert Paul, who made available to me the archives of the United States Olympic Committee, including the Official Reports of the Organizing Committees of the various Olympic Games, which form the basis of the statistics in this book. In addition to the people acknowledged in previous editions of *The Complete Book of the Olympics,* I would like to thank Dr. Bill Mallon, author of *The Unofficial Summary of the 1920 Games;* Ian Buchanan, author of *British Olympians;* Volker Kluge, author of *Winter Olympia Kompakt;* Dr. Karel Wendl, former director of the Olympic Research Department of the International Olympic Committee; Benjamin Wright, chairman of the Hall of Fame and Museum Committee of The United States Figure Skating Association; Dale Mitch, director of the World Figure Skating Museum; Ove Karlsson; Arild Gjerde; Brynjar Selseth; Jeff Matlock; Martin Rix; Bob Edelman; the staff of the library of the Amateur Athletic Foundation in Los Angeles; the staff of the Public Information and Media Department of the United States Olympic Committee; the Olympic research staff of CBS Sports; the overworked and underappreciated sports journalists who cover the Olympic Games; and my Olympics research assistants, Alexandra Hesse, Pauline Ploquin and Cheryl Mick.

THE CHARTS

SOURCES

Although the primary sources for the information included in the charts are the Official Reports of the various Olympics, these reports are often incomplete or incorrect. The man who has done the most to correct these inadequacies is Erich Kamper of Austria, coauthor with Bill Mallon of *The Golden Book of the Olympics.* My search for correct spellings and accent marks also led me to *Die Olympischen Spiele von 1896 bis 1980* by Volker Kluge of East Germany; *Starozytme i Nowozytne Igrazyska Olimpyskie* by Zbigniew Porada of Poland; *Meet the Bulgarian Olympians* by Kostadinov, Georgiev, and Kambourov; *Az Olimpiajátékokon Indult Magyar Versenyzök Névsora 1896–1980; Die Deutschen Sportler der Olympischen Spiele 1896 bis 1968;* and *Sveriges Deltagare i de Olympiska Spelen 1896–1952.* I am particularly indebted to Bill Mallon of the United States, and to Benjamin Wright who provided me with those figure skating protocols that were not included in the Official Reports.

HOW TO READ THEM

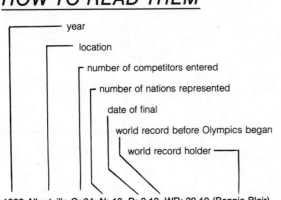

Numbers in the charts indicate times unless otherwise noted. Whenever possible I have included an athlete's first and last names. If the first name was unavailable, I have included the first initial. If that was unavailable I have just included the surname. If a female athlete competed under her maiden name, then married and took part in a second Olympics using her married name, I have included her maiden name in brackets.

In 1956, 1960, and 1964, West Germany (GER) and East Germany (GDR) entered combined teams. Nevertheless, as a matter of historical interest, I have indicated which athletes were actually from each country.

For this edition I have added the nations for each athlete according to current boundaries. SOV/RUS, for example, indicates a Russian athlete representing the Soviet Union, CZE/SVK a Slovak athlete representing Czechoslovakia, and YUG/SLO a Slovenian athlete representing Yugoslavia. In team sports and events, "SOV" without a second designation means that the team included athletes from more than one republic.

KEY TO ABBREVIATIONS

NATIONS

ARG	Argentina	ITA	Italy
AUS	Australia	JPN	Japan
AUT	Austria	KAZ	Kazakhstan
BEL	Belgium	KOR	South Korea
BLR	Belarus	LAT	Latvia
BUL	Bulgaria	LIE	Liechtenstein
CAN	Canada	LIT	Lithuania
CHN	China	LUX	Luxembourg
CZE	Czech Republic (Czechoslovakia 1920–1992)	NOR	Norway
		NZL	New Zealand
DEN	Denmark	POL	Poland
EST	Estonia	PRK	North Korea (People's Republic of Korea)
FIN	Finland		
FRA	France	ROM	Romania
GBR	Great Britain and Northern Ireland	RUS	Russia
		SLO	Slovenia
GDR	East Germany (German Democratic Republic)	SOV	Soviet Union (Unified Team, 1992)
		SPA	Spain
GER	Germany, West Germany (Federal Republic of Germany, 1952–1988)	SVK	Slovakia
		SWE	Sweden
		SWI	Switzerland
		UKR	Ukraine
HOL	Holland (Netherlands)	USA	United States of America
HUN	Hungary	UZB	Uzbekistan
		YUG	Yugoslavia

TERMS

C:	Number of competitors entered
CD	Compulsory dances
CF	Compulsory figures
D:	Date of final
DISQ	Disqualified
DNF	Did not finish
EOR	Equaled Olympic record
EWR	Equaled world record
F.I.S.	International Ski Federation
GA	Goals against
GF	Goals for
I.O.C.	International Olympic Committee
kg.	Kilograms
KM	Kilometers
L	Lost
lbs.	Pounds
M	Meters
N:	Number of nations entered
OD	Original (set pattern) dance
OR	Olympic record
PTS.	Points
SP	Short program
T:	Number of teams entered
T	Tied
W	Won
WR	World record

THE
COMPLETE
BOOK OF THE
WINTER
OLYMPICS

BIATHLON

MEN	WOMEN
10 Kilometers	7.5 Kilometers
20 Kilometers	15 Kilometers
4 × 7.5-Kilometer Relay	4 × 7.5-Kilometer Relay

Biathlon is a combination of cross-country skiing and rifle shooting. The first skiing and shooting competition was held in Norway in 1767. The first modern race was organized by the Norwegian military in 1912, and the first World Biathlon Championships were held at Saalfelden, Austria, in 1958. Competitors may use either the classical or skating method of skiing. They are restricted to .22-caliber small-bore rifles. Automatic or semi-automatic rifles are not allowed. The rifle with all accessories except the magazine and ammunition must weigh at least 7.7 pounds. All targets are set at a distance of 50 meters. The prone target is 4.5 centimeters (1¾ inches) in diameter; the standing target is 11.5 centimeters (4½ inches) in diameter. In individual races, competitors start at one-minute intervals and race against the clock.

MEN

10 KILOMETERS
Each contestant stops twice during the course, once after 3.75 kilometers to shoot five shots prone and once after 7.5 kilometers to shoot five shots standing. Each missed target is penalized by forcing the skier to ski a 150-meter penalty loop.

1924–1976 not held

1980 Lake Placid C: 50, N: 17, D: 2.19.

			MISSED TARGETS	TIME
1.	Frank Ullrich	GDR	2	32:10.69
2.	Vladimir Alikin	SOV/RUS	0	32:53.10
3.	Anatoly Alyabyev	SOV/RUS	1	33:09.16
4.	Klaus Siebert	GDR	2	33:32.76
5.	Kjell Søbak	NOR	1	33:34.64
6.	Peter Zelinka	CZE	1	33:45.20
7.	Odd Lirhus	NOR	2	34:10.39
8.	Peter Angerer	GER	4	34:13.43

1984 Sarajevo C: 64, N: 25, D: 2.14.

			MISSED TARGETS	TIME
1.	Eirik Kvalfoss	NOR	2	30:53.8
2.	Peter Angerer	GER	1	31:02.4
3.	Matthias Jacob	GDR	0	31:10.5
4.	Kjell Söbak	NOR	1	31:19.7
5.	Algimantas Šalna	SOV/LIT	2	31:20.8
6.	Yvon Mougel	FRA	2	31:32.9
7.	Frank-Peter Roetsch	GDR	2	31:49.8
8.	Friedrich Fischer	GER	2	32:04.7

Kvalfoss grew up competing in cross-country skiing. One day when he was 12 years old he showed up for an event and discovered that he wasn't entered. There was an opening in a separate biathlon competition, so he entered that instead. Kvalfoss borrowed a rifle, won the race, and changed sports.

1988 Calgary-Canmore C: 72, N: 22, D: 2.23.

			MISSED TARGETS	TIME
1.	Frank-Peter Roetsch	GDR	1	25:08.1
2.	Valery Medvedtsev	SOV/RUS	0	25:23.7
3.	Sergei Chepikov	SOV/RUS	0	25:29.4
4.	Birk Anders	GDR	2	25:51.8
5.	André Sehmisch	GDR	2	25:52.3
6.	Frank Luck	GDR	1	25:57.6
7.	Tapio Piipponen	FIN	1	26:02.2
8.	Johann Passler	ITA	2	26:07.7

Roetsch became the first biathlete to win both individual events.

1992 Albertville-Les Saisies C: 94, N: 27, D: 2.12.

			MISSED TARGETS	TIME
1.	Mark Kirchner	GER	0	26:02.3
2.	Ricco Gross	GER	1	26:18.0
3.	Harri Eloranta	FIN	0	26:26.6
4.	Sergei Chepikov	SOV/RUS	0	26:27.5
5.	Valery Kirienko	SOV/RUS	3	26:31.8
6.	Jens Steinigen	GER	0	26:34.8
7.	Andreas Zingerle	ITA	1	26:38.6
8.	Steve Cyr	CAN	0	26:46.4

Kirchner, the world champion in 1990 and 1991, was only 21 years old, as was silver medalist Gross. Both of them had been shooting poorly during the pre-Olympic season. After their Olympic success, Gross turned to Kirchner and said, "Imagine, we two blind men won." Back home in Scheibe-Alsbach, Kirchner received 10,000 letters of congratulations and sent out more than 6000 autographed photos.

1994 Lillehammer C: 68, N: 28, D: 2.23.

			MISSED TARGETS	TIME
1.	Sergei Chepikov	RUS	0	28:07.0
2.	Ricco Gross	GER	0	28:13.0
3.	Sergei Tarasov	RUS	1	28:27.4
4.	Vladimir Dratchev	RUS	1	28:28.9
5.	Ludwig Gredler	AUT	2	29:05.4
6.	Frank Luck	GER	2	29:09.7
7.	Sven Fischer	GER	1	29:16.0
8.	Hervé Flandin	FRA	1	29:33.8

Chepikov moved to Norway eight months before the Olympics after being offered sponsorship by a local club. He was 5.8 seconds behind Gross's time after the final shooting round, but skied a powerful final leg to secure the victory. This was the first time that the defending world champion did not win the Olympic 10-kilometer race. The 1993 champion, Mark Kirchner, finished twelfth.

20 KILOMETERS

Each skier stops four times—twice to take five shots prone and twice to take five shots standing. The prone stops are at 5 and 12.5 kilometers; the standing at 8.75 and 17.5. In 1960 and 1964 each missed target incurred a two-minute penalty. In 1968 the penalty was reduced to one minute.

1924–1956 not held

1960 Squaw Valley C: 30, N: 9, D: 2.21.

		TIME	MISSED TARGETS	ADJUSTED TIME
1. Klas Lestander	SWE	1:33:21.6	0	1:33:21.6
2. Antti Tyrväinen	FIN	1:29:57.7	2	1:33:57.7
3. Aleksandr Privalov	SOV/RUS	1:28:54.2	3	1:34:54.2
4. Vladimir Melanin	SOV/RUS	1:27:42.4	4	1:35:42.4
5. Valentin Pshenitsin	SOV/RUS	1:30:45.8	3	1:36:45.8
6. Dmitri Sokolov	SOV/RUS	1:28:16.7	5	1:38:16.7
7. Ola Wärhang	NOR	1:36:35.8	1	1:38:35.8
8. Martti Meinila	FIN	1:29:17.0	5	1:39:17.0

Lestander was only the 15th fastest skier of 30, but he was also the only one to hit all 20 targets. The fastest man was Victor Arbez of France, who clocked in at 1:25:58.4. However, he missed 18 of 20 targets and placed 25th. In fact, the entire four-man French team seemed ill-prepared for the shooting portion of the event: of 80 shots taken, they missed 68.

1964 Innsbruck-Seefeld C: 50, N: 14, D: 2.4.

		TIME	MISSED TARGETS	ADJUSTED TIME
1. Vladimir Melanin	SOV/RUS	1:20:26.8	0	1:20:26.8
2. Aleksandr Privalov	SOV/RUS	1:23:42.5	0	1:23:42.5
3. Olav Jordet	NOR	1:22:38.8	1	1:24:38.8
4. Ragnar Tveiten	NOR	1:19:52.5	3	1:25:52.5
5. Wilhelm György	ROM	1:22:18.0	2	1:26:18.0
6. József Rubiś	POL	1:22:31.6	2	1:26:31.6
7. Valentin Pshenitsin	SOV/RUS	1:22:59.0	2	1:26:59.0
8. Hannu Posti	FIN	1:25:16.5	1	1:27:16.5

1968 Grenoble-Autrans C: 60, N: 18, D: 2.12.

		TIME	MISSED TARGETS	ADJUSTED TIME
1. Magnar Solberg	NOR	1:13:45.9	0	1:13:45.9
2. Aleksandr Tikhonov	SOV/RUS	1:12:40.4	2	1:14:40.4
3. Vladimir Gundartsev	SOV/RUS	1:16:27.4	2	1:18:27.4
4. Stanislaw Szczepaniak	POL	1:17:56.8	1	1:18:56.8
5. Arve Kinnari	FIN	1:17:47.9	2	1:19:47.9
6. Nikolai Pusanov	SOV/RUS	1:17:14.5	3	1:20:14.5
7. Victor Mamatov	SOV/RUS	1:19:20.8	1	1:20:20.8
8. Stanislaw Lukaszczyk	POL	1:16:28.1	4	1:20:28.1

Magnar Solberg, a 31-year-old policeman, was practically unknown in the world of biathlon. He attained his victory by achieving a perfect shooting score—the first time he had ever accomplished such a feat. As photographers crowded around the surprised champion, he told them, "I am very happy, but too tired to smile."

1972 Sapporo-Makomanai C: 54, N: 14, D: 2.9.

		TIME	MISSED TARGETS	ADJUSTED TIME
1. Magnar Solberg	NOR	1:13:55.50	2	1:15:55.50
2. Hansjörg Knauthe	GDR	1:15:07.60	1	1:16:07.60
3. Lars-Göran Arwidson	SWE	1:14:27.03	2	1:16:27.03
4. Aleksandr Tikhonov	SOV/RUS	1:12:48.65	4	1:16:48.65
5. Yrjö Salpakari	FIN	1:14:51.43	2	1:16:51.43
6. Esko Saira	FIN	1:12:34.80	5	1:17:34.80
7. Victor Mamatov	SOV/RUS	1:16:16.26	2	1:18:16.26
8. Tor Svendsberget	NOR	1:15:26.54	3	1:18:26.54

1976 Innsbruck-Seefeld C: 51, N: 19, D: 2.6.

		TIME	MISSED TARGETS	ADJUSTED TIME
1. Nikolai Kruglov	SOV/RUS	1:12:12.26	2	1:14:12.26
2. Heikki Ikola	FIN	1:13:54.10	2	1:15:54.10
3. Aleksandr Yelizarov	SOV/RUS	1:13:05.57	3	1:16:05.57
4. Willy Bertin	ITA	1:13:50.36	3	1:16:50.36
5. Aleksandr Tikhonov	SOV/RUS	1:10:18.33	7	1:17:18.33
6. Esko Saira	FIN	1:15:32.84	2	1:17:32.84
7. Lino Jordan	ITA	1:15:49.83	2	1:17:49.83
8. Sune Adolfsson	SWE	1:16:00.50	2	1:18:00.50

1980 Lake Placid C: 49, N: 18, D: 2.16.

		TIME	MISSED TARGETS	ADJUSTED TIME
1. Anatoly Alyabyev	SOV/RUS	1:08:16.31	0	1:08:16.31
2. Frank Ullrich	GDR	1:05:27.79	3	1:08:27.79
3. Eberhard Rösch	GDR	1:09:11.73	2	1:11:11.73
4. Svein Engen	NOR	1:08:30.25	3	1:11:30.25
5. Erkki Antila	FIN	1:07:32.32	4	1:11:32.32
6. Yvon Mougel	FRA	1:08:33.60	3	1:11:33.60
7. Vladimir Barnashov	SOV/RUS	1:07:49.49	4	1:11:49.49
8. Vladimir Alikin	SOV/RUS	1:06:05.30	6	1:12:05.30

1984 Sarajevo C: 63, N: 25, D: 2.11.

		TIME	MISSED TARGETS	ADJUSTED TIME
1. Peter Angerer	GER	1:09:52.7	2	1:11:52.7
2. Frank-Peter Roetsch	GDR	1:10:21.4	3	1:13:21.4
3. Eirik Kvalfoss	NOR	1:09:02.4	5	1:14:02.4
4. Yvon Mougel	FRA	1:10:53.1	4	1:14:53.1
5. Frank Ullrich	GDR	1:11:53.7	3	1:14:53.7
6. Rolf Storsveen	NOR	1:11:23.9	4	1:15:23.9
7. Friedrich Fischer	GER	1:11:49.7	4	1:15:49.7
8. Leif Andersson	SWE	1:13:19.3	3	1:16:19.3

1988 Calgary-Canmore C: 71, N: 21, D: 2.20.

		TIME	MISSED TARGETS	ADJUSTED TIME
1. Frank-Peter Roetsch	GDR	53:33.3	3	56:33.3
2. Valery Medvedtsev	SOV/RUS	54:54.6	2	56:54.6

3.	Johann Passler	ITA	55:10.1	2	57:10.1
4.	Sergei Chepikov	SOV/RUS	56:17.5	1	57:17.5
5.	Yuri Kashkarov	SOV/RUS	55:43.1	2	57:43.1
6.	Eirik Kvalfoss	NOR	54:54.6	3	57:54.6
7.	André Sehmisch	GDR	55:11.4	3	58:11.4
8.	Tapio Piipponen	FIN	55:18.3	3	58:18.3

1992 Albertville-Les Saisies C: 94, N: 27, D: 2.20.

			TIME	MISSED TARGETS	ADJUSTED TIME
1.	Yevgeny Redkin	SOV/RUS	57:34.4	0	57:34.4
2.	Mark Kirchner	GER	54:40.8	3	57:40.8
3.	Mikael Löfgren	SWE	55:40.8	2	57:59.4
4.	Aleksandr Popov	SOV/RUS	56:02.9	2	58:02.9
5.	Harri Eloranta	FIN	57:15.7	1	58:15.7
6.	Vesa Hietalahti	FIN	57:24.6	1	58:24.6
7.	Johann Passler	ITA	54:25.9	4	58:25.9
8.	Frode Løberg	NOR	57:32.4	1	58:32.4

Andreas Zingerle of Italy led by over a minute after 17.5 kilometers, but missed four of his last five shots and finished 17th. Kirchner, Löfgren, and Popov each had a shot at the gold, but each missed once in the last shooting sequence. When the snow settled, the victory went to unheralded 21-year-old Yevgeny Redkin. Redkin, a former junior champion, was not even listed in the Unified Team teambook, and he learned that he was entered in the race only two days before it took place. Redkin's time was only the 18th fastest, but his shooting was perfect. The course was actually 563 meters short of 20 kilometers, leading to speculation that Kirchner, who finished strongly, might have caught Redkin if the course had been a full 20 kilometers.

1994 Lillehammer C: 70, N: 28, D: 2.20.

			TIME	MISSED TARGETS	ADJUSTED TIME
1.	Sergei Tarasov	RUS	54:25.3	3	57:25.3
2.	Frank Luck	GER	54:28.7	3	57:28.7
3.	Sven Fischer	GER	55:41.9	2	57:41.9
4.	Aleksandr Popov	BLR	57:53.1	0	57:53.1
5.	Jens Steningen	GER	56:18.1	2	58:18.1
6.	Andreas Zingerle	ITA	55:54.1	3	58:54.1
7.	Mark Kirchner	GER	55:16.4	4	59:16.4
8.	Sergei Chepikov	RUS	54:31.4	5	59:31.4

In 1992 Sergei Tarosov arrived in Albertville as one of the favorites. However, just before the biathlon competitions were to begin, he was hospitalized with what team officials claimed was a life-threatening case of food poisoning. Other observers were more suspicious. The fact that he was treated with a kidney dialysis machine and given corticosteroids led some to believe he had been the victim of blood doping gone wrong. (Blood doping is a procedure whereby athletes remove their own blood, preserve it and then reinject it after normal blood levels have returned. In 1984, U.S. cyclists added a ghoulist twist, injecting other people's blood.) In Lillehammer Tarasov denied ever having "competed" after blood doping, but refused to discuss his 1992 illness.

In the race itself, Tarasov missed twice at the first series of shots. He later explained that he was so disheartened by his misses that "my nerves lost their grips and I just let go and almost didn't care." More relaxed, he missed only once more, skied faster than any of his 69 opponents and earned a razor-thin victory when Frank Luck missed his final shot. Luck was the brother-in-law of bronze medalist Sven Fischer, having married Fischer's sister.

By competing in this race, 40-year-old Alfred Eder of Austria tied the record for competing in the most Winter Olympics (6). He also achieved his best finish ever in an individual race, shooting a perfect 20 for 20 to place tenth.

4 × 7.5-KILOMETER RELAY

Each skier shoots twice, once prone and once standing, and has eight shots to make five hits. However, only five rounds can be loaded into the magazine. The three extra must be loaded one at a time. For each miss beyond three, the skier has to ski a penalty loop of 150 meters. Unlike the individual events, in which the competitors race against the clock, one after another, in the biathlon relay all teams start at the same time.

1924–1964 not held

1968 Grenoble-Autrans T: 14, N: 14, D: 2.15.

		MISSED TARGETS	TIME
1. SOV/RUS	(Aleksandr Tikhonov, Nikolai Pusanov, Victor Mamatov, Vladimir Gundartsev)	2	2:13:02.4
2. NOR	(Ola Wärhang, Olav Jordet, Magnar Solberg, Jon Istad)	5	2:14:50.2
3. SWE	(Lars-Göran Arwidson, Tore Eriksson, Olle Petrusson, Holmfrid Olsson)	0	2:17:26.3
4. POL	(Józef Rózak, Andrzej Fiedor, Stanislaw Lukaszczyk, Stanislaw Szczepaniak)	4	2:20:19.6
5. FIN	(Juhani Suutarinen, Heikki Flöjt, Kalevi Vähäkylä, Arve Kinnari)	5	2:20:41.8
6. GDR	(Heinz Kluge, Hans-Gert Jahn, Horst Koschka, Dieter Speer)	4	2:21:54.5
7. ROM	(Gheorghe Cimpoia, Constant Carabela, Nicolae Barbarescu, Wilhelm Gyorgy)	4	2:25:39.8
8. USA	(Ralph Wakely, Edward Williams, William Spencer, John Ehrensbeck)	8	2:28:35.5

1972 Sapporo-Makomanai T: 13, N: 13, D: 2.11.

		MISSED TARGETS	TIME
1. SOV/RUS	(Aleksandr Tikhonov, Rinnat Safine, Ivan Biakov, Victor Mamatov)	3	1:51:44.92
2. FIN	(Esko Saira, Juhani Suutarinen, Heikki Ikola, Mauri Röppänen)	3	1:54:37.25
3. GDR	(Hansjörg Knauthe, Joachim Meischner, Dieter Speer, Horst Koschka)	4	1:54:57.67
4. NOR	(Tor Svendsberget, Kåre Hovda, Ivar Nordkild, Magnar Solberg)	7	1:56:24.41
5. SWE	(Lars-Göran Arwidson, Olle Petrusson, Torsten Wadman, Holmfrid Olsson)	6	1:56:57.40
6. USA	(Peter Karns, Dexter Morse, Dennis Donahue, William Bowerman)	1	1:57:24.32
7. POL	(Józef Rózak, Józef Stopka, Andrzej Rapacz, Aleksander Klima)	4	1:58:09.92
8. JPN	(Isao Ohno, Shozo Sasaki, Miki Shibuya, Kazuo Sasakubo)	5	1:59:09.48

1976 Innsbruck-Seefeld T: 15, N: 15, D: 2.13.

		MISSED TARGETS	TIME
1. SOV	(Aleksandr Yelizarov, Ivan Biakov, Nikolai Kruglov, Aleksandr Tikhonov)	0	1:57:55.64
2. FIN	(Henrik Flöjt, Esko Saira, Juhani Suutarinen, Heikki Ikola)	2	2:01:45.58
3. GDR	(Karl-Heinz Menz, Frank Ullrich, Manfred Beer, Manfred Geyer)	5	2:04:08.61
4. GER	(Heinrich Mehringer, Gerd Winkler, Josef Keck, Claus Gehrke)	4	2:04:11.86
5. NOR	(Kjell Hovda, Terje Hanssen, Svein Engen, Tor Svendsberget)	6	2:05:10.28
6. ITA	(Lino Jordan, Pierantonio Clementi, Luigi Weiss, Willy Bertin)	3	2:06:16.55
7. FRA	(Rene Arpin, Yvon Mougel, Marius Falquy, Jean Claude Viry)	5	2:07:34.42
8. SWE	(Mats-Åke Lantz, Torsten Wadman, Sune Adolfsson, Lars Göran Arwidson)	8	2:08:46.90

1980 Lake Placid T: 15, N: 15, D: 2.22.

		MISSED TARGETS	TIME
1. SOV/RUS	(Vladimir Alikin, Aleksandr Tikhonov, Vladimir Barnashov, Anatoly Alyabyev)	0	1:34:03.27
2. GDR	(Mathias Jung, Klaus Siebert, Frank Ullrich, Eberhard Rösch)	3	1:34:56.99
3. GER	(Franz Bernreiter, Hans Estner, Peter Angerer, Gerd Winkler)	2	1:37:30.26
4. NOR	(Svein Engen, Kjell Søbak, Odd Lirhus, Sigleif Johansen)	3	1:38:11.76
5. FRA	(Yvon Mougel, Denis Sandona, André Geourjon, Christian Poirot)	0	1:38:23.36
6. AUT	(Rudolf Horn, Franz-Josef Weber, Josef Koll, Alfred Eder)	4	1:38:32.02
7. FIN	(Keijo Kuntola, Erkki Antila, Kari Saarela, Raimo Seppanen)	6	1:38:50.84
8. USA	(Martin Hagen, Lyle Nelson, Donald Nielsen, Peter Hoag)	0	1:39:24.29

Thirty-three-year-old Aleksandr Tikhonov announced his retirement after winning his fourth straight biathlon relay gold medal.

1984 Sarajevo T: 17, N: 17, D: 2.17.

		MISSED TARGETS	TIME
1. SOV	(Dmitri Vasilyev, Yuri Kashkarov, Algimantas Šalna, Sergei Buligin)	2	1:38:51.7
2. NOR	(Odd Lirhus, Eirik Kvalfoss, Rolf Storsveen, Kjell Söbak)	2	1:39:03.9
3. GER	(Ernst Reiter, Walter Pichler, Peter Angerer, Friedrich Fischer)	1	1:39:05.1
4. GDR	(Holger Wick, Frank-Peter Roetsch, Matthias Jacob, Frank Ullrich)	1	1:40:04.7
5. ITA	(Adriano Darioli, Gottlieb Taschler, Johann Passler, Andreas Zingerle)	0	1:42:32.8
6. CZE	(Jaromir Šimůnek, Zdeněk Hák, Petr Zelinka, Jan Matouš)	4	1:42:40.5
7. FIN	(Keijo Tiitola, Toivo Makikyro, Arto Jaaskelainen, Tapio Piipponen)	2	1:43:16.0
8. AUT	(Rudolf Horn, Walter Hoerl, Franz Schuler, Alfred Eder)	1	1:43:28.1

Sergei Buligin of Siberia began the final leg 18.4 seconds behind the leading East Germans. While East German anchor Frank Ullrich faded badly, Buligin caught him at the first firing range and moved ahead steadily for the rest of the race.

1988 Calgary-Canmore T: 16, N: 16, D: 2.26.

		MISSED TARGETS	TIME
1. SOV/RUS	(Dmitri Vasilyev, Sergei Chepikov, Aleksandr Popov, Valery Medvedtsev)	0	1:22:30.0
2. GER	(Ernst Reiter, Stefan Höck, Peter Angerer, Friedrich Fischer)	0	1:23:37.4
3. ITA	(Werner Kiem, Gottlieb Taschler, Johann Passler, Andreas Zingerle)	0	1:23:51.5
4. AUT	(Anton Lengauer-Stockner, Bruno Hofstätter, Franz Schuler, Alfred Eder)	0	1:24:17.6
5. GDR	(Jürgen Wirth, Frank-Peter Roetsch, Matthias Jacob, André Sehmisch)	3	1:24:28.4
6. NOR	(Geir Einang, Frode Løberg, Gisle Fenne, Eirik Kvalfoss)	0	1:25:57.0
7. SWE	(Peter Sjödén, Mikael Löfgren, Roger Westling, Leif Andersson)	3	1:29:11.9
8. BUL	(Vasil Bozhilov, Vladimir Velichkov, Krasimir Videnov, Hristo Vodenicharov)	7	1:29:24.9

The East Germans took four of the top six places in the 10-kilometer individual event and thus were expected to give the Soviet team a stiff challenge. However, leadoff skier Jürgen Wirth, who had test-fired in windy conditions, failed to readjust the sight on his rifle when the wind died down and missed three of his first five shots, leaving East Germany in twelfth place with an insurmountable deficit of almost two minutes.

1992 Albertville-Les Saisies T: 21, N: 21, D: 2.16.

		MISSED TARGETS	TIME
1. GER	(Ricco Gross, Jens Steinigen, Mark Kirchner, Friedrich Fischer)	0	1:24:43.5
2. SOV/RUS	(Valery Medvedtsev, Aleksandr Popov, Valery Kirienko, Sergei Chepikov)	0	1:25:06.3
3. SWE	(Ulf Johansson, Leif Andersson, Tord Wiksten, Mikael Löfgren)	0	1:25:38.2
4. ITA	(Hubert Leitgeb, Johann Passler, Pieralberto Carrara, Andreas Zingerle)	2	1:26:18.1
5. NOR	(Geir Einang, Frode Loberg, Gisle Fenne, Eirik Kvalfoss)	1	1:26:32.4
6. FRA	(Xavier Blond, Thierry Gerbier, Christian Dumont, Hervé Flandin)	0	1:27:13.3
7. CZE	(Martin Rypl, Tomas Kos, Jiří Holubeč, Ivan Masrik)	0	1:27:15.7
8. FIN	(Vesa Hietalahti, Jaakko Niemi, Harri Eloranta, Kari Kataja)	1	1:27:39.5

The German team got off to a rough start when France's Xavier Blond crashed into Ricco Gross on the first downhill and knocked him down. Gross handed over to Steinigen in only 13th place. As he watched the rest of the race, Gross commented, "If we don't win this I will be the most hated man in Germany." He needn't have worried. Steinigen pulled the Germans up to fifth, and Kirchner put them into the lead. The 35-year-old German anchor, Fritz Fischer, carried a German flag for the last 50 meters as the Soviet win streak in this event was finally broken.

1994 Lillehammer T: 18, N: 18, D: 2.26.

		MISSED TARGETS	TIME
1. GER	(Ricco Gross, Frank Luck, Mark Kirchner, Sven Fischer)	0	1:30:22.1
2. RUS	(Valery Kirienko, Vladimir Dratchev, Sergei Tarasov, Sergei	2	1:31:23.6

Chepikov)

3.	FRA	(Thierry Dusserre, Patrice Bailly-Salins, Lionel Laurent, Hervé Flandin)	1	1:32:31.3
4.	BLR	(Victor Maigourov, Igor Khokhriakov, Oleg Ryzhenkov, Aleksandr Popov)	0	1:32:57.2
5.	FIN	(Erkki Latvala, Harri Eloranta, Timo Seppälä, Vesa Hietalahti)	1	1:33:11.9
6.	ITA	(Patrick Favre, Johann Passler, Pieralberto Carrara, Andreas Zingerle)	5	1:33:17.3
7.	NOR	(Ole Einar Bjørndalen, Ivar Michal Ulekleiv, Halvard Hanevold, Jon Åge Tyldum)	0	1:33:32.8
8.	POL	(Tomasz Sikora, Jan Ziemianin, Wieslaw Ziemianin, Jan Wojtas)	0	1:33:49.3

The four Germans, all of whom hailed from East Germany, earned a clear, wire-to-wire victory.

WOMEN

7.5 KILOMETERS
Each contestant stops twice during the course, once after 2.5 kilometers, to shoot five shots prone, and once after 5 kilometers, to shoot five shots standing. Each missed target is penalized by forcing the skier to ski a 150-meter penalty loop.

1924–1988 not held

1992 Albertville-Les Saisies C: 69, N: 20, D: 2.11.

		MISSED TARGETS	TIME
1. Anfisa Reztsova	SOV/RUS	3	24:29.2
2. Antje Miserky	GER	2	24:45.1
3. Yelena Belova	SOV/RUS	2	24:50.8
4. Nadezda Aleksieva	BUL	0	24:55.8
5. Jirina Adamičková	CZE	0	24:57.6
6. Petra Schaaf	GER	1	25:10.4
7. Anne Briand	FRA	2	25:29.8
8. Silvana Blagoeva	BUL	2	25:33.5

In the 1988 Calgary Olympics, Anfisa Reztsova, of Sverdlovsk, Russia, won a gold medal in the cross-country relay and then earned a silver in the 20-kilometer individual event. After the Games, she took two years off to have a baby. Her husband, a former member of the Soviet biathlon team, encouraged her to return to competition and switch to biathlon. In 1992, at the age of 27, Reztsova became the first woman to win gold medals in two winter sports. For the record, all three medalists in this, the first-ever women's biathlon event, had blue eyes.

1994 Lillehammer C: 69, N: 28, D: 2.23.

		MISSED TARGETS	TIME
1. Myriam Bédard	CAN	2	26:08.8
2. Svetlana Paramygina	BLR	2	26:09.9
3. Valentyna Tserbe	UKR	0	26:10.0

		MISSED TARGETS	TIME
4. Inna Sheshikl	KAZ	2	26:13.9
5. Petra Schaaf	GER	2	26:33.6
6. Irina Kokueva	BLR	2	26:38.4
7. Nathalie Santer	ITA	3	26:38.8
8. Simon Greiner-Petter-Memm	GER	3	26:46.5

This was an unusually exciting race, the closest in Olympic biathlon history. A late addition to the Ukrainian team, Valentyna Tserbe was almost unknown in the world of biathlon, having never placed higher than 21st in a World Cup race. But she shot two clear rounds and was still in first place after more than 50 of the 69 entrants had finished the race. However, two of the favorites were still on the course with good times. Svetlana Paramygina, who had won the last two World Cup races in the month before the Olympics, strained across the finish line and stopped the clock one-tenth of a second faster than Tserbe's time. Myriam Bédard, who had won the 15-kilometer event five days earlier and was the defending world champion at 7.5 kilometers, entered the Birkeleineren Ski Stadium one minute after Paramygina. As the crowd of 30,000 glanced back and forth between Bédard and the clock, Bédard crossed the line and beat Paramygina's time—by 1.1 seconds. That should have settled the medals, but there was more suspense to come. Inna Sheshikl of Kazakhstan struggled desperately to match the leaders' times. With a medal within reach, and the crowd roaring, and the seconds ticking down, Sheshikl, completely exhausted, stumbled and fell—a mere two meters from the finish line. She struggled to her feet and plunged across the line—four seconds too late to earn a medal.

Later, Bédard revealed that after the race had begun, she discovered that she was using mismatched skis. In the wax room before the race she had inadvertently grabbed one ski from one pair and another from a different pair. Although they were the same length, they had been waxed differently. The right ski glided smoothly, but she had trouble with the left one throughout the race. Because she won, the mistake was just a footnote to her story of glory, but, as Bédard pointed out, "When you consider it, I won the race by only 1.1 seconds. If I had not won, I would have thought about this the rest of my life."

15 KILOMETERS

Each skier stops four times during the course, twice to shoot five shots prone and twice to shoot five shots standing. The prone stops are at 3.75 and 10 kilometers, the standing at 6.25 and 12.5 kilometers. One minute is added to a competitor's elapsed time for each missed shot.

1924-1988 not held

1992 Albertville–Les Saisies C: 68, N: 20, D: 2.19.

		TIME	MISSED TARGETS	ADJUSTED TIME
1. Antje Misersky	GER	50:47.2	1	51.47.2
2. Svetlana Pecherskaya	SOV/RUS	50:58.5	1	51:58.5
3. Myriam Bédard	CAN	50:15.0	2	52:15.0
4. Véronique Claudel	FRA	50:21.2	2	52:21.2
5. Nadezda Aleksieva	BUL	51:30.2	1	52:30.2
6. Delphine Burlet	FRA	50:00.8	3	53:00.8
7. Corinne Niogret	FRA	51:06.6	2	53:06.6
8. Nathalie Santer	ITA	50:10.3	3	53:10.3

Misersky's father, Henner, was a cross-country coach in East Germany who objected to the training methods of the sports establishment. The East German leaders wanted all their Nordic skiers to concentrate solely on the freestyle "skating" technique. Henner Misersky believed that it was healthier to continue to practice the traditional "diagonal" stride as well. When Henner was ousted from his position in 1985, his daughter Antje, who was the reigning East German national champion at 5 and 10 kilometers, quit in protest. After four years away from sports, she took up biathlon in 1989. At the Albertville Games she won one gold medal and two silvers. A rarity among biathletes, bronze medalist Bédard had competed as a figure skater until the age of 12. Nadezda Aleksieva came painfully close to winning Bulgaria's first Winter Olympics gold medal. After 18 straight hits, she missed her next-to-last shot by 3.5 millimeters. The resultant one-minute penalty dropped her from first to fifth.

1994 Lillehammer C: 69, N: 28, D: 2.18.

			TIME	MISSED TARGETS	ADJUSTED TIME
1.	Myriam Bédard	CAN	50:06.6	2	52:06.6
2.	Anne Briand	FRA	49:53.3	3	52:53.2
3.	Ursula Disl	GER	50:15.3	3	53:15.3
4.	Svetlana Paramygina	BLR	49:21.3	4	53:21.3
5.	Corinne Niogret	FRA	51:38.1	2	53:38.1
6.	Martina Jasicová	SVK	51:56.4	2	53:56.4
7.	Natalia Permiakova	BLR	51:59.2	2	53:59.2
8.	Kerryn Rim	AUS	52:10.1	2	54:10.1

Twenty-four-year-old Myriam Bédard of Loretteville, Québec won the first of her two gold medals.

4 × 7.5-KILOMETER RELAY

Each skier shoots twice, once prone and once standing, and has eight shots to make five hits. However, only five rounds can be loaded into the magazine. The other three have to be loaded one at a time. For each miss beyond three, the competitor must ski a 150-meter penalty loop. Unlike the individual races, in which the competitors race against the clock, in the relay all teams start at the same time. In 1992 there were only three skiers per team.

1924-1988 not held

1992 Albertville-Les Saisies T: 16, N: 16, D: 2.14.

			MISSED TARGETS	TIME
1.	FRA	(Corinne Niogret, Véronique Claudel, Anne Briand)	0	1:15:55.6
2.	GER	(Uschi Disl, Antje Misersky, Petra Schaaf)	1	1:16:18.4
3.	SOV/RUS	(Yelena Belova, Anfisa Reztsova, Yelena Melnikova)	2	1:16:54.6
4.	BUL	(Silvana Blagoeva, Nadezda Aleksieva, Iwa Schkodreva)	0	1:18:54.8
5.	FIN	(Mari Lampinen, Tuija Sikiö, Terhi Markkanen)	0	1:20:17.8
6.	SWE	(Christina Eklund, Inger Björkbom, Mia Stadig)	0	1:20:56.6
7.	NOR	(Signe Trosten, Hildegunn Fossen, Elin Kristiansen)	1	1:21:20.0
8.	CZE	(Gabriela Suvová, Jana Kulhavá, Jirina Adamičková)	3	1:23:12.7

Since world championships were inaugurated in women's biathlon in 1984, the Soviet Union had won every relay—eight in a row. In addition, three days before the Olympic championship, ex-Soviet skiers Reztsova and Belova had finished first and third in the individual 7.5-kilometer race. However, it was Germany that had won the first World Cup relay of the season and France the last on January 26. The French victory in Anterselva, Italy, had been considered an unexpected breakthrough. At Les Saisies, Corinne Niogret gave France a surprise lead after the first leg with Bulgaria 4.2 seconds behind. Belova of the Unified Team and Disl of Germany each had to ski a penalty loop and trailed by 27.2 seconds and 39 seconds, respectively. The second leg saw blazing performances by Misersky and Reztsova. At the final exchange, the Unified Team led Germany by 7.2 seconds and France by 30 seconds. Melnikova, competing in her only race of the Olympics, gradually fell behind, and the contest developed into a duel between Petra Schaaf and Anne Briand, who had finished sixth and seventh in the individual race, 19.4 seconds apart. Briand caught Schaaf as they entered the shooting range for the last time. Although she missed her third and fourth shots, Briand sensed that Schaaf, who was only a few feet away at the next shooting lane, was more nervous than she was. Indeed, the German missed twice as well, and Briand was able to return to the course first and then pull away. There were only nine certified female biathletes in France, but by the end of the day three of them were Olympic champions. One of the French team members, Corinne Niogret, received a special prize in addition to her gold medal—a cow. Local farmers had offered the prize to France's youngest medalist. The 19-year-old Niogret needn't really need a cow, but was able to sell it for $1100.

1994 Lillehammer T: 17, N: 17, D: 2.25.

			MISSED TARGETS	TIME
1.	RUS	(Nadezhda Talanova, Natalya Snytina, Louiza Noskova, Anfisa Reztsova)	0	1:47:19.5
2.	GER	(Ursula Disl, Antje Harvey [Misersky], Simone Greiner-Petter-Memm, Petra Schaaf)	6	1:51:16.5
3.	FRA	(Corinne Niogret, Véronique Claudel, Delphyne Heymann [Burlet], Anne Briand)	1	1:52:28.3
4.	NOR	(Ann-Elen Skjelbreid, Annette Sikveland, Hildegunn Fossen, Elin Kristiansen)	2	1:54:08.1
5.	UKR	(Valentyna Tserbe, Maryna Skolota, Olena Petrova, Olena Ogurtsova)	3	1:54:26.5
6.	BLR	(Irina Kokueva, Natalya Permiakova, Natalya Ryzhenkova, Svetlana Paramygina)	8	1:54:55.1
7.	CZE	(Jana Kulhavá, Jiřina Pelcová, Iveta Knížková, Eva Háková)	3	1:57:00.8
8.	USA	(Beth Coats, Joan Smith, Laura Tavares, Joan Guetschow)	3	1:57:35.9

Midway through the race, the German team led the Russians by 1 minute 11.2 seconds. Then the third German skier, Simone Greiner-Petter-Memm, missed six of her ten targets and had to ski 900 meters worth of penalty loops. Louiza Noskova zoomed ahead of her. Then Russian anchor Anfisa Reztsova skied a 25:34.0 leg—a full minute faster than any of the 67 others in the race, and the Russians achieved the largest winning margin Olympic biathlon history. In fact, their margin was so huge that they would have won even if Greiner-Petter-Memm had shot clear.

BOBSLED

Two-Man
Four-Man

Bobsleds were invented in the 1880s by lashing together two toboggans. Current rules limit the length and weight of the sleds. Two-man bobs must not exceed 2.70 meters and 390 kilograms (including the riders). The four-man limitations are 3.80 meters and 630 kilos. The driver steers the bobsled by means of nylon cords connected to the front runners. Sleds do have brakes, but braking during a run is grounds for immediate disqualification. Women are not allowed to compete. The reason for this prohibition has nothing to do with lack of ability: in 1938 Katherine Dewey won the U.S. National Championship. In order to avoid chewing up of the course by lesser teams, a seeding system like that used in alpine skiing was instituted in 1992. This allows the top 15 teams to go down first. The final time is the combined total of four separate runs, two on one day, two more on the next.

TWO-MAN

1924–1928 not held

1932 Lake Placid T: 12, N: 8, D: 2.10.

1.	USA	(J. Hubert Stevens, Curtis Stevens)	8:14.74
2.	SWI	(Reto Capadrutt, Oscar Geier)	8:16.28
3.	USA	(John Heaton, Robert Minton)	8:29.15
4.	ROM	(Papana Alexandru, Hubert Dumitru)	8:32.47
5.	GER	(Hanns Kilian, Sebastian Huber)	8:35.36
6.	ITA	(Teofilo Rossi di Montelera, Italo Casini)	8:36.33
7.	GER	(Werner Huth, Max Ludwig)	8:45.05
8.	ITA	(Agostini Lanfranchi, Gaetano Lanfranchi)	8:50.66

J. Hubert Stevens and his brother, Curtis, were local residents of Lake Placid. They trailed Capadrutt and Geier by 6.32 seconds after the first run, but registered the fastest times in each of the other three runs to overtake the Swiss team for the victory. The Stevens brothers, aged 41 and 33, attributed part of their success to the fact that they heated their runners with blowtorches for 25 minutes prior to hitting the snow, a tactic that is now highly illegal, but which was then considered unusual but acceptable.

1936 Garmisch-Partenkirchen T: 23, N: 13, D: 2.15.

1.	USA	(Ivan Brown, Alan Washbond)	5:29.29
2.	SWI	(Fritz Feierabend, Joseph Beerli)	5:30.64
3.	USA	(Gilbert Colgate, Richard Lawrence)	5:33.96
4.	GBR	(Frederick McEvoy, James Cardno)	5:40.25
5.	GER	(Hanns Kilian, Hermann von Valta)	5:42.01
6.	GER	(Fritz Grau, Albert Brehme)	5:44.71
7.	SWI	(Reto Capadrutt, Charles Bouvier)	5:46.23
8.	BEL	(Rene Lunden, Eric de Spoelberch)	5:46.28

Ivan Brown of Keene Valley, New York, was an especially superstitious competitor. One of his quirks was a need to find at least one hairpin on the ground every day. Fortunately he had been able to accomplish this feat for 24 consecutive days prior to the Olympics. Brown was also the only driver to compete without goggles; he claimed they dulled his eyesight and added wind resistance.

1948 St. Moritz T: 16, N: 9, D: 1.31.

1.	SWI	(Felix Endrich, Friedrich Waller)	5:29.2
2.	SWI	(Fritz Feierabend, Paul Hans Eberhard)	5:30.4
3.	USA	(Frederick Fortune, Schuyler Carron)	5:35.3
4.	BEL	(Max Houben, Jacques Mouvet)	5:37.5
5.	GBR	(William Coles, Raymond Collings)	5:37.9
6.	ITA	(Mario Vitali, Dario Poggi)	5:38.0
7.	NOR	(Arne Holst, Ivar Johansen)	5:38.2
8.	ITA	(Nino Bibbia, Ediberto Campadese)	5:38.6

In 1953 Felix Endrich won the two-man bobsled world championship at Garmisch-Partenkirchen. Less than a week later he was leading a four-man bob down the same course when his sled hurtled over the wall at "dead man's curve" and crashed into a tree. The 31-year-old Endrich was killed almost instantly.

1952 Oslo T: 18, N: 9, D: 2.15.

1.	GER	(Andreas Ostler, Lorenz Nieberl)	5:24.54
2.	USA	(Stanley Benham, Patrick Martin)	5:26.89
3.	SWI	(Fritz Feierabend, Stephan Waser)	5:27.71
4.	SWI	(Felix Endrich, Werner Spring)	5:29.15
5.	FRA	(André Robin, Henri Rivière)	5:31.98
6.	BEL	(Marcel Leclef, Albert Casteleyns)	5:32.51
7.	USA	(Frederick Fortune, John Helmer)	5:33.82
8.	SWE	(Olle Axelsson, Jan de Man Lapidoth)	5:35.77

Ostler and Nieberl recorded the best time on each of the four runs despite the fact that they were using a 16-year-old bobsled.

1956 Cortina T: 25, N: 14, D: 1.28.

1.	ITA	(Lamberto Dalla Costa, Giacomo Conti)	5:30.14
2.	ITA	(Eugenio Monti, Renzo Alverà)	5:31.45
3.	SWI	(Max Angst, Harry Warburton)	5:37.46
4.	SPA	(Alfonso de Portago, Vicente Sartorius y Cabeza de Vaca)	5:37.60
5.	USA	(Waightman Washbond, Patrick Biesiadecki)	5:38.16
6.	USA	(Arthur Tyler, Edgar Seymour)	5:40.08
7.	SWI	(Franz Kapus, Heinrich Angst)	5:40.11
8.	GER	(Andreas Ostler, Hans Hohenester)	5:40.13

Dalla Costa and Monti finished first and second respectively on each of the four runs. Dalla Costa was a 35-year-old jet pilot who had never raced anywhere but Cortina.

1960 not held

1964 Innsbruck-Igls T: 19, N: 11, D: 2.1.

1.	GBR	(Anthony Nash, T. Robin Dixon)	4:21.90
2.	ITA	(Sergio Zardini, Romano Bonagura)	4:22.02
3.	ITA	(Eugenio Monti, Sergio Siorpaes)	4:22.63
4.	CAN	(Victor Emery, Peter Kirby)	4:23.49
5.	USA	(Lawrence McKillip, James Ernest Lamy)	4:24.60
6.	GER	(Franz Wörmann, Hubert Braun)	4:24.70
7.	USA	(Charles McDonald, Charles Pandolph)	4:25.00
8.	AUT	(Erwin Thaler, Josef Nairz)	4:25.51

Nash and Dixon came from behind to defeat Zardini and Bonagura on the final run, a remarkable achievement considering they came from a nation without a bobsled run.

1968 Grenoble-Alpe d'Huez T: 22, N: 11, D: 2.6.
1. ITA (Eugenio Monti, Luciano De Paolis) 4:41.54
2. GER (Horst Floth, Pepi Bader) 4:41.54
3. ROM (Ion Panţuru, Nicolae Neagoe) 4:44.46
4. AUT (Erwin Thaler, Reinhold Durnthaler) 4:45.13
5. GBR (Anthony Nash, T. Robin Dixon) 4:45.16
6. USA (Paul Lamey, Robert Huscher) 4:46.03
7. GER (Wolfgang Zimmerer, Peter Utzschneider) 4:46.40
8. AUT (Max Kaltenberger, Fritz Dinkhauser) 4:46.63

"Now I can retire a happy man," said Eugenio Monti after completing his 12-year quest for an Olympic gold medal. But his victory did not come easily. Trailing by one-tenth of a second after three runs, Monti drove his bob to a course record of 1:10.05, only to watch Floth race down in 1:10.15. This left the Italians and Germans in a tie for first place, and it was announced that both teams would be awarded gold medals. However, the judges later reversed their decision, invoking world bobsled rules. Sole possession of first place was given to the team that recorded the fastest single heat time—and 40-year-old Eugenio Monti had finally won his Olympic gold medal.

1972 Sapporo-Taineyama T: 21, N: 11, D: 2.5.
1. GER (Wolfgang Zimmerer, Peter Utzschneider) 4:57.07
2. GER (Horst Floth, Pepi Bader) 4:58.84
3. SWI (Jean Wicki, Edy Hubacher) 4:59.33
4. ITA (Gianfranco Gaspari, Mario Armano) 5:00.45
5. ROM (Ion Panţuru, Ion Zangor) 5:00.53
6. SWE (Carl-Erik Eriksson, Jan Johansson) 5:01.40
7. SWI (Hans Candrian, Heinz Schenker) 5:01.44
8. AUT (Herbert Gruber, Josef Oberhauser) 5:01.60

1976 Innsbruck-Igls T: 24, N: 13, D: 2.6.
1. GDR (Meinhard Nehmer, Bernhard Germeshausen) 3:44.42
2. GER (Wolfgang Zimmerer, Manfred Schumann) 3:44.99
3. SWI (Erich Schärer, Josef Benz) 3:45.70
4. AUT (Fritz Sperling, Andreas Schwab) 3:45.74
5. GER (Georg Heibl, Fritz Ohlwärter) 3:46.13
6. AUT (Dieter Delle Karth, Franz Köfel) 3:46.37
7. GDR (Horst Schönau, Raimund Bethge) 3:46.97
8. ITA (Giorgio Alvera, Franco Perruquet) 3:47.30

Nehmer and Germeshausen earned four Olympic medals each in 1976 and 1980, including three golds. A former javelin thrower, Nehmer was 35 years old when he earned his first medal.

1980 Lake Placid T: 20, N: 11, D: 2.16.
1. SWI (Erich Schärer, Josef Benz) 4:09.36
2. GDR (Bernhard Germeshausen, Hans Jürgen Gerhardt) 4:10.93
3. GDR (Meinhard Nehmer, Bogdan Musiol) 4:11.08
4. SWI (Hans Hildebrand, Walter Rahm) 4:11.32
5. USA (Howard Silher, Dick Nalley) 4:11.73
6. USA (Brent Rushlaw, Joseph Tyler) 4:12.12
7. AUT (Fritz Sperling, Kurt Oberhöller) 4:13.58
8. GER (Peter Hell, Heinz Busche) 4:13.74

1984 Sarajevo T: 28, N: 16, D: 2.11.

1.	GDR	(Wolfgang Hoppe, Dietmar Schauerhammer)	3:25.56
2.	GDR	(Bernhard Lehmann, Bogdan Musiol)	3:26.04
3.	SOV	(Zintis Ekmanis, Vladimir Alexandrov)	3:26.16
4.	SOV/LAT	(Jānis Kipurs, Aiwar Šnepsts)	3:26.42
5.	SWI	(Hans Hiltebrand, Meinrad Müller)	3:26.76
6.	SWI	(Ralph Pichler, Rico Freiermuth)	3:28.23
7.	ITA	(Guerrino Ghedina, Andrea Meneghin)	3:29.09
8.	GER	(Anton Fischer, Hans Metzler)	3:29.18

Fifty-three-year-old Carl-Erik Eriksson of Sweden became the first person to compete in six Winter Olympics. His best performance was a sixth-place finish in the 1972 two-man event. In 1984 he finished 19th in the two-man and 21st in the four-man.

1988 Calgary T: 41, N: 23, D: 2.22.

1.	SOV	(Jānis Kipurs, Vladimir Kozlov)	3:53.48
2.	GDR	(Wolfgang Hoppe, Bogdan Musiol)	3:54.19
3.	GDR	(Bernhard Lehmann, Mario Hoyer)	3:54.64
4.	SWI	(Gustav Weder, Donat Acklin)	3:56.06
5.	AUT	(Ingo Appelt, Harald Winkler)	3:56.49
6.	SWI	(Hans Hiltebrand, André Kiser)	3:56.52
7.	GER	(Anton Fischer, Christoph Langen)	3:56.62
8.	AUT	(Peter Kienast, Christian Mark)	3:56.91

Defending Olympic champion Wolfgang Hoppe registered the fastest time of the first run, but finished only eighth best in the second run. Hoppe complained bitterly about the poor racing conditions, comparing his slide down the dirt- and dust-covered track to "running on sandpaper." Hoppe, who was tied for second place after the first day, was not alone in his criticism. Six nations, including the first-place Soviet Union, filed a protest asking that the results of the first two runs be disallowed. The protest was denied and the next day the competition continued. However, the third run was finally canceled—after 28 sleds had already raced—because of excessive sand on the track due to warm weather and high winds.

The competition was resumed one day later. Hoppe clocked the fastest times in both the third and fourth runs, but the 1.21-second deficit he had incurred in the second run was too much to overcome. The upset victory went to Jānis Kipurs, a 30-year-old Latvian who had taken up bobsledding when he answered a newspaper ad in 1980. In Calgary, Kipurs painted his sled with the Latvian colors as a protest against Soviet occupation of his country. (By 1992, Latvia had regained its independence and entered a separate team in Albertville.)

Meanwhile, Hoppe continued to fume about the racing conditions. Besides the failure to protect the run from poor weather, his main objection was that the field was too large. Because bobsled competitions did not, until 1992, allow the top 15 seeds to race first, the course was often badly chewed up before one or more of the favorites got to it. This was precisely what had happened to Hoppe in the second run.

Hoppe's criticisms were not completely unjustified. The 1988 competition did include some unusual entrants, several of whom came from countries with little or no snow. In fact, the snowless nations organized their own informal "Caribbean Cup." Among the warm-weather sledders were the four Tames Perea brothers, who represented Mexico, although they earned their living as waiters in Dallas, Texas; the popular Jamaican bobsled team, which helped finance its training by selling tee-shirts, sweatshirts, and a reggae record; 52-year-old Harvey Hook of the U.S. Virgin Islands; and John Foster, who had previously represented the Virgin

Islands in yachting and did so again in 1988. The "Caribbean Cup" was won by New Zealand's Alexander Peterson and Peter Henry, who tied for twentieth place overall. The top finish by a team from a truly snow-free country was the twenty-ninth place earned by Bart Carpentier Alting and Bart Dreschsel of the Netherlands Antilles. Carpentier Alting, attempting a rare double, also finished thirty-sixth of thirty-eight in the one-man luge.

1992 Albertville-La Plagne T: 46, N: 25, D: 2.16.

1. SWI (Gustav Weder, Donat Acklin) 4:03.26
2. GER (Rudolf Lochner, Markus Zimmermann) 4:03.55
3. GER (Christoph Langen, Günther Eger) 4:03.63
4. AUT (Ingo Appelt, Thomas Schroll) 4:03.67
5. ITA (Günther Huber, Stefano Ticci) 4:03.72
6. GBR (Mark Tout, Lenox Paul) 4:03.87
7. USA (Brian Shimer, Herschel Walker) 4:03.95
8. AUT (Gerhard Rainer, Thomas Bachler) 4:04.00

For the first time in Olympic bobsled history, none of the eventual medal winners were in first, second, or third place after the first day's two runs. The surprise leaders at the halfway point of the competition were Tout and Paul. Close behind them were Huber and Ticci and Appelt and Schroll. On the second day, the favorites, Weder and Acklin, roared back from fifth place to record the fastest times of both runs and earn Switzerland's only victory of the Albertville Games. Lochner and Zimmermann staged an even more dramatic recovery, moving up from tenth to second. Lochner, who didn't take up bobsledding until he was 27 years old, was a notorious cigarette smoker whose motto was "Smoke openly, train secretly." Weder was such an intense competitor that he videotaped every meter of every bobsled run he raced and studied the videos for hours. Sometimes he could be a bit too intense. At the 1989 world championships in St. Moritz he was caught one night scraping ice off of a difficult corner in the course. He was allowed to compete anyway and won his first world championship in the four-man event.

1994 Lillehammer-Hunderfosser T: 43, N: 30, D: 2.20.

1. SWI (Gustav Weder, Donat Acklin) 3:30.81
2. SWI (Reto Götschi, Guido Acklin) 3:30.86
3. ITA (Günther Huber, Stefano Ticci) 3:31.01
4. GER (Rudolf Lochner, Markus Zimmermann) 3:31.78
5. AUT (Hubert Schösser, Thomas Schroll) 3:31.93
6. GBR (Mark Tout, Lenox Paul) 3:32.15
7. CZE (Jiri Dzmura, Pavel Polomsky) 3:32.18
8. CAN (Pierre Lueders, David MacEachern) 3:32.18

Gustav Weder and Donat Acklin became the first repeat winners of the two-man bob. They trailed Reto Gotschi and Guido Acklin (Donat's younger brother) after three runs. Last to come down the track on the final run, Gotschi was dead-even with Weder's time with about 200 meters to go, but faltered slightly at the end, giving Weder the victory by .05 seconds. This was the first time in 30 years that Germany failed to win at least one medal.

Among the also-rans, in 36th place, were Joe Almasian and Ken Topalian, New Englanders competing for Armenia. Armenia had first hoped to take part in the 1920 Olympics, but was prevented by Russia, which had occupied Armenia. Almasian and Topalian were the first athletes to represent an independent Armenia. When they marched in the Parade of Nations at the Opening Ceremony in Lillehammer, they wore replicas of the 1920 Armenian team uniform.

FOUR-MAN

1924 Chamonix T: 9, N: 5, D: 2.3.

1. SWI	(Eduard Scherrer, Alfred Neveu, Alfred Schläppi, Heinrich Schläppi)	5:45.54
2. GBR	(Ralph Broome, Thomas Arnold, Alexander Richardson, Rodney Soher)	5:48.83
3. BEL	(Charles Mulder, René Mortiaux, Paul van den Broeck, Victor Verschueren, Henri Willems)	6:02.29
4. FRA	(André Berg, Henri Aldebert, Gérard André, Jean de Suarez D'Aulan)	6:22.95
5. GBR	(William Horton, Archibald Crabbe, Francis Fairlie, George Cecil Pim)	6:40.71
6. ITA	(Lodovico Obexer, Massimo Fink, Paolo Herbert, Giuseppe Steiner, Aloise Trenker)	7:15.41

1928 St Moritz T: 23, N: 14, D: 2.18.

1. USA	(William Fiske, Nion Tucker, Geoffrey Mason, Clifford Gray, Richard Parke)	3:20.5
2. USA	(Jennison Heaton, David Granger, Lyman Hine, Thomas Doe, Jay O'Brien)	3:21.0
3. GER	(Hanns Kilian, Valentin Krempel, Hans Hess, Sebastian Huber, Hans Nägle)	3:21.9
4. ARG	(Arturo Gramajo, Ricardo Gonzales Moreno, Mariano Domari, Rafael Iglesias, J. Nash)	3:22.6
5. ARG	(Eduardo Hope, Jorge del Caril, Hector Milberg, Horacio Iglesias, Horacio Gramajo)	3:22.9
6. BEL	(Ernest Lambert, Marcel Sedille-Courbon, Léon Tom, Max Houben, Walter Ganshof van der Meersch)	3:24.5
7. ROM	(Grigore Socolescu, Ion Gavrat, Traian Nitescu, Petre Ghitulescu, Mircea Socolescu)	3:24.6
8. SWI	(Charles Stoffel, Henry Höhnes, René Fonjallez, E. Coppetti, Louis Koch)	3:25.7

The competition was limited to two runs due to heavy thawing. For the only time in Olympic history, there were five men on each team rather than four. Three members of the winning team—Tucker, Mason, and Parke—were chosen after they answered an ad in the Paris edition of the *New York Herald Tribune*. None of them had ever seen a bobsled before. Mason showed up for practice on February 1, won a gold medal 18 days later, and never rode in an international bobsled race again.

1932 Lake Placid T: 7, N: 5, D: 2.15.

1. USA	(William Fiske, Edward Eagan, Clifford Gray, Jay O'Brien)	7:53.68
2. USA	(Henry Homburger, Percy Bryant, F. Paul Stevens, Edmund Horton)	7:55.70
3. GER	(Hanns Kilian, Max Ludwig, Hans Melhorn, Sebastian Huber)	8:00.04
4. SWI	(Reto Capadrutt, Hans Eisenhut, Charles Jenny, Oscar Geier)	8:12.18
5. ITA	(Teofilo Rossi Di Montelera, Agostino Lanfranchi, Gaetano Lanfranchi, Italo Casini)	8:24.21
6. ROM	(Papana Alexandru, Ionescu Alexandru, Ulise Petrescu, Hubert Dumitru)	8:24.22
7. GER	(Walther von Mumm, Hasso von Bismarck, Gerhard Hessert, Georg Gyssling)	8:25.45

Eddie Eagan is the only person to have won a gold medal in both the Summer and Winter Olympics. Eagan came from a poor family in Denver, but made his way through Yale, Harvard Law School, and Oxford, became a successful lawyer, and married an heiress. He lived his life according to the precepts of Frank Merriwell, the fictional hero of dime novels. In 1932 he wrote, "To this day I have never used tobacco, because Frank didn't. My first glass of wine, which I do not care for, was taken under social compulsion in Europe. Frank never drank." Back in 1920, Eddie Eagan won the Light Heavyweight boxing championship at the Antwerp Olympics. Later he won the U.S. amateur Heavyweight title and became the first American to win the amateur championship of Great Britain. In 1932 he showed up as a member of the four-man bob team led by boy wonder Billy Fiske, who had driven a U.S.

The 1932 U.S. four-man bobsled team: (left to right) *Jay O'Brien, Eddie Eagan, Clifford Gray, and Billy Fiske. Eight years later, only Eagan was still alive.*

team to victory at the 1928 Olympics when he was only 16 years old. The other members of the 1932 squad were St. Moritz veterans 48-year-old Jay O'Brien, who happened to be the head of the U.S. Olympic Bobsled Committee, and 40-year-old Clifford "Tippy" Gray, a songwriter who was actually a citizen of Great Britain. Their main rivals were the team driven by civil engineer Henry Homburger, which was known as the Saranac Lake Red Devils.

The weather was so poor during the Olympics that the four-man bob had to be delayed until after the official closing ceremony. The officials in charge of the bobsled competitions ordered that all four heats be run on February 14. But after the second round, Paul Stevens of the Red Devils protested the poor racing conditions and stalked off. Most of the competitors followed him, and the officials were forced to reschedule runs 3 and 4 the next day. Fiske's team recorded the fastest time for each of the first three runs. The Red Devils picked up 2.31 seconds on their final run, but it wasn't enough.

Fiske and his partners never raced together again. In fact, three of them died within a one-year period starting in 1940. Jay O'Brien died of a heart attack at the age of 57. Billy Fiske was the first American to join the British Royal Air Force in 1939 and was wounded over southern England during the Battle of Britain, while flying a Hurricane fighter. He died on August 17, 1940, when he was only 29 years old. Tippy Gray, whose 3000 songs included "Got a Date with an Angel" and "If You Were the Only Girl in the World," died in 1941. Gray was such a modest man that his children never even knew that he had won two Olympic gold medals until after he died. Eddie Eagan, the only team member to survive World War II, died on June 14, 1967, and was buried with both of his gold medals.

1936 Garmisch-Partenkirchen T: 18, N: 10, D: 2.12.

1.	SWI	(Pierre Musy, Arnold Gartmann, Charles Bouvier, Joseph Beerli)	5:19.85
2.	SWI	(Reto Capadrutt, Hans Aichele, Fritz Feierabend, Hans Bütikofer)	5:22.73

3.	GBR	(Frederick McEvoy, James Cardno, Guy Dugdale, Charles Green)	5:23.41
4.	USA	(J. Hubert Stevens, Crawford Merkel, Robert Martin, John Shene)	5:24.13
5.	BEL	(Max Houben, Martial van Schelle, Louis de Ridder, Paul Graeffe)	5:28.92
6.	USA	(Francis Tyler, James Bickford, Richard Lawrence, Max Bly)	5:29.00
7.	GER	(Hanns Kilian, Sebastian Huber, Fritz Schwarz, Hermann von Valta)	5:29.07
8.	BEL	(Rene Lunden, Eric de Spoelberch, Philippe de Pret Roose, Gaston Braun)	5:29.82

Again the bobsled competition was disrupted by bad weather—this time heavy rain. The first day's two runs were dangerous and unpredictable, but the next day the course was fast and smooth. Musy, a 25-year-old Swiss Army lieutenant, was the son of a former president of Switzerland.

1948 St. Moritz T: 15, N: 9, D: 2.7.

1.	USA	(Francis Tyler, Patrick Martin, Edward Rimkus, William D'Amico)	5.20.1
2.	BEL	(Max Houben, Freddy Mansveld, Louis-Georges Niels, Jacques Mouvet)	5:21.3
3.	USA	(James Bickford, Thomas Hicks, Donald Dupree, William Dupree)	5:21.5
4.	SWI	(Fritz Feierabend, Friedrich Waller, Felix Endrich, Heinrich Angst)	5:22.1
5.	NOR	(Arne Holst, Ivar Johansen, Reidar Berg, Alf Large)	5:22.5
6.	ITA	(Nino Bibbia, Giancarlo Ronchetti, Edilberto Campadese, Luigi Cavalieri)	5:23.0
7.	GBR	(William Coles, William McLean, R.W. Pennington Collings, George Holliday)	5:23.9
8.	SWI	(Franz Kapus, Rolf Spring, B. Schilter, Paul Eberhard)	5:25.4

The competition was halted in the middle of the second round when a water pipe burst, flooding the bob run. The winning team from Lake Placid, New York, weighed a total of 898 pounds.

1952 Oslo T: 15, N: 9, D: 2.22.

1.	GER	(Andreas Ostler, Friedrich Kuhn, Lorenz Nieberl, Franz Kemser)	5:07.84
2.	USA	(Stanley Benham, Patrick Martin, Howard Crossett, James Atkinson)	5:10.48
3.	SWI	(Fritz Feierabend, Albert Madörin, André Filippini, Stephan Waser)	5:11.70
4.	SWI	(Felix Endrich, Fritz Stöckli, Franz Kapus, Werner Spring)	5:13.98
5.	AUT	(Karl Wagner, Franz Eckhart, Hermann Palka, Paul Aste)	5:14.74
6.	SWE	(Kjell Holmström, Felix Fernström, Nils Landgren, Jan de Man Lapidoth)	5:15.01
7.	SWE	(Gunnar Åhs, Börje Ekedahl, Lennart Sandin, Gunnar Garpö)	5:17.86
8.	ARG	(Carlos Tomasi, Roberto Bordeau, Hector Tomasi, Carlos Sareistian)	5:18.85

The four members of the winning German team weighed in at 1041½ pounds. At a meeting held prior to the Olympics, the International Bobsled and Toboganning Federation passed a rule limiting future teams from weighing more than 880 pounds.

1956 Cortina T: 21, N: 13, D: 2.4.

1.	SWI	(Franz Kapus, Gottfried Diener, Robert Alt, Heinrich Angst)	5:10.44
2.	ITA	(Eugenio Monti, Ulrico Giardi, Renzo Alverà, Renato Mocellini)	5:12.10
3.	USA	(Arthur Tyler, William Dodge, Charles Butler, James Lamy)	5:12.39
4.	SWI	(Max Angst, Albert Gartmann, Harry Warburton, Rolf Gerber)	5:14.27
5.	ITA	(Dino DeMartin, Giovanni DeMartin, Giovanni Tabacchi, Carlo Da Prà)	5:14.66
6.	GER	(Hans Rösch, Martin Pössinger, Lorenz Nieberl, Silvester Wackerle, Sr.)	5:18.02
7.	AUT	(K. Loserth, K. Thurner, W. Schwarzböck, F. Dominik)	5:18.29
8.	GER	(Franz Schelle, Jakob Nirschel, Hans Henn, Edmund Koller)	5:18.50

Franz Kapus was 46 years old when he drove the Swiss team to victory by scoring the fastest times in all but the first run.

1960 not held

1964 Innsbruck-Igls T: 18, N: 11, D: 2.7.
1.	CAN	(Victor Emery, Peter Kirby, Douglas Anakin, John Emery)	4:14.46
2.	AUT	(Erwin Thaler, Adolf Koxeder, Josef Nairz, Reinhold Durnthaler)	4:15.48
3.	ITA	(Eugenio Monti, Sergio Siorpaes, Benito Rigoni, Gildo Siorpaes)	4:15.60
4.	ITA	(Sergio Zardini, Romano Bonagura, Sergio Mocellini, Ferruccio Dalla Torre)	4:15.89
5.	GER	(Franz Schelle, Otto Göbl, Ludwig Siebert, Josef Sterff)	4:16.19
6.	USA	(William Hickey, Charles Pandolph, Reginald Benham, William Dundon)	4:17.23
7.	AUT	(Paul Aste, Hans Stoll, Herbert Gruber, Andreas Arnold)	4:17.73
8.	SWI	(Herbert Kiessel, Oskar Lory, Bernhard Wild, Hansrudi Beuggar)	4:18.12

The winning Canadian team was made up of four bachelors from Montreal. Canada had never before entered an Olympic bobsled competition.

1968 Grenoble-Alpe d'Huez T: 19, N: 11, D: 2.15.
1.	ITA	(Eugenio Monti, Luciano De Paolis, Roberto Zandonella, Mario Armano)	2:17.39
2.	AUT	(Erwin Thaler, Reinhold Durnthaler, Herbert Gruber, Josef Eder)	2:17.48
3.	SWI	(Jean Wicki, Hans Candrian, Willi Hofmann, Walter Graf)	2:18.04
4.	ROM	(Ion Panţuru, Nicolae Neagoe, Petre Hristovici, Gheorghe Maftei)	2:18.14
5.	GER	(Horst Floth, Pepi Bader, Willi Schäfer, Frank Lange)	2:18.33
6.	ITA	(Gianfranco Gaspari, Leonardo Cavallini, Giuseppe Rescigno, Andrea Clemente)	2:18.36
7.	FRA	(Francis Luiggi, Maurice Grether, Andre Patey, Gerard Monrazel)	2:18.84
8.	GBR	(Anthony Nash, Robin Dixon, Guy Renwick, Robin Widdows)	2:18.84

The danger of a sudden thaw forced the officials to limit the contest to only two runs. Eugenio Monti won two silver medals in 1956, two bronze medals in 1964, and two gold medals in 1968.

1972 Sapporo-Teineyama T: 18, N: 10, D: 2.11.
1.	SWI	(Jean Wicki, Edy Hubacher, Hans Leutenegger, Werner Carmichel)	4:43.07
2.	ITA	(Nevio De Zordo, Gianni Bonichon, Adriano Frassinelli, Corrado Dal Fabbro)	4:43.83
3.	GER	(Wolfgang Zimmerer, Peter Utzschneider, Stefan Gaisreiter, Walter Steinbauer)	4:43.92
4.	SWI	(Hans Candrian, Heinz Schenker, Erwin Juon, Gaudenz Beeli)	4:44.56
5.	GER	(Horst Floth, Pepi Bader, Donat Ertel, Walter Gilik)	4:45.09
6.	AUT	(Herbert Gruber, Josef Oberhauser, Utz Chwalla, Josef Eder)	4:45.77
7.	AUT	(Werner Dellekarth, Fritz Sperling, Werner Moser, Walter Dellekarth)	4:46.66
8.	ITA	(Gianfranco Gaspari, Luciano De Paolis, Roberto Zandonella, Mario Armano)	4:46.73

1976 Innsbruck-Igls T: 21, N: 12, D: 2.14.
1.	GDR	(Meinhard Nehmer, Jochen Babock, Bernhard Germeshausen, Bernhard Lehmann)	3:40.43
2.	SWI	(Erich Schärer, Ulrich Bächli, Rudolf Marti, Josef Benz)	3:40.89
3.	GER	(Wolfgang Zimmerer, Peter Utzschneider, Bodo Bittner, Manfred Schumann)	3:41.37
4.	GDR	(Horst Schönau, Horst Bernhard, Harald Seifert, Raimund Bethge)	3:42.44
5.	GER	(Georg Heibl, Hans Morant, Siegfried Radant, Fritz Ohlwärter)	3:42.47
6.	AUT	(Werner Delle Karth, Andreas Schwab, Otto Breg, Franz Köfel, Heinz Krenn)	3:43.21
7.	AUT	(Fritz Sperling, Kurt Oberholler, Gerd Zaunschirm, Dieter Gehmacher)	3:43.79
8.	ROM	(Dragos Panaitescu, Paul Neagu, Costel Ionescu, Gheorghe Lixandru)	3:43.91

1980 Lake Placid T: 17, N: 10, D: 2.24.

1.	GDR	(Meinhard Nehmer, Bogdan Musiol, Bernhard Germeshausen, Hans-Jürgen Gerhardt)	3:59.92
2.	SWI	(Erich Schärer, Ulrich Bächli, Rudolf Marti, Josef Benz)	4:00.87
3.	GDR	(Horst Schönau, Ronald Wetzig, Detlef Richter, Andreas Kirchner)	4:00.97
4.	AUT	(Fritz Sperling, Heinrich Bergmüller, Franz Rednak, Bernhard Purkrabek)	4:02.62
5.	AUT	(Walter Delle Karth, Franz Paulweber, Gerd Zaunschirm, Kurt Oberhöller)	4:02.95
6.	SWI	(Hans Hiltebrand, Ulrich Schindler, Walter Rahm, Armin Baumgartner)	4:03.69
7.	GER	(Peter Hell, Hans Wagner, Heinz Busche, Walter Barfuss)	4:04.40
8.	ROM	(Dragos Panaitescu, Dorel Critudor, Sandu Mitrofan, Gheorghe Lixandru)	4:04.68

1984 Sarajevo T: 24, N: 15, D: 2.18.

1.	GDR	(Wolfgang Hoppe, Roland Wetzig, Dietmar Schauerhammer, Andreas Kirchner)	3:20.22
2.	GDR	(Bernhard Lehmann, Bogdan Musiol, Ingo Voge, Eberhard Weise)	3:20.78
3.	SWI	(Silvio Giobellina, Heinz Stettler, Urs Salzmann, Rico Freiermuth)	3:21.39
4.	SWI	(Ekkehard Fasser, Hans Märchy, Kurt Poletti, Rolf Strittmatter)	3:22.90
5.	USA	(Jeff Jost, Joe Briski, Thomas Barnes, Hal Hoye)	3:23.33
6.	SOV/ LAT	(Jānis Kipurs, Maris Poikans, Ivar Berzups, Aiwar Šnepsts)	3:23.51
7.	ROM	(Dorin Degan, Cornel Popescu, Georghe Lixandru, Costel Petrariu)	3:23.76
8.	ITA	(Guerrino Ghedina, Stefano Ticci, Paolo Scaramuzza, Andrea Meneghin)	3:23.77

The top three teams finished 1, 2, 3 in each of the four runs.

1988 Calgary T: 26, N: 17, D: 2.28.

1.	SWI	(Ekkehard Fasser, Kurt Meier, Marcel Fässler, Werner Stocker)	3:47.51
2.	GDR	(Wolfgang Hoppe, Dietmar Schauerhammer, Bogdan Musiol, Ingo Voge)	3:47.58
3.	SOV	(Jānis Kipurs, Guntis Osis, Juris Tone, Vladimir Kozlov)	3:48.26
4.	USA	(Brent Rushlaw, Hal Hoye, Michael Wasko, William White)	3:48.28
5.	SOV/LAT	(Maris Poikans, Olafs Klyavinch, Ivars Bersups, Juris Judzems)	3:48.35
6.	AUT	(Peter Kienast, Franz Siegl, Christian Mark, Kurt Teigl)	3:48.65
7.	AUT	(Ingo Appelt, Josef Muigg, Gerhard Redl, Harald Winkler)	3:48.95
8.	GDR	(Detlef Richter, Bodo Ferl, Ludwig Jahn, Alexander Szelig)	3:49.06

Third after two runs and second after three, 35-year-old Ekkehard Fasser eked out an upset victory in the final competition of his career. Fasser and his crew gained their advantage over Hoppe and the East Germans in the first 50 meters of the 1475-meter course, picking up a combined time of one sixteen-hundredth of a second over four runs.

1992 Albertville-La Plagne T: 31, N: 20, D: 2.22.

1.	AUT	(Ingo Appelt, Harald Winkler, Gerhard Haidacher, Thomas Schroll)	3:53.90
2.	GER	(Wolfgang Hoppe, Bogdan Musiol, Axel Kühn, René Hannemann)	3:53.92
3.	SWI	(Gustav Weder, Donat Acklin, Lorenz Schindelholz, Curdin Morell)	3:54.13
4.	CAN	(Christopher Lori, Kenneth LeBlanc, Cal Langford, David MacEachern)	3:54.24
5.	SWI	(Christian Meili, Bruno Gerber, Christian Reich, Gerold Löffler)	3:54.38
6.	GER	(Harald Czudaj, Tino Bonk, Axel Jang, Alexander Szelig)	3:54.42
7.	GBR	(Mark Tout, George Farrell, Paul Field, Lenox Paul)	3:54.89
8.	FRA	(Christophe Flacher, Claude Dasse, Thierry Tribondeau, Gabriel Fourmigue)	3:54.91

Ingo Appelt, a 30-year-old jeweler from Stubaital, overcame a 10th place finish in the second run to win the closest four-man contest in Olympic history. The competition was brightened by unexpected moments of comic relief. During the second run, Soviet team member Aleksandr Bortyuk slipped at the start, dived into his sled, and found himself facing the wrong way. The Soviets completed the course

During the second run of the 1992 four-man bob, Soviet team member Aleksandr Bortyuk slipped at the start and ending up facing the wrong direction.

convulsed in laughter with Bortyuk nose-to-nose with one of his teammates. At least they did better than Canada's number two team: Chris Farstad slipped while trying to jump into the sled and ended up in the seat that was supposed to be occupied by Jack Pyc. Pyc hesitated, missed the sled entirely, and slid down the run behind the sled until he was saved by a spectator. The Canadians were disqualified, but gained satisfaction from the fact that they finished first in the *three*-man bob.

1994 Lillehammer-Hunderfossen T: 30, N: 21, D: 2.27.

1.	GER	(Harald Czudaj, Karsten Brannasch, Olaf Hampel, Alexander Szelig)	3:27.78
2.	SWI	(Gustav Weder, Donat Acklin, Kurt Meier, Domenico Semeraro)	3:27.84
3.	GER	(Wolfgang Hoppe. Ulf Hielscher, René Hannemann, Carsten Embach)	3:28.01
4.	AUT	(Hubert Schösser, Gerhard Redl, Harald Winkler, Gerhard Haidacher)	3:28.40
5.	GBR	(Mark Tout, George Farrell, Jason Wing, Lenox Paul)	3:28.87
6.	AUT	(Kurt Einberger, Thomas Bachler, Carsten Nentwig, Martin Schützenauer)	3:28.91
7.	SWI	(Christian Meili, Rene Schmidheiny, Gerold Löffler, Christian Reich)	3:29.33
8.	GBR	(Sean Olsson, John Herbert, Dean Ward, Paul Field)	3:29.41

Harald Czudaj was a medal favorite in 1992, but the day before the Opening Ceremony, it was publicly revealed that, during the Communist period, in exchange for the dropping of drunken driving charges, he had served as an informer for the Stasi, the East German secret police. His fellow bobsledders forgave him, but, distracted, he finished only sixth. By 1994 the story was old news. He recorded the fastest time of the first run, while the favorite, Gustav Weder, faltered at the bottom of the course and placed fourth, 0.13 seconds behind Czudaj. Weder recovered to win each of the remaining three runs. However Czudaj was almost as consistent and Weder was only able to pick up seven of the thirteen hundredths of a second that he needed.

By finishing third, Wolfgang Hoppe brought his Olympic total to two golds, three silver and one bronze.

In 1988 the Jamaican bobsled team had been considered comic relief, but six years later no one was laughing anymore. With Dudley Stokes driving, the Jamaicans finished 14th—ahead of both teams from the United States, one of which had the dubious distinction of being the first bob crew to be disqualified for overheated runners.

In last place (except for the disqualified Americans) was the team from Bosnia, which used a sled donated by the Dutch. While their homeland was wracked by deadly ethnic warfare, the Bosnians tried to show that there was a peaceful side to their country. Their four-man bob team was made up of a Serb, a Croat and two Muslims.

CURLING

MEN
WOMEN

Although some people may snicker at curling's inclusion in the Olympics, it does further the International Olympic Committee's movement towards democracy by allowing non-athletes to take part in the Winter Olympics. Curling was included as a demonstration sport in 1924, 1932, 1936, 1964, 1988 and 1992 before finally achieving medal status in 1998.

Curling is played by four-player teams on a *rink* 146 feet (44.5 meters) long and 15 feet 7 inches (4.75 meters) wide. The object is to deliver a stone with a handle on top as close as possible to a *tee* on the opposite side of the rink and to knock away the stones of the opposing team. In this sense, curling is similar to shuffleboard, petanque and lawn bowling. The path of the *running stone,* that is a stone that has been delivered but has not yet stopped, may be guided by team members who sweep the ice with a brush or a broom. Most stones come from a quarry on the Aisla Craig in the Firth of Clyde in the west of Scotland. Stones may weigh no more than 44 pounds (19.96 kilograms) and may be no more than 36 inches (91.44 centimeters) in circumference and 4½ inches (11.43 centimeters) high.

An *end* is that part of a game in which each player on each team delivers two stones, for a total of 16 stones per end. A point or *shot* is scored for each stone that is nearer to the tee than any stone of the opposing team. However, for a stone to be scored it must lie within six feet (1.83 meters) of the tee. This area is known as the *house.* A game consists of ten ends. Each team is allowed a total of 75 minutes to deliver its stones in a ten-end game. If the teams are tied, extra ends are played until the tie is broken.

MEN

This event will be held for the first time in 1998.

WOMEN

This event will be held for the first time in 1998.

ICE HOCKEY

MEN

The teams in Olympic ice hockey tournaments are divided into two round-robin pools. According to rules instituted in 1992, the winner of each pool plays the fourth-place team in the opposing pool, and the second-place teams play the other pool's third-place team. The winners advance to the semifinals. Matches are divided into three 20-minute periods. In pool play, ties are allowed to stand, but in the playoff rounds, regulation play is followed by a 10-minute sudden-death overtime and then by a shoot-out.

PROFESSIONALS IN THE OLYMPICS

The question of whether professionals should be allowed to play in the Olympics is not a new one. The U.S. team of 1920 included one player, Jerry Geran, who had played in the NHL, and the team that represented the U.S. in 1948 was paid a weekly salary. Still, Olympic ice hockey remained basically a sport for amateurs until Communist Czechoslovakia joined in 1948 and the Soviet Union followed in 1956. The Soviet and Czechoslovak team members were all full-time ice hockey players, but because their salaries were paid by governments and not by profit-making clubs, they were considered amateurs. This gave an enormous advantage to the USSR and Czechoslovakia, who were able to use their countries' best players, while the rest of the world had to make due with players who weren't good enough to earn a living at the sport. In 1972, Canada refused to take part in the Olympic ice hockey tournament. In 1976, Sweden joined the boycott. Both teams returned to the Olympics in 1980, but their point had been made. In 1987, the International Ice Hockey Federation voted to make all professionals, including players from the NHL, eligible for the Olympics. The NHL owners refused to allow their best players to leave in the middle of the season. But when they saw the success of the inclusion of NBA professionals in the 1992 Olympic basketball tournament, the NHL agreed to suspend the season for the period of the Winter Olympics. The 1998 Games will be the first in which the best professional players in the world will take part.

Although 29 nations have taken part in the 18 Olympic ice hockey tournaments, only 7 nations have achieved a cumulative winning record and only 6 have a cumulative positive goal differential.

1920 Antwerp T: 7, N: 7, D: 4.26.

			W	L	GF	GA
1.	CAN	(Robert Benson, Walter Byron, Frank Frederickson, Chris Fridfinnson, Magnus "Mike" Goodman, Haldor Halderson, Konrad Johannesson, Allan "Huck" Woodman)	3	0	29	1

				W	L	GF	GA

2. USA (Raymond Bonney, Anthony Conroy, Herbert Drury, J. Edward Fitzger- 3 1 52 2
ald, George Geran, Frank Goheen, Joseph McCormick, Lawrence
McCormick, Frank Synott, Leon Tuck, Cyril Weidenborner)
3. CZE (Karel Hartmann, Karel Kotrbá, Josef Loos, Vilém Loos, Jan Peka, 1 2 1 31
Karel Pešek-Kadă, Josef Šroubek, Otakar Vindyš, Jan Palouš, Karel
Wälzer)
4. SWE (Wilhelm Arwe, Erik Burman, Seth Howander, Albin Jansson, Georg 3 3 17 20
Johansson, Einar Lindqvist, Einar Lundell, Hansjacob Mattsson, Nils
Molander, Sven Säfwenberg, Einar Svensson)

The 1920 ice hockey tournament was played by seven-man teams rather than six-man ones. Each match consisted of two 20-minute periods and there were no substitutions. If a player was injured, the opposing team was required to pull one of its players. The Europeans were in awe of the North American style of play. In the words of Oscar Söderlund of the *Stockholms-Tidninger,* "Every single player on the rink [during the Canada-USA match] was a perfect acrobat on skates, skated at tremendous speed without regard to himself or anyone else, jumped over sticks and players with ease and grace, turned sharply with perfect ease and without losing speed, and skated backwards just as easily as forwards. And during all this, the puck was held down on the ice and was dribbled forwards by means of short shoves of the stick."

Canada scored victories of 15–0 over Czechoslovakia, 2–0 over the United States, and 12–1 over Sweden. According to the rules of the tournament, the three teams that lost to Canada then played off for second place. The United States beat Sweden, 7–0, and Czechoslovakia, 16–0. Then Czechoslovakia defeated Sweden, 1–0, to win the bronze medal, even though the Czechs had been outscored 1 to 31 in their three matches. Canada was represented by the Winnipeg Falcons, who had just defeated the University of Toronto for the Canadian championship. The invitation to the Olympics came at such short notice that the Falcons didn't have time to return home to Winnipeg. Funds had to be raised to buy the players new clothes for the overseas journey. All of the Canadian players were of Icelandic origin except goalie Wally Byron. The U.S. team, for its part, included four Canadian citizens who played for U.S. clubs: Drury, Synott and the McCormick brothers—as well as one player, Jerry Geran, who had played professional ice hockey in the NHL. The most lopsided match of the tournament was the U.S.'s 29–0 defeat of Switzerland. The Americans scored a goal a minute for the first 13 minutes and scored one goal while two men short. Tony Conroy led the scoring with 8 goals.

1924 Chamonix T: 8, N: 8, D: 2.8.

				W	L	GF	GA
1.	CAN	(Jack Cameron, Ernest Collett, Albert McCaffery, Harold McMunn, Duncan Munro, W. Beattie Ramsay, Cyril Slater, Reginald Smith, Harry Watson)		5	0	110	3
2.	USA	(Clarence Abel, Herbert Drury, Alphonse Lacroix, John Langley, John Lyons, Justin McCarthy, Willard Rice, Irving Small, Frank Synott)		4	1	73	6
3.	GBR	(William Anderson, Lorne Carr-Harris, Colin Carruthers, Eric Carruthers, George "Guy" Clarkson, Cuthbert Ross Cuthbert, George Holmes, Hamilton Jukes, Edward Pitblado, Blane Sexton)		3	2	40	38
4.	SWE	(Ruben Allinger, Vilhelm Arwe, Erik Burman, Birger Holmqvist, Gustaf Johansson, Hugo Johansson, Karl Josefson, Ernst Karlberg, Nils Molander, Einar Ohlsson)		2	3	21	49
5.	CZE	(Jaroslav Stransky, Jaroslav Rezač, Otakar Vindyš, Vilém Loos, Josef Šroubek, Jaraslav Jirkovsky, Josef Malecek, Jaroslav Fleischmann, Miroslav Fleischmann, Jan Palouš, Johann Josef Krasl)		1	2	14	41

		W	L	GF	GA
5. FRA	(B. Poule, P.E. Bouillon, L. Brasseur, André Charlet, Pierre Charpentier, Jacques Chaudron, H. Couttet, Raoul Couvert, Maurice Del Valle, Alred De Rauch, Georges De Wilde, Albert Hassler, Charles Lavaivre, H. Levy-Grunwald, Jean Monnard, J. Nard, Calixte Payot, Philippe Payot, Léonhard Quaglia, G. Simond)	1	2	9	42
7. BEL	(Victor Verschueren, Paul Van den Broeck, Henri Louette, Frederick ·Rudolph, Andre Poplimont, Gaston Van Volckxsom, Charles Van den Driessche, Louis de Ridder)	0	3	8	35
7. SWI	(Bruno Leuzinger, Wilhelm de Siebenthal, Donald Unger, Ernest Mottier, René Savoie, Marius Jaccard, Fred Auckenthaler, Emile Jacquet, Peter Müller, André Verdeil, Emil Filliol)	0	3	2	53

The Canadian team, the Toronto Granites, displayed extraordinary superiority. After defeating Czechoslovakia, 30–0, and Sweden, 22–0, they outscored Switzerland, 18–0 in the first period alone and then breezed to a 33–0 victory, before crushing Great Britain, 19–2. Meanwhile the U.S. team had beaten Belgium 19–0, France 22–0, Great Britain 11–0, and Sweden 20–0. The final match between Canada and the United States was a rough battle that saw Canada's Harry Watson knocked cold after only 20 seconds of play. Watson recovered, however, and, with blood in his eyes, scored the first two goals of the game. Canada led 2–1 after the first period and 5–1 after the second. A single third-period goal accounted for the final score of 6–1. Taffy Abel, the captain of the U.S. team, was a Chippewa Indian. All but two members of the British team were born in Canada.

1928 St. Moritz T: 11, N: 11, D: 2.19.

		W	L	T	GF	GA
1. CAN	(Charles Delahay, Frank Fisher, Louis Hudson, Norbert Mueller, Herbert Plaxton, Hugh Plaxton, Roger Plaxton, John Porter, Frank ˙Sullivan, Joseph Sullivan, Ross Taylor, David Trottier)	3	0	0	38	0
2. SWE	(Carl Abrahamsson, Emil Bergman, Birger Holmqvist, Gustaf Johansson, Henry Johansson, Nils Johansson, Ernst Karlberg, Erik Larsson, Bertil Linde, Sigurd Öberg, Vilhelm Petersen, Kurt Sucksdorf)	3	1	1	12	14
3. SWI	(Gianni Andreossi, Murezzan Andreossi, Robert Breiter, Louis Dufour, Charles Fasel, Albert Geromini, Fritz Kraatz, Adolf Martignoni, Heinrich Meng, Anton Morosani, Luzius Rüedi, Richard Torriani)	2	2	1	9	21
4. GBR	(Blane Sexton, Eric Carruthers, Cuthbert Ross Cuthbert, Frederick Melland, Victor Tait, Charles Wyld, Colin Carruthers, William Speechley, Harold Greenwood, William Brown, G.E.F. Rogers, Bernard Fawcett)	2	4	0	11	27

Canada was represented by the 1926 Toronto University team, which had stayed together and, renamed the Toronto Graduates, had won the Canadian championships. They arrived in Switzerland ten days before the opening of the Games. When Olympic officials saw the Canadians practice they realized that the rest of the teams would be completely outclassed. Consequently, they devised an unusual organization for the tournament. Canada was advanced straight to the final round, while the other ten nations were divided into three pools. The winners of the three pools then joined Canada in the final round. This odd system turned out to be well justified, as Canada obliterated Sweden 11–0, Great Britain 14–0, and Switzerland 13–0.

1932 Lake Placid T: 4, N: 4, D: 2.13.

			W	L	T	GF	GA
1.	CAN	(William Cockburn, Clifford Crowley, Albert Duncanson, George Garbutt, Roy Hinkel, Victor Lundquist, Norman Malloy, Walter Monson, Kenneth Moore, N. Romeo Rivers, Harold Simpson, Hugh Sutherland, W. Stanley Wagner, J. Aliston Wise)	5	0	1	32	4
2.	USA	(Osborn Anderson, John Bent, John Chase, John Cookman, Douglas Everett, Franklin Farrell, Joseph Fitzgerald, Edward Frazier, John Garrison, Gerard Hallock, Robert Livingston, Francis Nelson, Winthrop Palmer, Gordon Smith)	4	1	1	27	5
3.	GER	(Rudi Ball, Alfred Heinrich, Erich Herker, Gustav Jaenecke, Werner Korff, Walter Leinweber, Erich Römer, Marquardt Slevogt, Martin Schröttle, Georg Strobl)	2	4	0	7	26
4.	POL	(Adam Kowalski, Aleksander Kowalski, Wlodzimierz Krygier, Albert Maurer, Roman Sabiński, Kazimierz Sokolowski, Jósef Stogowski, Witalis Ludwiczak, Czeslaw Marchewczyk, Kazimierz Materski)	0	6	0	3	34

Because of the worldwide Depression, only four nations appeared for the Olympic hockey tournament. Consequently, it was decided that each team would play each other team twice. The Canadian team from Winnipeg won their first five matches, including a 2–1 victory over the United States. This meant that a win or a tie in the second match against the United States would assure Canada of first place. If the United States won, then a third match would be required. The United States took a 2–1 lead, but with 50 seconds to play, Rivers shot a bouncing puck into the net to tie the score. Three scoreless overtimes later, Canada was declared the tournament winner.

1936 Garmisch-Partenkirchen T: 15, N: 15, D: 2.16.

			W	L	T	GF	GA
1.	GBR	(Alexander "Sandy" Archer, James Borland, Edgar Brenchley, James Chappell, John Coward, Gordon Dailley, John Davey, Carl Erhardt, James Foster, John Kilpatrick, Archibald Stinchcombe, James Wyman)	5	0	2	17	3
2.	CAN	(Maxwell Deacon, Hugh Farquharson, Kenneth Farmer, James Haggarty, Walter Kitchen, Raymond Milton, Francis Moore, Herman Murray, Arthur Nash, David Neville, Ralph St. Germain, Alexander Sinclair, William Thomson)	7	1	0	54	7
3.	USA	(John Garrison, August Kammer, Philip LaBatte, John Lax, Thomas Moone, Eldrige Ross, Paul Rowe, Francis Shaugnessy, Gordon Smith, Francis Spain, Frank Stubbs)	5	2	1	10	4
4.	CZE	(Josef Boháč, Alois Cetkovsky, Karel Hromádka, Drahos Jirotka, Zdenek Jirotka, Jan Košek, Oldřich Kučera, Josef Maleček, Jan Peka, Jaroslav Pusbauer, Jiři Tožička, Ladislav Troják, Walter Ullrich)	5	3	0	16	16
5.	GER	(Wilhelm Egginger, Joachim Albrecht von Bethmann-Hollweg, Gustav Jaenecke, Phillip Schenk, Rudi Ball, Karl Kögel, Anton Wiedemann, Herbert Schibukat, Alois Kuhn, Werner George, Georg Strohl, Paul Trautmann)	3	2	1	10	9
5.	SWE	(Hermann Carlsson, Sven Bergquist, Bertil Lundell, Holger Engberg, Torsten Jöhncke, Yngve Liljeberg, Bertil Norberg, Vilhelm Petersen, Åke Ericson, Stig Andersson, Lennart Hellman, Vilhelm Larsson, Ruben Carlsson)	2	3	0	5	7

		W	L	T	GF	GA
7. AUT	(Hermann Weiss, Hans Trauttenberg, Rudolf Vojta, Oskar No-wak, Friedrich Demmer, Franz Csöngei, Hans Tatzer, Willibald Stanek, Lambert Neumaier, Franz Schüssler, Emil Seidler, Josef Göbl)	2	4	0	12	11
7. HUN	(István Csak, Ferenc Monostori, Miklós Barcza, László Róna, Frigyes Helmeczi, Sándor Magyar, András Gergely, László Gergely, Béla Háray, Zoltán Jeney, Sándor Miklós, Ferenc Szamosi, Mátyás Farkas)	2	4	0	16	77

Germany's leading hockey player was Rudi Ball, a Jew who fled the country when the Nazis began their campaign of anti-Semitism. One month before the Games began, he returned to lead the German team after being invited back by the Nazi leadership. He was the only Jewish member of the German Winter Olympics team.

Canada's Olympic undefeated streak was halted at 20 by Great Britain in the semifinal round, when Edgar Brenchley scored a rebound goal in the 14th minute of the final period to give the British a 2–1 victory. Great Britain remained unbeaten by surviving a 0–0 triple overtime tie with the United States in their final match. Nine of the 12 members of the British team were born in Great Britain, but moved to Canada as children and learned to play ice hockey there. A tenth player, Gordon Dailley, was actually born in Canada and served in the Canadian Army.

1948 St. Moritz T: 9, N: 9, D: 2.8.

		W	L	T	GF	GA
1. CAN	(Murray Dowey, Bernard Dunster, Jean Orval Gravelle, Patrick Guzzo, Walter Halder, Thomas Hibbert, Henri-André Laperrière, John Lecompte, George Mara, Albert Renaud, Reginald Schroeter, Irving Taylor)	7	0	1	69	5
2. CZE	(Vladimir Bouzek, Augustin Bubnik, Jaroslav Drobny, Přemysl Hajny, Zdenek Jarkovský, Stanislav Konopásek, Bohumil Modry, Miloslav Pokorny, Václav Rozinák, Moroslav Sláma, Karel Stibor, Vilibald Štovik, Ladislav Troják, Josef Trousilek, Oldřich Zábrodsky, Vladimir Zábrodský, Vladimir Kobranov)	7	0	1	80	18
3. SWI	(Hans Bänninger, Alfred Bieler, Heinrich Boller, Ferdinand Cattini, Hans Cattini, Hans Dürst, Walter Dürst, Emil Handschin, Heini Lohrer, Werner Lohrer, Reto Perl, Gebhard Poltera, Ulrich Poltera, Beat Rüedi, Otto Schubiger, Richard Torriani, Hans Trepp)	6	2	0	67	21
—USA	(Robert Baker, Ruben Bjorkman, Robert Boeser, Bruce Cunliffe, John Garrity, Donald Geary, Goodwin Harding, Herbert Van Ingen, John Kirrane, Bruce Mather, Allan Opsahl, Fred Pearson, Stanton Priddy, Jack Riley, Ralph Warburton)	5	3	0	86	33
4. SWE	(Stig Andersson, Åke Andersson, Stig Carlsson, Åke Ericson, Rolf Ericson, Svante Granlund, Arne Johansson, Rune Johansson, Gunnar Landelius, Klas Lindström, Lars Ljungman, Holger Nurmela, Bror Pettersson, Rolf Pettersson, Kurt Svanberg, Sven Thunman)	4	4	0	55	28
5. GBR	(Leonard Baker, George Baillie, James Chappell, J. Gerry Davey, Frederick Dunkelman, Arthur Green, Frank Green, Frank Jardine, John Murray, John Oxley, Stanley Simon, William Smith, Archibald Stinchcombe, Thomas Syme)	3	5	0	39	47
6. POL	(Henryk Bromer, Mieczyslaw Burda, Stefan Csorich, Tadeusz Dolewski, Alfred Gansiniec, Thomas Jasiński, Mieczslaw Kasprzycki, Boleslaw Kolasa, Adam Kowalski, Eugeniusz Lewacki, Jan Maciejko, Czeslaw Marchewczyk, Mieczyslaw Palus, Henryk Przeździecki, Hilary Skarzyński, Maksymilian Wiecek, Ernest Ziaja)	2	6	0	20	97

7. AUT (Albert Böhm, Franz Csöngei, Friedrich Demmer, Egon Engel, Walter Feistritzer, Gustav Gross, Adolf Hafner, Alfred Huber, Julius Juhn, Oskar Nowack, Jörg Reichel, Johann Schneider, Willibald Stanek, Herbert Ulrich, Fritz Walter, Helfried Winger, Rudolf Wurmbrandt) 1 7 0 33 77

8. ITA (Claudio Apollonio, Giancarlo Bazzi, Mario Bedogni, Luigi Bestagini, Carlo Bulgheroni, Ignacio Dionisi, Arnaldo Fabbris, Vincenzo Fardella, Aldo Federici, Umberto Gerli, Dino Innocenti, Caistanzo Mangini, Dino Menardi, Otto Rauth, Franco Rossi, Gianantonio Zopegni) 0 8 0 24 156

The controversy that engulfed the 1948 ice hockey tournament actually began a year earlier, when the International Ice Hockey Federation ruled that the Amateur Athletic Union was being replaced as the governing body for amateur ice hockey in the United States by the American Hockey Association (A.H.A.). Avery Brundage, chairman of the American Olympic Committee (A.O.C.), accused the A.H.A. of being under commercial sponsorship and refused to sanction its team. Consequently, two U.S. teams arrived in Switzerland prepared to play in the Olympic tournament. Two days before the opening ceremony, the executive committee of the International Olympic Committee (I.O.C.) voted to bar both U.S. teams from competition. However, the Swiss Olympic Organizing Committee, siding with the International Ice Hockey Federation, defied the International Olympic Committee and announced that the A.H.A. team would be allowed to play. The A.O.C. team got to take part in the opening-day parade, while the A.H.A. team watched from the stands. But after that, the A.O.C. team had nothing to do but enjoy their paid vacation.

Meanwhile, the A.H.A. players raked up a couple of amazing scores, beating Poland 23–4 and Italy 31–1. Their coach justified these thrashings because the rules stated that if two teams were tied at the end of the tournament, the one with the largest cumulative scoring margin would be declared the winner.

The I.O.C. disowned the ice hockey tournament, but later gave it official approval on the condition that the A.H.A. team not be included in the placings.

With one day left in the competition, three nations—Canada, Czechoslovakia, and Switzerland—all had a chance to finish in first place. In the morning Czechoslovakia defeated the United States, 4–3, which eliminated Switzerland's hopes of placing higher than second. The final match pitted Canada against the Swiss. Two days earlier the Czechs and the Canadians had played a 0–0 tie. Consequently, Canada needed to beat Switzerland by at least two goals to win the gold medal on the basis of the goal differential tie-breaker. About 5000 Swiss perched on mountain cliffs and watched the game, pelting officials with snowballs whenever they disagreed with a call. Their enthusiasm did little good, as the Canadian team tallied a goal in each period and won, 3–0. A final note about the Italian team: in addition to their 31–1 loss to the United States, they lost to Sweden 23–0, Canada 21–1, Czechoslovakia 22–3, and Switzerland 16–0.

1952 Oslo T: 9, N: 9, D: 2.24.

		W	L	T	GF	GA
1. CAN	(George Abel, John Davies, William Dawe, Robert Dickson, Donald Gauf, William Gibson, Ralph Hansch, Robert Meyers, David Miller, Eric Paterson, Thomas Pollock, Allan Purvis, Gordon Robertson, Louis Secco, Francis Sullivan, Robert Watt)	7	0	1	71	14
2. USA	(Ruben Bjorkman, Leonard Ceglarski, Joseph Czarnota, Richard Desmond, Andre Gambucci, Clifford Harrison, Gerald Kilmartin, John Mulhern, John Noah, Arnold Oss, Robert Rompre, James Sedin, Allen Van, Donald Whiston, Kenneth Yackel)	6	1	1	43	21

		W	L	T	GF	GA
3. SWE	(Göte Almqvist, Hans Andersson, Stig "Tvilling" Andersson, Åke Andersson, Lars Björn, Göte Blomqvist, Thord Flodqvist, Erik Johansson, Gösta Johansson, Rune Johansson, Sven Johansson, Åke Lassas, Holger Nurmela, Hans Öberg, Lars Pettersson, Lars Svensson, Sven Thunman)	7	2	0	53	22
4. CZE	(Slavomir Barton, Miloslav Blažek, Václav Bubnik, Vlastimil Bubnik, Miloslav Charouzd, Bronislav Danda, Karel Gut, Vlastimil Hajšman, Jan Lidral, Miroslav Nový, Miloslav Ošmera, Zdenek Pýcha, Miroslav Rejman, Jan Richter, Oldrich Sedlak, Jiri Sekyra, Josef Záhorsky)	6	3	0	50	23
5. SWI	(Gian Bazzi, Hans Bänninger, François Blank, Bixio Celio, Reto Delnon, Walter Dürst, Emil Golaz, Emil Handschin, Paul Hofer, Willy Pfister, Gebhard Poltera, Ulrich Poltera, Otto Schläpfer, Otto Schubiger, Alfred Streun, Hans Trepp, Paul Wyss)	4	4	0	40	40
6. POL	(Michal Antuszewicz, Henryk Bromowicz, Kazimierz Chodakowski, Stefan Csorich, Rudolf Czech, Alfred Gansiniec, Jan Hampel, Marian Jezak, Eugeniusz Lewacki, Roman Pęczek, Hilary Skarzyński, Konstanty Świcarz, Stanislaw Szlendak, Zdzislaw Trojanowski, Adolf Wróbel, Alfred Wróbel)	2	5	1	21	56
7. FIN	(Yrjo Hakala, Aarne Honkavaara, Erkki Hytonen, Pentti Isotalo, Matti Karumaa, Ossi Kauppi, Keijo Kuusela, Kauko Makinen, Pekka Myllyla, Christian Rapp, Esko Rehoma, Matti Rintakoski, Eero Saari, Eero Salisma, Lauri Silvan, Unto Vitala, Jukka Vuolio)	2	6	0	21	60
8. GER	(Karl Bierschel, Markus Egen, Karl Enzler, Georg Guggemos, Alfred Hoffmann, Engelbert Holderied, Walter Kremershof, Ludwig Kuhn, Dieter Niess, Hans Georg Pescher, Fritz Poitsch, Herbert Schibukat, Xaver Unsinn, Heinz Wackers, Karl Wild)	1	6	1	21	53

Canada, represented by the Edmonton Mercurys, won their first seven games. A final 3–3 tie with the United States gave them the championship. The Americans were just as thrilled by the outcome, since it meant they would finish second instead of fourth. The U.S. team was not popular with the spectators because of their rough style of play. In fact, three of the U.S. players, Czarnota, Yackel, and Gambucci, spent more time in the penalty box than the team totals of any of the other eight teams in the tournament.

Between 1920 and 1952, Canadian ice hockey teams compiled an extraordinary Olympic record of 37 wins, 1 loss, and 3 ties. In those 41 games they scored 403 goals while allowing only 34.

1956 Cortina T: 10, N: 10, D: 2.4.

		W	L	T	GF	GA
1. SOV/RUS	(Yevgeny Babich, Usevolod Bobrov, Nikolai Chlystov, Aleksei Guryshev, Yuri Krylov, Alfred Kuchevsky, Valentin Kusin, Grigory Mkrtchan, Viktor Nikiforov, Yuri Pantyuchov, Nikolai Puchkov, Viktor Shuvalov, Genrich Sidorenkov, Nikolai Sologubov, Ivan Tregubov, Dmitri Ukolov, Aleksandr Uvarov)	7	0	0	40	9
2. USA	(Wendell Anderson, Wellington Burnett, Eugene Campbell, Gordon Christian, William Cleary, Richard Dougherty, Willard Ikola, John Matchefts, John Mayasich, Daniel McKinnon, Richard Meredith, Weldon Olson, John Petroske, Kenneth Purpur, Donald Rigazio, Richard Rodenheiser, Edward Sampson)	5	2	0	33	16

		W	L	T	GF	GA

3. CAN (Denis Brodeur, Charles Brooker, William Colvin, Alfred Horne, Arthur Hurst, Byrle Klinck, Paul Knox, Kenneth Laufman, Howard Lee, James Logan, Floyd Martin, Jack McKenzie, Donald Rope, Georges Scholes, Gérald Théberge, Robert White, Keith Woodall) — 6 2 0 53 12

4. SWE (Lars Björn, Sigurd Bröms, Stig Carlsson, Yngve Casslind, Sven Johansson, Vilgot Larsson, Åke Lassas, Lars-Erik Lundvall, Ove Malmberg, Nils Nilsson, Holger Nurmela, Hans Öberg, Ronald Pettersson, Lars Svensson, Hans Tvilling [Andersson], Stig "Tvilling" Andersson, Bertz Zetterberg) — 2 4 1 17 27

5. CZE (Stanislav Bacilek, Stavomir Barton, Václav Bubnik, Vlastimil Bubnik, Jaromir Bünter, Otto Čimrman, Bronislav Danda, Karel Gut, Jan Jendek, Jan Kasper, Miroslav Kluc, Ždenek Návrat, Václav Pantuček, Bohumil Prošek, František Vaněk, Jan Vodička, Vladimir Zábrodsky) — 3 4 0 32 36

6. GER (Paul Ambros, Martin Beck, Toni Biersack, Karl Bierschel, Markus Egen, Arthur Endress, Bruno Guttowski, Alfred Hoffmann, Hans Huber, Ulrich Jansen, Günther Jochems, Rainer Kossmann, Rudolf Pittrich, Hans Rampf, Kurt Sepp, Ernst Trautwein, Martin Zach) — 1 5 2 15 41

7. ITA (Carmine Tucci, Carlo Montemurro, Aldo Federici, Mario Bedogni, Bernardo Tomei, Giovanni Furlani, Giampiero Branduardi, Aldo Maniacco, Ernesto Crotti, Giancarlo Agazzi, Gianfranco Darin, Rino Alberton, Giulio Oberhammer, Francesco Macchietto) — 3 1 2 26 14

8. POL (Janusz Zawadzki, Kazimierz Chodakowski, Stanislaw Olczyk, Mieczyslaw Chmura, Henryk Bromowicz, Józef Kurek, Zdzislaw Nowak, Szymon Janiczko, Adolf Wróbel, Kazimierz Bryniarski, Marian Herda, Hilary Skarżyński, Bronislaw Gosztyla, Rudolf Czech, Alfred Wróbel, Edward Kocząb, Wladyslaw Pabisz) — 2 3 0 15 22

The Soviet team made a great impression, not only with their excellent play, but with their good sportsmanship and clean style as well.

1960 Squaw Valley T: 9, N: 9, D: 2.28.

	W	L	T	GF	GA
1. USA	7	0	0	48	17
2. CAN	6	1	0	55	15
3. SOV/RUS	4	2	1	40	23

1. USA (Roger Christian, William Christian, Robert Cleary, William Cleary, Eugene Grazia, Paul Johnson, John Kirrane, John Mayasich, Jack McCartan, Robert McVey, Richard Meredith, Weldon Olson, Edwyn Owen, Rodney Paavola, Lawrence Palmer, Richard Rodenheiser, Thomas Williams)

2. CAN (Robert Attersley, Maurice "Moe" Benoit, James Connelly, Jack Douglas, Fred Etcher, Robert Forhan, Donald Head, Harold Hurley, Kenneth Laufman, Floyd Martin, Robert McKnight, Clifford Pennington, Donald Rope, Robert Rousseau, George Samolenko, Harry Sinden, Darryl Sly)

3. SOV/RUS (Veniamin Aleksandrov, Aleksandr Alyimetov, Yuri Baulin, Mikhail Bychkov, Vladimir Grebennikov, Yevgeny Groshev, Viktor Yakushev, Yevgeny Yerkin, Nikolai Karpov, Alfred Kuchevsky, Konstantin Loktev, Stanislav Petuchov, Viktor Prjazhnikov, Nikolai Puchkov, Genrich Sidorenkov, Nikolai Sologubov, Yuri Tsitsinov)

		W	L	T	GF	GA
4. CZE	(Vlastimil Bubnik, Josef Černy, Bronislav Danda, Vladimir Dvořaček, Josef Golonka, Karel Gut, Jaroslav Jiřik, Jan Kasper, František Maslan, Vladimir Nadrchal, Vaclav Pantuček, Rudolf Potsch, Jan Starsi, František Tikal, František Vanek, Miroslav Vlach, Jaroslav Volf)	3	4	0	44	31
5. SWE	(Anders Andersson, Lars Björn, Gert Blomé, Sigurd Bröms, Einar Granath, Sven Johansson, Bengt Lindqvist, Lars-Erik Lundvall, Nils Nilsson, Bert-Ola Nordlander, Carl-Göran Öberg, Ronald Pettersson, Ulf Sterner, Roland Stoltz, Hans Svedberg, Kjell Svensson, Sune Wretling)	2	4	1	40	24
6. GER	(Paul Ambros, Georg Eberl, Markus Egen, Ernst Eggerbauer, Michael Hobelsberger, Hans Huber, Uli Jansen, Hans Rampf, Josef Reif, Otto Schneitberger, Siegfried Schubert, Horst Schuldes, Kurt Sepp, Ernst Trautwein, Xaver Unsinn, Leonhard Waitl, Horst Metzer)	1	6	0	9	54
7. FIN	(Yrjo Hakala, Raimo Kilpiö, Kolso, Lampainen, Esko Luostarinen, Niemii, Nieminen, Kalevi Numminen, Heino Pulli, Rassa, Rastio, Jouni Seistamo, Sonio, Vainio, Juhani Wahlsten)	3	2	1	63	23
8. JPN	(Shikashi Akazawa, Shinichi Honma, Toshiei Honma, Hidenori Inatsu, Atsuo Irie, Yuji Iwaoka, Takashi Kakihara, Yoshikiro Miyasaki, Masao Murano, Isao Ono, Akiyoshi Segawa, Shigeru Shimada, Kunito Takagi, Mamuru Takashima, Masamu Tanabu, Shoichi Tomita, Toshihiko Yamada)	2	3	1	34	68

When they first started playing together, the U.S. squad hardly seemed to be the "Team of Destiny" that they were to become. Before leaving for Squaw Valley, they played an 18-game training tour and compiled an unimpressive record of ten wins, four losses, and four ties. Not only did they lose to Michigan Tech and Denver University, but less than three weeks before the Olympics began, the U.S. team actually lost, 7–5, to the Warroad Lakers of Warroad, Minnesota. However their first Olympic match set the tone for the rest of the tournament. Trailing Czechoslovakia 4–3 after two periods, they scored four straight goals in the final period and won, 7–5. This was followed by three convincing victories over Australia (12–1), Sweden (6–3), and Germany (9–1).

On February 25 they faced the cofavorite Canadian team. Bob Cleary of Westwood, Massachusetts, took a pass from John Mayasich and scored the first goal after 12 minutes and 47 seconds. Paul Johnson, formerly of the University of Minnesota, scored an unassisted goal in the second period, and the United States held on to win, 2–1. The real star of the game was goalie Jack McCartan, who turned back 39 shots, including 20 in the second period alone.

Two days later the United States went up against the defending champions from the U.S.S.R. The Americans drew first blood after 4:04 of the first period, when Bill Cleary scored after taking a pass from his brother Bob. However the Soviets tied the score a minute later on a goal by Aleksandrov. At the 9:37 mark Bychkov struck from 15 feet in front of the cage and the U.S.S.R. led 2–1. Their lead held for the rest of the first period and most of the second until Billy Christian, with an assist from *his* brother, Roger, fired a shot past Puchkov, the Soviet goalie, to make the score 2–2. The two teams fought on even terms for the next 24 minutes. Then, with five minutes to play, the Christian brothers teamed up for another goal. From there on McCartan took over and heroically protected the U.S. goal, while the partisan overflow crowd screamed with joy. It was the first time that the United States had beaten the U.S.S.R. at ice hockey.

All that stood between the U.S. team and the Olympic championship was an eight a.m. game the next day against the same Czechoslovakian team they had beaten to open the tournament. But the Americans were so emotionally spent that they were unable to sleep, and they arrived at the arena exhausted and tense. The Czechs wasted no time, scoring their first goal after only eight seconds. After two periods, Czechoslovakia led 4–3. During the break between periods, Nikolai Sologubov, the captain of the U.S.S.R. team, entered the U.S. dressing room to give the Americans a piece of advice. Since he didn't speak English, Sologubov pantomimed that the U.S. players should take some oxygen. A tank was obtained, and the revived Americans went back on the ice with visions of the gold medals that were almost within their grasp. After almost six scoreless minutes, the U.S. team went on a rampage, as the Clearys and Christians scored six straight goals to win 9–4. The very same team that had lost to the Warroad, Minnesota, Lakers had won the Olympic gold medal.

A few words about the 1960 Australian team: They lost all six of their matches, giving up 88 goals while scoring only ten. Even when things went right for the Australians they went wrong. Trailing in the first period of a consolation match against Finland, Cunningham scored Australia's only goal of the game. In his excited attempt to follow through the shot, Australian center Ivor Vesley went straight into the net, smashed his head on the iron crossbar, and had to be taken to the hospital. Finland won, 14–1.

1964 Innsbruck T: 16, N: 16, D: 2.8.

		W	L	T	GF	GA
1. SOV/RUS	(Veniamin Aleksandrov, Aleksandr Alyimetov, Vitaly Davydov, Anatoly Firsov, Eduard Ivanov, Viktor Konovalenko, Viktor Kuzkin, Konstantin Loktev, Boris Mayorov, Yevgeny Mairov, Stanislav Petuchov, Aleksandr Ragulin, Vyacheslav Starshinov, Leonid Volkov, Victor Yakushev, Boris Zaitsev)	7	0	0	54	10
2. SWE	(Anders Andersson, Gert Blomé, Lennart Häggroth, Lennart Johansson, Nils Johansson, Sven "Tumba" Johansson, Lars Lundvall, Eilert Määttä, Hans Mild, Nils Nilsson, Bert Nordlander, Carl Öberg, Uno Öhrlund, Ronald Pettersson, Ulf Sterner, Roland Stoltz, Kjell Svensson)	5	2	0	47	16
3. CZE	(Vlastimil Bubnik, Josef Černý, Jiři Dolana, Vladimir Dzurilla, Josef Golonka, František Gregor, Jiři Holik, Jaroslav Jiřik, Jan Klapáč, Vladimir Nadrchal, Rudolf Potsch, Stanislav Pryl, Ladislav Smid, Stanislav Sventek, František Tikal, Miroslav Vlach, Jaroslav Walter)	5	2	0	38	19
4. CAN	(Henry Akervall, Gary Begg, Roger Bourbonnais, Kenneth Broderick, Raymond Cadieux, Terrence Clancy, Brian Conacher, Paul Conlin, Gary Dineen, Robert Forhan, Larry Johnston, Seth Martin, John McKenzie, Terrence O'Malley, Rodney-Albert Seiling, George-Raymond Swarbrick)	5	2	0	32	17
5. USA	(David Brooks, Herbert Brooks, Roger Christian, William Christian, Paul Coppo, Daniel Dilworth, Dates Fryberger, Paul Johnson, Thomas Martin, James McCoy, Wayne Meredith, William Reichart, Donald Ross, Patrick Rupp, Gary Schmaltzbauer, James Westby, Thomas Yurkovich)	2	5	0	29	33
6. FIN	(Raimo Kilpiö, Juhani Lahtinen, Rauno Lehtiö, Esko Luostarinen, Ilka Mäsikämmen, Seppo Nikkilä, Kalevi Numminen, Lasse Oksanen, Jorma Peltonen, Heino Pulli, Matti Reunamäki, Jouni Seistamo, Jorma Suokko, Juhani Wahlsten, Jarmo Wasama)	2	5	0	10	31

			W	L	T	GF	GA
7.	GER	(Paul Ambros, Bernd Herzig, Michael Hobelsberger, Ernst Köpf, Albert Loibl, Josef Reif, Otto Schneitberger, Georg Scholz, Siegfried Schubert, Dieter Schwimmbeck, Ernst Trautwein, Leonhard Waitl, Helmut Zanghellini)	2	5	0	13	49
8.	SWI	(Franz Berry, Roger Chappot, Rolf Diethelm, Elvin Friedrich, Gaston Furrer, Oskar Jenny, René Kiener, Pio Parolini, Kurt Pfammatter, Gerald Rigolet, Max Ruegg, Walter Salzmann, Herold Truffer, Peter Wespi, Otto Wittwer)	0	7	0	9	57

The tournament was actually much closer than the standings make it appear. If Canada had been able to defeat the U.S.S.R. in their final match, they would have finished first instead of fourth. The Canadians did in fact take a 2–1 lead, but the well-balanced Soviet team tied the score with a goal by Starshinov at the end of the second period. The U.S.S.R. gained a 3–2 victory, thanks to an early third-period goal by Veniamin Aleksandrov. During the Canada-Sweden match (won by Canada 3–1), Sweden's Karl Oberg bashed the Canadian coach, Father David Bauer, on the head with his stick. Bauer ordered his players not to retaliate. They grudgingly obeyed. The referee was suspended for two games for failing to give Oberg a 10-minute misconduct penalty.

1968 Grenoble T: 14, N: 14, D: 2.17.

			W	L	T	GF	GA
1.	SOV/RUS	(Viktor Konovalenko, Viktor Zinger, Viktor Blinov, Aleksandr Ragulin, Viktor Kuzkin, Oleg Zaitsev, Igor Romichevsky, Vitaly Davydov, Yevgeny Zymin, Vyacheslav Starshinov, Boris Mayorov, Viktor Polupanov, Anatoly Firsov, Yuri Moiseyev, Anatoly Ionov, Yevgeny Michakov, Veniamin Aleksandrov, Vladimir Vikulov)	6	1	0	48	10
2.	CZE	(Vladimir Dzurilla, Vladimir Nadrchal, Josef Horešovský, Karel Masopust, Jan Suchý, František Pospišil, Jan Hrbatý, Jiři Kochta, Jan Klapáč, Jiři Holik, František Sevčik, Jaroslav Jiřik, Josef Černý, Jan Havel, Petr Hejma, Václav Nedomanský, Jozef Golonka, Oldřich Machač, Petr Hejma)	5	1	1	33	17
3.	CAN	(Wayne Stephenson, Kenneth Broderick, Terrence O'Malley, Paul Conlin, John Barry MacKenzie, Brian Glennie, Marshall Johnstone, Francis Huck, Morris Mott, Raymond Cadieux, Gerry Pinder, Stephen Monteith, Dan O'Shea, Roger Bourbonnais, William McMillan, Ted Hargreaves, Gary Dineen, Herbert Pinder)	5	2	0	28	15
4.	SWE	(Leif Holmqvist, Hans Dahllöf, Lars-Erik Sjöberg, Arne Carlsson, Lennart Svedberg, Roland Stoltz, Nils Johansson, Björn Palmqvist, Folke Bengtsson, Carl-Göran Öberg, Håkan Wickberg, Tord Lundström, Henric Hedlund, Svante Granholm, Roger Olsson, Leif Henriksson, Lars-Göran Nilsson)	4	2	1	23	18
5.	FIN	(Urpo Ylönen, Pentti Koskela, Paavo Tirkonen, Juha Rantasila, Ilpa Koskela, Pekka Kuusisto, Lalli Partinen, Seppo Lindström, Matti Reunamäki, Juhani Wahlsten, Matti Keinonen, Lasse Oksanen, Jorma Peltonen, Esa Peltonen, Karl Johanson, Veli-Pekka Ketola, Matti Harju, Pekka Leimu)	4	3	1	28	25
6.	USA	(Herbert Brooks, John Cunniff, John Dale, Craig Falkman, Robert Paul Hurley, Thomas Hurley, Leonard Lilyholm, James Logue, John Morrison, Louis Nanne, Robert Paradise, Lawrence Pleau, Bruce Riutta, Donald Ross, Patrick Rupp, Larry Stordahl, Douglas Volmar, Patrick Loyne)	2	4	1	23	28

| 7. GER | (Ernst Köpf, Bernd Kuhn, Lorenz Funk, Gustav Hanig, Horst Meindl, Heinz Weisenbach, Leonhard Waitl, Heinz Bader, Josef Schramm, Günther Knauss, Hans Schichtl, Josef Völk, Rudolf Thanner, Manfred Gmeiner, Peter Lax, Josef Reif, Alois Schloder) | 2 | 6 | 0 | 20 | 39 |
| 8. GDR | (Ullrich Noack, Bernd Karrenbauer, Hartmut Nickel, Helmut Novy, Wolfgang Plotka, Wilfried Sock, Dieter Pürschel, Klaus Hirche, Dieter Kratzsch, Dieter Voigt, Manfred Buder, Lothar Fuchs, Peter Prusa, Joachim Ziesche, Bernd Poindl, Dietmar Peters, Bernd Hiller, Rüdiger Noack) | 1 | 7 | 0 | 16 | 49 |

The final outcome of the 1968 competition was still in doubt with only two matches left to be played. The heavily favored Soviet team had received a shocking 5–4 defeat at the hands of Czechoslavakia, their first loss since 1963. This meant that the championship hinged on the games between Czechoslovakia and Sweden and the U.S.S.R. and Canada, all of whom had records of five wins and one loss. A Czech win combined with a Soviet win would give the gold medal to Czechoslovakia. However, the overcautious Czechoslovakian players, physically and emotionally exhausted by their upset victory over the U.S.S.R. in their previous game, fell behind the determined Swedes 2–1 late in the second period. They managed to score one goal to tie in the seventh minute of the final period, but that was all. The game ended in a 2–2 draw, which closed the door on Czechoslovakia's chances for first place. This left the Canada-U.S.S.R. match to decide the winner. Firsov scored first for the Soviets after 14:51. Michakov made it 2–0 after 12:44 of the second period. Three more Soviet goals in the final period settled the issue, 5–0 for the U.S.S.R.

1972 Sapporo T: 11, N: 11, D: 2.13.

		W	L	T	GF	GA
1. SOV/RUS	(Vladislav Tretiak, Aleksandr Pachkov, Vitaly Davydov, Vladimir Lutchenko, Aleksandr Ragulin, Viktor Kuzkin, Gennady Tsygankov, Valery Vasilyev, Valery Kharlamov, Yuri Blinov, Vladimir Petrov, Anatoly Firsov, Aleksandr Maltsev, Vladimir Chadrin, Boris Mikhailov, Vladimir Vikulov, Aleksandr Yakushev)	4	0	1	33	13
2. USA	(Michael Curran, Peter Sears, James McElmury, Thomas Mellor, Frank Sanders, Charles Brown, Richard McGlynn, Walter Olds, Kevin Ahearn, Stuart Irving, Mark Howe, Henry Boucha, Keith Christiansen, Robbie Ftorek, Ronald Naslund, Craig Sarner, Timothy Sheehy)	4	2	0	23	18
3. CZE	(Vladimir Dzurilla, Jiři Holeček, František Pospišil, Karel Vohralik, Josef Horešovský, Oldřich Machač, Vladimir Bednář, Rudolf Tajcnár, Josef Černý, Jiři Holik, Bohuslav Štastný, Richard Farda, Ivan Hlinka, Vacláv Nedomanský, Jiři Kochta, Vladimir Martinec, Eduard Novák, Jaroslav Holik)	4	2	0	34	15
4. SWE	(Leif Holmqvist, Christer Abrahamsson, Thomas Abrahamsson, Lars-Erik Sjöberg, Kjell-Rune Milton, Stig Östling, Bert-Ola Nordlander, Kenneth Ekman, Tord Lundstrom, Lars-Göran Nilsson, Håkan Pettersson, Håkan Wickberg, Mats Åhlberg, Björn Palmqvist, Hans Hansson, Inge Hammarström, Hans Lindberg, Thomas Bergman, Stig-Göran Johansson, Mats Lindh)	3	2	1	25	14

		W	L	T	GF	GA
5. FIN	(Jorma Valtonen, Stig Wetzell, Ilpo Koskela, Seppo Lindström, Heikki Riihiranta, Heikki Järn, Juha Rantasila, Pekka Marjamäki, Jorma Vehmanen, Jorma Peltonen, Veli-Pekka Ketola, Matti Murto, Matti Keinonen, Harri Linnonmaa, Juhani Tamminen, Lasse Oksanen, Esa Peltonen, Jorma Peltonen, Seppo Repo, Lauri Mononen, Timo Turunen)	3	3	0	27	25
6. POL	(Andrzej Tkacz, Walery Kosyl, Ludwik Czachowski, Stanislaw Fryźlewicz, Jerzy Potz, Marian Feter, Adam Kopczyński, Andrzej Szczepaniec, Feliks Góralczyk, Tadeusz Kacik, Krzysztof Bialynicki, Józef Slowakiewicz, Leszek Tokarz, Wieslaw Tkacz, Józef Batkiewicz, Tadeusz Oblój, Walenty Ziętara, Robert Góralczyck, Stefan Chowaniec)	1	5	0	13	39
7. GER	(Anton Kehle, Rainer Makatsch, Otto Schneitberger, Josef Völk, Werner Modes, Paul Langner, Rudolf Thanner, Karl Egger, Rainer Phillip, Bernd Kuhn, Reinhold Bauer, Johann Eimannsberger, Lorenz Funk, Erich Kühnhackl, Alois Schloder, Anton Hofherr, Hans Rothkirch)	3	2	0	22	14
8. NOR	(Kåre Østensen, Tore Wålberg, Øyvind Berg, Jan Kinder, Svein Hansen, Terje Steen, Birger Jansen, Thor Martinsen, Tom Røymark, Thom Kristensen, Steinar Bjølbakk, Svein Haagensen, Roy Jansen, Bjørn Johansen, Morten Sethereng, Terje Thoen, Arne Mikkelsen)	3	2	0	17	27

Again the championship was decided by the final match—this time between the U.S.S.R. and Czechoslovakia. The winner-take-all game turned out to be an anticlimax, as the Soviet team took a 4–0 lead in the second period and coasted to a 5–2 victory. The United States was awarded second place because they had beaten Czechoslovakia, 5–1. For the first time since the Winter Olympics began, Canada did not take part in the ice hockey tournament. The Canadians withdrew from international amateur competition in 1969 because they objected to facing the professional amateurs of the U.S.S.R. and other Communist countries. Sweden joined the Olympic ice hockey boycott in 1976, but both nations returned in 1980.

1976 Innsbruck T: 12, N: 12, D: 2.14.

		W	L	GF	GA
1. SOV/RUS	(Vladislav Tretiak, Aleksandr Sidelnikov, Boris Aleksandrov, Sergei Babinov, Aleksandr Gusiev, Valery Kharlamov, Aleksandr Yakushev, Viktor Zlukov, Sergei Kapustin, Vladimir Lutchenko, Yuri Lyapkin, Aleksandr Maltsev, Boris Mikhailov, Vladimir Petrov, Vladimir Chadrin, Viktor Szalimov, Gennady Tsygankov, Valery Vasilyev)	5	0	40	11
2. CZE	(Jiři Holeček, Jiři Crha, Oldřich Machač, Milan Chalupa, František Pospišil, Miroslav Dvořák, Milan Kajkl, Jiři Bubla, Milan Nový, Vladimir Martinec, Jiři Novák, Bohuslav Šťastný, Jiri Holik, Ivan Hlinka, Eduard Novák, Jaroslav Pouzar, Bohuslav Ebermann, Josef Augusta)	2	2	17	10
3. GER	(Erich Weishaupt, Anton Kehle, Rudolf Thanner, Josef Völk, Udo Kiessling, Stefan Metz, Klaus Auhuber, Ignaz Berndaner, Rainer Philipp, Lorenz Funk, Wolfgang Boos, Ernst Köpf, Ferenc Vozar, Walter Köberle, Erich Kühnhackl, Alois Schloder, Martin Hinterstocker, Franz Reindl)	2	3	21	24
4. FIN	(Matti Hagman, Reijo Laksola, Antti Leppänen, Henry Leppä, Seppo Lindström, Pekka Marjamäki, Matti Murto, Timo Nummelin, Esa Peltonen, Timo Saari, Jorma Vehmanen, Urpo Ylönen, Hannu Haapalainen, Seppo Ahokainen, Tapio Koskinen, Pertti Koivulahti, Hannu Kapanen, Matti Rautiainen)	2	3	19	18

		W	L	T	GF	GA

5. USA (Steven Alley, Daniel Bolduc, Blane Comstock, Robert Dobek, Robert Harris, Jeffrey Hymanson, Paul Jensen, Steven Jensen, Richard Lamby, Robert Lundeen, Robert Miller, Douglas Ross, Gary Ross, William "Buzz" Schneider, Stephen Sertich, John Taft, Theodore Thorndike, James Warden) 2 3 15 21

6. POL (Stefan Chowaniec, Andrzej Tkacz, Andrzej Iskrzycki, Marek Marciń- czak, Josef Matiewicz, Tadeusz Obój, Jerzy Potz, Andrzej Slowakie- wicz, Andrzej Zabawa, Walenty Ziętara, Karol Żurek, Walery Kosyl, Robert Góralczyk, Kordian Jajszczok, Wieslaw Jobezyk, Leszek Ko- koszka, Henryk Pytel, Mieczyslaw Jaskierski, Marian Kajzerek) 0 4 9 37

7. ROM (Valerian Netedu, Vasile Morar, Elöd Antal, Sandor Gall, George Justinian, Ion Ionita, Desideriu Varga, Doru Morosan, Doru Tureanu, Dumitru Axinte, Eduard Pana, Vasile Hutanu, Ion Gheorghiu, Tibri Miclos, Alexandru Halauca, Marian Pisaru, Nicolae Visan) 4 1 23 15

8. AUT (Daniel Gritsch, Franz Schilcher, Walter Schneider, Gerhard Hausner, Johann Schuller, Michael Herzog, Günther Oberhuber, Othmar Russ, Max Moser, Rudolf Koenig, Josef Ruschnig, Franz Voves, Josef Schwitzer, Peter Cini, Josef Kriechbaum, Alexander Sadjina, Herbert Poek, Herbert Moertl) 3 2 18 14

The tournament was thrown into confusion when Czechoslovakia's captain, František Pospišil, was chosen for a random drug test after a victory over Poland. The team trainer immediately admitted that Pospišil had been given codeine to combat a virus infection. The I.O.C. expelled Pospišil and ordered the game against Poland declared null and void. The final decision on the case was actually delayed, so as not to spoil the drama of the winner-take-all game between Czecho- slovakia and the U.S.S.R. In that match, the Czechs led 3–2 in the final period. But with five minutes to play Aleksandr Yakushev tied the score. Twenty-four seconds later Valery Kharlamov knocked the puck into the net again to give the U.S.S.R. their fourth straight set of gold medals in ice hockey.

1980 Lake Placid T: 12, N: 12, D: 2.24.

		W	L	T	GF	GA

1. USA (James Craig, Kenneth Morrow, Michael Ramsey, William Baker, John O'Callahan, Bob Suter, David Silk, Neal Broten, Mark John- son, Steven Christoff, Mark Wells, Mark Pavelich, Eric Strobel, Michael Eruzione, David Christian, Robert McClanahan, William "Buzz" Schneider, Philip Verchota, John Harrington) 6 0 1 33 15

2. SOV (Vladimir Myshkin, Vladislav Tretiak, Vyacheslav Fetisov, Vasily Pervukhin, Valery Vasilyev, Aleksei Kasatonov, Sergei Starikov, Zinetula Bilyaletdinov, Vladimir Krutov, Aleksandr Maltsev, Yuri Lebedev, Boris Mikhailov, Vladimir Petrov, Valery Kharlamov, Hel- mūts Balderis, Viktor Zlukov, Aleksandr Golikov, Sergei Makarov, Vladimir Golikov, Aleksandr Skvortsov) 6 1 0 63 17

3. SWE (Per-Eric "Pelle" Lindbergh, William Löfqvist, Tomas Jonsson, Sture Andersson, Ulf Weinstock, Jan Eriksson, Tommy Samuel- sson, Mats Waltin, Thomas Eriksson, Per Lundqvist, Mats Åhlberg, Håkan Eriksson, Mats Näslund, Lennart Norberg, Bengt Lundholm, Leif Holmgren, Dan Söderström, Harald Lückner, Lars Mohlin, Bo Berglund) 4 1 2 31 19

4. FIN (Antero Kivelä, Jorma Valtonen, Seppo Suoraniemi, Olli Saari- nen, Hannu Haapalainen, Tapio Levo, Kari Eloranta, Lasse Litma, Esa Peltonen, Ismo Villa, Mikko Leinonen, Markku Kiimalainen, Jari Kurri, Jukka Koskilahti, Hannu Koskinen, Reijo Leppänen, Markku Hakulinen, JUkka Porvari, Jarmo Mäkitalo, Timo Susi) 3 3 1 31 25

			W	L	T	GF	GA
5.	CZE	(Jiři Kralik, Karel Lang, Jan Neliba, Vitezslav Duras, Milan Chalupa, Arnold Kadleč, Miroslav Dvořak, František Kaberle, Jiři Bubla, Milan Nový, Jiři Novák, Miroslav Frycer, Marian Štastný, Anton Štastný, Vincent Lukač, Karel Holy, Jaroslav Pouzar, Bohuslav Ebermann, Peter Štastný)	4	2	0	40	17
6.	CAN	(Robert Dupuis, Paul Pageau, Warren Anderson, J. Bradley Pirie, Randall Gregg, Timothy Watters, D. Joseph Grant, Donald Spring, Terrence O'Malley, Ronald Davidson, Glenn Anderson, Kevin Maxwell, James Nill, John Devaney, Paul Maclean, Daniel D'Alvise, Ken Berry, David Hindmarch, Kevin Primeau, Stelio Zupancich)	3	3	0	29	18
7.	POL	(Henryk Wojtynek, Pawel Lukaszka, Andrzej Ujwary, Henryk Janiszewski, Henryk Gruth, Andrzej Jańczy, Jerzy Potz, Ludwik Synowiec, Marek Marcińczak, Stefan Chowaniec, Wieslaw Jobczyk, Tadeusz Oblój, Dariusz Sikora, Leszek Kokoszka, Andrzej Zabawa, Henryk Pytel, Stanislaw Klocek, Leszek Jachna, Bogdan Dziubiński, Andrzej Malysiak)	2	3	0	15	23
7.	ROM	(Valerian Netedu, Gheorghe Hutan, Mihail Popescu, Ion Berdila, Sandor Gall, Elöd Antal, Istvan Antal, Doru Morosan, George Justinian, Doru Tureanu, Dumitru Axinte, Marian Costea, Constantin Nistor, Alexandru Halauca, Laszlo Solyom, Bela Nagy, Traian Cazacu, Adrian Olenici, Marian Pisaru, Zoltan Nagy)	1	3	1	13	29

Just as Canada dominated Olympic ice hockey from 1920 through 1952, so the Soviet Union took control after that. Between 1956 and 1992 the U.S.S.R. played 68 games, tallying 60 victories, six defeats, and two ties. In those 68 games they scored 457 goals while giving up only 125. The only nation to break the Soviet monopoly was the United States, which won the ice hockey tournament the two times during that period that the Winter Olympics were held in the United States—in 1960 and 1980. The 1960 and 1980 U.S. squads were remarkably similar. Both were patchwork teams whose success was completely unexpected. Both teams put together a series of upsets and come-from-behind wins, culminating in a come-from-behind victory over the favored Soviet team followed by one final come-from-behind performance against a lesser opponent, who almost spoiled the whole drama.

But there *were* two important differences. The first was television. In 1960 appreciation of the thrilling victories of the U.S. team was limited mostly to sports fans. In 1980 the excitement of the tournament reached into almost every U.S. household and united the country in a remarkable manner. The other difference was the mood of the country. In 1960 most Americans were feeling prosperous and proud. The victory of the Olympic ice hockey team was basically perceived as a pleasant surprise. In 1980 the United States was in the midst of an identity crisis. It is difficult for most people in the world to understand that Americans, as a nation, could ever feel persecuted and mistreated, but that was the case in 1980. With hostages in Iran, Russians in Afghanistan, and inflation on the rise, it seemed that nothing was going right. When President Jimmy Carter ordered a boycott of the Summer Olympics, Americans were left with the Winter Olympics as their only vehicle for regaining a sense of pride in the world arena. The problem was that speed skater Eric Heiden was the only likely prospect for a gold medal that the U.S. had. Then, with theatrically perfect timing, the 20 young men who comprised the U.S. ice hockey team showed up to offer the ideal tonic to cure the American malaise.

Nine of the U.S. players were from the University of Minnesota, as was the coach, two-time Olympian Herb Brooks. Known as "The Khomeini of Ice Hockey," Brooks was a fanatic disciplinarian who told his young team (average age: 22), "Gentlemen, you don't have enough talent to win on talent alone." Instead they played 63 exhibition games, including a final match, three days before the Olympics opened, against the same U.S.S.R. team that had beaten the National Hockey League All-Stars. The U.S. Olympic team was crushed by the Soviets, 10–3. When the tournament began, the United States was seeded seventh out of 12 teams.

The teams were split into two round-robin divisions. The first- and second-place teams in each division would then advance to a final round-robin of four teams. Favored to advance from the division in which the United States had been placed were Czechoslovakia and Sweden, who happened to be the Americans' first two opponents. In the opening game between the United States and Sweden, the Swedes scored first and led 2–1 as the contest entered its final minute. In desperation, Brooks pulled goalie Jim Craig and put in an extra skater. The gamble paid off as Bill Baker slammed in a shot from 55 feet with 27 seconds left in the game, allowing the United States to escape with a tie. Next came the powerful Czech team. Again the United States gave up the first goal, this time after only 2:23 of the first period. However, the Americans had the game tied up 2–2 by the end of the period. Then, surprisingly, they forged ahead to a shocking 7–3 victory. By this time the U.S. ice hockey team had attracted the nation's attention. In their third game, they spotted Norway a 1–0 lead and then scored five goals in the last two periods to win 5–1. Their next match, against Romania, a 7–2 victory, was notable because it was the only one of seven games in which the Americans scored first. Against West Germany they fell behind 2–0 and then won 4–2.

This put the United States into the medal round along with Sweden, Finland, and the U.S.S.R. The 2–2 tie with Sweden was carried over as part of the final round-robin, as was the Soviets' 4–2 victory over Finland. At five p.m. on Friday, February 22, the U.S. team went out onto the ice to face the best ice hockey team in the world, professional or amateur. That morning Coach Brooks had given his team an uncharacteristic pep talk. "You're born to be a player," he said. "You're meant to be here. This moment is yours. You're meant to be here at this time." Not surprisingly, the U.S.S.R. scored the first goal, as Vladimir Krutov cut off a slap shot by Aleksei Kasatonov and deflected it into the net. Buzz Schneider evened the score five minutes later, but three and a half minutes after that Sergei Makorov put the Soviets ahead again. It looked like the period would end with the score 2–1, but Mark Johnson knocked in a blocked shot with one second left, to bring the United States even once more.

When the second period began, Vladislav Tretiak, considered by many to be the best goalie in the world, had been replaced by Vladimir Myshkin. The U.S.S.R. quickly moved back into the lead on a power-play goal by Aleksandr Maltsev at 2:18, and the period ended with the Soviets ahead 3–2. Amazed to find themselves only one goal behind with 20 minutes to play, the U.S. players sensed their destiny. After 8:39 of the third period Mark Johnson picked up the puck as it slipped away from a Soviet defender and shoveled it past Myshkin from five feet out. The United States was tied again. Less than one and a half minutes later, at the ten-minute mark, team captain Mike Eruzione, using a Soviet defender as a screen, fired off a 30-foot shot that went through Myshkin and into the net. The partisan crowd burst into wild cheering that continued for the rest of the game. For the final 10 minutes goalie Jim Craig (who recorded 39 saves in the game) and the rest of the U.S. team fought off a seemingly endless barrage of attacks by the Soviets. When the last seconds had finally ticked off, the emotional excitement that filled the arena was so great that even many of the Soviet players had to smile as they congratulated their American counterparts. Back in the dressing room, the U.S. team sang "God Bless America," even though they couldn't remember all the words. Meanwhile, Coach Brooks had locked himself in the men's room with his emotions. "Finally I snuck out into the hall," he said, "and the state troopers were all standing there crying."

But there was still one more game to be played. In fact, if the United States lost to Finland on February 24, they would only finish in third place, and the U.S.S.R. would win the tournament anyway. And the Finns were not prepared to roll over and concede defeat. They scored first and led 2–1 after two periods. But the Americans had come too far to lose it all in the final match. Dave Christian, whose father and uncle had been members of the 1960 U.S. squad, sent a pass to Phil Verchota, who sped down the left side of the ice and tied the score with a 15-foot shot at 2:25. At 6:05 Rob McClanahan put the United States in the lead with a stuff shot, and at 16:25 Mark Johnson scored an insurance goal. When the game ended three and a half minutes later, the score was 4–2. American TV viewers were treated to two more emotional moments. While the rest of the team jumped for joy and hugged each other, Jim Craig skated around the rink until he found in the crowd the one person with whom he most wanted to share this moment—his widowed father. Later, at the medal ceremony, Mike Eruzione took the stand as the captain of his team. But after the playing of "The Star-Spangled Banner," he called his teammates onto the platform to join him in accepting the cheers of the crowd. Twelve years later, Jim Craig was still receiving 600 fan letters a year.

The 1980 U.S. ice hockey team celebrates its final victory over Finland.

1984 Sarajevo T: 12, N: 12, D: 2.19.

		W	L	T	GF	GA
1. SOV/RUS	(Zinatula Bilyaletdinov, Sergei Chepelev, Nikolai Drozdetsky, Vyacheslav Fetisov, Aleksandr Gerasimov, Aleksei Kasatonov, Andrei Komutov, Vladimir Kovin, Aleksandr Kozhernikov, Vladimir Krutov, Igor Larionov, Sergei Makarov, Vladimir Myshkin, Vasily Pervukhin, Aleksandr Skvortsov, Sergei Starikov, Igor Stelnov, Vladislav Tretiak, Victor Tumenev, Michail Vasiliev)	7	0	0	48	5
2. CZE	(Jaroslav Benák, Vladimir Caldr, František Cernik, Milan Chalupa, Miloslav Horava, Jiří Hrdina, Arnold Kadlec, Jaroslav Korbela, Jiří Králik, Vladimir Kynos, Jiří Lála, Igor Liba, Vincent Lukáč, Dušan Pašek, Pavel Richter, Darius Rusnák, Vladimir Růzička, Jaromir Sindel, Radoslav Svoboda, Eduard Uvíra)	6	1	0	40	9
3. SWE	(Thomas Ahlen, Per-Erik Eklund, Thomas Eklund, Bo Ericsson, Lars Erikson, Peter Gradin, Mats Hessel, Peter Michael Hjälm, Göran Lindblom, Tommy Mörth, Leif Nordin, Jens Öhling, Rolf-Lennart Riddervall, Thomas Rundquist, Tomas Sandström, Karl Södergren, Mats Thelin, Arne Thelvén, Göte Wälitalo, Mats Waltin)	4	2	1	36	17
4. CAN	(Warren Anderson, Robin Bartel, Russ Courtnall, Jean Daigneault, Kevin Dineen, Dave Donnelly, Bruce Driver, Darren Eliot, Pat Flatley, Dave Gagner, Mario Gosselin, Vaugh Karpan, Doug Lidster, Darren Lowe, Kirk Muller, James Patrick, Craig Redmond, Dave Tippett, Carey Wilson, Dan Wood)	4	3	0	24	16
5. GER	(Manfred Ahne, Ignaz Berndaner, Michael Betz, Bernhard Englbrecht, Karl Friesen, Dieter Hegen, Ulrich Hiemer, Ernst Höfner, Udo Kiessling, Harold Kreis, Marcus Kuhl, Erich Kühnhackl, Andreas Niederberger, Joachim Reil Franz Reindl, Roy Roedger, Peter Scharf, Helmut Steiger, Gerhard Truntschka, Manfred Wolf)	4	1	1	34	21
6. FIN	(Raimo Helminen, Risto Jalo, Arto Javanainen, Timo Jutila, Erkki Laine, Markus Lehto, Mika Lehto, Pertti Lehtonen, Jarmo Mäkitalo, Anssi Melametsä, Hannu Oksanen, Arto Ruotanen, Simo Saarinen, Ville Siren, Arto Sirviö, Perti Skriko, Raimo Summanen, Kari Takko, Juka Tammi, Harri Tuohimaa, Jorma Valtonen)	2	3	1	31	26
7. USA	(Marc Behrend, Barry Scott Bjugstad, Robert Brooke, Chris Chelios, Richard Costello, Mark Fusco, Scott Fusco, Steven Griffith, Paul Guay, Gary Haight, John Harrington, Tomas Hirsch, Al Iafrate, David A. Jensen, David H. Jensen, Kurt Kleinendorst, Mark Kumpel, Pat Lafontaine, Robert Mason, Corey Millen, Edward Olczyk, Gary Sampson, Tim Thomas, Philip Verchota)	2	2	2	23	21
8. POL	(Janusz Adamiec, Marek Cholewa, Andrzey Chowaniec, Jerzy Christ, Jozef Chrzastek, Czeslaw Drozd, Bogdan Gebczyk, Henrik Gruth, Andrzej Hachula, Andrzej Hanisz, Leszek Jachna, Wieslaw Jobszyk, Stanislaw Klocek, Andrzey Nowak, Wlodzimierz Olszewski, Bogdan Pawlik, Jan Piecko, Henryk Pytel, Gabriel Samolej, Dariusz Sikora, Krystian Sikorski, Jan Stopczyk, Ludwik Synowiec, Robert Szopinski, Andrzej Ujwary, Andrzey Zabawa)	1	5	0	20	44

With the Winter Olympics once again being held outside the United States, the ice hockey tournament returned to normalcy. As usual, the Soviets overwhelmed every team they played. Even their final 2–0 victory over Czechoslovakia was never really in doubt. The U.S. team, seeded seventh, finished seventh.

1988 Calgary T: 12, N: 12, D: 2.28.

		W	L	T	GF	GA
1. SOV/RUS	(Ilya Byakin, Igor Stelnov, Vyacheslav Fetisov, Aleksei Gusarov, Aleksei Kasatonov, Sergei Starikov, Vyacheslav Bykov, Sergei Yashin, Valery Kamensky, Sergei Svetlov, Aleksandr Chernykh, Andrei Khomutov, Vladimir Krutov, Igor Larionov, Andrei Lomakin, Sergei Makarov, Aleksandr Mogilny, Anatoly Semenov, Aleksandr Kozhevnikov, Igor Kravchuk, Vitaly Samoylov, Sergei Mylnikov)	7	1	0	45	13
2. FIN	(Timo Blomqvist, Kari Eloranta, Jyrki Lumme, Jukka Virtanen, Arto Ruotanen, Reijo Ruotsalainen, Simo Saarinen, Kai Suikkanen, Raimo Helminen, Iiro Järvi, Esa Keskinen, Erkki Lehtonen, Reijo Mikkolainen, Janne Ojanen, Timo Susi, Pekka Tuomisto, Teppo Numminen, Jari Torkki, Jukka Tammi, Jarmo Myllys)	5	2	1	34	14
3. SWE	(Peter Andersson, Anders Eldebrink, Lars Ivarsson, Lars Karlsson, Mats Kihlström, Tommy Samuelsson, Mikael Andersson, Bo Berglund, Jonas Bergqvist, Peter Eriksson, Michael Hjälm, Mikael Johansson, Lars Molin, Lars-Gunnar Pettersson, Thomas Rundqvist, Ulf Sandström, Håkan Södergren, Jens Öhling, Thomas Eriksson, Thom Eklund, Peter Åslin, Anders Bergman, Peter Lindmark)	4	1	3	33	21
4. CAN	(Chris Felix, Randy Gregg, Timothy Watters, Anthony Stiles, Trent Yawney, Zarley Zalapski, Claude Vilgrain, Kenneth Berry, Serge Boisvert, Brian Bradley, Ken Yaremchuk, Marc Habscheid, Robert Joyce, Vaughn Karpan, Merlin Malinowski, Steven Tambellini, Wallace Schreiber, Gordon Sherven, Serge Roy, Jim Peplinski, Sean Burke, Andrew Moog)	5	2	1	31	21
5. GER	(Ron Fischer, Udo Kiessling, Horst-Peter Kretschmer, Dieter Medicus, Andreas Niederberger, Harold Kreis, Manfred Schuster, Manfred Wolf, Christian Brittig, Peter Draisaitl, Georg Franz, Dieter Hegen, Georg Holzmann, Peter Obresa, Roy Roedger, Peter Schiller, Helmut Steiger, Gerd Truntschka, Bernd Truntschka, Joachim Reil, Helmut de Raaf, Karl-Heinz Friesen, Josef Schlickenrieder)	5	3	0	25	27
6. CZE	(Jaroslav Benák, Mojmir Božik, Rudolf Suchánek, Miloslav Hořava, Bedrich Ščerban, Antonin Stavjaňa, Jiří Sejba, Jiří Doležal, Oto Haščák, Jiří Hrdina, Rostislav Vlach, Jiří Lála, Igor Liba, Petr Vlk, David Volek, Dušan Pašek, Petr Rosol, Vladimir Růžička, Radim Raděvic, Eduard Uvíra, Dominik Hašek, Jaromir Šindel, Petr Bříza)	4	4	0	33	28
7. USA	(Greg Brown, Guy Gosselin, Peter Laviolette, Jeffrey Norton, Eric Weinrich, Dave Snuggerud, Allen Bourbeau, Kevin Stevens, John Donatelli, Scott Fusco, Tony Granato, Craig Janney, James Johannson, Scott Young, Stephen Leach, Bradley MacDonald, Cory Millen, Kevin Miller, Brian Leetch, Todd Okerlund, Michael Richter, Chris Terreri, John Blue)	3	3	0	35	31
8. SWI	(Patrice Brasey, André Künzi, Jakob Kölliker, Fausto Mazzoleni, Andreas Ritsch, Bruno Rogger, Philipp Neuenschwander, Gaëtan Boucher, Manuele Celio, Thomas Vrabec, Jörg Eberle, Felix Hollenstein, Peter Jaks, Roman Wäger, Markus Leuenberger, Fredy Lüthi, Gil Montandon, Peter Schlagenhauf, Urs Burkart, Andreas Zehnder, Thomas Mueller, Pietro Cunti, Olivier Anken, Richard Bucher, Renato Tosio)	3	3	0	23	18

In the weeks leading up to the Calgary Olympics, the international press was filled with articles declaring the end of the Soviet ice hockey dynasty. Perhaps the team from the U.S.S.R. was still favored, but only by a slight margin. But once the tournament began, it was clear that nothing had changed. The Soviets cruised through the preliminary round, then crushed Canada 5–0 and Sweden 7–1. They did lose 2–1 to Finland in their final match, but by that time they had already clinched first place.

1992 Albertville-Méribel T: 12, N: 12, D: 2.23.

			W	L	T	GF	GA
1.	SOV	(Sergei Bautin, Igor Boldin, Nikolai Borchevsky, Vyacheslav Butsayev, Vyacheslav Bykov, Mikhail Shtalenkov, Yevgeny Davydov, Aleksei Zhamnov, Aleksei Zhitnik, Darus Kasparaitis, Yuri Khmylev, Andrei Khomutov, Andrei Kovalenko, Aleksei Kovalev, Igor Kravchuk, Vladimir Malakhov, Dmitri Mironov, Sergei Petrenko, Vitaly Prokhorov, Andrei Trefilov, Dmitri Yuchkevich, Sergei Zubov)	7	1	0	46	14
2.	CAN	(David Archibald, Todd Brost, Sean Burke, Kevin Dahl, Curt Giles, David Hannan, Gordon Hynes, Fabian Joseph, Joe Juneau, Trevor Kidd, Patrick Lebeau, Chris Lindberg, Eric Lindros, Kent Manderville, Adrian Plavsic, Dan Ratushny, Brad Schlegel, Wallace Schreiber, Randy Smith, David Tippett, Brian Tutt, Jason Wooley)	6	2	0	37	17
3.	CZE	(Petr Bríza, Oldrich Svoboda, Leo Gudas, Miloslav Horava, Drahomir Kadlec, Bedrich Scerban, Richard Smehlik, Frantisek Prochazka, Robert Svehla, Petr Rosol, Robert Lang, Kamil Kasták, Richard Zemlicka, Ladislav Lubina, Radek Toupal, Peter Veselovsky, Petr Hrbek, Otakar Janecky, Patrick Augusta, Jirí Slegr, Tomas Jelinek, Igor Liba)	6	2	0	36	21
4.	USA	(Greg Brown, Clark Donatelli, Theodore Donato, Thedore Drury, David Emma, Scott Gordon, Guy Gosselin, Bret Hedican, Steve Heinze, Sean Hill, James Johannson, Scott Lachance, Ray LeBlanc, Moe Mantha, Shawn McEachern, Marty McInnis, Joe Sacco, Tim Sweeney, Keith Tkachuk, David Tretowicz, Carl Young, Scott Young)	5	3	0	25	19
5.	SWE	(Peter Andersson, Peter Andersson, Charles Berglund, Patrik Carnbäck, Lars Edström, Patrik Erickson, Bengt-Åke Gustavsson, Mikael Johansson, Kenneth Kennholt, Patric Kjellberg, Petri Liimatainen, Håkan Loob, Roger Nordström, Mats Näslund, Peter Ottosson, Thomas Rundqvist, Daniel Rydmark, Börje Salming, Tommy Sjödin, Fredrik Stillman, Tommy Söderström, Jan Viktorsson)	5	3	0	30	19
6.	GER	(Richard Amann, Thomas Brandl, Andreas Brockmann, Peter Draisaitl, Ronald Fischer, Karl Friesen, Dieter Hegen, Michael Heidt, Joseph Heiss, Ulrich Hiemer, Raimond Hilger, Georg Holzmann, Axel Kammerer, Udo Kiessling, Ernst Köpf, Jörg Mayr, Andreas Niederberger, Helmut De Raaf, Jürgen Rumrich, Michael Rumrich, Michael Schmidt, Bernd Truntschka, Gerd Truntschka)	3	5	0	22	24
7.	FIN	(Pekka Tuomisto, Markus Ketterer, Jukka Tammi, Timo Blomqvist, Kari Eloranta, Timo Jutila, Janne Laukkanen, Harri Laurila, Arto Ruotanen, Simo Saarinen, Ville-Jussi Siren, Raimo Helminen, Hannu Järvenpää, Jari Lindroos, Mikko Mäkelä, Mika Nieminen, Timo Peltomaa, Timo Saarikoski, Teemu Selänne, Petri Skriko, Raimo Summanen, Keijo Säilynoja)	4	3	1	29	21

			W	L	T	GF	GA
8. FRA	(Peter Almasy, Michaël Babin, Stéphane Barin, Stépane Botteri, Philippe Bozon, Arnaud Briand, Yves Crettenand, Jean-Marc Djian, Patrick Dunn, Gerald Guennelon, Benoît Laporte, Michel Leblanc, Jean-Philippe Lemoine, Pascal Margerit, Denis Perez, Serge Poudrier, Christian Pouget, Pierre Pousse, Antoine Richer, Bruno Saunier, Christophe Ville, Petri Ylonen)		2	6	0	20	36

Final: SOV 3–1 CAN
3rd Place: CZE 6–1 USA
5th Place: SWE 4–3 GER
7th Place: FIN 4–1 FRA

In 1992, the ex–Soviet Union, now known as the Unified Team, was again considered vulnerable, especially after finishing only third at the 1991 Swedish-won world championship. The warnings seemed justified when Czechoslovakia beat them 4–3 in a preliminary match. It was only the fourth loss by a Soviet team in the last eight Olympics. But then the Czechoslovaks were beaten 5–1 by Canada, and the Unified Team came back to defeat the Canadians 5–4. This left Canada, the Unified Team, and Czechoslovakia in a three-way tie for first place in pool B. The tie-breaking rule—goal differential in games played among the three—put Canada on top of the pool and gave them the right to play Germany, which had placed fourth in pool A with a mediocre record of two wins and three losses, in the quarter-finals.

However, what should have been an easy victory for Canada turned out to be a thrilling and memorable contest. Trailing 2–3, the Germans scored with 2:22 to go in the third period and sent the game into sudden-death overtime. When neither team scored after 10 minutes, a five-man shoot-out was called for. Canada took a 2–0 lead, but the Germans made their last two shots to put the match into a new phase: sudden-death shoot-out. Eric Lindros shot first for Canada and scored. Peter Draisaitl came up for Germany. If he scored, the shoot-out would continue. If he missed, Canada would advance to the semifinals. Draisaitl squeezed the puck through goalie Sean Burke's legs, but Burke managed to slow it down with his pads. The puck rolled toward the goal, wobbled, and landed *on* the goal line. According to the rules of hockey, a point isn't scored unless the puck goes *past* the goal line. Canada escaped a possible major upset by one inch. One of the other quarter-finals saw the world champion Swedish team defeated 3–1 by Czechoslovakia.

In the first semifinal, the Unified Team broke open a 2–2 tie with the United States midway through the third period by scoring three goals in 6¼ minutes. In the second semi, Canada scored twice in the final period to beat Czechoslovakia 4–2.

The final was scoreless after two periods. Vyacheslav Butsayev struck first at the 1:01 mark of the third period. Igor Boldin made it 2–0 at 15:54. Lindberg of Canada scored at 17:20, but a final goal by Vyacheslav Bykov sealed another Olympic championship for the ex–Soviets. The victors were the youngest team in the tournament as well as the least penalized. Although the team was overwhelmingly Russian, one member, Darus Kasparaitis, was actually from Lithuania even though Lithuania was competing as a separate nation in Albertville.

1994 Lillehammer T: 12, N: 12, D: 2.27.

			W	L	T	GF	GA
1. SWE	(Håken Algotsson, Tomas Jonsson, Christian Due-Boje, Patrik Juhlin, Leif Rohlin, Magnus Svensson, Roger Hansson, Håken Loob, Fredrik Stillman, Stefan Ørnskog, Niklas Eriksson, Daniel Rydmark, Jonas Bergkvist, Kenny Jönsson, Jörgen Jönsson, Peter Forsberg, Charles Berglund, Andreas Dackell, Mats Näslund, Patric Kjellberg, Roger Johansson, Tommy Salo)		6	1	1	32	18

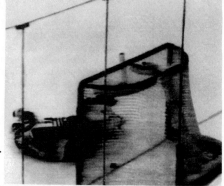

During the 1992 quarterfinal shootout between Canada and Germany, the German-shot puck stops on the line without going over, thus preserving the victory for Canada.

2. CAN (Corey Hirsch, Adrian Aucoin, Derek Mayer, Ken Lovsin, Todd **5 2 1 27 18** Hlushko, Brad Warenka, Fabian Joseph, Paul Kariya, Dwayne Norris, Greg Johnson, Brian Savage, Wallace Schreiber, Todd Warriner, Greg Parks, Mark Astley, Jean Yves Roy, Christopher Kontos, David Harlock, Chris Therien, Bradley Schlegel, Peter Nedved)

3. FIN (Marko Kiprusov, Vesa Erik Hämäläinen, Timo Jutila, Pasi **7 1 0 38 10** Sormunen, Janne Ojanen, Esa Keskinen, Saku Koivu, Janne Laukkanen, Marko Palo, Raimo Helminen, Mika Alatalo, Ville Peltonen, Jere Lehtinen, Hannu Virta, Sami Kapanen, Mika Strömberg, Tero Lehterä, Petri Varis, Jukka Tammi, Jarmo Myllys, Mika Nieminen, Mikko Mäkelä)

4. RUS (Andrei Zuyev, Oleg Davydov, Sergei Tertychny, Sergei Sorokin, **4 4 0 26 24** Aleksandr Smirnov, Vladimir Tarasov, Aleksei Kudachov, Igor Ivanov, Georgi Yevtiukhin, Sergei Berezin, Valery Karpov, Igor Varitski, Aleksandr Vinogradov, Valery Ivannikov, Dmitri Denisov, Sergei Chendelev, Pavel Torgayev, Andrei Nikolichin, Vyacheslav Bezukladnikov, Oleg Chargorodski, Andrei Tarasenko, Ravil Gusmanov, Sergei Abramov)

5. CZE (Petr Bríza, Roman Turek, Jirí Vykoukal, Drahomir Kadlec, **5 3 0 30 18** Bedrich Scerban, Antonin Stavjana, Miloslav Horava, Jirí Veber, Kamil Kasták, Richard Zemlicka, Roman Horak, Jan Alinc, Tomas Srsen, Petr Hrbek, Tomas Kapusta, Otakar Janecky, Jirí Kucera, Martin Hostak, Pavel Geffert, Jirí Dolezal, Radek Toupal, Jan Vopat)

6. SVK (Eduard Hartmann, Jaromír Dragan, Jergus Baca, Marían **4 2 2 35 30** Smerciak, Miroslav Marcinko, Lubomír Sekerás, Vlastimil Plavucha, Oto Hascák, Vladimir Búril, Dusan Pohorelec, René Pucher, Miroslav Satan, Branislav Janós, Roman Kontsek, Miroslav Michalek, Stanislav Medrík, Peter Stastny, Ján Varholík, Lubomír Kolník, Jozef Dano, Róbert Petrovicky, Róbert Svehla, Zigmund Pálffy)

7. GER (Helmut De Raaf, Mirko Lüdemann, Torsten Kienass, Jörg Mayr, **4 4 0 20 26** Thomas Brandl, Alexander Serikow, Leo Stefan, Bernhard Truntschka, Raimund Hilger, Benoit Doucet, Andreas Niederberger, Richard Amann, Wolfgang Kummer, Georg Franz, Dieter Hegen, Stefan Ustorf, Ulrich Hiemer, Michael Rumrich, Klaus Merk, Joseph Heiss, Jan Benda, Jörg Handrick, Jayson Meyer)

		W	L	T	GF	GA
8. USA	(Michael Dunham, Matthew Martin, Christopher Imes, Brett Hauer, Peter Laviolette, Jeffrey Lazaro, David Roberts, Brian Rolston, Peter Ciavaglia, Craig Johnson, David Sacco, Peter Ferraro, Theodore Drury, John Lilley, Mark Beaufait, Travis Richards, Todd Marchant, James Campbell, Barron Richter, Darby Hendrickson, Garth Snow, Edward Crowley)	1	4	3	28	32

Final: SWE 2–2 CAN
      Penalties: Sweden 3 (of 7), Canada 2 (of 7).
3rd Place: FIN 4–0 RUS
5th Place: CZE 7–1 SVK
7th Place: GER 4–3 USA

The long-awaited collapse of the Russian ice hockey dynasty finally took place in 1994. It wasn't the breakup of the Soviet Union that did it—123 of the 126 players who represented the USSR between 1956 and 1992 were from Russia—it was the disintegration of the Soviet sports system, as almost 200 of the leading Russian players sought employment in other countries. Russia won its first game against Norway, but in its second outing, it was crushed by Finland 5–0. Not only was this the worst Russian loss in Olympic history, it was the first time in 70 matches that they had been shut out. The Finns dominated group A, winning all five of their matches and conceding only four goals. Group B was more competitive. Following a 4–4 tie between Sweden and Slovakia, Slovakia beat Canada 3–1 and Canada beat Sweden 3–2. This left Slovakia in first place in the pool, followed by Canada and Sweden.

In the quarterfinals, Finland easily defeated the U.S. 6–1 and Sweden shut out Germany 3–0. Russia ended Slovakia's dream run 3–2 in overtime and Canada did the same to the Czech Republic on a goal by Paul Kariya.

The first semifinal pitted Finland against Canada. The Finns took a 2–0 lead early in the second period. But then the Canadians took charge. The Finns had allowed only five goals in almost 396 minutes of Olympic play, but in 18 minutes 20 seconds, the Canadians beat them for five more. A late goal for Finland made the final score 5–3. In the second semi, Sweden held off a late surge to defeat Russia 4–3.

Canada had defeated Sweden 6–5 in Stockholm nine days before the Olympics and then 3–2 in the preliminary play at the Olympics. The final was as close a contest as might be expected. Six minutes 10 seconds into the match, Tomas Jonsson scored on a power play to give Sweden a 1–0 lead. There was no more scoring for the rest of the period and the second period was scoreless as well. But with 10:52 to play in the third period, Paul Kariya tied the score and two minutes 35 seconds after that Derek Mayer scored with a slapshot to put Canada ahead. It looked like a Canadian victory, but with 2:10 to play, Canada's Brad Werenka was penalized for hooking. Twenty-one seconds into the power play, Magnus Svensson scored to force the game into overtime.

When the ten-minute overtime period passed without a goal, hockey fans were forced to watch the Olympic Championship decided by a shootout. No matter who won, it seemed an unsatisfactory ending to a well-played match.

The rules called for each of five players from each team to rush from center ice and shoot. Peter Nedved and Paul Kariya gave Canada a 2–0 lead, but Magnus Svensson and Peter Torsberg brought Sweden even. Swedish goalie Tommy Salo stopped a shot by Greg Johnson and Canadian goalie Corey Hirsch stopped one by Roger Hansson. With the score still tied, the shootout moved into a second phase: modified sudden death, with each team taking a shot until one side led. The Swedes went first with Svensson, but Hirsch blocked his shot. With a chance to win for Canada, Nedved shot wide. Then Forsberg attacked to Hirsch's right, slipped the puck back the other way and nudged it just past the goalie's glove and into the goal. Kariya tried to even the score with the same high wrist shot he had used successfully earlier in the shootout, but Salo, down on the ice, kicked up his leg and knocked the puck away. Sweden, playing in its sixteenth Olympic tournament, had finally earned gold medals.

Sweden's Peter Forsberg scores the winning shootout goal in the 1994 ice hockey final against Canada

WOMEN

This event will be held for the first time in 1998.

COMMON ICE HOCKEY PENALTIES

Charging—Applying a body check after taking more than two steps toward the opposing player.

Cross checking—Hitting an opponent while holding the stick in the air with both hands.

Elbowing—Applying a check with the arms or elbows instead of the body.

High sticking—Holding the stick above shoulder level while moving toward an opponent.

Holding—Using the hands to grab an opposing player or his stick.

Hooking—Using the stick to restrain an opponent.

Slashing—Using the stick to try to hit an opponent.

Spearing—Using the stick to stab an opponent.

Tripping—Using an arm, foot, leg, or stick to knock down an opposing player.

LUGE (TOBOGGAN)

MEN	WOMEN	MIXED
Single	Single	Two-Seater
Discontinued Event		

Luge sleds are similar to toboggans. A singles sled can weigh no more than 22 kilograms (48.4 lbs.), a doubles sled no more than 25 kg (55.1 lbs.). The runners may be no more than 18 inches apart. It is forbidden to heat the runners before the competition. Participants, known as sliders, careen down the course feet first, guiding the luge with their legs and shoulders. Luge has the reputation of being one of the most dangerous sports in the Olympics. The two-seater event is decided on the basis of two runs, the singles on a total of four. The first organized luge competition was a four-kilometer race held in Davos, Switzerland, in 1883; the first world championships were held in Oslo in 1955. All 81 medals awarded in luge since its permanent inclusion in the Olympic program in 1964 have been won by four nations: Germany, Austria, Italy, and the U.S.S.R. Twenty-six of the 27 gold medals have been won by German-speaking athletes.

MEN
SINGLE

1924–1960 not held

1964 Innsbruck-Igls C: 36, N: 10, D: 2.1.

1.	Thomas Köhler	GDR	3:26.77
2.	Klaus Bonsack	GDR	3:27.04
3.	Hans Plenk	GER	3:30.15
4.	Rolf Greger Ström	NOR	3:31.21
5.	Josef Feistmantl	AUT	3:31.34
6.	Mieczyslaw Pawelkiewicz	POL	3:33.02
7.	Carlo Prinoth	ITA	3:33.49
8.	Franz Tiefenbacher	AUT	3:33.86

Critics who had contended that luge was too dangerous a sport to be included in the Olympics gained sad support for their arguments when Polish-born British slider Kazimierz Kay-Skrzypeski was killed during a trial run on the Olympic course at Igls two weeks before the Games began. German sliders Josef Fleischmann and Josef Lenz were also severely injured in a separate accident.

1968 Grenoble-Villard de Lans C: 50, N: 15, D: 2.15.

1.	Manfred Schmid	AUT	2:52.48
2.	Thomas Köhler	GDR	2:52.66
3.	Klaus Bonsack	GDR	2:53.33
4.	Zbigniew Gawior	POL	2:53.51
5.	Josef Feistmantl	AUT	2:53.57
6.	Hans Plenk	GER	2:53.67
7.	Horst Hörnlein	GDR	2:54.10
8.	Jerzy Wojnar	POL	2:54.62

After the East German women were disqualified for heating the runners on their sleds, the coaches of seven of the men's teams signed a petition saying they would all walk out if the East German men were allowed to continue in the contest, which still had one round to go. The International Luge Federation decided against suspending the East German men, but bad weather intervened and the competition was ended after three runs anyway.

1972 Sapporo-Teineyama C: 45, N: 13, D: 2.7.

1.	Wolfgang Scheidel	GDR	3:27.58
2.	Harald Ehrig	GDR	3:28.39
3.	Wolfram Fiedler	GDR	3:28.73
4.	Klaus Bonsack	GDR	3:29.16
5.	Leonhard Nagenrauft	GER	3:29.67
6.	Josef Fendt	GER	3:30.03
7.	Manfred Schmid	AUT	3:30.05
8.	Paul Hildgartner	ITA	3:30.55

1976 Innsbruck-Igls C: 43, N: 15, D: 2.7.

1.	Dettlef Günther	GDR	3:27.688
2.	Josef Fendt	GER	3:28.196
3.	Hans Rinn	GDR	3:28.574
4.	Hans-Heinrich Wickler	GDR	3:29.454
5.	Manfred Schmid	AUT	3:29.511
6.	Anton Winkler	GER	3:29.520
7.	Reinhold Sulzbacher	AUT	3:30.398
8.	Dainis Bremze	SOV/LAT	3:30.576

During the 1975 Olympic Test Competition on the same course that would be used for the Olympics, the East Germans set up cameras and timers all along the run to help determine the fastest routes through each of the straightaways and curves.

1980 Lake Placid C: 30, N: 13, D: 2.16.

1.	Bernhard Glass	GDR	2:54.796
2.	Paul Hildgartner	ITA	2:55.372
3.	Anton Winkler	GER	2:56.545
4.	Dettlef Günther	GDR	2:57.163
5.	Gerhard Sandbichler	AUT	2:57.451
6.	Franz Wilhelmer	AUT	2:57.483
7.	Gerd Böhmer	GER	2:57.769
8.	Anton Wembacher	GER	2:58.012

After two runs Dettlef Günther seemed to be well on his way to a repeat victory. However, he crashed near the end of his third run and, although he was able to climb back aboard and finish, the three seconds he had lost effectively removed him from the competition for first place. This left Italy's Ernst Haspinger in the lead, with one run to go. Unfortunately, he fell victim to the same turn as Günther and lost nine seconds, which dropped him to 21st place. Bernhard Glass ended up with the gold medal even though he didn't place first in a single run.

1984 Sarajevo C: 32, N: 16, D: 2.12.

1.	Paul Hildgartner	ITA	3:04.258
2.	Sergei Danilin	SOV/RUS	3:04.962
3.	Valery Dudin	SOV/RUS	3:05.012
4.	Michael Walter	GDR	3:05.031
5.	Torsten Görlitzer	GDR	3:05.129
6.	Ernst Haspinger	ITA	3:05.327
7.	Yuri Kharchenko	SOV/RUS	3:05.548
8.	Markus Prock	AUT	3:05.839

Görlitzer led after the first two runs, but 31-year-old Paul Hildgartner of Kiens (Chienes) in the Südtyrol region of Italy recorded the fastest time in both of the final two runs. Hildgartner had previously won a gold medal in the 1972 two-seater event and a silver in the 1980 single competition.

1988 Calgary C: 38, N: 18, D: 2.15.

1.	Jens Müller	GDR	3:05.548
2.	Georg Hackl	GER	3:05.916
3.	Yuri Kharchenko	SOV/RUS	3:06.274
4.	Thomas Jacob	GDR	3:06.358
5.	Michael Walter	GDR	3:06.933
6.	Sergei Danilin	SOV/RUS	3:07.098
7.	Johannes Schettel	GER	3:07.371
8.	Hansjörg Raffl	ITA	3:07.525

Müller, second to Hackl at the European championship two weeks prior to the Olympics, won three of the four runs and was three one-thousandths of a second out of first in the other.

1992 Albertville-La Plagne C: 34, N: 18, D: 2.10.

1.	Georg Hackl	GER	3:02.363
2.	Markus Prock	AUT	3:02.669
3.	Markus Schmid	AUT	3:02.942
4.	Norbert Huber	ITA	3:02.973
5.	Jens Müller	GER	3:03.197
6.	Robert Manzenreiter	AUT	3:03.267
7.	Oswald Haselrieder	ITA	3:03.276
8.	René Friedl	GER	3:03.543

Georg Hackl grew up four miles from the Königssee luge course in the Bavarian town of Berchtesgaden. After being pipped for the gold medal in 1988 because of problems with his start, a start range was built for him at Königssee. The increased practice paid off. In 1992, the 25-year-old army sergeant posted the fastest time in three of the four runs to win the closest men's single competition in 24 years.

1994 Lillehammer-Hunderfossen C: 33, N: 18, D: 2.14.

1. Georg Hackl	GER	3:21.571
2. Markus Prock	AUT	3:21.584
3. Armin Zöggeler	ITA	3:21.833
4. Arnold Huber	ITA	3:22.418
5. Wendel Suckow	USA	3:22.424
6. Norbert Huber	ITA	3:22.474
7. Gerhard Gleirscher	AUT	3:22.569
8. Jens Müller	GER	3:22.580

This repeat duel between Georg Hackl and Markus Prock was even closer than the one at the 1992 Olympics. Hackl won the first two runs, but at the end of the first day he led Prock by only one one-hundredth of a second. Prock set a course record on the third run and took a lead of .048 seconds. But his final run was only seventh-best and Hackl, more consistent, slipped ahead to win by thirteen one-thousandths of a second—the closest finish in the event's history. The contest was so close that if the four runs had been a single race, Hackl would have won by less than 14 inches after 3½ miles of sliding.

Discontinued Event

SKELETON (CRESTA RUN)

The skeleton is a heavy sled which is ridden head first in a prone position and steered by dragging one's feet and shifting one's weight. The event is held only when the Olympics are in St. Moritz.

1928 St. Moritz C: 10, N: 6, D: 2.17.

1. Jennison Heaton	USA	3:01.8
2. John Heaton	USA	3:02.8
3. David Northesk	GBR	3:05.1
4. Agostino Lanfranchi	ITA	3:08.7
5. Alexander Berner	SWI	3:08.8
6. Franz Unterlechner	AUT	3:13.5
7. Alessandro del Torso	ITA	3:14.9
8. Louis Hasenknopf	AUT	3:36.7

The Heaton brothers recorded the two fastest times in each of the three runs.

1932–1936 not held

1948 St. Moritz C: 15, N: 6, D: 2.4.

1. Nino Bibbia	ITA	5:23.2
2. John Heaton	USA	5:24.6
3. John Crammond	GBR	5:25.1
4. William Martin	USA	5:28.0
5. Gottfried Kägi	SWI	5:29.9
6. Richard Bott	GBR	5:30.4
7. James Coates	GBR	5:31.9
8. Fairchilds MacCarthy	USA	5:35.5

John Heaton of New Haven, Connecticut, had the rare experience of winning consecutive silver medals in the same event—20 years apart. The first time he was 19, the second time 39.

WOMEN

SINGLE

1924–1960 not held

1964 Innsbruck-Igls C: 16, N: 6, D: 2.4.

1.	Ortrun Enderlein	GDR	3:24.67
2.	Ilse Geisler	GDR	3:27.42
3.	Helene Thurner	AUT	3:29.06
4.	Irena Pawelczyk	POL	3:30.52
5.	Barbara Gorgón-Flont	POL	3:32.73
6.	Oldřiska Tylová	CZE	3:32.76
7.	Friederike Matejka	AUT	3:34.68
8.	Helena Macher	POL	3:35.87

1968 Grenoble-Villard de Lans C: 26, N: 10, D: 2.15.

1.	Erica Lechner	ITA	2:28.66
2.	Christa Schmuck	GER	2:29.37
3.	Angelika Dünhaupt	GER	2:29.56
4.	Helena Macher	POL	2:30.05
5.	Jadwiga Damse	POL	2:30.15
6.	Dana Beldová	CZE	2:30.35
7.	Anna Mąka	POL	2:30.40
8.	Ute Gaehler	GER	2:30.42

DISQ: Ortrun Enderlein (GDR) 2:28.04, Anna-Maria Müller (GDR) 2:28.06, Angela Knösel (GDR) 2:28.93

The weather-shortened competition ended with defending champion Ortrun Enderlein in first place and East German teammates Anna-Maria Müller and Angela Knösel in second and fourth. However the East German women aroused suspicion by consistently showing up at the last minute and then disappearing as soon as they finished a run. Their toboggans were examined, and it was discovered that their runners had been illegally heated. The three East Germans were disqualified by unanimous vote of the Jury of Appeal. The East German Olympic Committee made a pathetic attempt to blame the affair on a "capitalist revanchist plot," but they failed to address the fact that the problem had been discovered by the Polish president of the Jury, Lucian Swiderski.

1972 Sapporo-Teineyama C: 22, N: 8, D: 2.7.

1.	Anna-Maria Müller	GDR	2:59.18
2.	Ute Rührold	GDR	2:59.49
3.	Margit Schumann	GDR	2:59.54
4.	Elisabeth Demleitner	GER	3:00.80
5.	Yuko Otaka	JPN	3:00.98
6.	Halina Kanasz	POL	3:02.33
6.	Wieslawa Martyka	POL	3:02.33
8.	Sarah Felder	ITA	3:02.90

After the 1968 scandal, I.O.C. president Avery Brundage had spoken with the disqualified East German women and encouraged them to win the medals next time around. Anna-Maria Müller took this advice to heart and did exactly that, winning a close battle with her two teenage teammates. Asked why she enjoyed such a dangerous sport, Müller replied, "I love this sport because it provides a harmonious counterbalance to my work as a pharmacist."

1976 Innsbruck-Igls C: 26, N: 12, D: 2.7.

1.	Margit Schumann	GDR	2:50.621
2.	Ute Rührold	GDR	2:50.846
3.	Elisabeth Demleitner	GER	2:51.056
4.	Eva-Maria Wernicke	GDR	2:51.262
5.	Antonia Mayr	AUT	2:51.360
6.	Margit Graf	AUT	2:51.459
7.	Monika Schefftschik	GER	2:51.540
8.	Angelika Schafferer	AUT	2:52.322

Undefeated since the 1972 Olympics, Lieutenant Margit Schumann was only in fifth place after the first two runs, but recorded the best times on each of the last two runs to take the victory. The unusually attractive Ute Rührold won her second straight silver medal, even though she was only 21 years old.

1980 Lake Placid C: 18, N: 8, D: 2.16.

1.	Vera Zozulya	SOV/LAT	2:36.537
2.	Melitta Sollmann	GDR	2:37.657
3.	Ingrīda Amantova	SOV/LAT	2:37.817
4.	Elisabeth Demleitner	GER	2:37.918
5.	Ilona Brand	GDR	2:38.115
6.	Margit Schumann	GDR	2:38.255
7.	Angelika Schafferer	AUT	2:38.935
8.	Astra Ribena	SOV/LAT	2:39.011

Latvian Vera Zozulya recorded the fastest time in each of the four runs to upset two-time world champion Melitta Sollmann. Zozulya is the only non-German-speaking athlete to win a luge medal.

1984 Sarajevo C: 27, N: 15, 2.12.

1.	Steffi Martin	GDR	2:46.570
2.	Bettina Schmidt	GDR	2:46.873
3.	Ute Weiss	GDR	2:47.248
4.	Ingrīda Amantova	SOV/LAT	2:48.480
5.	Vera Zozulya	SOV/LAT	2:48.641
6.	Marie Luise Rainer	ITA	2:49.138
7.	Annefried Goellner	AUT	2:49.373
8.	Andrea Hatle	GER	2:49.491

World champion Steffi Martin recorded the fastest time in each of the four runs.

1988 Calgary C: 24, N: 14, D: 2.16.

1.	Steffi Walter [Martin]	GDR	3:03.973
2.	Ute Oberhoffner [Weiss]	GDR	3:04.105
3.	Cerstin Schmidt	GDR	3:04.181
4.	Veronika Bilgeri	GER	3:05.670
5.	Yulia Antipova	SOV/RUS	3:05.787
6.	Bonny Warner	USA	3:06.056

7.	Marie-Claude Doyon	CAN	3:06.211
8.	Nadezhda Danilina	SOV/RUS	3:06.364

Defending champion Steffi Walter trailed teammate Ute Oberhoffner by thirty-eight thousandths of a second after two runs. The final two runs were delayed for one day because of heavy winds. When the competition resumed, Walter picked up one hundred eighty-one thousandths of a second on the third run, giving her the margin of victory. The East German women clocked the three fastest times for each of the four runs.

1992 Albertville-La Plagne C: 24, N: 12, D: 2.12.

1.	Doris Neuner	AUT	3:06.696
2.	Angelika Neuner	AUT	3:06.769
3.	Susi Erdmann	GER	3:07.115
4.	Gerda Weissensteiner	ITA	3:07.673
5.	Cammy Myler	USA	3:07.973
6.	Gabriele Kohlisch	GER	3:07.980
7.	Andrea Tagwerker	AUT	3:08.018
8.	Natalja Yakushenko	SOV/UKR	3:08.383

After the Austrians stood 1-2-3 following the first day's two runs, the U.S. and Italian coaches filed a protest claiming that the Austrians' suits were illegally strapped to the heels of their boots, causing their toes to point inside. This scandalous flouting of the rules could have led to the Austrians' disqualification, but the Jury of Appeal rejected the protest. Doris Neuner, a 20-year-old secretary from Innsbruck, took a huge lead (two-tenths of a second) after the first run and held on for the victory despite not winning another run. Her sister, Angelika, a 22-year-old bank clerk, closed the gap with each of her remaining runs, but fell seventy-three thousandths of a second short.

1994 Lillehammer-Hunderfossen C: 25, N: 14, D: 2.16.

1.	Gerda Weissensteiner	ITA	3:15.517
2.	Susi Erdmann	GER	3:16.276
3.	Andrea Tagwerker	AUT	3:16.652
4.	Angelika Neuner	AUT	3:16.901
5.	Natalie Obkircher	ITA	3:16.937
6.	Gabriele Kohlisch	GER	3:17.197
7.	Irina Gubkina	RUS	3:17.198
8.	Natalja Yakushenko	UKR	3:17.378

Defending world champion Gerda Weissensteiner recorded the fastest time in each of the four runs to earn the gold medal. She didn't keep that medal for long: less than three weeks later, while she was attending her brother's funeral, thieves broke into her house in Bolzano and stole the medal. The Lillehammer Olympic Organizing Committee provided her with a replacement.

MIXED

TWO-SEATER

Theoretically the doubles event changed from men-only to coed after the 1992 Olympics, however no women have yet entered.

1924–1960 not held

1964 Innsbruck-Igls T: 14, N: 8, D: 2.1.
1. AUT (Josef Feistmantl, Manfred Stengl) 1:41.62
2. AUT (Reinhold Senn, Helmut Thaler) 1:41.91
3. ITA (Walter Aussendorfer, Sigisfredo Mair) 1:42.87
4. GDR (Walter Eggert, Helmut Vollprecht) 1:43.08
5. ITA (Giampaolo Ambrosi, Giovanni Graber) 1:43.77
5. POL (Lucjan Kudzia, Ryszard Pędrak) 1:43.77
7. POL (Edward Fender, Mieczyslaw Pawelkiewicz) 1:45.13
8. CZE (Jan Hamrik, Jiři Hujer) 1:45.41

1968 Grenoble-Villard de Lans T: 14, N: 8, D: 2.18.
1. GDR (Klaus Bonsack, Thomas Köhler) 1:35.85
2. AUT (Manfred Schmid, Ewald Walch) 1:36.34
3. GER (Wolfgang Winkler, Fritz Nachmann) 1:37.29
4. GER (Hans Plenk, Bernhard Aschauer) 1:37.61
5. GDR (Horst Hörnlein, Reinhard Bredow) 1:37.81
6. POL (Zbigniew Gawior, Ryszard Gawior) 1:37.85
7. AUT (Josef Feistmantl, Wilhelm Biechl) 1:38.11
8. ITA (Giovanni Graber, Enrico Graber) 1:38.15

1972 Sapporo-Teineyama T: 20, N: 11, D: 2.10.
1. GDR (Horst Hörnlein, Reinhard Bredow) 1:28.35
1. ITA (Paul Hildgartner, Walter Plaikner) 1:28.35
3. GDR (Klaus Bonsack, Wolfram Fiedler) 1:29.16
4. JPN (Satoru Arai, Masatoshi Kobayashi) 1:29.63
5. GER (Hans Brandner, Balthasar Schwarm) 1:29.66
5. POL (Miroslaw Więckowski, Wojciech Kubik) 1:29.66
7. AUT (Manfred Schmid, Ewald Walch) 1:29.75
8. ITA (Sigisfredo Mair, Ernst Mair) 1:30.26

The results of the first run, which had been won by Hildgartner and Plaikner, were cancelled due to a malfunctioning starting gate. The Italians argued that the run should be counted, since all contestants had suffered equally. Their protest was denied. The tie which resulted from the two official runs caused a sticky problem. Finally the International Luge Federation, in consultation with I.O.C. president Avery Brundage, decided to award gold medals to both teams.

1976 Innsbruck-Igls T: 25, N: 15, D: 2.10.
1. GDR (Hans Rinn, Norbert Hahn) 1:25.604
2. GER (Hans Brandner, Balthasar Schwarm) 1:25.889
3. AUT (Rudolf Schmid, Franz Schachner) 1:25.919
4. GER (Stefan Hölzlwimmer, Rudolf Grösswang) 1:26.238
5. AUT (Manfred Schmid, Reinhold Sulzbacher) 1:26.424
6. CZE (Jindřich Zeman, Vladimir Resl) 1:26.826
7. ITA (Karl Feichter, Ernst Haspinger) 1:27.171
8. SOV/LAT (Dainis Bremze, Aigars Krikis) 1:27.407

1980 Lake Placid T: 19, N: 12: D: 2.19.
1. GDR (Hans Rinn, Norbert Hahn) 1:19.331
2. ITA (Peter Gschnitzer, Karl Brunner) 1:19.606

3.	AUT	(Georg Fluckinger, Karl Schrott)	1:19.795
4.	GDR	(Bernd Hahn, Ulrich Hahn)	1:19.914
5.	ITA	(Hansjörg Raffl, Alfred Silginer)	1:19.976
6.	GER	(Anton Winkler, Anton Wembacher)	1:20.012
7.	GER	(Hans Brandner, Balthasar Schwarm)	1:20.063
8.	CZE	(Jindřich Zeman, Vladimir Resl)	1:20.142

Hans Rinn and Norbert Hahn became the first repeat winners of an Olympic luge event. Norbert was no relation to Bernd and Ulrich Hahn, two brothers who finished fourth.

1984 Sarajevo T: 15, N: 9, D: 2.15.

1.	GER	(Hans Stanggassinger, Franz Wembacher)	1:23.620
2.	SOV/RUS	(Yevgeny Belousov, Aleksandr Belyakov)	1:23.660
3.	GDR	(Jörg Hoffmann, Jochen Pietzsch)	1:23.887
4.	AUT	(Georg Fluckinger, Franz Wilhelmer)	1:23.902
5.	AUT	(Günther Lemmerer, Franz Lechleitner)	1:24.133
6.	ITA	(Hansjörg Raffl, Norbert Huber)	1:24.353
7.	SOV/LAT	(Yuris Eyssak, Eynar Veykcha)	1:24.366
8.	GER	(Thomas Schwab, Wolfgang Staudinger)	1:24.634

Belousov and Belyakov led after the first run and were on their way to the best time of the second run when they faltered just before the end, losing about one-sixth of a second in the last few meters. This gave Stanggassinger and Wembacher the victory by four one-hundredths of a second.

1988 Calgary T: 18, N: 11, D: 2.19.

1.	GDR	(Jörg Hoffmann, Jochen Pietzsch)	1:31.940
2.	GDR	(Stefan Krausse, Jan Behrendt)	1:32.039
3.	GER	(Thomas Schwab, Wolfgang Staudinger)	1:32.274
4.	GER	(Stefan Ilsanker, Georg Hackl)	1:32.298
5.	AUT	(Georg Fluckinger, Robert Manzenreiter)	1:32.364
6.	SOV/RUS	(Vitaly Melnik, Dmitri Alexeev)	1:32.459
7.	ITA	(Kurt Brugger, Wilfried Huber)	1:32.553
7.	SOV/RUS	(Yevgeny Belousov, Aleksandr Belyakov)	1:32.553

1992 Albertville-La Plagne T: 20, N: 15, D: 2.14.

1.	GER	(Stefan Krausse, Jan Behrendt)	1:32.053
2.	GER	(Yves Mankel, Thomas Rudolph)	1:32.239
3.	ITA	(Hansjörg Raffl, Norbert Huber)	1:32.298
4.	ROM	(Ioan Apostol, Constantin-Liviu Cepoi)	1:32.649
5.	ITA	(Kurt Brugger, Wilfried Huber)	1:32.810
6.	SWE	(Hans Kohala, Carl-Johan Lindqvist)	1:33.134
7.	AUT	(Gerhard Gleirscher, Markus Schmid)	1:33.257
8.	SOV/RUS	(Albert Demchenko, Aleksei Zelensky)	1:33.299

The two Italian teams dominated the pre-Olympic season, finishing one-two in every World Cup event they entered, but both faltered on the course at La Plagne. Krausse and Behrendt were childhood friends who grew up in Ilmenau, the hometown of both 1988 individual gold medalists, Jens Müller and Ute Oberhoffner.

1994 Lillehammer-Hunderfosser T: 20, N: 15, D: 2.18.

1.	ITA	(Kurt Brugger, Wilfried Huber)	1:36.720
2.	ITA	(Hansjörg Raffl, Norbert Huber)	1:36.769
3.	GER	(Stefan Krausse, Jan Behrendt)	1:36.945

4.	USA	(Mark Grimmette, Jonathan Edwards)	1:37.289
5.	USA	(Christopher Thorpe, Gordon Sheer)	1:37.296
6.	ROM	(Ioan Apostol, Constantin-Liviu Cepoi)	1:37.323
7.	RUS	(Albert Demchenko, Aleksei Zelensky)	1:37.477
8.	CAN	(Robert Gasper, Clay Ives)	1:37.691
8.	UKR	(Ihor Urbansky, Andrij Mukhin)	1:37.691

For five years Raffl and Norbert Huber had finished ahead of Brugger and Wilfried Huber in every major event they had entered. But in Norway Brugger and Wilfried came from behind on the second run to score a narrow victory. All in all it was quite a successful Olympics for the Huber brothers. Wilfried (23) earned the gold, Norbert (29) earned silver and also placed sixth in the singles event, and Gunther (28) took home a bronze medal in the two-man bobsled.

FIGURE SKATING

MEN
WOMEN
Pairs
Ice Dance
Discontinued Event

"I can't comprehend speed skaters, whose whole life comes down to four inches over 500 meters. And yet, I seem to be able to comprehend leaving my future happiness in the hands of nine people who I don't know. So it's a strange sport, but you've got to admit, it's exciting."

Kurt Browning
February 19, 1994

The first international figure skating competition was held in Vienna in 1882 and the first world championship in St. Petersburg in 1896. A separate event for women's singles was not created until 1906, and the first world championship for pairs took place in 1908. According to current rules, each skater or pair appears twice, performing a two-minute and forty-second short or original program with eight required moves (33⅓ percent of the total score) and a freestyle long program (66⅔ percent of the score). The men's and pairs' long programs last four and a half minutes, the women's only four. Prior to 1992, singles skaters were also required to perform compulsory (or special) figures.

In singles and pairs competitions, the nine judges assign each entrant two scores from 0 to 6 points, one for technical merit and one for artistic impression. More important, in both the short program and the long program, each judge ranks the skaters according to the points awarded. The numerical equivalents for each place (1 for first, 2 for second, etc.) are called ordinals or place numbers. At the end of each stage of the competition, the skaters are ranked in consensus order. If one skater receives a majority of first-place votes, that skater is ranked first. If no one receives a majority of first-place votes, then the second-place votes are added to the first-place votes. If there is still no one with a majority of votes, then the person with the lowest ordinal total is ranked first. If a tie still exists, the skater with the most points is awarded first place. The same procedure is used to determine all other places. To determine final scores, a skater's short-program ranking is multiplied by 0.5 and added to the long-program ranking. Until 1984, the ordinals were based on total scores, not on separate programs.

MEN

1908 London C: 9, N: 5, D: 10.29.

		JUDGES' RANKINGS					
		GBR	SWE	SWI	RUS	GER	ORDINALS
1. Ulrich Salchow	SWE	1	1	2	2	1	7
2. Richard Johansson	SWE	2	2	3	1	2	10

3.	Per Thorén	SWE	4	3	1	3	3	14
4.	John Keiller Greig	GBR	3	4	4	4	4	19
5.	A. Albert March	GBR	5	5	7	6	6	29
6.	Irving Brokaw	USA	6	7	5	5	7	30
7.	Henri Torromé	ARG	7	6	6	7	5	31

Early in 1908 Salchow suffered his first defeat in six years, losing to Nicolai Panin (Kolomenkin) of Russia. At the London Olympics, the two met again. Salchow was given three first-place votes for his compulsory figures to Panin's two. Panin withdrew in protest, claiming that the judging was stacked against him. Salchow was the originator of the jump which now bears his name. To perform a Salchow, a skater must take off from the back inside edge of one skate, make a complete turn in the air, and land on the back outside edge of the opposite skate.

1920 Antwerp C: 9, N: 6, D: 4.27.

JUDGES' RANKINGS

			SWE	FRA	BEL	NOR	GBR	BEL	FIN	ORDINALS
1.	Gillis Grafström	SWE	1	1	1	1	1	1	1	7
2.	Andreas Krogh	NOR	3	2	2	2	4	3	2	18
3.	Martin Stixrud	NOR	2	3	3.5	3	5	5	3	24.5
4.	Ulrich Salchow	SWE	4	4	3.5	5	2	2	5	25.5
5.	Sakari Ilmanen	FIN	5	5	5	4	3	4	4	30
6.	Nathaniel Niles	USA	6	9	6	6	8	8	6	49
7.	Basil Williams	GBR	8	6	7	8	6	7	7.5	49.5
8.	Alfred Mégroz	SWI	7	8	8	9	7	6	7.5	52.5

Bronze medalist Stixrud was 44 years old.

1924 Chamonix C: 11, N: 9, D: 1.30.

JUDGES' RANKINGS

			FRA	FRA	CZE	SWI	GBR	AUT	AUT	ORDINALS
1.	Gillis Grafström	SWE	1	1	2	1	1	2	2	10
2.	Willy Böckl	AUT	2	2	3	2	2	1	1	13
3.	Georges Gautschi	SWI	3	4	4	3	3	3	3	23
4.	Josef Sliva	CZE	4	3	1	4	5	4	7	28
5.	John Page	GBR	5	5	7	6	4	5	4	36
6.	Nathaniel Niles	USA	7	6	9	5	7	6	6	46
7.	Melville Rogers	CAN	6	7	8	7	6	9	8	51
8.	Pierre Brunet	FRA	8	8	5	9	8	7	9	54

The Czech judge ranked Sliva of Czechoslovakia first, the two Austrian judges voted for Böckl of Austria, and the other four judges, none of whom was Swedish, gave first place to Gillis Grafström.

1928 St. Moritz C: 17, N: 10, D: 2.17.

JUDGES' RANKINGS

			GER	AUT	BEL	USA	FIN	GBR	CZE	ORDINALS
1.	Gillis Grafström	SWE	1	3	3	2	1	1	1	12
2.	Willy Böckl	AUT	2	1	2	1	2	2	3	13
3.	Robert von Zeebroeck	BEL	3	4	1	7	3	4	5	27
4.	Karl Schäfer	AUT	4	2	4	3	6	7	9	35
5.	Josef Sliva	CZE	5	6	8	4	5	6	2	36
6.	Marcus Nikkanen	FIN	7	5	7	8	4	10	6	46
7.	Pierre Brunet	FRA	10	7	5	9	7	8	4	50
8.	Ludwig Wrede	AUT	8	8	7	10	8	5	7	53

The 34-year-old Grafström won his third straight gold medal despite suffering from a badly swollen knee. Grafström's smooth, orthodox, and perfectly executed routines appealed to the judges more than Böckl's more aggressive performance and von Zeebroeck's spectacular leaps and spins.

1932 Lake Placid C: 12, N: 8, D: 2.9.

		NOR	GBR	AUT	FIN	CAN	HUN	USA	ORDINALS
1. Karl Schäfer	AUT	1	2	1	2	1	1	1	9
2. Gillis Grafström	SWE	3	1	2	1	2	2	2	13
3. Montgomery Wilson	CAN	4	3	4	4	3	3	3	24
4. Marcus Nikkanen	FIN	2	4	3	3	5	5	6	28
5. Ernst Baier	GER	5	5	5	5	4	4	7	35
6. Roger Turner	USA	6	6	6	6	6	6	4	40
7. James Madden	USA	7	7	8	8	8	9	5	52
8. Gail Borden II	USA	8	8	7	7	9	7	8	54

JUDGES' RANKINGS

This competition marked a changing of the guard, as 38-year-old three-time Olympic champion Gillis Grafström lost to 22-year-old, soon-to-be two-time Olympic champion Karl Schäfer. Grafström suffered a sudden mental lapse at the very beginning of his performance, evidently starting to trace a different figure than the one that was required. He recovered and skated smoothly thereafter, but he was penalized an average of almost eight points by each judge.

1936 Garmisch-Partenkirchen C: 25, N: 12, D: 2.14.

		USA	GBR	FIN	CAN/GER	AUT	HUN	CZE	ORDINALS
1. Karl Schäfer	AUT	1	1	1	1	1	1	1	7
2. Ernst Baier	GER	4	4	4	2	3	5	2	24
3. Felix Kaspar	AUT	3	3	2	4	2	7	3	24
4. Montgomery Wilson	CAN	2	5	3	3	4	8	5	30
5. Henry Graham Sharp	GBR	6	2	6	7	5	4	4	34
6. John Dunn	GBR	5	6	7	6	6	6	6	42
7. Marcus Nikkanen	FIN	7	7	5	5	12	9	9	54
8. Elemer Tardonfalvi	HUN	10	9	9	8	9	3	8	56

JUDGES' RANKINGS

An extreme example of national prejudice by a judge was committed by Judge von Orbán of Hungary, who placed the two Hungarian skaters, Dénes Pataky and Elemer Tardonfalvi, second and third, while none of the other judges ranked them higher than seventh and eighth. Being a judge could be a dangerous job in the days of outdoor rinks. After six hours of judging figures in inclement weather, Canadian judge John Machado contracted pneumonia and had to be replaced.

1948 St. Moritz C: 16, N: 10, D: 2.5.

		GBR	SWI	USA	CZE	AUT	BEL	CAN	DEN	HUN	ORDINALS
1. Richard Button	USA	1	2	1	1	1	1	1	1	1	10
2. Hans Gerschwiler	SWI	2	1	5	2	3	2	3	2	3	23
3. Edi Rada	AUT	7	3	3	3	2	3	4	6	2	33
4. John Lettengarver	USA	3	4	2	5	6	4	2	3	7	36
5. Ede Király	HUN	5	5	6	4	4	5	5	4	4	42
6. James Grogan	USA	6	7	4	8	10	6	6	5	10	62
7. Henry Graham Sharp	GBR	4	9	10	7	8	10	7	7	5	67
8. Hellmut May	AUT	8	6	9	6	5	9	11	8	6	68

JUDGES' RANKINGS

Dick Button, men's figure skating champion of 1948 and 1952.

Two days before the free-skating portion of the competition, 18-year-old Dick Button, a Harvard freshman from Englewood, New Jersey, successfully completed a double axel for the first time. He was anxious to include this new move in his program but, as the leader going into the final round, he was hesitant to risk his position by trying a move with which he was not yet fully confident. In his book *Dick Button on Skates,* he recalled, "I disliked being so unprepared. But the cravenness of backing away from something because of the pressure of the Olympic games repulsed me and, once I had made up my mind, I could not divert the steps that culminated in the double axel." The jump went perfectly and Button was awarded first place by eight of the nine judges. Only the Swiss judge voted a first for world champion Hans Gerschwiler of Switzerland.

1952 Oslo C: 14, N: 11, D: 2.21.

		USA	GER	ITA	AUT	DEN	CAN	FIN	FRA	HUN	ORDINALS
1.	Richard Button	USA	1	1	1	1	1	1	1	1	1	9
2.	Helmut Seibt	AUT	4	2	2	2	2	3	2	4	2	23
3.	James Grogan	USA	2	3	3	3	3	2	3	2	3	24
4.	Hayes Alan Jenkins	USA	3	5	5	5	5	5	4	3	5	40
5.	Peter Firstbrook	CAN	5	4	6	6	4	4	5	5	4	43
6.	Carlo Fassi	ITA	6	6	4	4	6	6	6	6	6	50
7.	Alain Giletti	FRA	7	7	7	7	7	7	7	7	7	63
8.	Freimut Stein	GER	8	8	8	8	8	8	8	8	8	72

JUDGES' RANKINGS

By 1952 Dick Button was a Harvard senior working on a thesis entitled "International Socialism and the Schumann Plan." Once again he had a new move to unveil at the Olympics—the triple loop, which required him to make three complete revolutions in the air and then come down smoothly. No one had ever performed a triple jump of any kind in competition. Button could have played it safe, skipped the triple loop, and probably won anyway, but he felt that this would have been a form of failure. Button was very anxious, and his parents were so nervous that they couldn't sit together. In his autobiography, Button describes the triple loop: "I forgot in momentary panic which shoulder should go forward and which back. I was extraordinarily conscious of the judges, who looked so immobile at rinkside. But this was it. . . . The wind cut my eyes, and the coldness caused tears to stream down my checks. Up! Up! Height was vital. Round and around again in a spin which took only a fraction of a second to complete before it landed on a clean steady back edge. I pulled away breathless, excited and overjoyed, as applause rolled from the far-away stands like the rumbling of a distant pounding sea."

All nine judges placed Button first, far ahead of the other skaters. Dick Button turned professional a few months later and toured with the Ice Capades. Later he became a lawyer, an actor, a TV sports commentator, and an entrepreneur. The seventh-place finisher in 1952, Alain Giletti, was only 12 years old.

1956 Cortina C: 16, N: 11, D: 2.1.

					JUDGES' RANKINGS					
		AUS	AUT	CAN	CZE	FRA	GER	GBR	USA	SWI	ORDINALS

		AUS	AUT	CAN	CZE	FRA	GER	GBR	USA	SWI	ORDINALS
1. Hayes Alan Jenkins	USA	3	1	1	1	2	2	1	1	1	13
2. Ronald Robertson	USA	1	2	2	2	1	1	3	2	2	16
3. David Jenkins	USA	2	3	4	3	3	4	2	3	3	27
4. Alain Giletti	FRA	4	5	3	5	4	3	5	4	4	37
5. Karol Divin	CZE/ SVK	7	4	5	4	5.5	5	6	8	5	49.5
6. Michael Booker	GBR	5	6	8	6	5.5	7	4	6	6	53.5
7. Norbert Felsinger	AUT	9	7	7	7	9	10	8	7	7	71
8. Charles Snelling	CAN	8	9	6	9	8	6	7	5	9	67

The three Americans finished in the same order as they had in the 1955 world championships. Twenty-two-year-old Hayes Alan Jenkins of Colorado Springs, Colorado, had practiced 40 hours a week, 10 months a year, for nine years. Silver medalist Ronnie Robertson was known as the "king of the spin." Taking advantage of an uncanny ability to avoid dizziness, he was able to revolve 240 times a minute. In the words of Canadian coach Louis Stong, "you'd see his face and the back of his head at the same time." It was said that if he held his arms out while he was spinning, blood would come out of his fingertips.

1960 Squaw Valley C: 19, N: 10, D: 2.26.

					JUDGES' RANKINGS					
		AUT	CAN	CZE	FRA	GER	GBR	JPN	SWI	USA	ORDINALS

		AUT	CAN	CZE	FRA	GER	GBR	JPN	SWI	USA	ORDINALS
1. David Jenkins	USA	1	1	1	1	1	2	1	1	1	10
2. Karol Divin	CZE/ SVK	2	3	2	4	3	1	2	3	2	22
3. Donald Jackson	CAN	5	2	3	3	4	3	4	4	3	31
4. Alain Giletti	FRA	3	4	4	2	2	4	5	2	5	31
5. Timothy Brown	USA	4	5	5	6	5	5	3	6	4	43
6. Alain Calmat	FRA	6	6	6	5	6	6	7	5	7	54
7. Robert Brewer	USA	7	8	8	8	7	7	6	9	6	66
8. Manfred Schnelldorfer	GER	8	7	7	7	10	9	9	8	10	75

Medical student David Jenkins, the younger brother of 1956 champion Hayes Alan Jenkins, trailed Karol Divin after the compulsory figures. However, his free-skating program won first-place votes from all nine judges, and he won eight of nine first places overall. At the 1962 world championships in Prague, Don Jackson became the first skater to land a triple lutz in competition. It would be twelve years before anyone else matched his feat.

1964 Innsbruck C: 24, N: 11, D: 2.6.

		GER	FRA	GBR	ITA	CAN	AUT	CZE	USA	SOV	ORDINALS
		JUDGES' RANKINGS									
1. Manfred Schnelldorfer	GER	1	2	1	3	1	1	1	2	1	13
2. Alain Calmat	FRA	3	1	2	1	3	2	4	3	3	22
3. Scott Allen	USA	2	3	3	2	2	5	3	1	5	26
4. Karol Divin	CZE/SVK	4	4	4	4	4	4	2	4	2	32
5. Emmerich Danzer	AUT	5	5	5	5	5	3	5	5	4	42
6. Thomas Litz	USA	10	8	11	6	6	6	6	12	12	77
7. Peter Jonas	AUT	6	6	6	13	14	8	10	9	7	79
8. Nobuo Sato	JPN	8	9	7	9	12	9	9	10	15	88

Manfred Schnelldorfer, a 20-year-old architecture student from Munich, was a former German roller skating champion. Two days shy of his 15th birthday, Scotty Allen of Smoke Rise, New Jersey, became the youngest person to win a medal in the Winter Olympics.

1968 Grenoble C: 28, N: 15, D: 2.16.

		AUT	CAN	CZE	FRA	GER	GBR	ITA	JPN	USA	ORDINALS
		JUDGES' RANKINGS									
1. Wolfgang Schwarz	AUT	1	1	1	2	1	1	2	2	2	13
2. Timothy Wood	USA	3	2	2	1	3	3	1	1	1	17
3. Patrick Pera	FRA	4	3	3	3	4	4	3	4	3	31
4. Emmerich Danzer	AUT	2	4	4	4	2	2	4	3	4	29
5. Gary Visconti	USA	7	6	8	5	5	5	5	5	6	52
6. John "Misha" Petkevich	USA	8	5	5	6	8	6	7	6	5	56
7. Jay Humphry	CAN	5	7	7	9	7	8	6	7	7	63
8. Ondrej Nepela	CZE/SVK	6	9	6	7	6	11	9	8	8	70

Wolfgang Schwarz, who was famous for consistently finishing second behind fellow Austrian Emmerich Danzer, won the narrowest of victories over Tim Wood. If either the Canadian judge or the British judge had given one more point to Wood, he would have won. Instead, Schwarz earned five first-place votes, while Wood was awarded only four. World champion Danzer had the best scores of the free-skating portion of the competition, but he was only fourth in the compulsories. He lost out on a bronze medal because of the placement rule, five to four, despite the fact that he had more points and fewer ordinals than Patrick Pera.

1972 Sapporo C: 17, N: 10, D: 2.11.

		FRA	GDR	CAN	GBR	AUT	CZE	JPN	USA	SOV	ORDINALS
		JUDGES' RANKINGS									
1. Ondrej Nepela	CZE/SVK	1	1	1	1	1	1	1	1	1	9
2. Sergei Chetveroukhin	SOV/RUS	3	2	3	2	2	2	2	2	2	20
3. Patrick Pera	FRA	2	3	2	3	3	3	3	6	3	28

		FRA	GDR	CAN	GBR	AUT	CZE	JPN	USA	SOV	ORDINALS
		JUDGES' RANKINGS									
4. Kenneth Shelley	USA	5	5	4	5	5	5	4	3	7	43
5. John "Misha" Petkevich	USA	4	6	5	8	6	4	5	4	5	47
6. Jan Hoffmann	GDR	9	4	8	7	4	6	6	7	4	55
7. Haig Oundjian	GBR	7	7	7	6	7	7	7	9	8	65
8. Vladimir Kovalev	SOV/ RUS	10	11	10	9	10	8	8	8	6	80

Ondrej Nepela first competed in the Olympics in 1964, when he was 13 years old. That year he placed 22nd out of 24. In 1968 he moved up to eighth place, and in 1972, a seasoned veteran of 21, he was the unanimous choice of the judges, despite falling during a competition for the first time in four years. He had been attempting a triple-toe loop jump. Nepela died of AIDS at the age of 38.

1976 Innsbruck C: 20, N: 13, D: 2.11.

		CAN	HUN	GBR	CZE	USA	FRA	JPN	SOV	GDR	ORDINALS
		JUDGES' RANKINGS									
1. John Curry	GBR	2	1	1	1	1	1	1	2	1	11
2. Vladimir Kovalev	SOV/ RUS	4	2	4	2	4	5	3	1	3	28
3. Toller Cranston	CAN	1	3	2	4	6	2	5	3	4	30
4. Jan Hoffman	GDR	3	5	5	3	3	3	4	6	2	34
5. Sergei Volkov	SOV/ RUS	6	4	6	5	7	12	2	4	7	53
6. David Santee	USA	5	7	3	7	2	6	6	7	6	49
7. Terry Kubicka	USA	7	6	8	6	5	4	7	8	5	56
8. Yuri Ovchinnikov	SOV/ RUS	9	8	10	8	10	9	8	5	8	75

Birmingham-born John Curry had two major obstacles to overcome on his way to a gold medal. The first was a lack of proper training facilities in England. This he solved by moving to Colorado in 1973. His second obstacle was the fact that the Soviet and Eastern European judges did not approve of his style of skating, which they considered too feminine. Actually Curry, who believed that figure skating was an art as well as a sport, felt that his style was in the tradition of three-time gold medalist Gillis Grafström. For the Olympics, however, Curry supplemented his natural elegance with enough "masculine" jumps, so that even the Communist judges could find no fault with his performance. The Soviet judge gave first place to Kovalev and the Canadian judge gave first place to Cranston, but even they placed Curry second. During his long program, Terry Kubicka became the only skater to perform a backflip during Olympic competition. The move was banned immediately afterward. John Curry died of an AIDS-related illness on April 15, 1994. He was 44 years old.

1980 Lake Placid C: 17, N: 10, D: 2.21.

		CAN	GDR	SOV	USA	FRA	SWE	GBR	GER	JPN	ORDINALS
		JUDGES' RANKINGS									
1. Robin Cousins	GBR	1	2	1	3	1	1	1	2	1	13
2. Jan Hoffman	GDR	2	1	2	1	2	2	2	1	2	15
3. Charles Tickner	USA	4	3	3	2	3	3	4	3	3	28
4. David Santee	USA	3	4	4	4	4	4	3	4	4	34
5. Scott Hamilton	USA	5	5	5	5	5	5	5	5	5	45
6. Igor Bobrin	SOV/ RUS	6	6	6	6	7	6	6	6	6	55

| 7. Jean-Christophe Simond | FRA | 7 | 8 | 7 | 9 | 6 | 7 | 7 | 7 | 6 | 64 |
| 8. Mitsuru Matsumura | JPN | 8 | 7 | 9 | 8 | 9 | 9 | 9 | 8 | 8 | 75 |

There were four favorites in the 1980 competition: world champion Vladimir Kovalev of the U.S.S.R., former world champions Charles Tickner and Jan Hoffman, and European champion Robin Cousins of Bristol, England. Hoffman was taking part in his fourth Olympics, having first competed in 1968 when he was 12 years old. Twenty-sixth in 1968, he moved up to sixth in 1972 and fourth in 1976. Cousins, like John Curry before him, trained in Colorado with Carlo and Christa Fassi, who had also coached Peggy Fleming and Dorothy Hamill. In Denver Cousins lived only a few blocks from Charles Tickner.

Kovalev dropped out after placing fifth in the compulsories. Hoffman was in first place, followed by Tickner, Santee, and Cousins. The next day Cousins skated a brilliant short program to move into second place. He made one slip at the beginning of his long program, but otherwise skated flawlessly. Six judges gave Cousins first place, while three voted for Hoffman. Actually Cousins' worst fall came at the awards ceremony, where, dazzled by the lights and the applause and the emotion, he stumbled while trying to negotiate the one and a half steps to the victory platform. In his book, *Skating for Gold,* Cousins recalls the raising of the British flag to honor his victory: "As it was slowly going up, I lost sight of [my parents] for a while. But when the Union Jack was finally above our heads, we were looking directly at each other. So I was able to know how they were feeling and they could see how I was feeling, but it is difficult to describe that to anyone else."

1984 Sarajevo C: 23, N: 14, D: 2.16.

				JUDGES' RANKINGS (FREE SKATING)								
		CF	SP	YUG	GER	FRA	USA	GDR	SWE	SOV	CZE	CAN	ORDINALS
1. Scott Hamilton	USA	1	2	3	2	1	2	2	5	5	2	2	3.4
2. Brian Orser	CAN	7	1	1	1	2	1	1	1	1	1	1	5.6
3. Josef Sabovčik	CZE	4	5	2	5	5	3	3	2	2	3	4	7.4
4. Rudi Cerne	GER	3	6	7	4	4	6	4	4	7	4	3	8.2
5. Brian Boitano	USA	8	3	5	5	3	4	6	3	3	5	9	11.0
6. Jean-Christophe Simond	FRA	2	4	9	7	6	11	9	8	10	8	7	11.8
7. Aleksandr Fadeyev	SOV/ RUS	5	8	10	3	10	10	5	7	4	6	11	13.2
8. Vladimir Kotin	SOV/ RUS	11	9	6	10	9	5	7	5	5	9	5	16.2

Scott Hamilton, the adopted son of two college professors in Bowling Green, Ohio, was considered a shoo-in to win at Sarajevo. Beginning in September 1980, the 5-foot 2½-inch, 108-pound Hamilton had won 16 straight tournaments including three world championships. But the pressure of great expectations got to him and the quality of his performance was below that of his usual brilliance. He finished second to Brian Orser in both the short and long programs. However, the big lead that Hamilton had built up during the compulsories, in which Orser placed seventh, carried him to the top platform at the medal ceremony. Despite his own disappointment with his performance, Hamilton's good nature and dry wit made him a most popular winner.

1988 Calgary C: 28, N: 21, D: 2.20.

				JUDGES' RANKINGS (FREE SKATING)								
		CF	SP	GER	USA	DEN	SOV	SWI	JPN	GDR	CAN	CZE	ORDINALS
1. Brian Boitano	USA	2	2	2	1	1	1	1	1	2	2	2	3.0
2. Brian Orser	CAN	3	1	1	2	2	2	2	2	1	1	1	4.2

		JUDGES' RANKINGS (FREE SKATING)										
		CF	SP	GER	USA	DEN	SOV	SWI	JPN	GDR	CAN	CZE	ORDINALS
3. Viktor Petrenko	SOV/ UKR	6	3	3	3	3	2	4	3	5	3	3	7.8
4. Aleksandr Fadeyev	SOV/ RUS	1	9	4	4	4	4	3	4	3	4	4	8.2
5. Grzegorz Filipowski	POL	7	4	7	6	5	8	8	6	6	6	6	10.8
6. Vladimir Kotin	SOV/ RUS	5	6	8	9	7	6	9	5	4	8	5	13.4
7. Christopher Bowman	USA	8	5	5	5	8	7	5	8	8	5	8	13.8
8. Kurt Browning	CAN	11	7	6	7	6	9	7	9	7	7	9	15.4

The North American media promoted this event as "The Battle of the Brians": Brian Orser of Penetanguishene, Ontario, and Brian Boitano of Sunnyvale, California. They had met 10 times in international competition, with Orser leading the series 7–3. However, by 1988 they were so evenly matched that it was impossible to choose a favorite. Over the years, Orser had developed a reputation as a nervous performer who stumbled at major championships. He placed second at the 1984 Olympics, second at the 1984 world championships, second at the 1985 world championships, and second again at the 1986 world championships. In 1987 he finally broke through his invisible barrier and won his first world title. Boitano, meanwhile, had been crowned world champion in 1986 before finishing second to Orser in 1987.

In Calgary, Orser placed first in the short program and trailed Boitano by a negligible margin going into the long program, which was worth 50 percent of the total score. Boitano skated first and gave a stunning performance, with only a barely perceptible bobble in a triple jump landing. In figure skating it is rare for a champion to do his best in a major competition because of the enormous pressure involved, but Boitano broke the rule. "I felt like angels were lifting and spinning me," he would later explain.

Despite Boitano's near-perfection, it was still possible for Orser, a superior artistic skater, to salvage the gold medal. But the pressure on Orser was even greater than that on Boitano. On top of the natural stress brought on by competing for an Olympic title, Orser carried with him the burden of being the host country's only gold medal hope. Ninety seconds into his routine, Orser nearly missed a triple flip jump, landing on two feet instead of one. Still, in the words of Dick Button, it was only "the slightest of slightest glitches," and not enough to settle the contest in Boitano's favor. But late in his routine, a fatigued Orser downgraded a triple axel to a double and his fate was sealed.

As it was, the judging could hardly have been closer. Four judges voted for Orser, three for Boitano, and two scored it a tie. In figure skating, judges are given the option of breaking ties based on the criterion of their choice. In this case, both judges who had scored the Brians evenly chose the score for technical merit as their tiebreaker. As both had awarded Boitano higher marks for technical merit, he ended up winning 5–4.

All of the hype about the "Battle of the Brians" aside, Boitano and Orser were actually good friends. At the medal ceremony, Boitano was plagued by contradictory emotions. "I almost felt guilty feeling great," he would later say. "I tried to hold it back, so me feeling great wouldn't make him feel worse."

The third-place winner, Viktor Petrenko, was the first Ukrainian to win a medal in an individual event at a Winter Olympics.

Brian Boitano (right) consoles Brian Orser after defeating him in the figure skating competition of 1988.

1992 Albertville C: 31, N: 23, D: 2.15.

		SP	AUS	FIN	SOV	ITA	CAN	CZE	JPN	USA	FRA	ORDINALS
		JUDGES' RANKINGS (FREE SKATING)										
1. Viktor Petrenko	SOV/ UKR	1	2	1	1	1	3	1	1	1	1	1.5
2. Paul Wylie	USA	3	1	2	4	3	1	5	3	2	2	3.5
3. Petr Barna	CZE	2	3	3	2	2	4	2	2	3	3	4.0
4. Christopher Bowman	USA	7	4	5	4	5	5	6	5	4	7	7.5
5. Aleksei Urmanov	SOV/ RUS	5	6	6	3	8	6	3	9	6	5	7.5
6. Kurt Browning	CAN	4	8	4	8	6	2	4	4	9	6	8.0
7. Elvis Stojko	CAN	6	7	7	7	4	7	7	6	7	9	10.0
8. Vyacheslav Zagorodniuk	SOV/ UKR	10	5	8	6	7	9	9	7	5	4	13.0

At the last two world championships, Viktor Petrenko had ranked first after the short program only to lose to Kurt Browning because he wilted toward the end of his long program. Once again Petrenko led after the short program, and once again he wilted in the second half of his long program, even falling once, but this time Browning, slow to recover from a back injury, was unable to match the performances that had earned him three straight world titles. The star of the competition was Harvard graduate Paul Wylie, at 27 the oldest skater on the ice. Wylie was the only one of the top six men to complete his long program without falling or touching the ice with his hand. However, his program was not as challenging as Petrenko's.

Bronze medalist Petr Barna became the first skater to successfully perform a quadruple jump in the Olympics.

1994 Lillehammer-Hamar C: 25, N: 17, D: 2.19.

JUDGES' RANKINGS (FREE SKATING)

		SP	ROM	RUS	BLR	JPN	FRA	DEN	USA	GBR	CAN	ORDINALS
1. Aleksei Urmanov	RUS	1	2	1	1	1	5	2	1	1	1	1.5
2. Elvis Stojko	CAN	2	3	5	3	3	1	3	2	2	2	3.0
3. Philippe Candeloro	FRA	3	5	3	5	6	2	1	3	4	4	6.5
4. Viktor Petrenko	UKR	9	1	4	4	4	3	4	5	3	5	8.5
5. Kurt Browning	CAN	12	4	2	2	2	4	5	4	5	3	9.0
6. Brian Boitano	USA	8	6	6	6	5	7	8	6	10	6	10.0
7. Erik Millot	FRA	6	8	8	7	7	6	6	11	7	8	10.0
8. Scott Davis	USA	4	7	7	10	8	8	9	9	9	7	10.0

For some years, skaters, led by Brian Boitano, lobbied the International Skating Union (ISU) to follow the lead of most other sports and open the Olympics to professionals. In 1990, the ISU grudgingly allowed current and future skaters to turn professional without losing their Olympic eligibility. But they refused to extend their welcome to Boitano and other past champions. Then, in June 1992, the ISU agreed to allow all professionals to compete in the Olympics, *if* the skater competed only in ISU-approved events. It wasn't what Boitano and others had wanted, but it would have to do for 1994. Boitano applied for reinstatement, as did defending Olympic champion Victor Petrenko. It looked like the Lillehammer Olympics would be a hot battle among Boitano, the 1988 gold medalist, Petrenko, the 1992 gold medalist, and four-time and defending world champion Kurt Browning. Even when Boitano lost to Scott Davis at the U.S. trials and Browning was beaten by Elvis Stojko at the Canadian trials, it was hard to imagine anyone other than the big three actually winning in Lillehammer.

Because Boitano and Petrenko had not taken part in the last world championship, they were seeded in the opening group with other "newcomers" for the short program. In fact Boitano was the very first skater on the ice, before the stands were even half full. Fifty seconds into his routine, he went too high on a triple axel, stumbled on the landing and touched both hands to the ice. What was worse, the triple axel was supposed to be the beginning of a combination, the second jump of which he was forced to abort. Four skaters later, Petrenko overrotated the landing of his triple axel and two-footed the landing of a triple lutz. Browning, skating last of the 25 entrants, saw a clear road to first place. But his performance was even worse than those of Boitano and Petrenko. He fell after a triple flip, reduced a double axel to a single and, disheartened, pulled out of his final spin. Instead of ending the technical program in first, second and third, Boitano, Petrenko and Browning found themselves in eighth, ninth and twelfth respectively.

First place in the technical program went to 20-year-old Aleksei Urmanov, a solid jumper whose clean and classical performance impressed the judges if not the audience. Second was the more popular Elvis Stojko, who performed to the techno-hip-hop number *Frogs in Space*, and third was crowd-pleasing Philippe Candeloro, who performed to *The Godfather*.

The old guard saved face in the free skate, with Browning earning third place and leaping to fifth overall, and Petrenko earning fourth place. However the medal places remained unchanged. Stojko swept the judges' scores for technical merit, but his radical kung-fu routine and his somewhat stiff performance led judges to mark him down for artistic impression. Candeloro might have won gold or silver, but, after completing seven triple jumps, he tried an eighth ten seconds before the end of his routine and fell. Although Urmanov's performance left most spectators bored, he landed eight triple jumps with only one stumble and, while Candeloro continued his Godfather theme and Stojko performed to the theme from *Dragon: The Bruce Lee Story,* Urmanov stuck to Rossini and won.

Urmanov was an unusual winner in that he had never won a major international competition before his Olympic victory, nor has he won one since. Such successes occur occasionally in certain other sports, such as alpine skiing and track and field, but are almost unheard of in a judged sport like figure skating. One month after the Olympics, Urmanov placed only fourth at the world championships (won by Stojko) to become the first Olympic champion ever to miss the medal podium in the same year's world championship. While the other leading skaters went on to lucrative tours and careers, Urmanov, who earned $30 a month, returned to live with his mother in a St. Petersburg apartment. By 1995 he was not even invited to participate in that year's Tour of World Champions. At the 1997 world championships, Urmanov was in first place after the short program, but a groin injury forced him to withdraw before the free skate.

WOMEN

1908 London C: 5, N: 3, D: 10.29.

			JUDGES' RANKINGS				
		GBR	SWE	SWI	RUS	GER	ORDINALS
1. Florence "Madge" Syers	GBR	1	1	1	1	1	5
2. Elsa Rendschmidt	GER	3	2	2	2	2	11
3. Dorothy Greenhough-Smith	GBR	2	3	4	3	3	15
4. Elna Montgomery	SWE	4	4	5	4	4	21
5. Gwendolyn Lycett	GBR	5	5	3	5	5	23

In 1902, 20-year-old Madge Syers caused a sensation by becoming the first woman to enter the world championships. Even more shocking was the fact that she placed second behind Ulrich Salchow. Figure skating authorities immediately banned women from international competitions, although Syers did take part in the British national championship, winning in 1903 and again in 1904, when she defeated her husband. In 1906 a separate women's event was introduced at the world championships, and Syers won easily. She won again the following year and then was the unanimous choice of the five judges at the Olympics.

1920 Antwerp C: 6, N: 4, D: 4.25.

			JUDGES' RANKINGS				
		SWE	FRA	BEL	NOR	GBR	ORDINALS
1. Magda Julin-Mauroy	SWE	2	3	2	3	2	12
2. Svea Norén	SWE	1	1.5	3	4	3	12.5
3. Theresa Weld	USA	3	1.5	1	6	4	15.5
4. Phyllis Johnson	GBR	4.5	4	4	5	1	18.5
5. Margot Moe	NOR	4.5	6	6	1	5	22.5
6. Ingrid Gulbrandsen	NOR	6	5	5	2	6	24

Magda Julin won the closest of all Olympic figure skating contests despite the fact that she received no first-place votes. The British judge voted for Johnson, the Swedish judge for Norén, and the Norwegian judge placed Moe and Gulbrandsen first and second, even though the other judges put them last. The Belgian judge voted for Weld and the French judge declared a tie between Norén and Weld. Julin did receive three second-place votes and won according to the placings countback rule. At one point Weld was cautioned by the judges for making jumps "unsuitable for a lady," because they caused her skirt to fly up to her knees.

1924 Chamonix C: 8, N: 6, D: 1.29.

				JUDGES' RANKINGS					
		AUT	FIN	GBR	AUT	FRA	BEL	FRA	ORDINALS
1. Herma Planck-Szabó	AUT	1	1	1	1	1	1	1	7
2. Beatrix Loughran	USA	2	2	2	2	2	2	2	14
3. Ethel Muckelt	GBR	4	3	3	4	4	5	3	26
4. Theresa Blanchard-Weld	USA	3	4	4	3	5	3	5	27
5. Andrée Joly	FRA	6	6	7	5	3	4	7	38
6. Cecil Smith	CAN	5	7	5	8	6	7	6	44
7. G. Kathleen Shaw	GBR	7	8	6	6	7	8	4	46
8. Sonja Henie	NOR	8	5	8	7	8	6	8	50

In retrospect, the 1924 competition was most notable for the appearance of the last-place finisher, 11-year-old Sonja Henie, who was to become the most famous figure skater of all time. In Chamonix, her free skating routine was punctuated by frequent visits to the sidelines to ask her teacher what she should do next.

1928 St. Moritz C: 20, N: 8, D: 2.18.

				JUDGES' RANKINGS					
		NOR	FRA	GBR	BEL	USA	GER	AUT	ORDINALS
1. Sonja Henie	NOR	1	1	1	1	2	1	1	8
2. Fritzi Burger	AUT	3	2	4	5	6	3	2	25
3. Beatrix Loughran	USA	7	3	2	4	1	6	5	28
4. Maribel Vinson	USA	4	5	5	3	3	4	8	32
5. Cecil Smith	CAN	6	4	3	2	5	5	7	32
6. Constance Wilson	CAN	5	6	6	6	4	2	6	35
7. Melitta Brunner	AUT	2	7	8	10	8	9	4	48
8. Ilse Hornung	AUT	8	9	10	8	9	7	3	54

Sonja Henie was born in Oslo on April 8, 1912. Her father was a wealthy furrier, the owner of Norway's largest fur company, as well as the owner of Oslo's first automobile. Sonja gained valuable experience at the 1924 Olympics. Two years later she had improved enough to finish second at the world championships. In 1927 the world championships were held on Henie's home rink in Oslo. Henie won the title, but not without some controversy concerning the judging. There were five judges: one Austrian, one German, and three from Norway. The Austrian and the German both gave their first-place votes to Herma Planck-Szabó. However, all three Norwegian judges voted for Sonja Henie, giving her the championship. The ensuing uproar prompted the International Skating Union to institute a rule, still in effect, allowing only one judge per country in international meets. At the 1928 Olympics there was no such controversy, as Henie was awarded first place by six of the seven judges. Only the American judge voted for Beatrix Loughran, who had the unusual distinction of receiving one vote for each of the first seven places.

1932 Lake Placid C: 15, N: 7, D: 10.9.

				JUDGES' RANKINGS					
		NOR	GBR	AUT	FIN	CAN	FRA	USA	ORDINALS
1. Sonja Henie	NOR	1	1	1	1	1	1	1	7
2. Fritzi Burger	AUT	2	4	2	3	2	2	3	18
3. Maribel Vinson	USA	4	2	3	4	5	3	2	23

Sonja Henie was only 23 years old when she earned her third consecutive figure skating gold medal.

4. Constance Wilson-Samuel	CAN	3	5	4	5	3	4	4	28
5. Vivi-Anne Hultén	SWE	5	3	5	2	4	5	5	29
6. Yvonne de Ligne	BEL	6	6	8	6	7	6	6	45
7. Megan Taylor	GBR	8	10	7	9	6	7	8	55
8. M. Cecilia Colledge	GBR	14	9	6	7	13	8	7	64

Sonja Henie was the unanimous choice of the seven judges. Already Sonja Henie imitators were springing up wherever figure skating was appreciated. Two 11-year-olds from Great Britain, Megan Taylor and Cecilia Colledge, placed seventh and eighth at Lake Placid. Bronze medalist Maribel Vinson later became the first female sportswriter for the *New York Times*.

1936 Garmisch-Partenkirchen C: 26, N: 13, D: 2.15.

		JUDGES' RANKINGS							
		USA	GBR	GER	BEL	SWE	AUT	CZE	ORDINALS
1. Sonja Henie	NOR	1	1	1	1	1	1.5	1	7.5
2. M. Cecilia Colledge	GBR	2	2	2	2	2	1.5	2	13.5
3. Vivi-Anne Hultén	SWE	4	4	3	4	3	7	3	28
4. Liselotte Landbeck	BEL	6	5	5	3	6	3	4	32
5. Maribel Vinson	USA	3	3	9	7	4	8	5	39
6. Hedy Stenuf	AUT	5	7	8	5	5	4	6	40
7. Emmy Putzinger	AUT	8	10	6	6	7	5	7	49
8. Viktoria Lindpaintner	GER	7	6	4	8	8	10	8	51

By 1936 Sonja Henie was so popular that police had to be called out to control the crowds around her in places as far apart as New York City and Prague. During an exhibition in Berlin in 1935 she prefaced her performance by skating up to Adolf Hitler, giving the Nazi salute and booming out, "Heil Hitler!" In Germany she was hailed as a heroine, but back in her native Norway she was denounced as a traitor. Henie had announced that she would retire from competition following the 1936 world championships, to be held one week after the Olympics. She wanted to close out her amateur career with a third Olympic gold medal, so she felt great tension preceding the competition. When the scoring totals were posted for the compulsory figures, Henie was only 3.6 points ahead of Colledge. When Henie was told the results she tore the offending sheet of paper off the announcements board and ripped it to shreds, stating that it was a misrepresentation. Fifteen-year-old Cecilia Colledge was the second skater to perform her free-skating program. As she glided onto the ice she gave the Nazi salute, which pleased the crowd. Just as she prepared to begin her routine, it was discovered that someone had put on the wrong music, and she was forced to endure a delay while the proper record was found. Not surprisingly, Colledge almost fell during the first minute of her performance. But she recovered sufficiently to earn an average score of 5.7. Sonja Henie, the last of the 26 skaters, appeared nervous, but skated with great vigor and precision. An average score of 5.8 assured her of her third gold medal. A week later she won her tenth straight world championship, a feat surpassed only by Ulrich Salchow, who won 11 consecutive world titles from 1901 through 1911.

During her competitive career, Sonja Henie accumulated 1473 cups, medals, and trophies. After she turned professional her parents convinced Twentieth Century-Fox to put her in the movies. Henie's first film, *One in a Million,* was a big success, and nine more films followed. By 1938, her box-office popularity was matched only by Shirley Temple and Clark Gable. In 1937 she earned more than $200,000. Her father died that year, but Sonja definitely inherited his business acumen. She made enough money to allow her to engage in an occasional indulgence. The only person she trusted to sharpen her skates was Eddie Pec. One time while Sonja was performing in Chicago, she needed her skates sharpened. So she called Eddie Pec in New York. Pec took the next train to Chicago, arriving the following day. He spent a couple minutes sharpening Henie's skates, then turned around and took the next train back to New York.

Sonja Henie became a U.S. citizen in 1941. After divorcing two Americans, the 44-year-old Henie married her childhood sweetheart, Norwegian shipowner Niels Onstad. Sonja Henie died of leukemia at the age of 57, while on an ambulance airplane flying her from Paris to Oslo. She was worth over $47 million at the time of her death.

Another future actress who took part in the 1936 figure skating competition was Vera Hruba of Czechoslovakia, who placed 17th. As Vera Hruba Ralston, she starred in numerous B pictures, including *The Lady and the Monster, Hoodlum Empire,* and *I, Jane Doe.* Her specialties were Westerns and pioneer films. She also married the president of Republic Pictures, Herbert Yates, who was sued by stockholders for using company profits to further his wife's career.

1948 St. Moritz C: 25, N: 10, D: 2.6.

		ITA	USA	SWI	GBR	CAN	AUT	FRA	HUN	CZE	ORDINALS
					JUDGES' RANKINGS						
1. Barbara Ann Scott	CAN	1	1	1	2	1	2	1	1	1	11
2. Eva Pawlik	AUT	2	2	3	3	4	1	2	2	5	24

In 1948, Barbara Ann Scott became the first North American to win a gold medal in figure skating.

3. Jeannette Altwegg	GBR	3	4	2	1	2	5	3	4	4	28
4. Jirina Nekolová	CZE	5	3	4	4	3	4	5	3	3	34
5. Alena Vrzánová	CZE	6	6	6	6	6	3	4	5	2	44
6. Yvonne Sherman	USA	9	7	7	8	5	6	6	7	7	62
7. Bridget Shirley Adams	GBR	7	8	5	5	11	7	11	6	9	69
8. Gretchen Merrill	USA	4	5	8	7	8	9	8	9	15	73

In 1947, 18-year-old Barbara Ann Scott became the first North American to win a figure skating world championship. Her hometown of Ottawa awarded her a yellow Buick convertible with the license 47-U-1. However, I.O.C. member Avery Brundage contended that such a gift would make her a professional and disqualify her from the Olympics. After weeping in public, she reluctantly returned the car. The day of the free-skating competition, the ice was badly chewed up by two hockey matches. Just before Scott went out to perform, one of the earlier skaters, Eileen Seigh of the United States, gave her a complete description of the location of all the ruts and clean spots all over the rink. Scott wore a hand-sewn cream-colored fur dress. On the inside, all the women who had worked on it had signed their names and a good luck message. Scott won seven of the nine first-place votes, with the Austrian judge voting for Pawlik and the British judge for Altwegg. Immediately after the Olympics, Scott turned professional and collected her convertible—but with a new license plate: 48-U-1.

1952 Oslo C: 25, N: 12, D: 2.20.

		USA	GBR	GER	SWI	NOR	CAN	AUT	FIN	FRA	ORDINALS
		JUDGES' RANKINGS									
1. Jeannette Altwegg	GBR	4	2	1	1	1	1	1	1	2	14
2. Tenley Albright	USA	1	1	3	5	2	2	3	2	3	22
3. Jacqueline du Bief	FRA	3	3	2	2	4	3	2	4	1	24
4. Sonya Klopfer	USA	2	5	4	4	3	4	4	5	5	36
5. Virginia Baxter	USA	5	4	7	9	5	6	7	3	4	50
6. Suzanne Morrow	CAN	6	6	6	8	8	5	5	6	6	56
7. Barbara Wyatt	GBR	7	7	5	6	6	9	9	7	7	63
8. Gundi Busch	GER	10	9	8	7	7	8	8	10	8	75

Jeannette Altwegg placed only fourth in free-skating. However she had built up such a large lead during the compulsory figures that she won anyway.

1956 Cortina C: 21, N: 11, D: 2.2.

		AUS	AUT	CAN	CZE	FRA	GER	GBR	ITA	HOL	USA	SWI	ORDINALS
		JUDGES' RANKINGS											
1. Tenley Albright	USA	1	1	1	1	1	1	1	1	1	2	1	12
2. Carol Heiss	USA	2	2	2	2	2	2	2	2	2	1	2	21
3. Ingrid Wendl	AUT	8	3	4	3	3	3	3	3	3	3	3	39
4. Yvonne de Monfort Sugden	GBR	3	5	8	4	4	7	4	4	4	5	5	53
5. Hanna Eigel	AUT	4	4	6	5	6	4	5	5	5	4	4	52
6. Carole Jane Pachl	CAN	5	7	3	6	5	10	8	9	8	6	6	73
7. Hannerl Walter	AUT	6	6	7	7	10	8.5	6	8	7	9	9	83.5
8. Catherine Machado	USA	10	8	5	9	8	8.5	7	10	6	7	8	86.5

Tenley Albright, a surgeon's daughter from Newton Center, Massachusetts, had been stricken by nonparalytic polio at the age of 11. Less than two weeks before the Cortina Olympics, Tenley was practicing when she hit a rut. As she fell, her left skate hit her ankle joint, cut through three layers of her right boot, slashed a vein, and severely scraped the bone. Her father arrived two days later and patched her up. In the Olympic competition she skated well enough to earn the first-place votes of ten of the 11 judges. Back in the United States she entered Harvard Medical School and eventually became a surgeon herself.

1960 Squaw Valley C: 26, N: 13, D: 2.23.

		AUT	CAN	CZE	GER	GBR	ITA	JPN	HOL	USA	ORDINALS
		JUDGES' RANKINGS									
1. Carol Heiss	USA	1	1	1	1	1	1	1	1	1	9
2. Sjoukje Dijkstra	HOL	2	2	2	2	2	2	3	2	3	20
3. Barbara Roles	USA	3	4	3	3	3	3	2	3	2	26
4. Jana Mrázková	CZE	5	7	4	5	4	4	10	5	9	53
5. Joan Haanappel	HOL	7	5	7	6	6	6	6	4	5	52
6. Laurence Owen	USA	6	3	6	13	7	5	4	9	4	57
7. Regine Heitzer	AUT	4	9	5	4	5	7	12	6	6	58
8. Anna Galmarini	ITA	9	10	9	7	8	8	11	7	10	79

In 1956, 16-year-old Carol Heiss of Ozone Park, Queens, traveled to Cortina with her mother, who was dying of cancer. She gained a silver medal at the Olympics, but two weeks later, she defeated Tenley Albright for the first time to win the world championship in Garmisch-Partenkirchen. In October her mother died, but Carol

Heiss took a vow to win an Olympic gold medal in her honor. This she did with extraordinary ease in 1960, earning the first-place votes of all nine judges. After the Olympics, Heiss attempted a Hollywood career, but understandably lost interest after making one film: *Snow White and the Three Stooges.*

1964 Innsbruck C: 30, N: 14, D: 2.2.

		GER	FRA	GBR	JPN	CAN	HOL	AUT	SWE	CZE	ORDINALS
						JUDGES' RANKINGS					
1. Sjoukje Dijkstra	HOL	1	1	1	1	1	1	1	1	1	9
2. Regine Heitzer	AUT	2	2	3	2	3	3	2	3	2	22
3. Petra Burka	CAN	3	4	2	4	2	2	3	2	3	25
4. Nicole Hassler	FRA	4	3	4	7	4	4	4	4	4	38
5. Miwa Fukuhara	JPN	7	5	7	3	5	5	5	8	5	50
6. Peggy Fleming	USA	5	7	11	5	8	6	6	5	6	59
7. Christine Haigler	USA	15	8	9	8	6	7	7	7	7	74
8. Albertina Noyes	USA	10	6	5	6	10	9	10	9	8	73

Two-time world champion Sjoukje Dijkstra was the third straight silver medalist to win a gold medal four years later. Her specialty was compulsory figures.

1968 Grenoble C: 32, N: 15, D: 2.11.

		CAN	CZE	GDR	GER	GBR	HUN	JPN	USA	SOV	ORDINALS
						JUDGES' RANKINGS					
1. Peggy Fleming	USA	1	1	1	1	1	1	1	1	1	9
2. Gabriele Seyfert	GDR	2	2	2	2	2	2	2	2	2	18
3. Hana Mašková	CZE	4	3	3	3	4	3	4	4	3	31
4. Albertina Noyes	USA	3	6	6	5	3	4	5	3	5	40
5. Beatrix Schuba	AUT	5	4	4	4	6	6	10	8	4	51

Peggy Fleming won an overwhelming victory in the 1968 women's figure skating competition.

		CAN	CZE	GDR	GER	GBR	HUN	JPN	USA	SOV	ORDINALS
					JUDGES' RANKINGS						
6. Zsuzsa Almássy	HUN	8	5	5	6	5	5	6	10	7	57
7. Karen Magnussen	CAN	7	8	7	7	7	8	8	5	6	63
8. Kumiko Ohkawa	JPN	6	7	8	8	8	7	3	6	8	61

Like Carol Heiss, Peggy Fleming came from a family which had sacrificed greatly to further her passion for figure skating. Peggy's father, who had moved the family from Cleveland to Pasadena, California, to Colorado Springs (and Carlo Fassi), died in 1966. Her mother designed and sewed all of Peggy's dresses. As a competition, the contest at Grenoble had little to offer. Fleming built up a huge lead after the compulsory figures and easily won all of the first-place votes, despite a shaky free skate in which she turned a double axel into a single and double-footed the landing of an incomplete double lutz. Likewise, Gaby Seyfert was awarded all of the second-place votes. Peggy Fleming was the only U.S. gold medal winner of the Grenoble Games. She signed a $500,000 contract with Ice Follies and appeared in TV commercials for vitamins, soap and panty hose. She later became a successful television commentator, often working with Dick Button.

1972 Sapporo C: 19, N: 14, D: 2.7.

		ITA	SOV	GDR	SWE	AUT	CAN	USA	JPN	HUN	ORDINALS
					JUDGES' RANKINGS						
1. Beatrix Schuba	AUT	1	1	1	1	1	1	1	1	1	9
2. Karen Magnussen	CAN	2	2	2	2	4	2	4	3	2	23
3. Janet Lynn	USA	3	3	3	3	3	3	3	2	4	27
4. Julie Holmes	USA	4	4	5	7	2	4	2	4	7	39
5. Zsuzsa Almássy	HUN	6	5	6	4	6	5	7	5	3	47
6. Sonja Morgenstern	GDR	7	6	4	5	7	7	5	6	6	53
7. Rita Trapanese	ITA	5	7	7	6	5	6	6	8	5	55
8. Christine Errath	GDR	8	9	8	8	9	9	9	9	9	78

World champion Trixi Schuba built up a large lead with her compulsory figures and coasted to victory with a seventh place in free-skating.

1976 Innsbruck C: 21, N: 15, D: 2.13.

		SOV	USA	GDR	JPN	HOL	CZE	CAN	GER	ITA	ORDINALS
					JUDGES' RANKINGS						
1. Dorothy Hamill	USA	1	1	1	1	1	1	1	1	1	9
2. Dianne de Leeuw	HOL	2	2	3	2	2	3	2	2	2	20
3. Christine Errath	GDR	3	3	2	3	3	4	4	3	3	28
4. Anett Pötzsch	GDR	4	4	4	4	4	2	3	4	4	33
5. Isabel de Navarre	GER	7	8	5	10	5	6	8	5	5	59
6. Wendy Burge	USA	5	5	7	7	10	7	6	8	8	63
7. Susanna Driano	ITA	8	7	6	6	8	9	5	7	7	63
8. Linda Fratianne	USA	9	6	9	8	6	8	9	6	6	67

For the fifth straight time the women's figure skating was decided by unanimous decision. Hamill was the last skater to earn a gold medal without performing a triple jump. Her victory was particularly exciting for her coach, Carlo Fassi, who achieved a unique double, having also coached the men's winner, John Curry. Hamill became the first female athlete to sign a $1 million-a-year contract—with the Ice Capades, which she later purchased and managed in 1993.

1980 Lake Placid C: 22, N: 15, D: 2.23.

		GER	AUT	JPN	USA	YUG	FIN	ITA	GDR	SWI	ORDINALS
					JUDGES' RANKINGS						
1. Anett Pötzsch	GDR	1	1	2	2	1	1	1	1	1	11
2. Linda Fratianne	USA	2	2	1	1	2	2	2	2	2	16
3. Dagmar Lurz	GER	3	3	4	3	3	3	3	3	3	28
4. Denise Biellmann	SWI	4	5	6	6	4	6	4	4	4	43
5. Lisa-Marie Allen	USA	5	4	5	4	6	5	5	5	6	45
6. Emi Watanabe	JPN	6	7	3	5	5	4	6	7	5	48
7. Claudia Kristofics- Binder	AUT	7	6	7	7	7	7	7	5	7	60
8. Susanna Driano	ITA	8	9	10	9	9	8	8	8	8	77

The closest Olympic women's figure skating competition in 60 years showcased the friendly rivalry between Linda Fratianne of Los Angeles and Anett Pötzsch of Karl-Marx Stadt. In 1977 Fratianne had won the world championship, but in 1978 she was defeated by Pötzsch. The following year, Linda won back the title, but at the Olympics, the pendulum swung Anett's way. Both 19-year-olds tried to increase their chances of victory by altering their appearance. Linda had cosmetic surgery to her nose and hired a coach to teach her how to smile while skating, while Anett lost ten pounds. Both tried to appear brighter, livelier, sexier. In the end, it turned out that glamour was unimportant, as Pötzsch gained a solid lead in the compulsory figures and Fratianne was unable to close the gap. Denise Biellmann ranked first in free-skating, but her 12th place in the compulsories kept her out of the medals.

1984 Sarajevo C: 23, N: 16, D: 2.18.

		CF	SP	SOV	YUG	GER	ITA	SWI	GDR	USA	CAN	BEL	ORDINALS
			JUDGES' RANKINGS (FREE SKATING)										
1. Katarina Witt	GDR	3	1	1	1	1	2	2	1	2	1	2	3.2
2. Rosalynn Sumners	USA	1	5	2	4	2	1	1	3	1	2	1	4.6
3. Kira Ivanova	SOV	5	3	4	3	5	6	8	5	5	8	5	9.2
4. Tiffany Chin	USA	12	2	3	2	3	3	4	2	3	3	3	11.0
5. Anna Kondrashova	SOV/ RUS	7	4	6	6	4	5	5	7	6	5	7	11.8
6. Elaine Zayak	USA	13	6	5	5	6	4	3	4	4	4	4	14.2
7. Manuela Ruben	GER	6	11	7	7	8	7	6	8	8	12	10	15.0
8. Yelena Vodorezova	SOV/ RUS	2	8	11	10	11	13	11	13	12	11	6	15.4

The 1984 Olympics pitted defending world champion Rosalynn Sumners against 1982 world champion Elaine Zayak and the beautiful up-and-coming East German, Katarina Witt. Zayak removed herself from the competition for the gold medal by placing 13th in the compulsories, which were won by Sumners, with Witt a strong third. Witt took a slight lead following the short program, and turned the free-skating into a head-to-head showdown. Witt, skating before Sumners, achieved high marks, but not high enough to put first place out of reach for Sumners. The Edmonds, Washington, native looked close to victory, but in the closing seconds of her routine, she let up slightly, turning a triple toe loop into a double and a double axel into a single. This lapse probably also turned her gold medal into silver. After her Olympic victory, Katarina Witt received 35,000 love letters. Among her admirers was East German dictator Erich Honecker. He made sure that the Stasi, East Germany's domestic spy organization, kept a close watch on all aspects of Witt's

Katarina Witt, who received 35,000 love letters following her victory in the 1984 women's figure skating competition. Four years later she became the event's first repeat champion since Sonja Henie.

life. Not only did they keep track of her lovers, they kept a log of the duration of her sexual encounters.

1988 Calgary C: 31, N: 23, D: 2.27.

					JUDGES' RANKINGS (FREE SKATING)							
		CF	SP	SWI	USA	GBR	JPN	GDR	GER	SOV	CAN	CZE	ORDINALS
1. Katarina Witt	GDR	3	1	2	2	3	3	1	3	1	2	2	4.2
2. Elizabeth Manley	CAN	4	3	1	1	1	1	2	1	2	1	1	4.6
3. Debra Thomas	USA	2	2	5	4	5	4	5	4	4	4	5	6.0
4. Jill Trenary	USA	5	6	4	5	4	5	4	5	5	5	4	10.4
5. Midori Ito	JPN	10	4	3	3	2	2	3	2	3	3	3	10.6
6. Claudia Leistner	GER	6	9	6	6	6	8	6	6	8	6	6	13.2
7. Kira Ivanova	SOV/ RUS	1	10	7	15	14	7	8	9	7	11	10	13.6
8. Anna Kondrashova	SOV/ RUS	9	7	8	7	8	6	7	7	6	9	9	15.2

The 1988 competition turned out to be a classic matchup between defending Olympic and world champion Katarina Witt and the only person to beat her in five years, the 1986 world champion, Stanford pre-medical student Debi Thomas. After the short program, Thomas held a slight lead over Witt, with local favorite Elizabeth Manley a distant third.

As it happened, both Witt and Thomas chose to perform their long program to Georges Bizet's *Carmen*. Witt, first on the ice, skated cautiously and tentatively. Having immersed herself in the character of Carmen, her artistic presentation was flawless, but because she took few risks, her marks for technical merit were unimpressive and she left the door open for Thomas to seize the gold medal. But Thomas was preceded by Elizabeth Manley. The 5-foot Canadian, who had a reputation for crumbling under pressure, brought down the house with a brilliant performance that would ultimately earn her an unexpected silver medal.

Thomas began her routine with a triple toe loop combination, but she underrotated the second jump and landed badly. Barely 20 seconds into her four-minute program, she gave up. "The whole reason I came here was to be great," she later explained, "and after that I couldn't be great." Thomas missed two more triples, once touching the ice with her hand to keep from falling. Despite her disappointing performance, Thomas made history by becoming the first black athlete to win a medal in the Winter Olympics. Witt, for her part, became the first repeat winner in singles figure skating since Sonja Henie.

1992 Albertville C: 29, N: 21, D: 2.21.

			JUDGES' RANKINGS (FREE SKATING)									
		SP	GER	CAN	CHN	FRA	JPN	DEN	CZE	GBR	SOV	ORDINALS
1. Kristi Yamaguchi	USA	1	1	1	1	1	2	1	2	1	1	1.5
2. Midori Ito	JPN	4	2	2	2	2	1	2	1	3	2	4.0
3. Nancy Kerrigan	USA	2	4	3	3	5	3	3	3	5	3	4.0
4. Tonya Harding	USA	6	5	7	4	4	4	8	6	7	4	7.0
5. Surya Bonaly	FRA	3	3	8	5	3	6	7	4	10	6	7.5
6. Chen Lu	CHN	11	6	5	6	7	8	4	5	4	5	10.5
7. Yuka Sato	JPN	7	10	4	7	6	5	6	9	2	8	10.5
8. Karen Preston	CAN	12	7	6	9	10	7	5	7	9	7	14.0

The two favorites were 4-foot 9-inch 22-year-old Midori Ito and 20-year-old Kristi Yamaguchi. As a 12-year-old, Ito had become the first female to land a triple-triple combination. At the Calgary Games she captivated the audience with an exuberant display of breathtaking jumps. Later that year she became the first woman to complete a triple axel in competition, a feat she repeated while winning the 1989 world championship. At the 1991 world championships in Munich, Ito was involved in a memorable incident. During the warm-up period before her short program, she was unintentionally broadsided by French skater Laetitia Hubert. Still dazed when she began her performance a few minutes later, Ito mistimed the takeoff of her double toe loop and went flying out of the rink. In Albertville, she had another unfortunate encounter with a French skater. Just as Ito was about to attempt the first jump in her routine during a practice session, Surya Bonaly cut in front of her and did a backflip—an illegal move. Rattled by this unsportsmanlike conduct, Ito missed seven of ten triple axel attempts. The next day, Ito dropped the triple axel from her short program and replaced it with the easier triple lutz. But she fell during the triple lutz and wound up only fourth going into the free skate. Ito's misfortune smoothed the path for Kristi Yamaguchi.

Yamaguchi, whose mother was born in a World War II internment camp for Japanese-Americans while her grandfather was serving as a lieutenant in the U.S.

Army, became obsessed with figure skating as a little girl. Her favorite toy was a Dorothy Hamill doll that she carried with her everywhere. Through 1990, Yamaguchi competed in both singles and pairs (with Rudy Galindo). That year she qualified for the world championships in both events, placing fourth and fifth respectively. Then she dropped out of pairs to concentrate on singles and was rewarded with her first world championship title in 1991.

In Albertville, Yamaguchi led after the original program, with her Olympic roommate, Nancy Kerrigan, in second and Bonaly third. But Yamaguchi had a history of placing first in the original program and then falling behind after the long program. This time she was the first of the leaders to skate. Backstage she was approached, for the first time, by none other than her childhood idol, Dorothy Hamill, who wished her luck and told her to go out and "have fun." Yamaguchi's relatively conservative program was marred by a touchdown at the end of a shaky triple loop. However, all the other contenders fell and Yamaguchi won a clear victory.

1994 Lillehammer-Hamar C: 27, N: 16, D: 2.25.

					JUDGES' RANKINGS (FREE SKATING)						
		SP	GBR	POL	CZE	UKR	CHN	USA	JPN	CAN	GER	ORDINALS
1. Oksana Baiul	UKR	2	3	1	1	1	1	2	2	3	1	2.0
2. Nancy Kerrigan	USA	1	1	2	2	2	2	1	1	1	2	2.5
3. Chen Lu	CHN	4	2	4	3	3	3	3	3	2	4	5.0
4. Surya Bonaly	FRA	3	4	3	4	4	4	5	5	5	5	5.5
5. Yuka Sato	JPN	7	6	5	5	5	5	7	4	4	3	8.5
6. Tanja Szewczenko	GER	5	5	6	7	6	6	4	6	8	6	8.5
7. Katarina Witt	GER	6	7	11	6	11	7	8	8	9	8	11.0
8. Tonya Harding	USA	10	8	6	8	7	8	6	7	6	7	12.0

It was the middle of the Lillehammer Olympics and the U.S. television network CBS was enjoying record-breaking ratings. Inside the CBS studios in Norway, buoyant executives posted a notice thanking all members of the staff and crew for making the ratings success possible. Underneath one of the notices, an anonymous CBS employee scrawled, "Don't thank us—thank Tonya."

From the ground-breaking days of Madge Syers until the Second World War, women's figure skating—"Ladies' " figure skating, as it is still known—was the domain of the wealthy. After World War II, a new model of skating champion developed: the young woman who came from a family that worked hard to make their daughter's dream come true. One heard frequent stories of mothers who sewed their daughters' costumes and fathers who worked two jobs and drove hundreds of miles to bring their little girls to practice and competition. This new breed of women skaters might not have come from wealthy families, but they were raised to act like ladies, and the old guard of skating had no cause to complain.

On the surface, Tonya Harding appeared to fit right into this new mold. Her parents were definitely not rich—her mother was a waitress and her father, her mother's fifth husband, bounced around from job to job. And her mother did in fact sew her costumes and drive her long distances to practice. But that was where the similarity between Tonya Harding and other skaters ended. Other mothers at the skating rink were appalled when Tonya's mom called her "scum," "bitch" and "stupid" and smacked her hard in public when she didn't perform well. Tonya's father taught her to fish and hunt (she killed her first deer at 14), how to chop wood, and how to replace a transmission, rebuild an engine and do a brake job. She could bench press 110 pounds and shoot a mean game of pool. She could also skate like no other girl in her hometown of Portland, Oregon. She was doing triple loops before the age of ten and she completed her first triple lutz at twelve.

When Harding was 16 years old, her mother moved out. When her father found work in Idaho, Tonya moved in with her mother and her mother's sixth husband. This was not a satisfying domestic arrangement and Tonya, who had already dropped out of high school, spent increasing amounts of time with her violent and controlling boyfriend, Jeff Gillooly. The two had started dating when Tonya was 15 and Jeff 18. Tonya moved in with Gillooly as soon as she turned 18 herself. A couple months later, Harding achieved her first major skating breakthrough, finishing third in the 1989 U.S. National Championships. She and Gillooly married on March 18, 1990. At both the 1992 and 1994 Olympics, Harding was the only women's singles competitor who had ever been married.

At the 1991 U.S. nationals, Harding hit seven triple jumps, including a triple axel, scoring an upset victory over Kristi Yamaguchi. In characteristic fashion, Harding stayed away from the traditional winners' gala and instead spent the evening shooting pool in a hotel bar. The following month she finished second to Yamaguchi at the world championships in Munich. Another skater completed the medal sweep for the United States: a reserved and beautiful 21-year-old from Stoneham, Massachusetts, named Nancy Kerrigan.

Nancy Kerrigan really did come from a classic post-War skating background. Her father, a welder, sometimes worked three jobs to keep up with his daughter's skating expenses. He also remortgaged his home and took out loans. Nancy's mother contracted a rare virus and lost her vision before Nancy's first birthday. But Kerrigan was blessed with a loving extended family and a decent, traditional community. When Nancy qualified for the 1992 Olympics, her father's coworkers collected money to send her parents to France. When she came home with a bronze medal, 40,000 people gathered for her welcome home parade. The population of Stoneham was 22,000.

When Tonya Harding called her mother for the first time after earning the silver medal at the 1991 world championships, her mother told Tonya her "routine was awful." "Your hair looked terrible," she said. "Have you gained weight?" In spite of her mother's opinion, the future looked promising for Tonya Harding in 1991. She was the second best female skater in the world. The only woman ahead of her, Kristi Yamaguchi, was certain to retire after a year.

The 1991–1992 season began well for Harding: she defeated Yamaguchi at the Skate America contest. Yamaguchi regained her form and in 1992 she won the U.S. national championship, the Olympic championship and the world championship. Tonya Harding was not too distressed by Yamaguchi's triumphs—Yamaguchi would be gone soon enough. But what was troublesome was the rise of Nancy Kerrigan. At the 1992 U.S. nationals, Kerrigan finished second. Harding was third. At the Olympics, Kerrigan finished third. Harding was fourth, missing the medal podium. At the world championships Kerrigan placed second. Harding dropped to sixth. The following season Kerrigan won the U.S. championship. Harding, fourth, didn't even qualify for the U.S. world championship team.

Nancy Kerrigan had trouble dealing with her own success. She had been comfortable as the second or third best American, but being the leader was more stressful. According to the rules of the International Skating Union, the number of entries each nation is allotted for the Olympics is determined by the nation's performance at the most recent world championships. According to the rules of the time, for the U.S. to earn three entries at the 1994 Olympics, Nancy Kerrigan had to win a medal at the 1993 world championships in Prague. If she placed fourth or worse, only two American women would compete at the Olympics. At least one U.S. woman had earned a medal at the last 23 world championships. In Prague, Kerrigan was in first place after the short program. But during the free skate she self-destructed, turning her first triple into a single, stumbling through another, taking an extra step in the middle of a combination and touching the ice with her hand. Ranked ninth in the free skate, she plummeted to fifth overall. For the first time in 70 years, the U.S. would have only two entrants in the women's singles at the Olympics. Kerrigan was humiliated. A television microphone caught her saying, "I just want to die."

Tonya Harding, in the meantime, was experiencing a crisis in her personal life. Fifteen months after marrying Jeff Gillooly, she filed for divorce and asked that a restraining order be issued to keep him away from her. Her friends were relieved that the relationship appeared over, but five months later they were back together. In the summer of 1993 Harding again filed for divorce, this time leaving so abruptly that all she took with her was her waterbed. Again a restraining order was issued and although the divorce did go through, again the ill-fated couple reconciled. In October police were called to separate Tonya and Jeff during a fight in which Tonya fired a handgun.

Amidst this chaos, the 1993–1994 Olympic season began. For Kerrigan, it began well. Determined to wipe out the memory of her Prague collapse, she pursued a much more rigorous training program and engaged in successful therapy with a sports psychologist. In her only pre-Olympic international competition—on the Olympic rink in Hamar—she defeated Chen Lu and Surya Bonaly, the bronze and silver medalists at the last world championships.

For Harding, the season did not begin well. At the Skate America competition, she was 50 seconds away from an impressive defeat of both Bonaly and world champion Oksana Baiul when one of her skate blades loosened. Harding screwed it back together, but when she resumed her performance, she had lost her momentum. She ended up in third place. On November 4, during the same week that a court issued a default judgment against Harding and Gillooly for nonpayment of a credit card bill, skating officials at a regional qualifying competition informed Harding that they had received a death threat against her. It would later turn out to be a self-contrived hoax. At the time, it convinced U.S. figure skating authorities to advance her to the national championships without having to deal with the bothersome regional. And, coming six months after the courtside knifing of tennis star Monica Seles, it gained sympathy for Harding. In fact, baseball owner George Steinbrenner donated $20,000 to the embattled skater. What Harding and Gillooly would do with that money would set off the biggest scandal in the history of the Winter Olympics.

At the NHK Trophy competition in Chiba, Japan, on December 11, Harding was beaten by Bonaly, Yuka Sato and Chen Lu. She returned to Portland in a bad mood, convinced that the judges were against her. It appeared that even if she skated two clean programs at the Olympics, as the second-best American the best she could hope for was about sixth place.

As their finances disintegrated, Harding and Gillooly's anger began to focus on one person: Nancy Kerrigan. It wasn't just that Kerrigan was winning medals that could have been Harding's, it was that she was winning endorsements and signing commercial contracts. Kerrigan was making money—big money. Beautiful and wholesome, Kerrigan had already appeared in commercials and advertisements for Coca-Cola, Reebok, Campbell's Soup, Northwest Airlines, Xerox, Seiko, Evian and the Massachusetts State Lottery. Tonya Harding wanted a piece of the action, but she couldn't get any as long as Nancy Kerrigan was in the way.

A few days after Harding's return from Japan, Gillooly asked childhood friend Shawn Eckardt, a 311-pound blowhard, if he knew anyone who could pave Harding's road to Olympic glory by acting against Nancy Kerrigan. Eckardt contacted Derrick Smith, who contacted his nephew, Shane Stant. At a meeting on December 28, the four men kicked around various ideas—like killing Kerrigan or cutting the tendon of her landing leg—before settling on "disabling" her leg by bashing her knee. Gillooly pledged $6500 for the hit, not much for such an important job, and he got what he paid for. Unbeknownst to Gillooly, the others, not trusting him to pay, tape-recorded the meeting.

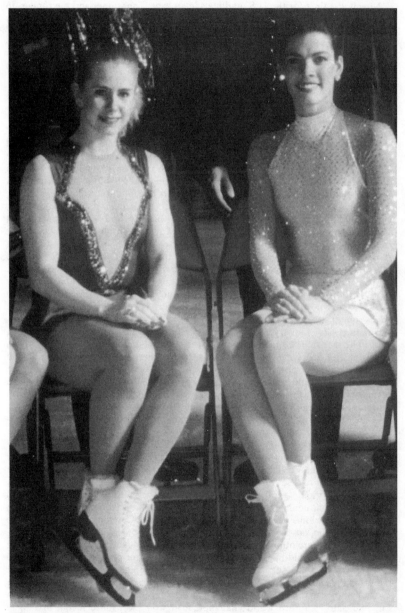

Tonya Harding and Nancy Kerrigan pose for a U.S. team photo on January 9, 1994—three days after the attack on Kerrigan.

Initially the conspirators planned to attack Kerrigan while she trained in Cape Cod. But the hitman, Stant, was so inept, that he couldn't find her even though Harding had made phone calls to locate her practice rink and times. On January 1, Harding complained to Eckardt because there had been no action.

Now it was time for the U.S. nationals in Detroit. The winner and the runner-up would go to the Olympics. Stant took a bus to Detroit, where he was joined by his uncle, who would drive the getaway car.

On January 6, Nancy Kerrigan, wearing a typically sexy yet wholesome lacy white costume, stepped off the ice after finishing a practice session at Detroit's Cobo Ice Arena. She was approached by Dana Scarton, a reporter from the *Pittsburgh Post-Gazette*. Suddenly a powerful man dressed in black pushed between them and, using a 21-inch ASP retractable baton, whacked Kerrigan with both hands just above the knee. It was Stant. He escaped by diving through a plexiglass door and running through the snow to the getaway car. Kerrigan collapsed in pain. Her father raced to her aid. "It hurts, Dad," she cried. "I'm so scared. Why me?"

Two days later Tonya Harding won the U.S. national championship and qualified for the Olympics. Nancy Kerrigan was given the second spot on the team despite being too "disabled" to compete. Fortunately, the attack missed her kneecap by an inch and her injuries were limited to severe bruising and a badly strained knee even though doctors had to drain 20 cubic centimeters of blood to reduce the swelling.

Initially it was assumed that the attack had been carried out by an insane nut, such as the man who had knifed Monica Seles. But it soon became apparent that there was more to the case, and the conspiracy quickly unraveled. The first break came when a friend of Shawn Eckardt's father told police about the tape-recording of the December 28th meeting. Four days after the attack, Eckardt and Smith were arrested and Stant turned himself in a couple of days later. All three confessed.

When Gillooly was asked if he had commissioned the attack, he replied, "I have more faith in my wife than to bump off her competition." Harding, appearing on ABC's "Good Morning America," declared, "I may be a little rough around the edges sometimes, but overall I think I'm a good person."

The next day, January 18, Harding was interrogated by the FBI for 10½ hours. When she was finished, she announced to the press that she was separating from Gillooly. The following day, he was arrested. Hung out to dry, Gillooly joined Eckardt in telling the authorities that Harding had been an active participant in the plot. Harding would only admit to knowing about the attack after it had been carried out. Questions were raised as to whether Harding should be allowed to represent the United States at the upcoming Olympics. Responsibility for the decision fell on the United States Olympic Committee (USOC). Leroy Walker, president of the USOC, was adamant. "We're not going to hedge on this," he declared, "simply because we might be sued." But when Harding's lawyers did sue to stop the USOC from barring her from the Olympics, the USOC capitulated immediately.

Nancy Kerrigan arrived in Lillehammer fully recovered from her injuries. Tonya Harding arrived to discover that Gillooly, bitter at her betrayal of him to the FBI, had sold to the media a copy of an explicit video of their wedding night, that showed that Harding's athleticism was not limited to the ice. Stills from the videotape were published in tabloids across Europe. As the Opening Ceremony approached, the American public, absorbed in the good versus evil tale of Nancy and Tonya, discovered that there were other skaters in the competition. In fact, Kerrigan and Harding weren't even the gold-medal favorites. There were after all, the four women who had finished ahead of Kerrigan at the 1993 world championships. Yuka Sato, whose father had placed 8th at the 1964 Olympics and whose mother had placed 8th at the 1968 Olympics, had earned fourth place at the Prague world championships. Chen Lu, like Sato, a future world champion, had won the bronze medal in Prague despite coming from a country where figure skating was almost unknown.

Surya Bonaly of France had earned the silver medal in Prague. Known for her athletic strength, she had worked hard on her artistic presentation and hoped to become the first black athlete to win a gold medal at the Winter Olympics. Her parents, who adopted her when she was 8 months old, had claimed for years that she had been born on the island of Réunion because it sounded exotic. In fact, she was born in Nice. It was true, however, that Bonaly was raised vegetarian and that she didn't cut her hair until she was 18 years old. She was born with the name Claudine, but her somewhat bohemian parents renamed her Surya after the Hindi word for "sun."

The real gold-medal favorite in Lillehammer was the defending world champion, 16-year-old Oksana Baiul of the Ukraine. The long-legged Baiul had a background that made Tonya Harding's look privileged. Her parents separated soon after her birth and her father disappeared from her life. Oksana was raised by her mother, a French teacher, and her mother's parents. It was a loving family. But then Oksana's grandmother died and then her grandfather. In 1991, her mother, who was only 36 years old, died of ovarian cancer. Oksana Baiul was 13 years old. Although her mother had remarried a year earlier, the stepfather felt little responsibility for Oksana. For a while she stayed with friends, for a while she slept on a cot at the ice rink in her hometown of Dnepropetrovsk. All she had was her coach, Stanislav Korytek. When Korytek accepted a job offer in Canada, he brought Baiul to another coach in Odessa, Galina Zmievskaya, whose student, Victor Petrenko, was the 1992 Olympic champion. When Zmievskaya heard Baiul's story, she knew that to take her on as a pupil meant also taking her on as a daughter. "She is only one girl," said Petrenko. "How much can she cost?" He agreed to pay for her skates and outfits. Since one of Zmievskaya's daughters was moving out to marry Petrenko, there was even a bed for her.

In some sports it is possible for a relative unknown to emerge from obscurity and earn an Olympic or world championship. In figure skating, such a development was unheard of. And yet that is exactly what happened to Oksana Baiul. In 1991 she had placed twelfth at the national championships of the Soviet Union. Two years later, in her first international competition, she surprised everyone by winning the silver medal behind Surya Bonaly at the European championships. Baiul was a competent jumper, but her balletic skills were superb. In addition, she was a natural performer who shamelessly mugged and flirted with the judges and the crowd. She went straight from the European championships to the world championships without returning to Odessa. Ranked second behind Nancy Kerrigan after the technical program, she held her form and moved up to first when Kerrigan fell apart. She had left the Ukraine a completely unknown 15-year-old. A mere few weeks later she was the world champion—the youngest since Sonja Henie in 1927. After sobbing convulsively following her victory, she told Zmievskaya, "The teardrops were God's kisses from my mother."

Despite her sensational upset, there was some question as to whether Baiul could win again at the Olympics. It was one thing to win the world championships when nothing was expected of her. It was quite another thing for the intensely emotional teenager to enter the pressure-cooker of the Olympics as the favorite. In October she defeated Bonaly and Harding at Skate America, but the following month she lost to Tanja Szewczenko and, one month before the Olympic competition, Bonaly beat her at the European championships.

At the Olympics, the International Skating Union insisted that Nancy Kerrigan and Tonya Harding practice at the same time because they were from the same country. Kerrigan made her statement by showing up at the first practice wearing the same lacy white skating dress she had been wearing when she was attacked.

The women's short program began at 7 p.m. Wednesday night, February 23. When it was broadcast on tape several hours later in the United States, it garnered the highest ratings of any show in 11 years and the 6th highest in American television history.

The first famous skater to perform was Katarina Witt, the two-time gold medalist from 1984 and 1988. As a returning professional, she was placed in the first group of skaters with the most lightly regarded entrants. Since Witt had left the competitive ranks, women's singles had turned into a battle of triple jumps and combinations. Witt could not compete with the leapers, but, dressed as Robin Hood, she impressed the judges enough to earn sixth place—and inclusion in the final group for the long program.

The next big name on the ice was Tonya Harding. Disdaining figure skating tradition, she wore the same scarlet dress she had worn at the U.S. nationals a year earlier. In the words of *Washington Post* columnist Tony Kornheiser, "Tonya came out in a red sleeveless dance hall dress. . . . She had on so much makeup, it looked like she rear-ended a Mary Kay Cadillac. I half expected her to skate over and take my drink order." Skating to the soundtrack of *Much Ado About Nothing,* Harding blew her medal hopes in only 30 seconds. She double-footed the landing of her first triple jump, took extra steps during a combo and even double-footed a relatively easy double flip. By the evening's end she was down in tenth place.

Surya Bonaly bobbled and hopped a bit, but her jumps were too powerful for any of the other skaters to match. Oksana Baiul had a sloppy landing on her triple lutz, but, as expected, her artistry was charming. Skating 26th of 27, Nancy Kerrigan skated a clean program, triumphantly putting to rest any doubts about her physical condition. When the judges' votes were tallied, Kerrigan was in first place, Baiul second and Bonaly third. Even though she ran into the sideboards once, Chen Lu remained within striking distance with a fourth place ranking.

Thursday was an off day in the competition, but it was not without its action. During practice, Baiul and Szewczenko started skating backwards from opposite directions. They both turned around at the last second, but it was too late and they collided forcefully. Katarina Witt was the first to come to their aid. Szewczenko had to be carried away, but mostly suffered from shock. Baiul needed three stitches to close a cut on her right shin and her tailbone was bruised as well. Both recovered enough to perform the following night.

The U.S. TV ratings for the free skate were not quite as high as they were for the technical program, but it was the most-watched Friday night show in American history.

Even though Tonya Harding was out of medal contention, she managed to cause a commotion anyway. When her name was announced, she failed to appear. Finally she dashed onto the ice just in time to avoid disqualification. But her performance appeared tentative. After 45 seconds she stopped and skated over to the judges in tears. The lace on her right boot had broken during warm-ups and her replacement lace was too short. Harding was granted a reskate. To the accompaniment of the soundtrack from *Jurassic Park* ("I think of myself as a tyrannosaurus rex, the powerful, strong beast"), she completed a solid program, but it was too little, too late. Her career was over.

It is a good bet that at this stage Nancy Kerrigan was more concerned with the memory of her world championship failure than with her memory of being attacked by Tonya Harding's goons. Skating to a medley of Neil Diamond songs, Kerrigan reduced her first jump, a triple flip, to a double, but after that her performance was flawless. She successfully, and brilliantly, erased the memory of Prague. As the heavily pro-Nancy crowd roared with delight, she skated off the ice convinced that she had won the gold medal.

Kerrigan was followed immediately by Oksana Baiul, who had received a painkilling injection only an hour earlier. Again Baiul skated with a beauty and soul that Kerrigan couldn't match, but she had trouble with the technical side of her program. As the seconds ticked down, she threw in a triple toe loop and a double axel-double toe loop combination. The gold medal decision would be a close call. In the press section reporters could see on their computer monitors that Baiul was ahead of Kerrigan five votes to four, but the results would not be final until Surya Bonaly skated. Bonaly needed a perfect performance, but the grace she had worked so hard to incorporate into her program wasn't there and she slipped off the medal podium, to be replaced by Chen Lu. The victory belonged to Oksana Baiul.

The final performer was Katarina Witt. Witt was out of the medal hunt, but, skating to "Where Have All the Flowers Gone?", she enchanted the crowd with a moving tribute to Sarejevo, the city where she had won her first gold medal, but which was now engulfed in a brutal civil war.

Nancy Kerrigan's supporters were peeved by the results. They were particularly upset by the inclusion on the judges' panel of Alfred Korytek, the father of Oksana Baiul's first coach. Korytek was included because the Ukraine had earned a spot on the panel and he was the only licensed judge in the entire country. As it happened, five judges from the old Communist bloc (including former East German Jan Hoffman) all voted for Baiul, while the four Western judges chose Kerrigan. However the split had more to do with style preferences than ideological prejudices. Kerrigan supporters were mystified that three of the judges awarded higher technical marks to Baiul, in spite of her inferior jumping. In a refreshing display of openness, the competition referee, Britta Lindgren of Sweden, who was in charge of judging the judges, met with members of the press and explained that scoring technical merit was not just a checklist of jumps, but also an evaluation of the quality of spins, spirals and footwork, and it was here that Baiul showed her superiority.

The medal ceremony was delayed for 26 minutes while officials searched frantically for a recording of the Ukrainian national anthem. Mistakenly informed that the delay was caused by Baiul redoing her makeup, a disgruntled Kerrigan complained to Chen Lu—within range of a TV microphone, "She's going to get out here and cry again. What's the difference?"

Indeed, Nancy Kerrigan's post-Olympic life had a rough start. While other athletes remained in Norway for the Closing Ceremony, she was whisked away to Disney World in Florida. While posing with Mickey Mouse, she was heard to say, "This is so dumb. I hate it. This is the most corny thing I've ever done." Many Americans were offended by Kerrigan's remarks, but she spoke the truth and who could blame her? In the coming years, Kerrigan would become a millionaire, marry and give birth, while continuing to perform and do charity work.

Tonya Harding's return to the United States was quite a bit less satisfying. Taking advantage of the Oregon judicial system's reluctance to incur the expense of a high profile trial, she was able to cop a plea. On March 16, she pleaded guilty to conspiring to hinder prosecution of a case. She was put on three years probation, ordered to perform 500 hours of community service and forced to pay a $100,000 fine as well as set up a $50,000 fund for the Special Olympics. She was also stripped of her national title and banned for life by the United States Figure Skating Association. She managed to stay away from Jeff Gillooly, but a marriage to a new husband was followed by another divorce and another restraining order.

And Oksana Baiul? She and her adopted family moved to the United States, where Oksana turned professional and learned the joys of being a material girl. In January 1997, she was charged with drunken driving and "driving unreasonably fast" when she drove her Mercedes off a Connecticut road while going almost 100 miles (160 kilometers) an hour. Although she was so intoxicated that she still had alcohol on her breath six hours later, her passenger, skater Ararat Zakarian, suggested that the accident occurred not because Baiul was drunk, but because "she got very emotional. There was a Madonna song playing and she loves Madonna."

Apparently Baiul began singing along and became so involved that she lost control of the steering wheel. Fortunately, no one was seriously injured.

PAIRS

Beginning in 1964, this event has been won nine straight times by pairs from Russia. Rather than an international battle for gold, pairs figure skating has been a contest between Moscow and St. Petersburg. Moscow has a narrow 5–4 lead with victories in 1972, 1976, 1980, 1988 and 1994. So dominant are the Russians that the last time even one judge voted in favor of a non-Russian pair was 1964.

1908 London T: 3, N: 2, D: 10.29.

		GER	SWI	GBR	GBR	RUS	ORDINALS
		\multicolumn{6}{c}{JUDGES' RANKINGS}
1. Anna Hübler Heinrich Burger	GER	1	1	1	1	1	5
2. Phyllis Johnson James Johnson	GBR	2	2	2	2	2	10
3. Florence "Madge" Syers Edgar Syers	GBR	3	3	3	3	3	13

1920 Antwerp T: 8, N: 6, D: 4.26.

		JUDGES' RANKINGS							
		SWE	FRA	BEL	NOR	FIN	GBR	SWI	ORDINALS
1. Ludovika Jakobsson-Eilers Walter Jakobsson	FIN	1	1	1	1	1	1	1	7
2. Alexia Bryn-Schøien Yngvar Bryn	NOR	2	2	2.5	2	2	2	2	15.5
3. Phyllis Johnson Basil Williams	GBR	3	3	6	3	4	3	3	25
4. Theresa Weld Nathaniel Niles	USA	4	4	2.5	6	3	4	4	28.5
5. Ethel Muckelt Sydney Wallwork	GBR	5	6	4	4	6	5	6	34
6. Georgette Herbos Georges Waegemans	BEL	6.5	5	5	8	5	7	5	41.5
7. Simone Sabouret Charles Sabouret	FRA	6.5	7	7	5	7	6	7	45.5
8. Madelon Beaumont Kenneth Macdonald Beaumont	GBR	8	8	8	7	8	8	8	55

1924 Chamonix T: 9, N: 7, D: 1.31.

		JUDGES' RANKINGS							
		AUT	GBR	SWI	FRA	AUT	FRA	BEL	ORDINALS
1. Helene Engelmann Alfred Berger	AUT	1	2	1	1	1	1	2	9
2. Ludovika Jakobsson-Eilers Walter Jakobsson	FIN	4	3	2	2	3.5	3	1	18.5
3. Andrée Joly Pierre Brunet	FRA	2	6	3	4	2	2	3	22
4. Ethel Muckelt John Page	GBR	6.5	1	7	3	3.5	5.5	4	30.5
5. Georgette Herbos Georges Waegemans	BEL	3	4	6	7	7	4	6	37

6. Theresa Blanchard-Weld Nathaniel Niles	USA	5	5	5	6	5.5	5.5	7	39
7. Cecil Smith Melville Rogers	CAN	6.5	8	4	5	5.5	7	5	41.5
8. F. Mildred Richardson Thomas Richardson	GBR	8	7	8	9	8	8	9	57

Because Canadians Smith and Rogers received the most enthusiastic applause, French newspapers quickly spread the news that they had won the competition. However, when the scores were finally tallied a few hours later, it turned out that they had placed only seventh.

1928 St. Moritz T: 13, N: 10, D: 2.19.

		JUDGES' RANKINGS								
		GER	FIN	SWI	USA	AUT	FRA	GBR	CZE	BEL	ORDINALS
1. Andrée Joly Pierre Brunet	FRA	4	1	1	1	2	1	2	1	1	14
2. Lilly Scholz Otto Kaiser	AUT	3	2	2	2	1	2	1	2	2	17
3. Melitta Brunner Ludwig Wrede	AUT	2	4	3	5	3	3	3	3	3	29
4. Beatrix Loughran Sherwin Badger	USA	1	9	5	3	5	4	5	7	4	43
5. Ludovika Jakobsson Walter Jakobsson	FIN	7	3	7	6	7	6	6	4	5	51
6. Josy van Leberghe Robert van Zeebroeck	BEL	6	7	4	4	6	7	7	5	8	54
7. Ethel Muckelt John Page	GBR	8.5	6	8	8	8	5	4	8	6	61.5
8. Ilse Kishauer Ernst Gaste	GER	5	5	6	9	4	9	8	6	11	63

Joly and Brunet dominated pairs figure skating from the time they won their first world championship on Valentine's Day, 1926, until they turned professional in 1936. Joly radicalized the sport by dressing in black like her partner. Previously, female pairs skaters always wore white.

1932 Lake Placid T: 7, N: 4, D: 2.12.

		JUDGES' RANKINGS							
		HUN	NOR	AUT	FIN	FRA	GBR	USA	ORDINALS
1. Andrée Brunet [Joly] Pierre Brunet	FRA	2.5	1	1.5	3	1	1	2	12
2. Beatrix Loughran Sherwin Badger	USA	4	2	4	1	2	2	1	16
3. Emília Rotter László Szollás	HUN	1	3	3	4	3	3	3	20
4. Olga Orgonista Sándor Szalay	HUN	2.5	5	1.5	5	5	4	5	28
5. Constance Wilson-Samuel Montgomery Wilson	CAN	5	6	5	6	4	5	4	35
6. Frances Claudet Chauney Bangs	CAN	6	4	6	2	6	6	6	36
7. Gertrude Meredith Joseph Savage	USA	7	7	7	7	7	7	7	49

1936 Garmisch-Partenkirchen T: 18, N: 12, D: 2.13.

		USA	GER	SWE	SWI	AUT	BEL	NOR	HUN	FIN	ORDINALS
1. Maxi Herber Ernst Baier	GER	1	1	1	1	2	1	1	2	1	11
2. Ilse Pausin Erik Pausin	AUT	3.5	2	2	2	1	2	2	3	2	19.5
3. Emília Rotter László Szollás	HUN	6	3	3.5	5	4	3	3	1	4	32.5
4. Piroska Szekrényessy Attila Szekrényessy	HUN	3.5	5	6	4	3	5	5	4	3	38.5
5. Maribel Vinson George Hill	USA	2	6	5	6	5	4	7	6.5	5	46.5
6. Louise Bertram Stewert Reburn	CAN	5	14	3.5	7	13	6	4	5	11	68.5
7. Violet Cliff Leslie Cliff	GBR	9	4	7	3	6	9	6	6.5	6	56.5
8. Eva Prawitz Otto Weiss	GER	8	7	9.5	10	8	8	8	8	7	74.5

JUDGES' RANKINGS

Thirty-year-old Berlin architect Ernst Baier and his 15-year-old protégée, Maxi Herber, were early exponents of "shadow skating," in which both skaters perform the exact same moves without touching. In an unusual reversal of normal procedure, the German government made a film of Baier and Herber's routine and commissioned a composer to create a piece to match their moves. The judges seemed to have trouble with the Canadian pair, Bertram and Reburn, who received a wide variety of scores, ranging from third and fourth place from the Swedish and Norwegian judges to 13th and 14th from the Austrian and German judges.

1948 St. Moritz T: 15, N: 11, D: 2.7.

		NOR	USA	AUT	SWI	CZE	BEL	GBR	CAN	HUN	FRA	ITA	ORDINALS
1. Micheline Lannoy Pierre Baugniet	BEL	1	2	2.5	1	1.5	1	1	1	4.5	1	1	17.5
2. Andrea Kékessy Ede Király	HUN	3	4	1	2	1.5	3	3	3	1	2.5	2	26
3. Suzanne Morrow Wallace Diestel- meyer	CAN	2	1	4	3	3	2	4	2	2.5	2.5	5	31
4. Yvonne Sherman Robert Swenning	USA	5	3	9	5	4	5	5	4.5	4.5	5	3	53
5. Winifred Silver- thorne Dennis Silver- thorne	GBR	6	5	6.5	4	5	4	2	6	2.5	6	6	53
6. Karol Kennedy Michael Kennedy	USA	4	6	2.5	8.5	6.5	6	6	4.5	7.5	4	4	59.5
7. Marianna Nagy László Nagy	HUN	7	7	6.5	6	8	10	10	10	6	7.5	11	89
8. Jennifer Nicks John Nicks	GBR	9	9.5	14	8.5	6.5	7	7	8	9	9.5	10	98

JUDGES' RANKINGS

Morrow and Diestelmeyer were the first pair to successfully perform the soon-to-be-ubiquitous death spiral.

1952 Oslo T: 13, N: 9, D: 2.22.

		CAN	USA	NOR	GBR	SWI	GER	SWE	HUN	AUT	ORDINALS
					JUDGES' RANKINGS						
1. Ria Falk	GER	1	2	2	1	1	1	1.5	1	1	11.5
Paul Falk											
2. Karol Kennedy	USA	2	1	1	2	2	2	1.5	3	3	17.5
Michael Kennedy											
3. Marianna Nagy	HUN	4	4	4	4	5	3	3	2	2	31
László Nagy											
4. Jennifer Nicks	GBR	5	5	3	3	4	4	5	4	6	39
John Nicks											
5. Frances Dafoe	CAN	3	3	5	6	6	7	7	7	4	48
Norris Bowden											
6. Janet Gerhauser	USA	6	6	6	5	7	6	4	6	8	54
John Nightingale											
7. Silvia Grandjean	SWI	8	7	7	7	3	5	6	5	5	53
Michel Grandjean											
8. Ingeborg Minor	GER	7	8	8	8	8	8	8	9	9.5	73.5
Hermann Braun											

1956 Cortina T: 11, N: 7, D: 2.3.

		AUS	AUT	CAN	CZE	GER	USA	GBR	HUN	SWI	ORDINALS
					JUDGES' RANKINGS						
1. Elisabeth Schwartz	AUT	1	1	2	1	1	2	2	2	2	14
Kurt Oppelt											
2. Frances Dafoe	CAN	2	2	1	2	3	1	1	3	1	16
Norris Bowden											
3. Marianna Nagy	HUN	5	3	6	3	4	4	3	1	3	32
László Nagy											
4. Marika Kilius	GER	3.5	4.5	4.5	5	2	3	4	5	4	35.5
Franz Ningel											
5. Carole Ormaca	USA	3.5	7	4.5	8	8	5	5	10	5	56
Robin Greiner											
6. Barbara Wagner	CAN	8	8.5	3	7	5.5	6	6.5	4	6	54.5
Robert Paul											
7. Lucille Ash	USA	7	6	9	5	5.5	7	6.5	6.5	7	59.5
Sully Kothmann											
8. Vera Suchanova	CZE	10	4.5	7	5	7	9	10	8	8	68.5
Zdenek Dolezal											

In this unusually close contest, both Schwarz and Oppelt and Dafoe and Bowden received four first-place votes, with the Hungarian judge voting for the Nagys. The Austrians won because they also received five second-place votes while the Canadians earned three seconds and two thirds. The decisive moment came when a tired Fran Dafoe lost her balance and faltered during a lift. The crowd, which had grumbled all along about the judging, became unruly when the popular German couple of 12-year-old Marika Kilius and 19-year-old Franz Ningel received scores only good enough for fourth place. Members of the audience pelted the judges and referee with oranges, and the ice had to be cleared three times before the competition could go on.

1960 Squaw Valley T: 13, N: 7, D: 2.19.

		JUDGES' RANKINGS							
		AUS	AUT	CAN	GER	ITA	SWI	USA	ORDINALS
1. Barbara Wagner Robert Paul	CAN	1	1	1	1	1	1	1	7
2. Marika Kilius Hans-Jürgen Bäumler	GER	4	2	3	2	2	2	4	19
3. Nancy Ludington Ronald Ludington	USA	3	3	2	6	6.5	4	3	27.5
4. Maria Jelinek Otto Jelinek	CAN	2	4	4	3	4	7	2	26
5. Margret Göbl Franz Ningel	GER	5	5	8	4	3	3	8	36
6. Nina Zhuk Stanislav Zhuk	SOV/ RUS	7	6	5	5	5	5	5	38
7. Rita Blumenberg Werner Mensching	GER	9	7.5	7	7	6.5	6	10	53
8. Diana Hinko Heinz Dopfl	AUT	10	7.5	6	8	8	9	6	54.5

Gold medal winner Bob Paul later gained further renown as a choreographer for Peggy Fleming, Dorothy Hamill, and Linda Fratianne, as well as for entertainers Donny and Marie Osmond.

1964 Innsbruck T: 17, N: 7, D: 1.29.

		JUDGES' RANKINGS								
		GER	FRA	ITA	CAN	AUT	SWI	CZE	USA	SOV	ORDINALS
1. Lyudmila Belousova Oleg Protopopov	SOV/ RUS	2	2	2	1	2	1	1	1	1	13
2. Marika Kilius Hans-Jürgen Bäumler	GER	1	1	1	3	1	2	2	2	2	15
3. Debbi Wilkes Guy Revell	CAN	4	5	4	2	4.5	3	4	3	6	35.5
4. Vivian Joseph Ronald Joseph	USA	3	3	3	4	4.5	4	5	5	4	35.5
5. Tatyana Zhuk Aleksandr Gavrilov	SOV/ RUS	6	6	5	9	3	6	3	4	3	45
6. Gerda Johner Rüdi Johner	SWI	5	7.5	7	7.5	7	5	6	6	5	56
7. Judianne Fotheringill Jerry Fotheringill	USA	7	7.5	8	5	12	7	9	7	7	69.5
8. Cynthia Kauffman Ronald Kauffman	USA	8	4	11	6	9	8	11	9	8	74.0

Oleg Protopopov was the son of a ballerina. As a child he traveled with his mother when she went on tour. Lyudmila Belousova, the daughter of a military officer, did not discover figure skating until she was 15 years old, when she saw Sonja Henie in the movie *Sun Valley Serenade*. Protopopov and Belousova met at a skating rink while he was on leave from the navy. They first competed at the Olympics in 1960, placing ninth. In 1966 Kilius and Bäumler returned their silver medals following allegations that they had signed a professional contract before the start of the Innsbruck Games. They were officially rehabilitated by the I.O.C. in 1987.

*Lyudmila Belousova and Oleg
Protopopov, winners of the pairs skating
in 1964 and 1968. "These pairs of
brother and sister, how can they convey
the emotion, the love, that exists
between a man and a woman? That is
what we try to show."*

1968 Grenoble T: 18, N: 8, D: 2.14.

					JUDGES' RANKINGS						
		AUT	CAN	CZE	FRA	GDR	GER	POL	USA	SOV	ORDINALS
1. Lyudmila Belousova	SOV/	1	1	2	1	1	1	1	1	1	10
Oleg Protopopov	RUS										
2. Tatyana Zhuk	SOV/	2	2	1	2	2	2	2	2	2	17
Aleksandr Gorelik	RUS										
3. Margot Glockshuber	GER	3	3	3	3	3	3	3	4	5	30
Wolfgang Danne											
4. Heidemarie Steiner	GDR	4	5	4	4	4	5	4	3	4	37
Heinz-Ulrich Walther											
5. Tamara Moskvina	SOV/	5	6	5	5	5	4	5	6	3	44
Aleksei Michine	RUS										
6. Cynthia Kauffman	USA	8	4	7	6	9	7	6	5	6	58
Ronald Kauffman											
7. Sandi Sweitzer	USA	7	7	6	7	8	8	7	7	7.5	64.5
Roy Wagelein											
8. Gudrun Hauss	GER	6	8	8	8	6	6	8	8	9	67
Walter Häfner											

Belousova and Protopopov, now 32 and 35 years old, respectively, climaxed their spectacular amateur career with an elegant display that earned them a second Olympic championship. Protopopov told the press, "Art cannot be measured by points. We skate from the heart. To us it is spiritual beauty that matters. . . . These pairs of brother and sister, how can they convey the emotion, the love, that exists between a man and a woman? That is what we try to show."

1972 Sapporo T: 16, N: 9, D: 2.6.

JUDGES' RANKINGS

		SOV	CAN	GDR	POL	USA	JPN	GBR	GER	FRA	ORDINALS
1. Irina Rodnina Aleksei Ulanov	SOV/ RUS	1	1	1	1	1	2	1	2	2	12
2. Lyudmila Smirnova Andrei Suraikin	SOV/ RUS	2	2	2	2	2	1	2	1	1	15
3. Manuela Gross Uwe Kagelmann	GDR	3	3	3	3	4	4	3	3	3	29
4. Alicia "Jojo" Starbuck Kenneth Shelley	USA	5	4	4	4	3	3	4	4	4	35
5. Almut Lehmann Herbert Wiesinger	GER	4	5	5	6	5	6	7	6	8	52
6. Irina Chernieva Vassily Blagov	SOV/ RUS	6	6	7	5	7	5	6	5	5	52
7. Melissa Militano Mark Militano	USA	9.5	7	8	9	6	8	5	7	6	65.5
8. Annette Kansy Axel Salzmann	GDR	7	9	6	7	8	7	8	9	7	68

At the 1969 European championships, Belousova and Protopopov were dethroned by Irina Rodnina (19) and Aleksei Ulanov (21). The younger couple, knowing they couldn't compete on the same terms with the elegant and sophisticated Olympic champions, had developed a new style, full of dazzling and complex leaps and stunts. Rodnina and Ulanov thrilled the audience and the judges in 1969 and continued undefeated for the next three years. However, as the Sapporo Olympics approached, the Soviet team was in great turmoil. Ulanov, tired of being spurned and mocked by Rodnina, had become romantically involved with Lyudmila Smirnova of the number-two U.S.S.R. team. The harmonious interaction between the partners of the two pairs was severely disrupted. Nevertheless, they finished first and second, with Rodnina leaving the ice in tears.

1976 Innsbruck T: 14, N: 9, D: 2.7.

JUDGES' RANKINGS

		SOV	AUT	CZE	CAN	SWI	GBR	GER	USA	GDR	ORDINALS
1. Irina Rodnina Aleksandr Zaitsev	SOV/ RUS	1	1	1	1	1	1	1	1	1	9
2. Romy Kermer Rolf Österreich	GDR	2	2	2	3	2	3	2	3	2	21
3. Manuela Gross Uwe Kagelmann	GDR	5	4	3	5	3	4	3	4	3	34
4. Irina Vorobieva Aleksandr Vlasov	SOV/ RUS	3	3	4	2	4	5	4	5	5	35
5. Tai Babilonia Randy Gardner	USA	4	5	5	4	5	2	5	2	4	36
6. Kerstin Stolfig Veit Kempe	GDR	8	6	6	7	7	7	6	6	6	59
7. Karin Künzle Christian Künzle	SWI	6	7	7	9	6	6	9	7	7	64
8. Corinna Halke Eberhard Rausch	GER	9	9	8	6	8	9	7	8	8	72

Following the 1972 season, Aleksei Ulanov married Lyudmila Smirnova and a nationwide search was begun to find a new partner for Irina Rodnina. The winner was Aleksandr Zaitsev of Leningrad. According to Beverley Smith in her book

Figure Skating: A Celebration, Zaitsev was so awestruck by Rodnina that he would stutter when he spoke to her. Before long though, the new pair had not only clicked as skaters, but they had also become wife and husband. Rodnina, still under the direction of the controversial Soviet trainer Stanislav Zhuk, continued her winning ways as if nothing had happened. American skater Tai Babilonia was the first black athlete to compete in the Winter Olympics.

1980 Lake Placid T: 11, N: 7, D: 2.17.

		GDR	USA	FRA	CAN	AUS	CZE	GER	JPN	SOV	ORDINALS
					JUDGES' RANKINGS						
1. Irina Rodnina	SOV/	1	1	1	1	1	1	1	1	1	9
Aleksandr Zaitsev	RUS										
2. Marina Cherkosova	SOV/	2	3	2	2	2	2	2	2	2	19
Sergei Shakrai	RUS										
3. Manuela Mager	GDR	3	5	3	4	3	4	3	3	5	33
Uwe Bewersdorff											
4. Marina Pestova	SOV/	4	2	4	3	4	3	4	4	3	31
Stanislav Lednovich	RUS										
5. Caitlin "Kitty" Carruthers	USA	5	4	5	5	5	6	5	5	6	46
Peter Carruthers											
6. Sabine Baess	GDR	6	6	7	6	7	5	6	6	4	53
Tassilo Thierbach											
7. Sheryl Franks	USA	7	7	6	7	6	8	8	7	8	64
Michael Botticelli											
8. Christina Riegel	GER	8	8	8	9	9	7	7	8	7	71
Andreas Nischwitz											

In 1978 Irina Rodnina won her tenth straight world championship. She took off the following year to have a baby and, in her absence, the world title was won by two young people from Los Angeles, Tai Babilonia and Randy Gardner. Tai and Randy had been skating together for over eight years, since they were 10 and 12. The stage was set for a dramatic confrontation as Rodnina and Zaitsev attempted a comeback, while Tai and Randy tried to end the Soviet domination of pairs skating. Unfortunately, Randy Gardner suffered a groin injury prior to his arrival in Lake Placid. With a shot of lidocaine to kill the pain, Randy went out on the ice to warm up before the Olympic short program. But he fell four times, and the disappointed pair were forced to withdraw. Rodnina and Zaitsev skated flawlessly and, for the second straight time, won the first-place votes of all nine judges. Thus Rodnina matched the accomplishments of Sonja Henie by winning ten world championships and three Olympic gold medals.

1984 Sarajevo T: 15, N: 7, D: 2.12.

		SP	GBR	FRA	CZE	USA	GDR	CAN	SOV	GER	JPN	ORDINALS
					JUDGES' RANKINGS (FREE SKATING)							
1. Yelena Valova	SOV/	1	1	1	1	1	1	1	1	1	1	1.4
Oleg Vasilyev	RUS											
2. Caitlin "Kitty" Carruthers	USA	2	2	3	2	2	4	2	3	3	4	2.8
Peter Carruthers												
3. Larissa Selezneva	SOV/	2	3	2	3	4	3	3	2	4	3	3.8
Oleg Makarov	RUS											
4. Sabine Baess	GDR	4	3	4	4	3	2	4	4	2	2	5.6
Tassilo Thierbach												

		JUDGES' RANKINGS (FREE SKATING)									
	SP	GBR	FRA	CZE	USA	GDR	CAN	SOV	GER	JPN	ORDINALS
5. Birgit Lorenz / Knut Schubert — GDR	5	5	6	5	5	5	5	6	5	5	7.0
6. Jill Watson / Burt Lancon — USA	8	5	5	7	6	6	7	7	7	6	9.2
7. Barbara Underhill / Paul Martini — CAN	6	7	7	6	8	7	6	5	6	7	9.4
8. Katerina Matousek / Lloyd Eisler — CAN	9	8	9	8	9	8	8	8	9	8	11.6

Peter and Kitty Carruthers were brother and sister, separately adopted by Charles and Maureen Carruthers of Burlington, Massachusetts.

1988 Calgary T: 15, N: 8, D: 2.16.

		JUDGES' RANKINGS (FREE SKATING)									
	SP	SOV	GER	USA	GBR	CAN	AUS	CZE	GDR	POL	ORDINALS
1. Yekaterina Gordeyeva / Sergei Grinkov — SOV/RUS	1	1	1	1	1	1	1	1	1	1	1.4
2. Yelena Valova / Oleg Vasilyev — SOV/RUS	2	2	2	2	2	2	2	2	2	2	2.8
3. Jill Watson / Peter Oppegard — USA	3	4	3	3	4	5	3	3	3	3	4.2
4. Larissa Selezneva / Oleg Makarov — SOV/RUS	6	3	5	6	6	3	4	4	4	4	6.4
5. Gillian Wachsman / Todd Waggoner — USA	4	5	7	4	8	6	5	5	8	8	6.6
6. Denise Benning / Lyndon Johnston — CAN	5	7	4	7	3	4	7	8	5	7	9.0
7. Peggy Schwarz / Alexander König — GDR	11	6	6	9	7	7	6	7	6	5	10.4
8. Christine Hough / Doug Ladret — CAN	8	9	8	10	4	8	9	6	7	9	11.2

Three months before the Olympics, Grinkov hit a rut on the ice and dropped Gordeyeva. She landed on her forehead and was hospitalized for six days. At the time of their Olympic victory, Gordeyeva was 16 years old and 4 feet 9 inches (145 centimeters) tall. Grinkov was 21 years old and 5-foot 10 inches (180 centimeters). They had been skating together for five years. In Calgary, they were the only pair to complete their long program without a major error. The next day the Soviet Skating Federation gave them each a surprise reward of $3860 in cash. Back home in Moscow, Katya Gordeyeva's father put her gold medal in a goblet of champagne and everyone drank from it.

1992 Albertville T: 18, N: 11, D: 2.11.

		JUDGES' RANKINGS (FREE SKATING)									
	SP	FRA	CZE	AUS	USA	GER	CAN	ITA	SOV	GBR	ORDINALS
1. Natalya Mishkutenok / Artur Dmitriev — SOV/RUS	1	1	1	1	1	1	1	1	1	1	1.5
2. Yelena Bechke / Denis Petrov — SOV/RUS	2	2	3	2	2	2	2	2	2	2	3.0
3. Isabelle Brasseur / Lloyd Eisler — CAN	3	5	4	3	3	5	3	3	3	6	4.5

4.	Radka Kovariková René Novotny	CZE	4	3	2	4	4	3	4	5	4	3	6.0
5.	Yevgenya Shishkova Vadim Naumov	SOV	5	6	5	5	5	4	5	4	6	4	7.5
6.	Natasha Kuchiki Todd Sand	USA	6	4	6	7	6	8	6	9	11	7	9.0
7.	Peggy Schwarz Alexander König	GER	8	10	7	8	12	6	7	8	5	5	11.0
8.	Mandy Wötzel Axel Rauschenbach	GER	10	8	8	9	8	7	9	7	9	8	13.0

There was so much stumbling and falling in the long program that it almost seemed that something was wrong with the ice. However, when Mishkutenok and Dmitriev performed, it became clear that the problem rested with the other skaters, not with the condition of the ice. Mishkutenok and Dmitriev, from Siberia, earned a standing ovation from the audience with their interpretation of Franz Liszt's "Liebesträume," the same music the Protopopovs had used in winning the 1964 gold medal. Both of the top two teams were trained in St. Petersburg by Tamara Moskvina.

1994 Lillehammer-Hamar T: 18, N: 10, D: 2.15.

			SP	CZE	UKR	GER	USA	CAN	BLR	GBR	RUS	AUS	ORDINAL
			JUDGES' RANKINGS (FREE SKATING)										
1.	Yekaterina Gordeyeva Sergei Grinkov	RUS	1	1	1	1	1	1	2	1	1	1	1.5
2.	Natalya Mishkutenok Artur Dmitriev	RUS	2	2	2	2	3	2	1	2	2	3	3.0
3.	Isabelle Brasseur Lloyd Eisler	CAN	3	4	3	4	2	3	3	4	4	2	4.5
4.	Yevgenya Shishkova Vadim Naumov	RUS	4	3	4	3	4	4	4	3	3	4	6.0
5.	Jenni Meno Todd Sand	USA	6	6	5	6	5	5	6	5	5	5	8.0
6.	Radka Kovariková Rene Novotny	CZE	5	5	6	5	6	6	5	6	6	6	8.5
7.	Peggy Schwarz Alexander König	GER	7	8	7	9	11	7	8	9	7	7	11.5
8.	Elena Berzhnaia Oleg Shliachov	LAT	9	9	9	13	9	8	10	10	8	11	13.5

The 1994 Olympics was blessed by a superb competition that displayed the talents of three world champion pairs. Gordeyeva and Grinkov retired from competition and turned professional for three years, until professionals were declared eligible for the Olympics. During that period they began dating in 1989, married in 1991 and Gordeyeva gave birth to a daughter in 1992. Mishkutenok and Dmitriev turned professional after winning their second world championship in 1992. Their post-Olympic years had been less romantic. On the bus back to the Olympic Village after earning the gold medal in 1992, Dmitriev stunned Mishhkutenok by informing her that he was engaged to be married and his fiancée was pregnant. Despite this shock, and Mishkutenok's struggle with her weight, they too decided to take another crack at the Olympics when professionals were offered reinstatement. Brasseur and Eisler were the defending world champions, but in Hamar the battle for Olympic gold was between the two Russian pairs.

Mishkutenok and Dmitriev skated two energetic and flawless programs and won over most of the crowd. Gordeyeva and Grinkov committed some minor mistakes but their elegance and harmony earned them the votes of eight of the nine judges. It would be easy to create a pseudo-rivalry between the pairs: Moscow (G and G) versus St. Petersburg (M and D), a dynamic performance by Mishkutenok and Dmitriev snubbed by traditionally-minded, pre-decided judges. In reality, Grinkov and Dmitriev, in particular, were good friends and even the "losing" coach, Tamara Moskina, shrugged off the judges' decision as a question of style preference.

The 1994 results were a confirmation of the "flea and gorilla" trend in pairs skating in which a tiny young woman is matched with a tall, strong man. The first such pair to achieve international success was Marina Cherkosova and Sergei Shakrai, the 1980 silver medalists. By 1994, the top six pairs all had height disparities of between nine and eleven inches.

After the Olympics, Gordeyeva and Grinkov returned to the professional ranks. But Grinkov, upset because he had made a mistake in the 1994 free skate, wanted to compete at the 1998 Olympics. It was not to be. On November 20, 1995, he and Gordeyeva were rehearsing for the Stars on Ice show at the Olympic Ice Arena in Lake Placid, when Grinkov suddenly collapsed. He died almost immediately, the victim of a heart attack caused by a closed artery. He was 28 years old. Three months later in Hartford, Connecticut, Gordeyeva, skating alone for the first time, performed a moving tribute to her husband. Her book, *My Sergei: A Love Story*, co-authored by E.M. Swift, was a number one bestseller.

ICE DANCE

Ice dance competitions consist of two compulsory dances that represent 10 percent of the final score each, a two-minute original set-pattern dance (30 percent), and a four-minute free dance, which accounts for 50 percent of the total. Judging is slightly different than for other figure skating events in that only a single mark is given for each compulsory dance. For the original dance, separate marks are given for composition and presentation, while the free dance is graded like singles and pairs: one mark for technical merit and one for artistic impression.

In 1998 the compulsory dances will be chosen among the golden waltz, the quickstep, the silver samba and the Argentine tango. The original dance will be jive and, for the first time, vocal music will be permitted.

Following the 1992 Olympics, the Technical Committee on Dance of the International Skating Union issued new restrictions to control dangerous tendencies that were threatening to poison their beloved sport. Among the moves and behavior that are now prohibited are:

1. lying on the ice
2. holding of the partner's skates
3. sitting or lying over the partner's leg without having at least one foot on the ice
4. jumping for more than one revolution
5. spinning or pirouetting for more than three revolutions
6. sitting or lying on the partner's shoulder or back (because it is considered "a feat of prowess")
7. the gentleman wearing tights instead of trousers
8. the lady not wearing a skirt

Had these rules been in effect in 1992, both the gold and silver medal winners would have been disqualified.

1924–1972 not held

1976 Innsbruck T: 18, N: 9, D: 2.9.

JUDGES' RANKINGS

		USA	ITA	SOV	GBR	POL	HUN	AUT	CZE	CAN	ORDINALS
1. Lyudmila Pakhomova Aleksandr Gorshkov	SOV/ RUS	1	1	1	1	1	1	1	1	1	9
2. Irina Moiseyeva Andrei Minenkov	SOV/ RUS	3	2	2	3	2	2	2	2	2	20
3. Colleen O'Conner James Millns	USA	2	3	4	2	4	3	3	3	3	27
4. Natalya Linichuk Gennady Karponosov	SOV/ RUS	5	4	3	4	3	4	4	4	4	35
5. Krisztina Regöczy András Sallay	HUN	4	6	5	6.5	5	5	5	5	7	48.5
6. Matilde Ciccia Lamberto Ceserani	ITA	8	5	6	6.5	6	7	6	6	8	58.5
7. Hilary Green Glyn Watts	GBR	6	7	7	5	7	6	7	7	5	57
8. Janet Thompson Warren Maxwell	GBR	9	9	9	8	9	8	8	8	10	78

Five-time world champions Lyudmila Pakhomova and Aleksandr Gorshkov sat out the 1975 world championships while Gorshkov recovered from a prolonged illness. He was completely recovered for the Olympics, and the husband-wife team from Moscow had little trouble captivating the judges and garnering all nine first-place votes.

1980 Lake Placid T: 12, N: 8, D: 2.19.

JUDGES' RANKINGS

		GER	USA	SOV	CZE	HUN	AUT	CAN	GBR	FRA	ORDINALS
1. Natalya Linichuk Gennady Karponosov	SOV/ RUS	2	2	1	1	2	1	1	1	2	13
2. Krisztina Regöczy András Sallay	HUN	1	1	3	2	1	2	2	1	1	14
3. Irina Moiseyeva Andrei Minenkov	SOV/ RUS	3	3	2	3	3	3	3	4	3	27
4. Liliana Rehakova Stanislav Drastich	CZE	4	5	4	4	4	4	4	5	5	39
5. Jayne Torvill Christopher Dean	GBR	5	4	5	5	5	5	6	3	4	42
6. Lorna Wighton John Dowding	CAN	7	6	6	6	6	6	5	6	6	54
7. Judy Blumberg Michael Seibert	USA	6	8	8	7	8	7	8	7	7	66
8. Natalya Bestemianova Andrei Bukin	SOV/ RUS	9	9	7	8	9	10	7	8	8	75

Four judges voted for the Soviet pair and four for the Hungarians. British judge Brenda Long awarded the same number of points to both couples. Given the option of breaking the tie, she refused. This meant that the gold and silver medals would be decided by total ordinals. Because Soviet judge Igor Kabanov placed Regöczy and Sallay third behind Moiseyeva and Minenkov, the victory went to Linichuk and Karponosov. The announcement of the results was greeted by catcalls and boos from the American audience, which preferred the lively, upbeat style of Regöczy and Sallay to the staid, traditional image of Linichuk and Karponosov.

1984 Sarajevo T: 19, N: 12, D: 2.14.

		CD	OD	HUN	SOV	GER	GBR	JPN	CZE	ITA	CAN	USA	ORDINALS
					JUDGES' RANKINGS (FREE DANCE)								
1.	Jayne Torvill Christopher Dean	GBR	1	1	1	1	1	1	1	1	1	1	1	2.0
2.	Natalya Bestemianova Andrei Bukin	SOV/ RUS	2	2	2	2	2	3	2	2	2	2	3	4.0
3.	Marina Klimova Sergei Ponomarenko	SOV/ RUS	4	4	3	3	3	4	4	3	3	4	4	7.0
4.	Judy Blumberg Michael Seibert	USA	3	3	4	4	4	2	3	4	4	3	2	7.0
5.	Carol Fox Richard Dalley	USA	6	5	6	9	5	6	6	5	6	6	5	10.6
6.	Karen Barber Nicholas Slater	GBR	5	6	5	5	6	5	6	7	5	7	6	11.4
7.	Olga Volozhinskaya Aleksandr Svinin	SOV	8	7	8	6	8	10	5	7	9	8	7	14.6
8.	Tracy Wilson Robert McCall	CAN	7	8	7	8	9	8	8	6	8	5	9	15.4

The first time that the Nottingham City Council voted to grant £14,000 to Jayne Torvill and Christopher Dean to help them while they trained to become world champions, there were protests that the expenditure was a frivolous waste. Three world championships later, no one was complaining anymore as "T&D" had brought the town more glory than D.H. Lawrence, though not quite as much as Robin Hood.

Dean, a former police trainee, and Torvill, a former insurance clerk, brought to the discipline of ice-dancing a new level of greatness, which earned them the first perfect scores of 6.0 in the event's history. In Sarajevo, Torvill and Dean decided to run through their routine the morning of the free dance final. In order to avoid having an audience watch them, they arrived at the arena at 6 AM. When they completed their performance they were surprised to hear applause. They looked up into the stands and discovered 20 to 30 workers who had been cleaning the seats. All of them had stopped their work, put down their cleaning tools and watched in awe. That evening Torvill and Dean mesmerized the audience with their interpretation of Ravel's *Bolero,* receiving from the judges 12 6.0s out of 18 marks including across-the-board perfect scores for artistic impression.

Christopher Dean's specialty was creatively pushing the rules to the limits. Typical was the story behind the development of the *Bolero* routine. Arranger Bob Stewart compressed *Bolero* from 17 minutes to 4 minutes 28 seconds. But the maximum time allowed for a free dance routine was 4 minutes 10 seconds and no one could figure out how to cut another 18 seconds without ruining the integrity of the presentation. Dean checked the rule book and discovered that the 4 minutes and 10 seconds didn't begin until the pair began skating. Dean proposed that he and Torvill begin the routine on their knees, moving their bodies for 18 seconds before they actually started skating. The result was a dance that revolutionized the sport.

1988 Calgary T: 20, N: 14, D: 2.23.

		CD	OD	SOV	CAN	USA	GER	ITA	AUT	GBR	HUN	FRA	ORDINALS
					JUDGES' RANKINGS (FREE DANCE)								
1.	Natalya Bestemianova Andrei Bukin	SOV/ RUS	1	1	1	1	1	1	1	1	1	1	1	2.0
2.	Marina Klimova Sergei Ponomarenko	SOV/ RUS	2	2	2	3	2	2	2	2	2	2	2	4.0

		CD	OD	SOV	CAN	USA	GER	ITA	AUT	GBR	HUN	FRA	ORDINALS
					JUDGES' RANKINGS (FREE DANCE)								
3.	Tracy Wilson Robert McCall	CAN	3	3	3	2	3	3	3	3	3	3	3	6.0
4.	Natalya Annenko Genrich Sretensky	SOV/ RUS	4	4	4	4	6	4	4	4	4	4	4	8.0
5.	Kathrin Beck Christoff Beck	AUT	5	5	5	5	5	5	5	6	5	5	10.0
6.	Suzanne Semanick Scott Gregory	USA	6	6	6	8	7	6	6	6	7	6	7	12.0
7.	Klára Engi Attila Tóth	HUN	7	7	7	7	8	7	7	7	8	7	8	14.0
8.	Isabelle Duchesnay Paul Duchesnay	FRA	8	8	10	6	4	9	8	10	5	10	5	16.0

As an athletic competition, the ice dancing tournament left much to be desired. The twenty teams were ranked in the same order in all three sections of the meet, except for the fifteenth- and fourteenth-placed pairs, who switched places after the compulsory dances. Bronze medalist Rob McCall died of AIDS-related brain cancer on November 15, 1991. He was 33 years old.

1992 Albertville T: 19, N: 12, D: 2.17.

			CD	OD	SOV	GBR	FIN	CAN	HUN	FRA	USA	CZE	ITA	ORDINALS
					JUDGES' RANKINGS (FREE DANCE)									
1.	Marina Klimova Sergei Ponomarenko	SOV/ RUS	1	1	1	2	2	1	2	3	1	1	1	2.0
2.	Isabelle Duchesnay-Dean Paul Duchesnay	FRA	3	2	3	1	1	2	1	1	2	2	2	4.4
3.	Maia Usova Aleksandr Zhulin	SOV/ RUS	2	3	2	3	3	3	3	2	3	3	3	5.6
4.	Oksana Grischuk Yevgeny Platov	SOV/ RUS	4	4	4	4	4	4	4	4	4	4	5	8.0
5.	Stefania Calegari Pasquale Camerlengo	ITA	5	5	5	5	5	5	5	5	5	5	4	10.0
6.	Susanna Rahkamo Petri Kokko	FIN	7	6	7	6	6	7	7	7	6	6	6	12.4
7.	Klára Engi Attila Tóth	HUN	6	7	6	7	7	9	6	6	8	7	7	13.6
8.	Dominique Yvon Frédéric Palluel	FRA	8	9	11	9	8	8	8	8	9	8	8	16.6

The normally calcified world of ice dancing was treated to a showdown between the 1989 and 1990 world champions, Klimova and Ponomarenko, and their 1991 usurpers, Paul and Isabelle Duchesnay. The Duchesnays were brother and sister who were raised in Quebec, trained in Germany, coached by a Slovak, and choreographed by an Englishman, Christopher Dean, who also happened to be Isabelle's husband. They gained fame by challenging the rigid rules of ice dancing with innovative and entertaining programs. For years the judges punished them for their rebelliousness, but at the 1991 Munich World Championships their great popularity finally intimidated the jury into awarding them top honors. Klimova and Ponomarenko, having patiently waited their turn to earn Olympic gold, were furious at this turn of events and lashed out at the Duchesnays, publicly accusing them of manipulating the judges. In February 1991, just before the Munich championships, they also had to fend off charges that Klimova had tested positive for steroids at the European championships. The positive result had been obtained at an unaccredited laboratory in Bulgaria. Klimova's "B" sample was sent to an accredited lab in Germany and she was cleared, raising the specter of sabotage.

In Albertville the Duchesnays appeared tense and flat while Klimova and Ponomarenko were smooth and polished. The competition was decided on the second day when Klimova and Ponomarenko, rather than the Duchesnays, pushed the rules in the original dance by wearing non-polka costumes while performing a polka. In addition, while the Duchesnays stuck to a traditional Bavarian polka, Klimova and Ponomarenko danced to Shostakovich's more waltzlike "Polka for 3 Ballet Suite." Going into the free dance, the Duchesnays needed to place first to win, and even then they would gain the victory only if Klimova and Ponomarenko placed third or worse. Instead, Klimova and Ponomarenko, a married couple, beat the Duchesnays at their own game by presenting a nontraditional, steamy interpretation of Bach that won over the French audience as well as five of the nine judges.

A political footnote: the breakup of the Soviet Union also threatened to break up the ice dancing partnership of Lithuanian Povilas Vanagas and his Ukrainian-born Russian wife, Margarita Drobiavko. Because Lithuania was competing as a separate nation, Olympic rules prevented them from entering as a pair. However, six days before the Opening Ceremony the I.O.C. granted Drobiavko a waiver to compete for Lithuania. The couple finished seventeenth, but happy.

1994 Lillehammer-Hamar T: 21, N: 15, D: 2.18.

JUDGES' RANKINGS (FREE DANCE)

		CD	SP	RUS	FIN	GBR	BLR	UKR	FRA	CZE	GER	CAN	ORDINALS
1. Oksana Grischuk Yevgeny Platov	RUS	1	3	1	2	3	3	3	1	1	1	1	3.4
2. Maia Usova Aleksandr Zhulin	RUS	1	2	2	1	2	1	1	2	2	2	2	3.8
3. Jayne Torvill Christopher Dean	GBR	3	1	3	3	1	2	2	3	3	3	3	4.8
4. Susanna Rahkamo Petri Kokko	FIN	4	4	4	4	5	4	5	5	5	4	4	8.0
5. Sophie Moniotte Pascal Lavanchy	FRA	5	5	5	5	4	5	4	4	4	5	5	10.0
6. Anzhelika Krylova Vladimir Fedorov	RUS	6	6	6	6	7	7	7	7	6	6	6	12.0
7. Iryna Romanova Igor Yaroshenko	UKR	7	7	8	7	6	6	6	6	8	8	7	14.0
8. Katerina Mrazova Martin Simecek	CZE	8	8	7	8	10	8	8	8	7	7	9	16.0

Maia Usova and Aleksandr Zhulin were 16 and 17 years old, respectively, when they were paired by Moscow coach Natalya Dubova. For Zhulin it was love at first sight, but it took six years for him to convince Usova to marry him. They soon developed a torrid and sensual style of dancing. In 1989 they placed second at the world championships behind another Dubova pair, Marina Klimova and Sergei Ponomarenko. The following two years they dropped to third, deferring as well to Isabelle and Paul Duchesnay. They also finished third at the 1992 Olympics. In the world of ice dancing, you wait your turn. When Klimova and Ponomarenko and the Duchesnays retired from competition in 1992, Usova and Zhulin's patience was rewarded and it was their turn at last. They won the 1993 world championships and seemed on track for Olympic gold when 1984 Olympic champions Jayne Torvill and Christopher Dean announced that they would apply for reinstatement and have another go at the Olympics.

As it turned out, the return of Torvill and Dean was a secondary obstacle compared to other problems brewing within the Russian camp. In 1989 Dubova took on another young pair from Odessa, Oksana Grischuk and Yevgeny Platov. Unlike Usova and Zhulin, Grischuk and Platov were not romantically attached. Grischuk, who was seven years younger than Usova, set her sights on Zhulin. The two did have an affair. Usova was not one to tolerate such behavior. After the 1992 Olympics, both pairs were touring in Los Angeles when Usova walked into Spago's restaurant in Hollywood, saw Grischuk sipping a margarita at the bar, came up behind her, grabbed her hair and smashed her head against the counter.

Dubova did not want her number one couple, Usova and Zhulin, to break up, so she dismissed Grischuk from her camp and found a new partner for Platov. Grischuk found her way back to her old coach, 1980 Olympic champion Natalya Linichuk. Platov rejected his new partnership and rejoined Grischuk.

The 1993 world championships would prove controversial. No one questioned Usova and Zhulin's right to first place, but eyebrows were raised when Grischuk and Platov and another Russian couple, Anzhelika Krylova and Vladimir Federov, were awarded second and third. Many observers felt that Grischuk and Platov had included illegal moves in their free dance that were penalized by only three of the nine judges. In addition, Grischuk annoyed many aficionados by smiling inappropriately throughout the routine, which was accompanied by dark and somewhat violent blues music. Afterwards, six of the judges were suspended for "protocol judging"—scoring based on reputation rather the performance itself—although all six were reinstated and three of them were on the judges' panel at the 1994 Olympics.

Meanwhile, Torvill and Dean were preparing their return—and feeling choked by new rules that forbid the use of classical music and favored ballroom dancing numbers. They also worried that several of the judges were resentful of their return from the world of show business.

The first—and only—pre-Olympic confrontation between Torvill and Dean and the Russians took place at the 1994 European championships in Copenhagen four weeks before the Olympic contest. It was unusually close and competitive for an ice dance tournament. Torvill and Dean and Usova and Zhulin were tied for first place after the compulsory dances and set pattern dance, with Grischuk and Platov close behind. It was Grischuk and Platov who stole the show during the decisive free dance, charming both the audience and the judges with an energetic display of 1950s rock and roll dancing inspired by "Rock Around the Clock." They were the last of the three favorites to perform. Before they came out, the judges had chosen Usova and Zhulin over Torvill and Dean 5 votes to 4. But Grischuk and Platov's surprise success vaulted them into first place in the free dance and threw the overall results into confusion. Torvill and Dean ended up winning with Usova and Zhulin second.

Although they had won the European championship, Torvill and Dean felt doomed by the results. They had won only one of the three parts of the competition—the original dance—and the free dance victory of Grischuk and Platov did not bode well for the Olympics. Frantically they revamped their routine, inserting livelier elements, some borrowed from their professional tour numbers.

In Hamar, at the Olympics, the compulsory dances were *Starlight Waltz* and the Blues. The two Russian pairs tied for first with Torvill and Dean third. The original dance, two nights later, was a rumba. Torvill and Dean took first place followed by Usova and Zhulin and Grischuk and Platov. With half of the scoring completed and only the free dance left, Torvill and Dean and Usova and Zhulin both had 1.8 points with Grischuk and Platov in third place at 2.4.

Tension was high among the three leading couples. During practices the two Russian pairs pretended to ignore each other while skating close to one another in a series of near-misses.

For their free dance, Usova and Zhulin who, like Torvill and Dean, were hampered by the exclusion of classical music, chose to dance a playful circus theme that contrasted with the presentations that had made their reputation over the years. They were followed a few minutes later by Torvill and Dean, who skated to "Let's Face the Music and Dance" by Irving Berlin. It was an exuberant performance that included Torvill lifting Dean and Torvill doing a back somersault up Dean's back and over his shoulder. The audience gave them a prolonged standing ovation. But the judges did not like what they saw. Most of them deemed the back somersault an infraction of the rule that forbids the man from raising his hands above shoulder level during a lift. Their posted marks were met by catcalls and booing.

Grischuk and Platov skated last. Prior to the Olympics, some judges, concerned about possible breaches of judgment by singles skaters Katarina Witt and Tonya Harding, warned that "bare stomachs, bare arms and unnecessary bare skin will not be permitted." Apparently, no one told the judges in charge of ice dancing. Oksana Grischuk appeared wearing a halter top and short jacket that revealed quite a bit of bare stomach, as well as a slitted mini-skirt that revealed other parts of her body that more severe judges might have found "unnecessary."

Her "Rock Around the Clock" presentation with Platov was as energetic as it had been at the Euros, but at the Olympics the audience reacted with controlled admiration rather than enthusiasm. The judges, however, were just as impressed as those in Copenhagen. First place: Grischuk and Platov; second place: Usova and Zhulin; third place: Torvill and Dean. In Great Britain, where the competition was watched on television by 23 million people, authorities noted a 1350 megawatt power surge as distressed viewers rushed to their stoves to prepare a calming cup of tea. This was almost twice the surge following a typical episode of *Coronation Street,* but only half that of the record set following England's loss to Argentina in the 1990 World Cup semifinals.

The British were not alone in their fury at the judges. Replays of Grischuk and Platov's free dance routine clearly showed that they had broken the rules without being penalized. Ice dancing rules prohibit couples from dancing apart for more than five seconds at a time. But the gold-medal winners separated for longer periods at least three times, once for 8 seconds, once for 9 seconds and once for 10 seconds. If all nine judges had penalized Grischuk and Platov for their separations, it would have dropped them to third place. Usova refused to attend the medalists' press conference. Before the year was out, she and Aleksandr Zhulin separated romantically, although they continued to skate together.

Discontinued Event

SPECIAL FIGURES

1908 London C: 3, N: 2, D: 10.29.

		JUDGES' RANKINGS					
		GBR	SWE	SWI	GER	RUS	ORDINALS
1. Nikolai Panin (Kolomenkin)	RUS	1	1	1	1	1	5
2. Arthur Cumming	GBR	2	2	2	2	2	10
3. Geoffrey Hall-Say	GBR	3	3	3	3	3	15

The first Russian Olympic gold medal winner, 35-year-old Nikolai Kolomenkin, competed under a pseudonym, Nikolai Panin, a common practice among wealthy Russians for whom participation in sports was considered undignified. Four years later in Stockholm, Kolomenkin was a member of the Russian military revolver team, which finished in fourth place. Later he founded the figure skating school that formed the basis for future Soviet and Russian successes.

GLOSSARY OF FIGURE SKATING TERMS

Axel Jump—One of the most difficult jumps, which takes off from the forward outside edge and is landed on the back outside edge of the opposite foot. A single axel consists of 1½ revolutions, a double is 2½ revolutions, and a triple is 3½ revolutions. Named for its inventor Axel Paulsen, it is easily recognizable as it is the only jump that takes off from the forward position.

Crossovers—A method of gaining speed and turning corners in which skaters cross one foot over the other. There are both forward and backward crossovers.

Death Spiral—A pair move in which the man spins in a pivot position while holding one hand of the woman, who is spinning in a horizontal position with her body parallel to the ice.

Edges—The two sides of the skate blade on either side of the grooved center. There is an inside edge—the edge on the inner side of the leg—and an outside edge—that on the outer side of the leg. There is a forward and backward for each edge, equaling a total of four different edges.

Flip Jump—A toe pick–assisted jump, taken off from the back inside edge of one foot, and landed on the back outside edge of the opposite foot.

Hand-to-Hand Loop Lift—A lift in which the man raises his partner, who is in front of him and facing the same direction, above his head. She remains facing the same direction, in the sitting position with her hands behind her, while her partner supports her by the hands.

Hydrant Lift—A lift in which the man throws his partner over his head while skating backwards, rotates one-half turn, and catches his partner facing him.

Jump Combination—The combining of several jumps such that the landing edge of one jump serves as the takeoff edge of the next jump.

Lateral Twist—A move in which the man throws his partner overhead. She rotates once, while in a lateral position to the ice, and is caught.

Layback Spin—Generally performed by women, the layback spin involves an upright spin position where the head and shoulders are dropped backward and the back arches.

Lifts—Pair moves in which the man lifts his partner above his head with arm(s) fully extended. Lifts consist of precise ascending, rotational, and descending movements.

Loop Jump—An edge jump, taken off from a back outside edge and landed on the same back outside edge.

Lutz Jump—A toe pick–assisted jump, taken off from a back outside edge and landed on the back outside edge of the opposite foot. The skater approaches on a wide curve, taps his toe pick into the ice, and rotates in the opposite direction of the curve.

Platter Lift—A lift in which the man raises his partner overhead, with his hands resting on her hips. She is horizontal to the ice, facing the back of the man. In a platter position.

Salchow—Another edge jump, taken off from the back inside edge of one foot and landed on the back outside edge of the opposite foot. Created by Ulrich Salchow.

Shadow Skating—Any movement in pair skating performed by both partners simultaneously while skating in close proximity.

Sit Spin—A spin which is done in a "sitting" position. The body is low to the ice with the skating (spinning) knee bent and the non-skating or "free" leg extended beside it.

Star Lift—A lift in which the man raises his partner by her hip, from his side into the air. She is in the scissor position, with either one hand touching his shoulder, or in a hands-free position.

Throw Jump—A pair move in which the male partner assists the woman into the air.

Toe Loop—A toe pick–assisted jump that takes off and lands on the same back outside edge.

Toe Overhead Lift—A lift in which the man swings his partner from one side of his body, around behind his head, and into a raised position. She is facing the same direction as the man, in a split position.

Toe Picks—The teeth at the front of the blade, used primarily for jumping and spinning.

Source: United States Figure Skating Association

SPEED SKATING

MEN
500 Meters
1000 Meters
1500 Meters
5000 Meters
10,000 Meters
Short Track: 500 Meters
Short Track: 1000 Meters
Short Track: 5000-Meter Relay
Discontinued Event

In speed skating, the competitors skate against the clock, although they race in pairs. They are required to change lanes in the back straightaway of each lap. The skater on the outside is considered to have the right of way. The skater leaving the inside lane is held responsible for a collision except in cases of obvious obstruction. The first world championships were held in Amsterdam in 1889, although racing records date back to the 18th century. All Olympic races are held on a 400-meter oval.

MEN

500 METERS

1924 Chamonix C: 27, N: 10, D: 1.26. WR: 43.4 (Oscar Mathisen)

1.	Charles Jewtraw	USA	44.0
2.	Oskar Olsen	NOR	44.2
3.	Roald Larsen	NOR	44.8
3.	A. Clas Thunberg	FIN	44.8
5.	Asser Vallenius	FIN	45.0
6.	Axel Blomqvist	SWE	45.2
7.	Charles Gorman	CAN	45.4
8.	Joseph Moore	USA	45.6
8.	Harald Ström	NOR	45.6

This was the first event to be decided in the first Olympic Winter Games. Figure skating and ice hockey competitions held prior to 1924 were incorporated in the regular Summer Games. Jewtraw came from a poor family in Lake Placid, New York, where his father was the caretaker of the speed skating rink on Mirror Lake. In the 1930s Jewtraw found himself unemployed at the height of the Depression. He returned to Lake Placid and asked for a job teaching skating. Instead, the first-ever Winter Olympics champion was given the task of sweeping floors. He later worked as a security guard in New York City. His gold medal is now in a drawer at the Smithsonian Institution in Washington, D.C.

1928 St. Moritz C: 33, N: 14, D: 2.13. WR: 43.1 (Roald Larsen)

1. Bernt Evensen	NOR	43.4	OR
1. A. Clas Thunberg	FIN	43.4	OR
3. John O'Neil Farrell	USA	43.6	
3. Jaako Friman	FIN	43.6	
3. Roald Larsen	NOR	43.6	
6. Håkon Pedersen	NOR	43.8	
7. Charles Gorman	CAN	43.9	
8. Bertel Backmann	FIN	44.4	

1932 Lake Placid C: 16, N: 4, D: 2.4. WR: 42.6 (A. Clas Thunberg)

1. John Shea	USA	43.4	EOR
2. Bernt Evensen	NOR	—	
3. Alexander Hurd	CAN	—	
4. Frank Stack	CAN	—	
5. William Logan	CAN	—	
6. John O'Neil Farrell	USA	—	

In 1932 the speed skating competitions were held as actual races, with five or six men in a heat, rather than the usual way of two skaters at a time racing against the clock. This new method, known as the North American Rules, so outraged world record holder and five-time Olympic champion Clas Thunberg that he refused to participate. New York Governor Franklin D. Roosevelt officially opened the Third Olympic Winter Games on the morning of February 4. A local speed skater, 21-year-old Jack Shea, recited the Olympic oath on behalf of the 306 assembled athletes. A short time later the three qualifying heats were held for the 500 meters speed skating. Not surprisingly, five of six qualifiers were North Americans. Following the heats, the first period of the Canada–U.S.A. ice hockey game was played. Then came the 500 meters final. Shea tore into the lead and finished five yards ahead of co-defending champion Bernt Evensen. Shea's victory was very popular, since he was a hometown boy from Lake Placid, as was 1924 winner Charles Jewtraw.

1936 Garmisch-Partenkirchen C: 36, N: 14, D: 2.11. WR: 42.4 (Allan Potts)

1. Ivar Ballangrud	NOR	43.4	EOR
2. George Krog	NOR	43.5	
3. Leo Freisinger	USA	44.0	
4. Shozo Ishihara	JPN	44.1	
5. Delbert Lamb	USA	44.2	
6. Karl Leban	AUT	44.8	
6. Allan Potts	USA	44.8	
8. Antero Ojala	FIN	44.9	
8. Jorma Ruissalo	FIN	44.9	
8. Birger Wasenius	FIN	44.9	

1948 St. Moritz C: 42, N: 15, D: 1.31. WR: 41.8 (Hans Engnestangen)

1. Finn Helgesen	NOR	43.1	OR
2. Kenneth Bartholomew	USA	43.2	
2. Thomas Byberg	NOR	43.2	
2. Robert Fitzgerald	USA	43.2	
5. Kenneth Henry	USA	43.3	
6. Sverre Farstad	NOR	43.6	
6. Torodd Hauer	NOR	43.6	
6. Delbert Lamb	USA	43.6	
6. Frank Stack	CAN	43.6	

1952 Oslo C: 41, N: 14, D: 2.16. WR: 41.2 (Yuri Sergeev)

1.	Kenneth Henry	USA	43.2
2.	Donald McDermott	USA	43.9
3.	Gordon Audley	CAN	44.0
3.	Arne Johansen	NOR	44.0
5.	Finn Helgesen	NOR	44.0
6.	Hroar Elvenes	NOR	44.1
6.	Kiyotaka Takabayashi	JPN	44.1
8.	Gerardus Maarse	HOL	44.2
8.	Toivo Salonen	FIN	44.2

The Norwegian Skating Union chose as one of their four entrants in this race Finn Hodt, who had served a sentence for collaborating with the Nazis, and who had gone so far as to fight for the Germans on the Eastern Front. One month before the Oslo Games, the Norwegian Olympic committee overruled the Skating Union, voting 25–2 to ban Hodt and all other collaborators from representing Norway in the Oslo Olympics. Helgesen was placed fifth despite his time because he was paired with Audley and finished behind him.

1956 Cortina C: 47, N: 17, D: 1.28. WR: 40.2 (Yevgeny Grishin)

1.	Yevgeny Grishin	SOV/RUS	40.2	EWR
2.	Rafael Gratch	SOV/RUS	40.8	
3.	Alv Gjestvang	NOR	41.0	
4.	Yuri Sergeyev	SOV/RUS	41.1	
5.	Toivo Salonen	FIN	41.7	
6.	William Carow	USA	41.8	
7.	Colin Hickey	AUS	41.9	
7.	Bengt Malmsten	SWE	41.9	

1960 Squaw Valley C: 46, N: 15, D: 2.24. WR: 40.2 (Yevgeny Grishin)

1.	Yevgeny Grishin	SOV/RUS	40.2	EWR
2.	William Disney	USA	40.3	
3.	Rafael Gratch	SOV/RUS	40.4	
4.	Hans Wilhelmsson	SWE	40.5	
5.	Gennady Voronin	SOV/RUS	40.7	
6.	Alv Gjestvang	NOR	40.8	
7.	Richard "Terry" McDermott	USA	40.9	
7.	Toivo Salonen	FIN	40.9	

Grishin's time was remarkable, considering that he stumbled and skidded in the homestretch, losing at least a second.

1964 Innsbruck C: 44, N: 19, D: 2.4. WR: 39.5 (Yevgeny Grishin)

1.	Richard "Terry" McDermott	USA	40.1	OR
2.	Alv Gjestvang	NOR	40.6	
2.	Yevgeny Grishin	SOV/RUS	40.6	
2.	Vladimir Orlov	SOV/RUS	40.6	
5.	Keiichi Suzuki	JPN	40.7	
6.	Edward Rudolph	USA	40.9	
7.	Heike Hedlund	FIN	41.0	
8.	William Disney	USA	41.1	
8.	Villy Haugen	NOR	41.1	

Terry McDermott, a 23-year-old barber from Essexville, Michigan, stunned the skating world with his surprise victory, the only U.S. gold medal of the 1964 Winter Games. McDermott used skates that he had borrowed from the U.S. coach, Leo Freisinger. He also got some help from Mrs. Freisinger. When Lydia Skoblikova won four speed skating gold medals in 1964, she wore a good-luck pin that had been given to her by Mrs. Freisinger. McDermott heard about this story and asked the coach's wife if he too could have such a pin. Freisinger gave McDermott her last pin, and he put it to good use. In 1968 Dianne Holum also received a Freisinger pin, although she didn't win her gold medal until 1972.

1968 Grenoble C: 48, N: 17, D: 2.14. WR: 39.2 (Erhard Keller)

1.	Erhard Keller	GER	40.3
2.	Richard "Terry" McDermott	USA	40.5
2.	Magne Thomassen	NOR	40.5
4.	Yevgeny Grishin	SOV/RUS	40.6
5.	Neil Blatchford	USA	40.7
5.	Arne Herjuaunet	NOR	40.7
5.	John Wurster	USA	40.7
8.	Seppo Hänninen	FIN	40.8
8.	Haakan Holmgren	SWE	40.8
8.	Keiichi Suzuki	JPN	40.8

In 1968 McDermott had the misfortune of being drawn in the last of 24 pairs on ice that had been badly melted by the sun. Keller, a dental student from Munich, was a gracious winner. He said of McDermott, "What he did today was just sheer guts. If he had started in the earlier heats while the ice was still good, I'd have lost. It's as simple as that."

1972 Sapporo C: 37, N: 16, D: 2.5. WR: 38.0 (Leo Linkovesi)

1.	Erhard Keller	GER	39.44	OR
2.	Hasse Börjes	SWE	39.69	
3.	Valery Muratov	SOV/RUS	39.80	
4.	Per Björang	NOR	39.91	
5.	Seppo Hänninen	FIN	40.12	
6.	Leo Linkovesi	FIN	40.14	
7.	Ove König	SWE	40.25	
8.	Masaki Suzuki	JPN	40.35	

This was the only one of the 1972 men's skating races that wasn't won by Ard Schenk, who fell after four steps and finished 34th.

1976 Innsbruck C: 29, N: 15, D: 2.10. WR: 37.00 (Yevgeny Kulikov)

1.	Yevgeny Kulikov	SOV/RUS	39.17	OR
2.	Valery Muratov	SOV/RUS	39.25	
3.	Daniel Immerfall	USA	39.54	
4.	Mats Wallberg	SWE	39.56	
5.	Peter Mueller	USA	39.57	
6.	Jan Bazen	HOL	39.78	
6.	Arnulf Sunde	NOR	39.78	
8.	Andrei Malikov	SOV/RUS	39.85	

1980 Lake Placid C: 37, N: 18, D: 2.15. WR: 37.00 (Yevgeny Kulikov)

1.	Eric Heiden	USA	38.03	OR
2.	Yevgeny Kulikov	SOV/RUS	38.37	
3.	Lieuwe de Boer	HOL	38.48	
4.	Frode Rönning	NOR	38.66	
5.	Daniel Immerfall	USA	38.69	
6.	Jarle Pedersen	NOR	38.83	
7.	Anatoly Medennikov	SOV/RUS	38.88	
8.	Gaétan Boucher	CAN	38.90	

Eric Heiden had won only three gold medals when he posed for this photo; he borrowed the other two. Later he won two more of his own.

As a 17-year-old, Eric Heiden had competed in the 1976 Olympics in Innsbruck, finishing seventh in the 1500 and 19th in the 5000. Thus it came as quite a shock the following year when he seemingly appeared from nowhere to win the overall title at the 1977 world championships. His victory was so unexpected that even Heiden wondered if his performance might have been a fluke. It wasn't. He successfully defended his world title in 1978 and 1979, and became a national hero—not in his native country, the United States, but in Norway and the Netherlands, where speed skating is taken more seriously.

The 1980 Olympics began with Heiden the favorite in all five men's speed skating events. If there was one distance at which he was thought to be shaky, it was the 500. A week earlier Heiden had lost at 500 meters to teammate Tom Plant at the world speed skating sprint championship. At Lake Placid Heiden was paired against world record holder Yevgeny Kulikov. The two favorites were the first pair to skate. Kulikov was slightly ahead at 100 meters, but they raced neck and neck most of the way. Coming out of the last curve, Kulikov slipped slightly and Heiden, who had a 32-inch waist but 27-inch thighs, pulled ahead and won.

1984 Sarajevo C: 42, N: 20, D: 2.10. WR: 36.57 (Pavel Pegov)

1.	Sergei Fokichev	SOV/RUS	38.19
2.	Yoshihiro Kitazawa	JPN	38.30
3.	Gaétan Boucher	CAN	38.39
4.	Daniel Jansen	USA	38.55
5.	K. Nick Thometz	USA	38.56
6.	Vladimir Kozlov	SOV/KAZ	38.57
7.	Frode Rönning	NOR	38.58
8.	Uwe-Jens Mey	GDR	38.65

Fokichev had not previously competed in a major international meet.

1988 Calgary C: 37, N: 15, D: 2.14. WR: 36.55 (K. Nick Thometz)

1.	Uwe-Jens Mey	GDR	36.45	WR
2.	Jan Ykema	HOL	36.76	
3.	Akira Kuroiwa	JPN	36.77	
4.	Sergei Fokichev	SOV/RUS	36.82	

5.	Bae Ki-tae	KOR	36.90
6.	Igor Zhelezovsky	SOV/BLR	36.94
7.	Guy Thibault	CAN	36.96
8.	K. Nick Thometz	USA	37.16

One of the favorites was Dan Jansen of West Allis, Wisconsin, who won the World Sprint Championship held in his hometown one week before the Olympics. At 6:00 a.m. on the day of the 500-meter event, Jansen received a phone call informing him that his sister, Jane Beres, was about to succumb to the leukemia she had been fighting for over a year. Dan spoke to her and although she could not respond, she indicated to him through another brother who was with her that she wanted Dan to remain in Calgary and compete. At noon, Dan Jansen's sister had died less than three hours after he had spoken to her. At 5:00 p.m. he was on the ice, preparing for his race. After false starting, he took off quickly, but at the first turn he slipped and fell, just as he had at the World Cup meet on the same track two months earlier. Four days later, Jansen took part in the 1000-meter race but fell again.

1992 Albertville C: 43, N: 17, D: 2.15. WR: 36.41 (Daniel Jansen)

1.	Uwe-Jens Mey	GER	37.14
2.	Toshiyuki Kuroiwa	JPN	37.18
3.	Junichi Inoue	JPN	37.26
4.	Daniel Jansen	USA	37.46
5.	Yasunori Miyabe	JPN	37.49
5.	Gerard van Velde	HOL	37.49
7.	Aleksandr Golubev	SOV/RUS	37.51
8.	Igor Zhelezovsky	SOV/BLR	37.57

The men's 500 meters looked to be the most hotly contested duel of the Albertville Olympics. Uwe-Jens Mey and Dan Jansen had met six times during the pre-Olympic season. Mey won three times, Jansen twice, and once they tied. In addition, they had taken turns breaking the world record. On January 19, in Davos, Switzerland, Mey clocked a 36.43 to beat his own 1988 record by two hundredths of a second. Six days later, on the same Davos oval, Jansen took the record down to 36.41. The stage was set in Albertville, but the tight contest was not to be. Skating in the second pair, Jansen, apparently haunted at a deep level by his falls four years earlier, hesitated entering the final turn and lost precious tenths of a second. Two pairs later, Mey skated a solid race and earned his second straight gold medal. Jansen ended up in fourth place, just as he had eight years earlier as an 18-year-old in Sarajevo.

1994 Lillehammer-Hamar C: 40, N: 16, D: 2.14. WR: 35.76 (Daniel Jansen)

1.	Aleksandr Golubev	RUS	36.33	OR
2.	Sergei Klevchenya	RUS	36.39	
3.	Manabu Horii	JPN	36.53	
4.	Liu Hongbo	CHN	36.54	
5.	Hiroyasu Shimizu	JPN	36.60	
6.	Junichi Inoue	JPN	36.63	
7.	Grunde Njøs	NOR	36.66	
8.	Daniel Jansen	USA	36.68	

Were it not for his unfortunate Olympic history, Dan Jansen would have been the prohibitive favorite in 1994. Not only had he won 6 of 8 races in the pre-Olympic season, but twice he had broken the world record. The first time he skated a 35.92 on the Olympic ice at Hamar on December 5. Then, On January 30, only two weeks before the Olympics, he stopped the clock at 35.76 at the World Sprint Championships in Calgary. By the opening of the Olympics, Dan Jansen had broken the 36-second barrier four times. No one else had done it once.

The Olympic race took place exactly six years after the day that Jansen's sister died and he experienced the first of his Olympic slips. In 1994, as in 1988 and 1992, he skated in the second pair. He was off his world record pace but skating well, when he entered the final turn leaning a bit too far back. His left skate slipped and he was forced to touch the ice with his hand. He had difficulty with his next two strokes and then recovered. But at 500 meters one slip is all it takes. Jansen ended up in eighth place.

Aleksandr Golubev of Kostroma, Russia, was known as a sprinter with an extremely fast start who faded in the final straightaway. Seventh in 1992, he concentrated his training on building his endurance for a strong finish. His training strategy worked. Skating in the ninth pair he clocked the fastest split for the first 100 meters (9.58 to Shimizu's second best 9.79) and held on to beat the final time of the fast-finishing Klevchenya.

1000 METERS

1924–1972 not held

1976 Innsbruck C: 31, N: 16, 2.12. WR: 1:16.92 (Valery Muratov)

1.	Peter Mueller	USA	1:19.32
2.	Jörn Didriksen	NOR	1:20.45
3.	Valery Muratov	SOV/RUS	1:20.57
4.	Aleksandr Safronov	SOV/RUS	1:20.84
5.	Hans van Helden	HOL	1:20.85
6.	Gaétan Boucher	CAN	1:21.23
7.	Mats Wallberg	SWE	1:21.27
8.	Pertti Niittylä	FIN	1:21.43

1980 Lake Placid C: 41, N: 19, D: 2.19. WR: 1:13.60 (Eric Heiden)

1.	Eric Heiden	USA	1:15.18	OR
2.	Gaétan Boucher	CAN	1:16.68	
3.	Vladimir Lobanov	SOV/RUS	1:16.91	
3.	Frode Rönning	NOR	1:16.91	
5.	Peter Mueller	USA	1:17.11	
6.	Bert de Jong	HOL	1:17.29	
7.	Andreas Dietel	GDR	1:17.71	
8.	Oloph Granath	SWE	1:17.74	

Boucher had the good fortune to be skating first, paired against Eric Heiden. The silver medals in the three shortest races in 1980 were won by whoever was paired with Heiden.

1984 Sarajevo C: 43, N: 20, D: 2.14. WR: 1:12.58 (Pavel Pegov)

1.	Gaétan Boucher	CAN	1:15.80
2.	Sergei Khlebnikov	SOV/RUS	1:16.63
3.	Kai Arne Engelstad	NOR	1:16.75
4.	K. Nick Thometz	USA	1:16.85
5.	André Hoffmann	GDR	1:17.33
6.	Viktor Chacherin	SOV/KAZ	1:17.42
7.	Andreas Dietel	GDR	1:17.46
7.	Hilbert van der Duim	HOL	1:17.46

1988 Calgary C: 40, N: 16, D: 2.18. WR: 1:12.58 (Pavel Pegov)

1. Nikolai Gulyaev	SOV/RUS	1:13.03	OR
2. Uwe-Jens Mey	GDR	1:13.11	
3. Igor Zhelezovsky	SOV/BLR	1:13.19	
4. Eric Flaim	USA	1:13.53	
5. Gaétan Boucher	CAN	1:13.77	
6. Michael Hadschieff	AUT	1:13.84	
7. Guy Thibault	CAN	1:14.16	
8. Peter Adeberg	GDR	1:14.19	

Two months before the Olympics, Gulyaev was caught passing a packet of anabolic steroids to a Norwegian skater. Gulyaev claimed that the packet had been given to him by a Soviet trainer and that he was unaware of its contents. The I.O.C. and the International Skating Union, although skeptical of his account, were unable to uncover evidence to disprove it. Two days before the Opening Ceremony, Gulyaev was cleared to compete.

1992 Albertville C: 46, N: 21, D: 2.18. WR: 1:12.58 (Pavel Pegov, Igor Zhelezovsky)

1. Olaf Zinke	GER	1:14.85
2. Kim Yoon-man	KOR	1:14.86
3. Yukinori Miyabe	JPN	1:14.92
4. Gerard van Velde	HOL	1:14.93
5. Peter Adeberg	GER	1:15.04
6. Igor Zhelezovsky	SOV/BLR	1:15.05
7. Guy Thibault	CAN	1:15.36
8. Nikolai Gulyaev	SOV/RUS	1:15.46

This was the closest speed skating race in Olympic history as Igor Zhelezovsky was relegated to sixth place even though he was only two-tenths of a second slower than the winner. The upset victory went to 25-year-old Olaf Zinke, an auto mechanic who was given a job by the city of Berlin so that he could train. Zinke's first love was soccer, but East German sports officials ordered him to switch to speed skating when he was 14 years old. Even more of an outsider than Zinke was silver medalist Kim, a Seoul University student whose goal had been to finish in the top ten. Actually, Kim's superb performance wasn't totally unexpected. On the morning of the race he spoke on the phone to his mother back in Ui Jung Bu City, and she told him she had dreamed about a dragon. "That was a good omen for me," explained Kim.

1994 Lillehammer-Hamar C: 43, N: 17, D: 2.18. WR: 1:12.54 (Kevin Scott)

1. Daniel Jansen	USA	1:12.43	WR
2. Igor Zhelezovsky	BLR	1:12.72	
3. Sergei Klevchenya	RUS	1:12.85	
4. Liu Hongbo	CHN	1:13.47	
5. Sylvain Bouchard	CAN	1:13.56	
6. Patrick Kelly	CAN	1:13.67	
7. Roger Strøm	NOR	1:13.74	
8. Junichi Inoue	JPN	1:13.75	

When 28-year-old Dan Jansen stepped to the starting line of the 1000 meters on February 18, 1994, he was already one of the greatest sprinters in speed skating history. He had won the world sprint championship twice, he had won seven overall World Cup titles and he had set seven world records. But, as sports fans knew all too well, he had never earned an Olympic medal. In 1984, Jansen had placed a surprising fourth in the 500 meters at the Sarajevo Olympics, missing a bronze medal by only .16 of a second. He was also 16th in the 1000. It was a bit disappoint-

Dan Jansen slips during the 1994 1000 meters—his last attempt at an Olympic medal.

ing to come so close to a medal in the 500, but he was 18 years old and his unexpected success seemed a forerunner of good things to come. By 1988, he was one of the favorites, but his sister (Jansen was the youngest of nine children) died of leukemia the morning of the 500-meter final. Jansen started the race anyway, but slipped and fell. Four days later he fell again in the 1000. At the 1992 Albertville Olympics, Jansen was co-favorite in the 500 meters, but skated tentatively and placed fourth. Discouraged, he raced all out at the beginning of the 1000, skated a powerful 600 meters, but then blew up, faded and ended up in 26th place. In 1994, Jansen was *the* favorite in the 500 meters, but he slipped again and only placed eighth. He had had an illustrious career, but in the Olympics he had started seven races over a ten-year period and had yet to mount the medal podium.

The 1994 1000 meters was his eighth and final chance. It looked like a long shot. Three times he had competed in the Olympic 1000 meters and never had he finished better than 16th. He had performed well at 1000 meters early in the pre-Olympic season, but had dropped to fourth at the World Sprint Championships two weeks before the Olympics. His personal best of 1:13.01 had been set on the Olympic oval, but six of his opponents had better times. And, of course, there was the burden of his long history of Olympic underachievement.

Jansen's travails received lots of attention from the world's media, particularly in the United States where his failures were the source of national empathy and anxiety. Only speed skating aficionados knew that there was a second skater in the race with an Olympic history almost as frustrating as that of Jansen's. Igor Zhelezovsky had won the World Sprint Championships six times, as early as 1985 and as recently as 1993. He won a bronze medal in the 1000 in Calgary at the 1988 Olympics, but other than that, his Olympic career had been nothing but one disappointment after another. In 1988 he was fourth in the 1500 and sixth in the 500. In 1992 he had been the favorite at 1000 meters, but could do no better than sixth, while placing eighth in the 500 and tenth in 1500. In 1994, he dropped to tenth in the 500. Like Jansen, the 30-year-old Zhelezovsky had achieved great non-Olympic success. Like Jansen he had raced in seven Olympic contests without winning, despite being the favorite. Like Jansen, he knew that the 1994 1000 meters was his last chance.

Zhelezovsky skated in the first pair against the other favorite, Sergei Klevchenya, who had come within one one-hundredth of a second of the world record on January 29, and who had already earned a silver medal at 500 meters at the Lillehammer Olympics. It was a great race, as expected. Klevchenya slipped slightly and Zhelezovsky took advantage to beat him 1:12.72 to 1:12.85. These were times that Jansen had not approached in competition. Two more pairs raced and then it was Jansen's turn. Lining up against Junichi Inoue, Jansen looked and felt uncomfortable. He felt his timing was off.

But, as Jansen later described in his autobiography, *Full Circle*, "Suddenly, right before I heard the gun, a jolt of energy came into my legs. . . . I knew I was ready." As he powered his way around the oval, the extremely supportive, mostly Norwegian crowd cheered him on. His 600-meter split time showed that he was on world record pace and the crowd of 12,000 roared its approval. Then, on the second-to-last turn, Jansen slipped yet again. His left hand brushed the ice and he came within one inch of stepping on a lane marker and falling. The audience gasped almost as one. But this time Jansen cooly regained his balance and drove on towards the finish. When he crossed the finish line he unzipped his top and peeled off his hood and, a bit disoriented, searched the arena for the clock. 1:12.43: not just a personal best and a great time, but a world record.

In the words of the Official Report of the 1994 Olympics, "At the moment there were no Norwegians, Dutch, Americans or people of other nationalities among the spectators, only fans of Dan Jansen." In the stands, Jansen's wife Robin was so overcome by emotion she had to seek medical care. Back in the skaters' locker room there was no television monitor. But when Jansen's time was announced on the loudspeaker, his "rivals" cheered and yelled and stomped their skates. In the shopping centers of Hamar and Lillehammer, Norwegians approached American visitors and congratulated them. Said Dan Jansen: "Finally I feel like I've made other people happy instead of having them feel sorry for me."

After receiving his gold medal and listening to the "Star-Spangled Banner," Jansen saluted the sky in honor of his late sister Jane. Then, with his 8½ month-old daughter, named Jane after his sister, in his arms, Jansen skated a victory lap while the Norwegian spectators sang along to Johann Strauss's "Skater's Waltz."

1500 METERS

1924 Chamonix C: 22, N: 9, D: 1.27. WR: 2:17.4 (Oscar Mathisen)

1.	A. Clas Thunberg	FIN	2:20.8
2.	Roald Larsen	NOR	2:22.0
3.	Sigurd Moen	NOR	2:25.6
4.	Julius Skutnabb	FIN	2:26.6
5.	Harald Ström	NOR	2:29.0
6.	Oskar Olsen	NOR	2:29.2
7.	Harry Kaskey	USA	2:29.8
8.	Charles Jewtraw	USA	2:31.6
8.	Joseph Moore	USA	2:31.6

In 1924 30-year-old A. Clas Thunberg won three gold medals, one silver, and one bronze. Four years later he followed up with two more gold medals.

1928 St. Moritz C: 30, N: 14, D: 2.14. WR: 2:17.4 (Oscar Mathisen)

1.	A. Clas Thunberg	FIN	2:21.1
2.	Bernt Evensen	NOR	2:21.9

3. Ivar Ballangrud   NOR   2:22.6
4. Roald Larsen   NOR   2:25.3
5. Edward Murphy   USA   2:25.9
6. Valentine Bialas   USA   2:26.3
7. Irving Jaffee   USA   2:26.7
8. John Farrell   USA   2:26.8

1932 Lake Placid C: 18, N: 6, D: 2.5. WR: 2:17.4 (Oscar Mathisen)

1. John Shea   USA   2:57.5
2. Alexander Hurd   CAN   —
3. William Logan   CAN   —
4. Frank Stack   CAN   —
5. Raymond Murray   USA   —
6. Herbert Taylor   USA   —

American officials, having already irritated the foreign teams with their strange mass starts, left them completely exasperated with a ruling in the second heat. In the middle of the race the judges suddenly stopped the contest, accused the skaters of "loafing," and ordered the race rerun. In the final Taylor was leading, but he lost his balance coming out of the last turn and tumbled across the track into a snowbank. Shea found himself in first place and crossed the finish line eight yards ahead of Hurd.

1936 Garmisch-Partenkirchen C: 37, N: 15, D: 2.13. WR: 2:17.4 (Oscar Mathisen)

1. Charles Mathisen   NOR   2:19.2   OR
2. Ivar Ballangrud   NOR   2:20.2
3. Birger Wasenius   FIN   2:20.9
4. Leo Freisinger   USA   2:21.3
5. Max Stiepl   AUT   2:21.6
6. Karl Wazulek   AUT   2:22.2
7. Harry Haraldsen   NOR   2:22.4
8. Hans Engnestangen   NOR   2:23.0

A brief note about the world record: Oscar Mathisen of Norway first broke the world record for the 1500 meters in 1908. By January 11, 1914, he had lowered his time to 2:19.4. One week later, in Davos, Switzerland, he skated a 2:17.4. This time remained a world record for 23 years, until Michael Staksrud, also skating at Davos, recorded a 2:14.9. Mathisen's performance was bettered only twice in the 38 years between 1914 and 1952.

1948 St. Moritz C: 45, N: 14, D: 2.2. WR: 2:13.8 (Hans Engnestangen)

1. Sverre Farstad   NOR   2:17.6   OR
2. Åke Seyffarth   SWE   2:18.1
3. Odd Lundberg   NOR   2:18.9
4. Lauri Parkkinen   FIN   2:19.6
5. Gustav Harry Jansson SWE   2:20.0
6. John Werket   USA   2:20.2
7. Kalevi Laitinen   FIN   2:20.3
8. Göthe Hedlund   SWE   2:20.7

Farstad was a 27-year-old cartoonist.

1952 Oslo C: 39, N: 13, D: 2.18. WR: 2:12.9 (Valentin Chaikin)

1. Hjalmar Andersen   NOR   2:20.4
2. Willem van der Voort HOL   2:20.6

3. Roald Aas	NOR	2:21.6
4. Carl-Erik Asplund	SWE	2:22.6
5. Cornelis "Kees" Broekman	HOL	2:22.8
6. Lauri Parkkinen	FIN	2:23.0
7. Kauko Salomaa	FIN	2:23.3
8. Sigvard Ericsson	SWE	2:23.4

Anderson won the second of his three gold medals.

1956 Cortina C: 54, N: 18, D: 1.30. WR: 2:09.1 (Yuri Mikhailov)

1. Yevgeny Grishin	SOV/RUS	2:08.6	WR
1. Yuri Mikhailov	SOV/RUS	2:08.6	WR
3. Toivo Salonen	FIN	2:09.4	
4. Juhani Järvinen	FIN	2:09.7	
5. Robert Merkulov	SOV/RUS	2:10.3	
6. Sigvard Ericsson	SWE	2:11.0	
7. Colin Hickey	AUS	2:11.8	
8. Boris Shilkov	SOV/RUS	2:11.9	

1960 Squaw Valley C: 48, N: 16, D: 2.26. WR: 2:06.3 (Juhani Järvinen)

1. Roald Aas	NOR	2:10.4
1. Yevgeny Grishin	SOV/RUS	2:10.4
3. Boris Stenin	SOV/RUS	2:11.5
4. Jouko Jokinen	FIN	2:12.0
5. Per Olov Brogren	SWE	2:13.1
5. Juhani Järvinen	FIN	2:13.1
7. Toivo Salonen	FIN	2:13.2
8. André Kouprianoff	FRA	2:13.3

Grishin registered his second straight tie for first place at 1500 meters and collected his fourth Olympic gold medal. In 1952 he had competed as a cyclist in the Summer Olympics.

1964 Innsbruck C: 54, N: 21, D: 2.6. WR: 2:06.3 (Juhani Järvinen)

1. Ants Antson	SOV/EST	2:10.3
2. Cornelis "Kees" Verkerk	HOL	2:10.6
3. Villy Haugen	NOR	2:11.2
4. Jouko Launonen	FIN	2:11.9
5. Lev Zaitsev	SOV/RUS	2:12.1
6. Ivar Eriksen	NOR	2:12.2
6. Edouard Matoussevich	SOV/BLR	2:12.2
8. Juhani Järvinen	FIN	2:12.4

1968 Grenoble C: 53, N: 18, D: 2.16. WR: 2:02.5 (Magne Thomassen)

1. Cornelis "Kees" Verkerk	HOL	2:03.4	OR
2. Ivar Eriksen	NOR	2:05.0	
2. Adrianus "Ard" Schenk	HOL	2:05.0	
4. Magne Thomassen	NOR	2:05.1	
5. Johnny Höglin	SWE	2:05.2	
5. Björn Tveter	NOR	2:05.2	
7. Svein-Erik Stiansen	NOR	2:05.5	
8. Edouard Matoussevich	SOV/BLR	2:06.1	

Kees Verkerk was a 25-year-old bartender from the village of Puttershoek who also played the trumpet on a Dutch television show.

1972 Sapporo C: 39, N: 16, D: 2.6. WR: 1:58.7 (Adrianus "Ard" Schenk)

1. Adrianus "Ard" Schenk	HOL	2:02.96	OR
2. Roar Grönvold	NOR	2:04.26	
3. Göran Claesson	SWE	2:05.89	
4. Björn Tveter	NOR	2:05.94	
5. Jan Bols	HOL	2:06.58	
6. Valery Lavrouchkin	SOV/RUS	2:07.16	
7. Daniel Carroll	USA	2:07.24	
8. Cornelis "Kees" Verkerk	HOL	2:07.43	

1976 Innsbruck C: 30, N: 19, D: 2.13. WR: 1:58.7 (Adrianus "Ard" Schenk)

1. Jan Egil Storholt	NOR	1:59.38	OR
2. Yuri Kondakov	SOV/RUS	1:59.97	
3. Hans van Helden	HOL	2:00.87	
4. Sergei Riabev	SOV/RUS	2:02.15	
5. Daniel Carroll	USA	2:02.26	
6. Piet Kleine	HOL	2:02.28	
7. Eric Heiden	USA	2:02.40	
8. Colin Coates	AUS	2:03.34	

Storholt and Kondakov raced head to head in the fourth pair. Storholt, an electrician from Trondheim, celebrated his 27th birthday the day he won the gold medal.

1980 Lake Placid C: 36, N: 16, D: 2.21. WR: 1:54.79 (Eric Heiden)

1. Eric Heiden	USA	1:55.44	OR
2. Kai Arne Stenshjemmet	NOR	1:56.81	
3. Terje Andersen	NOR	1:56.92	
4. Andreas Dietel	GDR	1:57.14	
5. Yuri Kondakov	SOV/RUS	1:57.36	
6. Jan Egil Storholt	NOR	1:57.95	
7. S. Tomas Gustafson	SWE	1:58.18	
8. Vladimir Lobanov	SOV/RUS	1:59.38	

Midway through his race against Stenshjemmet, Heiden almost fell when he hit a rut in the ice. But he was able to steady himself before he had lost more than a few hundredths of a second, and he went on to win his fourth gold medal.

1984 Sarajevo C: 40, N: 20, D: 2.16. WR: 1:54.26 (Igor Zhelezovsky)

1. Gaétan Boucher	CAN	1:58.36
2. Sergei Khlebnikov	SOV/RUS	1:58.83
3. Oleg Bozhyev	SOV/RUS	1:58.89
4. Hans van Helden	FRA	1:59.39
5. Andreas Ehrig	GDR	1:59.41
6. Andreas Dietel	GDR	1:59.73
7. Hilbert van der Duim	HOL	1:59.77
8. Viktor Chacherin	SOV/KAZ	1:59.81

Boucher, a 25-year-old marketing student from St. Hubert, Quebec, left Sarajevo with two gold medals and one bronze. He had already won a silver in the 1000 meters in 1980.

1988 Calgary C: 40, N: 20, D: 2.20. WR: 1:52.50 (Igor Zhelezovsky)

1. André Hoffmann	GDR	1:52.06	WR
2. Eric Flaim	USA	1:52.12	
3. Michael Hadschieff	AUT	1:52.31	

4. Igor Zhelezovsky	SOV/BLR	1:52.63
5. Toru Aoyanagi	JPN	1:52.85
6. Aleksandr Klimov	SOV/RUS	1:52.97
7. Nikolai Gulyaev	SOV/RUS	1:53.04
8. Peter Adeberg	GDR	1:53.57

1992 Albertville C: 46, N: 21, D: 2.16. WR: 1:52.06 (André Hoffman)

1. Johann Koss	NOR	1:54.81
2. Ådne Sønderål	NOR	1:54.85
3. Leo Visser	HOL	1:54.90
4. Rintje Ritsma	HOL	1:55.70
5. Bart Veldkamp	HOL	1:56.33
6. Olaf Zinke	GER	1:56.74
7. Falko Zandstra	HOL	1:56.96
8. Geir Karlstad	NOR	1:56.98

On February 8, the day of the Opening Ceremony of the Albertville Games, Johann Olav Koss, the son of two doctors, and a medical student himself, was lying in a hospital bed in Bavaria suffering from an inflamed pancreas. After passing a gallstone, he was released the next day and resumed training immediately. On Thursday the thirteenth he placed seventh in the 5000 meters, an event in which he held the world record, and promptly vomited. By Sunday the sixteenth he was back in perfect shape and earned a gold medal in the 1500.

1994 Lillehammer-Hamar C: 44, N: 17, D: 2.16. WR: 1:51.60 (Rintje Ritsma)

1. Johann Koss	NOR	1:51.29	WR
2. Rintje Ritsma	HOL	1:51.99	
3. Falko Zandstra	HOL	1:52.38	
4. Ådne Sønderål	NOR	1:53.13	
5. Andrei Anufrienko	RUS	1:53.16	
6. Peter Adeberg	GER	1:53.50	
7. Neal Marshall	CAN	1:53.56	
8. Martin Hersman	HOL	1:53.59	

Koss defended his 1500-meter title and earned the second of his three world record victories in Hamar. His time was only the fifth best at 700 meters, but each of his last two laps was the fastest recorded. Zandstra and Ritsma both skated after Koss and both were ahead of his time with one lap to go, but neither could match Koss's closing power. Less than six weeks earlier, Ritsma, skating on the Olympic oval, had broken André Hoffman's almost six-year-old world record while winning the European championship.

5000 METERS

1924 Chamonix C: 22, N: 10, D: 1.26. WR: 8:26.5 (Harald Ström)

1. A. Clas Thunberg	FIN	8:39.0
2. Julius Skutnabb	FIN	8:48.4
3. Roald Larsen	NOR	8:50.2
4. Sigurd Moen	NOR	8:51.0
5. Harald Ström	NOR	8:54.6
6. Valentine Bialas	USA	8:55.0
7. Fridtjof Paulsen	NOR	8:59.0
8. Richard Donovan	USA	9:05.3

Thunberg won the first of his five Olympic gold medals.

1928 St. Moritz C: 33, N: 14, D: 2.13. WR: 8:26.5 (Harald Ström)

1.	Ivar Ballangrud	NOR	8:50.5
2.	Julius Skutnabb	FIN	8:59.1
3.	Bernt Evensen	NOR	9:01.1
4.	Irving Jaffee	USA	9:01.3
5.	Armand Carlsen	NOR	9:01.5
6.	Valentine Bialas	USA	9:06.3
7.	Michael Staksrud	NOR	9:07.3
8.	Otto Polacsek	AUT	9:08.9

This was the first of Ballangrud's seven Olympic medals.

1932 Lake Placid C: 18, N: 6, D: 2.4. WR: 8:21.6 (Ivar Ballangrud)

1.	Irving Jaffee	USA	9:40.8
2.	Edward Murphy	USA	—
3.	William Logan	CAN	—
4.	Herbert Taylor	USA	—
5.	Ivar Ballangrud	NOR	—
6.	Bernt Evensen	NOR	—
7.	Frank Stack	CAN	—
8.	C. Harry Smyth	CAN	—

1936 Garmisch-Partenkirchen C: 37, N: 16, D: 2.12. WR: 8:17.2 (Ivar Ballangrud)

1.	Ivar Ballangrud	NOR	8:19.6	OR
2.	Birger Wasenius	FIN	8:23.3	
3.	Antero Ojala	FIN	8:30.1	
4.	Jan Langedijk	HOL	8:32.0	
5.	Max Stiepl	AUT	8:35.0	
6.	Ossi Blomqvist	FIN	8:36.6	
7.	Charles Mathisen	NOR	8:36.9	
8.	Karl Wazulek	AUT	8:38.4	

1948 St. Moritz C: 40, N: 14, D: 2.1. WR: 8:13.7 (Åke Seyffarth)

1.	Reidar Liaklev	NOR	8:29.4
2.	Odd Lundberg	NOR	8:32.7
3.	Göthe Hedlund	SWE	8:34.8
4.	Gustav Jansson	SWE	8:34.9
5.	Jan Langedijk	HOL	8:36.2
6.	Cornelis "Kees" Broekman	HOL	8:37.3
7.	Åke Seyffarth	SWE	8:37.9
8.	Pentti Lammio	FIN	8:40.7

Åke Seyffarth, who had set the world record seven years earlier, lost precious seconds on the final lap when he brushed against a photographer who had jumped onto the ice to take a picture. Liaklev and Lundberg were both born and raised in the small village of Brandbu.

1952 Oslo C: 35, N: 13, D: 2.17. WR: 8:03.7 (Nikolai Mamonov)

1.	Hjalmar Andersen	NOR	8:10.6	OR
2.	Cornelis "Kees" Broekman	HOL	8:21.6	
3.	Sverre Haugli	NOR	8:22.4	
4.	Anton Huiskes	HOL	8:28.5	
5.	Willem van der Voort	HOL	8:30.6	
6.	Carl-Erik Asplund	SWE	8:30.7	
7.	Pentti Lammio	FIN	8:31.9	
8.	Arthur Mannsbarth	AUT	8:36.2	

Spurred on by a standing ovation from the crowd of 24,000, 28-year-old Trondheim truck driver Hjalmar Andersen achieved the largest winning margin in the history of the 5000 meters.

1956 Cortina C: 46, N: 17, D: 1.29. WR: 7:45.6 (Boris Shilkov)

1. Boris Shilkov	SOV/RUS	7:48.7	OR
2. Sigvard Ericsson	SWE	7:56.7	
3. Oleg Goncharenko	SOV/RUS	7:57.5	
4. Willem de Graaf	HOL	8:00.2	
4. Cornelis "Kees" Broekman	HOL	8:00.2	
6. Roald Aas	NOR	8:01.6	
7. Olof Dahlberg	SWE	8:01.8	
8. Knut Johannesen	NOR	8:02.3	

1960 Squaw Valley C: 37, N: 15, D: 2.25. WR: 7:45.6 (Boris Shilkov)

1. Viktor Kosichkin	SOV/RUS	7:51.3
2. Knut Johannesen	NOR	8:00.8
3. Jan Pesman	HOL	8:05.1
4. Torstein Seiersten	NOR	8:05.3
5. Valery Kotov	SOV/RUS	8:05.4
6. Oleg Goncharenko	SOV/RUS	8:06.6
7. Ivar Nilsson	SWE	8:09.1
7. Keijo Tapiovaara	FIN	8:09.1

1964 Innsbruck C: 44, N: 19, D: 2.5. WR: 7:34.3 (Jonny Nilsson)

1. Knut Johannesen	NOR	7:38.4	OR
2. Per Ivar Moe	NOR	7:38.6	
3. Fred Anton Maier	NOR	7:42.0	
4. Victor Kosichkin	SOV/RUS	7:45.8	
5. Herman Strutz	AUT	7:48.3	
6. Jonny Nilsson	SWE	7:48.4	
7. Ivar Nilsson	SWE	7:49.0	
8. Rutgerus Liebrechts	HOL	7:50.9	

Skating in the fifth pair, 19-year-old Per Ivar Moe recorded the second-fastest 5000 meters ever. Then he watched as Olympic veteran Knut Johannesen assaulted his time as part of the 14th pair. With five of 12½ laps to go, Johannesen was three seconds behind Moe's pace. But he caught up with two laps left and pushed for the finish with the crowd on its feet, rooting him on. Unfortunately, as he crossed the finish line, the clock stopped at 7:38.7—one-tenth of a second slower than Moe. But then the scoreboard was revised to match the official time—7:38.4—and Johannesen had won his second gold medal. Between 1956 and 1964 he won two gold, two silver, and one bronze.

1968 Grenoble C: 38, N: 17, D: 2.15. WR: 7:26.2. (Fred Anton Maier)

1. Fred Anton Maier	NOR	7:22.4	WR
2. Cornelis "Kees" Verkerk	HOL	7:23.2	
3. Petrus Nottet	HOL	7:25.5	
4. Per-Willy Guttormsen	NOR	7:27.8	
5. Johnny Höglin	SWE	7:32.7	
6. Örjan Sandler	SWE	7:32.8	
7. Jonny Nilsson	SWE	7:32.9	
8. Jan Bols	HOL	7:33.1	

Verkerk broke Maier's world record by three seconds and then watched as the 29-year-old clerk won it back 20 minutes later.

1972 Sapporo C: 28, N: 14, D: 2.4. WR: 7:12.0 (Adrianus "Ard" Schenk)

1.	Adrianus "Ard" Schenk	HOL	7:23.61
2.	Roar Grönvold	NOR	7:28.18
3.	Sten Stensen	NOR	7:33.39
4.	Göran Claeson	SWE	7:36.17
5.	Willy Olsen	NOR	7:36.47
6.	Cornelis "Kees" Verkerk	HOL	7:39.17
7.	Valery Lavrouchkin	SOV/RUS	7:39.26
8.	Jan Bols	HOL	7:39.40

Schenk skated first, while it was snowing, but he still managed to outstrip the field.

1976 Innsbruck C: 31, N: 17, D: 2.11. WR: 7:07.82 (Hans van Helden)

1.	Sten Stensen	NOR	7:24.48
2.	Piet Kleine	HOL	7:26.47
3.	Hans van Helden	HOL	7:26.54
4.	Viktor Varlamov	SOV/KAZ	7:30.97
5.	Klaus Wunderlich	GDR	7:33.82
6.	Daniel Carroll	USA	7:36.46
7.	Vladimir Ivanov	SOV/RUS	7:37.73
8.	Örjan Sandler	SWE	7:39.69

1980 Lake Placid C: 29, N: 15, D: 2.16. WR: 6:56.9 (Kai Arne Stenshjemmet)

1.	Eric Heiden	USA	7:02.29	OR
2.	Kai Arne Stenshjemmet	NOR	7:03.28	
3.	Tom-Erik Oxholm	NOR	7:05.59	
4.	Hilbert van der Duim	HOL	7:07.97	
5.	Öyvind Tveter	NOR	7:08.36	
6.	Piet Kleine	HOL	7:08.96	
7.	Michael Woods	USA	7:10.39	
8.	Ulf Ekstrand	SWE	7:13.13	

Stenshjemmet, skating two pairs after Eric Heiden, stayed ahead of his pace for ten and a half laps, but began his arm swinging too early and couldn't keep it up. It was Heiden's second gold medal.

1984 Sarajevo C: 42, N: 20, D: 2.12. WR: 6:54.66 (Aleksandr Baranov)

1.	S. Tomas Gustafson	SWE	7:12.28
2.	Igor Malkov	SOV/RUS	7:12.30
3.	René Schöfisch	GDR	7:17.49
4.	Andreas Ehrig	GDR	7:17.63
5.	Oleg Bozhyev	SOV/RUS	7:17.96
6.	Pertti Niittylä	FIN	7:17.97
7.	Björn Nyland	NOR	7:18.27
8.	Werner Jaeger	AUT	7:18.61

Skating in the first pair, Gustafson, who had trained in Wisconsin with Diane Holum and Eric Heiden, came off the ice thinking his time would be good enough for fifth or sixth place. Three pairs later, Malkov, not realizing how close he was to Gustafson's time, faded in the last 400 meters and lost by one-fiftieth of a second.

1988 Calgary C: 38, N: 18, D: 2.17. WR: 6:43.59 (Geir Karlstad)

1.	S. Tomas Gustafson	SWE	6:44.63	OR
2.	Leo Visser	HOL	6:44.98	
3.	Gerard Kemkers	HOL	6:45.92	
4.	Eric Flaim	USA	6:47.09	

5. Michael Hadschieff	AUT	6:48.72	
6. David Silk	USA	6:49.95	
7. Geir Karlstad	NOR	6:50.88	
8. Roland Freier	GDR	6:51.42	

Defending champion Tomas Gustafson, skating seven pairs after Leo Visser, was eight tenths of a second behind Visser's pace with 400 meters to go. The public-address announcer informed the audience that Gustafson was going for the silver or bronze medal. But the 28-year-old Swede, who had struggled through knee surgery, meningitis, and the death of his father since his last Olympic victory, had set his sights higher. His final lap was an amazing 31.86. "How do you describe happiness?" he said afterward. "I'd have to write a poem."

1992 Albertville C: 36, N: 20, D: 2.13. WR: 6:41.73 (Johann Olav Koss)

1. Geir Karlstad	NOR	6:59.97
2. Falko Zandstra	HOL	7:02.28
3. Leo Visser	HOL	7:04.96
4. Frank Dittrich	GER	7:06.33
5. Bart Veldkamp	HOL	7:08.00
6. Eric Flaim	USA	7:11.15
7. Johann Koss	NOR	7:11.32
8. Yevgeny Sanarov	SOV/KAZ	7:11.38

In 1988 Geir Karlstad was one of the big disappointments of the Calgary Games. After he set world records in the 5000 and 10,000, he was overwhelmed by media attention in speed skating-crazed Norway. In addition to this distraction, he was involved in a steroids scandal after he was asked to pass a mysterious package from Nikolai Gulyaev to fellow Norwegian skater Stein Krosby. Although he had been favored in both distance events, Karlstad placed only seventh in the 5000 and fell in the 10,000 and failed to finish. Another controversy involving Karlstad came up before the Albertville Games. Norway's chief medical officer, Ingard Lerheim, who was also a member of the I.O.C.'s medical committee, told the press that Karlstad had an abnormally high testosterone level and that he had been issued a "Doping Certificate" proving that his high test levels were a result of natural causes. Prince Alexandre de Merode, the I.O.C. medical commission chairman, denied that such a certificate existed. One good thing that happened to Karlstad between Olympics was the emergence of Johann Olav Koss, who drew away most of the media attention and allowed Karlstad to train in peace. The 5000-meter race in Albertville was run in a steady rain. After his victory, Karlstad told the press, "I didn't like soft ice up to now, but now I do."

1994 Lillehammer-Hamar C: 32, N: 17, D: 2.13. WR: 6:35.53 (Johann Koss)

1. Johann Koss	NOR	6:34.96	WR
2. Kjell Storelid	NOR	6:42.68	
3. Rintje Ritsma	HOL	6:43.94	
4. Falko Zandstrra	HOL	6:44.58	
5. Bart Veldkamp	HOL	6:49.00	
6. Toshihiko Itokawa	JPN	6:49.36	
7. Jaromir Radke	POL	6:50.40	
8. Frank Dittrich	GER	6:52.27	

On December 4, 1993, skating at the Olympic Vikingskipet arena in Hamar, Johann Koss set his fourth world record at 5000 meters. But the following month, with the Olympics only weeks away, he began to fall apart. Suffering from a sprained knee ligament, as well as self-doubt, he dropped to fourth at the European championships and then fifth at a World Cup 5000-meter race only three weeks before the

Olympics. Unfortunately for the Dutch team, who had set their sights on beating Koss, he recovered completely before the Games began. Skating in the fourth pair, Koss set another world record.

10,000 METERS

1924 Chamonix C: 16, N: 6, D: 1.27. WR: 17:22.6 (Oscar Mathisen)

1.	Julius Skutnabb	FIN	18:04.8
2.	A. Clas Thunberg	FIN	18:07.8
3.	Roald Larsen	NOR	18:12.2
4.	Fritjof Paulsen	NOR	18:13.0
5.	Harald Ström	NOR	18:18.6
6.	Sigurd Moen	NOR	18:19.0
7.	Léon Quaglia	FRA	18:25.0
8.	Valentine Bialas	USA	18:34.0

Skutnabb defeated Thunberg head-on, since they were paired together. This reversed the order of finish of the 5000, which had been held the previous day.

1928 St. Moritz C: 10, N: 6, D: 2.14. WR: 17:17.4 (Armand Carlsen)

1.	Irving Jaffee	USA	18:36.5
2.	Bernt Evensen	NOR	18:36.6
3.	Otto Polacsek	AUT	20:00.9
4.	Rudolf Riedl	AUT	20:21.5
5.	Keistutis Bulota	LIT	20:22.2
6.	Armand Carlsen	NOR	20:56.1
7.	Valentine Bialas	USA	21:05.4

Officially, this race never took place. After seven of the ten entrants had completed their heats, the temperature rose suddenly, and the officials in charge ordered the day's times cancelled and the races rerun. By the time a final decision had been reached, the Norwegians, who had already made it clear that they considered Jaffee the champion, had gone home, so the contest was cancelled. As far as the skaters were concerned, the matter had been settled after the first heat, when Jaffee came from behind to nip Evensen just before the finish line. However sports historians generally consider the 1928 10,000 meters to have been a non-event.

1932 Lake Placid C: 18, N: 6, D: 2.8. WR: 17:17.4 (Armand Carlsen)

1.	Irving Jaffee	USA	19:13.6
2.	Ivar Ballangrud	NOR	—
3.	Frank Stack	CAN	—
4.	Edwin Wedge	USA	—
5.	Valentine Bialas	USA	—
6.	Bernt Evensen	NOR	—
7.	Alexander Hurd	CAN	—
8.	Edward Schroeder	USA	—

The turmoil that marred the 1932 speed skating competitions culminated in disputes that broke out during the heats of the 10,000 meters. For this contest the North Americans tacked on a rule that required each skater to do his share in setting the pace. After the first heat, Alex Hurd, who won the race, as well as Edwin Wedge of the United States and Shozo Ishihara of Japan, were disqualified for not doing their share. In the second heat Frank Stack was disqualified for interference after a

Irving Jaffee stumbles across the finish line of the 1932 10,000-meter speed skating race.

protest by Bernt Evensen. After much haggling and many threats it was decided to rerun the two races the following day. The same eight men who had originally qualified for the final qualified again. The final race was slow and tactical, as all eight stayed in a bunch until the last lap. Jaffee won by five yards, but the finish was so close that only two yards separated Ballangrud in second place from Evensen in sixth. During the Depression, Jaffee was forced to pawn his two gold medals. Unfortunately, times were so tough that even the pawnshop went out of business and Jaffee never saw his medals again. Bronze medalist Frank Stack was still competing in the Olympics in 1952 when, at the age of 46, he finished 12th in the 500 meters.

1936 Garmisch-Partenkirchen C: 30, N: 14, D: 2.14. WR: 17:17.4 (Armand Carlsen)

1. Ivar Ballangrud	NOR	17:24.3	OR
2. Birger Wasenius	FIN	17:28.2	
3. Max Stiepl	AUT	17:30.0	
4. Charles Mathisen	NOR	17:41.2	
5. Ossi Blomqvist	FIN	17:42.4	
6. Jan Langedijk	HOL	17:43.7	
7. Antero Ojala	FIN	17:46.6	
8. Edward Schroeder	USA	17:52.0	

Ballangrud and Wasenius, paired together, raced neck and neck for 4000 meters before the Norwegian began to pull away. Ballangrud completed his Olympic career with four gold medals, two silver, and one bronze.

1948 St. Moritz C: 27, N: 11, D: 2.3. WR: 17:05.5 (Charles Mathisen)

1. Åke Seyffarth	SWE	17:26.3
2. Lauri Parkkinen	FIN	17:36.0

3.	Pentti Lammio	FIN	17:42.7
4.	Kornel Pajor	HUN	17:45.6
5.	Cornelis "Kees" Broekman	HOL	17:54.7
6.	Jan Langedijk	HOL	17:55.3
7.	Odd Lundberg	NOR	18:05.8
8.	Harry Jansson	SWE	18:08.0

1952 Oslo C: 30, N: 12, D: 2.19. WR: 16:32.6 (Hjalmar Andersen)

1.	Hjalmar Andersen	NOR	16:45.8	OR
2.	Cornelis "Kees" Broekman	HOL	17:10.6	
3.	Carl-Erik Asplund	SWE	17:16.6	
4.	Pentti Lammio	FIN	17:20.5	
5.	Anton Huiskes	HOL	17:25.5	
6.	Sverre Haugli	NOR	17:30.2	
7.	Kazuhiko Sugawara	JPN	17:34.0	
8.	Lauri Parkkinen	FIN	17:36.8	

Hjalmar "Hjallis" Andersen's unusually large margin of victory, the most decisive in Olympic history, earned him his third gold medal in three days.

1956 Cortina C: 32, N: 15, D: 1.31. WR: 16:32.6 (Hjalmar Andersen)

1.	Sigvard Ericsson	SWE	16:35.9	OR
2.	Knut Johannesen	NOR	16:36.9	
3.	Oleg Goncharenko	SOV/RUS	16:42.3	
4.	Sverre Haugli	NOR	16:48.7	
5.	Cornelius "Kees" Broekman	HOL	16:51.2	
6.	Hjalmar Andersen	NOR	16:52.6	
7.	Boris Yakimov	SOV/RUS	16:59.7	
8.	Olof Dahlberg	SWE	17:01.3	

Skating three pairs after Johannesen, 25-year-old woodchopper Sigge Ericsson kept a steady pace and held on for the victory despite losing two seconds to the fast-finishing Norwegian on the final lap.

1960 Squaw Valley C: 30, N: 15, D: 2.27. WR: 16:32.6 (Hjalmar Andersen)

1.	Knut Johannesen	NOR	15:46.6	WR
2.	Viktor Kosichkin	SOV/RUS	15:49.2	
3.	Kjell Bäckman	SWE	16:14.2	
4.	Ivar Nilsson	SWE	16:26.0	
5.	Terence Monaghan	GBR	16:31.6	
6.	Torstein Seiersten	NOR	16:33.4	
7.	Olof Dahlberg	SWE	16:34.6	
8.	Juhani Järvinen	FIN	16:35.4	

Since February 10, 1952, the world record for 10,000 meters had been Hjallis Andersen's 16:32.6. But with the ice perfect and the weather sunny and calm, five different skaters bettered Andersen's mark. Skating in the second pair, Kjell Bäckman chopped over 18 seconds off the record with a 16:14.2. Two pairs later, Knut Johannesen, a 26-year-old carpenter, became the first person to break the 16-minute barrier with a phenomenal 15:46.6. Johannesen's world record lasted for three years, but it almost didn't survive the rest of the day. Two pairs after Johannesen came Viktor Kosichkin, who stayed ahead of Johannesen's pace for 6400 meters and was still even after 7600 meters. After that, though, Kosichkin began to tire and crossed the finish line 2.6 seconds too late. He did, however, have the rare experience of breaking the world record by more than 43 seconds and earning only a silver medal.

1964 Innsbruck C: 33, N: 19, D: 2.7. WR: 15:33.0 (Jonny Nilsson)

1. Jonny Nilsson	SWE	15:50.1	
2. Fred Anton Maier	NOR	16:06.0	
3. Knut Johannesen	NOR	16:06.3	
4. Rutgerus Liebrechts	HOL	16:08.6	
5. Ants Antson	SOV/EST	16:08.7	
6. Victor Kosichkin	SOV/RUS	16:19.3	
7. Gerhard Zimmermann	GER	16:22.5	
8. Alfred Malkin	GBR	16:35.2	

1968 Grenoble C: 28, N: 13, D: 2.17. WR: 15:20.3 (Fred Anton Maier)

1. Johnny Höglin	SWE	15:23.6	OR
2. Fred Anton Maier	NOR	15:23.9	
3. Örjan Sandler	SWE	15:31.8	
4. Per-Willy Guttormsen	NOR	15:32.6	
5. Cornelis "Kees" Verkerk	HOL	15:33.9	
6. Jonny Nilsson	SWE	15:39.6	
7. Magne Thomassen	NOR	15:44.9	
8. Petrus Nottet	HOL	15:54.7	

Höglin, who had never before gone faster than 15:40, was one of the surprise winners of the 1968 Winter Games. Maier had the advantage of skating first, but Höglin, in the seventh pair, moved ahead of Maier's pace with three of 25 laps to go.

1972 Sapporo C: 24, N: 14, D: 2.7. WR: 14:55.9 (Adrianus "Ard" Schenk)

1. Adrianus "Ard" Schenk	HOL	15:01.35	OR
2. Cornelis "Kees" Verkerk	HOL	15:04.70	
3. Sten Stensen	NOR	15:07.08	
4. Jan Bols	HOL	15:17.99	
5. Valery Lavrouchkin	SOV/RUS	15:20.08	
6. Göran Claesson	SWE	15:30.19	
7. Kimmo Koskinen	FIN	15:38.87	
8. Gerhard Zimmermann	GER	15:43.92	

Handsome Ard Schenk won his third gold medal to match the single Olympics record of Ivar Ballangrud and Hjalmar "Hjallis" Andersen. Two weeks later in Norway, Schenk became the first person in 60 years to sweep all four events at the world championships. The last person to achieve the feat had been Oscar Mathisen in 1912. Schenk was considered such a hero in Holland that a tulip was named after him.

1976 Innsbruck C: 20, N: 13, D: 2.14. WR: 14:50.31 (Sten Stensen)

1. Piet Kleine	HOL	14:50.59	OR
2. Sten Stensen	NOR	14:53.30	
3. Hans van Helden	HOL	15:02.02	
4. Victor Varlamov	SOV/KAZ	15:06.06	
5. Örjan Sandler	SWE	15:16.21	
6. Colin Coates	AUS	15:16.80	
7. Daniel Carroll	USA	15:19.29	
8. Franz Krienbuhl	SWI	15:36.43	

Stensen had set a world record of 14:50.31 three weeks earlier. In Innsbruck, skating sixth, he was able to do only 14:53.30. Two pairs later, Piet Kleine, a 6-foot 5-inch 24-year-old unemployed carpenter, attacked Stensen's pace in steady fashion. He moved ahead at the halfway mark and stayed at least two seconds faster for the last eight laps.

1980 Lake Placid C: 25, N: 12, D: 2.23. WR: 14:34.33 (Viktor Leskin)

1.	Eric Heiden	USA	14:28.13	WR
2.	Piet Kleine	HOL	14:36.03	
3.	Tom-Erik Oxholm	NOR	14:36.60	
4.	Michael Woods	USA	14:39.53	
5.	Öyvind Tveter	NOR	14:43.53	
6.	Hilbert van der Duim	HOL	14:47.58	
7.	Viktor Leskin	SOV/RUS	14:51.72	
8.	Andreas Ehrig	GDR	14:51.94	

Having already become the first male speed skater to win four gold medals in one Olympics, Eric Heiden took the night off before his final race to attend the United States-U.S.S.R. ice hockey match. The U.S. team included two friends of Heiden's from Madison, Wisconsin, Mark Johnson and Bobby Suter. Heiden was so excited by the U.S. victory—more excited than by his own accomplishments—that he had trouble falling asleep and ended up oversleeping in the morning. Snatching a few pieces of bread for breakfast, he rushed to the track and, skating in the second pair, calmly broke the world record by over six seconds. He had become the first person in Olympic history to win five individual gold medals at one games (three of Mark Spitz's seven gold medals had been in relay events). Repelled by the instant celebrity that followed his feats, Eric Heiden announced that he would retire at the end of the season. "Maybe if things had stayed the way they were," he told the press, "and I could still be obscure in an obscure sport, I might want to keep skating. I really liked it best when I was a nobody." After the Olympics, Heiden turned to cycling and competed in the 1986 Tour de France. Later, he continued to shun the world of endorsement deals and, following in his father's footsteps, became an orthopedic surgeon.

1984 Sarajevo C: 32, N: 17, D: 2.18. WR: 14:23.59 (S. Tomas Gustafson)

1.	Igor Malkov	SOV/RUS	14:39.90
2.	S. Tomas Gustafson	SWE	14:39.95
3.	René Schöfisch	GDR	14:46.91
4.	Geir Karlstad	NOR	14:52.40
5.	Michael Hadschieff	AUT	14:53.78
6.	Dmitri Bochkarov	SOV/RUS	14:55.65
7.	Michael Woods	USA	14:57.30
8.	Henry Nilsen	NOR	14:57.81

Six days after 19-year-old Igor Malkov narrowly missed beating Tomas Gustafson for the 5000-meter gold medal, he again found himself skating after the Swede. This time he paced himself well and finished strongly to win by one-twentieth of a second.

1988 Calgary C: 32, N: 19, D: 2.21. WR: 13:48.51 (Geir Karlstad)

1.	S. Tomas Gustafson	SWE	13:48.20	WR
2.	Michael Hadschieff	AUT	13:56.11	
3.	Leo Visser	HOL	14:00.55	
4.	Eric Flaim	USA	14:05.57	
5.	Gerard Kemkers	HOL	14:08.34	

6. Yuri Klyuyev	SOV/RUS	14:09.68	
7. Roberto Sighel	ITA	14:13.60	
8. Roland Freier	GDR	14:19.60	

Tomas Gustafson brought his career Olympic medal total to three golds and one silver. Gerard Kemkers finished fifth despite falling in the fifth lap. Colin Coates of Australia, competing in his sixth Olympics, placed twenty-sixth, twenty years after his first appearance.

1992 Albertville C: 30, N: 15, D: 2.20. WR: 13:43.54 (Johann Olav Koss)

1. Bart Veldkamp	HOL	14:12.12
2. Johann Koss	NOR	14:14.58
3. Geir Karlstad	NOR	14:18.13
4. Robert Vunderink	HOL	14:22.92
5. Kazuhiro Sato	JPN	14:28.30
6. Michael Hadschieff	AUT	14:28.80
7. Per Bengtsson	SWE	14:35.58
8. Steinar Johansen	NOR	14:36.09

Veldkamp's victory, the first by a Dutch male skater in 16 years, set off wild celebrations among the many Dutch fans in the stands. Veldkamp himself was so excited that he danced on the podium at the medal ceremony and sprayed champagne on the reporters and photographers at his press conference.

1994 Lillehammer-Hamar C: 16, N: 10, D: 2.20. WR: 13:43.54 (Johann Koss)

1. Johann Koss	NOR	13:30.55	WR
2. Kjell Storelid	NOR	13.49.25	
3. Bart Veldkamp	HOL	13:56.73	
4. Falko Zandstra	HOL	13:58.25	
5. Jaromir Radke	POL	14:03.84	
6. Frank Dittrich	GER	14:04.33	
7. Rintje Ritsma	HOL	14:09.28	
8. Jonas Schön	SWE	14:10.15	

Johann Koss had already won the 5000 and the 1500, setting world records in each, when he started his specialty, the 10,000 meters. After an opening lap of 35.12, he thrilled the hometown crowd—and demoralized his opponents—by reeling off 24 straight sub-33-second laps to break his own world record by 12.99 seconds. At the medal ceremony, the man who placed the gold around Koss's neck was Hjalmar Andersen, the last Norwegian skater to earn three gold medals—42 years earlier. At the post-race press conference, the Dutch team presented Koss with a golden butterfly, normally reserved for Dutch gold medal winners.

Johann Koss came away from the Lillehammer Olympics as a sports superhero, but, refreshingly for a star athlete, he was a man with a life outside sports. An active supporter of the Olympic Aid project to help children in Sarajevo and other war-torn countries, he donated his $30,000 bonus money for winning the 1500 meters to Olympic Aid. He also allowed his skates to be auctioned on national television, gaining another $85,000 for Olympic Aid. A few months before the Olympics, Koss visited Eritrea, the East African nation still recovering from decades of civil war. He promised to return after the Olympics with sports equipment for Eritrea's children. On the final day of the Lillehammer Games, Koss appealed to the children of Norway to donate extra soccer balls, sports clothes and other equipment to the children of Eritrea. As promised, Johann Koss did return to Eritrea—with twelve tons of equipment.

Short Track

Short track is the exciting younger cousin of staid long-track speed skating. Instead of racing in pairs against the clock, the skaters race in a pack, usually four at a time. The first person across the finish line is the winner. Elimination heats lead to semifinals and finals. In individual races, semifinal losers take part in a "B" final to decide places 5 through 8. In relays, fifth through eighth places are determined by semifinal placings and times. The track is only 111.12 meters around. The course is marked by four rubber blocks in the corners. Skaters may cross into the infield, but they must come back outside to go around the blocks. They are allowed to touch the ice inside the blocks with their hands. Although the sport is often compared to roller derby, pushing, colliding, and obstructing are grounds for immediate disqualification. Passing must be done without body contact.

Pack-style speed skating first appeared in the 1932 Olympics, although it was held on a normal 400-meter oval with a different set of rules. The first short-track world championship was held at Meudon-la-Forêt, France, in 1981, and the sport was included as a demonstration at the 1988 Olympics.

SHORT TRACK: 500 METERS

1924-1992 not held

1994 Lillehammer-Hamar C: 31, N: 16, D: 2.26. WR: 43.08 (Mirko Vuillermin)

1.	Chae Ji-hoon	KOR	43.45
2.	Mirko Vuillermin	ITA	43.47
3.	Nicholas Gooch	GBR	43.68
4.	Marc Gagnon	CAN	52.74
5.	Frédéric Blackburn	CAN	44.97
6.	Lee Jun-ho	KOR	45.13
7.	Martin Johnsson	SWE	45.24
8.	Steven Bradbury	AUS	45.33

Chae Ji-hoon's specialty was the 3000-meter race, an event not included in the Olympic program. The 19-year-old from Seoul, who had already earned a silver medal at 1000 meters four days earlier, slipped ahead of world record holder Mirko Vuillermin just as they reached the finish line.

SHORT TRACK: 1000 METERS

1924-1988 not held

1992 Albertville C: 28, N: 16, D: 2.20. WR: 1:31.80 (Tsutomu Kawasaki)

1.	Kim Ki-hoon	KOR	1:30.76 WR
2.	Frédéric Blackburn	CAN	1:31.11
3.	Lee Joon-ho	KOR	1:31.16
4.	Michael McMillen	NZL	1:31.32
5.	Wilfred O'Reilly	GBR	1:36.24
6.	Geert Blanchart	BEL	1:36.28

7. Mark Lackie	CAN	1:36.28
8. Michel Daignault	CAN	1:37.10

World record holder Tsutomu Kawasaki was eliminated in the quarterfinals. Wilf O'Reilly, winner of the 1988 Olympic demonstration event and the defending world champion, fell in his semifinal heat and was also eliminated. That race was won by Lee Joon-ho in a world record time of 1:31.27. The other semi was won by Lee's countryman, Kim Ki-hoon. Kim, the 1989 world champion, had spent four months in the hospital that same year after being spiked in an artery during a race. In the final, the two Koreans went out fast. Blackburn caught Lee, but Kim eluded him, as all four skaters broke the pre-Olympic world record. Kim returned to Korea as a national hero and was awarded a $30,000 annual stipend for the rest of his life.

1994 Lillehammer-Hamar C: 31, N: 16, D: 2.22. WR: 1:28.47 (Michael McMillen)

1. Kim Ki-hoon	KOR	1:34.57
2. Chae Ji-hoon	KOR	1:34.92
3. Marc Gagnon	CAN	1:33.03
4. Satoru Terao	JPN	1:33.39
5. Lee Jun-ho	KOR	1:44.99
6. Derrick Campbell	CAN	DNF
7. Nicholas Gooch	GBR	DISQ
8. Frédéric Blackburn	CAN	DISQ

Kim Ko-hoon successfully defended his Olympic title, but the real excitement happened behind him. Derrick Campbell led the final for six laps, but with three laps to go Nicholas Gooch tried to pass him on the inside. He pushed Campbell as he went by, sending the Canadian skidding into the sideboards. Gooch crossed the finish line in second place, but 20 minutes later, officials announced his disqualification. Chae Ji-hoon was moved up to the silver medal spot. And for the bronze medal, at first it appeared that it would go to Campbell, who had risen after his spill and continued the race. But then it was determined that he had stopped skating one lap too soon, so he too was disqualified. Next in line was Campbell's teammate, Marc Gagnon, who had won the consolation final. Thus Gagnon had the strange experience of winning a bronze medal even though he didn't take part in the final.

SHORT TRACK: 5000-METER RELAY

Short-track relay racing is probably the most exciting spectator event at the Winter Olympics. Each team includes four skaters. There are no rules regulating who skates when and for how long, except that no changeover may be made in the final two laps. Changeovers are performed by touch, although in actual practice the retiring skater vigorously pushes the new skater. If a racer falls, a new skater may take over by touching his or her fallen comrade. An alternate is allowed to mill around in the infield to replace an injured skater.

1924-1988 not held

1992 Albertville T: 9, N: 9, D: 2.22. WR: 7:22.12 (HOL—Mos, Sagten, Van de Velde, Veldhoven)

1. KOR	(Kim Ki-hoon, Lee Joon-ho, Song Jae-kun, Mo Ji-su)	7:14.02 WR
2. CAN	(Frédéric Blackburn, Mark Lackie, Michel Daignault, Sylvain Gagnon)	7:14.06

3.	JPN	(Tatsuyoshi Ishihara, Tsutomu Kawasaki, Toshinobu Kawai, Yuichi Akasaka)	7:18.18
4.	NZL	(Michael McMillen, Christopher Nicholson, Andrew Nicholson, Tony Smith)	7:18.91
5.	FRA	(Marc Bella, Arnaud Drouet, Rémi Ingres, Claude Nicouleau)	7:26.09
6.	GBR	(Nicky Gooch, Stuart Horsepool, Jasper Matthew, Wilf O'Reilly)	7:29.40
7.	AUS	(Kieran Hansen, John Kah, Andrew Murtha, Richard Nizielski)	7:32.57
8.	ITA	(Orazio Fagone, Hugo Herrnhof, Roberto Peretti, Mirko Vuillermin)	7:32.80

The South Korean team set a world record of 7:14.07 in the first preliminary heat. The final was a spectacular dual between the Koreans and the Canadians. The lead changed hands five times during the first 30 laps. Then Canada took over while the Koreans tucked in behind them for the next 1500 meters. Michel Daignault slipped slightly midway through the final lap, then went a bit wide on the final turn. Kim Ki-hoon took advantage of the opening to slither by on the inside. He edged ahead of Daignault in the final stride to win in a photo finish and set another world record. Chris Nicholson of the fourth-place New Zealand team competed as a cyclist five months later at the Barcelona Summer Olympics. He placed tenth in the team time trial event.

1994 Lillehammer-Hamar T: 8, N: 8, D: 2.26. WR: 7:10.95 (NZL-Biggs, McMillen, A. Nicholson, C. Nicholson)

1.	ITA	(Maurizio Carnino, Orazio Fagone, Hugo Herrnhof, Mirko Vuillermin)	7:11.74	OR
2.	USA	(Randall Bartz, John Coyle, Eric Flaim, Andrew Gabel)	7:13.68	
3.	AUS	(Steven Bradbury, Kieran Hansen, Andrew Murtha, Richard Nizielski)	7:13.68	
4.	CAN	(Frédéric Blackburn, Derrick Campbell, Marc Gagnon, Stephen Gough)	7:20.40	
5.	JPN	(Yuichi Akasaka, Tatsuyoshi Ishihara, Satoru Terao, Jun Uematsu)	7:19.11	
6.	NOR	(Bjørnar Elgetun, Gisle Elvebakken, Tore Klevstuen, Morten Staubo)	7:24.29	
7.	CHN	(Li Jiajun, Li Lianli, Yang He, Zhang Hongbo)	DISQ	
8.	NZL	(Michael McMillen, Andrew Nicholson, Christopher Nicholson, Tony Smith)	DISQ	

At the 1993 world championships that served as the qualifier for the 1994 Olympics, South Korea, the defending Olympic champion, was eliminated when their star, Kim Ki-hoon, fell in a preliminary heat, broke his skate and was unable to finish the race. With the South Koreans gone, the Olympic final was wide open. Just after the halfway mark, Orazio Fagone pulled away and the Italians could not be caught. By finishing third, the Australian team earned their nation's first Winter Olympics medal. Eric Flaim of the United States became the first person to win medals in both long-track and short-track speed skating. In 1988 he had won a silver medal in the 1500-meter long-track event.

Discontinued Event

FOUR RACES COMBINED EVENT

1924 Chamonix C: 22, N: 9, D: 1.27.

			PTS.
1.	A. Clas Thunberg	FIN	5.5
2.	Roald Larsen	NOR	9.5
3.	Julius Skutnabb	FIN	11

			PTS.
4.	Sigurd Moen	NOR	17
4.	Harald Ström	NOR	17
6.	León Quaglia	FRA	25
7.	Alberts Rumba	LAT	27
8.	Leon Jucewicz	POL	32

The concept of an all-around champion has continued to be a matter of major importance in world championships, but was never included again in the Olympics.

SPEED SKATING

WOMEN
500 Meters
1000 Meters
1500 Meters
3000 Meters
5000 Meters
Short Track: 500 Meters
Short Track: 1000 Meters
Short Track: 3000-Meter Relay

WOMEN

500 METERS

Twenty-eight of the 31 medals awarded in this event have been won by skaters from only three nations: the U.S.S.R. (10), the U.S.A. (10), and Germany (8).

1924–1956 not held

1960 Squaw Valley C: 23, N: 10, D: 2.20. WR: 45.6 (Tamara Rylova)

1. Helga Haase	GDR	45.9	
2. Natalya Donchenko	SOV/RUS	46.0	
3. Jeanne Ashworth	USA	46.1	
4. Tamara Rylova	SOV	46.2	
5. Hatsue Takamizawa	JPN	46.6	
6. Klara Guseva	SOV/RUS	46.8	
6. Elwira Seroczyńska	POL	46.8	
8. Fumie Hama	JPN	47.4	

Haase was the first East German to win an Olympic gold medal.

1964 Innsbruck C: 28, N: 14, D: 1.30. WR: 44.9 (Inga Voronina)

1. Lydia Skoblikova	SOV/RUS	45.0	OR
2. Irina Yegorova	SOV/RUS	45.4	
3. Tatyana Sidorova	SOV/RUS	45.5	
4. Jeanne Ashworth	USA	46.2	
4. Janice Smith	USA	46.2	
6. Gunilla Jacobsson	SWE	46.5	
7. Janice Lawler	USA	46.6	
8. Helga Haase	GDR	47.2	

On January 27, 1962, Inga Voronina of the U.S.S.R. set world records for the 500 meters and 1500 meters. The next day she broke the world record at 3000 meters. However, the following year it was another Soviet skater, Lydia Skoblikova, a teacher from Chelyabinsk, who won the gold medal for all four distances at the world championships in Karuizawa, Japan. Voronina, not fully recovered from a bad stomach ailment, failed to make the Soviet Olympic team in 1964. Skoblikova, on the other hand, entered the competition as the favorite in three of the four events. Only in the 500 meters, the first distance to be contested, was she expected to have a tough time. Yegorova opened the day with a 45.4. This held up as the best time until Skoblikova, skating in the 13th of 14 pairs, zipped past the finish line in 45.0. Before the week was out she had duplicated her world championship feat by sweeping all four women's events.

1968 Grenoble C: 28, N: 11, D: 2.9. WR: 44.7 (Tatyana Sidorova)

1.	Lyudmila Titova	SOV/RUS	46.1
2.	Jennifer Fish	USA	46.3
2.	Dianne Holum	USA	46.3
2.	Mary Meyers	USA	46.3
5.	Elisabeth van den Brom	HOL	46.6
6.	Kaija Mustonen	FIN	46.7
6.	Sigrid Sundby	NOR	46.7
8.	Kirsti Biermann	NOR	46.8

On February 3, Tatyana Sidorova set a world record of 44.7, but six days later in Grenoble she could do no better than 46.9 and finished in a tie for ninth place. The unusual triple American tie for second place was accomplished by Mary Meyers of St. Paul, Minnesota (the day before her 22nd birthday), 16-year-old Dianne Holum of Northbrook, Illinois, and 18-year-old Jennifer Fish of Strongville, Ohio.

1972 Sapporo C: 29, N: 12, D: 2.10. WR: 42.5 (Anne Henning)

1.	Anne Henning	USA	43.33	OR
2.	Vera Krasnova	SOV/RUS	44.01	
3.	Lyudmila Titova	SOV/RUS	44.45	
4.	Sheila Young	USA	44.53	
5.	Monika Pflug	GER	44.75	
6.	Atje Keulen-Deelstra	HOL	44.89	
7.	Kay Lunda	USA	44.95	
8.	Alla Boutova	SOV/RUS	45.17	

Sixteen-year-old Anne Henning of Northbrook, Illinois, the world record holder and heavy favorite, was paired against Canada's Sylvia Burka, who had impaired vision in one eye. At the crossover Burka didn't see Henning and headed toward a collision. Rather than push her way past Burka, Henning stood up, let her pass, and then dug in faster than ever. Despite losing a full second because of the mishap (which caused Burka's disqualification), Henning still won the gold medal with a time of 43.70. The officials allowed her another run at the end of the competition and she improved to 43.33. Henning was undoubtedly aided by her superstitious mother, who watched the race while holding a clutch of good-luck charms, including a four-leaf clover, Japanese beads, a Christmas ornament, and two U.S. flags. Afterward Henning told reporters, "I just can't wait to be normal again. But, you know, I suppose people will never really let me be normal again, will they?"

1976 Innsbruck C: 27, N: 13, D: 2.6. WR: 40.91 (Sheila Young)

1.	Sheila Young	USA	42.76	OR
2.	Cathy Priestner	CAN	43.12	
3.	Tatyana Averina	SOV/RUS	43.17	
4.	Leah Poulos	USA	43.21	
5.	Vera Krasnova	SOV/RUS	43.23	
6.	Lyubov Sachikova	SOV/RUS	43.80	
7.	Makiko Nagaya	JPN	43.88	
8.	Paula Halonen	FIN	43.99	

Sheila Young, who began skating when she was two years old, won a complete set of medals at the 1976 Games. She was the first U.S. athlete to win three medals at a single Winter Olympics. In 1973 Young won the sprint world championship in both speed skating and cycling. She earned another cycling world championship in 1976, a few months after her Olympic gold medal in speed skating.

1980 Lake Placid C: 31, N: 15, D: 2.15. WR: 40.68 (Sheila Young)

1.	Karin Enke	GDR	41.78	OR
2.	Leah Mueller [Poulos]	USA	42.26	
3.	Natalya Petruseva	SOV/RUS	42.42	
4.	Ann-Sofie Järnström	SWE	42.47	
5.	Makiko Nagaya	JPN	42.70	
6.	Cornelia Jacob	GDR	42.98	
7.	Beth Heiden	USA	43.18	
8.	Tatyana Tarasova	SOV/KAZ	43.26	

Eighteen-year-old Karin Enke was practically unknown in speed skating circles until a week before the Olympics, when she won the world sprint championship in West Allis, Wisconsin, after qualifying for the East German team as an alternate. She showed that her victory was no fluke when she took the Olympic gold medal at Lake Placid.

1984 Sarajevo C: 33, N: 16, D: 2.10. WR: 39.67 (Christa Rothenburger)

1.	Christa Rothenburger	GDR	41.02	OR
2.	Karin Enke	GDR	41.28	
3.	Natalya Chive	SOV/RUS	41.50	
4.	Irina Kuleshova	SOV/UKR	41.70	
5.	Skadi Walter	GDR	42.16	
6.	Natalya Petruseva	SOV/RUS	42.19	
7.	Monika Holzner [Pflug]	GER	42.40	
8.	Bonnie Blair	USA	42.53	

Two years after earning her Olympic gold medal, Christa Rothenburger of Dresden won the women's match sprint title at the 1986 world cycling championships.

1988 Calgary C: 30, N: 15, D: 2.22. WR: 39.39 (Christa Rothenburger)

1.	Bonnie Blair	USA	39.10	WR
2.	Christa Rothenburger	GDR	39.12	
3.	Karin Kania [Enke]	GDR	39.24	
4.	Angela Stahnke	GDR	39.68	
5.	Seiko Hashimoto	JPN	39.74	
6.	Shelley Rhead	CAN	40.36	
7.	Monika Holzner-Gawenus [Pflug]	GER	40.53	
8.	Shoko Fusano	JPN	40.61	

Defending champion Christa Rothenburger, skating in the second pair, blasted her own world record by a quarter of a second. Two pairs later, Bonnie Blair of Champaign, Illinois, who began skating at the age of two, and competing at the age of four, got off to the best start of her life, clocking 10.55 seconds for the first 100 meters to Rothenburger's 10.57. That difference of two one-hundredths of a second turned out to be Blair's final margin of victory.

1992 Albertville C: 34, N: 13, D: 2.10. WR: 39.10 (Bonnie Blair)

1.	Bonnie Blair	USA	40.33
2.	Ye Qiaobo	CHN	40.51
3.	Christa Luding [Rothenburger]	GER	40.57
4.	Monique Garbrecht	GER	40.63

5. Christine Aaftink	HOL	40.66
6. Susan Auch	CAN	40.83
7. Kyoko Shimazaki	JPN	40.98
8. Angela Hauck [Stahnke]	GER	41.10

The first person to tell Bonnie Blair that she would someday win a gold medal was her father, Charlie. After Charlie Blair died on Christmas Day, 1989, Bonnie's skating began to lose its intensity. In 1990 she lost the world sprint championship to Angela Hauck, and in 1991 she slipped to fifth. But then she decided to dedicate her Olympic performance to her father. She swept through the 1991-92 season undefeated at both 500 meters and 1000 meters and went to Albertville as the favorite in both events. Almost fifty family members and friends traveled to France to watch Blair compete. Once there, they lined the side of the track with pro-Blair posters.

The start of the competition was delayed one hour in order to let the outdoor oval harden. Blair's leading challenger, Ye Qiaobo, skated in the second pair against Yelena Tiushniakova of Russia. At the crossover, Tiushniakova, on the inside, failed to make way for Ye as she moved to the outside and Ye was forced to rise out of her crouch to avoid a collision. Three pairs later, Blair quickly pulled away from Angela Hauck and beat Ye's time by eighteen hundredths of a second. Chinese officials asked that Ye be given a rerun, but surprisingly, their protest was rejected.

At the postrace press conference, Ye told her "long, sad story," as she put it. In 1987, her team doctor began giving all the female speed skaters medicine that made her put on 14 kilograms (31.5 lbs.). In 1988, just before the start of the Calgary Olympics, Ye was informed that she and a teammate had tested positive for anabolic sterioids. Ye, who had no idea that she had been taking a banned substance, was sent home in disgrace. She served a 15-month suspension. She considered quitting, but a friend told her she was "a little flower that didn't open. And if I quit skating, as I thought of quitting everything, I would never open." So Ye, who had switched from running to skating at age ten because she wanted "to capture the joy" she saw in the eyes of skaters, decided to keep competing. In Albertville she became the first Asian woman and the first Chinese athlete of either sex to win a Winter Olympic medal.

Bonnie Blair, for her part, became the first U.S. woman to win a gold medal in two different Olympics, while Christa Luding, at age 32, matched Karen Kania's feat of winning a complete set of medals at 500 meters.

1994 Lillehammer-Hamar C: 34, N: 12, D: 2.19. WR: 39.10 (Bonnie Blair)

1. Bonnie Blair	USA	39.25
2. Susan Auch	CAN	39.61
3. Franziska Schenk	GER	39.70
4. Xue Ruihong	CHN	39.71
5. Yoo Sun-hee	KOR	39.92
6. Monique Garbrecht	GER	39.95
7. Svetlana Boyarkina	RUS	40.17
8. Edel Høiseth	NOR	40.20

Prior to the 1994 Olympics Bonnie Blair had won three gold medals by a combined total of twenty-two one-hundredths of a second. In Hamar she outclassed the field by thirty-six one-hundredths to become the first speed skater ever to win the same event three times. Five weeks later she became the first woman to break 39 seconds. The surprise bronze medalist, 19-year-old Franziska Schenk, improved her personal best by .74 seconds.

1000 METERS

1924–1956 not held

1960 Squaw Valley C: 22, N: 10, D: 2.22. WR: 1:33.4 (Tamara Rylova)

1. Klara Guseva	SOV/RUS	1:34.1
2. Helga Haase	GDR	1:34.3
3. Tamara Rylova	SOV/RUS	1:34.8
4. Lydia Skoblikova	SOV/RUS	1:35.3
5. Helena Pilejczyk	POL	1:35.8
5. Hatsue Takamizawa	JPN	1:35.8
7. Fumie Hama	JPN	1:36.1
8. Jeanne Ashworth	USA	1:36.5

Elwira Seroczyńska of Poland had the fastest time going into the final curve, but with 100 meters to go, one of her skates hit the dividing line, and she fell.

1964 Innsbruck C: 28, N: 13, D: 2.1. WR: 1:31.8 (Lydia Skoblikova)

1. Lydia Skoblikova	SOV/RUS	1:33.2	OR
2. Irina Yegorova	SOV/RUS	1:34.3	
3. Kaija Mustonen	FIN	1:34.8	
4. Helga Haase	GDR	1:35.7	
5. Valentina Stenina	SOV/RUS	1:36.0	
6. Gunilla Jacobsson	SWE	1:36.5	
7. Janice Smith	USA	1:36.7	
8. Kaija-Liisa Keskivitikka	FIN	1:37.6	

With this race Skoblikova became the first woman to win three gold medals at one Winter Olympics and the first person of either sex to win five Winter gold medals.

1968 Grenoble C: 29, N: 12, D: 2.11. WR: 1:31.8 (Lydia Skoblikova)

1. Carolina Geijssen	HOL	1:32.6	OR
2. Lyudmila Titova	SOV/RUS	1:32.9	
3. Dianne Holum	USA	1:33.4	
4. Kaija Mustonen	FIN	1:33.6	
5. Irina Yegorova	SOV/RUS	1:34.4	
6. Sigrid Sundby	NOR	1:34.5	
7. Jeanne Ashworth	USA	1:34.7	
8. Kaija-Liisa Keskivitikka	FIN	1:34.8	

Geijssen was a 21-year-old Amsterdam secretary who skated to work each day. She was the first Dutch skater to win an Olympic gold medal.

1972 Sapporo C: 33, N: 12, D: 2.11. WR: 1:27.3 (Anne Henning)

1. Monika Pflug	GER	1:31.40	OR
2. Atje Keulen-Deelstra	HOL	1:31.61	
3. Anne Henning	USA	1:31.62	
4. Lyudmila Titova	SOV/RUS	1:31.85	
5. Nina Statkevich	SOV/RUS	1:32.21	
6. Dianne Holum	USA	1:32.41	
7. Elly van den Brom	HOL	1:32.60	
8. Sylvia Burka	CAN	1:32.95	

Seventeen-year-old Monika Pflug was a surprise winner. A bookbinding apprentice from Munich, she false-started twice. Threatened with disqualification if she jumped the gun again, she started slowly, but was able to make up lost time after the first 200 meters.

1976 Innsbruck C: 27, N: 10, D: 2.7. WR: 1:23.46 (Tatyana Averina)

1. Tatyana Averina	SOV/RUS	1:28.43	OR
2. Leah Poulos	USA	1:28.57	
3. Sheila Young	USA	1:29.14	
4. Sylvia Burka	CAN	1:29.47	
5. Monika Holzner [Pflug]	GER	1:29.54	
6. Cathy Priestner	CAN	1:29.66	
7. Lyudmila Titova	SOV/RUS	1:30.06	
8. Heike Lange	GDR	1:30.55	

1980 Lake Placid C: 37, N: 16, D: 2.17. WR: 1:23.46 (Tatyana Averina)

1. Natalya Petruseva	SOV/RUS	1:24.10	OR
2. Leah Mueller [Poulos]	USA	1:25.41	
3. Silvia Albrecht	GDR	1:26.46	
4. Karin Enke	GDR	1:26.66	
5. Beth Heiden	USA	1:27.01	
6. Annie Borckink	HOL	1:27.24	
7. Sylvia Burka	CAN	1:27.50	
8. Ann-Sofie Järnström	SWE	1:28.10	

Petruseva and Mueller were the second pair to skate. Mueller was ahead at 200 meters, but Petruseva took the lead and eventually pulled away to win by 40 feet. For Mueller, it was her third Olympic silver medal. A couple of weeks earlier, Petruseva had won the world sprint championship in Norway, but then had taken seven hours to produce a urine sample, leading to rumors that she had taken illegal drugs. Suspicions seemed confirmed when she finished only eighth in the 1500 meters, the opening Olympic event. But after taking the bronze medal in the 500 meters, she won the 1000 meters and passed the urine test for drugs without any problems. Part of the Soviet success in speed skating had to be due to the fact that, by 1980, there were 1202 Olympic-size speed skating rinks in the U.S.S.R., whereas in the United States, a nation of comparable population, there were only two.

1984 Sarajevo C: 38, N: 17, D: 2.13. WR: 1:19.31 (Natalya Petruseva)

1. Karin Enke	GDR	1:21.61	OR
2. Andrea Schöne [Mitscherlich]	GDR	1:22.83	
3. Natalya Petruseva	SOV/RUS	1:23.21	
4. Valentina Lalenkova	SOV/UKR	1:23.68	
5. Christa Rothenburger	GDR	1:23.98	
6. Yvonne van Gennip	HOL	1:25.36	
7. Erwina Rys-Ferens	POL	1:25.81	
8. Monika Holzner [Pflug]	GER	1:25.87	

Enke, skating one pair after Schöne, won her second gold medal of the Sarajevo Games and her third overall.

1988 Calgary C: 27, N: 12, D: 2.22. WR: 1:18.11 (Karin Kania [Enke])

1. Christa Rothenburger	GDR	1:17.65	WR
2. Karin Kania [Enke]	GDR	1:17.70	
3. Bonnie Blair	USA	1:18.31	
4. Andrea Ehrig	GDR	1:19.32	
[Mitscherlich, Schöne]			

5. Seiko Hashimoto	JPN	1:19.75
6. Angela Stahnke	GDR	1:20.05
7. Leslie Bader	USA	1:21.09
8. Katie Class	USA	1:21.10

Seven months after earning the gold medal at 1000 meters, Christa Rothenburger took a silver in the cycling sprint race in Seoul to become the only athlete in Olympic history to win medals in winter and summer in the same year.

1992 Albertville C:36, N: 14, D: 2.14. WR: 1:17.65 (Christa Luding [Rothenburger])

1. Bonnie Blair	USA	1:21.90
2. Ye Qiaobo	CHN	1:21.92
3. Monique Garbrecht	GER	1:22.10
4. Christine Aaftink	HOL	1:22.60
5. Seiko Hashimoto	JPN	1:22.63
6. Mihaela Dascalu	ROM	1:22.85
7. Yelena Tiushniakova	SOV	1:22.97
8. Christa Luding [Rothenburger]	GER	1:23.06

Bonnie Blair took advantage of a strong start to become the first U.S. woman to win three gold medals in the Winter Olympics. Her total margin of victory for all three wins was twenty-two one-hundredths of a second. Ye and Garbrecht skated head-to-head three pairs after Blair.

1994 Lillehammer-Hamar C: 36, N: 12, D: 2.23. WR: 1.17.65 (Christa Luding [Rothenburger])

1. Bonnie Blair	USA	1:18.74
2. Anke Baier	GER	1:20.12
3. Ye Qiaobo	CHN	1:20.22
4. Franziska Schenk	GER	1:20.25
5. Monique Garbrecht	GER	1:20.32
6. Shiho Kusunose	JPN	1:20.37
7. Emese Hunyady	AUT	1:20.42
8. Susan Auch	CAN	1:20.72

Skating her fastest 1000-meter time since the 1988 Olympics, 29-year-old Bonnie Blair achieved the largest winning margin in the event's history. She also became the first American to earn six medals in the Winter Olympics and the first American woman in either winter or summer to win five gold medals.

1500 METERS

1924–1956 not held

1960 Squaw Valley C: 23, N: 10, D: 2.21. WR: 2:25.5 (Khalida Schegoleyeva)

1. Lydia Skoblikova	SOV/RUS	2:25.2	WR
2. Elwira Seroczyńska	POL	2:25.7	
3. Helena Pilejczyk	POL	2:27.1	
4. Klara Guseva	SOV/RUS	2:28.7	
5. Valentina Stenina	SOV/RUS	2:29.2	
6. Iris Sihvonen	FIN	2:29.7	
7. Christina Scherling	SWE	2:31.5	
8. Helga Haase	GDR	2:31.7	

This was the first of Skoblikova's six career gold medals.

1964 Innsbruck C: 30, N: 14, D: 1.31. WR: 2:19.0 (Inga Voronina)

1. Lydia Skoblikova	SOV/RUS	2:22.6	OR
2. Kaija Mustonen	FIN	2:25.5	
3. Berta Kolokoltseva	SOV/RUS	2:27.1	
4. Kim Song-soon	PRK	2:27.7	
5. Helga Haase	GDR	2:28.6	
6. Christina Scherling	SWE	2:29.4	
7. Valentina Stenina	SOV/RUS	2:29.9	
8. Kaija-Liisa Keskivitikka	FIN	2:30.0	

1968 Grenoble C: 30, N: 13, D: 2.10. WR: 2:19.0 (Inga Artamonova [Voronina])

1. Kaija Mustonen	FIN	2:22.4	OR
2. Carolina Geijssen	HOL	2:22.7	
3. Christina Kaiser	HOL	2:24.5	
4. Sigrid Sundby	NOR	2:25.2	
5. Lasma Kaouniste	SOV/LAT	2:25.4	
6. Kaija-Liisa Keskivitikka	FIN	2:25.8	
7. Lyudmila Titova	SOV/RUS	2:26.8	
8. Ruth Schleiermacher	GDR	2:27.1	

Defending champion Lydia Skoblikova finished 11th, while future champion Dianne Holum was 13th.

1972 Sapporo C: 31, N: 12, D: 2.9. WR: 2:15.8 (Christina Baas-Kaiser)

1. Dianne Holum	USA	2:20.85	OR
2. Christina Baas-Kaiser	HOL	2:21.05	
3. Atje Keulen-Deelstra	HOL	2:22.05	
4. Elisabeth van den Brom	HOL	2:22.27	
5. Rosemarie Taupadel	GDR	2:22.35	
6. Nina Statkevich	SOV/RUS	2:23.19	
7. Connie Carpenter	USA	2:23.93	
8. Sigrid Sundby	NOR	2:24.07	

As a 16-year-old in 1968, Dianne Holum had won a silver medal in the 500 meters and a bronze in the 1000. In 1972 she added a gold in the 1500 meters and a silver in the 3000. The success of the Dutch system of training was shown not only by the fact that Dutch skaters finished second, third, and fourth, but by the fact that Dianne Holum used a Dutch coach as well. The following year she took on a young pupil of her own—14-year-old Eric Heiden—and coached him all the way to the 1976 and 1980 Olympics.

1976 Innsbruck C: 26, N: 12, D: 2.5. WR: 2:09.90 (Tatyana Averina)

1. Galina Stepanskaya	SOV/RUS	2:16.58	OR
2. Sheila Young	USA	2:17.06	
3. Tatyana Averina	SOV/RUS	2:17.96	
4. Lisbeth Korsmo	NOR	2:18.99	
5. Karin Kessow	GDR	2:19.05	
6. Leah Poulos	USA	2:19.11	
7. Ines Bautzmann	GDR	2:19.63	
8. Erwina Ryś	POL	2:19.69	

1980 Lake Placid C: 31, N: 14, D: 2.14. WR: 2:07.18 (Halida Vorobieva)

1. Annie Borckink	HOL	2:10.95	OR
2. Ria Visser	HOL	2:12.35	
3. Sabine Becker	GDR	2:12.38	

4. Bjørg Eva Jensen	NOR	2:12.59	
5. Sylvia Filipsson	SWE	2:12.84	
6. Andrea Mitscherlich	GDR	2:13.05	
7. Beth Heiden	USA	2:13.10	
8. Natalya Petruseva	SOV/RUS	2:14.15	

Borckink, a 28-year-old nursing student, had never before finished in the top three in an international meet.

1984 Sarajevo C: 32, N: 15, D: 2.9. WR: 2:04.04 (Natalya Petruseva)

1. Karin Enke	GDR	2:03.42	WR
2. Andrea Schöne [Mitscherlich]	GDR	2:05.29	
3. Natalya Petruseva	SOV/RUS	2:05.78	
4. Gabi Schönbrunn	GDR	2:07.69	
5. Erwina Ryś-Ferens	POL	2:08.08	
6. Valentina Lalenkova	SOV/UKR	2:08.17	
7. Natalya Kurova	SOV/RUS	2:08.41	
8. Björg Eva Jensen	NOR	2:09.53	

A converted figure skater from Dresden, Karin Enke, the 1980 Olympic champion at 500 meters, had set a world record of 2:03.40 on December 8. However the International Skating Union refused to recognize her record because they had received insufficient advance notice of the meet in which she was competing. Determined to prove herself at the Olympics, Enke again broke Petruseva's world record, which had been set at high-altitude.

1988 Calgary C: 28, N: 13, D: 2.27. WR: 1:59.30 (Karin Kania [Enke])

1. Yvonne van Gennip	HOL	2:00.68	OR
2. Karin Kania [Enke]	GDR	2:00.82	
3. Andrea Ehrig [Mitscherlich, Schöne]	GDR	2:01.49	
4. Bonnie Blair	USA	2:04.02	
5. Yelena Lapuga	SOV/RUS	2:04.24	
6. Seiko Hashimoto	JPN	2:04.38	
7. Gunda Kleemann	GDR	2:04.68	
7. Erwina Ryś-Ferens	POL	2:04.68	

Van Gennip bettered her personal best by almost four seconds to earn the second of her three gold medals. At her post-race press conference van Gennip inadvertently caused a sensation. Asked to describe her feelings, she replied, "I am not emotional here, but in my bed, I am emotional." When reporters began to laugh, she made it clear that they had misinterpreted her words. Karin Kania's second-place finish gave her a career total of three gold medals, four silvers, and one bronze.

1992 Albertville C: 33, N: 14, D: 2.12. WR: 1:59.30 (Karin Kania [Enke])

1. Jacqueline Börner	GER	2:05.87
2. Gunda Niemann [Kleemann]	GER	2:05.92
3. Seiko Hashimoto	JPN	2:06.88
4. Natalya Polozkova	SOV/RUS	2:07.12
5. Monique Garbrecht	GER	2:07.24
6. Svetlana Bazhanova	SOV/RUS	2:07.81
7. Emese Hunyady	AUT	2:08.29
8. Heike Warnicke	GER	2:08.52

On August 15, 1990, Jacqueline Börner, the reigning all-around speed skating champion, was cycling with nine teammates on the streets of Wandlitz, an East Berlin suburb known as the home of many Communist Party officials. A car drove by and grazed two of Börner's male companions. Words were exchanged with the driver, who continued down the road, then turned around and drove straight at Börner. She woke up in a hospital with a broken foot, torn knee ligaments, and head injuries. Fortunately, the hit-and-run driver was driving a Trabant, the notoriously weak East German automobile. Otherwise Börner might have died. As it was, she spent four months in the hospital and four more months in a rehabilitation center. Under the old East German system, Börner would have been discarded as an athlete, but while she was recuperating, the two Germanys reunited and her new club continued to support her. Börner returned to competition on November 24, 1991, but placed no higher than third during the pre-Olympic World Cup series. In Albertville, Börner skated in the first pair after a one-hour warm weather delay. Her time of 2:05.87 withstood the challenge, five pairs later, of the favorite, Gunda Niemann.

Bronze medalist Seiko Hashimoto, the first Japanese woman to win a Winter medal, also competed as a cyclist at the 1988, 1992 and 1996 Summer Olympics. Her best placement was eleventh in the 1992 pursuit event. Fourth-place finisher Natalya Polozkova was the daughter-in-law of Lydia Skoblikova, the only woman to win the 1500-meter event twice.

1994 Lillehammer-Hamar C: 30, N: 11, D: 2.21. WR: 1:59.30 (Karin Kania [Enke])

1.	Emese Hunyady	AUT	2:02.19
2.	Svetlana Fedotkina	RUS	2:02.69
3.	Gunda Niemann [Kleemann]	GER	2:03.41
4.	Bonnie Blair	USA	2:03.44
5.	Annamarie Thomas	HOL	2:03.70
6.	Svetlana Bazhanova	RUS	2:03.99
7.	Natalya Polozkova	RUS	2:04.00
8.	Mihaela Dascalu	ROM	2:04.02

Emese Hunyady was born and raised in Budapest and represented Hungary at the 1984 Olympics. The following year, at age 18, she followed her coach to Vienna and became an Austrian citizen. She earned a bronze medal at 3000 meters in 1992 and moved up to silver in 1994, four days before winning gold at 1500 meters. Skating late, in the ninth pair, Svetlana Fedotkina, a six-foot tall medical student from Siberia, stayed ahead of Hunyady's pace until the final lap, then held on for a surprise silver. After receiving her gold medal, Hunyady, a former figure skater performed pirouettes and other spins during her victory lap. The public address announcer wryly proclaimed, "Marks for artistic impression: 6.0." Later Hunyady told the press, "I thank Austria for everything. But deep inside, privately, I'm Hungarian." As for Fedotkina, she failed a drug test in 1996 and was banned from competition for two years.

3000 METERS

1924–1956 not held

1960 Squaw Valley C: 20, N: 10, D: 2.23. WR: 5:13.8 (Rimma Zukova)

1.	Lydia Skoblikova	SOV/RUS	5:14.3
2.	Valentina Stenina	SOV/RUS	5:16.9
3.	Eevi Huttunen	FIN	5:21.0
4.	Hatsue Takamizawa	JPN	5:21.4
5.	Christina Scherling	SWE	5:25.5
6.	Helena Pilejczyk	POL	5:26.2
7.	Elwira Seroczyńska	POL	5:27.3
8.	Jeanne Ashworth	USA	5:28.5

Lydia Skoblikova won six speed skating gold medals in
1960 and 1964, more than any other athlete in the
history of the Winter Olympics.

1964 Innsbruck C: 28, N: 13, D: 2.2. WR: 5:06.0 (Inga Voronina)

1.	Lydia Skoblikova	SOV/RUS	5:14.9
2.	Han Pil-hwa	PRK	5:18.5
2.	Valentina Stenina	SOV/RUS	5:18.5
4.	Klara Nesterova [Guseva]	SOV/RUS	5:22.5
5.	Kaija Mustonen	FIN	5:24.3
6.	Hatsue Nagakubo	JPN	5:25.4
7.	Kim Song-soon	KOR	5:25.9
8.	Doreen McCannel	CAN	5:26.4

With this race Lydia Skoblikova became the first person to win four gold medals in a single Winter Olympics and the first to win six gold medals all together. Further excitement was caused by the last skater, tiny Han Pil-hwa, a previously unknown North Korean who kept up Skoblikova's pace for four of the seven laps before falling back to a tie for second place.

1968 Grenoble C: 26, N: 12, D: 2.12. WR: 4:54.6 (Christina Kaiser)

1.	Johanna Schut	HOL	4:56.2	OR
2.	Kaija Mustonen	FIN	5:01.0	
3.	Christina Kaiser	HOL	5:01.3	
4.	Kaija-Liisa Keskivitikka	FIN	5:03.9	
5.	Wilhelmina Burgmeijer	HOL	5:05.1	
6.	Lydia Skoblikova	SOV/RUS	5:08.0	

7. Christina Lindblom	SWE	5:09.8
8. Anna Sablina	SOV/RUS	5:12.5

1972 Sapporo C: 22, N: 10, D: 2.12. WR: 4:46.5 (Christina Baas-Kaiser)

1. Christina Baas-Kaiser	HOL	4:52.14	OR
2. Dianne Holum	USA	4:58.67	
3. Atje Keulen-Deelstra	HOL	4:59.91	
4. Sippie Tigelaar	HOL	5:01.67	
5. Nina Statkevich	SOV/RUS	5:01.79	
6. Kapitolina Sereguina	SOV/RUS	5:01.88	
7. Tuula Vilkas	FIN	5:05.92	
8. Lyudmila Savroulina	SOV/RUS	5:06.61	

Baas-Kaiser's margin of victory was the largest ever by a woman skater. After the race, the two Dutch medalists, both of whom were 33 years old, were asked by a reporter if they were planning to retire. Baas-Kaiser replied, "What's the matter, don't we skate fast enough?"

1976 Innsbruck C: 26, N: 12, D: 2.8. WR: 4:44.69 (Tamara Kuznyetsova)

1. Tatyana Averina	SOV/RUS	4:45.19	OR
2. Andrea Mitscherlich	GDR	4:45.23	
3. Lisbeth Korsmo	NOR	4:45.24	
4. Karin Kessow	GDR	4:45.60	
5. Ines Bautzmann	GDR	4:46.67	
6. Sylvia Filipsson	SWE	4:48.15	
7. Nancy Swider	USA	4:48.46	
8. Sylvia Burka	CAN	4:49.04	

If the top three skaters had actually been on the ice at the same time, only 16 inches would have separated them at the finish.

1980 Lake Placid C: 29, N: 14, D: 2.20. WR: 4:31.00 (Galina Stepanskaya)

1. Bjørg Eva Jensen	NOR	4:32.13	OR
2. Sabine Becker	GDR	4:32.79	
3. Beth Heiden	USA	4:33.77	
4. Andrea Mitscherlich	GDR	4:37.69	
5. Erwina Ryś-Ferens	POL	4:37.89	
6. Mary Docter	USA	4:39.29	
7. Sylvia Filipsson	SWE	4:40.22	
8. Natalya Petruseva	SOV/RUS	4:42.59	

1984 Sarajevo C: 26, N: 14, D: 2.15. WR: 4:21.70 (Gabi Schönbrunn)

1. Andrea Schöne [Mitscherlich]	GDR	4:24.79	OR
2. Karin Enke	GDR	4:26.33	
3. Gabi Schönbrunn	GDR	4:33.13	
4. Olga Pleshkova	SOV/RUS	4:34.42	
5. Yvonne van Gennip	HOL	4:34.80	
6. Mary Docter	USA	4:36.25	
7. Bjørg Eva Jensen	NOR	4:36.28	
8. Valentina Lalenkova	SOV/UKR	4:37.36	

Twenty-three-year-old Andrea Schöne of Dresden skated first and recorded a time that no one else could match.

1988 Calgary C: 29, N: 16, D: 2.23. WR: 4:16.76 (Gabi Zange [Schönbrunn])

1.	Yvonne van Gennip	HOL	4:11.94 WR
2.	Andrea Ehrig	GDR	4:12.09
	[Mitscherlich, Schöne]		
3.	Gabi Zange [Schönbrunn]	GDR	4:16.92
4.	Karin Kania [Enke]	GDR	4:18.80
5.	Erwina Ryś-Ferens	POL	4:22.59
6.	Svetlana Boyko	SOV/RUS	4:22.90
7.	Seiko Hashimoto	JPN	4:23.29
7.	Yelena Lapuga	SOV/RUS	4:23.29

The first pair on the ice were East German veterans Karin Kania and defending champion Andrea Ehrig. Kania, overanxious to win a gold medal, went out too fast, suffered a muscle cramp, and became so exhausted that she barely finished the race. Ehrig, on the other hand, kept to a steady pace and ripped over 4½ seconds off teammate Gabi Zange's world record. But three pairs later, 23-year-old Yvonne van Gennip, trailing Ehrig's pace for 2600 meters, made up eight tenths of a second on the final lap to score an upset victory.

1992 Albertville C: 26, N: 12, D: 2.09. WR: 4:10.80 (Gunda Niemann [Kleemann])

1.	Gunda Niemann [Kleemann]	GER	4:19.90
2.	Heike Warnicke	GER	4:22.88
3.	Emese Hunyady	AUT	4:24.64
4.	Carla Zijlstra	HOL	4:27.18
5.	Svetlana Boyko	SOV/RUS	4:28.00
6.	Yvonne van Gennip	HOL	4:28.10
7.	Svetlana Bazhanova	SOV/RUS	4:28.19
8.	Jacqueline Börner	GER	4:28.52

Niemann and Warnicke were training partners from Erfurt. The top four skaters took the same places as they had at the pre-Olympic test competition on the Albertville oval two months earlier.

1994 Lillehammer-Hamar C: 27, N: 14, D: 2.17. WR: 4:10.80 (Gunda Niemann [Kleemann])

1.	Svetlana Bazhanova	RUS	4:17.43
2.	Emese Hunyady	AUT	4:18.14
3.	Claudia Pechstein	GER	4:18.34
4.	Lyudmila Prokasheva	KAZ	4:19.33
5.	Annamarie Thomas	HOL	4:19.82
6.	Seiko Hashimoto	JPN	4:21.07
7.	Hiromi Yamamoto	JPN	4:22.37
8.	Mihaela Dascalu	ROM	4:22.42

Gunda Niemann had not lost a 3000-meter race in three years and was the overwhelming favorite to defend her Olympic title. But in the middle of a curve 450 meters after the start, her left skate hit a lane marker and she fell. Three days earlier, the same turn had proved the undoing of Dan Jansen at 500 meters, in a race then won by Alexsandr Golubev. The beneficiary of Neimann's misfortune was another Russian, Svetlana Bazhanova, who acknowledged that there might be "a ghost" on that turn who helped Russians.

5000 METERS

1924–1984 not held

1988 Calgary C: 25, N: 14, D: 2.28. WR: 7:20.36 (Yvonne van Gennip)

1. Yvonne van Gennip	HOL	7:14.13	WR
2. Andrea Ehrig [Mitscherlich, Schöne]	GDR	7:17.12	
3. Gabi Zange [Schönbrunn]	GDR	7:21.61	
4. Svetlana Boyko	SOV/RUS	7:28.39	
5. Yelena Lapuga	SOV/RUS	7:28.65	
6. Seiko Hashimoto	JPN	7:34.43	
7. Gunda Kleeman	GDR	7:34.59	
8. Jasmin Krohn	SWE	7:36.56	

Two months before the Olympics, Yvonne van Gennip was lying in a hospital bed recovering from surgery to her right foot, which had become infected after she cut it by tying her skate lace too tightly. After two weeks in the hospital, van Gennip's Olympic expectations had been reduced to a bronze medal or two. But when she arrived in Calgary, she discovered that she was well rested and in the best condition of her life. Inspired by Bonnie Blair's defeat of the supposedly unbeatable East Germans in the 500-meter race, van Gennip scored upset victories in both the 3000 and the 1500.

Andrea Ehrig, skating in the first pair of the 5000 meters, bettered van Gennip's world record by 3.24 seconds. Four pairs later, van Gennip fell behind Ehrig's pace but finished strongly to earn her third gold medal of the Calgary games. Ehrig, competing in her fourth Olympics and using her third name, brought her combined medal total to one gold, five silvers, and one bronze. After van Gennip's Olympic triumph, 60,000 fans turned out to welcome her back to her hometown of Haarlem.

1992 Albertville C:24, N: 11, D: 2.17. WR: 7:14.13 (Yvonne van Gennip)

1. Gunda Niemann [Kleemann]	GER	7:31.57
2. Heike Warnicke	GER	7:37.59
3. Claudia Pechstein	GER	7:39.80
4. Carla Zijlstra	HOL	7:41.10
5. Lyudmila Prokasheva	SOV/KAZ	7:41.65
6. Svetlana Boyko	SOV/RUS	7:44.19
7. Svetlana Bazhanova	SOV/RUS	7:45.55
8. Lia van Schie	HOL	7:46.94

As expected, Gunda Niemann used her 23½-inch (60-cm) thighs and her 17-inch (43-cm) calves to power her to her second gold medal of the Albertville Games.

1994 Lillehammer-Hamar C: 16, N: 9, D: 2.25. WR: 7:13.29 Gunda Niemann [Kleemann])

1. Claudia Pechstein	GER	7:14.37
2. Gunda Niemann [Kleemann]	GER	7:14.88
3. Hiromi Yamamoto	JPN	7:19.68
4. Elena Belci	ITA	7:20.33
5. Svetlana Bazhanova	RUS	7:22.68
6. Lyudmila Prokasheva	KAZ	7:28.58
7. Carla Zijlstra	HOL	7:29.42
8. Seiko Hashimoto	JPN	7:29.79

Gunda Niemann was the prohibitive favorite in this event. She won the 1991 world championship by 5.30 seconds, the 1992 Olympics by 6.02 seconds and the 1993 world championship by 6.55 seconds. In addition, at the European championships in Hamar on December 6, 1993, she broke Yvonne van Gennip's 1988 world record with a time of 7:13.29. But her 1994 Olympic week had been disappointing—she fell in the 3000 meters and placed third in the 1500 meters. Skating two pairs after compatriot Claudia Pechstein, Neimann got off to a fast start and was 4.04 seconds ahead of Pechstein's pace after 2200 meters. She was still ahead by .44 seconds with one lap to go, but couldn't hold on. Eleven of the 16 entrants set personal records, including bronze medalist Hiromi Yamamoto by 11 seconds and winner Pechstein by an incredible 19.21 seconds.

Short Track

SHORT TRACK: 500 METERS

1924-1988 not held

1992 Albertville C: 27, N: 14, D: 2.22. WR: 46.72 (Sylvie Daigle)

1.	Cathy Turner	USA	47.04
2.	Li Yan	CHN	47.08
3.	Hwang Ok-sil	PRK	47.23
4.	Monique Velzeboer	HOL	47.28
5.	Marina Pylayeva	SOV/RUS	48.42
6.	Nathalie Lambert	CAN	48.50
7.	Yulia Vlasova	SOV/RUS	48.70
8.	Wang Xiulan	CHN	1:34.12

This volatile event saw some early surprises in the opening-round heats. In the first heat, former world record holder Zhang Yammei fell and was disqualified. In the second heat, the current world record holder, Sylvie Daigle of Quebec, was eliminated after a clash with Cathy Turner of Rochester, New York, entering the first turn. The seventh heat was won by Italy's Marinella Canclini in 47.00. In the first semifinal, Li Yan, winner of the 1000-meter demonstration race at the 1988 Olympics, was beaten by Hwang Ok-sil. In the second semi, Cathy Turner edged Monique Velzeboer, the winner of the 500-meter race in 1988. Turner let Hwang take the lead in the final, then took over after two laps. In the final straightaway, Li came up on the inside and clipped Turner's skate, causing the American to totter. Li inched ahead as they approached the finish line. Turner threw her skate forward at the end, but thought she had lost. When she realized she had won, she rushed over to her mother, who draped her in a gold-trimmed American flag. Turner's path to the Olympic victory podium was an unusual one. She gave up speed skating in 1980 and pursued a career as a songwriter and a lounge singer. In 1988, after an eight-year absence from the sport, the 25-year-old Turner traded in her microphone for skates. Turner's kamikaze style of racing was legendary in short-track circles. At the 1991 world championships, her preliminary heat had to be restarted six times because of crashes in which she was involved as the skaters entered the first turn. Fourth-place finisher Velzeboer was paralyzed for life after crashing headfirst into a restraining barrier while training on December 23, 1993.

1994 Lillehammer-Hamar C: 30, N: 15, D: 2.24. WR: 45.60 (Zhang Yanmei)

1. Cathy Turner	USA	45.98	OR
2. Zhang Yanmei	CHN	46.44	
3. Amy Peterson	USA	46.76	
4. Won Hye-kyong	KOR	47.60	
5. Kim So-hee	KOR	49.01	
6. Wang Xiulan	CHN	49.03	
7. Isabelle Charest	CAN	47.25	
8. Yang Yang	CHN	47.25	

After her victory at the Albertville Olympics, Cathy Turner was hired to skate with Ice Capades. When she lost that job, she returned to short track. Not unexpectedly, Turner, who once served a three-month suspension for screaming obscenities at U.S. coaches and officials, placed herself in the middle of controversy at the 1994 Olympics. Turner's leading rivals were Zhang Yanmei of China and Nathalie Lambert and Isabelle Charest of Canada. Before the competition was over, Turner would clash with all of them. In her quarterfinal heat, Turner bumped Lambert twice. Then the two clipped skates and Lambert went down—and out of the competition. In the semifinals, Turner was involved in a three-skater pileup with Charest and China's Wang Xiulan. Charest was disqualified; Turner won the rerun. In the final, Zhang was leading with two laps to go when Turner moved to pass her on the outside. Turner brushed Zhang's right leg with her left hand and went on to cross the finish line first. Zhang immediately protested that Turner had not merely brushed her leg, but had actually grabbed her. Video replays were inconclusive and the protest was denied.

The Chinese were furious. Only two days earlier, their relay team had finished second, only to be disqualified following a U.S. protest. At the 500-meter medal ceremony, Zhang appeared sullen, to say the least. After the playing of the "Star-Spangled Banner," Turner pulled fellow American Amy Peterson onto the top platform. Then she turned to Zhang, but Zhang was no longer there. As soon as the music ended, she stepped off the platform, took her silver medal off her neck and stuffed it in her pocket, threw down her honorary bouquet and stomped off the ice. After the ceremony, Turner entertained reporters by singing a song of her own composition: "Sexy Kinky Tomboy."

SHORT TRACK: 1000 METERS

1924-1992 not held

1994 Lillehammer-Hamar C: 30, N: 15, D: 2.26. WR: 1:34.07 (Nathalie Lambert)

1. Chun Lee-kyung	KOR	1:36.87	OR
2. Nathalie Lambert	CAN	1:36.97	
3. Kim So-hee	KOR	1:37.09	
4. Zhang Yanmei	CHN	1:37.80	
5. Yang Yang	CHN	1:47.10	
6. Isabelle Charest	CAN	1:37.49	
7. Sylvie Daigle	CAN	DISQ	
8. Cathy Turner	USA	DISQ	

Two nights after Chinese and Canadian skaters accused American Cathy Turner of being "the dirtiest skater in short track," it was Turner herself who was finally disqualified. With two laps to go in her semifinal heat, Turner cut in front of Kim So-hee to prevent her from passing. Although the judges cited her for "cross-tracking," it appeared that in this particular race she had done nothing wrong. Rather her disqualification was more of a Lifetime Achievement Award.

The final included five skaters instead of four because, in the second semifinal, Yang Yang was knocked down in a collision that led to the disqualification of veteran Sylvie Daigle. Eighteen-year-old Chun Lee-kyung slid ahead of Nathalie Lambert entering the final lap and held on for the victory. Silver medalist Lambert was 30 years old; bronze medalist Kim was only sixteen.

SHORT TRACK: 3000-METER RELAY

1924-1988 not held

1992 Albertville T: 8, N: 8, D: 2.20. WR: 4:33.49 (CHN—Li C., Wang, Li Y., Zhang)

1.	CAN	(Angela Cutrone, Sylvie Daigle, Nathalie Lambert, Annie Perreault)	4:36.62
2.	USA	(Darcie Dohnal, Amy Peterson, Cathy Turner, Nicole Ziegelmeyer)	4:37.85
3.	SOV/ RUS	(Yulia Allagulova, Natalya Ishahova, Viktoria Taranina, Yulia Vlasova)	4:42.69
4.	JPN	(Mie Naito, Rie Sato, Hiromi Takeuchi, Nobuko Yamada)	4:44.50
5.	FRA	(Valerie Barizza, Sandrine Daudet, Morielle Leyssieux, Karine Rubini)	
6.	HOL	(Priscilla Ernst, Van Ankere Van Koetsveld, Monique Velzeboer, Simone Velzeboer)	
7.	ITA	(Marinella Canclini, Maria Candidu, Concetta LaTorre, Cristina Sciolla)	
8.	CHN	(Li Changxiang, Li Yan, Wang Xiulan, Zhang Yanmei)	

This event had the makings of a classic Olympic duel between the Canadians, who had won six straight world championships and ten of the last eleven, and the Chinese, who had set a world record in beating the Canadians at the Olympic test event in Albertville on November 16, 1991. Because there were only eight teams entered at the Olympics, the competition consisted of two semifinal heats with the top two teams in each heat advancing to the final. Canada won the first semi. In the second semi, China pulled out to a huge lead. When Zhang Yanmei began the 27th and final lap, she was on world record pace. The other teams were far behind, and all she had to do to qualify China for the final was to stay on her feet. But midway through the final turn Zhang suddenly lost her footing and crashed into the sideboards. The audience was shocked into a stunned silence. Zhang, who had also fallen in a preliminary heat in the individual event, cried for two hours straight. In the final, the four skaters from Quebec easily beat back every challenge from the U.S. team.

1994 Lillehammer-Hamar T: 8, N: 8, D: 2.22. WR: 4:26.56 (CAN—Boudrias, Charest, Cutone, Lambert)

1.	KOR	(Chun Lee-kyung, Kim So-hee, Kim Yoon-mi, Won Hye-kyung)	4:26.64	OR
2.	CAN	(Christine-Isabel Boudrias, Isabelle Charest, Sylvie Daigle, Nathalie Lambert)	4:32.04	
3.	USA	(Karen Cashman, Amy Peterson, Cathy Turner, Nicole Ziegelmeyer)	4:39.34	
4.	ITA	(Barbara Baldissera, Marinella Canclini, Katia Colturi, Katia Mosconi)	4:36.46	
5.	RUS	(Yekaterina Mikhailova, Marina Pylayeva, Yelena Tikhanina, Viktoria Troitskaya)	4:34.60	
6.	HOL	(Penelope Di Lella, Priscilla Ernst, Anke Landman, Esmeralda Ossendrijver)	4:45.40	
7.	FRA	(Valerie Barizza, Sandrine Daudet, Sandra Deleglise, Laure Drovet)	4:59.94	
8.	CHN	(Su Xiaohua, Wang Xiulan, Yang Yang, Zhang Yanmei)	DISQ	

Again this was expected to be a duel between the Canadians, who hadn't lost a major race in six years, and the Chinese, with the young South Korean team ready to move up if Canada or China met with disaster. The fourth team in the final, the United States, didn't find out they were going to the Olympics until three days before the Opening Ceremony. Because of a fall at the 1993 world championships, the U.S. found themselves in eleventh place with only the top eight qualifying for the 1994 Olympics. At the last moment, North Korea decided not to send a team. The Japanese and Australians were each offered the open spot, but both declined. Next in line, the Americans said yes.

In the final, Cathy Turner took the early lead for the U.S., but the Canadians quickly took over and pulled away with the Chinese giving chase. At the halfway mark Canada was on world record pace. But then Charest and Lambert had a bad exchange and China was able to close the gap. Three laps later, under great pressure from behind, Christine Boudrias slipped and crashed into the boards. With Canada out of the running, the Koreans moved up, passed the Chinese and won the race. The Chinese were then disqualified because one of their skaters loitered too long on the track after passing off, causing Nikki Ziegelmeyer to bump into her and fall. So Ziegelmeyer and fellow American Karen Cashman went from getting ready to watch the Olympics on television to standing on the medal platform in less than two weeks.

One of the members of the Korean team was 13-year-old Kim Yoon-mi, who became the youngest medalist in the history of the Winter Olympics and the youngest female gold medalist in either the Summer or the Winter Games. The other Koreans were only 14, 17 and 18. Their average age of 15½ contrasted with the Canadian average, 27½.

ALPINE SKIING

MEN
Downhill
Slalom
Giant Slalom
Super Giant Slalom
Alpine Combined

MEN

DOWNHILL

The first crude downhill race was held in Kitzbühel, Austria, in 1905. A more formal contest was held in Crans-Montana, Switzerland, in 1911. It was organized by an Englishman, Arnold Lunn, who also invented the modern slalom in 1922 and was the main force in obtaining Olympic recognition for alpine skiing in 1936. Downhill races are decided on the basis of a single run.

Of the 40 medals that have been awarded in the men's downhill race, 36 have gone to Western Europeans; of these, thirteen went to Austria, ten to Switzerland and eight to France.

1924–1936 not held

1948 St. Moritz C: 112, N: 25, D: 2.2.

1.	Henri Oreiller	FRA	2:55.0
2.	Franz Gabl	AUT	2:59.1
3.	Karl Molitor	SWI	3:00.3
3.	Rolf Olinger	SWI	3:00.3
5.	Egon Schöpf	AUT	3:01.2
6.	Silvio Alverà	ITA	3:02.4
6.	Carlo Gartner	ITA	3:02.4
8.	Fernand Grosjean	SWI	3:03.1

A member of the French underground during World War II, Henri Oreiller was a cocky, clowning fellow who warned the other skiers he was so confident of victory that they needn't bother racing against him. He careened down the two-mile course like an acrobat, flying over bumps without caution and then regaining his balance in midair. Oreiller later turned to race car driving and was killed at the wheel of his Ferrari on October 7, 1962, at the age of 36.

1952 Oslo-Norefjell C: 81, N: 27, D: 2.16.

1.	Zeno Colò	ITA	2:30.8
2.	Othmar Schneider	AUT	2:32.0
3.	Christian Pravda	AUT	2:32.4
4.	Fredy Rubi	SWI	2:32.5
5.	William Beck	USA	2:33.3
6.	Stein Eriksen	NOR	2:33.8
7.	Gunnar Hjeltnes	NOR	2:35.9
8.	Carlo Gartner	ITA	2:36.5

Zeno Colò was a colorful 31-year-old restaurant owner from Tuscany, whose form on the slopes was almost as unorthodox as that of Oreiller. In 1954 he was banned from competition because he openly endorsed ski equipment.

1956 Cortina C: 75, N: 27, D: 2.3.

1. Anton Sailer   AUT   2:52.2
2. Raymond Fellay   SWI   2:55.7
3. Andreas Molterer   AUT   2:56.2
4. Roger Staub   SWI   2:57.1
5. Hans-Peter Lanig   GER   2:59.8
6. Gino Burrini   ITA   3:00.2
7. Kurt Hennrich   CZE   3:01.5
8. Charles Bozon   FRA   3:01.9

Toni Sailer had already won the giant slalom and the slalom and was confident of completing his alpine sweep, since he held the course record of 2:46.2 for the downhill. However, as he tightened the straps that tied his boots to his skis, one of the straps broke. "That had never happened to me before," he later wrote. "I had not even thought it possible that such straps could break and had therefore not taken along a spare." It was almost his turn to race. If he couldn't find a strap, he would have to withdraw. Unfortunately, the problem was so rare that none of the other skiers had brought along spare straps either. Then Hansl Senger, the trainer of the Italian team, walked by and noticed the Austrians in panic. Senger immediately took the straps from his own bindings and handed them to Sailer. Sailer later claimed that he himself was never worried. After all, "I had at least ten minutes to find another strap." Strong winds and a glassy course prevented 28 of the 75 starters from reaching the finish line, and sent eight men to the hospital. But Sailer was able to survive one near spill and complete the course three and a half seconds faster than anyone else.

After the victory ceremony, Sailer joined his parents and, holding his three gold medals in his hand, said, "It's a good thing there are three medals. One for you, Father, one for you, Mother. Then there is a third one for me." Sailer later became an actor and singer, and then went into business as a hotel owner and an investor in a textile company, before settling in as the operator of a children's ski school. He also coached the Austrian national team during the 1970s.

1960 Squaw Valley C: 63, N: 21, D: 2.22.

1. Jean Vuarnet   FRA   2:06.0
2. Hans-Peter Lanig   GER   2:06.5
3. Guy Périllat   FRA   2:06.9
4. Willy Forrer   SWI   2:07.8
5. Roger Staub   SWI   2:08.9
6. Bruno Alberti   ITA   2:09.1
7. Karl Schranz   AUT   2:09.2
8. Charles Bozon   FRA   2:09.6

In 1960 the downhill race was postponed for three days because of heavy snow. Vuarnet was the first Olympic gold medalist to use metal skis and no wax. He is also credited with inventing the aerodynamically efficient "egg position" for skiing, now known as the tuck. At his press conference after the race, Vuarnet, who was clocked at speeds as high as 80 miles per hour, apologized in English for breaking the California speed limit of 65 miles per hour.

1964 Innsbruck C: 84, N: 27, D: 1.30.

1. Egon Zimmermann   AUT   2:18.16
2. Léo Lacroix   FRA   2:18.90

3.	Wolfgang Bartels	GER	2:19.48
4.	Joos Minsch	SWI	2:19.54
5.	Ludwig Leitner	GER	2:19.67
6.	Guy Périllat	FRA	2:19.79
7.	Gerhard Nenning	AUT	2:19.98
8.	Willi Favre	SWI	2:20.23

The downhill competition was held under a cloud of gloom following the death of 19-year-old Ross Milne of Australia, who was killed during a practice run on January 25 when he flew off the course and smashed into a tree. Twenty-four-year-old Egon Zimmermann was the third alpine gold medalist to come from Lech, a hamlet of less than 200 people that had been converted to a ski resort following World War II. Also from Lech were Orthmar Schneider, the 1952 slalom winner, and Trude Beiser, who won the women's downhill the same year.

1968 Grenoble-Chamrousse C: 86, N: 29, D: 2.9.

1.	Jean-Claude Killy	FRA	1:59.85
2.	Guy Périllat	FRA	1:59.93
3.	John-Daniel Dätwyler	SWI	2:00.32
4.	Heinrich Messner	AUT	2:01.03
5.	Karl Schranz	AUT	2:01.89
6.	Ivo Mahlknecht	ITA	2:02.00
7.	Gerhard Prinzing	GER	2:02.10
8.	Bernard Orcel	FRA	2:02.22

Jean-Claude Killy grew up in the resort village of Val d'Isère in the French Savoy Alps, hometown of 1948 Olympic champion Henri Oreiller. Killy's mother abandoned her family, and his father was forced to send Jean-Claude to boarding school at age 11. Killy dropped out of school at the age of 15 in order to join the French ski team, and soon became known for his fun-loving attitude. Once he entered a ski-jump competition in Wengen, Switzerland, and caused a sensation by dropping his pants after takeoff and finishing his jump in longjohns. Apparently he dropped his pants in other places as well, since he also contracted VD in Sun Valley and was named in a paternity suit in Austria. He was declared innocent. While serving with the French Army in Algeria, Killy contracted amoebic parasitosis, but he regained his health sufficiently to qualify for the 1964 French Olympic team in all three alpine events. At Innsbruck he placed fifth in the giant slalom, but failed to finish the downhill and slalom. Killy started to pick up speed after the 1964 Olympics, however, and by 1967 he was on top of the world. During the 1966–67 season he won 12 of 16 World Cup meets, and the following summer he won a sports car race in Sicily. Despite some troubles at the start of the 1967–68 season, Killy went to the 1968 Olympics confident of victory.

There was certainly a lot of pressure on Killy to win in Grenoble. French fans were anxious for him to duplicate the 1952 triple-gold performance of Austria's Toni Sailer. In addition, a huge Jean-Claude Killy industry was waiting to spring into production if Killy won three gold medals. Ski-makers, boot-makers, binding-makers, glove-makers, and others were ready with fat contracts for Killy's product endorsements, which he had already been giving out as readily as he could within the restrictions set up by the International Ski Federation. But these restrictions weren't good enough for I.O.C. President Avery Brundage. Shortly before the games, Killy signed a contract with an Italian ski pole manufacturer. The International Ski Federation informed Killy that the contract violated the rules of amateurism, so Killy backed off, whereupon the ski pole manufacturer threatened to sue him. The French Ski Federation and the French Sports Ministry undertook hasty negotiations with the Italian ski pole manufacturer in an attempt to settle the issue before the Olympics. "Payments for damages"—sums never revealed—satisfied the Italians.

Brundage demanded that all trade names and trademarks be removed from the skis used by competitors in the 1968 Olympics. The International Ski Federation, the team managers, and the skiers themselves rejected the ban, claiming that the entire sport of alpine skiing was dependent on the financial support of ski-makers. On the eve of the Games an awkward compromise was reached whereby the skiers would be allowed to keep the trade names and trademarks on their skis, but their skis would be taken away from them before they could be photographed. The policemen in charge of this unpleasant task were particularly on edge when Jean-Claude Killy, the favorite, shot down the slopes as the 14th contestant in the opening alpine race—the downhill. Killy slashed across the finish line eight one-hundredths of a second faster than his teammate, yoga practitioner Guy Périllat. Immediately, Michel Arpin, Killy's friend and adviser, rushed out and embraced Killy, making sure that the photographers got a good view of the pouch on his back, which was emblazoned with the word "Dynamic," the brand of skis that Killy used, and his gloves, which bore the Dynamic trademark—two yellow bars. When a policeman, surrounded by a horde of photographers, confiscated Killy's skis, Michel Arpin took one of his own skis and planted it in the snow so that the two yellow bars on the tip were right next to Killy's head.

Eventually Killy gave up competitive skiing and traveled to the United States, where he signed commercial contracts with Chevrolet, United Air Lines, Bristol-Myers, *Ladies' Home Journal,* Head Skis, Lange boots, Mighty Mac sportswear, Wolverine gloves and after-ski boots, and over 100 other companies. Killy later served as copresident of the organizing committee of the 1992 Albertville Olympics.

1972 Sapporo-Eniwadake C: 55, N: 20, D: 2.7.

1.	Bernhard Russi	SWI	1:51.43
2.	Roland Collombin	SWI	1:52.07
3.	Heinrich Messner	AUT	1:52.40
4.	Andreas Sprecher	SWI	1:53.11
5.	Erik Håker	NOR	1:53.16
6.	Walter Tresch	SWI	1:53.19
7.	Karl Cordin	AUT	1:53.32
8.	Robert Cochran	USA	1:53.39

Most people in the sports world breathed a sigh of relief when Avery Brundage announced that he would retire after the completion of the 1972 Olympics. But the 84-year-old Brundage decided to go out with a bang by staging one final attack against commercialism in alpine skiing. Although he considered at least 30 or 40 skiers to be in violation of the rules of amateurism, Brundage chose to concentrate his attack on Austrian hero Karl Schranz, who was reputedly earning at least $40,000 to $50,000 a year as a "tester and designer" for various ski product manufacturers. Schranz was not alone in receiving such income, but he had also committed the crime of being outspoken in his criticism of Brundage.

Karl Schranz was the son of a poor railway worker in St. Anton in the Arlberg Mountains. His father died of work-related tuberculosis at an early age. In 1962 Schranz won the world downhill and combined championships and in 1964 he earned a silver medal in the Olympic giant slalom. In 1968 he appeared to have won the Olympic slalom until his disqualification for missing a gate was announced. By 1972 he had won every honor that is offered in international alpine skiing—except an Olympic gold medal. The 33-year-old Schranz delayed his retirement in the hope of achieving that final goal. But three days before the opening of the Sapporo Games, Avery Brundage got his way, and the I.O.C. voted 28–14 to ban Schranz from participating in the Olympics. Austrian Olympic officials announced that their ski team would withdraw from the games, but the Austrian skiers decided to compete anyway. While Brundage accused the alpine skiers of being "trained seals of the merchandisers," Schranz told the press, "If Mr. Brundage had been poor, as I was, and as were many other athletes, I wonder if he wouldn't have a different attitude. . . . If we followed Mr. Brundage's recommendations to their true end, then the Olympics would be a competition only for the very rich. No man of ordinary means could ever afford to excel in his sport."

When Schranz returned to Vienna he was met by 100,000 Austrian supporters and treated to a tickertape parade. It was the largest demonstration in Austria since World War II. Because Brundage was an American (he was known in Austria as "the senile millionaire from Chicago"), the U.S. embassy in Vienna was subjected to bomb threats and protests. The hypocrisy of the I.O.C's decision against Schranz was shown by the fact that the eventual downhill gold medalist, Bernhard Russi, had allowed his photo and name to be used on matchboxes, car stickers, and newspaper advertisements as part of a large-scale pre-Olympic publicity campaign for a Swiss insurance company. Karl Schranz announced his retirement from competitive skiing as soon as the 1972 Olympics ended. In 1988, the I.O.C. awarded Schranz a symbolic medal as a participant in the Sapporo Games.

1976 Innsbruck C: 74, N: 27, D: 2.5.

1.	Franz Klammer	AUT	1:45.73
2.	Bernhard Russi	SWI	1:46.06
3.	Herbert Plank	ITA	1:46.59
4.	Philippe Roux	SWI	1:46.69
5.	Ken Read	CAN	1:46.83
6.	Andy Mill	USA	1:47.06
7.	Walter Tresch	SWI	1:47.29
8.	David Irwin	CAN	1:47.41

In 1975 Franz Klammer of Mooswald in Carinthia won eight of nine World Cup downhill races. When the Olympics came to Innsbruck the following year there was great pressure on the 22-year-old Klammer as an Austrian favorite competing in Austria. Further pressure was exerted by defending champion Bernhard Russi, who sped down the 3145-meter (1.95-mile) Olympic hill in 1:46.06. The 15th starter of the day, Klammer fell one-fifth of a second off Russi's pace, but fought back wildly in the last 1000 meters to nip Russi by one-third of a second. Flushed with excitement, Klammer told reporters that at one point he skied so close to the fence lining the course that "I heard a shout or scream from a lady. I thought I was hitting her with a pole. . . . I thought I was going to crash all the way. . . . Now I've got everything. I don't need anything else."

1980 Lake Placid C: 47, N: 22, D: 2.14.

1.	Leonhard Stock	AUT	1:45.50
2.	Peter Wirnsberger	AUT	1:46.12
3.	Steve Podborski	CAN	1:46.62
4.	Peter Müller	SWI	1:46.75
5.	Pete Patterson	USA	1:47.04
6.	Herbert Plank	ITA	1:47.13
7.	Werner Grissmann	AUT	1:47.21
8.	Valery Tsyganov	SOV/RUS	1:47.34

The Austrian alpine team was so strong that they had seven men ranked in the top 20 in the world. When it was decided to leave Franz Klammer behind, team manager Karl "Downhill Charlie" Kahr had to explain the decision on national television. Leonhard Stock, who had broken a collarbone in December, was chosen to go to Lake Placid as an alternate. But when he recorded the fastest time in two of the three pre-Olympic trial runs, Austrian alpine officials changed their minds and declared that Stock was now a starter, along with Harti Weirather, but that the other three Austrians—Wirnsberger, Grissmann, and Sepp Walcher—would have to have a race-off for the final two spots. Walcher lost out. The four remaining Austrians all placed in the top nine, as Leonhard Stock went from being an alternate who had never won a World Cup race to being an Olympic champion in less than 30 hours. After the 1980 Olympics, he didn't win another downhill race until 1989.

1984 Sarajevo C: 61, N: 25, D: 2.16.

1.	William Johnson	USA	1:45.59
2.	Peter Müller	SWI	1:45.86
3.	Anton Steiner	AUT	1:45.95
4.	Pirmin Zurbriggen	SWI	1:46.05
5.	Helmut Höflehner	AUT	1:46.32
5.	Urs Räber	SWI	1:46.32
7.	Sepp Wildgruber	GER	1:46.53
8.	Steve Podborski	CAN	1:46.59

When Bill Johnson was seventeen years old, he was caught red-handed trying to steal a car. The judge in charge of his case, upon learning that Johnson was an excellent skier, sent him not to prison, but to a ski academy. The judge's decision turned out to be a fine advertisement for creative sentencing. Not only did Johnson never steal another car, but his skiing led him all the way to the Olympics. Still, two months before the Sarajevo Games, Bill Johnson seemed an unlikely candidate to win a gold medal. No U.S. male skier had ever won an Olympic downhill medal. And there was nothing in the least bit impressive about Johnson's record on the World Cup circuit. But then, in mid-January, he won the prestigious Lauberhorn downhill at Wengen, Switzerland. A couple of undistinguished performances were followed by a fourth at Cortina and Johnson suddenly looked like a serious contender, particularly considering that the Olympic course on Mt. Bjelašnica was relatively free of turns—perfect for a "glider" like Bill Johnson, who was able to keep his tuck longer than other skiers. When he scored the best series of places during the five practice runs, Johnson actually found himself the betting favorite.

Not the modest type, Johnson agreed with the emerging consensus. "I don't even know why everyone else is here," he announced to reporters. "They should hand [the gold medal] to me. Everyone else can fight for second place."

Heavy snow and powerful winds caused the downhill to be postponed three times, but Johnson seemed unperturbed by the delays. "Everyone knows it's my kind of course," he said.

When the weather finally cleared on the mountain, Johnson made good on his boasts. When told afterwards that the beaten skiers of the "downhill mafia," Austria and Switzerland, had grumbled that he had won because the course was an easy one, Johnson snapped, "If it's so easy, why didn't *they* win it?"

1988 Calgary-Nakiska C: 51, N: 18, D: 2.15.

1.	Pirmin Zurbriggen	SWI	1:59.63
2.	Peter Müller	SWI	2:00.14
3.	Franck Piccard	FRA	2:01.24
4.	Leonhard Stock	AUT	2:01.56
5.	Gerhard Pfaffenbichler	AUT	2:02.02
6.	Markus Wasmeier	GER	2:02.03
7.	Anton Steiner	AUT	2:02.19
8.	Martin Bell	GBR	2:02.49

The two favorites in the 1988 downhill, Peter Müller and Pirmin Zurbriggen, were both Swiss and they had both won a world championship in the event (Müller in 1987, Zurbriggen in 1985). But there the similarities ended. Müller was a "flatlander" from the Zurich suburb of Adliswil; Zurbriggen was from the tiny village of Saas Almagell (population 300) in the Valais Alps. Müller, age 30, fit the stereotype of the wild, high-living alpine ski champion; Zurbriggen, age 25, was every Swiss parent's dream son, a homebody who helped his mother do the dishes, prayed three times a day, and made pilgrimages to Lourdes. Müller was a downhill specialist; Zurbriggen was an all-arounder entered in all five alpine events in Calgary. Zurbriggen was also the overall World Cup champion in 1984 and 1987 and runner-up to Marc Girardelli in 1985 and 1986.

Müller, who had a history of skiing well in North America, was the first skier down the course. The next six skiers failed to come within three seconds of Müller's time and it became clear that he had had a great run. By the time Zurbriggen, skiing 14th, started, Müller still led by 1.42 seconds. Zurbriggen had watched the first two turns of Müller's run and knew immediately that he would need the race of his life to beat him. He tried to avoid hearing Müller's final time, but heard it anyway, which increased his nervousness. Nevertheless, Zurbriggen exploded down the course with an aggressiveness that belied his gentle exterior and Müller was forced to settle for his second straight silver medal.

1992 Albertville-Val d'Isère C: 55, N: 24, D: 2.9.

1.	Patrick Ortlieb	AUT	1:50.37
2.	Franck Piccard	FRA	1:50.42
3.	Günther Mader	AUT	1:50.47
4.	Markus Wasmeier	GER	1:50.62
5.	Jan Einar Thorsen	NOR	1:50.79
6.	Franz Heinzer	SWI	1:51.39
7.	Hansjörg Tauscher	GER	1:51.49
8.	Lasse Arnesen	NOR	1:51.63

The big story of the 1992 downhill was the course itself. Designed by 1972 Olympic champion Bernhard Russi, it was unusually steep and filled with curves and turns. Classical downhillers criticized the course as being more like a Super G than a downhill and hinted that it had been designed especially for local favorite Franck Piccard, the defending Super G champion. Technical specialists defended the course by saying that the race would be won "by skiers not by skis." The big loser in the controversy was popular Franz Heinzer, one of the classicists. Known in Switzerland as "Franz the Fourth" because he finished fourth in seven different World Cup downhills, Heinzer fianlly came into his own in 1991, winning the world championship and the World Cup. He also took four of six World Cup downhills in the 1991-1992 pre-Olympic season. In Val d'Isère, Heinzer could do no better than sixth, his worst placing in his last 13 downhill races.

Surprisingly, the Olympic championship was won by one of the course's critics, 6-foot 2½-inch Patrick Ortlieb. In the words of *Ski Racing* magazine, the 216-pound Ortlieb hurtled down the slope "like a cement truck with power steering," to register his first-ever World Cup victory. Like 1964 winner Egon Zimmermann, Ortlieb came from the village of Lech. Because his father was French, Ortlieb grew up with dual citizenship and turned down an offer to join the French team in 1989.

Despite the loss of Ortlieb, the French had cause for celebration when Franck Piccard, skiing in the 23rd position, took second place in the closest-ever alpine race in Olympic history. If Ortlieb, Piccard, and bronze medalist Günther Mader had been on the course at the same time, they would have finished only 9 feet (2.76 meters) apart.

1994 Lillehammer-Kvitfjell C: 55, N: 26, D: 2.13.

1.	Tommy Moe	USA	1:45.75
2.	Kjetil André Aamodt	NOR	1:45.79
3.	Edward Podivinsky	CAN	1:45.87
4.	Patrick Ortlieb	AUT	1:46.01
5.	Marc Girardelli	LUX	1:46.09
6.	Nicolas Burtin	FRA	1:46.22
6.	Hannes Trinkl	AUT	1:46.22
8.	Luc Alphand	FRA	1:46.25

Thirty thousand Norwegians ski fans roared with delight as the seventh skier, their own Kjetil André Aamodt, crossed the finish line with the fastest time of the day. Their joy was short-lived: the very next skier, Tommy Moe, beat Aamodt's time by four one-hundredths of a second. Later the Norwegians' disappointment turned to happiness again when they learned that Moe's great-great grandfather was Norwegian.

A skiing prodigy from Montana, Tommy Moe was banned from local competitions when, at age 13, he was caught smoking marijuana. At 16, he was training with the U.S. team when he was caught smoking again and put on probation: one more transgression and he would be removed from the team. Moe's father brought him up to Alaska's Aleutian Islands to make him work 12 hours and more a day on a construction site shoveling gravel and making wooden frames for cement foundations. And periodically he asked Tommy if he preferred practicing with the U.S. ski team. Tommy got the message and concentrated on his ski training from then on. Still, Moe's victory was a surprise because he had never before won a World Cup race.

The 1994 downhill field was so well-balanced that Armin Assinger of Austria finished less than a second slower than Moe (.93 seconds to be exact) and placed only fifteenth. The most unusual competitor was Connor O'Brien, a 33-year-old Wall Street investment banker, skiing for his fourth country. Born in Canada, O'Brien represented Great Britain at the 1984 Olympics because his father was born and raised in Belfast. He placed 33rd in the downhill. While a student at Middlebury College in Vermont, he represented the United States and then he skied in World Cup events for Canada until injury forced him to retire in 1985. At his mother's urging, he returned to competition to represent the country of her birth: Estonia. He even visited Estonia for the first time on his way to the 1994 Olympics. Starting 53rd of 55 in the downhill, O'Brien lost a ski entering the second turn and was unable to finish the race.

As for Tommy Moe, like Bill Johnson, the only other American to win an Olympic downhill, he never again won a World Cup downhill race.

SLALOM

Whereas the downhill requires pure speed, the slalom (or "special slalom") is more a test of control. Each skier is required to weave in and out of blue- and red-flagged double poles, or "gates." Missing a gate results in immediate disqualification. There are two runs on different courses. Times for the two runs are added to determine final places.

1924–1936 not held

1948 St. Moritz C: 76, N: 22, D: 2.5.

1.	Edi Reinalter	SWI	2:10.3
2.	James Couttet	FRA	2:10.8

3. Henri Oreiller	FRA	2:12.8
4. Silvio Alverà	ITA	2:13.2
5. Olle Dahlman	SWE	2:13.6
6. Egon Schöpf	AUT	2:14.2
7. Jack Reddish	USA	2:15.5
8. Karl Molitor	SWI	2:16.2

Alverà led after the first run, followed by Couttet, Reinalter, and Oreiller. Reinalter's second run of 1:02.6 was a half second faster than the next best skier, Egon Schöpf.

1952 Oslo C: 86, N: 27, D: 2.19.

1. Othmar Schneider	AUT	2:00.0
2. Stein Eriksen	NOR	2:01.2
3. Guttorm Berge	NOR	2:01.7
4. Zeno Colò	ITA	2:01.8
5. Stig Sollander	SWE	2:02.6
6. James Couttet	FRA	2:02.8
7. Fredy Rubi	SWI	2:03.3
8. Per Rollum	NOR	2:04.5

The fastest time of the first run, 59.2, was first posted by Stein Eriksen, who had won the giant slalom four days earlier, and then equaled by Hans Senger of Austria. Downhill silver medalist Othmar Schneider was third in 59.5. The second run saw Senger fall, while Schneider's 1:00.5 was beaten only by Fredy Rubi's 59.7. Antoin Miliordos of Greece, disgusted by the fact that he fell 18 times, sat down and crossed the finish line backward. His time for one run was 26.9 seconds slower than Schneider's time for two runs.

1956 Cortina C: 89, N: 29, D: 1.31.

1. Anton Sailer	AUT	3:14.7
2. Chiharu Igaya	JPN	3:18.7
3. Stig Sollander	SWE	3:20.2
4. Joseph Brooks Dodge	USA	3:21.8
5. Georges Schneider	SWI	3:22.6
6. Gérard Pasquier	FRA	3:24.6
7. Charles Bozon	FRA	3:26.2
8. Bernard Perret	FRA	3:26.3

Sailer recorded the fastest times in both runs and won his second gold medal.

1960 Squaw Valley C: 63, N: 21, D: 2.24.

1. Ernst Hinterseer	AUT	2:08.9
2. Matthias Leitner	AUT	2:10.3
3. Charles Bozon	FRA	2:10.4
4. Ludwig Leitner	GER	2:10.5
5. Josef "Pepi" Stiegler	AUT	2:11.1
6. Guy Périllat	FRA	2:11.8
7. Hans-Peter Lanig	GER	2:14.3
8. Paride Milianti	ITA	2:14.4

Eighteen-year-old Willi Bogner of Germany, whose father was the first designer of stretch pants, had the fastest time of the first run, 1:08.8. Hinterseer and Leitner, fifth and ninth after the first run, led the way on the second course in 58.2 and 59.2. Bogner, meanwhile, had fallen and was disqualified. In last place was Kyung Soonyim of South Korea, whose time of 2:35.2 for the second run was slower than the combined run times of 22 of the 39 other skiers who completed both runs. Kyung had a good excuse: he had never skied on snow before arriving in Squaw Valley, He had learned to ski by reading books and practicing on grass. The other skiers gave him equipment and lessons. When he crossed the finish line in the slalom competition, the final alpine race of the Olympics, Kyung was met by the other racers, who threw a celebration for him.

A historical footnote to the 1960 men's slalom: at one point, race officials asked CBS-TV if they could review a tape of the race because of a controversy about one skier who was alleged to have missed a gate. It was this incident that gave CBS producers the idea to invent the instant replay.

1964 Innsbruck C: 96, N: 28, D: 2.8.

1.	Josef "Pepi" Stiegler	AUT	2:11.13
2.	William Kidd	USA	2:11.27
3.	James Heuga	USA	2:11.52
4.	Michel Arpin	FRA	2:12.91
5.	Ludwig Leitner	GER	2:12.94
6.	Adolf Mathis	SWI	2:12.99
7.	Gerhard Nenning	AUT	2:13.20
8.	Wallace "Bud" Werner	USA	2:13.46

Pepi Stiegler, a 26-year-old photographer, had twice been removed from the Austrian team and replaced by Egon Zimmermann. Both times he was reinstated after public pressure. After the first run, Stiegler led by a second over Karl Schranz, who was followed by Heuga, Nenning, Mathis, and Kidd. Stiegler skied cautiously the second time around, registering the 8th best time, but his first-round performance turned out to be good enough to edge the Americans. Eighth-place finisher Buddy Werner was killed two months after the Olympics while trying to out-ski a sudden avalanche at St. Moritz.

1968 Grenoble-Chamrousse C: 100, N: 33, D: 2.17.

1.	Jean-Claude Killy	FRA	1:39.73
2.	Herbert Huber	AUT	1:39.82
3.	Alfred Matt	AUT	1:40.09
4.	Dumeng Giovanoli	ITA	1:40.22
5.	Vladimir Sabich	USA	1:40.49
6.	Andrzej Bachleda	POL	1:40.61
7.	James Heuga	USA	1:40.97
8.	Alain Penz	FRA	1:41.14

With two gold medals down and one to go for Jean-Claude Killy, the slalom was held in bad weather, with fog, mist, and shadows prevailing. The skiers pleaded that the contest be postponed, but the officials in charge refused. Appropriately, the sun shone through only once—during Killy's first run, which was good enough to put him in first place. Killy was the first skier of the second round, so he was forced to wait anxiously as the others came down the hill. Håkon Mjöen of Norway bettered Killy's time, but was disqualified for missing two gates. Then came the turn of Karl Schranz, the biggest threat to Killy's goal of a triple crown. But something curious happened as Schranz sped through the fog, something that has never been fully explained. According to Schranz, as he approached the 21st gate, a mysterious figure in black crossed the course. Schranz skidded to a halt and, with three witnesses in tow, walked back to the starting point to ask for a rerun. Colonel Robert Readhead, the British referee, granted Schranz's request. This time Schranz achieved an almost perfect run, beat

Killy's time, and was declared the unofficial winner. Schranz was allowed to enjoy the postrace press conference, while Killy sulked in the corner. But two hours later it was announced that Schranz had been disqualified for missing two gates just prior to his encounter with the mysterious interloper.

The Austrians were outraged. Schranz claimed that if he did miss a gate or two it was because he had already been distracted by the sight of someone on the course. His supporters contended that the mystery man had been a French policeman or soldier who had purposely interfered with Schranz in order to insure Killy's victory. The French, on the other hand, hinted that Schranz had made up the whole story after he had missed a gate. A final four-hour meeting of the Jury of Appeal ended with a 3–1 vote against Schranz, with two Frenchmen and a Swiss voting to give the gold medal to Killy, while Colonel Readhead abstained and a Norwegian supported Schranz. Because of this incident, the 1968 Winter Olympics ended in a rather ugly mood, but back home in Val d'Isère Killy had no trouble putting it out of his mind. "The party went on for two and a half days," he later recalled, "and the whole time I never saw the sun once."

1972 Sapporo-Teineyama C: 72, N: 31, D: 2.13.

1.	Francisco Fernández Ochoa	SPA	1:49.27
2.	Gustav Thöni	ITA	1:50.28
3.	Roland Thöni	ITA	1:50.30
4.	Henri Duvillard	FRA	1:50.45
5.	Jean-Noël Augert	FRA	1:50.51
6.	Eberhard Schmalzl	ITA	1:50.83
7.	David Zwilling	AUT	1:51.97
8.	Edmund Bruggmann	SWI	1:52.03

The biggest surprise of the 1972 Winter Games was the sensational victory of 21-year-old Paquito Ochoa of Spain, who had never before finished higher than sixth in an international meet. Not only was Ochoa's gold medal the first ever won by Spain in the Winter Olympics, but it was the first Spanish victory of any kind since the equestrian team jumping competition of 1928. From Japan, Ochoa had written to his mother saying, "Mama, pray not for me, but for you. I will win and for you it is very emotional. So pray for your own strength." In fact, Ochoa was so overcome by emotion that he was unable to speak to reporters except to say, "I can't believe it. It can't be true." An hour later, referring to Spain's leading matador, he said, "El Cordobés is a little man compared with me. I am the champion." Ochoa did run into one problem. When it came time for the medal presentation, he was not allowed into the stadium because he had forgotten his credentials. "I told the Japanese at the entry," he would recall, " 'But I am the Olympic champion!' They didn't believe me. And they were right, it was incredible. Imagine, if you will, a Spanish Olympic ski champion. It's as if a Japanesee became king of the bullring." Eventually Juan-Antonio Samaranch, then vice-president of the IOC, was summoned and Ochoa was allowed to enter.

1976 Innsbruck C: 94, N: 31, D: 2.14.

1.	Piero Gros	ITA	2:03.29
2.	Gustav Thöni	ITA	2:03.73
3.	Willy Frommelt	LIE	2:04.28
4.	Walter Tresch	SWI	2:05.26
5.	Christian Neureuther	GER	2:06.56
6.	Wolfgang Junginger	GER	2:07.08
7.	Alois Morgenstern	AUT	2:07.18
8.	Peter Lüscher	SWI	2:08.10

Fifth after the first run, Gros was "as sure as I could be that I could never beat Thöni. In my opinion at that time Gustavo had the gold medal in his pocket." But Gros gained the victory with a superb second run, over a second faster than that of Thöni, his teammate and mentor.

1980 Lake Placid C: 79, N: 28, D: 2.22.

1.	Ingemar Stenmark	SWE	1:44.26
2.	Phillip Mahre	USA	1:44.76
3.	Jacques Lüthy	SWI	1:45.06
4.	Hans Enn	AUT	1:45.12
5.	Christian Neureuther	GER	1:45.14
6.	Petar Popangelov	BUL	1:45.40
7.	Anton Steiner	AUT	1:45.41
8.	Gustav Thöni	ITA	1:45.99

Skiing with a three-inch metal plate and four screws in his left ankle joint, the result of a bad fall 11 months earlier, Phil Mahre of White Pass, Washington, whizzed down the first run in 53.31. Because he was the first skier to compete, there was no way to judge if this was a good time or a bad time. But by the time the 13th skier, favorite Ingemar Stenmark, had completed the course over a half second slower than Mahre, it was clear that the 22-year-old American would enter the second round in first place. However Stenmark, in fourth place, had come from behind three days earlier to win the giant slalom, and he was known for his lightning second runs. Sure enough, he tore down the course in 50.37, a time that no one could beat. Three skiers later, Phil Mahre, needing a 50.94 to win the gold medal, never gained his rhythm and could only manage 51.45. Ingemar Stenmark, the Silent Swede, had completed his slalom double, but was not impressed by his accomplishment. "History is not important," he said. "The important thing is that I am satisfied with myself." As for Phil Mahre, he was back on the slopes the next day—filming an American Express commercial.

1984 Sarajevo C: 101, N: 37, D: 2.19.

1.	Phillip Mahre	USA	1:39.41
2.	Steven Mahre	USA	1:39.62
3.	Didier Bouvet	FRA	1:40.20
4.	Jonas Nilsson	SWE	1:40.25
5.	Oswald Tötsch	ITA	1:40.48
6.	Petar Popangelov	BUL	1:40.68
7.	Bojan Križaj	YUG/SLO	1:41.51
8.	Lars-Göran Halvarsson	SWE	1:41.70

Of the seven World Cup slalom events held prior to the Olympics, six had been won by either Ingemar Stenmark or Marc Girardelli, neither of whom was allowed to take part in the Sarajevo Games. Stenmark's punishment was a result of his being a professional, a rather ludicrous charge considering the huge amounts of money being earned by numerous other skiers. Girardelli's problem was that he competed for Luxembourg even though he was an Austrian citizen.

With Stenmark and Girardelli gone, the natural favorites seemed to be three-time defending World Cup champion Phil Mahre and his twin brother Steve. But after a decade on the circuit, the Mahres seemed to have lost their competitive edge. They were already thinking ahead to their post-Olympic retirement. Phil was also concerned about his pregnant wife, Dolly, who was back in the United States with a due date of February 27. The 1983–84 season had been a disaster for the Mahres. Steve stood 45th in the World Cup standings, Phil 62nd. Even when things went right, they went wrong. On January 16, Steve had won the slalom at Parpan,

Switzerland, with Phil placing sixth. Then it was discovered that the twins had inadvertently switched their number bibs and both were disqualified. Girardelli was awarded the victory. The situation did not improve for the Mahres in Sarajevo. In the giant slalom, held five days before the slalom, Phil finished eighth and Steve seventeenth.

At a press conference, Phil tried to put things in perspective. "I'm pretty mellow about Sarajevo," he said. "I have nothing to prove, nothing to escape. I've enjoyed myself, and that's the essence of sport." Then he added, "I think it is unfortunate that all the emphasis is on coming here and winning medals. The problem with gold medals is that it sets you for life or it doesn't. Well, I'm set for life, so I don't care."

The U.S. press did not take kindly to Phil Mahre's relativist attitude. Referring to his eighth place giant slalom finish, Dan Barreiro of the *Dallas Morning News* ranted, "That's the good news. The bad news is Mahre gets another chance Sunday in the slalom. I hope he chokes again. Or that he doesn't even show up. Phil Mahre is America's best skier, but he could do us all a favor by getting out of town. Right now." Not to be outdone by his crosstown rival, Skip Bayless of the *Dallas Times Herald* referred to Phil as the "ugly American skier." "Perhaps Mahre never sat in front of a free-enterprise TV and got caught up in some Yank beating some communist at some foreign game."

The slalom course on Mt. Bjelašnica turned out to be a difficult one, as only 47 of the 101 starters managed to complete both runs. But while other skiers were literally falling by the wayside and Texas sportswriters were sniffing the odor of crow in their kitchens, the Mahre twins were back to their old form. At the end of the first run, Steve was in first place with a big lead of almost seven-tenths of a second, and Phil was in third. In second place was Jonas Nilsson, who was not considered a threat, due to his inexperience.

Phil Mahre executed an excellent second run and then immediately grabbed a walkie-talkie radio to pass on some final advice to the only person who stood between him and a gold medal—his brother Steve. Steve could have skied a safe race and still won. Instead he attacked the course, made too many mistakes, and had to settle for the silver medal.

For two brothers to win the gold and silver in the same event certainly makes for a fine day, but there was more good news for the Mahres. As they left the Olympic Village to attend the medal ceremony, Phil was informed that his wife had just given birth to their second child and first son. At a press conference after the ceremony, Phil was asked what part his wife had played in his career. He tried to answer, but was stopped by tears. Steve put his arm around his brother, who then recovered enough to say, "Heck, there she was, doing all the work while I was out there playing."

1988 Calgary-Nakiska C: 109, N: 37, D: 2.27.

1. Alberto Tomba	ITA	1:39.47
2. Frank Wörndl	GER	1:39.53
3. Paul Frommelt	LIE	1:39.84
4. Bernhard Gstrein	AUT	1:40.08
5. Ingemar Stenmark	SWE	1:40.22
6. Jonas Nilsson	SWE	1:40.23
7. Pirmin Zurbriggen	SWI	1:40.48
8. Oswald Tötsch	ITA	1:40.55

World champion Frank Wörndl recorded the fastest time of the first run, with Jonas Nilsson second and Alberto Tomba, who had won the giant slalom two days earlier, third. The winner of the second run was the legend: Ingemar Stenmark, but his eleventh place earlier in the day kept him out of the medals. Tomba, who had skied with relative caution in the first run, went all out to register the second fastest time of the second run. Then he watched as Wörndl suffered a momentary lapse of concentration in the middle of the course, allowing Tomba to gain the victory.

1992 Albertville-Les Ménuires C: 119, N: 44, D: 2.22.

1.	Finn Christian Jagge	NOR	1:44.39
2.	Alberto Tomba	ITA	1:44.67
3.	Michael Tritscher	AUT	1:44.85
4.	Patrick Staub	SWI	1:45.44
5.	Thomas Fogdö	SWE	1:45.48
6.	Paul Accola	SWI	1:45.62
7.	Michael von Grünigen	SWI	1:46.42
8.	Jonas Nilsson	SWE	1:46.57

An estimated 15,000 Italians made the long trip north to Les Ménuires to cheer on their hero, Alberto Tomba, in his attempt to become the first alpine skier to win four gold medals. Included in the army of fans was a 400-car convoy from Tomba's hometown of Bologna. They avoided the prohibition against private vehicles by arriving 12 hours early and sleeping in their cars (if they slept at all). In eight pre-Olympic slaloms, Tomba had registered five firsts, two seconds, and a third. In addition, he was the defending Olympic champion and had already won his second giant slalom title four days earlier. But it was 25-year-old Finn Christian Jagge, whose mother, Liv, had placed seventh in the 1964 slalom, who recorded the best time of the first run. Tomba could do no better than sixth, 1.58 seconds behind.

Still, there was no reason for Tomba's fans to give up hope. Not only was their idol known for his strong second runs, but the gates on the second course had been set by none other than Tomba's personal coach, Gustavo Thöni. Tomba did have a sensational run, but was able to make up only 1.30 seconds on Jagge. Referring to Tomba's boisterous fans, *Ski Racing*'s Bruce Stoff wrote, "Alberto Tomba's silver medal was perfect. Had he won, there would have been a riot. Had he fallen, there also would have been a riot. With a silver, everyone went home happy and police intervention wasn't required."

The good sport award in the slalom went to Robert Scott Detlof, a Brazilian-born American representing Brazil. Detlof sprained his knee while training and was prepared to withdraw until he learned that the Brazilian Ski Federation would have to pay $2500 to cover his expenses if he didn't compete. Knowing that Brazil was strapped for cash, Detlof put on his skis and hit the piste. Although his time was slow—3:18.58—he did complete both runs, which was more than could be said for 54 of the 119 entrants.

But even Detlof was a whiz kid compared to Costa Rica's Julian Munoz Aia, whose combined time was 3:44.11. And then there was Munoz Aia's teammate, Alejandro Preinfalk Lavagni, who seemed to walk down the mountain, testing each step like a bather putting his bare foot into freezing water. His two runs were so slow, 2:09.83 and 2:19.93, that he would have lost to a runner going uphill. When Preinfalk Lavagni finally reached the finish line, he was met by Jagge and Tomba, who hoisted him onto their shoulders.

1994 Lillehammer-Hafjell C: 57, N: 25, D: 2.27.

1.	Thomas Stangassinger	AUT	2:02.02
2.	Alberto Tomba	ITA	2:02.17
3.	Jure Košir	SLO	2:02.53
4.	Mitja Kunc	SLO	2:02.62
5.	Thomas Fogdö	SWE	2:03.05

6.	Finn Christian Jagge	NOR	2:03.19
7.	P. Casey Puckett	USA	2:03.47
8.	Angelo Weiss	ITA	2:03.72

Despite missing a gate in the giant slalom four days earlier, Alberto Tomba was the favorite to win the slalom. He dominated the pre-Olympic season, garnering four firsts, a second and a third in eight races. But his first run was not impressive and he found himself in twelfth place, 1.84 seconds behind the leader, Thomas Stangassinger. Tomba was known for his strong second runs, such as the one that had earned him silver at the 1992 Olympics, but to win a medal this time seemed unlikely. Not only would he have to ski a near-perfect course, he would have to hope that nine of the eleven skiers ahead of him faltered.

Tomba did produce a great run, although how great was not immediately apparent. One by one, those skiers who had beaten Tomba in the first run, came down a second time. Kunc of Slovenia—too slow, Weiss of Italy—too slow, Miklavc of Slovenia—too slow, Košir of Slovenia—close but too slow, Marila of Finland—much too slow, Jagge of Norway—too slow. Now there were only four skiers left, but they were the four with the best times. Sykora of Austria—lost a ski at the fourth gate, Roth of Germany—fell at the second gate, Aamodt of Norway—fell at the second gate. Incredibly, Alberto Tomba was assured at least a silver medal. All that stood between him and gold was Stangassinger. A slalom specialist, the 28-year-old Austrian had placed ninth in the event in both 1988 and 1992. With the big lead to cushion him, he skied cautiously, almost lost form at the end, but managed to cross the finish line a mere .15 seconds ahead of Tomba. A close call, but enough to salvage an otherwise disappointing Olympics for the Austrian alpine team.

GIANT SLALOM

The giant slalom is similar to the slalom except the course is longer, the gates are farther apart, and the corners are not so sharp.

1924–1948 not held

1952 Oslo-Norefjell C: 83, N: 26, D: 2.15.

1.	Stein Eriksen	NOR	2:25.0
2.	Christian Pravda	AUT	2:26.9
3.	Toni Spiss	AUT	2:28.8
4.	Zeno Colò	ITA	2:29.1
5.	Georges Schneider	SWI	2:31.2
6.	Joseph Brooks Dodge	USA	2:32.6
6.	Stig Sollander	SWE	2:32.6
8.	Bernhard Perren	SWI	2:33.1

Stein Eriksen, whose father competed as a gymnast at the 1912 Olympics, was the first of only seven skiers from outside of the Alps to win an Olympic men's alpine gold medal. He was also the first skiing superstar. He was handsome, stylish, and glamorous. At the Oslo Games he proved to be a modest winner, declaring, "I had a great advantage over most of the others because I knew the course by heart." In 1954 Eriksen won three gold medals at the world alpine championships. Immediately afterward, he became a ski school director at Boyne Mt., Michigan. He moved on to Heavenly Valley, California, in 1957, Aspen Highlands, Colorado, in 1959, Sugarbush, Vermont, in 1965, Snowmass, Colorado, in 1969, and Park City, Utah, in 1973. Everywhere he went Stein Eriksen became the inspiration for the stereotypical ski instructor of the 1950s and 1960s—rich, good-looking, an outdoors-

The 1952 giant slalom champion, Stein Eriksen, was the inspiration for the stereotype of the suave and handsome ski instructor.

man who made women melt, and, above all, an Olympic champion. Eriksen's formula for success? "Be tough, be confident. But you will never be a whole and happy person if you aren't humble."

1956 Cortina C: 95, N: 29, D: 1.29.

1. Anton Sailer	AUT	3:00.1
2. Andreas Molterer	AUT	3:06.3
3. Walter Schuster	AUT	3:07.2
4. Adrien Duvillard	FRA	3:07.2
5. Charles Bozon	FRA	3:08.4
6. Ernst Hinterseer	AUT	3:08.5
7. Hans-Peter Lanig	GER	3:08.6
8. Sepp Behr	GER	3:11.4

The 1956 giant slalom was held on the "Ilio Colli" course at Cortina. Ilio Colli was a local skier who had crashed into a tree at 50 m.p.h. during a race. He broke his skull and died instantly. Each participant in the giant slalom was handed a souvenir picture of Colli. In his book *My Way to the Triple Olympic Victory*, Toni Sailer wrote, "It is a beautiful thought to name such a famous course . . . after a dead racer, even if it is not exactly encouraging for those starting to be handed such a death notice." When the sixth skier, Andreas "Anderl" Molterer, came down in 3:06.3, he was mobbed and congratulated. But Molterer waved everyone away, telling them, "Toni hasn't come yet." When Toni did come, he came really fast—in 3:00.1, over six seconds better than any of the other 94 skiers. Over the next five days Sailer also won the slalom and the downhill.

1960 Squaw Valley C: 65, N: 21, D: 2.21.

1. Roger Staub	SWI	1:48.3
2. Josef "Pepi" Stiegler	AUT	1:48.7

3. Ernst Hinterseer	AUT	1:49.1
4. Thomas Corcoran	USA	1:49.7
5. Bruno Alberti	ITA	1:50.1
6. Guy Périllat	FRA	1:50.7
7. Karl Schranz	AUT	1:50.8
8. Paride Milianti	ITA	1:50.9

1964 Innsbruck C: 96, N: 29, D: 2.2.

1. François Bonlieu	FRA	1:46.71
2. Karl Schranz	AUT	1:47.09
3. Josef "Pepi" Stiegler	AUT	1:48.05
4. Willy Favre	SWI	1:48.69
5. Jean-Claude Killy	FRA	1:48.92
6. Gerhard Nenning	AUT	1:49.68
7. William Kidd	USA	1:49.97
8. Ludwig Leitner	GER	1:50.04

François Bonlieu engaged in a running battle with the French coaches and officials and refused to listen to their advice. His rebelliousness turned out to be wisdom, as he upset the Austrians on their own course. However, it later proved his undoing. After working as a mountain guide, he dropped out of conventional society and was eventually murdered on the boardwalk in Cannes on August 18, 1973.

1968 Grenoble-Chamrousse C: 99, N: 36, D: 2.12.

1. Jean-Claude Killy	FRA	3:29.28
2. Willy Favre	SWI	3:31.50
3. Heinrich Messner	AUT	3:31.83
4. Guy Périllat	FRA	3:32.06
5. William Kidd	USA	3:32.37
6. Karl Schranz	AUT	3:33.08
7. Dumeng Giovanoli	SWI	3:33.55
8. Gerhard Nenning	AUT	3:33.61

For the first time the giant slalom was decided by a combination of two runs on separate days, rather than by a single run. This was the second of Killy's three gold medals. He had the fastest time of the first run and extended his winning margin over the second run.

1972 Sapporo-Teineyama C: 73, N: 27, D: 2.10.

1. Gustavo Thöni	ITA	3:09.62
2. Edmund Bruggmann	SWI	3:10.75
3. Werner Mattle	SWI	3:10.99
4. Alfred Hagn	GER	3:11.16
5. Jean-Noël Augert	FRA	3:11.84
6. Max Rieger	GER	3:11.96
7. David Zwilling	AUT	3:12.32
8. Reinhard Tritscher	AUT	3:12.42

Erik Håker of Norway had the fastest time of the first run, followed by Alfred Hagn and Gustavo Thöni. When Håker opened the second run by falling and Hagn skied too cautiously, the way was open for the 20-year-old Thöni to become the first Italian to win an alpine gold medal since Zeno Colò won the downhill in 1952.

1976 Innsbruck C: 97, N: 32, N: 2.9.

1. Heini Hemmi	SWI	3:26.97
2. Ernst Good	SWI	3:27.17

3.	Ingemar Stenmark	SWE	3:27.41
4.	Gustavo Thöni	ITA	3:27.67
5.	Phillip Mahre	USA	3:28.20
6.	Engelhard Pargätzi	SWI	3:28.76
7.	Fausto Radici	ITA	3:30.09
8.	Franco Bieler	ITA	3:30.24

Neither Hemmi nor Good had ever won a World Cup race. They had been placed third and second after the first run, behind Gustavo Thöni. However, Thöni's second run was only the eighth best of the day, while Hemmi's and Good's were second and third best. Ingemar Stenmark, ninth after the first run, stormed back with the fastest second-round time to take the bronze medal and establish a pattern that was to make him extremely famous in the years to come.

1980 Lake Placid C: 78, N: 28, D: 2.19.

1.	Ingemar Stenmark	SWE	2:40.74
2.	Andreas Wenzel	LIE	2:41.49
3.	Hans Enn	AUT	2:42.51
4.	Bojan Križaj	YUG/SLO	2:42.53
5.	Jacques Lüthy	SWI	2:42.75
6.	Bruno Nöckler	ITA	2:42.95
7.	Joel Gaspoz	SWI	2:43.05
8.	Boris Strel	YUG/SLO	2:43.24

Born in the small village of Tärnaby in Swedish Lapland, about 100 miles south of the Arctic Circle, Ingemar Stenmark learned to ski at an early age because, "It was a thing I could do alone." When he was 10 years old he wrote a school essay on "How I See My Future." Stenmark wrote that he wanted to be a ski racer. When the teacher returned his paper she told him that his dream was "unrealistic . . . impossible to achieve." She was wrong. Ingemar Stenmark grew up to become the most successful ski racer in history. He was the overall World Cup leader three times and he won the slalom and giant slalom titles eight times each. When he retired in 1989, he had won a record 86 World Cup races. Only Marc Girardelli has won half that many.

On September 14, 1979, Stenmark, then 23 years old, was practicing his downhill technique in the Italian Alps when he lost control and tumbled violently down the hill for 200 meters. Lying unconscious on the snow, he began foaming at the mouth and experiencing spasms. He had suffered a major concussion. But five months later he was in top shape again for the Olympics, although he did skip the downhill race. As usual, Stenmark skied somewhat cautiously on his first run of the giant slalom, placing third behind Andreas Wenzel and Bojan Križaj. But on the second day Stenmark roared down the course almost a full second faster than anyone else. "I'm not disappointed," said silver medalist Wenzel. "I had an idea this would happen."

1984 Sarajevo C: 108, N: 38, D: 2.14.

1.	Max Julen	SWI	2:41.18
2.	Jure Franko	YUG/SLO	2:41.41
3.	Andreas Wenzel	LIE	2:41.75
4.	Franz Gruber	AUT	2:42.08
5.	Boris Strel	YUG/SLO	2:42.36
6.	Hubert Strolz	AUT	2:42.71
7.	Alex Giorgi	ITA	2:43.00
8.	Phillip Mahre	USA	2:43.25

Twenty-two-year-old Max Julen of Zermatt led after the first run and clocked the second fastest time of the second run to hold off the powerful finish of hometown favorite Jure Franko. Franko, the first Yugoslav to win a Winter Olympics medal, became a national hero, his performance touching off boisterous celebrations in Sarajevo.

1988 Calgary-Nakiska C: 117, N: 39, D: 2.25.

1.	Alberto Tomba	ITA	2:06.37
2.	Hubert Strolz	AUT	2:07.41
3.	Pirmin Zurbriggen	SWI	2:08.39
4.	Ivano Camozzi	ITA	2:08.77
5.	Rudolf Nierlich	AUT	2:08.92
6.	Andreas Wenzel	LIE	2:09.03
7.	Helmut Mayer	AUT	2:09.09
8.	Frank Wörndl	AUT	2:09.22

Alberto Tomba, the son of a wealthy textile merchant, didn't win his first World Cup race until November 27, 1987, but in the two and a half months before the Olympics he won seven slalom and giant slalom races. His sudden success catapulted the boisterous Italian from being an unknown into the role of favorite.

Just before taking off on his first run, Tomba turned to his rivals and said, "Okay boys, keep calm. And good luck to all." Then he obliterated the field, registering a time 1.14 seconds faster than Hubert Strolz in second place. While waiting for the second run, Tomba impulsively walked up to a pay phone and placed a collect call to his startled family in Lazzaro di Savenna, a suburb of Bologna. Perhaps he just wanted to remind his father of the elder Tomba's promise to buy his son a Ferrari if he won a gold medal in Calgary.

Two other incidents occurred during the break between runs. Race officials disqualified the entire Canadian team for wearing ski suits that had not been submitted for safety inspection. Having punished the Canadians, they went down the line and eliminated the Bolivians, the Moroccans, the Lebanese, and the Taiwanese, as well. On a darker note, Austria's leading orthopedic surgeon, Jörg Oberhammer, collided with another skier, fell beneath a snow-grooming machine, and was killed instantly. This horrible incident was witnessed by Swiss skiers Pirmin Zurbriggen and Martin Hangl, who happened to be passing overhead in a chairlift. A shaken Zurbriggen still managed to capture the bronze medal, but Hangl collapsed near the starting gate and had to withdraw.

When the competition resumed, Strolz picked up one tenth of a second over Tomba, but it wasn't nearly enough to prevent the latter from qualifying for his Ferrari. "I want it red," he told reporters.

1992 Albertville-Val d'Isère C: 131, N: 47, D: 2.18.

1.	Alberto Tomba	ITA	2:06.98
2.	Marc Girardelli	LUX	2:07.30
3.	Kjetil André Aamodt	NOR	2:07.82
4.	Paul Accola	SWI	2:08.02
5.	Ole Kristian Furuseth	NOR	2:08.16
6.	Günther Mader	AUT	2:08.80
7.	Rainer Salzgeber	AUT	2:08.83
8.	Fredrik Nyberg	SWE	2:09.00

The 1992 men's giant slalom attracted more entrants from more nations than any other event in the history of the Winter Olympics. But for all the color and variety, in the end it was the four favorites who battled for the medals. The man to beat was the defending champion, Alberto Tomba. Following his 1988 triumphs, he put on weight, became distracted by his celebrity, and lost his competitive focus. In the

Alberto Tomba is cheered on by his supporters in 1992 after becoming the first alpine skier to win the same event twice.

next two years he won only four races, fell often, and broke his collarbone. Finally the Italian Ski Federation stepped in and assigned 1972 gold medalist Gustavo Thöni to be Tomba's personal coach. They also added a full-time fitness coach, a masseur, a psychologist, and an equipment technician. By 1991 Tomba was back on track, winning giant slalom after giant slalom. He continued to dominate the 1991-92 pre-Olympic season. When asked if he was altering his training for the Olympics, Tomba replied, "I used to have a wild time with three women until 5 a.m. In the Olympic Village, I will live it up with five women until 3 a.m."

Tomba's only serious challengers in the giant slalom were thought to be World Cup leader Paul Accola, Super G gold medal winner Kjetil Aamodt, and, most especially, Super G silver medalist Marc Girardelli. Girardelli was known as the skier without a country because he was born in Austria, lived in Switzerland, and acquired citizenship in Luxembourg after his father had a dispute with Austrian ski authorities. Girardelli was one of only three male skiers to win the overall World Cup four times (the others were Gustavo Thöni and Pirmin Zurbriggen), and he ranked third in total World Cup victories, with 36, behind Ingemar Stenmark and Zurbriggen. Until the Albertville Games, Girardelli's best Olympic performance was a ninth in the Calgary downhill.

Aamodt was first down the hill in the 1992 giant slalom. He laid down the challenge with a fine 1:04.81. Tomba, racing sixth, topped him at 1:04.57. Accola followed with a 1:04.88 and Girardelli with 1:04.70. Because the leaders raced the second run in reverse order of their times in the first run, Tomba started immediately after Girardelli and knew that he needed a near-perfect performance to overcome his rival. He got off to a sloppy start and quickly fell behind Girardelli's pace. As his fans watched his intermediate splits in horror, Tomba gradually found his rhythm and ripped through the final third of the course. When he crossed the finish line he didn't know if he had succeeded until he saw the crowd cheering and waving their arms. Only then did he realize that he had made Olympic history by becoming the first alpine skier to win the same event twice. In 1993 Girardelli claimed a bit of history himself, by winning a fifth World Cup title.

Olympic history of a stranger sort was made earlier in the competition at the end of the first run. The skiers took off at 40-second intervals, but the 129th starter, Raymond Kayrouz of Lebanon, was so slow that he was actually passed by the next starter, El Hassan Matha of Morocco. Unfortunately, both Matha and Kayrouz missed a gate and were disqualified.

1994 Lillehammer-Hafjell C: 61, N: 29, D: 2.23.

1.	Markus Wasmeier	GER	2:52.46
2.	Urs Kälin	SWI	2:52.48
3.	Christian Mayer	AUT	2:52.58
4.	Jan Einar Thorsen	NOR	2:52.71
5.	Rainer Salzgeber	AUT	2:52.87
6.	Norman Berganelli	ITA	2:53.12
7.	Lasse Kjus	NOR	2:53.23
8.	Bernhard Gstrein	AUT	2:53.35

Christian Mayer recorded the fastest time of the first run, followed by Urs Kälin and Markus Wasmeier. Six days earlier Wasmeier had won his specialty, the super giant slalom, providing a happy ending to the 30-year-old's long career. Having achieved his goal, he found himself unusually relaxed for the giant slalom, an event he had not won in any competition for nine years. His second run was even better than his first. Kälin stopped the clock only two one-hundredths of a second slower than Wasmeier—tying Barbara Cochran's 1972 slalom victory as the slimmest winning margin in Olympic alpine history.

SUPER GIANT SLALOM

The Super G, first held in 1981 and first included in the World Cup in 1983, is an attempt to combine the speed of the downhill with the technical skills of the giant slalom. Like the downhill, it is decided on the basis of a single run.

1924–1984 not held

1988 Calgary-Nakiska C: 94, N: 34, D: 2.21.

1.	Franck Piccard	FRA	1:39.66
2.	Helmut Mayer	AUT	1:40.96
3.	Lars-Börje Eriksson	SWE	1:41.08
4.	Hubert Strolz	AUT	1:41.11
5.	Günther Mader	AUT	1:41.96
5.	Pirmin Zurbriggen	SWI	1:41.96
7.	Luc Alphand	FRA	1:42.27
8.	Leonhard Stock	AUT	1:42.36

Franck Piccard, a 23-year-old from Albertville, the hub of the 1992 Winter Games, had never won a World Cup race. He had, however, picked up a bronze medal in the downhill six days before the Super G. When he reached the end of the latter race, he felt he had blown it. "I was really angry with myself," he said. But one by one he watched the favorites fall or at least commit worse mistakes than he had, and before he knew it, he had earned France's first alpine gold in twenty years. Piccard was named after Frank Sinatra, who sent him a congratulatory telegram after he won the gold medal.

1992 Albertville-Val d'Isère C: 118, N: 43, D: 2.16.

1.	Kjetil André Aamodt	NOR	1:13.04
2.	Marc Girardelli	LUX	1:13.77
3.	Jan Einar Thorsen	NOR	1:13.83
4.	Ole Kristian Furuseth	NOR	1:13.87
5.	Josef Polig	ITA	1:13.88
6.	Marco Hangl	SWI	1:13.90
7.	Günther Mader	AUT	1:14.08
8.	Tom Stiansen	NOR	1:14.51

In 1990, Kjetil André Aamodt finished first or second in all five events at the junior world championships. In 1991 he moved up to the senior division and earned a Super G silver medal at the world championships. But on November 4, 1991, Aamodt was hospitalized with mononucleosis. He was so ill that he lost 11 kilograms (24 lbs.) and had to be drip-fed. Despite being told that he wouldn't be able to ski again for six months, the 20-year-old Aamodt recovered quickly and returned to training on January 4. Six weeks later he became Norway's first Olympic alpine medalist since Stein Eriksen in 1952. It was also a happy day for Marc Girardelli, who until then was the greatest skier never to have won an Olympic medal.

1994 Lillehammer-Kvitfjell C: 69, N: 28, D: 2.17.

1.	Markus Wasmeier	GER	1:32.53
2.	Tommy Moe	USA	1:32.61
3.	Kjetil André Aamodt	NOR	1:32.93
4.	Marc Girardelli	LUX	1:33.07
5.	Werner Perathoner	ITA	1:33.10
6.	Atle Skårdal	NOR	1:33.31
7.	Jan Einar Thorsen	NOR	1:33.37
8.	Luc Alphand	FRA	1:33.39

Before the Lillehammer Olympics, German ski trainer Sylvester Neidhardt announced that if Markus Wasmeier won a gold medal, Neidhardt would shave off his shoulder-length blond hair. It didn't appear to be much of a gamble on Neidhardt's part. For one thing, only one German man had ever won an alpine gold medal—and that was back in 1936. In addition, Wasmeier himself had not won a major race since the 1985 world championships. Two days before the men's super G, Wasmeier ran into Diane Roffe-Steinrotter, who had just won the women's super G after a similar nine-year drought following her own 1985 world championship victory. "You can win the super G too," she told him. Wasmeier laughed. "It was just a joke," he thought.

But on a day when the good-spirited crowd sang "Happy Birthday" to Norwegian skier Atle Skårdal and honorary Norwegian Tommy Moe, Markus Wasmeier skied the race of his life and did earn the gold medal. In fact, he won another one six days later in the giant slalom.

Wasmeier did not fit the wildman stereotype of Olympic alpine champions. A married man, when the Lillehammer Olympic Organizing Committee asked him to list his hobbies, Wasmeier wrote, "family." He also restored old paintings in his spare time and played Mozart on his viola and zither.

ALPINE COMBINED

This event combines one downhill run and, another day, two slalom runs. Since 1994 final results have been determined by adding the times from the three runs. Prior to 1994, points for each half of the competition were determined by computing the percentage difference between the racer and the leader and then multiplying by a fixed number. In the 1992 combined slalom, for example, that number was 570. Thus, if skier A won the downhill and skier B's time was one percent slower, skier A's score for the downhill would be 0 and skier B's would be 5.70. The scores for the downhill and slalom were added to create the final score.

1924–1932 not held

1936 Garmisch-Partenkirchen C: 66, N: 21, D: 2.9.

			DOWNHILL	SLALOM	PTS.
1.	Franz Pfnür	GER	4:51.8 (2)	2:26.6 (1)	99.25
2.	Gustav Lantschner	GER	4:58.2 (3)	2:32.5 (2)	96.26
3.	Emile Allais	FRA	4:58.8 (4)	2:37.3 (3)	94.69
4.	Birger Ruud	NOR	4:47.4 (1)	2:49.0 (6)	93.38
5.	Roman Wörndle	GER	5:01.2 (6)	2:47.7 (5)	91.16
6.	Rudolf Cranz	GER	5:04.0 (8)	2:47.5 (4)	91.03
7.	Giacinto Sertorelli	ITA	5:05.0 (9)	2:49.4 (7)	90.39
8.	Alf Konningen	NOR	5:00.4 (5)	2:53.6 (9)	90.06

Franz Pfnür, a 27-year-old woodcarver and cabinetmaker from Bavaria, was second to Birger Ruud in the downhill and first in both runs of the slalom. Silver medalist Gustav "Guzzi" Lantschner was described by Albion Ross of the *New York Times* as "a violent Nazi." Born and raised in Innsbruck, Austria, Lantschner moved to Germany and became a cameraman for the Nazi party. Resat Erçes of Turkey showed great patience when he completed the downhill course in 22:44.4—18 minutes slower than Birger Ruud. But, then again, Ruud, a versatile athlete who won the ski jump gold in both 1932 and 1936, had an advantage over Erçes, as well as all the other athletes. Although there was no telephone communication between the start and finish, Ruud knew that the local tram company had its own line connected to the top station a quarter mile from the starting gate. While all the other skiers were waxing their skis for the cold weather appropriate to the gloomy conditions at the top of the two-mile run, Ruud went down to the phone and learned from a friend that the sun had broken through at the bottom of the course and that the snow was turning soft. He changed his wax and outraced the field by 4.4 seconds.

In 1936, skiers were penalized six seconds for each gate missed during the slalom competition rather than being disqualified. Ruud and Wörndle each lost six seconds, while Cranz lost 12.

1948 St. Moritz C: 78, N: 24, D: 2.4.

			DOWNHILL	SLALOM	PTS.
1.	Henri Oreiller	FRA	2:55.0 (1)	2:22.3 (5)	3.27
2.	Karl Molitor	SWI	3:00.3 (2)	2:22.5 (6)	6.44
3.	James Couttet	FRA	3:07.3 (8)	2:14.9 (1)	6.95
4.	Edi Mall	AUT	3:09.3 (13)	2:16.0 (2)	8.54
5.	Silvio Alverà	ITA	3:02.4 (3)	2:24.9 (11)	8.71
6.	Hans Hansson	SWE	3:05.0 (6)	2:23.5 (9)	9.31
7.	Vittorio Chierroni	ITA	3:10.0 (15)	2:18.1 (3)	9.69
8.	Hans Nogler	AUT	3:03.2 (5)	2:27.0 (14)	9.96

1952–1984 not held

1988 Calgary-Nakiska C: 56, N: 20, D: 2.17.

			DOWNHILL		SLALOM		PTS.
1.	Hubert Strolz	AUT	1:48.51	(5)	1:27.31	(7)	36.55
2.	Bernhard Gstrein	AUT	1:50.20	(15)	1:25.82	(3)	43.45
3.	Paul Accola	SWI	1:51.27	(24)	1:24.93	(1)	48.24
4.	Luc Alphand	FRA	1:49.60	(13)	1:28.47	(10)	57.73
5.	Peter Jurko	CZE	1:50.29	(19)	1:27.61	(8)	58.56
6.	Jean-Luc Cretier	FRA	1:50.04	(14)	1:28.52	(11)	62.98
7.	Markus Wasmeier	GER	1:49.32	(8)	1:29.84	(13)	65.44
8.	Adrian Bíreš	CZE	1:50.24	(16)	1:28.94	(12)	68.50

Pirmin Zurbriggen recorded the fastest time in the downhill and led by over two seconds after the first run of the slalom. He seemed well on his way to his second gold of the Calgary Games when he hooked a tip on the 39th of 57 gates on the second slalom run, ran right into the 40th gate, spun around, and landed on his back. Hubert Strolz, a 25-year-old policeman and a good friend of Zurbriggen's, was the immediate beneficiary of the Swiss star's mistake.

Paul Accola took the bronze despite placing only twenty-fourth in the downhill. He did record the best combined time in the slalom. Only 26 of the 56 starters completed all three runs.

1992 Albertville-Val d'Isère C: 66, N: 27, D: 2.11.

			DOWNHILL		SLALOM		PTS.
1.	Josef Polig	ITA	1:45.78	(6)	1:42.16	(5)	14.58
2.	Gianfranco Martin	ITA	1:45.48	(2)	1:42.76	(7)	14.90
3.	Steve Locher	SWI	1:46.53	(12)	1:41.44	(2)	18.16
4.	Jean-Luc Cretier	FRA	1:46.25	(9)	1:42.09	(4)	18.97
5.	Markus Wasmeier	GER	1:45.91	(7)	1:45.15	(13)	32.77
6.	Kristian Ghedina	ITA	1:46.65	(15)	1:44.91	(11)	38.96
7.	Ole Kristian Furuseth	NOR	1:48.94	(33)	1:41.04	(1)	40.47
8.	Xavier Gigandet	SWI	1:45.61	(4)	1:47.19	(15)	41.21

The favorites were Paul Accola, who had won all three pre-Olympic alpine combined competitions, and Marc Girardelli, the 1991 World Cup leader. The downhill portion of the event was delayed 2¼ hours to allow course workers to prepare the piste after a night of heavy snowfall. The first competitor, Girardelli, fell spectacularly. After the twelfth skier, there was another delay while race officials considered canceling the run. After they decided to go ahead, Accola got in a cautious but solid run that left him in fifth place by day's end. Because the four skiers ahead of him were considered weak at the slalom, it looked like the gold medal was Accola's for the taking. But the next day he missed a gate almost immediately. He climbed back and completed the run, but the precious seconds that he lost put him out of contention. Accola was so disgusted that he finished the second run facing backward and buried his race bib in the snow.

Meanwhile, defending champion Hubert Strolz, after placing thirteenth in the downhill, crushed the field on the first slalom run and found himself poised to make history by becoming the first repeat winner of an alpine event. But barely 100 feet from victory in the final run, he lost his balance, missed a gate, and was disqualified. "I was already at the finish in my thoughts," he explained sheepishly. Suddenly the gold medal was up for grabs. When the computer spit out the results, the winner turned out to be unheralded 23-year-old Josef Polig, who had never before placed higher than fifth in a World Cup event. The silver medal went to his even-less-heralded Italian teammate Gianfranco Martin.

In a weird footnote to the event, the French team formally protested the results on the basis that the logos on the racing suits of the Italian team exceeded the Olympic-approved maximum of 50 square centimeters. They were right, but the French, having made their point, withdrew their protest.

1994 Lillehammer-Kvitfjell, Hafjell C: 56, N: 27, D: 2.25.

		DOWNHILL		SLALOM		TOTAL
1.	Lasse Kjus	NOR	1:36.95	(1)	1:40.58	(7)	3:17.53
2.	Kjetil André Aamodt	NOR	1:37.49	(6)	1:41.06	(9)	3:18.55
3.	Harald Christian Strand Nilsen	NOR	1:39.05	(21)	1:40.09	(4)	3:19.14
4.	Günther Mader	AUT	1:38.46	(13)	1:40.77	(8)	3:19.23
5.	Tommy Moe	USA	1:37.14	(3)	1:42.27	(15)	3:19.41
6.	Paul Accola	SWI	1:39.41	(24)	1:40.03	(3)	3:19.44
7.	Mitja Kunc	SLO	1:40.01	(27)	1:39.54	(2)	3:19.55
8.	Fredrik Nyberg	SWE	1:38.40	(11)	1:41.90	(13)	3:20.30

In 1991 Lasse Kjus crashed during a training run, severing the nerve to his deltoid muscle. He was only able to regain use of his left arm by training surrounding muscles to do the work that the deltoid could no longer do. Kjus and his best friend, Kjetil André Aamodt, finished one-two at the 1993 world championships. In January's two pre-Olympic World Cup combined events, the two traded first and seecond place. At the Olympics, Kjus led after the downhill, with Americans Kyle Rasmussen and Tommy Moe in second and third. Aamodt was well-placed in sixth. The slalom portion of the event was held eleven days after the downhill. Kjus maintained his lead through both slalom runs. Aamodt moved into second place after the first slalom, while Nilsen brought joy to the hometown crowd by leapfrogging from twenty-first to sixth to third to give Norway the first home country Winter Olympics sweep since the Japanese victory in the 1972 normal hill ski jump. Aamodt became the first alpine skier to win five medals, beating Vreni Schneider by one day and Alberto Tomba by two.

ALPINE SKIING

WOMEN
Downhill
Slalom
Giant Slalom
Super Giant Slalom
Alpine Combined

WOMEN

DOWNHILL
Of the 13 gold medals awarded in this event, all but one have been earned by Austria, Switzerland and Germany. Of the 26 gold *and* silver medals, 23 have gone to Austria (8), Switzerland (7), Germany (5) and the United States (3).

1924–1936 not held

1948 St. Moritz C: 37, N: 11, D: 2.2.
1.	Hedy Schlunegger	SWI	2:28.3
2.	Trude Beiser	AUT	2:29.1
3.	Resi Hammer	AUT	2:30.2
4.	Celina Seghi	ITA	2:31.1
5.	Lina Mittner	SWI	2:31.2
6.	Suzanne Thiollière	FRA	2:31.4
7.	Françoise Gignoux	FRA	2:32.4
7.	Laila Schou Nilsen	NOR	2:32.4

1952 Oslo-Norefjell C: 42, N: 13, D: 2.17.
1.	Trude Jochum-Beiser	AUT	1:47.1
2.	Annemarie Buchner	GER	1:48.0
3.	Giuliana Minuzzo	ITA	1:49.0
4.	Erika Mahringer	AUT	1:49.5
5.	Dagmar Rom	AUT	1:49.8
6.	Madeleine Berthod	SWI	1:50.7
7.	Margit Hvammen	NOR	1:50.9
8.	Joanne Hewson	CAN	1:51.3

1956 Cortina C: 47, N: 16, D: 2.1.
1.	Madeleine Berthod	SWI	1:40.7
2.	Frieda Dänzer	SWI	1:45.4
3.	Lucile Wheeler	CAN	1:45.9
4.	Giuliana Chenal-Minuzzo	ITA	1:47.3
4.	Hilde Hofherr	AUT	1:47.3
6.	Carla Marchelli	ITA	1:47.7
7.	Dorothea Hochleitner	AUT	1:47.9
8.	Josette Neviere	FRA	1:49.2

Madeleine Berthod, the favorite in the event, celebrated her 25th birthday the day she won the downhill gold medal. Her margin of victory was four times larger than any other winner's in this event.

1960 Squaw Valley C: 42, N: 14, D: 2.20.

1. Heidi Biebl	GER	1:37.6
2. Penelope Pitou	USA	1:38.6
3. Traudl Hecher	AUT	1:38.9
4. Pia Riva	ITA	1:39.9
5. Jerta Schir	ITA	1:40.5
6. Anneliese Meggl	GER	1:40.8
7. Sonja Peril	GER	1:41.0
8. Erika Netzer	AUT	1:41.1

As a first-year student in high school, Penny Pitou made the boys' varsity ski team and finished fifth in the New Hampshire state slalom championship before being banned from further competition by the local school board. At the age of 15 she qualified for the U.S. Olympic team, finishing 31st, 34th, and 34th. Four years later she was the favorite at Squaw Valley, but the pressure on her was great. "The predictions that I'm going to win make me nervous," she said. "America is putting its hopes on me and it's a terrible feeling. . . . I'd be much happier being a normal girl, sitting at home or going to school." A near-fall three gates from the finish cost her about two seconds and the gold medal. Later she was married for a few years to Austrian downhill gold medalist Egon Zimmermann. And later still she became New Hampshire's first female bank director.

1964 Innsbruck C: 43, N: 15, D: 2.6.

1. Christl Haas	AUT	1:55.39
2. Edith Zimmermann	AUT	1:56.42
3. Traudl Hecher	AUT	1:56.66
4. Heidi Biebl	GER	1:57.87
5. Barbara Henneberger	GER	1:58.03
6. Madeleine Bochatay	FRA	1:59.11
7. Nancy Greene	CAN	1:59.23
8. Christine Terraillon	FRA	1:59.66

When she was three years old, Christl Haas told her parents that she wanted to become a ski racer. Seventeen years later the 5-foot 10-inch Haas, skiing in the 13th position, had no trouble living up to her role of an Austrian favorite competing in Austria.

1968 Grenoble-Chamrousse C: 39, N: 14, D: 2.10.

1. Olga Pall	AUT	1:40.87
2. Isabelle Mir	FRA	1:41.33
3. Christl Haas	AUT	1:41.41
4. Brigitte Seiwald	AUT	1:41.82
5. Annie Famose	FRA	1:42.15
6. Felicity Field	GBR	1:42.79
7. Fernande Bochatay	SWI	1:42.87
8. Marielle Goitschel	FRA	1:42.95

The Austrians went 1, 3, 4 despite the absence of one of their leading performers: 1966 world champion Erica Schinegger. During routine medical testing prior to the Grenoble Games, doctors were surprised to discover that the saliva of the 20-year-old ski star contained only male hormones. Further examination revealed that Schinegger, who was raised as a girl, actually had male sex organs which had grown inside instead of outside. Schinegger eventually underwent corrective surgery, changed his name to Eric, married and became a father. In 1988, he handed over his world championship gold medal to second-place finisher Marielle Goitschel, although it took the International Ski Federation another eight years to officially change the results.

1972 Sapporo-Eniwadake C: 41, N: 13, D: 2.5.

1.	Marie-Theres Nadig	SWI	1:36.68
2.	Annemarie Pröll	AUT	1:37.00
3.	Susan Corrock	USA	1:37.68
4.	Isabelle Mir	FRA	1:38.62
5.	Rosi Speiser	GER	1:39.10
6.	Rosi Mittermaier	GER	1:39.32
7.	Bernadette Zurbriggen	SWI	1:39.49
8.	Annie Famose	FRA	1:39.70

The first noteworthy time was 1:38.62, registered by the eighth skier, Isabelle Mir. Next on the course was French heroine Annie Famose, who was having an exhausting time defending her eligibility from accusations of "commercialism" by the International Ski Federation. Famose finished in eighth place. The tenth skier, unheralded Susan Corrock of Ketchum, Idaho, surprised the experts by taking the lead in 1:37.68. Three skiers later came an even bigger surprise. Seventeen-year-old Marie-Theres Nadig of Flums, Switzerland, who had never won a World Cup race, beat Corrock's time by exactly one second. The 15th skier was the pre-Olympic favorite, 18-year-old Annemarie Pröll. The previous year she had become the youngest-ever overall winner of the World Cup. Pröll skied an excellent race, but finished one third of a second slower than Nadig. Disappointed and angry, she refused to attend the postrace press conference.

According to *Ski* magazine, after her victory Marie-Theres Nadig told the following story to her coach: "I was on the last flat stretch that leads into the steep wall before the finish, when I thought suddenly of a film [*The Love Bug*] I had seen last summer. It was about a funny little car that dreamed of racing in the Grand Prix. The little car was called Herbie. In each race it would start ahead of the other champions who would chase it. Suddenly I saw myself in the role of Herbie. I was being chased by hordes of other racers. A voice inside me said, 'Go, Herbie, go, go, go.' At each 'go,' I would lower my body still further to cut the wind resistance. In my whole life I never skied in such a low crouch. I could easily have fallen. But inside me, I always heard the voice crying out, 'Go, Herbie, go.' "

1976 Innsbruck C: 38, N: 15, D: 2.8.

1.	Rosi Mittermaier	GER	1:46.16
2.	Brigitte Totschnigg	AUT	1:46.68
3.	Cynthia Nelson	USA	1:47.50
4.	Nicola-Andrea Spiess	AUT	1:47.71
5.	Danielle Debernard	FRA	1:48.48
6.	Jacqueline Rouvier	FRA	1:48.58
7.	Bernadette Zurbriggen	SWI	1:48.62
8.	Marlies Oberholzer	SWI	1:48.68

Rosi Mittermaier had never before won a major downhill race, even though she was competing in her tenth World Cup season and her third Olympics.

1980 Lake Placid C: 28, N: 13, D: 2.17.

1.	Annemarie Moser-Pröll	AUT	1:37.52
2.	Hanni Wenzel	LIE	1:38.22

3.	Marie-Theres Nadig	SWI	1:38.36
4.	Heidi Preuss	USA	1:39.51
5.	Kathy Kreiner	CAN	1:39.53
6.	Ingrid Eberle	AUT	1:39.63
7.	Torill Fjeldstad	NOR	1:39.69
7.	Cynthia Nelson	USA	1:39.69

Winning two Olympic silver medals would probably be a dream come true for most skiers, but when Annemarie Pröll won two silvers at Sapporo in 1972, losing both times to Marie-Theres Nadig, she considered it a failure and a humiliation. She was back to her winning ways before long, but in March 1975, after marrying ski salesman Herbert Moser, she retired from competitive skiing and bypassed the 1976 Olympics. After her father died later that year, Annemarie Pröll returned to the circuit. By 1979 she had won six of the last nine annual World Cups and finished second twice. However, the 1980 season had seen her win only one downhill race to Nadig's six. Motivated by the only achievement that had eluded her, Moser-Pröll, the sixth skier, sped down the course on Whiteface Mountain in 1:37.52. Her time withstood the onslaughts of Nadig and Wenzel and earned her the final jewel in her champion's crown. Moser-Pröll holds the record for most World Cup victories by a woman: 62, including 36 downhills.

1984 Sarajevo C: 32, N: 13, D: 2.16.

1.	Michela Figini	SWI	1:13.36
2.	Maria Walliser	SWI	1:13.41
3.	Olga Charvátová	CZE	1:13.53
4.	Ariane Ehrat	SWI	1:13.95
5.	Jana Gantnerová	CZE	1:14.14
6.	Marina Kiehl	GER	1:14.30
6.	Gerry Sorensen	CAN	1:14.30
8.	Lea Sölkner	AUT	1:14.39

Michela Figini scored her first World Cup victory only two weeks before the Olympics. At Sarajevo she recorded the fastest time in three of the five practice runs and was leading the real race on February 15th when it was cancelled because of fog. The next day she confirmed her new consistency by becoming, at age 17, the youngest skier ever to win an Olympic gold medal.

1988 Calgary-Nakiska C: 35, N: 14, D: 2.19.

1.	Marina Kiehl	GER	1:25.86
2.	Brigitte Oertli	SWI	1:26.61
3.	Karen Percy	CAN	1:26.62
4.	Maria Walliser	SWI	1:26.89
5.	Laurie Graham	CAN	1:26.99
6.	Petra Kronberger	AUT	1:27.03
7.	Regine Mösenlechner	GER	1:27.16
8.	Elisabeth Kirchler	AUT	1:27.19

Marina Kiehl, a 23-year-old millionaire's daughter from Munich, had a reputation for having a lofty and generally unpleasant personality. Her manager and her sponsors finally convinced her to control her sharp tongue and to make an effort to be friendly to those around her. Kiehl succeeded in making herself more likable, but her race results declined dramatically. Things got so bad that a popular German sports writer urged her, in print, to "go ahead and be rude again, because when you are bad you are better." When German Olympic officials threatened to drop her from the roster for the Super G, her best event, Kiehl exploded at them, much to the relief of her fans. A deal was worked out: if Kiehl finished in the top six of the downhill, she could also take part in the Super G. If she failed, she would be bumped from the starting lineup.

In seven years on the World Cup circuit, Kiehl had never won a downhill race. In Calgary she had a wild run, almost falling twice. "I was out of control up there," she explained afterward, "so I just let the skis go faster and faster." Because she had twice lost races to unheralded, late-starting skiers, Kiehl refused to celebrate her victory until the final Argentinian had skied off the course. Three days later Kiehl competed in the Super G—and finished in a tie for twelfth place.

1992 Albertville-Méribel C: 30, N: 12, D: 2.15.

1.	Kerrin Lee-Gartner	CAN	1:52.55
2.	Hilary Lindh	USA	1:52.61
3.	Veronika Wallinger	AUT	1:52.64
4.	Katja Seizinger	GER	1:52.67
5.	Petra Kronberger	AUT	1:52.73
6.	Katharina Gutensohn	GER	1:53.71
7.	Barbara Sadleder	AUT	1:53.81
8.	Svetlana Gladicheva	SOV/RUS	1:53.85

The course, designed by Bernhard Russi, was universally acknowledged to be the most difficult women's course ever. At 2770 meters (1⅔ miles) it was also the longest and, with a vertical drop of 828 meters, the steepest. In addition, an impending snowstorm prompted race officials to move up the start of the contest and to send the racers down the slope at shorter-than-usual intervals. Intermittent fog made the course more challenging for some than for others.

Kerrin Lee-Gartner grew up in Rossland, British Columbia, five doors down from the parents of 1968 giant slalom medalist Nancy Greene. In 1990 Lee-Gartner had a dream in which she heard an announcer say, "*Médaille d'or,* Kerrin Lee-Gartner, Canada." She didn't speak French, but she knew enough of the language to know that "*médaille d'or*" meant "gold medal." It seemed as much a fantasy as a dream since ten years of World Cup races had earned her only a single third-place finish. Although she had placed eighth in the Calgary combined, she had finished only fifteenth in the downhill.

But some dreams do come true. In Méribel, Lee-Gartner had the race of her life and really did get to hear an announcer say, "*Médaille d'or,* Kerrin Lee-Gartner, Canada." She is the only winner of the women's downhill to have come from a non-German-speaking country. The silver medalist was also an outsider: Hilary Lindh of Juneau, Alaska, whose best placing in a World Cup event had been a sixth in 1989. The 1992 women's downhill was by far the tightest women's alpine race in Olympic history. Only eighteen one-hundredths of a second separated Lee-Gartner in first from Petra Kronberger in fifth.

1994 Lillehammer-Kvitfjell C: 48, N: 19, D: 2.19.

1.	Katja Seizinger	GER	1:35.93
2.	Picabo Street	USA	1:36.59
3.	Isolde Kostner	ITA	1:36.85
4.	Marina Ertl	GER	1:37.10
5.	Catherine Pace	CAN	1:37.17
6.	Mélanie Suchet	FRA	1:37.34
7.	Hilary Lindh	USA	1:37.44
8.	Varvara Zelenskaya	RUS	1:37.48

Originally the women's downhill was scheduled for the slalom hill at Hafjell, but the leading skiers from Germany, Austria, Switzerland and France protested that the course was too flat. To their credit, the Lillehammer organizers listened to the skiers' arguments, decided they were right, and moved the downhill to the men's course at Kvitfjell, but with a lower starting gate.

Exactly three weeks before the Olympic race, the downhill world was shocked and sobered when Ulrike Maier of Austria, fifth overall in the 1992–1993 World Cup, was killed during a downhill race in Garmisch-Partenkirchen.

Under this cloud, the Olympic championship was won by the favorite, 21-year-old Katja Seizinger. Seizinger was an oddity in German skiing because she was not from the mountains of Bavaria, but from the industrial Ruhr region of northern Germany. Her father was a steel executive and Seizinger learned to ski during vacations in the Savoy region of France, home of the 1992 Winter Olympics. She won the World Cup downhill for the 1992–1993 season and the 1993–1994 Olympic season before being supplanted by Lillehammer silver medalist Picabo (PEEK-a-boo) Street, who was born in the appropriately-named Triumph, Idaho.

SLALOM

1924–1936 not held

1948 St. Moritz C: 28, N: 10, D: 2.5.

1.	Gretchen Fraser	USA	1:57.2
2.	Antoinette Meyer	SWI	1:57.7
3.	Erika Mahringer	AUT	1:58.0
4.	Georgette Miller-Thiollière	FRA	1:58.8
5.	Renée Clerc	SWI	2:05.8
6.	Anneliese Schuh-Proxauf	AUT	2:06.7
7.	Rese Hammerer	AUT	2:08.6
8.	Andrea Mead	USA	2:08.8

Gretchen Fraser of Vancouver, Washington, had qualified for the U.S. team for the 1940 Olympics that were never held. Eight years later she was considered an unknown quantity. Skiing in the first position she clocked the fastest time of the first run—59.7. Erika Mahringer was one-tenth of a second behind her. As Fraser prepared to lead off the second round, a problem suddenly developed in the telephone timing system between the top and the bottom of the hill. Despite a 17-minute delay at such a critical time, Fraser finished the second run in 57.5, a time beaten only by Antoinette Meyer (57.0.)

1952 Oslo C: 40, N: 14, D: 2.20.

1.	Andrea Mead Lawrence	USA	2:10.6
2.	Ossi Reichert	GER	2:11.4
3.	Annemarie Buchner	GER	2:13.3
4.	Celina Seghi	ITA	2:13.8
5.	Imogene Anna Opton	USA	2:14.1
6.	Madeleine Berthod	SWI	2:14.9
7.	Agnel Marysette	FRA	2:15.6
8.	Trude Jochum-Beiser	AUT	2:15.9
8.	Giuliana Minuzzo	ITA	2:15.9

Nineteen-year-old Andrea Mead Lawrence of Rutland, Vermont, fell early in her first run, but got up, and showed her superiority by finishing the course with the fourth best time. She overhauled the leaders with a second run that was two seconds faster than anyone else's. Lawrence became the first American skier to win two gold medals. By the time of the opening of the 1956 Games, she had given birth to three children.

1956 Cortina C: 48, N: 16, D: 1.30.

1.	Renée Colliard	SWI	1:52.3
2.	Regina Schöpf	AUT	1:55.4
3.	Yevgenya Sidorova	SOV/RUS	1:56.7
4.	Giuliana Chenal-Minuzzo	ITA	1:56.8
5.	Josefine Frandl	AUT	1:57.9
6.	Inger Björnbakken	NOR	1:58.0
6.	Astrid Sandvik	NOR	1:58.0
8.	Josette Neviere	FRA	1:58.3

Renée Colliard, a pharmacy student from Geneva, was making her first appearance as a member of the Swiss team. Racing in the number-one position, she registered the fastest time in each run.

1960 Squaw Valley C: 43, N: 14, D: 2.26.

1.	Anne Heggtveit	CAN	1:49.6
2.	Betsy Snite	USA	1:52.9
3.	Barbara Henneberger	GER	1:56.6
4.	Thérèse Leduc	FRA	1:57.4
5.	Hilde Hofherr	AUT	1:58.0
5.	Liselotte Michel	SWI	1:58.0
7.	Stalian Korzukhina	SOV/RUS	1:58.4
8.	Sonja Sperl	GER	1:58.8

Bronze medalist Barbara Henneberger was killed by an avalanche while filming a movie in St. Moritz on April 12, 1964.

1964 Innsbruck C: 48, N: 16, D: 2.1.

1.	Christine Goitschel	FRA	1:29.86
2.	Marielle Goitschel	FRA	1:30.77
3.	Jean Saubert	USA	1:31.36
4.	Heidi Biebl	GER	1:34.04
5.	Edith Zimmermann	AUT	1:34.27
6.	Christl Haas	AUT	1:35.11
7.	Liv Jagge	NOR	1:36.38
8.	Patricia du Roy de Blicquy	BEL	1:37.01

Christine and Marielle Goitschel, teenaged sisters from Val d'Isère, the home of Jean-Claude Killy, were the stars of the 1964 ski contests. Marielle, the favorite, had the fastest time of the first run, 43.09, with her older sister, Christine, in second place at 43.85. Christine prevailed in the second round, giving the Goitschels a one-two finish. That same day, back in France, their younger sister, Patricia, won a National Junior title.

1968 Grenoble-Chamrousse C: 49, N: 18, D: 2.13.

1.	Marielle Goitschel	FRA	1:25.86
2.	Nancy Greene	CAN	1:26.15
3.	Annie Famose	FRA	1:27.89
4.	Georgina Hathorn	GBR	1:27.92
5.	Isabelle Mir	FRA	1:28.22
6.	Burgl Färbinger	GER	1:28.90
7.	Glorianda Cipolla	ITA	1:29.74
8.	Bernadette Rauter	AUT	1:30.44

Sixteen-year-old Judy Nagel of Enumclaw, Washington, was the surprise leader of the first run, but she fell at the beginning of her second run. Although she finished the course, she was disqualified for missing a gate.

1972 Sapporo-Teineyama C: 42, N: 13, D: 2.11.

1.	Barbara Cochran	USA	1:31.24
2.	Danièlle Debernard	FRA	1:31.26
3.	Florence Steurer	FRA	1:32.69
4.	Judy Crawford	CAN	1:33.95
5.	Annemarie Pröll	AUT	1:34.03
6.	Pamela Behr	GER	1:34.27
7.	Monika Kaserer	AUT	1:34.36
8.	Patricia Boydstun	USA	1:35.59

Back home in Richmond, Vermont, Barbara Cochran's father had taught his talented children how to save a tenth of a second by setting their bodies in motion before pushing open the starting wand that sets off the timing mechanism. That one-tenth second turned out to be the difference between gold and silver for Barbara Cochran. Her time for the first run was three one-hundredths of a second faster than Danièlle Debernard. In the final run Debernard was able to pick up only one of the three-hundredths of a second. Only 19 of 42 starters made it through both runs without falling or missing a gate. Cochran's brother, Robert, and her sister, Marilyn, also competed at the 1972 Olympics. Her youngest sister, Linda, placed sixth in the 1976 slalom.

1976 Innsbruck C: 42, N: 14, D: 2.11.

1.	Rosi Mittermaier	GER	1:30.54
2.	Claudia Giordani	ITA	1:30.87
3.	Hanni Wenzel	LIE	1:32.20
4.	Danièlle Debernard	FRA	1:32.24
5.	Pamela Behr	GER	1:32.31
6.	Linda Cochran	USA	1:33.24
7.	Christa Zechmeister	GER	1:33.72
8.	Wanda Bieter	ITA	1:35.66

For the second straight time, 42 women started the Olympic slalom, but only 19 finished both courses without missing a gate. Rosi Mittermaier recorded the fastest time of the second run after trailing teammate Pamela Behr by nine-hundredths of a second after the first run. Mittermaier had already won the downhill race three days earlier.

1980 Lake Placid C: 47, N: 21, D: 2.23.

1.	Hanni Wenzel	LIE	1:25.09
2.	Christa Kinshofer	GER	1:26.50
3.	Erika Hess	SWI	1:27.89
4.	Mariarosa Quario	ITA	1:27.92
5.	Claudia Giordani	ITA	1:29.12
6.	Nadezhda Patrakeyeva	SOV/RUS	1:29.20
7.	Daniela Zini	ITA	1:29.22
8.	Christin Cooper	USA	1:29.28

German-born Hanni Wenzel moved to tiny Liechtenstein (population 25,000) when she was one year old. She was granted Liechtenstein citizenship after winning the slalom at the 1974 world championships in St. Moritz. Having already finished second in the downhill and first in the giant slalom at the 1980 Olympics, Wenzel breezed through the slalom, registering the best time in both the first and second runs. By earning two gold medals and one silver in one Olympics, she matched the 1976 feat of Rosi Mittermaier. Hanni's brother, Andreas, won the silver medal in the downhill, to give Liechtenstein four medals at the Lake Placid Games, one for every 6250 people. If the U.S. had won the same number of medals per capita it would have won 36,000 medals. Actually there were only 114 medals awarded.

Winner of the 1980 slalom and giant slalom, Hanni Wenzel was the first-ever Olympic gold medalist from the tiny nation of Liechtenstein.

1984 Sarajevo C: 45, N: 19, D: 2.17.

1.	Paoletta Magoni	ITA	1:36.47
2.	Perrine Pelen	FRA	1:37.38
3.	Ursula Konzett	LIE	1:37.50
4.	Roswitha Steiner	AUT	1:37.84
5.	Erika Hess	SWI	1:37.91
6.	Malgorzata Tlalka	POL	1:37.95
7.	Maria Rosa Quario	ITA	1:37.99
8.	Anni Kronbichler	AUT	1:38.05

The first run leader was unheralded Christelle Guignard of France; however, she missed a turn on the top half of the second run and failed to finish. In fact, only 21 of the 45 starters completed both runs without missing a gate. The winner was 19-year-old Paoletta Magoni, a bricklayer's daughter from Selvino who had never before finished better than sixth in a World Cup race.

1988 Calgary-Nakiska C: 57, N: 25, D: 2.26.

1.	Vreni Schneider	SWI	1:36.69
2.	Mateja Svet	YUG/SLO	1:38.37
3.	Christa Kinshofer-Güthlein	GER	1:38.40
4.	Roswitha Steiner	AUT	1:38.77
5.	Blanca Fernández Ochoa	SPA	1:39.44
6.	Ida Ladstätter	AUT	1:39.59
7.	Paoletta Magoni Sforza	ITA	1:39.76
8.	Dorota Tlalka-Mogore	FRA	1:39.86

Schneider, who had already won the giant slalom two days earlier, recorded the fastest time in both runs. Camilla Nilsson of Sweden trailed Schneider by only one one-hundredth of a second after the first run, but fell early in the second run and was eliminated. In 1988-89, Schneider won 14 World Cup events, breaking Ingemar Stenmark's 10-year-old season record of 13.

1992 Albertville-Méribel C: 63, N: 31, D: 2.20.

1.	Petra Kronberger	AUT	1:32.68
2.	Annelise Coberger	NZL	1:33.10
3.	Blanca Fernández Ochoa	SPA	1:33.35
4.	Julie Parisien	USA	1:33.40
5.	Karin Buder	AUT	1:33.68
6.	Patricia Chauvet	FRA	1:33.72
7.	Vreni Schneider	SWI	1:33.96
8.	Anne Berge	NOR	1:34.22

Julie Parisien, who had lost three teeth and fractured her wrist in separate accidents less than a month before the start of the Olympics, led the first run with a time of 48.22. Close behind were Blanca Fernández Ochoa at 48.25 and Petra Kronberger at 48.28. But Parisien faltered after the three-hour break between runs and recorded only the eighth-fastest time of the second run. Kronberger, who had won the combined event seven days earlier, did not falter. Coberger was the first athlete from the Southern Hemisphere to win a Winter Olympic medal. Competing in her fourth Olympics, Fernández Ochoa, whose brother Paco won the 1972 slalom, was the first Spanish woman to win an Olympic medal in either winter or summer.

1994 Lillehammer-Hafjell C: 55, N: 22, D: 2.26.

1.	Vreni Schneider	SWI	1:56.01
2.	Elfriede Eder	AUT	1:56.35
3.	Katja Koren	SLO	1:56.61
4.	Pernilla Wiberg	SWE	1:56.68
5.	Babriela Zingre	SWI	1:57.80
6.	Christine von Grünigen	SWI	1:57.86
7.	Robeta Serra	ITA	1:57.88
8.	Urška Hrovat	SLO	1:58.07

Vreni Schneider, a 29-year-old shoemaker's daughter from the small village of Elm in Glarus, had dominated the slalom since her victory at the 1988 Olympics. She won the World Cup in four of five years between 1989 and 1993 and the one year she didn't win (1991) she won the world championship instead. However, at the 1992 Olympics she had been hampered by a herniated disc and only finished seventh and at the 1993 world championships she went out on the first run. For this reason, some were predicting that the 1994 gold would go to Schneider's rival, Pernilla Wiberg. In the eight pre-Olympic World Cup slaloms, Schneider recorded five firsts and two seconds, Wiberg two firsts and four seconds. In Lillehammer, prior to the slalom, Wiberg won the combined event, with Schneider in second, while Schneider added a bronze in the giant slalom.

First out of the gate in the first run, Schneider skied a 59.68. Immediately after her, Wiberg stopped the clock at 59.05. It appeared that the morning run would end with Wiberg in first and Schneider in fourth, when 18-year-old Katja Koren, skiing out of the 33rd spot, suddenly came down the hill in 59.00.

In the afternoon Schneider attacked the second run with such intensity that she was almost a half second faster than all the other skiers. "I went so hard," she later explained, "that I was unprepared when the finish line came up. Before I knew it the race was over." Schneider was the first female alpine skier to win three gold medals and the first to win five total medals. Only 28 of the 55 starters completed both runs without falling or missing a gate.

GIANT SLALOM

1924–1948 not held

1952 Oslo-Norefjell C: 45, N: 15, D: 2.14.

1.	Andrea Mead Lawrence	USA	2:06.8
2.	Dagmar Rom	AUT	2:09.0
3.	Annemarie Buchner	GER	2:10.0
4.	Trude Klecker	AUT	2:11.4
5.	Katy Rodolph	USA	2:11.7
6.	Borghild Niskin	NOR	2:11.9
7.	Celina Seghi	ITA	2:12.5
8.	Ossi Reichert	GER	2:13.2

Silver medalist Dagmar Rom was a well-known Austrian film actress.

1956 Cortina C: 49, N: 16, D: 1.27.

1.	Ossi Reichert	GER	1:56.5
2.	Josefine Frandl	AUT	1:57.8
3.	Dorothea Hochleitner	AUT	1:58.2
4.	Madeleine Berthod	SWI	1:58.3
4.	Andrea Mead Lawrence	USA	1:58.3
6.	Lucile Wheeler	CAN	1:58.6
7.	Borghild Niskin	NOR	1:59.0
8.	Marysette Agnel	FRA	1:59.4

1960 Squaw Valley C: 44, N: 14, D: 2.23.

1.	Yvonne Rügg	SWI	1:39.9
2.	Penelope Pitou	USA	1:40.0
3.	Giuliana Chenal-Minuzzo	ITA	1:40.2
4.	Betsy Snite	USA	1:40.4
5.	Carla Marchelli	ITA	1:40.7
5.	Anneliese Meggl	GER	1:40.7
7.	Thérèse Leduc	FRA	1:40.8
8.	Anne-Marie Leduc	FRA	1:41.5

1964 Innsbruck C: 46, N: 15, D: 2.3.

1.	Marielle Goitschel	FRA	1:52.24
2.	Christine Goitschel	FRA	1:53.11
2.	Jean Saubert	USA	1:53.11
4.	Christl Haas	AUT	1:53.86
5.	Annie Famose	FRA	1:53.89
6.	Edith Zimmermann	AUT	1:54.21
7.	Barbara Henneberger	GER	1:54.26
8.	Traudl Hecher	AUT	1:54.55

On February 1, Christine Goitschel had won the slalom with her younger sister, Marielle, second and Jean Saubert third. Christine was the first of the three to go down the course of the giant slalom two days later. Her time of 1:53.11 looked good. Three skiers later Jean Saubert clocked the exact same time despite the introduction of timing to the hundredth of a second. When Marielle Goitschel, the 14th skier, heard that Saubert had equaled her sister's time, she attacked the course with extra determination and earned herself the gold medal.

After her victory, 18-year old Marielle announced to the press that she had just become engaged to a 20-year-old French skier by the name of Jean-Claude Killy, who had finished fifth in the giant slalom the day before. "I am happy and I am in love," she enthused. "This evening, on television, I will give him my first public kiss." While the more gullible reporters scurried away to spread the exciting news around the world, Marielle and Christine sat back and enjoyed their little hoax. When the press caught up with Killy, he smiled and spilled out the truth. "The joke of a tomboy," he said. "Marielle talks too much." It says a lot about the fully justified self-confidence of the Goitschel sisters that they had actually planned their practical joke the night before the race, on the assumption that one of them would win the gold medal.

1968 Grenoble-Chamrousse C: 47, N: 18, D: 2.15.

1.	Nancy Greene	CAN	1:51.97
2.	Annie Famose	FRA	1:54.61
3.	Fernande Bochatay	SWI	1:54.74
4.	Florence Steurer	FRA	1:54.75
5.	Olga Pall	AUT	1:55.61
6.	Isabelle Mir	FRA	1:56.07
7.	Marielle Goitschel	FRA	1:56.09
8.	Divina Galica	GBR	1:56.58

In 1967 Nancy Greene of Rossland, British Columbia, won the inaugural World Cup despite missing three of the nine meets. The following year she participated in her third Olympics. After finishing tenth in the downhill and second in the slalom, she realized that the giant slalom was her last chance to win a gold medal. The Canadian coaches brought her to the top of the slope 45 minutes early and suggested that they fill the time by eating a snack at a nearby restaurant. Over tea and rolls they became involved in a spirited discussion about ski politics. Suddenly one of the coaches realized that the race had already started. When they reached the start hut, the fifth skier, Annie Famose, was already in the gate. Green was number nine. In fact, the coaches had planned the whole thing so that Greene would be distracted from her nervousness. When it came her turn to start in the gate, she told herself, "Anne Heggtveit won a slalom gold when I was on the team in 1960, and she washes her clothes the same way I do." Green skied a perfect race, but when she turned around to look at the electronic clock, the numbers were still moving. "My heart almost stopped," she later recalled. "I thought, I've just skied the race of my life and they missed my time." After two or three seconds the clock malfunction was corrected and her time appeared. "But that's all it took for my blood pressure to shoot out of sight. I had a headache for the next two days."

1972 Sapporo-Teineyama C: 42, N: 13, D: 2.8.

1.	Marie-Theres Nadig	SWI	1:29.90
2.	Annemarie Pröll	AUT	1:30.75
3.	Wiltrud Drexel	AUT	1:32.35
4.	Laurie Kreiner	CAN	1:32.48
5.	Rosi Speiser	GER	1:32.56
6.	Florence Steurer	FRA	1:32.59
7.	Divina Galica	GBR	1:32.72
8.	Brit Lafforgue	FRA	1:32.80

Hoping to avenge her upset defeat at the hands of Marie-Theres Nadig in the downhill, Annemarie Pröll, the second skier, slammed down the course in 1:30.75. Her time held up until Nadig, in the tenth spot, clocked 1:29.90. Pröll, bearing the burden of being the favorite, was bitterly disappointed. "Two silver medals don't equal one gold medal," she said. Nadig attributed her victory to the fact that she was relaxed while Pröll had been under enormous pressure. After the Olympics, however, Nadig learned firsthand what her rival had had to endure. "After

In 1976 Rosi Mittermaier came within thirteen one-hundredths of a second of becoming the first woman to win all three alpine skiing events.

Sapporo," Nadig later said, "people expected everything from me. They expected me to win all the time, and after a while I didn't know where I was."

1976 Innsbruck C: 45, N: 17, D: 2.13.

1.	Kathy Kreiner	CAN	1:29.13
2.	Rosi Mittermaier	GER	1:29.25
3.	Danièlle Debernard	FRA	1:29.95
4.	Lise-Marie Morerod	SWI	1:30.40
5.	Marie-Theres Nadig	SWI	1:30.44
6.	Monika Kaserer	AUT	1:30.49
7.	Wilma Gatta	ITA	1:30.51
8.	Evi Mittermaier	GER	1:30.64

There was great excitement before the running of the giant slalom because everyone wanted to know if Rosi Mittermaier would become the first woman to sweep the three alpine races. They didn't have to wait long to find out. The first skier on the course, 18-year-old Kathy Kreiner of Timmins, Ontario, had an excellent run and flashed across the finish line in 1:29.13. Three skiers later it was Rosi Mittermaier's turn. A half-second ahead of Kreiner's pace at the halfway mark, Mittermaier lost precious fractions of a second when she approached one of the lower gates too directly. Her final time was one-eighth of a second slower than Kreiner's.

1980 Lake Placid C: 46, N: 21, D: 2.21.

1.	Hanni Wenzel	LIE	2:41.66
2.	Irene Epple	GER	2:42.12
3.	Perrine Pelen	FRA	2:42.41
4.	Fabienne Serrat	FRA	2:42.42

5.	Christa Kinshofer	GER	2:42.63
6.	Annemarie Moser-Pröll	AUT	2:43.19
7.	Christin Cooper	USA	2:44.71
8.	Maria Epple	GER	2:45.56

For the first time, the women's giant slalom was held as a two-run competition. Wenzel had the fastest time of the first run and the third fastest of the second. She was Liechtenstein's first Olympic gold medal winner.

1984 Sarajevo C: 54, N: 21, D: 2.13.

1.	Debbie Armstrong	USA	2:20.98
2.	Christin Cooper	USA	2:21.38
3.	Perrine Pelen	FRA	2:21.40
4.	Tamara McKinney	USA	2:21.83
5.	Marina Kiehl	GER	2:22.03
6.	Blanca Fernández Ochoa	SPA	2:22.14
7.	Erika Hess	SWI	2:22.51
8.	Olga Charvátová	CZE	2:22.57

With hundreds of sports journalists crowding around and pestering the world's leading skiers from the moment they arrived in Sarajevo, 20-year-old Debbie Armstrong of Seattle, Wash., was blessed with anonymity. The night before the giant slalom, she watched Peter and Kitty Carruthers win silver medals for pairs figure skating and then stayed up late indulging her addiction to peanut butter. The next day, relaxed and "having fun," she recorded the second fastest time of the first run, only one-tenth of a second behind teammate Christin Cooper. During the 2½ hour break before the final run, Armstrong, who had never won a World Cup race, was more than a little excited.

"I felt so good at the top," she would say afterwards. "I was so happy waiting for that second run. It was so much fun. I knew it was a good hill for me. I knew if I stayed relaxed the skiing would take care of itself. I didn't feel the pressure."

According to Cooper, who would hit the course immediately after Armstrong, "She was so hyped up, it was really funny. She kept coming up to me and bouncing all over me and telling me to have a good time. She would say, 'I'm just going to have fun out there, just have fun, have fun!' And when she was in the gate, I could hear her talking to herself. She was saying, 'Okay, De . . . have a good run, have a good run. Just have a good time.' And then she turned to me and said, 'You too, Coop. Have the run of your life.' " With that, Armstrong was out of the starting gate and down the slope. Her time was the fourth best of the second run, but when Cooper slipped at the fifth gate, losing valuable moments, the gold medal went to the ebullient Armstrong.

At the post-race press conference she was asked what she had sacrificed to become a champion skier. She replied, "Nothing. Skiing is my life. That's what I love to do." Then she added characteristically, "It's fun." Armstrong, who finished 13th in the 1988 giant slalom, never won another international race.

Years later, when Sarajevo was engulfed by war, Christin Cooper decided that Olympic athletes owed the people of Sarajevo for being such gracious hosts. She co-founded The Spirit of HOPE—Humanitarian Olympians for Peace, and arranged for more than ten tons of new winter clothing and sports equipment to be sent to the beseiged citizens of Sarajevo.

1988 Calgary-Nakiska C: 64, N: 26, D: 2.24.

1.	Vreni Schneider	SWI	2:06.49
2.	Christa Kinshofer-Güthlein	GER	2:07.42
3.	Maria Walliser	SWI	2:07.72
4.	Mateja Svet	YUG/SLO	2:07.80

5. Christine Meier	GER	2:07.88
6. Ulrike Maier	AUT	2:08.10
7. Anita Wachter	AUT	2:08.38
8. Catherine Quittet	FRA	2:08.84

The first-round leader was Spain's Blanca Fernández Ochoa. She was followed by 1980 slalom silver medalist Christa Kinshofer-Güthlein, Anita Wachter, Christine Meier, and, in fifth place, the favorite, world champion and World Cup champion Vreni Schneider. Fernández Ochoa fell early in her second run. Schneider, on the other hand, registered the fastest time of the round to score one of her patented come-from-behind victories.

Only 29 of the 64 starters completed both runs. In 28th place was Seba Johnson of the U.S. Virgin Islands, the first black skier to take part in the Olympics and, at age 14, the youngest competitor at the Calgary Games.

1992 Albertville-Méribel C: 69, N: 32, D: 2.19.

1. Pernilla Wiberg	SWE	2:12.74
2. Diann Roffe	USA	2:13.71
2. Anita Wachter	AUT	2:13.71
4. Ulrike Maier	AUT	2:13.77
5. Julie Parisien	USA	2:14.10
6. Carole Merle	FRA	2:14.24
7. Eva Twardokens	USA	2:14.47
8. Katja Seizinger	GER	2:14.96

Wiberg, the defending world champion, finished second in the first run. The second run was set by the Swedish alpine coach, Jarl Svanberg. Wiberg took advantage of this psychological boost to record the fastest time of the run. Co-silver medalist Diann Roffe had won the 1985 world championship at age 17 but hadn't won an international race since. The first-run leader was Uli Maier, the only mother on the World Cup circuit. However, like Julie Parisien in the slalom the following day, she faltered in the second run and missed a medal by less than one-tenth of a second. On January 29, 1994, while competing in Garmisch-Partenkirchen, Maier crashed and broke her neck. She died almost immediately. She was 26 years old; her daughter was four.

1994 Lillehammer-Hafjell C: 47, N: 19, D: 2.24.

1. Deborah Compagnoni	ITA	2:30.97
2. Martina Ertl	GER	2:32.19
3. Vreni Schneider	SWI	2:32.97
4. Anita Wachter	AUT	2:33.06
5. Carole Merle	FRA	2:33.44
6. Eva Twardokens	USA	2:34.44
7. Lara Magoni	ITA	2:34.67
8. Marianne Kjørstad	NOR	2:34.79

Campagnoni skied the best time of both runs and earned a giant slalom gold medal to go with the Super G one she won in 1992. Only 24 of the 47 starters completed both courses.

SUPER GIANT SLALOM

1924–1984 not held

1988 Calgary-Nakiska C: 46, N: 20, D: 2.22.

1. Sigrid Wolf	AUT	1:19.03
2. Michela Figini	SWI	1:20.03

3. Karen Percy	CAN	1:20.29
4. Regine Mösenlechner	GER	1:20.33
5. Anita Wachter	AUT	1:20.36
6. Maria Walliser	SWI	1:20.48
7. Zoë Haas	SWI	1:20.91
7. Micaela Marzola	ITA	1:20.91

Five weeks before the Olympics, Sigrid Wolf won a Super G race in Lech, Austria, but was disqualified for wearing a safety pin on her number bib to keep it from flapping in the wind. In Calgary, Wolf again raced with a safety pin—but this time it was attached to a necklace for good luck.

1992 Albertville-Méribel C: 59, N: 26, D: 2.18.

1. Deborah Compagnoni	ITA	1:21.22
2. Carole Merle	FRA	1:22.63
3. Katja Seizinger	GER	1:23.19
4. Petra Kronberger	AUT	1:23.20
5. Ulrike Maier	AUT	1:23.35
6. Kerrin Lee-Gartner	CAN	1:23.76
7. Michaela Gerg-Leitner	GER	1:23.77
8. Eva Twardokens	USA	1:24.19

The three pre-Olympic World Cup Super G races had been won by Seizinger, Merle, and Compagnoni. The other major contender was Maier, who had won two world championships, one in 1989 while she was pregnant and the other in 1991 after she was a mother. Racing in the fourth position, Merle, under intense pressure as France's leading medal hope, skied beautifully and took a big lead. The French crowd watched with glee as Seizinger, Maier, and nine others fell far short of Merle's time. But then came Italy's heroine, 21-year-old Deborah Compagnoni. In addition to the usual severe knee injuries common to alpine skiers, Compagnoni survived emergency surgery in October 1990, during which a 27-inch length of her intestines was removed. Doctors told her father that had they waited twenty minutes longer, Compagnoni might have died. In Méribel, she didn't believe she could win a gold medal, even during the race, which she won handily. The very next day, during the first run of the giant slalom, she leaned too heavily on her inner ski, fell, tore ligaments in her left knee, and ended up back in the hospital.

1994 Lillehammer-Kvitfjell C: 55, N: 23, D: 2.15.

1. Diann Roffe	USA	1:22.15
2. Svetlana Gladisheva	RUS	1:22.44
3. Isolde Kostner	ITA	1:22.45
4. Pernilla Wiberg	SWE	1:22.67
5. Morena Gallizio	ITA	1:22.73
6. Katharina Gutensohn	GER	1:22.84
7. Katja Koren	SLO	1:22.96
8. Kerrin Lee-Gartner	CAN	1:22.98

When Diann Roffe won the giant slalom at the 1985 world championships at the age of 17, it appeared that she had a long future of victories ahead of her. She won one more World Cup giant slalom that season and then went nine years without an international victory. She did, however, earn a silver medal in the giant slalom at the 1992 Olympics. For the Lillehammer Super G, she drew the number one starting spot, just as she had two years earlier in Albertville. That time she had crashed. This time she was so nervous at the starting gate she was sick to her stomach. But as soon as she started skiing, her fears vanished and she dominated the course. At the bottom everyone complimented her on a nice run. It would be quite a while before it became apparent just how nice a run it had been. Several of the favorites were ahead of her pace two-thirds of the way down, but none could hold on over the steep lower section. Skiing in the 35th spot, Svetlana Gladisheva came the closest and earned the silver, Russia's first alpine medal since 1956.

ALPINE COMBINED

1924–1932 not held

1936 Garmisch-Partenkirchen C: 37, N: 13, D: 2.8.

			DOWNHILL		SLALOM		PTS.
1.	Christl Cranz	GER	5:23.4	(6)	2:22.1	(1)	97.06
2.	Käthe Grasegger	GER	5:11.0	(3)	2:33.4	(2)	95.26
3.	Laila Schou Nilsen	NOR	5:04.4	(1)	2:43.4	(5)	93.48
4.	Erna Steuri	SWI	5:20.4	(4)	2:38.4	(3)	92.36
5.	Hadi Pfeiffer	GER	5:21.6	(5)	2:39.6	(4)	91.85
6.	Lisa Resch	GER	5:08.4	(2)	3:00.4	(8)	88.74
7.	Johanne Dybwad	NOR	5:32.0	(8)	2:57.4	(7)	85.90
8.	Jeannette Kessler	GBR	6:05.4	(12)	2:47.9	(6)	83.97

Christl Cranz was only sixth in the downhill, but her times in the two slalom runs were so superior that she won anyway. Her first run was 4 seconds faster than her closest competitor and her second run was 7.2 seconds better than any of her rivals. The times of Schou Nilsen and Dybwad include 6-second penalties for missing a gate in the slalom. Resch's time includes a 12-second penalty for missing two gates. Diana Gordon-Lennox, representing Canada, received an ovation because she skied both the downhill and slalom with one arm in a cast and using only one pole. She also wore a monocle while competing. Gordon-Lennox finished 29th.

In 1937, bronze medalist Laila Schou Nilsen set four world records—in speed skating—all of which lasted for at least 12 years.

1948 St. Moritz C: 28, N: 10, D: 2.4.

			DOWNHILL		SLALOM		PTS.
1.	Trude Beiser	AUT	2:29.1	(2)	2:10.5	(8)	6.58
2.	Gretchen Fraser	USA	2:37.1	(11)	2:11.0	(2)	6.95
3.	Erika Mahringer	AUT	2:39.3	(15)	1:58.1	(1)	7.04
4.	Celina Seghi	ITA	2:31.1	(4)	2:09.7	(7)	7.46
5.	Françoise Gignoux	FRA	2:32.4	(7)	2:09.0	(5)	8.14
6.	Rosmarie Bleuer	SWI	2:33.3	(9)	2:09.3	(6)	8.80
7.	Anneliese Schuh-Proxauf	AUT	2:39.0	(13)	2:04.3	(3)	9.76
8.	Hedy Schlunegger	SWI	2:28.3	(1)	2:18.5	(15)	10.20

1952–1984 not held

1988 Calgary-Nakiska C: 39, N: 14, D: 2.21.

			DOWNHILL		SLALOM		PTS.
1.	Anita Wachter	AUT	1:17.14	(3)	1:22.97	(2)	29.25
2.	Brigitte Oertli	SWI	1:18.37	(11)	1:20.71	(1)	29.48
3.	Maria Walliser	SWI	1:16.98	(2)	1:25.92	(11)	51.28
4.	Karen Percy	CAN	1:18.22	(9)	1:24.00	(3)	54.47
5.	Lenka Kebrlová	CZE	1:18.43	(13)	1:24.38	(5)	60.87
6.	Lucia Medzihradská	CZE/SVK	1:18.62	(15)	1:24.35	(4)	63.56

7. Michelle McKendry	CAN	1:17.58	(4)	1:26.44	(13)	64.85
8. Kerrin Lee	CAN	1:18.15	(8)	1:25.43	(9)	65.26

Wachter's surprising third-place finish in the downhill run set her up as the overnight favorite. Oertli, the pre-Olympic favorite, picked up 2.26 seconds in the two slalom runs, but it wasn't enough to overcome her eleventh-place finish in the downhill.

1992 Albertville-Méribel C: 40, N: 18, D: 2.13.

			DOWNHILL		SLALOM		PTS.
1. Petra Kronberger	AUT		1:25.84	(1)	1:09.60	(3)	2.55
2. Anita Wachter	AUT		1:27.25	(12)	1:09.51	(2)	19.39
3. Florence Masnada	FRA		1:27.08	(10)	1:10.01	(5)	21.38
4. Chantal Bournissen	SWI		1:26.92	(7)	1:10.69	(6)	24.98
5. Anne Berge	NOR		1:28.67	(22)	1:09.29	(1)	35.28
6. Michelle McKendry	CAN		1:27.32	(14)	1:11.79	(7)	39.02
7. Natasa Bokal	SLO		1:29.02	(25)	1:09.65	(4)	42.60
8. Lucia Medzihradská	CZE/SVK		1:27.89	(17)	1:11.95	(9)	47.43

Petra Kronberger was the overwhelming favorite in this event, especially after her most serious challenger, teammate Sabine Ginther, fell on the downhill course the day before the competition and fractured a disk. Kronberger was such a well-rounded skier that in December 1990 she won a World Cup event in each of the four alpine disciplines and then added a combined victory the following month. She easily won the downhill run at the Olympics, but the next day she skied conservatively on the first slalom run and placed only sixth. Two months earlier, the Austrian women's slalom coach, Aloïs Kahr, had been killed in a car crash. Just before her second run, Kronberger sensed Kahr talking to her and giving her advice. This time she attacked the course and recorded a faster time than any of the other skiers.

1994 Lillehammer-Kvitfjell, Hafjell C: 41, N: 20, D: 2.21.

		DOWNHILL		SLALOM		TOTAL
1. Pernilla Wiberg	SWE	1:28.70	(5)	1:36.46	(2)	3:05.16
2. Vreni Schneider	SWI	1:28.91	(7)	1:36.38	(1)	3:05.29
3. Alenka Dovžan	SLO	1:28.67	(4)	1:37.97	(3)	3:06.64
4. Morena Gallizio	ITA	1:28.71	(6)	1:38.00	(4)	3:06.71
5. Martina Ertl	GER	1:29.38	(13)	1:39.40	(6)	3:08.78
6. Katja Koren	SLO	1:30.59	(25)	1:39.00	(5)	3:09.59
7. Florence Masnada	FRA	1:29.11	(10)	1:40.91	(10)	3:10.02
8. Hilde Gerg	GER	1:29.02	(9)	1:41.08	(11)	3:10.10

The three medalists in the downhill, Katja Seizinger, Picabo Street and Isolde Kostner, finished 1-2-3 again in the downhill portion of the combined event the following day. But the new scoring method for 1994—combining the downhill and slaloms times—gave the advantage to slalom specialists who could hold their own in the downhill. Fifth after the downhill, Pernilla Wiberg took the lead after the first slalom run and then held on despite a great final run by Vreni Schneider. Wiberg's victory saved face for Sweden which had failed to win a single medal in the first week of the Olympics. Sweden's problems had greatly amused the Norwegian hosts. One newspaper headline had gloated, "Norway Leads Medal Count; Sweden Tied With Fiji." Alenka Dovžan's medal was the first for independent Slovenia and touched off wild celebrations back home. So many people sent congratulations to the Slovenian team in Lillehammer that their fax machine broke down.

FREESTYLE SKIING

MEN	WOMEN
Aerials	Aerials
Moguls	Moguls

The first freestyle skiing competition was held in Attitash, New Hampshire, in 1966. The International Ski Federation (F.I.S.) recognized the sport in 1979, and the following year a World Cup series was organized. In 1986 the first world championship was held in Tignes, France, site of the 1992 Olympic competition. There are three freestyle disciplines: moguls, aerials, and ballet, all of which were included as demonstration events at the 1988 Calgary Olympics. Moguls was awarded medal status in 1992 and aerials was added in 1994.

MEN

AERIALS

Competitors perform two acrobatic jumps in the qualifying round. Twelve finalists perform two more jumps. Qualifying scores are not carried over to the final round. Jumps range from the relatively simple front tuck, a front somersault performed in the tuck position, to the doublefull full full, a backward triple somersault, the first somersault with two twists, and the second and third with single full twists. A panel of judges score the skiers for three elements: height and distance, known as "air," account for 20 percent of the score; execution and precision, known as "form," for 50 percent; and landing for 30 percent. Aerials is the "highest" of Olympic events: competitors often fly 60 feet above the ground. Ski jumpers are rarely more than 20 feet above the ramp and even platform divers barely rise more than 40 feet above the water.

1924-1992 not held

1994 Lillehammer C: 24, N: 14, D: 2.24.

			PTS.
1.	Andreas "Sonny" Schönbächler	SWI	234.67
2.	Philippe LaRoche	CAN	228.63
3.	Lloyd Langlois	CAN	222.44
4.	Andrew Capicik	CAN	219.07
5.	Trace Worthington	USA	218.19
6.	Nicolas Fontaine	CAN	210.81
7.	Eric Bergoust	USA	210.48
8.	Mats Johansson	SWE	207.52

As expected, the North Americans dominated the final, claiming six of the first seven places. The problem was that the place they missed was first. The unexpected winner was 27-year-old Sonny Schönbächler, who came out of retirement when aerials was included as a medal event. He finished only tenth in the qualifying round, but three days later he put together what he described as "my best two jumps ever," a full-full-full—three flips with three twists, and a full-double full-

Andreas Schönbächler scores an upset victory in the 1994 aerials event

full—three flips with four twists. Silver medalist Philippe LaRoche had won the demonstration aerials event at the 1992 Games. When fellow Canadian Lloyd Langlois took third place, it marked the first time since 1932 that Canada had won two medals in the same Winter Olympics event. Trace Worthington, who placed fifth, was the great-grandson of Harry Worthington, who finished fourth in the long jump at the 1912 Stockholm Olympics.

MOGULS

Moguls are snow bumps. Competitors ski on a run filled with high-speed turns on a heavily moguled course. Sixteen finalists perform a second run. Qualifying scores are not carried over to the final round. Turns account for 50 percent of a competitor's score and are judged according to the skier's ability to keep a clean, controlled line down the course. Two aerial maneuvers performed during the run are judged on the criteria of height, distance, landing, execution, and degree of difficulty. They account for 25 percent of the score and are blessed with such poetic names as the back scratcher, the mule kick, the daffy, and the zadnik. The remaining 25 percent is based on time from start to finish. Moguls competitions are accompanied by loud rock and roll music.

1924-1988 not held

1992 Albertville-Tignes C: 47, N: 17, D: 2.13.

			PTS.
1.	Edgar Grospiron	FRA	25.81
2.	Olivier Allamand	FRA	24.87
3.	Nelson Carmichael	USA	24.82
4.	Eric Berthon	FRA	24.79
5.	John Smart	CAN	24.15
6.	Jörgen Pääjärvi	SWE	24.14
7.	Jean-Luc Brassard	CAN	23.71
8.	Leif Persson	SWE	22.99

Grospiron recorded the fastest time of the final and the second best scores for turns and air to earn a popular hometown victory. His fans broke down the security fence lining the course to embrace the gregarious champion and hoist him on their shoulders. When asked if he followed a special diet while training, the 22-year-old Grospiron replied, "Yes. One week red wine and the next week white wine."

1994 Lillehammer C: 29, N: 16, D: 2.16.

			PTS.
1.	Jean-Luc Brassard	CAN	27.24
2.	Sergei Shupletsov	RUS	26.90
3.	Edgar Grospiron	FRA	26.64
4.	Olivier Cotte	FRA	25.79
5.	Jörgen Pääjärvi	SWE	25.51
6.	Olivier Allamand	FRA	25.28
7.	John Smart	CAN	24.96
8.	Troy Benson	USA	24.86

With Edgar Grospiron all but out of the competition because of a knee injury, Jean-Luc Brassard dominated the 1992–1993 season, winning both the world championship and the World Cup. When Grospiron returned, he returned with a vengeance, winning four of five World Cup contests in the month before the Olympic competition. In Lillehammer Brassard finished first in the qualifying round and earned the right to ski last in the final the following day—immediately after Grospiron. In the final Grospiron skied by far the fastest run of the Olympics, but attempting to go even faster, he lost control in the last ten meters and lost valuable points for form. Brassard wore fluorescent yellow patches on his knees to make sure the judges didn't miss his smooth and constant movement down the course. The strategy worked. Although Brassard's time was only the 14th fastest of the 16 finalists, four of the five judges scoring turns gave him a perfect score of 5.0

WOMEN

AERIALS

1924-1992 not held

1994 Lillehammer C: 22, N: 13, D: 2.24.

			PTS.
1.	Lina Cheryazova	UZB	166.84
2.	Marie Lindgren	SWE	165.88
3.	Hilde Synnøve Lid	NOR	164.13
4.	Maja Schmid	SWI	156.90
5.	Natalija Sherstnyova	UKR	154.88
6.	Kirstie Marshall	AUS	150.76
7.	Tracy Evans	USA	139.77
8.	Caroline Olivier	CAN	138.96

The overwhelming favorite was 25-year-old Lina Cheryazova. An ethnic Russian from Tashkent, Cheryazova was the defending world champion, the winner of five straight World Cup events in the weeks before the Olympics, and the only female aerialist to consistently perform successful triple flips. The elimination round was full of surprises. Two of the medal favorites, Colette Brand of Switzerland and Nikki

Stone of the United States, placed 15th and 13th respectively and failed to qualify for the final. Cheryazova herself barely made it. Sixteenth after the first jump, she squeezed into the final in 12th place. The final was another story. Cheryazova earned 92.92 points for her first jump, a single twisting triple flip, and held on to win despite a poor landing or her second jump. When Cheryazova tried to telephone her parents in Uzbekistan, Uzbeki Olympic officials stopped her and broke the news that her mother had died of gangrene—and inadequate medical care—12 days earlier. Her mother's dying wish had been that Lina not be told until after she had completed her competition at the Olympics. On July 13, less than five months after earning her gold medal, Cheryazova was critically injured when she slammed her head against a ski jumping ramp while training with the U.S. team in Lake Placid, New York. Although her brain was damaged and she was kept in a coma for more than a week, she returned to World Cup competition in late 1995.

MOGULS

1924-1988 not held

1992 Albertville-Tignes C: 24, N: 11, D: 2.13.

			PTS.
1.	Donna Weinbrecht	USA	23.69
2.	Yelizaveta Kozhevnikova	SOV/RUS	23.50
3.	Stine Lise Hattestad	NOR	23.04
4.	Tatjana Mittermayer	GER	22.33
5.	Birgit Stein	GER	21.44
6.	Elizabeth McIntyre	USA	21.24
7.	Silvia Marciandi	ITA	19.66
8.	Raphaelle Monod	FRA	15.57

Skiing in a snowstorm to the accompaniment of "Rock 'n' Roll High School" by the Ramones, heavy favorite Donna Weinbrecht completed a conservative but clean run and waited nervously at the bottom of the course for the final competitor, local favorite Raphaelle Monod. Monod began strong but lost control two-thirds of the way down and skidded home in last place.

1994 Lillehammer C: 24, N: 13, D: 2.16.

			PTS.
1.	Stine Lise Hattestad	NOR	25.97
2.	Elizabeth McIntrye	USA	25.89
3.	Yelizaveta Kozhevnikova	RUS	25.81
4.	Raphaelle Monod	FRA	25.17
5.	Candice Gilg	FRA	24.82
6.	Tatjana Mittermayer	GER	24.43
7.	Donna Weinbrecht	USA	24.38
8.	Ann Battelle	USA	23.71

Donna Weinbrecht won six straight World Cup contests before being beaten by Stine Lise Hattestad in Sweden two weeks before the Olympic competition. In Lillehammer Weinbrecht had her worst performance in years. Hattestad and McIntyre received equal marks for turns and air, but Hattestad completed the course .32 seconds faster. All of the leading contenders reported having difficulty sleeping the night before the final, but Kozhevnikova had the best story. "Three times in the night I had the same dream," she explained at the medalists' press conference, "that I finished in 40th place. But then I told myself that there were only sixteen competitors. I was in such a good mood in the morning, I wanted to sing."

NORDIC SKIING

MEN

10 Kilometers (Classical)
Combined Pursuit
30 Kilometers (Classical)
50 Kilometers (Freestyle)
4 × 10-Kilometer Relay
Ski Jump, Normal Hill, Individual

Ski Jump, Large Hill, Individual
Ski Jump, Large Hill, Team
Nordic Combined, Individual
Nordic Combined, Team
Discontinued Event

Cross-country, or *langlauf,* races are run against the clock with the skiers leaving the starting line at 30-second intervals. The only exceptions are the relays, in which the first racers for each team start together, and the second half of the combined pursuit events.

Two skiing techniques are used in nordic events. The "classical" requires a diagonal stride; the "freestyle" has no restrictions and employs the faster "skating" style. The choice of skis and ski wax is extremely important and based on the course profile and daily weather conditions. The leading nordic nations employ computers to help decide the ideal skis and wax for each race. Skis may not be switched once a race has begun except in a relay, where one broken or damaged ski may be changed. Skiers are allowed to be handed new wax or other accessories on the course, but they must apply them without aid. If a skier is about to be passed, he or she must give way as soon as the passing skier calls out "Track!"

MEN

Since the Winter Olympics began in 1924, 58 of the 61 gold medals awarded in men's cross-country skiing have been won by only four nations: Norway (19, including all five in 1992), Sweden (18), the U.S.S.R. (11), and Finland (10). The Scandinavians and Soviets and ex-Soviets have also won 166 of 183 total medals. Of the 17 remaining medals, ten have been won by Italy.

10 KILOMETERS (CLASSICAL)

1924-1988 not held

1992 Albertville-Les Saisies C: 110, N: 39, D: 2.13.

1.	Vegard Ulvang	NOR	27:36.0
2.	Marco Albarello	ITA	27:55.2
3.	Christer Majbäck	SWE	27:56.4
4.	Bjørn Dahlie	NOR	28:01.6
5.	Niklas Jonsson	SWE	28:03.1
6.	Harri Kirvesniemi	FIN	28:23.3
7.	Giorgio Vanzetta	ITA	28:26.9
8.	Alois Stadlober	AUT	28:27.5

*Vegard Ulvang (right) won the 1992 10-kilometer race
after ignoring the advice of his coaches and listening
instead to one of his opponents, Ebbe Hartz (left).*

Ulvang won the second of his three gold medals, but not without difficulty. Heavy snow began falling shortly before the race and continued throughout. Ulvang picked out his skis literally at the last minute and, for the first time in his career, he chose to ski without wax. In doing so he followed the advice not of his coaches, but of a Danish competitor, Ebbe Hartz. Shortly after the five-kilometer mark, Ulvang fell and broke the handle of his ski pole. Five hundred meters later, a nonracing teammate handed him a slightly shorter replacement. Fourth midway in the race, Ulvang finished strongly and posted a clear victory.

Silver medalist Albarello also had problems. Unable to avoid a fallen Austrian skier, he too fell and lost his goggles four kilometers from the finish. The last-place finisher, architectural student Faissal Cherradi of Morocco, completed the course in 1:11:07.4. Seventy-three of the other 109 competitors finished the race in less time than it took Cherradi to reach the halfway point.

1994 Lillehammer C: 88, N: 33, D: 2.17.

1.	Bjørn Dahlie	NOR	24:20.1
2.	Vladimir Smirnov	KAZ	24:38.3
3.	Marco Albarello	ITA	24:42.3
4.	Mikhail Botvinov	RUS	24:58.9
5.	Sture Siversten	NOR	24:59.7
6.	Mika Myllylä	FIN	25:05.3
7.	Vegard Ulvang	NOR	25:08.0
8.	Silvio Fauner	ITA	25:08.1

At the post-race press conference, Bjørn Dahlie presented Norwegian journalists with glasses of cherry brandy made from cherries picked by Dahlie and his father from their orchard.

COMBINED PURSUIT

On the first day of the combined pursuit event, skiers race 10 kilometers, using the classical technique. On the second day, setting out from a staggered start based on the results of the previous day, they race another 15 kilometers freestyle.

1924-1988 not held

1992 Albertville-Les Saisies C: 102, N: 39, D: 2.15.

			10KM CLASSICAL		15KM FREESTYLE		TOTAL
1.	Bjørn Dahlie	NOR	28:01	(4)	37:36.9	(1)	1:05:37.9
2.	Vegard Ulvang	NOR	27:36	(1)	38:55.3	(13)	1:06:31.3
3.	Giorgio Vanzetta	ITA	28:26	(7)	38:06.2	(3)	1:06:32.2
4.	Marco Albarello	ITA	27:55	(2)	38:38.3	(8)	1:06:33.3
5.	N. Torgny Mogren	SWE	28:37	(9)	38:00.4	(2)	1:06:37.4
6.	Christer Majbäck	SWE	27:56	(3)	39:21.0	(23)	1:07:17.0
7.	Silvio Fauner	ITA	28:53	(10)	38:41.9	(9)	1:07:34.9
8.	Vladimir Smirnov	SOV/KAZ	29:13	(13)	38:22.8	(5)	1:07:35.8

Dahlie, the defending world champion of the 15-kilometer freestyle, spotted Ulvang 25 seconds at the start of the second day's race, passed him after four kilometers, and pulled away to an easy victory. Ulvang was also passed by Albarello at the eight-kilometer mark, but regained second place two kilometers later and fought off the two Italians in an exciting finish. The pursuit format proved a success with the spectators, but was less popular with the skiers themselves. The three medalists took advantage of the postrace press conference to criticize the concept and the rules. Their main complaint concerned the requirement that the leaders ski first. In normal cross-country races, the leading skiers get to choose if they ski early or late. Because the freestyle was held during a snowfall, Dahlie, Ulvang, and others felt they should have been given the option of starting later, after the course had been packed down, rather than early, according to the order of their finish in the classical race. Odd Martinsen, president of the Nordic Skiing commission of the International Ski Federation, and himself an Olympic gold medalist from Norway, rose to point out that the rules did not permit such a change and that rules are rules. In fact, race officials did bend the rules in one instance. According to the rule book, each skier's starting time in the 15-kilometer freestyle is determined by how far behind the leader he was in the 10-kilometer classical. This meant that Faissal Cherradi of Morocco should have started 43 minutes and 31 seconds after Vegard Ulvang. Because a women's race was scheduled immediately after the men's race, Cherradi was allowed to take off only 20 minutes after Ulvang. As it was, he crossed the finish line 52 minutes after the next-to-last competitor, his teammate Mohamed Oubahim.

1994 Lillehammer C: 76, N: 31, D: 2.19.

			10KM CLASSICAL		15KM FREESTYLE		TOTAL
1.	Bjørn Dahlie	NOR	24:20	(1)	35:48.8	(1)	1:00:08.8
2.	Vladimir Smirnov	KAZ	24:38	(2)	36:00.0	(2)	1:00:38.0
3.	Silvio Fauner	ITA	25:08	(7)	36:40.6	(4)	1:01:48.6
4.	Mika Myllylä	FIN	25:05	(6)	36:50.9	(7)	1:01:57.8
5.	Mikhail Botinov	RUS	24:58	(4)	36:59.8	(8)	1:01:57.8
6.	Jari Räsänen	FIN	25:31	(10)	36:32.7	(3)	1:02:03.7
7.	Sture Sivertsen	NOR	24:59	(5)	37:10.7	(9)	1:02:09.7
8.	Johann Mühlegg	GER	25:50	(15)	36:41.2	(5)	1:02:31.2

At the 1993 world championships, Dahlie and Smirnov finished in a photo finish so close that Smirnov was originally declared the winner and had already been interviewed by the press when the results were reversed. The same two fought for the gold medal in Lillhammer, but this time it was no contest. With this race Bjørn Dahlie became the first male cross-country skier to win five gold medals.

30 KILOMETERS (CLASSICAL)

1924–1952 not held

1956 Cortina C: 54, N: 18, D: 1.27.

1.	Veikko Hakulinen	FIN	1:44:06
2.	Sixten Jernberg	SWE	1:44:30
3.	Pavel Kolchin	SOV	1:45:45
4.	Anatoly Shelyukin	SOV	1:45:46
5.	Vladimir Kuzin	SOV	1:46:09
6.	Fedor Terentyev	SOV	1:46:43
7.	Per-Erik Larsson	SWE	1:46:51
8.	Lennart Larsson	SWE	1:46:56

1960 Squaw Valley C: 48, N: 17, D: 2:19.

1.	Sixten Jernberg	SWE	1:51:03.9
2.	Rolf Rämgård	SWE	1:51:16.9
3.	Nikolai Anikin	SOV/RUS	1:52:28.2
4.	Gennady Vaganov	SOV/RUS	1:52:49.2
5.	Lennart Larsson	SWE	1:53:53.2
6.	Veikko Hakulinen	FIN	1:54:02.0
7.	Toimo Alatalo	FIN	1:54:06.5
8.	Aleksei Kuznetsov	SOV/RUS	1:54:23.9

1964 Innsbruck-Seefeld C: 69, N: 22, D: 1.30.

1.	Eero Mäntyranta	FIN	1:30:50.7
2.	Harald Grönningen	NOR	1:32:02.3
3.	Igor Voronchikin	SOV/RUS	1:32:15.8
4.	Janne Stefansson	SWE	1:32:34.8
5.	Sixten Jernberg	SWE	1:32:39.6
6.	Kalevi Laurila	FIN	1:32:41.4
7.	Assar Rönnlund	SWE	1:32:43.6
8.	Einar Östby	NOR	1:32:54.6

1968 Grenoble-Autrans C: 66, N: 22, D: 2.6.

1.	Franco Nones	ITA	1:35:39.2
2.	Odd Martinsen	NOR	1:36:28.9
3.	Eero Mäntyranta	FIN	1:36:55.3
4.	Vladimir Voronkov	SOV/RUS	1:37:10.8
5.	Giulio De Florian	ITA	1:37:12.9
6.	Kalevi Laurila	FIN	1:37:29.8
7.	Kalevi Oikarainen	FIN	1:37:34.4
8.	Gunnar Larsson	SWE	1:37:48.1

Franco Nones, a 27-year-old customs officer from the village of Ziano di Fiemme in the Dolomite Mountains, was the first skier from a non-Nordic nation to win a gold medal in cross-country skiing. It is true that Nones was trained in northern Sweden by a Swedish coach, but his victory was nonetheless a major surprise, particularly coming as it did in the first event of the 1968 Winter Games.

1972 Sapporo-Makomanal C: 59, N: 19, D: 2.4.

1.	Vyacheslav Vedenine	SOV/RUS	1:36:31.15
2.	Pål Tyldum	NOR	1:37:25.30
3.	Johs Harviken	NOR	1:37:32.44
4.	Gunnar Larsson	SWE	1:37:33.72
5.	Walter Demel	GER	1:37:45.33
6.	Fedor Simashev	SOV/RUS	1:38:22.50
7.	Alois Kälin	SWI	1:38:40.72
8.	Gert-Dietmar Klause	GDR	1:39:15.54

The 5-foot 4¼-inch Vedenine was the first Soviet skier to win an individual Olympic gold medal.

1976 Innsbruck-Seefeld C: 69, N: 21, D: 2.5.

1.	Sergei Savelyev	SOV/RUS	1:30:29.38
2.	William Koch	USA	1:30:57.84
3.	Ivan Garanin	SOV/KAZ	1:31:09.29
4.	Juha Mieto	FIN	1:31:20.39
5.	Nikolai Bazhukov	SOV/RUS	1:31:33.14
6.	Gert-Dietmar Klause	GDR	1:32:00.91
7.	Albert Giger	SWI	1:32:17.71
8.	Arto Koivisto	FIN	1:32:23.11

Not a single American reporter was present to see Bill Koch of Guilford, Vermont, become the only American ever to have won an Olympic nordic skiing medal. When they finally caught up with him, Koch responded to his sudden celebrity in a typically Vermont manner. When a reporter asked, "Have you lived in Vermont all your life?" Koch replied, "Not yet." In 1982 Koch revolutionized cross-country skiing by introducing the skating technique to Olympic distances. The technique had previously been used only in marathon races. Skating was banned in 1983. Four years later, however, separate skating or "freestyle" events were included in the world championships and then at the 1988 Olympics. In 1982, Koch also pioneered the technique of "going hairies," in which the ski bottom is scuffed rather than waxed.

1980 Lake Placid C: 57, N: 20, D: 2.14.

1.	Nikolai Zimyatov	SOV/RUS	1:27:02.80
2.	Vassily Rochev	SOV/RUS	1:27:34.22
3.	Ivan Lebanov	BUL	1:28:03.87
4.	Thomas Wassberg	SWE	1:28:40.35
5.	Jósef Luszczek	POL	1:29:03.64
6.	Matti Pitkänen	FIN	1:29:35.03
7.	Juha Mieto	FIN	1:29:45.08
8.	Ove Aunli	NOR	1:29:54.02

Zimyatov won the first of his three gold medals at Lake Placid. Lebanov is the only Bulgarian to win a medal in the Winter Olympics.

1984 Sarajevo C: 72, N: 26, D: 2.10.

1.	Nikolai Zimyatov	SOV/RUS	1:28:56.3
2.	Aleksandr Zavyalov	SOV/RUS	1:29:23.3

3. Gunde Svan	SWE	1:29:35.7
4. Vladimir Sakhnov	SOV/KAZ	1:30:30.4
5. Aki Karvonen	FIN	1:30:59.7
6. Lars-Erik Eriksen	NOR	1:31:24.8
7. Harri Kirvesniemi	FIN	1:31:37.4
8. Juha Mieto	FIN	1:31:48.3

Soviet army captain Nikolai Zimyatov struggled through blizzard conditions to win his fourth Olympic gold medal.

1988 Calgary-Canmore C: 90, N: 32, D: 2.15.

1. Aleksei Prokurorov	SOV/RUS	1:24:26.3
2. Vladimir Smirnov	SOV/KAZ	1:24:35.1
3. Vegard Ulvang	NOR	1:25:11.6
4. Mikhail Devyatyarov	SOV/RUS	1:25:31.3
5. Giorgio Vanzetta	ITA	1:25:37.2
6. Pål Gunnar Mikkelsplass	NOR	1:25:44.6
7. Gianfranco Polvara	ITA	1:26:02.7
8. Marco Albarello	ITA	1:26:09.1

1992 Albertville-Les Saisies C: 87, N: 34, D: 2.10.

1. Vegard Ulvang	NOR	1:22:27.8
2. Bjørn Dahlie	NOR	1:23:14.0
3. Terje Langli	NOR	1:23:42.5
4. Marco Albarello	ITA	1:23:55.7
5. Erling Jevne	NOR	1:24:07.7
6. Christer Majbäck	SWE	1:24:12.1
7. Niklas Jonsson	SWE	1:25:17.6
8. Jyrki Ponsiluoma	SWE	1:25:24.4

Ulvang earned the first of his three gold medals. He was the first Norwegian man to win an Olympic cross-country race in 16 years. The Norwegians broke their losing streak in a big way, winning all five events at the 1992 Olympics. In the 30-kilometer race, the first of the Albertville Games, the Norwegian skiers achieved the first sweep of a men's cross-country race since 1948. Ulvang came from Kirkenes, an iron-mining town 300 miles north of the Arctic Circle, near the Russian border. In addition to his competitive exploits, Ulvang was something of an adventurer. In the year preceding the Olympics, he climbed Mt. Denali (McKinley) in Alaska and spent 15 days skiing across Greenland in the footsteps of explorer Fridtjof Nansen.

1994 Lillehammer C: 74, N: 28, D: 2.14.
(Freestyle)

1. Thomas Alsgaard	NOR	1:12:26.4
2. Bjørn Dahlie	NOR	1:13:13.6
3. Mika Myllylä	FIN	1:14:14.0
4. Mikhail Botvinov	RUS	1:14:43.8
5. Maurilio De Zolt	ITA	1:14:55.5
6. Jari Isometsä	FIN	1:15:12.5
7. Silvio Fauner	ITA	1:15:27.7
8. Egil Kristiansen	NOR	1:15:37.7

Alsgaard's win was a complete surprise, even to himself. Only 22 years old, he had never won a senior-level international race.

50 KILOMETERS (FREESTYLE)

1924 Chamonix C: 33, N: 11, D: 1.30.

1.	Thorleif Haug	NOR	3:44:32
2.	Thoralf Strömstad	NOR	3:46:23
3.	Johan Gröttumsbråten	NOR	3:47:46
4.	Jon Maardalen	NOR	3:49:48
5.	Torkel Persson	SWE	4:05:59
6.	Ernst Alm	SWE	4:06:31
7.	Matti Raivio	FIN	4:06:50
8.	Oscar Lindberg	SWE	4:07:44

1928 St. Moritz C: 41, N: 11, D: 2.14.

1.	Per Erik Hedlund	SWE	4:52:03
2.	Gustaf Jonsson	SWE	5:05:30
3.	Volger Andersson	SWE	5:05:46
4.	Olav Kjelbotn	NOR	5:14:22
5.	Ole Hegge	NOR	5:17:58
6.	Tauno Lappalainen	FIN	5:18:33
7.	Anders Ström	SWE	5:21:54
8.	Johan Stöa	NOR	5:25:30

This race was accompanied by freakish weather. At the beginning of the race the temperature was near zero; however, by the end it had risen to 77° Fahrenheit (25° Centigrade). Hedlund's phenomenal margin of victory is unequaled in Olympic history. Although the other Swedish skiers dressed in blue, Hedlund insisted on wearing a white outfit and red cap. In honor of his win, Swedish nordic skiers wore white uniforms and red caps at every Olympics for the next 48 years.

1932 Lake Placid C: 32, N: 9, D: 2.13.

1.	Veli Saarinen	FIN	4:28:00
2.	Väinö Likkanen	FIN	4:28:20
3.	Arne Rustadstuen	NOR	4:31:53
4.	Ole Hegge	NOR	4:32:04
5.	Sigurd Vestad	NOR	4:32:40
6.	Sven Utterström	SWE	4:33:25
7.	Tauno Lappalainen	FIN	4:45:02
8.	Karl Lindberg	SWE	4:47:22

The 1932 race was held in a raging blizzard. The start was delayed three hours while contestants and officials argued about the course.

1936 Garmisch-Partenkirchen C: 36, N: 11, D: 2.15.

1.	Elis Wiklund	SWE	3:30:11
2.	Axel Wikström	SWE	3:33:20
3.	Nils-Joel Englund	SWE	3:34:10
4.	Hjalmar Bergström	SWE	3:35:50
5.	Klaes Karppinen	FIN	3:39:33
6.	Arne Tuft	NOR	3:41:18
7.	Frans Heikkinen	FIN	3:42:44
8.	Pekka Niemi	FIN	3:44:14

1948 St. Moritz C: 28, N: 9, D: 2.6.

1.	Nils Karlsson	SWE	3:47:48
2.	Harald Eriksson	SWE	3:52:20

3. Benjamin Vanninen	FIN	3:57:28
4. Pekka Vanninen	FIN	3:57:58
5. Anders Törnkvist	SWE	3:58:20
6. Edi Schild	SWI	4:05:37
7. Pekka Kuvaja	FIN	4:10:02
8. Jaroslav Cardal	CZE	4:14:34

1952 Oslo C: 36, N: 13, D: 2.20.

1. Veikko Hakulinen	FIN	3:33:33
2. Eero Kolehmainen	FIN	3:38:11
3. Magnar Estenstad	NOR	3:38:28
4. Olav Ökern	NOR	3:38:45
5. Kalevi Mononen	FIN	3:39:21
6. Nils Karlsson	SWE	3:39:30
7. Edvin Landsem	NOR	3:40:43
8. Harald Maartmann	NOR	3:43:43

This was the first of woodchopper Veikko Hakulinen's seven Olympic medals.

1956 Cortina C: 33, N: 13, D: 2.2.

1. Sixten Jernberg	SWE	2:50:27
2. Veikko Hakulinen	FIN	2:51:45
3. Fedor Terentyev	SOV/RUS	2:53:32
4. Eero Kolehmainen	FIN	2:56:17
5. Anatoly Shelyukin	SOV/RUS	2:56:40
6. Pavel Kolchin	SOV/RUS	2:58:00
7. Victor Baranov	SOV	3:03:55
8. Antti Sivonen	FIN	3:04:16

1960 Squaw Valley C: 31, N: 10, D: 2.27.

1. Kalevi Hämäläinen	FIN	2:59:06.3
2. Veikko Hakulinen	FIN	2:59:26.7
3. Rolf Rämgård	SWE	3:02:46.7
4. Lennart Larsson	SWE	3:03:27.9
5. Sixten Jernberg	SWE	3:05:18.0
6. Pentti Pelkonen	FIN	3:05:24.5
7. Gennady Vaganov	SOV/RUS	3:05:27.6
8. Veikko Rasanen	FIN	3:06:04.4

Finland, Norway, Sweden, and the U.S.S.R. took the first 15 places.

1964 Innsbruck-Seefeld C: 41, N: 14, D: 2.5.

1. Sixten Jernberg	SWE	2:43:52.6
2. Assar Rönnlund	SWE	2:44:58.2
3. Arto Tiainen	FIN	2:45:30.4
4. Janne Stefansson	SWE	2:45:36.6
5. Sverre Steinsheim	NOR	2:45:47.2
6. Harald Grönningen	NOR	2:47:03.6
7. Einar Östby	NOR	2:47:20.6
8. Ole Ellefsäter	NOR	2:47:45.8

In 1956 Sixten Jernberg had predicted that whoever started the course last in the 50-kilometer race would win. Instead Jernberg, who started next to last, was the winner. At Innsbruck in 1964 he was the next to last starter again, and again he finished in first place. Three days later he earned another gold medal by skiing the

Sixten Jernberg won nine medals (four gold, three silver, two bronze) in nordic skiing between 1956 and 1964.

second leg on Sweden's relay team. He closed out his Olympic career two days after his 35th birthday, having won nine medals: four gold, three silver, and two bronze.

1968 Grenoble-Autrans C: 51, N: 17, D: 2.15.

1.	Ole Ellefsäter	NOR	2:28:45.8
2.	Vyacheslav Vedenine	SOV/RUS	2:29:02.5
3.	Josef Haas	SWI	2:29:14.8
4.	Pål Tyldum	NOR	2:29:26.7
5.	Melcher Risberg	SWE	2:29:37.0
6.	Gunnar Larsson	SWE	2:29:37.2
7.	Jan Halvarsson	SWE	2:30:05.9
8.	Reidar Hjermstad	NOR	2:31:01.8

Ole Ellefsäter, a forestry technician and pop singer, celebrated his 29th birthday by winning the 50-kilometer gold medal.

1972 Sapporo-Makomanai C: 40, N: 13, D: 2.10.

1.	Pål Tyldum	NOR	2:43:14.75
2.	Magne Myrmo	NOR	2:43:29.45
3.	Vyacheslav Vedenine	SOV/RUS	2:44:00.19
4.	Reidar Hjermstad	NOR	2:44:14.51
5.	Walter Demel	GER	2:44:32.67
6.	Werner Geeser	SWI	2:44:34.13
7.	Lars-Arne Bölling	SWE	2:45:06.80
8.	Fedor Simashev	SOV/RUS	2:45:08.93

Tyldum, the next to last starter, was placed only 18th after 15 kilometers, 78½ seconds behind the leader, Werner Geeser. By the 25-kilometer mark he had moved up to tenth place, but he was now 103½ seconds slower than Geeser. At 40 kilometers Geeser was still in first, but fading, while Tyldum had moved up to third, less than 26 seconds off Geeser's pace. While Geeser and Simachev tired dramatically in the last 10 kilometers, Tyldum plowed on to victory.

1976 Innsbruck-Seefeld C: 59, N: 15, D: 2.14.

1.	Ivar Formo	NOR	2:37:30.05
2.	Gert-Dietmar Klause	GDR	2:38:13.21
3.	Benny Södergren	SWE	2:39:39.21
4.	Ivan Garanin	SOV/KAZ	2:40:38.94
5.	Gerhard Grimmer	GDR	2:41:15.46
6.	Per Knut Aaland	NOR	2:41:18.06
7.	Pål Tyldum	NOR	2:42:21.86
8.	Tommy Limby	SWE	2:42:43.58

1980 Lake Placid C: 51, N: 14, D: 2.23.

1.	Nikolai Zimyatov	SOV	2:27:24.60
2.	Juha Mieto	FIN	2:30:20.52
3.	Alexandr Zavyalov	SOV/RUS	2:30:51.52
4.	Lars Erik Eriksen	NOR	2:30:53.00
5.	Sergei Savelyev	SOV/RUS	2:31:15.82
6.	Yevgeny Belyaev	SOV/RUS	2:31:21.19
7.	Oddvar Brå	NOR	2:31:46.83
8.	Sven-Åke Lundbäck	SWE	2:31:59.65

Zimyatov won this third gold medal in ten days, having skied a total of 105 kilometers.

1984 Sarajevo C: 54, N: 21, D: 2.19.

1.	Thomas Wassberg	SWE	2:15:55.8
2.	Gunde Svan	SWE	2:16:00.7
3.	Aki Karvonen	FIN	2:17:04.7
4.	Harri Kirvesniemi	FIN	2:18:34.1
5.	Jan Lindvall	NOR	2:19:27.1
6.	Andreas Grünenfelder	SWI	2:19:46.2
7.	Aleksandr Zavyalov	SOV/RUS	2:20:27.6
8.	Vladimir Sakhnov	SOV/KAZ	2:20:53.7

1988 Calgary-Canmore C: 70, N: 23, D: 2.27.

1.	Gunde Svan	SWE	2:04:30.9
2.	Maurilio De Zolt	ITA	2:05:36.4
3.	Andreas Grünenfelder	SWI	2:06:01.9
4.	Vegard Ulvang	NOR	2:06:32.3
5.	Holger Bauroth	GDR	2:07:02.4
6.	Jan Ottosson	SWE	2:07:34.8
7.	Kari Ristanen	FIN	2:08:08.1
8.	Uwe Bellmann	GDR	2:08:18.6

The 69th of 70 starters, Gunde Svan earned his second gold medal of the Calgary Games to match the two he won in Sarajevo in 1984.

Roberto Alvarez of Mexico, who had never skied more than 20 kilometers, was the last of the 61 finishers in a time of 3:22:25.1—almost 52 minutes slower than the man in sixtieth place, Battulga Dambajamtsyn of Mongolia. Alvarez was so far behind that race officials became worried that he had gotten lost and sent out a delegation to find him. In 1992, Alvarez was again the last of the finishers, this time in 3:09:04.7, only 31½ minutes behind the rest of the field.

1992 Albertville-Les Saisies C: 73, N: 29, D: 2.22.

1.	Bjørn Dahlie	NOR	2:03:41.5
2.	Maurilio De Zolt	ITA	2:04:39.1
3.	Giorgio Vanzetta	ITA	2:06:42.1
4.	Aleksei Prokurorov	SOV/RUS	2:07:06.1
5.	Hervé Balland	FRA	2:07:17.7
6.	Radim Nyc	CZE	2:07:41.5
7.	Johann Mühlegg	GER	2:07:45.2
8.	Pavel Benc	CZE	2:08:13.6

Dahlie led from the start and closed out the Albertville Olympics with three gold medals and one silver. De Zolt, at age 41, won his second straight silver medal. When Dahlie returned to his parents' home in Nannestad, he was presented with 1568 red roses arranged in the shape of the Olympic rings, as well as a book containing the names of 1568 people, each of whom had contributed one rose.

1994 Lillehammer C: 66, N: 25, D: 2.27.
(Classical)

1.	Vladimir Smirnov	KAZ	2:07:20.3
2.	Mika Myllylä	FIN	2:08:41.9
3.	Sture Sivertsen	NOR	2:08:49.0
4.	Bjørn Dahlie	NOR	2:09:11.4
5.	Erling Jevne	NOR	2:09:12.2
6.	Christer Majbäck	SWE	2:10:03.8
7.	Maurilio De Zolt	ITA	2:10:12.1
8.	Giorgio Vanzetta	ITA	2:10:16.4

Norway's prime minister, Gro Harlem Brundstad, summed up the feelings of most Norwegians when she said that the results of the 50-kilometer race were "the perfect ending to a great Olympics." One might assume from this that the winner was Norwegian. Not at all. He was a Russian from Kazakhstan who lived in Sweden. Vladimir Smirnov was, in his own words, "a citizen of the world."

At the 1988 Olympics, Smirnov earned two silver medals and one bronze. In 1991, a Swedish club offered to sponsor him and he moved with his family to Sundsvall, Sweden. Smirnov soon endeared himself to Scandinavians by quickly learning the Swedish language. Nonetheless, it was a difficult transition and his athletic performances suffered. At the 1992 Olympics he could do no better than eighth in an individual event.

The following year Smirnov regained his form, leading to the incident that made him a true favorite for Norwegians. At the 1993 world championships in Falun, Sweden, Smirnov and Norway's Bjørn Dahlie crossed the finish line in a near dead-heat in the combined pursuit event. Because his body reached the finish first, Smirnov was declared the winner. But cross-country races are actually decided by crossing an electronic beam 25 centimeters (9¾ inches) above the ground. When officials reviewed the finish, they discovered that Dahlie's foot had crossed the line before Smirnov's. Norwegian ski fans were thrilled that their hero had won, but they also appreciated that Smirnov was just as deserving of victory and they took him to heart. In fact, he became so popular in Norway that he was chosen to appear in a television commercial for coffee.

The Lillehammer Games were Smirnov's last chance for Olympic gold. Most observers, including Smirnov himself, thought that his best shot would be at 30 kilometers. But he finished a disappointing tenth. Then he placed second behind Dahlie in the 10-kilometer race and the pursuit and all that was left was the 50 kilometers. Unfortunately, this had always been Smirnov's weakest race. At the 1992 Olympics, for example, he had finished 35th and at the 1993 world championships 21st. Always the pattern was the same: after about 40 kilometers he would tie up or tire. This time, however, Smirnov reached the 40-kilometer mark and discovered something amazing: he felt fine. Spurred on by the large and enthusiastic crowd lining the trail, he held his pace and won easily.

4 × 10-KILOMETER RELAY

In 1988 this was a freestyle event; however, since 1992 two skiers on each team use the classical technique and two use the skating technique.

1924–1932 not held

1936 Garmisch-Partenkirchen T: 16, N: 16, D: 2.10.

1.	FIN	(Sulo Nurmela, Klaes Karppinen, Matti Lähde, Kalle Jalkanen)	2:41:33
2.	NOR	(Oddbjörn Hagen, Olaf Hoffsbakken, Sverre Brodahl, Bjarne Iversen)	2:41:39
3.	SWE	(John Berger, Erik Larsson, Arthur Häggblad, Martin Matsbo)	2:43:03
4.	ITA	(Giulio Gerardi, Severino Menardi, Vincenzo Demetz, Giovanni Kasebacher)	2:50:05
5.	CZE	(Cyril Musil, Gustav Berauer, Lukas Mihalak, František Simunek)	2:51:56
6.	GER	(Friedel Däuber, Willi Bogner, Herbert Leupold, Anton Zeller)	2:54:54
7.	POL	(Michal Górski, Marian Woyna-Orlewicz, Stanislaw Karpiel, Bronislaw Czech)	2:58:50
8.	AUT	(Alfred Robner, Harald Bosio, Erich Gallwitz, Hans Baumann)	3:02:48

Kalle Jalkanen, the last Finnish skier, staged a spectacular come-from-behind victory. Trailing Bjarne Iversen of Norway by 82 seconds when he took over the baton, he caught him as they entered the ski stadium and won by only 20 yards.

1948 St. Moritz T: 11, N: 11, D: 2.3.

1.	SWE	(Nils Östensson, Nils Täpp, Gunnar Eriksson, Martin Lundström)	2:32:08
2.	FIN	(Lauri Silvennoinen, Teuvo Laukkanen, Sauli Rytky, August Kiuru)	2:41:06
3.	NOR	(Erling Evensen, Olav Ökern, Reidar Nyborg, Olav Hagen)	2:44:33
4.	AUT	(Josl Gstrein, Josef Deutschmann, Engelbert Hundertpfund, Karl Rafreider)	2:47:18
5.	SWI	(Niklaus Stump, Robert Zurbriggen, Max Müller, Edi Schild)	2:48:07
6.	ITA	(Vincenzo Perruchon, Silvio Confortola, Rizzieri Rodighiero, Severino Compagnoni)	2:51:00
7.	FRA	(René Jeandel, Gerard Perrier, Marius Mora, Benoit Carrara)	2:51:53
8.	CZE	(Stefan Kovalcik, František Balvin, Jaroslav Zejicek, Jaroslav Cardal)	2:54:56

1952 Oslo T: 13, N: 13, D: 2.23.

1.	FIN	(Heikki Hasu, Paavo Lonkila, Urpo Korhonen, Tapio Mäkelä)	2:20:16
2.	NOR	(Magnar Estenstad, Mikal Kirkholt, Martin Stokken, Hallgeir Brenden)	2.23:13
3.	SWE	(Nils Täpp, Sigurd Andersson, Enar Josefsson, Martin Lundström)	2:24:13
4.	FRA	(Gerard Perrier, Benoit Carrara, Jean Mermet, René Mandrillon)	2:31:11
5.	AUT	(Hans Eder, Friedrich Krischan, Karl Rafreider, Josef Schneeberger)	2:34:36
6.	ITA	(Arrigo Delladio, Nino Anderlini, Frederico de Florian, Vincenzo Perruchon)	2:35:33
7.	GER	(Hubert Egger, Albert Mohr, Heinz Hauser, Rudi Kopp)	2:36:37
8.	CZE	(Vladimir Simunek, Stefan Kovalcik, Vlastimil Melich, Jaroslav Cardal)	2:37:12

Martin Stokken of the silver medal winning Norwegian team had placed fourth in the 10,000-meter run at the 1948 Summer Olympics.

1956 Cortina T: 14, N: 14, D: 2.4.

1. SOV/RUS	(Fedor Terentyev, Pavel Kolchin, Nikolai Anikin, Vladimir Kuzin)	2:15:30
2. FIN	(August Kiuru, Jormo Kortalainen, Arvo Viitanen, Veikko Hakulinen)	2:16:31
3. SWE	(Lennart Larsson, Gunnar Samuelsson, Per-Erik Larsson, Sixten Jernberg)	2:17:42
4. NOR	(Håkon Brusveen, Per Olsen, Marten Stokken, Hallgeir Brenden)	2:21:16
5. ITA	(Pompeo Fattor, Ottavio Compagnoni, Innocenzo Chatrian, Frederico De Florian)	2:23:28
6. FRA	(Victor Arbez, René Mandrillon, Benoit Carrara, Jean Mermet)	2:24:06
7. SWI	(Werner Zwingli, Victor Kronig, Fritz Kocher, Marcel Huguenin)	2:24:30
8. CZE	(Emil Okuliar, Vlastimil Melich, Josef Prokes, Ilja Matous)	2:24:54

The first two Soviet skiers, Terentyev and Kolchin, built up an insurmountable lead of two and three-quarter minutes.

1960 Squaw Valley T: 11, N: 11, D: 2.25.

1. FIN	(Toimi Alatalo, Eero Mäntyranta, Väinö Huhtala, Veikko Hakulinen)	2:18:45.6
2. NOR	(Harald Grönningen, Hallgeir Brenden, Einar Östby, Håkon Brusveen)	2:18:46.4
3. SOV/RUS	(Anatoly Shelyukin, Gennady Vaganov, Aleksei Kuznetsov, Nikolai Anikin)	2:21:21.6
4. SWE	(Lars Olsson, Janne Stefansson, Lennart Larsson, Sixten Jernberg)	2:21:31.8
5. ITA	(Giulio De Florian, Giuseppe Steiner, Pompeo Fattor, Marcello De Dorigo)	2:22:32.5
6. POL	(Andrzej Mateja, Józef Rysula, Józef Gut-Misiaga, Kazimierz Zelek)	2:26:25.3
7. FRA	(Victor Arbez, René Mandrillon, Benoit Carrara, Jean Mermet)	2:26:30.8
8. SWI	(Fritz Kocher, Marcel Huguenin, Lorenz Possa, Alphonse Baume)	2:29:36.8

Until the introduction of the pursuit race in 1992, the relay was the only skiing event in which the participants actually raced against each other. It was also the only event that had the potential for a truly exciting finish. Such a finish occurred in 1960. Lars Olsson gave Sweden a seven-second lead at the end of the first leg, but the second Swedish skier, Janne Stefansson, was quickly overtaken by Brenden and Mäntyranta. At the halfway mark, Norway and Finland were tied. Then Norway's Einar Östby pulled away to a 20-second lead. Håkon Brusveen, winner of the 15-kilometer race two days earlier, took over the last leg for Norway, followed by six-time Olympic medalist, 35-year-old Veikko Hakulinen. After eight kilometers Hakulinen overhauled Brusveen, but the Norwegian pulled back into the lead. With 100 meters to go, Hakulinen began to pass Brusveen again. Edging ahead in the final strides, the great Finnish veteran managed to win by three feet. It was a fitting ending to Hakulinen's marvelous Olympic career, during which he earned three gold medals, each in a different event and each in a different Olympics, as well as three silver medals and one bronze.

1964 Innsbruck-Seefeld T: 15, N: 15, D: 2.8.

1. SWE	(Karl Åke Asph, Sixten Jernberg, Janne Stefansson, Assar Rönnlund)	2:18:34.6
2. FIN	(Väinö Huhtala, Arto Tiainen, Kalevi Laurila, Eero Mäntyranta)	2:18:42.4
3. SOV/RUS	(Ivan Utrobin, Gennady Vaganov, Igor Voronchikin, Pavel Kolchin)	2:18:46.9
4. NOR	(Magnar Lundemo, Erling Steineidet, Einar Östby, Harald Grönningen)	2:19:11.9
5. ITA	(Giuseppe Steiner, Marcello De Dorigo, Giulio De Florian, Franco Nones)	2:21:16.8
6. FRA	(Victor Arbez, Felix Mathieu, Roger Pires, Paul Romand)	2:26:31.4

7. GDR/ (Heinz Seidel, Helmut Weidlich, Enno Röder, Walter Demel)   2:26:34.4
   GER
8. POL (Józef Gut-Misiaga, Tadeusz Jankowski, Edward Budny, Józef Rysula)   2:27:27.0

Another thrilling finish, in which Väinö Huhtala gave Finland a 5.9-second lead after the first lap with the U.S.S.R. in second, Norway third, and Sweden fourth. By the halfway mark, Vaganov of the Soviet Union had moved into an 11.6-second lead over second-place Norway, with Italy in third, followed by Sweden and Finland. Pavel Kolchin took over the last leg for the Soviet Union, followed 13.4 seconds later by Grönningen of Norway, 31.5 seconds later by Assar Rönnlund of Sweden, and 32.3 seconds later by Eero Mäntyranta. Grönningen passed Kolchin to take the lead, but he exhausted himself by his effort and was passed shortly afterward by Mäntyranta, Rönnlund, and Kolchin. A few hundred meters short of the finish line Rönnlund summoned an extra reserve of energy, pushed ahead of Mäntyranta, and won by 7.8 seconds.

1968 Grenoble-Autrans T: 15, N: 15, D: 2.14.
1. NOR (Odd Martinsen, Pål Tyldum, Harald Grönningen, Ole Ellefsäter)   2:08:33.5
2. SWE (Jan Halvarsson, Bjarne Andersson, Gunnar Larsson, Assar Rönnlund)   2:10:13.2
3. FIN (Kalevi Oikarainen, Hannu Taipale, Kalevi Laurila, Eero Mäntyranta)   2:10:56.7
4. SOV/ (Vladimir Voronkov, Anatoly Akentiev, Valery Tarakanov, Vyacheslav   2:10:57.2
   RUS Vedenine)
5. SWI (Konrad Hischier, Josef Haas, Florian Koch, Alois Kälin)   2:15:32.4
6. ITA (Giulio De Florian, Franco Nones, Palmiro Serafini, Aldo Stella)   2:16:32.2
7. GDR (Gerhard Grimmer, Axel Lesser, Peter Thiel, Gert-Dietmar Klause)   2:19:22.8
8. GER (Helmut Gerlach, Walter Demel, Herbert Steinbeisser, Karl Buhl)   2:19:37.6

Eero Mäntyranta made up over 26 seconds on the final leg to nip Vedenine at the finish line for the bronze medal. This gave Mäntyranta an Olympic medal total of three gold, two silver, and two bronze.

1972 Sapporo-Makomanai T: 14, N: 14, D: 2.13.
1. SOV/ (Vladimir Voronkov, Yuri Skobov, Fedor Simashev, Vyacheslav   2:04:47.94
   RUS Vedenine)
2. NOR (Oddvar Brå, Pål Tyldum, Ivar Formo, Johs Harviken)   2:04:57.06
3. SWI (Alfred Kälin, Albert Giger, Alois Kälin, Eduard Hauser)   2:07:00.06
4. SWE (Thomas Magnusson, Lars-Göran Åslund, Gunnar Larsson, Sven-Åke   2:07:03.60
   Lundbäck)
5. FIN (Hannu Taipale, Juha Mieto, Juhani Repo, Osmo Karjalainen)   2:07:50.19
6. GDR (Gerd Hessler, Axel Lesser, Gerhard Grimmer, Gert-Dietmar Klause)   2:10:03.73
7. GER (Franz Betz, Urban Hettich, Hartmut Dopp, Walter Demel)   2:10:42.85
8. CZE (Stanislav Henych, Jan Fajstavr, Jan Michalko, Jan Ilavsky)   2:11:27.55

Vedenine began the final leg 61½ seconds behind Johs Harviken, but he overtook the Norwegian one kilometer from the finish and won by over nine seconds.

1976 Innsbruck-Seefeld T: 16, N: 16, D: 2.12.
1. FIN (Matti Pitkänen, Juha Mieto, Pertti Teurajärvi, Arto Koivisto)   2:07:59.72
2. NOR (Pål Tyldum, Einar Sagstuen, Ivar Formo, Odd Martinsen)   2:09:58.36
3. SOV (Yevgeny Belyaev, Nikolai Bazhukov, Sergei Savelyev, Ivan Garanin)   2:10:51.46
4. SWE (Benny Södergren, Christer Johansson, Thomas Wassberg, Sven-Åke   2:11:16.88
   Lundbäck)
5. SWI (Franz Renggli, Edi Hauser, Heinz Gähler, Alfred Kälin)   2:11:28.53
6. USA (Douglas Peterson, Timothy Caldwell, William Koch, Ronny Yaeger)   2:11:41.35

| 7. ITA | (Renzo Chiocchetti, Tonio Biondini, Ulrico Kostner, Giulio Capitanio) | 2:12:07.12 |
| 8. AUT | (Rudolf Horn, Reinhold Feichter, Werner Vogel, Herbert Wachter) | 2:12:22.80 |

East Germany was in second place when their second skier, Axel Lesser, ran into a spectator, injured his knee, and had to abandon the race.

1980 Lake Placid T: 10, N: 10, D: 2.20.

1. SOV/ RUS	(Vassily Rochev, Nikolai Bazhukov, Yevgeny Belyaev, Nikolai Zimyatov)	1:57:03.46
2. NOR	(Lars Erik Eriksen, Per Knut Aaland, Ove Aunli, Oddvar Brå)	1:58:45.77
3. FIN	(Harri Kirvesniemi, Pertti Teurajärvi, Matti Pitkänen, Juha Mieto)	2:00:00.18
4. GER	(Peter Zipfel, Wolfgang Müller, Dieter Notz, Jochen Behle)	2:00:27.74
5. SWE	(Sven-Åke Lundbäck, Thomas Eriksson, Benny Kohlberg, Thomas Wassberg)	2:00:42.71
6. ITA	(Maurilio De Zolt, Benedetto Carrara, Giulio Capitanio, Giorgio Vanzetta)	2:01:09.93
7. SWI	(Hansüli Kreuzer, Konrad Hallenbarter, Edi Hauser, Gaudenz Ambühl)	2:03:36.57
8. USA	(William Koch, Timothy Caldwell, James Galanes, Stanley Dunklee)	2:04:12.17

1984 Sarajevo T: 17, N: 17, D: 2.16.

1. SWE	(Thomas Wassberg, Benny Kohlberg, Jan Ottosson, Gunde Svan)	1:55:06.3
2. SOV	(Aleksandr Batyuk, Aleksandr Zavyalov, Vladimir Nikitin, Nikolai Zimyatov)	1:55:16.5
3. FIN	(Kari Ristanen, Juha Mieto, Harri Kirvesniemi, Aki Karvonen)	1:56:31.4
4. NOR	(Lars-Erik Eriksen, Jan Lindvall, Ove Aunli, Tor Håkon Holte)	1:57:27.6
5. SWI	(Giachem Guidon, Konrad Hallenbarter, Joos Ambühl, Andreas Grünenfelder)	1:58:06.0
6. GER	(Jochen Behle, Stefan Dotzler, Franz Schöbel, Peter Zipfel)	1:59:30.2
7. ITA	(Maurilio De Zolt, Alfred Runggaldier, Giulio Capitanio, Giorgio Vanzetta)	1:59:30.3
8. USA	(Dan Simoneau, Timothy Caldwell, James Galanes, William Koch)	1:59:52.3

The anchor leg matched 15-kilometer gold medalist Gunde Svan against 30-kilometer gold medalist Nikolai Zimyatov. Zimyatov took off with a lead of a fraction of a second. Svan tracked him the whole way and then, as planned, launched his successful attack one kilometer from the finish.

1988 Calgary-Canmore T: 16, N: 16, D: 2.22.

1. SWE	(Jan Ottosson, Thomas Wassberg, Gunde Svan, N. Torgny Mogren)	1:43:58.6
2. SOV	(Vladimir Smirnov, Vladimir Sakhnov, Mikhail Devyatyarov, Aleksei Prokurorov)	1:44:11.3
3. CZE	(Radim Nyc, Vaclav Korunka, Pavel Benc, Ladislav Švanda)	1:45:22.7
4. SWI	(Andreas Grünenfelder, Jürg Capol, Giachem Guidon, Jeremias Wigger)	1:46:16.3
5. ITA	(Silvano Barco, Albert Walder, Giorgio Vanzetta, Maurilio De Zolt)	1:46:16.7
6. NOR	(Pål Gunnar Mikkelsplass, Oddvar Brå, Vegard Ulvang, Terje Langli)	1:46:48.7
7. GER	(Walter Kuss, Georg Fischer, Jochen Behle, Herbert Fritzenwenger)	1:48:05.0
8. FIN	(Jari Laukkanen, Harri Kirvesniemi, Jari Räsänen, Kari Ristanen)	1:48:24.0

The U.S.S.R. and Sweden were virtually even at the halfway point. Midway through the third leg, Gunde Svan pulled away from Mikhail Devyatyarov, who then fell, trying to maintain contact. By the time he passed off to Torgny Mogren, Svan had given Sweden a 27-second lead. Aleksei Prokurorov cut the deficit to 7 seconds with 5 kilometers to go. But he, too, fell, and he was never able to pick up the challenge again.

Torgny Mogren crosses the finish line in the 1988 4 x 10-kilometer nordic ski relay.

1992 Albertville-Les Saisies T: 16, N: 16, D: 2.18.

1.	NOR	(Terje Langli, Vegard Ulvang, Kristen Skjeldal, Bjørn Dahlie)	1:39:26.0
2.	ITA	(Giuseppe Pulié, Marco Albarello, Giorgio Vanzetta, Silvio Fauner)	1:40:52.7
3.	FIN	(Mika Kuusisto, Harri Kirvesniemi, Jari Räsänen, Jari Isometsä)	1:41:22.9
4.	SWE	(Jan Ottosson, Christer Majbäck, Henrik Forsberg, N. Torgny Mogren)	1:41:23.1
5.	SOV	(Andrei Kirillov, Vladimir Smirnov, Mikhail Botvinov, Aleksei Prokurorov)	1:43:03.6
6.	GER	(Holger Bauroth, Jochen Behle, Torald Rein, Johann Mühlegg)	1:43:41.7
7.	CZE	(Radim Nyc, Lubomir Buchta, Pavel Benc, Vaclav Korunka)	1:44:20.0
8.	FRA	(Patrick Rémy, Philippe Sanchez, Stéphane Azambre, Hervé Balland)	1:44:51.1

Ottosson gave Sweden the early lead, but Ulvang pulled away during the second leg and Norway won easily. Anchorman Bjørn Dahlie celebrated by turning around and crossing the finish line backward. Sweden's anchor, Torgny Mogren, skied the second-fastest leg of the day, but Isometsä caught him in the final strides to give Finland the bronze.

1994 Lillehammer T: 14, N: 14, D: 2.22.

1.	ITA	(Maurilio De Zolt, Marco Albarello, Giorgio Vanzetta, Silvio Fauner)	1:41:15.0
2.	NOR	(Sture Sivertsen, Vegard Ulvang, Thomas Alsgaard, Bjørn Dahlie)	1:41:15.4
3.	FIN	(Mika Myllylä, Harri Kirvesniemi, Jari Räsänen, Jari Isometsä)	1:42:15.6
4.	GER	(Torald Rein, Jochen Behle, Peter Schlickenrieder, Johann Mühlegg)	1:44:26.7
5.	RUS	(Andrei Kirilov, Aleksei Prokurorov, Gennadi Lazutin, Mikhail Botvinov)	1:44:29.2
6.	SWE	(Jan Ottosson, Christer Majbäck, Anders Bergström, Henrik Forsberg)	1:45:22.7
7.	SWI	(Jeremias Wigger, Hans Diethelm, Jürg Capol, Giachem Guidon)	1:47:12.2
8.	CZE	(Lubomír Buchta, Václav Korunka, Jirí Teply, Pavel Benc)	1:47:12.6

Italy's Sylvio Fauner (left) tries to hold off Norway's Bjørn Dahlie 100 meters from the finish of the 1994 4 × 10-kilometer relay.

In nordic skiing-crazed Norway, the hottest ticket of the 1994 Olympics was for the men's 4×10-kilometer relay. When ticket sales began, 31,000 inside-the-stadium tickets were made available. More than 203,000 people applied—almost five percent of Norway's population. Including those spectators who lined the trail outside the stadium, over 100,000 people showed up on race day. Although the result was not what they had hoped for, they saw what was probably the most exciting race in the history of the Winter Olympics.

For the first one hour and twenty minutes, it was an incredibly close three-team contest among Norway, Italy and Finland. In retrospect, the turning point came in the very first leg. At the 1993 world championships, Norway defeated Italy by 9.6 seconds after leadoff skier Sture Sivertsen pulled away to a 48-second lead over Maurilio De Zolt. In Lillehammer, the Italians stuck with De Zolt, a former fireman who once finished second in ladder climbing in the World Fireman Championships. This time De Zolt was able to keep within 10 seconds of Sivertsen, while Finland's Mika Myllyla handed off only a stride behind Sivertsen.

Italy's second skier, Marco Albarello, closed the gap and took the lead at the halfway mark with Norway a half second behind and Finland another six tenths of a second behind Norway. Jari Räsänen pulled Finland ahead with one leg to go, but the Finns had put their slowest man, Jari Isometsä, last, and he soon fell behind.

The final duel would be between Norway's Bjørn Dahlie, who had already won the individual 10-kilometer gold medal and Italy's Silvio Fauner, who had finished eighth in that same race, but who was confident he could beat Dahlie in a relay. Dahlie tried to pull away, but Fauner wouldn't let him go. On the last hill, Dahlie almost stopped completely in an attempt to make Fauner pass him, but Fauner stopped too. Finally Fauner edged ahead as they came around the final turn. With

100 meters to go, Dahlie tried to sprint past the Italian, but Fauner matched him stride for stride and reached the finish line about one ski-length ahead of Dahlie. The Norwegian crowd was stunned into silence, but then burst into applause in honor of a great race.

At age 43, Maurilio De Zolt had finally won an Olympic gold medal. Of the ten winter athletes who have earned gold medals after their 40th birthdays, only De Zolt was not a bobsledder.

SKI JUMP, NORMAL HILL, INDIVIDUAL

The first ski-jumping contest was held in Trysil, Norway, in 1862. Jumps are scored according to two criteria: distance and style. Style points are determined by five judges. The highest and lowest scores are dropped and the points awarded by the remaining three judges are added together. Each contestant takes two jumps. In 1964 the ski jump was split into two events: the small hill, or 70-meter jump, and the big hill, or 90-meter jump. The hills vary in size from Olympics to Olympics and the events are now known as normal hill and large hill.

In 1985, Swedish jumper Jan Boklöv began spreading the tips of his skis into a V shape. Initially he was laughed at and penalized. But when wind tunnel tests proved that the V provided 28 percent more lift than the traditional, parallel style, and when Boklöv won the 1989 World Cup, ski jumpers started changing their style en masse. By 1992, all the individual medal winners used the V style.

1924–1960 not held

1964 Innsbruck-Seefeld C: 53, N: 15, D: 1.31.

			FIRST JUMP (M)	SECOND JUMP (M)	TOTAL PTS.
1.	Veikko Kankkonen	FIN	80.0	79.0	229.9
2.	Toralf Engan	NOR	79.0	79.0	226.3
3.	Torgeir Brandtzäg	NOR	79.0	78.0	222.9
4.	Josef Matous	CZE	80.5	77.0	218.2
5.	Dieter Neuendorf	GDR	78.5	77.0	214.7
6.	Helmut Recknagel	GDR	77.0	75.5	210.4
7.	Kurt Elima	SWE	76.0	75.0	208.9
8.	Hans Olav Sörensen	NOR	76.0	74.5	208.6

In 1964 the competitors were allowed to use the best two of three jumps. This rule saved Kankkonen, whose mediocre first jump landed him in 29th place. However his second and third leaps were masterpieces.

1968 Grenoble-Autrans C: 58, N: 18, D: 2.11.

			FIRST JUMP (M)	SECOND JUMP (M)	TOTAL PTS.
1.	Jiři Raška	CZE	79.0	72.5	216.5
2.	Reinhold Bachler	AUT	77.5	76.0	214.2
3.	Baldur Preiml	AUT	80.0	72.5	212.6
4.	Björn Wirkola	NOR	76.5	72.5	212.0
5.	Topi Mattila	FIN	78.0	72.5	211.9
6.	Anatoly Zheglanov	SOV/RUS	79.5	74.5	211.5
7.	Dieter Neuendorf	GDR	76.5	73.0	211.3
8.	Vladimir Belousov	SOV/RUS	73.5	73.0	207.5

(Left to right) *Seiji Aochi (bronze), Yukio Kasaya (gold), and Akitsugu Konno (silver), popular winners of the 1972 normal hill ski jump.*

1972 Sapporo-Miyanomori C: 56, N: 16, D: 2.6.

			FIRST JUMP (M)	SECOND JUMP (M)	TOTAL PTS.
1.	Yukio Kasaya	JPN	84.0	79.0	244.2
2.	Akitsugu Konno	JPN	82.5	79.0	234.8
3.	Seiji Aochi	JPN	83.5	77.5	229.5
4.	Ingolf Mork	NOR	78.0	78.0	225.5
5.	Jiří Raška	CZE	78.5	78.0	224.8
6.	Wojciech Fortuna	POL	82.0	76.5	222.0
7.	Karel Kodejska	CZE	80.0	75.5	220.2
7.	Gari Napalkov	SOV/RUS	79.5	76.0	220.2

Before 1972 Japan had won a total of one medal in the Winter Olympics. Consequently, when 28-year-old Yukio Kasaya won three straight meets in Europe one month before the Sapporo Games, Japan's hopes for a gold medal in the first Winter Olympics to be held in Asia were concentrated on Kasaya. The excitement was particularly great because Kasaya was a hometown boy from Japan's northernmost island of Hokkaido, where the games were being held. Kasaya's teammates, Akitsugu Konno and Seiji Aochi, were also from Hokkaido. Scattered among the 100,000 people at the bottom of the jumping hill were old schoolmates of Kasaya's waving the flag of Yoichimachi High School, Kasaya's alma mater. Despite the enormous pressure, Kasaya produced the best jump of each round. While the nation rejoiced over the stunning Japanese sweep, Kasaya, who had made 10,000 jumps since he was 11 years old, reminded the press of his personal motto, "Challenge not your rivals, but yourself."

1976 Innsbruck-Seefeld C: 55, N: 15, D: 2.7.

			FIRST JUMP (M)	SECOND JUMP (M)	TOTAL PTS.
1.	Hans-Georg Aschenbach	GDR	84.5	82.0	252.0
2.	Jochen Danneberg	GDR	83.5	82.5	246.2

3.	Karl Schnabl	AUT	82.5	81.5	242.0
4.	Jaroslav Balcar	CZE	81.0	81.5	239.6
5.	Ernst von Grüningen	SWI	80.5	80.5	238.7
6.	Reinhold Bachler	AUT	80.5	80.5	237.2
7.	Anton Innauer	AUT	80.5	81.5	233.5
7.	Rudolf Wanner	AUT	79.5	79.5	233.5

Aschenbach later admitted to having taken anabolic steroids for eight years. He described his victory in 1976 as his greatest moment in sports, but also his most anxious. "Those were the worst hours of my life. I had won at the Olympic Winter Games on the small tower. Then the doping control. My God, what I went through. Will they catch you? Or was the timing correct once again? Was everything for nothing? Will you be the one they place the blame on, the idiot that is the butt of laughter for everybody? Nobody can imagine what you go through. You even forget that you have won."

1980 Lake Placid C: 48, N: 16, D: 2.17.

			FIRST JUMP (M)	SECOND JUMP (M)	TOTAL PTS.
1.	Anton Innauer	AUT	89.0	90.0	266.3
2.	Manfred Deckert	GDR	85.0	88.0	249.2
2.	Hirokazu Yagi	JPN	87.0	83.5	249.2
4.	Masahiro Akimoto	JPN	83.5	87.5	248.5
5.	Pentti Kokkonen	FIN	86.0	83.5	247.6
6.	Hubert Neuper	AUT	82.5	88.5	245.5
7.	Alfred Groyer	AUT	85.5	83.5	245.3
8.	Jouko Törmänen	FIN	83.0	85.5	243.5

Toni Innauer, a 21-year-old vegetarian, used his superb form to win by a huge margin.

1984 Sarajevo C: 58, N: 17, D: 2.12.

			FIRST JUMP (M)	SECOND JUMP (M)	TOTAL PTS.
1.	Jens Weissflog	GDR	90.0	87.0	215.2
2.	Matti Nykänen	FIN	91.0	84.0	214.0
3.	Jari Puikkonen	FIN	81.5	91.5	212.8
4.	Stefan Stannarius	GDR	84.0	89.5	211.1
5.	Rolf Åge Berg	NOR	86.0	86.5	208.5
6.	Andreas Felder	AUT	84.0	87.0	205.6
7.	Piotr Fijas	POL	87.0	88.0	204.5
8.	Vegard Opaas	NOR	86.0	87.0	203.8

Nineteen-year-old World Cup leader Jens Weissflog overcame his rival Matti Nykänen with a solid, though unspectacular, second jump.

1988 Calgary C: 58, N: 19, D: 2.14.

			FIRST JUMP (M)	SECOND JUMP (M)	TOTAL PTS.
1.	Matti Nykänen	FIN	89.5	89.5	229.1
2.	Pavel Ploc	CZE	84.5	87.0	212.1

		FIRST JUMP (M)	SECOND JUMP (M)	TOTAL PTS.
3. Jiří Malec	CZE	88.0	85.5	211.8
4. Miran Tepeš	YUG	84.0	83.5	211.2
5. Jiří Parma	CZE	83.5	82.5	203.8
6. Heinz Kuttin	AUT	87.0	80.5	199.7
7. Jari Puikkonen	FIN	84.0	80.0	199.1
8. Staffan Tällberg	SWE	83.0	81.0	198.1

Matti Nykänen outclassed the opposition to win the first of his three Calgary gold medals. In last place was the popular English plasterer, Michael "Eddie the Eagle" Edwards, who scored less than half the points of any other jumper. Edwards once summed up the mental challenge of ski jumping with this description of his first encounter with the sport: "When I looked from the top of the jump, I was so frightened that my bum shriveled up like a prune."

1992 Albertville-Courcheval C: 58, N: 16, D: 2.9.

		FIRST JUMP (M)	SECOND JUMP (M)	TOTAL PTS.
1. Ernst Vettori	AUT	88.0	87.5	222.8
2. Martin Höllwarth	AUT	90.5	83.0	218.1
3. Toni Nieminen	FIN	88.0	84.5	217.0
4. Heinz Kuttin	AUT	85.5	86.0	214.4
5. Mika Laitinen	FIN	85.5	85.5	213.6
6. Andreas Felder	AUT	87.0	83.0	213.5
7. Heiko Hunger	GER	87.0	84.0	211.6
8. Didier Mollard	FRA	84.5	85.0	209.7

Twenty-seven-year-old Ernst Vettori, in third place after the first round, proved more consistent than the two teenagers ahead of him, Höllwarth (17) and Nieminen (16). Competing in his third Olympics, Vettori had been on the verge of retirement when the new V style revived his interest and his jumping career. Jan Boklöv, the inventor of the V, finished only 47th.

1994 Lillehammer C: 58, N: 19, D: 2.25.

		FIRST JUMP (M)	SECOND JUMP (M)	TOTAL PTS.
1. Espen Bredesen	NOR	100.5	105.0	282.0
2. Lasse Ottesen	NOR	102.5	98.0	268.0
3. Dieter Thoma	GER	98.5	102.5	260.5
4. Jens Weissflog	GER	98.0	96.5	260.0
5. Koriaki Kasai	JPN	98.0	93.0	259.0
6. Jani Markus Soininen	FIN	95.0	100.5	258.5
7. Andreas Goldberger	AUT	98.0	93.5	258.0
8. Jinya Nishikata	JPN	99.0	94.0	253.0

In 1992 Espen Bredesen finished dead last in the normal hill event and 57th of 59 in the large hill. He was viciously ridiculed by Norwegian sportswriters, who dubbed him "Espen the Eagle" after the clownish "Eddie the Eagle" Edwards, who had placed last in 1988. Bredesen felt humiliated, but, in his words, "I had more patience than they had jokes." One year later he won two gold medals at the 1993 world championships and in Lillehammer, before a wildly enthusiastic crowd of

40,000, he earned the gold medal in the same event in which he had finished last at the last Olympics.

The Norwegian team coach, Trond Joran Pedersen, supplemented the usual training exercises by forcing Bredesen and his other charges to engage in some unusual pursuits. To help their balance he made them study rock climbing and ballet. To help them feel comfortable in the air he made them parachute from an airplane at 11,500 feet and dangle from a cliff at 4,800 feet.

SKI JUMP, LARGE HILL, INDIVIDUAL

1924 Chamonix C: 27, N: 9, D: 2.4.

			FIRST JUMP (M)	SECOND JUMP (M)	TOTAL PTS.
1.	Jacob Tullin Thams	NOR	49.0	49.0	18.960
2.	Narve Bonna	NOR	47.5	49.0	18.689
3.	Anders Haugen	USA	49.0	50.0	17.916
4.	Thorleif Haug	NOR	44.0	44.5	17.821
5.	Einar Landvik	NOR	42.0	44.5	17.521
6.	Axel Nilsson	SWE	42.5	44.0	17.146
7.	Menotti Jacobsen	SWE	43.0	42.0	17.083
8.	Alexander Girardbille	SWI	40.5	41.5	16.794

Jacob Tullin Thams is one of only three athletes to earn medals in both the Winter and Summer Olympics. In 1936 he won a silver medal in the 8-meter class yachting event. The final results of this event were not decided until 50 years after it took place. In 1924 it appeared that the great Thorleif Haug had finished third, thus winning two medals at one time: a bronze in the ski jump and a gold in the nordic combined, to go with the two gold medals he had already won in the 50-kilometer and 15-kilometer races. However, in 1974 Toralf Strömstad, who had earned a silver medal in the 1924 nordic combined, discovered an error in the computation of the scores. Haug, who had been dead for 40 years, was demoted to fourth place, while Norwegian-born Anders Haugen, who, at age 36, had paid his own way to the Olympics, was moved up to third. Haugen, the only American ever to win a medal in ski-jumping, was awarded his medal in a special ceremony in Oslo. He was 83 years old.

1928 St. Moritz C: 38, N: 13, D: 2:18.

			FIRST JUMP (M)	SECOND JUMP (M)	TOTAL PTS.
1.	Alf Andersen	NOR	60.0	64.0	19.208
2.	Sigmund Ruud	NOR	57.5	62.5	18.542
3.	Rudolf Burkert	CZE	57.0	59.5	17.937
4.	Axel Nilsson	SWE	53.5	60.0	16.937
5.	Sven Lundgren	SWE	48.0	59.0	16.708
6.	Rolf Monsen	USA	53.0	59.5	16.687
7.	Sepp Muhlbauer	SWI	52.0	58.0	16.541
8.	Ernst Feuz	SWI	52.5	58.5	16.458

An argument developed between the Swiss hosts and the Norwegian favorites. The Norwegians claimed that the high starting point chosen by the Swiss gave an unfair boost to mediocre jumpers who would have been unable to jump as far as the more skilled entrants if the start was farther down. Defending champion Jacob Thulin Thams became outraged when the Norwegians were accused of being "cowards." Tied for fifth after the first jump, he made his point with his second jump by flying all the way to the flat area beyond the landing zone. He stretched out to 73 meters—·at that time the longest jump ever recorded—but he fell when he hit the ground. The consequent loss of style points dropped him to 28th place.

In 1931, silver medalist Sigmund Ruud became the first person to break the 80-meter barrier when he soared 81.5 meters at Davos.

1932 Lake Placid C: 34, N: 10, D: 2.12.

		FIRST JUMP (M)	SECOND JUMP (M)	TOTAL PTS.
1.	Birger Ruud	NOR	66.5	69.0	228.1
2.	Hans Beck	NOR	71.5	63.5	227.0
3.	Kaare Wahlberg	NOR	62.5	64.0	219.5
4.	Sven Eriksson	SWE	65.5	64.0	218.9
5.	Caspar Oimen	USA	63.0	67.5	216.7
6.	Fritz Kaufmann	SWI	63.5	65.5	215.8
7.	Sigmund Ruud	NOR	63.0	62.5	215.1
8.	Goro Adachi	JPN	60.0	66.0	210.7

Hans Beck and the Ruud brothers were brought up together in the mining town of Kongsberg. Confusion concerning the scoring computations caused a four-hour delay in the announcement of the placings, and even then it was orginally stated that Beck had won.

1936 Garmisch-Partenkirchen C: 48, N: 14, D: 2.16.

		FIRST JUMP (M)	SECOND JUMP (M)	TOTAL PTS.
1.	Birger Ruud	NOR	75.0	74.5	232.0
2.	Sven Eriksson	SWE	76.0	76.0	230.5
3.	Reidar Andersen	NOR	74.0	75.0	228.9
4.	Kaare Wahlberg	NOR	73.5	72.0	227.0
5.	Stanislaw Marusarz	POL	73.0	75.5	221.6
6.	Lauri Valonen	FIN	73.5	67.0	219.4
7.	Masaji Iguro	JPN	74.5	72.5	218.2
8.	Arnold Kongsgaard	NOR	74.5	72.5	217.7

Birger Ruud was one of the greatest Olympic athletes of all time—the only person to earn medals in both nordic and alpine skiing. In 1936 he won his second gold medal in ski jumping as well as a silver in the inaugural alpine event, the combined downhill and slalom. Considering that he won another silver 12 years later in the ski jump, one can only imagine what he might have achieved if the 1940 and 1944 Olympics had not been canceled because of war. Despite his great athletic feats, Ruud is most revered for his courageous anti-Nazi stand during the German occupation of Norway. After refusing to cooperate with the Nazi order to organize competitions under their auspices, he helped stage illegal competitions. He was arrested and spent 18 months in a Nazi prison camp. He was released in the summer of 1944 and immediately joned the Resistance. He put his skiing skills to good use by finding and hiding ammunition that was dropped from British airplanes. At the age of 82, Ruud was chosen to be one of the athletes who carried the Olympic flag at the 1994 Opening Ceremony.

1948 St. Moritz C: 49, N: 14, D: 2.7.

		FIRST JUMP (M)	SECOND JUMP (M)	TOTAL PTS.
1. Petter Hugsted	NOR	65.0	70.0	228.1
2. Birger Ruud	NOR	64.0	67.0	226.6
3. Thorleif Schjelderup	NOR	64.0	67.0	225.1
4. Matti Pietikainen	FIN	69.5	69.0	224.6
5. Gordon Wren	USA	68.0	68.5	222.8
6. Leo Laakso	FIN	66.0	69.5	221.7
7. Asbjörn Ruud	NOR	58.0	67.5	220.2
8. Aatto Pietikainen	FIN	69.0	68.0	215.4

Two-time gold medalist Birger Ruud, now 36 years old, went to St. Moritz as a coach. But when he saw the poor weather the night before the competition, he decided to compete in place of the less experienced George Thrane. Ruud's confidence in himself paid off with a silver medal. Peter Hugsted, like Ruud, was from the small town of Kongsberg.

1952 Oslo C: 44, N: 13, D: 2.24.

		FIRST JUMP (M)	SECOND JUMP (M)	TOTAL PTS.
1. Arnfinn Bergmann	NOR	67.5	68.0	226.0
2. Torbjörn Falkanger	NOR	68.0	64.0	221.5
3. Karl Holmström	SWE	67.0	65.5	219.5
4. Toni Brutscher	GER	66.5	62.5	216.5
4. Halvor Naes	NOR	63.5	64.5	216.5
6. Arne Hoel	NOR	66.5	63.5	215.5
7. Antti Hyvärinen	FIN	66.5	61.5	213.5
8. Sepp Weiler	GER	67.0	63.0	213.0

This contest was witnessed by approximately 150,000 people, the largest crowd ever to attend an Olympic event. Between 1924 and 1952 Norway won 14 of the 18 medals awarded in the ski jumps. Since 1952, the Norwegians have earned only 9 of a possible 60 medals in individual events, 3 of them at home in 1994.

1956 Cortina C: 51, N: 16, D: 2.5.

		FIRST JUMP (M)	SECOND JUMP (M)	TOTAL PTS.
1. Antti Hyvärinen	FIN	81.0	84.0	227.0
2. Aulis Kallakorpi	FIN	83.5	80.5	225.0
3. Harry Glass	GDR	83.5	80.5	224.5
4. Max Bolkart	GER	80.0	81.5	222.5
5. Sven Pettersson	SWE	81.0	81.5	220.0
6. Andreas Däscher	SWI	82.0	82.0	219.5
7. Eino Kirjonen	FIN	78.0	81.0	219.0
8. Werner Lesser	GDR	77.5	77.5	210.0

The Norwegian win streak in this event was finally broken by Hyvarinen and Kallakorpi, the first jumpers to refine the new, aerodynamically superior style of jumping with the arms pinned to the sides and the body leaning far forward.

1960 Squaw Valley C: 45, N: 15, D: 2.28.

		FIRST JUMP (M)	SECOND JUMP (M)	TOTAL PTS.
1.	Helmut Recknagel	GDR	93.5	84.5	227.2
2.	Niilo Halonen	FIN	92.5	83.5	222.6
3.	Otto Leodolter	AUT	88.5	83.5	219.4
4.	Nikolai Kamensky	SOV/RUS	90.5	79.0	216.9
5.	Thorbjörn Yggeseth	NOR	88.5	82.5	216.1
6.	Max Bolkart	GER	87.5	81.0	212.6
7.	Ansten Samuelstuen	USA	90.0	79.0	211.5
8.	Juhani Karkinen	FIN	87.5	82.0	211.4

1964 Innsbruck C: 52, N: 15, D: 2.9.

		FIRST JUMP (M)	SECOND JUMP (M)	TOTAL PTS.
1.	Toralf Engan	NOR	93.5	90.5	230.7
2.	Veikko Kankkonen	FIN	95.5	90.5	228.9
3.	Torgeir Brandtzäg	NOR	92.0	90.0	227.2
4.	Dieter Bokeloh	GDR	92.0	83.5	214.6
5.	Kjell Sjöberg	SWE	90.0	85.0	214.4
6.	Aleksandr Ivannikov	SOV/RUS	90.0	83.5	213.3
7.	Helmut Recknagel	GDR	89.0	86.5	212.8
8.	Dieter Neuendorf	GDR	92.5	84.5	212.6

A second ski jump event was added in 1964 in order to give more competitors a chance to win medals in a sport where a sudden gust of wind or a split-second mistake can send the best jumper down to defeat. As it turned out, however, the same three men took the medals in both events. The 1964 competition was the only one in which the contestants were allowed to use the two best of three jumps.

1968 Grenoble-St. Nizler C: 58, N: 17, D: 2:18.

		FIRST JUMP (M)	SECOND JUMP (M)	TOTAL PTS.
1.	Vladimir Belousov	SOV/RUS	101.5	98.5	231.3
2.	Jiři Raška	CZE	101.0	98.0	229.4
3.	Lars Grini	NOR	99.0	93.5	214.3
4.	Manfred Queck	GDR	96.5	98.5	212.8
5.	Bent Tomtum	NOR	98.5	95.0	212.2
6.	Reinhold Bachler	AUT	98.5	95.0	210.7
7.	Wolfgang Stöhr	GDR	96.5	92.5	205.9
8.	Anatoly Zheglanov	SOV/RUS	99.0	92.0	205.7

1972 Sapporo-Okurayama C: 52, N: 15, D: 2.11.

		FIRST JUMP (M)	SECOND JUMP (M)	TOTAL PTS.
1.	Wojciech Fortuna	POL	111.0	87.5	219.9
2.	Walter Steiner	SWI	94.0	103.0	219.8
3.	Rainer Schmidt	GDR	98.5	101.0	219.3
4.	Tauno Käyhkö	FIN	95.0	100.5	219.2
5.	Manfred Wolf	GDR	107.0	89.5	215.1
6.	Gari Napalkov	SOV/RUS	99.5	92.0	210.1

| 7. Yukio Kasaya | JPN | 106.0 | 85.0 | 209.4 |
| 8. Danilo Pudgar | YUG/SLO | 92.5 | 97.5 | 206.0 |

Fortuna's first jump was so spectacular that he was able to win the gold medal even though his second jump was only the 22nd best of the round.

1976 Innsbruck C: 54, N: 15, D: 2.15.

		FIRST JUMP (M)	SECOND JUMP (M)	TOTAL PTS.
1. Karl Schnabl	AUT	97.5	97.0	234.8
2. Anton Innauer	AUT	102.5	91.0	232.9
3. Henry Glass	GDR	91.0	97.0	221.7
4. Jochen Danneberg	GDR	102.0	89.5	221.6
5. Reinhold Bachler	AUT	95.0	91.0	217.4
6. Hans Wallner	AUT	93.5	92.5	216.9
7. Bernd Eckstein	GDR	94.0	91.5	216.2
8. Hans-Georg Aschenbach	GDR	92.5	89.0	212.1

1980 Lake Placid C: 50, N: 16, D: 2.23.

		FIRST JUMP (M)	SECOND JUMP (M)	TOTAL PTS.
1. Jouko Törmänen	FIN	114.5	117.0	271.0
2. Hubert Neuper	AUT	113.0	114.5	262.4
3. Jari Puikkonen	FIN	110.5	109.5	248.5
4. Anton Innauer	AUT	110.0	107.0	245.7
5. Armin Kogler	AUT	110.0	108.0	245.6
6. Roger Ruud	NOR	110.0	109.0	243.0
7. Hansjörg Sumi	SWI	117.0	110.0	242.7
8. James Denney	USA	109.0	104.0	239.1

1984 Sarajevo C: 53, N: 17, D: 2.18.

		FIRST JUMP (M)	SECOND JUMP (M)	TOTAL PTS.
1. Matti Nykänen	FIN	116.0	111.0	231.2
2. Jens Weissflog	GDR	107.0	107.5	213.7
3. Pavel Ploc	CZE	103.5	109.0	202.9
4. Jeffrey Hastings	USA	102.5	107.0	201.2
5. Jari Puikkonen	FIN	103.5	102.0	196.6
6. Armin Kogler	AUT	106.0	99.5	195.6
7. Andreas Bauer	GER	105.0	100.5	194.6
8. Vladimir Podzimek	CZE	98.5	108.0	194.5

Notoriously ill-tempered Matti Nykänen of Jyväsklä put together two near-perfect jumps to achieve the largest winning margin in Olympic jumping history.

1988 Calgary C: 55, N: 18, D: 2.23.

		FIRST JUMP (M)	SECOND JUMP (M)	TOTAL PTS.
1. Matti Nykänen	FIN	118.5	107.0	224.0
2. Erik Johnsen	NOR	114.5	102.0	207.9
3. Matjaž Debelak	YUG/SLO	113.0	108.0	207.7

			FIRST JUMP (M)	SECOND JUMP (M)	TOTAL PTS.
4.	Thomas Klauser	GER	114.5	102.5	205.1
5.	Pavel Ploc	CZE	114.5	102.5	204.1
6.	Andreas Felder	AUT	113.5	103.0	203.9
7.	Horst Bulau	CAN	112.5	99.5	197.6
8.	Staffan Tällberg	SWE	110.0	102.0	196.6

In a competition that was postponed four times because of dangerous winds, Nykänen, mellowed somewhat by fatherhood, became the first ski jumper to win two gold medals in one Olympics. He earned a third in the team event. Unable to control his alcoholism and self-destructive tendencies, Nykanen ended up selling all of his gold medals.

1992 Albertville-Courcheval C: 59, N: 17, D: 2.16.

			FIRST JUMP (M)	SECOND JUMP (M)	TOTAL PTS.
1.	Toni Nieminen	FIN	122.0	123.0	239.5
2.	Martin Höllwarth	AUT	120.5	116.5	227.3
3.	Heinz Kuttin	AUT	117.5	112.0	214.8
4.	Masahiko Harada	JPN	113.5	116.0	211.3
5.	Jiří Parma	CZE	111.5	108.5	198.0
6.	Steeve Delaup	FRA	106.0	105.5	185.6
7.	Ivan Lunardi	ITA	110.5	102.5	185.2
8.	Franci Petek	SLO	107.0	99.5	177.1

Nieminen earned the two highest scores of the competition. At age 16, he became the youngest male to win a Winter Olympics gold in an individual event. The previous record holder was figure skater Dick Button, who was 18 when he won his first gold medal in 1948. At the other end of the standings was Germany's Heiko Hunger, who fell in his first jump and then withdrew. When asked for a comment, Hunger replied, "My horoscope said I shouldn't take any risks."

When Toni Niemenen returned to Finland after the Olympics, he needed a police escort to guide him through the crowd of teenage girls that awaited him. A week later, at a minor competition, the girls broke through a line of security guards and mobbed him. Niemenen's sponsor, Toyota, gave him a $50,000 sports car. He was not old enough to have a driver's license, but he was so popular that he was issued a special permit to drive anyway. All this was heady stuff for an unaffected young man. In fact, it proved to be too much. A mere two years later, he could do no better than 20th at the Norwegian national championships and he failed to qualify for the Olympic team in 1994. The same fate befell 1992 silver medalist Martin Hollworth, who was 17 when he won his medal, but was unable to make the Austrian team in 1994.

1994 Lillehammer C: 58, N: 19, D: 2.20.

			FIRST JUMP (M)	SECOND JUMP (M)	TOTAL PTS.
1.	Jens Weissflog	GER	129.5	133.0	274.5
2.	Espen Bredesen	NOR	135.5	122.0	266.5
3.	Andreas Goldberger	AUT	128.5	121.5	255.0
4.	Takanobu Okabe	JPN	117.0	128.0	243.5

5. Jani Markus Soininen	FIN	117.0	122.5	231.1
6. Lasse Ottesen	NOR	117.0	120.0	226.0
7. Jaroslav Sakala	CZE	117.0	115.5	222.0
8. Jinya Nishikata	JPN	123.5	110.5	218.3

At the 1984 Olympics Jens Weissflog won a gold medal on the normal hill and a silver on the large hill. Injuries and difficulties adjusting to the new V style meant that Weissflog's next few years were a series of ups and downs. Unfortunately, his downs coincided with the next two Olympics. In 1988 he was 9th on the normal hill and 31st on the large hill. In 1992 he again placed 9th on the normal hill and dropped to 33rd on the large hill. But ten years after his initial Olympic triumph he was definitely back in form and it was clear that barring unforeseen circumstances, the gold medal fight would be between Weissflog and local favorite Espen Bredesen. With his first jump, Bredesen set an Olympic record of 135.5 meters, while Weissflog was 10.3 points behind in second place. Jumping next to last in the second round, Weissflog launched such a beautiful jump that even the partisan Norwegian crowd roared its approval. Bredesen followed with the third best jump of the round, but it wasn't enough to top Weissflog, who became the only Sarajevo gold medal winner to repeat in Lillehammer.

SKI JUMP, LARGE HILL, TEAM
Each team member takes two jumps. All eight jumps are added to determine the final team total. Prior to 1994 the lowest score of each round was dropped for each team.

1924–1984 not held

1988 Calgary T: 11, N: 11, D: 2.24.

			TOTAL PTS.
1.	FIN	(Matti Nykänen 228.8, Ari-Pekka Nikkola 207.9, Jari Puikkonen 193.6, Tuomo Ylipulli 192.3)	634.4
2.	YUG	(Matjaž Zupan 211.5, Matjaž Debelak 207.5, Primož Ulaga 207.1, Miran Tepeš 192.8)	625.5
3.	NOR	(Erik Johnsen 218.7, Ole Gunnar Fidjestøl 193.9, Ole Christian Eidhammer 177.2, Jon Inge Kjørum 128.4)	596.1
4.	CZE	(Pavel Ploc 204.1, Jiří Malec 193.4, Jiří Parma 189.3, Ladislav Dluhoš 165.4)	586.8
5.	AUT	(Günter Stranner 197.5, Heinz Kuttin 193.3, Ernst Vettori 186.0, Andreas Felder 176.3)	577.6
6.	GER	(Thomas Klauser 197.6, Josef Heumann 180.9, Andreas Bauer 175.1, Peter Rohwein 174.3)	559.0
7.	SWE	(Jan Boklöv 180.1, Staffan Tällberg 178.7, Anders Daun 174.2, Per-Inge Tällberg 161.5)	539.7
8.	SWI	(Gérard Balanche 175.0, Christian Hauswirth 175.0, Fabrice Piazzini 166.2, Christoph Lehmann 156.7)	516.1

Matti Nykänen won his third gold medal of the Calgary Games to give him a two-Olympics total of four golds and one silver. Tuomo Ylipulli was the younger brother of Jukka Ylipulli, who won a bronze medal in the 1984 nordic combined.

1992 Albertville-Courcheval T: 14, N: 14, D: 2.14.

			TOTAL PTS.
1.	FIN	(Toni Nieminen 245.0, Ari-Pekka Nikkola 225.0, Risto Laakkonen 221.0, Mika Laitinen 216.0)	644.4
2.	AUT	(Martin Höllwarth 241.0, Heinz Kuttin 227.0, Andreas Felder 224.5, Ernst Vettori 224.0)	642.9
3.	CZE	(Jiří Parma 234.0, Tomas Goder 227.0, Frantisek Jez 218.0, Jaroslav Sakala 215.0)	620.1
4.	JPN	(Masahiko Harada 227.0, Jiro Kamiharako 215.0, Kenji Suda 206.5, Noriaki Kasai 203.5)	571.0
5.	GER	(Dieter Thoma 213.5, Heiko Hunger 212.0, Jens Weissflog 211.0, Christof Duffner 194.5)	544.6
6.	SLO	(Samo Gostisa 218.5, Franci Petek 212.5, Matjaž Zupan 207.5, Primoz Kipac 195.0)	543.3
7.	NOR	(Espen Bredesen 223.5, Magne Johansen 206.5, Rune Olijnyk 205.0, Lasse Ottesen 199.0)	538.0
8.	SWI	(Markus Gähler 214.5, Stefan Zünd 214.5, Sylvain Freiholz 209.5, Martin Trunz 198.5)	537.9

In ski-jumping contests the jury reserves the right to restart the competition if it believes the jumpers are going too far and endangering themselves. In such cases the scores for all completed jumps are erased and the starting point is moved. This is exactly what happened after Austria's second jumper, Ernst Vettori, uncorked a dazzling leap of 125.5 meters (411 feet). Martin Höllwarth then recorded what was then the longest official jump in Olympic history—123.5 meters—to lead Austria to a one-point lead over Finland after the first round. In the second round, with only Toni Nieminen and Andreas Felder left to jump, the Austrians led by 30 points. But Nieminen came through with a magnificent 122-meter leap that earned 119.8 points. Felder could respond with only a 109.5-meter jump that ended up being dropped from the final tally. At the age of 16 years and 259 days, Nieminen became the youngest male winter gold medalist ever, breaking bobsledder Billy Fiske's record by one day.

1994 Lillehammer T: 12, N: 12, D: 2.22.

			TOTAL PTS.
1.	GER	(Jens Weissflog 277.7, Dieter Thoma 254.1, Hansjörg Jäkle 231.8, Christof Duffner 206.5)	970.1
2.	JPN	(Takanobu Okabe 262.0, Jinya Nishikata 254.4, Noriaki Kasai 248.9, Masahiko Harada 191.6)	956.9
3.	AUT	(Andreas Goldberger 254.3, Stefan Horngacher 236.6, Heinz Kuttin 218.5, Christian Moser 209.5)	918.9
4.	NOR	(Espen Bredesen 257.7, Lasse Ottesen 239,8, Øyvind Berg 215.5, Roar Ljøkelsøy 185.8)	898.8
5.	FIN	(Raimo Ylipulli 231.6, Jani Markus Soininen 231.0, Janne Petteri Ahonen 214.9, Janne Väätäinen 212.0)	889.5
6.	FRA	(Nicolas Jean-Prost 224.0, Steeve Delaup 203.2, Nicolas Dessum 202.4, Didier Mollard 192.5)	822.1
7.	CZE	(Zbynek Krompolc 221.9, Jaroslav Sakala 203.9, Ladislav Dluhos 199.8, Jirí Parma 175.1)	800.7
8.	ITA	(Roberto Cecon 236.2, Ivo Pertile 199.8, Ivan Lunardi 188.5, Andrea Cecon 157.8)	782.3

The surprisingly solid German team led the Japanese by eight tenths of a point after the first round. But after three of the four second round jumps, Japan had taken a seemingly insurmountable lead of 54.9 points. The last German jumper, Jens Weissflog, launched a huge leap of 133.5 meters that tied the longest jump in Olympic history. Japan's final jumper was team leader Masahiko Harada. Harada's first jump had been 122 meters and he needed to go only 105 meters with reasonable style to ensure victory for Japan. However, two days earlier he had mistimed his second leap in the individual large hill event and gone only 101 meters. Sure enough, Harada made the same mistake in the second round of the team event. His distance was only 97.5 meters, the shortest of any of the 64 jumps by the top eight teams. In 1988 and 1992 each team had been allowed to drop its lowest score in each round, but the rules were changed for 1994 and Harada's 73-point jump dropped Japan to second place.

NORDIC COMBINED, INDIVIDUAL

Nordic combined contests were held in Norway as early as the mid-19th century. On the first day of competition, the competitors take three jumps on a normal hill with only the two best jumps counting. The second day they ski 15 kilometers. Since 1988 the start order of the cross-country race has been based on the result of the ski jumping. The leader of the ski jumping starts first. The others follow. According to the rules to be used at the 1998 Games, for each point behind the leader, they must wait 6 seconds, 10 points being equal to one minute. Whoever crosses the finish line first is the winner.

1924 Chamonix C: 30, N: 9, D: 2.4.

			18 KM		SKI JUMP		TOTAL PTS.
1.	Thorleif Haug	NOR	1:14:31.0	(1)	17.821	(1)	18.906
2.	Thoralf Strömstad	NOR	1:17:03.0	(3)	17.687	(2)	18.219
3.	Johan Gröttumsbråten	NOR	1:15:51.0	(2)	16.333	(8)	17.854
4.	Harald Ökern	NOR	1:20:30.0	(4)	17.395	(3)	17.260
5.	Axel Nilsson	SWE	1:25:29.0	(6)	16.500	(7)	14.063
6.	Josef Adolf	CZE	1:31:17.0	(5)	12.833	(18)	13.729
7.	Vincenz Buchberger	CZE	1:32:32.0	(7)	16.250	(9)	13.625
8.	Menotti Jacobsson	SWE	1:37:10.0	(15)	16.896	(4)	12.823

1928 St. Moritz C: 35, N: 14, D: 2.18.

			18 KM		SKI JUMP		TOTAL PTS.
1.	Johan Gröttumsbråten	NOR	1:37:01.0	(1)	15.667	(8)	17.833
2.	Hans Vinjarengen	NOR	1:41:44.0	(2)	12.856	(19)	15.303
3.	John Snersrud	NOR	1:50:51.0	(9)	16.917	(3)	15.021
4.	Paavo Nuotio	FIN	1:48:46.0	(4)	15.729	(7)	14.927
5.	Esko Järvinen	FIN	1:46:33.0	(3)	14.286	(16)	14.810
6.	Sven Eriksson	SWE	1:52:20.0	(11)	16.312	(5)	14.593
7.	Ludwig Böck	GER	1:48:56.0	(5)	11.812	(21)	13.260
8.	Ole Kolterud	NOR	1:50:17.0	(7)	13.500	(18)	13.146

1932 Lake Placid C: 33, N: 10, D: 2.11.

			18 KM		SKI JUMP	TOTAL PTS.
1.	Johan Gröttumsbråten	NOR	1:27:15.0	(1)	206.0 (6)	446.00
2.	Ole Stenen	NOR	1:28:05.0	(2)	200.3 (12)	436.05

		18 KM		SKI JUMP		TOTAL PTS.
3. Hans Vinjarengen	NOR	1:32:40.0	(4)	221.6	(2)	434.60
4. Sverre Kolterud	NOR	1:34:36.0	(7)	214.7	(5)	418.70
5. Sven Eriksson	SWE	1:39:32.0	(12)	220.8	(3)	402.30
6. Antonin Barton	CZE	1:33:39.0	(6)	188.6	(19)	397.10
7. Bronislaw Czech	POL	1:36:37.0	(8)	197.0	(14)	392.00
8. František Simunek	CZE	1:39:58.0	(14)	196.8	(15)	375.30

Gröttumsbråten closed out his Olympic career with three gold medals, one silver, and one bronze.

1936 Garmisch-Partenkirchen C: 51, N: 16, D: 2.13.

		18 KM		SKI JUMP		TOTAL PTS.
1. Oddbjörn Hagen	NOR	1:15:33.0	(1)	190.3	(16)	430.3
2. Olaf Hoffsbakken	NOR	1:17:37.0	(2)	192.0	(13)	419.8
3. Sverre Brodahl	NOR	1:18:01.0	(3)	182.6	(28)	408.1
4. Lauri Valonen	FIN	1:26:34.0	(26)	222.6	(1)	401.2
5. František Simunek	CZE	1:19:09.0	(4)	175.3	(33)	394.3
6. Bernt Østerkløft	NOR	1:21:37.0	(6)	188.7	(21)	393.8
7. Stanislaw Marusarz	POL	1:25:27.0	(18)	208.9	(3)	393.3
7. Timo Murama	FIN	1:24:52.0	(13)	205.8	(5)	393.3

1948 St. Moritz C: 39, N: 13, D: 2.1.

		18 KM		SKI JUMP		TOTAL PTS.
1. Heikki Hasu	FIN	1:16:43.0	(1)	208.8	(8)	448.80
2. Martti Huhtala	FIN	1:19:28.0	(2)	209.5	(6)	433.65
3. Sven Israelsson	SWE	1:21:35.0	(4)	221.9	(1)	433.40
4. Niklaus Stump	SWI	1:21:44.0	(7)	213.0	(5)	421.50
5. Olavi Sihvonen	FIN	1:21:50.0	(8)	209.2	(7)	416.20
6. Eilert Dahl	NOR	1:22:12.0	(10)	208.8	(8)	414.30
7. Pauli Salonen	FIN	1:22:15.0	(9)	206.3	(10)	413.30
8. Olav Dufseth	NOR	1:22:26.0	(5)	201.1	(16)	412.60

1952 Oslo C: 25, N: 11, D: 2.18.

		SKI JUMP		18 KM		TOTAL PTS.
1. Simon Slåttvik	NOR	223.5	(1)	1:05:40.0	(3)	451.621
2. Heikki Hasu	FIN	207.5	(5)	1:02:24.0	(1)	447.500
3. Sverre Stenersen	NOR	223.0	(2)	1:09:44.0	(9)	436.335
4. Paavo Korhonen	FIN	206.0	(6)	1:05:30.0	(2)	434.727
5. Per Gjelten	NOR	212.0	(3)	1:07:40.0	(6)	432.848
6. Ottar Gjermundshaug	NOR	206.0	(6)	1:06:13.0	(5)	432.121
7. Aulis Sipponen	FIN	198.5	(12)	1:06:03.0	(4)	425.227
8. Eeti Nieminen	FIN	206.0	(6)	1:08:24.0	(7)	424.181

February 18, 1952, was a great day in the history of Norwegian sports. Hjallis Andersen won the 1500-meter skating event, Hallgeir Brenden won the 18-kilometer cross-country race, and Simon Slåttvik won the nordic combined. People all over Oslo left their jobs and spilled into the streets to celebrate. The *New York Times* reported, with some annoyance, that at the Hotel Viking, where the press was staying, half of the waiters walked out, and "It took more than an hour to order food and another two hours to get it." The year 1952 was the first time that the jumping half of the nordic combined was held before the skiing.

1956 Cortina C: 36, N: 12, D: 1.31.

		SKI JUMP		15 KM		TOTAL PTS.
1. Sverre Stenersen	NOR	215.0	(2)	56:18.0	(1)	455.000
2. Bengt Eriksson	SWE	214.0	(3)	1:00:36.0	(15)	437.400
3. Franciszek Gasienica-Groń	POL	203.0	(10)	57:55.0	(7)	436.800
4. Paavo Korhonen	FIN	196.5	(17)	56:32.0	(2)	435.597
5. Arne Barhaugen	NOR	199.0	(15)	57:11.0	(3)	435.581
6. Tormod Knutsen	NOR	203.0	(11)	58:22.0	(9)	435.000
7. Nikolai Gusakov	SOV/RUS	200.0	(14)	58:17.0	(8)	432.300
8. Alfredo Prucker	ITA	201.0	(12)	58:52.0	(10)	431.100

1960 Squaw Valley C: 33, N: 13, D: 2.22.

		SKI JUMP		15 KM		TOTAL PTS.
1. Georg Thoma	GER	221.5	(1)	59:23.8	(4)	457.952
2. Tormod Knutsen	NOR	217.0	(4)	59:31.0	(5)	453.000
3. Nikolai Gusakov	SOV/RUS	212.0	(10)	58:29.4	(1)	452.000
4. Pekka Ristola	FIN	214.0	(6)	59:32.8	(6)	449.871
5. Dmitri Kochkin	SOV/RUS	219.5	(2)	1:01:32.1	(11)	444.694
6. Arne Larsen	NOR	215.0	(5)	1:01:10.1	(10)	444.613
7. Sverre Stenersen	NOR	205.5	(14)	1:00:24.0	(8)	438.081
8. Lars Dahlqvist	SWE	201.5	(19)	59:46.0	(7)	436.532

1964 Innsbruck-Seefeld C: 32, N: 11, D: 2.3.

		SKI JUMP		15 KM		TOTAL PTS.
1. Tormod Knutsen	NOR	238.9	(2)	50:58.6	(4)	469.28
2. Nikolai Kiselyov	SOV/RUS	233.0	(3)	51:49.1	(8)	453.04
3. Georg Thoma	GER	241.1	(1)	52:31.2	(10)	452.88
4. Nikolai Gusakov	SOV/RUS	223.4	(7)	51:19.8	(5)	449.36
5. Arne Larsen	NOR	198.3	(17)	50:49.6	(3)	430.63
6. Arne Barhaugen	NOR	191.3	(20)	50:40.4	(2)	425.63
7. Vyacheslav Driagin	SOV/RUS	216.2	(10)	52:58.3	(12)	422.75
8. Ezio Damolin	ITA	198.1	(18)	51:42.3	(7)	419.54

1968 Grenoble-Autrans C: 41, N: 13, D: 2.11.

		SKI JUMP		15 KM		TOTAL PTS.
1. Franz Keller	GER	240.1	(1)	50:45.2	(13)	449.04
2. Alois Kälin	SWI	193.2	(24)	47:21.5	(1)	447.99
3. Andreas Kunz	GDR	216.9	(10)	49:19.8	(3)	444.10
4. Tomáš Kučera	CZE	217.4	(9)	50:07.7	(6)	434.14
5. Ezio Damolin	ITA	206.0	(13)	49:36.2	(4)	429.54
6. Jósef Gąsienica	POL	217.7	(8)	50:34.5	(11)	428.78
7. Robert Makara	SOV/RUS	222.8	(5)	51:09.3	(17)	426.92
8. Vyacheslav Driagin	SOV/RUS	222.8	(5)	51:22.0	(19)	424.38

Had Kälin been able to finish the cross-country race 2.3 seconds sooner, he would have won the gold medal.

1972 Sapporo-Miyanomori/Makomanai C: 39, N: 14, D: 2.5.

		SKI JUMP		15 KM		TOTAL PTS.
1. Ulrich Wehling	GDR	200.9	(4)	49:15.3	(3)	413.340
2. Rauno Miettinen	FIN	210.0	(2)	51:08.2	(15)	405.505
3. Karl-Heinz Luck	GDR	178.8	(17)	48:24.9	(1)	398.800
4. Erkki Kilpinen	FIN	185.0	(9)	49:52.6	(4)	391.845
5. Yuji Katsuro	JPN	195.1	(6)	51:10.9	(18)	390.200
6. Tomáš Kučera	CZE	191.8	(7)	51:04.0	(14)	387.935
7. Aleksandr Nossov	SOV/RUS	201.3	(3)	52:08.7	(27)	387.730
8. Kåre Olav Berg	NOR	180.4	(16)	50:08.9	(7)	384.800

Hideki Nakano of Japan had the unusual distinction of finishing first among the competitors in the nordic combined in the ski jump, but last in the 15-kilometer race. This left him in 13th place overall.

1976 Innsbruck-Seefeld C: 34, N: 14, D: 2.8.

		SKI JUMP		15 KM		TOTAL PTS.
1. Ulrich Wehling	GDR	225.5	(1)	50:28.95	(13)	423.39
2. Urban Hettich	GER	198.9	(11)	48:01.55	(1)	418.90
3. Konrad Winkler	GDR	213.9	(4)	49:51.11	(7)	417.47
4. Rauno Miettinen	FIN	219.9	(2)	51:12.21	(19)	411.30
5. Claus Tuchscherer	GDR	218.7	(3)	51:16.12	(20)	409.51
6. Nikolai Nagovitzin	SOV/RUS	196.1	(16)	49:05.97	(3)	406.44
7. Valery Kapayev	SOV/RUS	202.9	(9)	49:53.26	(8)	406.14
8. Tom Sandberg	NOR	195.7	(17)	49:09.34	(4)	405.53

1980 Lake Placid C: 31, N: 9, D: 2.18.

		SKI JUMP		15 KM		TOTAL PTS.
1. Ulrich Wehling	GDR	227.2	(1)	49:24.5	(9)	432.200
2. Jouko Karjalainen	FIN	209.5	(7)	47:44.5	(1)	429.500
3. Konrad Winkler	GDR	214.5	(5)	48:45.7	(8)	425.320
4. Tom Sandberg	NOR	203.7	(9)	48:19.4	(5)	418.465
5. Uwe Dotzauer	GDR	217.6	(4)	49:52.4	(13)	418.415
6. Karl Lustenberger	SWI	212.7	(6)	50:01.1	(14)	412.210
7. Aleksandr Maiorov	SOV/RUS	194.4	(13)	48:19.6	(6)	409.135
8. Gunter Schmieder	GDR	201.7	(11)	49:42.0	(11)	404.075

The 27-year-old Wehling became the first non–figure skater to win three consecutive gold medals in the same individual Winter event.

1984 Sarajevo C: 28, N: 11, D: 2.12.

		SKI JUMP		15 KM		TOTAL PTS.
1. Tom Sandberg	NOR	214.7	(1)	47:52.7	(2)	422.595
2. Jouko Karjalainen	FIN	196.9	(15)	46:32.0	(1)	416.900
3. Jukka Ylipulli	FIN	208.3	(5)	48:28.5	(5)	410.825
4. Rauno Miettinen	FIN	205.5	(6)	49:02.2	(9)	402.970
5. Thomas Müller	GER	209.1	(3)	49:32.7	(12)	401.995
6. Aleksandr Prosvirnin	SOV/UKR	199.4	(13)	48:40.1	(6)	400.185
7. Uwe Dotzauer	GDR	199.5	(12)	48:56.8	(7)	397.780
8. Hermann Weinbuch	GER	201.6	(10)	49:13.4	(10)	397.390

1988 Calgary-Canmore C: 42, N: 13, D: 2.28.

		SKI JUMP		15 KM		TIME BEHIND
1. Hippolyt Kempf	SWI	217.9	(3)	38:16.8	(2)	0
2. Klaus Sulzenbacher	AUT	228.5	(1)	39:46.5	(17)	19.0
3. Allar Levandi	SOV/EST	216.6	(4)	39:12.4	(12)	1:04.3
4. Uwe Prenzel	GDR	207.6	(13)	38:18.8	(4)	1:10.7
5. Andreas Schaad	SWI	207.2	(14)	38:18.0	(3)	1:12.5
6. Torbjørn Løkken	NOR	199.4	(19)	37:39.0	(1)	1:15.5
7. Miroslav Kopal	CZE	208.7	(12)	38:48.0	(8)	1:32.5
8. Marko Frank	GDR	209.4	(10)	39:08.2	(11)	1:48.1

Nineteen eighty-eight marked the first time that nordic combined used the Gundersen Method, in which the starting order and intervals in the cross-country race are based on the results of the ski jump. World Cup leader Klaus Sulzenbacher earned the right to start first, with Hippolyt Kempf in third place 1:10.7 behind. Kempf caught Sulzenbacher 2.3 kilometers from the finish and pulled away to win by 19 seconds.

Because of delays caused by poor weather, the ski jump and cross-country race were held on the same day.

1992 Albertville-Courcheval C: 45, N: 12, D: 2.12.

		SKI JUMP		15 KM		TIME BEHIND
1. Fabrice Guy	FRA	222.1	(3)	43:45.4	(6)	0
2. Sylvain Guillaume	FRA	208.1	(13)	43:00.5	(3)	48.4
3. Klaus Sulzenbacher	AUT	221.6	(4)	44:48.4	(13)	1:06.3
4. Fred Børre Lundberg	NOR	211.9	(9)	44:04.1	(9)	1:26.7
5. Klaus Ofner	AUT	228.5	(1)	45:57.9	(21)	1:29.8
6. Allar Levandi	EST	206.4	(14)	43:34.8	(6)	1:34.1
7. Kenji Ogiwara	JPN	215.3	(6)	44:57.5	(16)	1:57.4
8. Stanislaw Ustupski	POL	202.6	(18)	44:03.5	(8)	2:28.1

Two months before the Olympics, 23-year-old Fabrice Guy was an obscure athlete in a sport with almost no following in his home country of France. But when he won four of five pre-Olympic World Cup events, he suddenly found himself a superstar in a host nation short on gold-medal prospects. Amazingly, he was able to live up to his compatriots' huge expectations. Guy knew that he had to keep close to Sulzenbacher in the jumping portion of the competition in order to take advantage of his superior skiing ability. In fact, he jumped so well that he outscored his Austrian rival. The next day, with almost half of the inhabitants of his hometown of Mouthe (population: 920) in attendance, he pulled away from Sulzenbacher after 5 kilometers and won easily. The French joy was multiplied by the surprise success of Sylvain Guillaume, who came from 13th place to grab the silver medal. Guy's fans were so deliriously happy that they gathered outside the doping control room and sang "La Marseillaise" while he tried to produce a urine sample. It took him an hour. A few months later, the town of Mouthe set up a display to honor Guy's victory and show off his gold medal. In one month 10,000 people viewed the medal.

1994 Lillehammer C: 53, N: 16, D: 2.19.

		SKI JUMP		15 KM		TIME BEHIND
1. Fred Børre Lundberg	NOR	247.0	(1)	39:07.9	(8)	0
2. Takanori Kono	JPN	239.5	(4)	39:35.4	(13)	1:17.5
3. Bjarte Engen Vik	NOR	240.5	(3)	39:43.2	(15)	1:18.3

		SKI JUMP		15 KM		TIME BEHIND
4. Kenji Ogiwara	JPN	231.0	(6)	39:30.7	(11)	2:08.8
5. Ago Markvardt	EST	243.5	(2)	41:26.8	(35)	2:41.9
6. Hippolyt Kempf	SWI	215.5	(9)	39:30.2	(10)	3:45.3
7. Jean-Yves Cuendet	SWI	222.0	(7)	40:17.5	(20)	3:55.6
8. Trond Einar Elden	NOR	201.5	(17)	38:07.7	(11)	4:02.8

Kenji Ogiwara was the overwhelming favorite, having dominated the event since the last Olympics. He won 6 of 8 races in the 1992–1993 World Cup, he was the defending world champion, and he had won 5 of 6 races in the pre-Olympic World Cup season. But, whereas he was normally the best nordic combined jumper, in Lillehammer he placed only sixth. On the other hand, Fred Børre Lundberg, who was born in Hammerfest, the northernmost town in Europe, put together two solid jumps and coasted to victory. "When the spectators started to sing the Norwegian victory song as I was on the final lap," he explained later, "I just floated towards the line."

NORDIC COMBINED, TEAM

In 1998 team sizes will be increased from three members to four. Each team member takes two jumps. (In 1988 and 1992, three jumps were allowed with only the best counting.) The next day, a 4 × 5-kilometer relay is held. The starting order is based on the results of the ski jump. According to rules to be used in 1998, each team's score is divided by four. The team with the best score starts first. The other teams follow with one point being equal to a 6⅔-second delay, or 9 points being equal to one minute. Prior to 1998, the relay was 3 × 10 kilometers rather than 4 × 5 kilometers.

1924–1984 not held

1988 Calgary-Canmore T: 11, N: 11, D: 2.23.

			SKI JUMP		10 KM		TIME BEHIND
1.	GER	Hans-Peter Pohl	204.7		27:26.7		0
		Hubert Schwarz	227.2		27:45.7		
		Thomas Müller	197.9	(1)	25:33.6	(8)	
2.	SWI	Andreas Schaad	195.4		25:34.7		3.4
		Hippolyt Kempf	199.8		25:12.9		
		Fredy Glanzmann	176.2	(6)	25:09.8	(1)	
3.	AUT	Günther Csar	193.7		26:39.7		30.9
		Hansjörg Aschenwald	204.5		28:33.7		
		Klaus Sulzenbacher	228.4	(2)	25:47.5	(9)	
4.	NOR	Hallstein Bøgseth	195.0		26:18.6		48.6
		Trond Arne Bredesen	201.1		27:04.0		
		Torbjørn Løkken	200.5	(3)	25:25.8	(3)	
5.	GDR	Thomas Prenzel	183.9		26:23.9		2:18.5
		Marko Frank	195.9		26:12.1		
		Uwe Prenzel	191.8	(5)	25:37.5	(2)	
6.	CZE	Ladislav Patraš	192.0		26:49.7		2:57.1
		Ján Klimko	184.7		26:30.4		
		Miroslav Kopal	196.8	(4)	25:42.0	(4)	
7.	FIN	Pasi Saapunki	165.0		26:29.7		4:52.3
		Jouko Parviainen	201.9		26:42.3		
		Jukka Ylipulli	194.4	(7)	26:44.3	(7)	

8. FRA	Jean Bohard	178.0		27:04.9		6:23.4
	Xavier Girard	187.2		26:43.2		
	Fabrice Guy	175.8	(8)	25:57.3	(5)	

The West Germans led after the ski jump, with Austria second and Switzerland back in sixth place. Günther Csar, starting 16 seconds after Hans-Peter Pohl, gave Austria a 31-second lead after the first leg of the relay, but Hubert Schwarz put West Germany back in the lead to stay. The Swiss, starting with a handicap of 4 minutes 52 seconds, staged a dramatic come-from-behind effort, but fell 3.4 seconds short of victory. "It's a very thrilling, frustrating feeling," said Swiss anchorman Fredy Glanzmann, who recorded the fastest leg of the day, "to be so near to the leader where you can almost touch him, but you can't touch him because your legs won't let you."

1992 Albertville-Courcheval T: 11, N: 11, D: 2.18.

		SKI JUMP		10 KM		TIME BEHIND
1. JPN	Reiichi Mikata	218.6		28:22.5		0
	Takanori Kono	199.0		28:40.2		
	Kenji Ogiwara	227.5	(1)	26:33.8	(6)	
2. NOR	Knut Tore Apeland	185.3		26:22.8		1:26.4
	Fred Børre Lundberg	185.7		26:19.7		
	Trond Einar Elden	198.9	(6)	26:04.4	(1)	
3. AUT	Klaus Ofner	195.5		27:56.6		1:40.1
	Stefan Kreiner	212.6		28:34.2		
	Klaus Sulzenbacher	207.5	(2)	26:18.8	(3)	
4. FRA	Francis Repellin	177.2		27:27.0		2:15.5
	Sylvain Guillaume	191.1		26:28.8		
	Fabrice Guy	210.1	(5)	26:23.2	(2)	
5. GER	Hans-Peter Pohl	180.1		28:01.2		4:45.4
	Jens Deimel	207.4		29:53.5		
	Thomas Dufter	222.2	(3)	27:30.2	(8)	
6. CZE	Josef Kovarik	166.0		27:47.8		9:04.7
	Milan Kucera	184.5		29:37.8		
	František Maka	196.2	(8)	27:03.6	(7)	
7. FIN	Pasi Saapunki	195.2		27:15.5		9:06.8
	Jari Mantila	166.4		30:23.1		
	Teemu Summanen	199.6	(7)	28:05.7	(9)	
8. USA	Joseph Holland	184.3		29:44.9		9:08.3
	Timothy Tetreault	198.1		28:48.6		
	Ryan Heckman	208.9	(4)	29:42.3	(10)	

The Japanese jumped so well that they put the gold medal out of reach after the first day. They began the relay 2 minutes and 27 seconds before second-place Austria and, more important, 6 minutes and 16 seconds before sixth-place Norway.

1994 Lillehammer T: 12, N: 12, D: 2.24.

		SKI JUMP		10 KM		TIME BEHIND
1. JPN	Takanori Kono	255.0		27:55.2		0
	Masashi Abe	233.0		27:48.1		
	Kenji Ogiwara	245.5	(1)	27:07.5	(3)	
2. NOR	Knut Tore Apeland	215.0		26:51.5		4.49.1
	Bjarte Engen Vik	249.5		28:28.8		
	Fred Børre Lundberg	207.5	(2)	27:13.6	(2)	

		SKI JUMP		10 KM		TIME BEHIND
3. SWI	Hippolyt Kempf	193.0		27:35.6		7.48.1
	Jean-Yves Cuendet	240.5		28:02.0		
	Andreas Schaad	210.0	(3)	27:32.3	(4)	
4. EST	Magnar Freimuth	193.5		28:09.5		10.15.6
	Allar Levandi	220.0		27:05.4		
	Ago Markvardt	205.5	(4)	28:20.5	(5)	
5. CZE	Zbynek Pánek	210.5		27:23.4		12.04.1
	Milan Kucera	206.5		28:45.0		
	Frantisek Máka	186.5	(6)	27:57.5	(6)	
6. FRA	Sylvain Guillaume	193.0		26:45.8		12.41.2
	Stéphane Michon	191.5		27:09.8		
	Fabrice Guy	173.0	(10)	26:57.4	(1)	
7. USA	John Jarrett	193.5		27:49.4		13.15.6
	Todd Lodwick	221.0		29:03.2		
	Ryan Heckman	187.5	(7)	28:17.4	(8)	
8. FIN	Topi Sarparanta	189.5		28:05.5		13.27.6
	Jari Mantila	202.0		28:44.7		
	Tapio Nurmela	200.5	(9)	27:42.2	(5)	

Again the Japanese put the gold medal out of reach on the first day with their superior jumping. This time they began the relay 5 minutes and 7 seconds ahead of Norway and had little trouble maintaining their lead.

Discontinued Event

15 KILOMETERS (CLASSICAL)

The 18- and 15-kilometer cross-country race was thoroughly dominated by four nations: Norway, Sweden, Finland, and the U.S.S.R. These four nations won all 45 medals, and only five other countries ever managed to finish in the top eight.

1924 Chamonix C: 41, N: 12, D: 2.2.
18 Kilometers

1. Thorleif Haug	NOR	1:14.31.0
2. Johan Gröttumsbråten	NOR	1:15.51.0
3. Tapani Niku	FIN	1:16.26.0
4. Jon Maardalen	NOR	1:16.56.0
5. Einar Landvik	NOR	1:17.27.0
6. Per Erik Hedlund	SWE	1:17.49.0
7. Matti Raivio	FIN	1:19.10.0
8. Elis Sandin	SWE	1:19.24.0

Thorleif Haug won the second of his three gold medals, having won the 50-kilometer race three days earlier. The Scandinavians took the first 11 places.

1928 St. Moritz C: 49, N: 15, D: 2.17.
18 Kilometers
1. Johan Gröttumsbråten   NOR   1:37.01.0
2. Ole Hegge   NOR   1:39.01.0
3. Reidar Ödegaard   NOR   1:40.11.0
4. Veli Saarinen   FIN   1:40:57.0
5. Hagbart Haakonsen   NOR   1:41:29.0
6. Per Erik Hedlund   SWE   1:41:51.0
7. Lars Theodor Johnsson   SWE   1:41:59.0
7. Martti Lappalainen   FIN   1:41:59.0

1932 Lake Placid C: 42, N: 11, D: 2.10.
18 Kilometers
1. Sven Utterström   SWE   1:23.07.0
2. Axel Wikström   SWE   1:25:07.0
3. Veli Saarinen   FIN   1:25:24.0
4. Martti Lappalainen   FIN   1:26:31.0
5. Arne Rustadstuen   NOR   1:27:06.0
6. Johan Gröttumsbråten   NOR   1:27:15.0
7. Valmari Toikka   FIN   1:27:51.0
8. Ole Stenen   NOR   1:28:05.0

Once again, Scandinavians took the first 11 places.

1936 Garmish-Partenkirchen C: 75, N: 22, D: 2.12.
18 Kilometers
1. Erik-August Larsson   SWE   1:14:38.0
2. Oddbjörn Hagen   NOR   1:15:33.0
3. Pekka Niemi   FIN   1:16:59.0
4. Martin Matsbo   SWE   1:17:02.0
5. Olaf Hoffsbakken   NOR   1:17:37.0
6. Arne Rustadstuen   NOR   1:18:13.0
7. Sulo Nurmela   FIN   1:18:20.0
8. Artur Häggblad   SWE   1:18:55.0

1948 St. Moritz C: 84, N: 15, D: 1.31.
18 Kilometers
1. Martin Lundström   SWE   1:13:50.0
2. Nils Östensson   SWE   1:14:22.0
3. Gunnar Eriksson   SWE   1:16:06.0
4. Heikki Hasu   FIN   1:16:43.0
5. Nils Karlsson   SWE   1:16:54.0
6. Sauli Rytky   FIN   1:18:10.0
7. August Kiuru   FIN   1:18:25.0
8. Teuvo Laukkanen   FIN   1:18:51.0

1952 Oslo C: 80, N: 18, D: 2.18.
18 Kilometers
1. Hallgeir Brenden   NOR   1:01:34.0
2. Tapio Mäkelä   FIN   1:02:09.0
3. Paavo Lonkila   FIN   1:02:20.0
4. Heikki Hasu   FIN   1:02:24.0
5. Nils Karlsson   SWE   1:02:56.0
6. Martin Stokken   NOR   1:03:00.0

7.	Nils Täpp	SWE	1:03:35.0
8.	Tauno Sipila	FIN	1:03:40.0

In an amazing display of regional dominance, Finland, Norway, and Sweden claimed the first 17 places. Hallgeir Brenden, a 23-year-old lumberjack and farmer from the small town of Trysil, was also Norway's national steeplechase champion.

1956 Cortina C: 62, N: 20, D: 1.30.

1.	Hallgeir Brenden	NOR	49:39.0
2.	Sixten Jernberg	SWE	50:14.0
3.	Pavel Kolchin	SOV/RUS	50:17.0
4.	Veikko Hakulinen	FIN	50:31.0
5.	Håkon Brusveen	NOR	50:36.0
6.	Martin Stokken	NOR	50:45.0
7.	Nikolai Anikin	SOV/RUS	50:58.0
8.	Lennart Larsson	SWE	51:03.0

Kolchin and Anikin were the first non-Scandinavians to crack the top eight in this event. This was also the first time that the race was conducted at 15 kilometers rather than 18.

1960 Squaw Valley C: 54, N: 19, D: 2.23.

1.	Håkon Brusveen	NOR	51:55.5
2.	Sixten Jernberg	SWE	51:58.6
3.	Veikko Hakulinen	FIN	52:03.0
4.	Einar Östby	NOR	52:18.0
4.	Gennady Vaganov	SOV	52:18.0
6.	Eero Mäntyranta	FIN	52:40.6
7.	Janne Stefansson	SWE	52:41.0
8.	Rolf Rämgård	SWE	52:47.3

Brusveen was considered past his prime and was originally not selected to go to the Olympics. However, public pressure forced Norwegian ski officials to change their minds. He later became a national institution as a radio announcer for cross-country races.

1964 Innsbruck-Seefeld C: 71, N: 24, D: 2.2.

1.	Eero Mäntyranta	FIN	50:54.1
2.	Harald Grönningen	NOR	51:34.8
3.	Sixten Jernberg	SWE	51:42.2
4.	Väinö Huhtala	FIN	51:45.4
5.	Janne Stefansson	SWE	51:46.4
6.	Pavel Kolchin	SOV/RUS	51:52.0
7.	Igor Voronchikin	SOV/RUS	51:53.9
8.	Magnar Lundemo	NOR	51:55.2

Mäntyranta and Grönningen took the same places they had taken in the 30-kilometer race three days earlier. Mäntyranta made his living on skis as a border patrol officer, a common vocation for state-supported skiers, while Grönningen earned his living fishing for salmon and growing strawberries.

1968 Grenoble-Autrans C: 75, N: 24, D: 2:10.

1.	Harald Grönningen	NOR	47:54.2
2.	Eero Mäntyranta	FIN	47:56.1
3.	Gunnar Larsson	SWE	48:33.7

4.	Kalevi Laurila	FIN	48:37.6
5.	Jan Halvarsson	SWE	48:39.1
6.	Bjarne Andersson	SWE	48:41.1
7.	Pål Tyldum	NOR	48:42.0
8.	Odd Martinsen	NOR	48:59.3

A three-time silver medalist, Grönningen finally beat his friend and rival Mäntyranta.

1972 Sapporo-Makomanai C: 62, N: 19, D: 2.7.

1.	Sven-Ake Lundbäck	SWE	45:28.24
2.	Fedor Simashev	SOV/RUS	46:00.84
3.	Ivar Formo	NOR	46:02.68
4.	Juha Mieto	FIN	46:02.74
5.	Yuri Skobov	SOV/RUS	46:04.59
6.	Axel Lesser	GDR	46:17.01
7.	Walter Demel	GER	46:17.36
8.	Gunnar Larsson	SWE	46:23.29

1976 Innsbruck-Seefeld C: 80, N: 25, D: 2.8.

1.	Nikolai Bazhukov	SOV/RUS	43:58.47
2.	Yevgeny Belyaev	SOV/RUS	44:01.10
3.	Arto Koivisto	FIN	44:19.25
4.	Ivan Garanin	SOV/KAZ	44:41.98
5.	Ivar Formo	NOR	45:29.11
6.	William Koch	USA	45:32.22
7.	Georg Zipfel	GER	45:38.10
8.	Odd Martinsen	NOR	45:41.33

1980 Lake Placid C: 63, N: 22, D: 2.17.

1.	Thomas Wassberg	SWE	41:57.63
2.	Juha Mieto	FIN	41:57.64
3.	Ove Aunli	NOR	42:28.62
4.	Nikolai Zimyatov	SOV/RUS	42:33.96
5.	Yevgeny Belyaev	SOV/RUS	42:46.02
6.	József Luszczek	POL	42:59.03
7.	Aleksandr Zavyalov	SOV/RUS	43:00.81
8.	Harri Kirvesniemi	FIN	43:02.01

Six-foot 5-inch Juha Mieto could be forgiven if he cursed the invention of electronic timing. In 1972 he missed winning a bronze medal because a clock registered his time as six one-hundredths of a second slower than that of Ivar Formo. Eight years later in Lake Placid, Mieto was the 54th skier to start and he finished 36 seconds faster than any of the other 53. But then he watched anxiously as Thomas Wassberg strained toward the finish line and crossed in 41 minutes and 57.63 seconds—one one-hundredth of a second faster than Juha Mieto. This incident led the rulemakers to decree that henceforth all times in cross-country races would be rounded to the nearest tenth of a second.

1984 Sarajevo C: 91, N: 34, D: 2.13.

1.	Gunde Svan	SWE	41:25.6
2.	Aki Karvonen	FIN	41:34.9
3.	Harri Kirvesniemi	FIN	41:45.6
4.	Juha Mieto	FIN	42:05.8

5. Vladimir Nikitin	SOV/RUS	42:31.6
6. Nikolai Zimyatov	SOV/RUS	42:34.5
7. Uwe Bellmann	GDR	42:35.8
8. Tor Håkon Holte	NOR	42:37.4
DISQ: Ove Aunli (NOR) 42:31.6		

At age 22, Gunde Svan became the youngest person ever to win an Olympic cross-country title. Ove Aunli, who finished in a tie for fifth place, was disqualified for using a skating step during the last 200 meters.

1988 Calgary-Canmore C: 90, N: 32, D: 2.19.

1. Mikhail Devyatyarov	SOV/RUS	41:18.9
2. Pål Gunnar Mikkelsplass	NOR	41:33.4
3. Vladimir Smirnov	SOV/KAZ	41:48.5
4. Oddvar Brå	NOR	42:17.3
5. Uwe Bellmann	GDR	42:17.8
6. Maurilio De Zolt	ITA	42:31.2
7. Vegard Ulvang	NOR	42:31.5
8. Harri Kirvesniemi	FIN	42:42.8

Devyatyarov attributed the success of the Soviet Nordic skiers at the Calgary Games to the fact that they trained on a course with the same profile as the one at Canmore and at the same altitude.

This race saw the unusual inclusion of an entrant from Fiji. Rusiate Rogoyawa learned to ski while studying electrical engineering in Oslo, Norway. He finished 83d. Rogoyawa skipped the 1992 Olympics, but returned in 1994 and finished last in the 10-kilometer race.

NORDIC SKIING

WOMEN
5 Kilometers (Classical)
Combined Pursuit
15 Kilometers (Classical)
30 Kilometers (Freestyle)
4 × 5-Kilometer Relay
Discontinued Events

Except for the combined pursuit, participants in the individual events start at 30-second intervals and race against the clock. In the relay all teams start at the same time.

WOMEN

5 KILOMETERS (CLASSICAL)

1924–1960 not held

1964 Innsbruck-Seefeld C: 32, N: 14, D: 2.5.
1. Klavdia Boyarskikh   SOV/RUS   17:50.5
2. Mirja Lehtonen   FIN   17:52.9
3. Alevtina Kolchina   SOV/RUS   18:08.4
4. Yevdokya Mekshilo   SOV/RUS   18:16.7
5. Toini Pöysti   FIN   18:25.5
6. Toini Gustaffson   SWE   18:25.7
7. Barbro Martinsson   SWE   18:26.4
8. Eeva Ruoppa   FIN   18:29.8

In 1964 Claudia Boyarskikh, a 24-year-old teacher from Siberia, swept all three women's nordic events.

1968 Grenoble-Autrans C: 34, N: 12, D: 2.13.
1. Toini Gustafsson   SWE   16:45.2
2. Galina Kulakova   SOV/RUS   16:48.4
3. Alevtina Kolchina   SOV/RUS   16:51.6
4. Barbro Martinsson   SWE   16:52.9
5. Marjatta Kajosmaa   FIN   16:54.6
6. Rita Achkina   SOV/RUS   16:55.1
7. Inger Aufles   NOR   16:58.1
8. Senja Pusula   FIN   17:00.3

Toini Gustafsson was the last skier to leave the starting line. Kept informed of Kulakova's time at each kilometer, she knew exactly what time she had to beat.

Four seconds off Kulakova's pace with only one kilometer to go, Gustafsson poured it on to win with three seconds to spare. A 30-year-old physical education teacher, Gustafsson also won the 10-kilometer contest and gained a silver medal in the relay after recording the fastest leg of the race.

1972 Sapporo-Makomanai C: 43, N: 12, D: 2.9.

1.	Galina Kulakova	SOV/RUS	17:00.50
2.	Marjatta Kajosmaa	FIN	17:05.50
3.	Helena Šikolová	CZE	17:07.32
4.	Alevtina Olunina	SOV/RUS	17:07.40
5.	Hilkka Kuntola	FIN	17:11.67
6.	Lyubov Mukhacheva	SOV/RUS	17:12.08
7.	Berit Mördre-Lammedal	NOR	17:16.79
8.	Aslaug Dahl	NOR	17:17.49

Kulakova, a 29-year-old physical education teacher from Izhevsk, matched Claudia Boyarskikh's feat of capturing all three women's nordic gold medals.

1976 Innsbruck-Seefeld C: 44, N: 14, D: 2.9.

1.	Helena Takalo	FIN	15:48.69
2.	Raisa Smetanina	SOV/RUS	15:49.73
3.	Nina Baldycheva	SOV/RUS	16:12.82
4.	Hilkka Kuntola	FIN	16:17.74
5.	Eva Olsson	SWE	16:27.15
6.	Zinaida Amosova	SOV/RUS	16:33.78
7.	Monika Debertshäuser	GDR	16:34.94
8.	Grete Kummen	NOR	16:35.43
DISQ (Drugs): Galina Kulakova (SOV/RUS) 16:07.36			

Defending champion Kulakova finished third, but was disqualified for having used a nasal spray that contained the banned drug ephedrine. She was, however, allowed to compete in the 10-kilometer race and the relay.

1980 Lake Placid C: 38, N: 12, D: 2.15.

1.	Raisa Smetanina	SOV/RUS	15:06.92
2.	Hilkka Riihivuori [Kuntola]	FIN	15:11.96
3.	Květoslava Jeriová	CZE	15:23.44
4.	Barbara Petzold	GDR	15:23.62
5.	Nina Baldycheva	SOV/RUS	15:29.03
6.	Galina Kulakova	SOV/RUS	15:29.58
7.	Veronika Hesse	GDR	15:31.83
8.	Helena Takalo	FIN	15:32.12

1984 Sarajevo C: 52, N: 14, D: 2.12.

1.	Marja-Liisa Hämäläinen	FIN	17:04.0
2.	Berit Aunli [Kvello]	NOR	17:14.1
3.	Květoslava Jeriová	CZE	17:18.3
4.	Lillemor Marie Risby [Johansson]	SWE	17:26.3
5.	Inger Helene Nybråten	NOR	17:28.2
6.	Brit Pettersen	NOR	17:33.6
7.	Anne Jahren	NOR	17:38.3
8.	Ute Noack	GDR	17:46.0

Hämäläinen won the second of her three gold medals.

1988 Calgary-Canmore C: 55, N: 17, D: 2.17.

1. Marjo Matikainen	FIN	15:04.0
2. Tamara Tikhonova	SOV/RUS	15:05.3
3. Vida Vencienė	SOV/LIT	15:11.1
4. Anne Jahren	NOR	15:12.6
5. Marja-Liisa Kirvesniemi [Hämäläinen]	FIN	15:16.7
6. Inger Helene Nybråten	NOR	15:17.7
7. Marie-Helene Westin	SWE	15:28.9
8. Svetlana Nageikina	SOV/RUS	15:29.9

Matikainen moved ahead after four kilometers, then used every last ounce of energy to push herself across the finish line 1.3 seconds faster than Tikhonova's time, before collapsing. The following year, Matikainen retired at the age of 23 in order to study engineering.

1992 Albertville-Les Saisies C: 62, N: 21, D: 2.13.

1. Marjut Lukkarinen	FIN	14:13.8
2. Lyubov Yegorova	SOV/RUS	14:14.7
3. Yelena Välbe	SOV/RUS	14:22.7
4. Stefania Belmondo	ITA	14:26.2
5. Inger Helene Nybråten	NOR	14:33.3
6. Olga Danilova	SOV/RUS	14:37.2
7. Larissa Lazutina	SOV/RUS	14:41.7
8. Solveig Pedersen	NOR	14:42.1

Whereas Marjo Matikainen retired early to pursue a career, Marjut Lukkarinen waited until she had completed her nursing studies before taking her racing seriously. She joined the World Cup circuit at age 24, two years before the Olympics, but continued to work twenty hours a week in an after-care ward in her hometown of Lohja. Skiing in a wet snowstorm, she won the fastest and closest women's nordic race in Olympic history. She did have to engage in unusual tactics to gain her victory. At one point she found herself behind Kateřina Neumannová of Czechoslovakia. She yelled, "Track," to get Neumannová to move over, as is the custom in cross-country skiing, but Neumannová did not respond. She tried again, but still Neumannová remained in her way. Finally Lukkarinen began hitting her on the legs with her ski pole. Neumannová moved over.

1994 Lillehammer C: 62, N: 19, D: 2.15.
(Freestyle)

1. Lyubov Yegorova	RUS	14:08.8
2. Manuela Di Centa	ITA	14:28.3
3. Marja-Liisa Kirvesniemi [Hämäläinen]	FIN	14:36.0
4. Anita Moen	NOR	14.39.4
5. Inger Helene Nybråten	NOR	14:43.6
6. Larissa Lazutina	RUS	14:44.2
7. Trude Dybendahl	NOR	14:48.1
8. Kateřina Neumannová	CZE	14:49.6

Yegorova won the first of her three gold medals in Lillehammer to go with the three she had won two years earlier in Les Saisies. The pre-Olympic favorite was Yegorova's teammate, Yelena Välbe. However, according to Russian officials, the Russian team had decided that whichever of the four Russians entered in the 15-kilometer race had the worst placing would be dropped from the 5-kilometer race and the pursuit. Välbe finished sixth at 15 kilometers. Unfortunately, three of the five skiers ahead of her were the other Russians. Välbe later dismissed this explanation, saying that her exclusion was due to the rivalry between competing coaches. Her replacement, Svetlana Nageikina, happened to be the girlfriend of Russian head coach Aleksandr Grushin. Nageikina placed 16th in the 5-kilometer race and 19th in the pursuit.

COMBINED PURSUIT

1928-1988 not held

1992 Albertville-Les Saisies C: 58, N: 21, D: 2.15.

		5 KM CLASSICAL		10 KM FREESTYLE		TOTAL
1. Lyubov Yegorova	SOV/RUS	14:14	(2)	25:53.7	(1)	40:07.7
2. Stefania Belmondo	ITA	14:26	(4)	26:05.8	(2)	40:31.8
3. Yelena Välbe	SOV/RUS	14:22	(3)	26:29.7	(3)	40:51.7
4. Marjut Lukkarinen	FIN	14:13	(1)	26:52.1	(7)	41:05.1
5. Elin Nilsen	NOR	14:50	(10)	26:36.9	(4)	41:26.9
6. Marie-Helene Westin	SWE	14:42	(8)	27:46.2	(6)	41:28.2
7. Inger Helene Nybråten	NOR	14:33	(5)	27:02.1	(8)	41:35.1
8. Larissa Lazutina	SOV/RUS	14:41	(7)	27:07.8	(10)	41:48.8

On the second day of the competition, Yegorova let Belmondo take the lead. She tracked her for 6.5 kilometers, then took off and ran away with the race.

1994 Lillehammer C: 55, N: 17, D: 2.17.

		5 KM CLASSICAL		10 KM FREESTYLE		TOTAL
1. Lyubov Yegorova	RUS	14:08	(1)	27:30.1	(3)	41:38.1
2. Manuela Di Centa	ITA	14:28	(2)	27:18.4	(2)	41:46.4
3. Stefania Belmondo	ITA	15:04	(12)	27:17.1	(1)	42:21.1
4. Larissa Lazutina	RUS	14:44	(5)	27:52.6	(5)	42:36.6
5. Nina Gavrilyuk	RUS	15:01	(10)	27:35.9	(4)	42:36.9
6. Katerina Neumannová	CZE	14:49	(7)	28:00.8	(6)	42:49.0
7. Trude Dybendahl	NOR	14:48	(6)	28:02.2	(7)	42:50.2
8. Anita Moen	NOR	14:39	(4)	28:42.2	(14)	43:21.2

Yegorova held off Di Centa to win the fifth of her record-tying six career gold medals. "If the race had been one kilometer longer," she said afterwards, "I would have lost." Yegorova's reputation was badly tarnished three years later when, at the 1997 world championships, she tested positive for the banned stimulant Bromantan, which is also used as a masking agent for other drugs.

15 KILOMETERS (CLASSICAL)

1928-1988 not held

1992 Albertville-Les Saisies C: 53, N: 21, D: 2.9.

1. Lyubov Yegorova	SOV/RUS	42:20.8
2. Marjut Lukkarinen	FIN	43:29.9
3. Yelena Välbe	SOV/RUS	43:42.3

4. Raisa Smetanina	SOV/RUS	44:01.5
5. Stefania Belmondo	ITA	44:02.4
6. Marja-Liisa Kirvesniemi [Hämäläinen]	FIN	44:02.7
7. Inger Helene Nybråten	NOR	44:18.6
8. Trude Dybendahl	NOR	44:31.5

Although she thought the course defeated her, Yegorova's intermediate times showed that she led from start to finish to win the first of her three gold medals.

1994 Lillehammer C: 54, N: 19, D: 2.13.
(Freestyle)

1. Manuela Di Centa	ITA	39:44.6
2. Lyubov Yegorova	RUS	41:03.0
3. Nina Gavrilyuk	RUS	41:10.4
4. Stefania Belmondo	ITA	41:33.6
5. Larissa Lazutina	RUS	41:57.6
6. Yelena Välbe	RUS	42:26.6
7. Antonina Ordina	SWE	42:29.1
8. Alžběta Havrancíková	SVK	42:34.4

Di Centa easily won the first gold medal of the Lillehammer Olympics. Before the Games were over she would earn medals in every cross-country event: two golds, two silvers and one bronze.

30 KILOMETERS (FREESTYLE)

1928-1988 not held

1992 Albertville-Les Saisies C: 57, N: 19, D: 2.21.

1. Stefania Belmondo	ITA	1:22:30.1
2. Lyubov Yegorova	SOV/RUS	1:22:52.0
3. Yelena Välbe	SOV/RUS	1:24:13.9
4. Elin Nilsen	NOR	1:26:25.1
5. Larissa Lazutina	SOV/RUS	1:26:31.8
6. Manuela Di Centa	ITA	1:27:04.4
7. Marie-Helene Westin	SWE	1:27:16.2
8. Simone Opitz	GER	1:27:17.4

Belmondo, only 5-foot 1-inch and 104 pounds, had placed fifth, fourth, second, and third before striking gold in the final women's cross-country event. Over half of her home village of Pontebernardo (population 160) traveled to Les Saisies to cheer her on to victory. Yegorova and Välbe both won medals in all five nordic events. Yegorova's final haul was three gold and two silver, while Välbe became the first female winter athlete to win four bronze medals.

1994 Lillehammer C: 53, N: 19, D: 2.24.
(Classical)

1. Manuela Di Centa	ITA	1:25:41.6
2. Marit Wold	NOR	1:25:57.8
3. Marja-Liisa Kirvesniemi [Hämäläinen]	FIN	1:26:13.6
4. Trude Dybendahl	NOR	1:26:52.6
5. Lyubov Yegorova	RUS	1:26:54.8
6. Yelena Välbe	RUS	1:26:57.4

7.	Inger Helene Nybråten	NOR	1:27:11.2
8.	Marjut Rolig [Lukkarinen]	FIN	1:27:51.4

Prior to the 1994 Olympics, 31-year-old Manuela Di Centa of Paluzza had competed in 23 Olympic and world championship races without winning a gold medal. She was particularly disheartened by her performance at the 1992 Olympics, where she felt exhausted all the time and could do no better than sixth in an individual event. One doctor told her she was suffering from "Belmonditis," a reference to her Italian rival, Stefania Belmondo, who starred in 1992, winning the 30 kilometers and finishing second in the pursuit. However, an endocrinologist discovered that Di Centa had a malfunctioning thyroid gland. After being hospitalized and treated, she earned medals in all five events in 1994, including gold at 15 kilometers and 30 kilometers.

Marja-Liisa Kirvesniemi's bronze medal brought her career total to three golds and three bronze.

4 × 5-KILOMETER RELAY

Through 1988 this was a freestyle event, but since 1992 two skiers on each team use the classical technique and two use the skating technique.

1924–1952 not held

1956 Cortina T: 10, N: 10, D: 2.1.
3 × 5-*Kilometer*

1.	FIN	(Sirkka Polkunen, Mirja Hietamies, Siiri Rantanen)	1:09.01.0
2.	SOV/ RUS	(Lyubov Kozyreva, Alevtina Kolchina, Radya Yeroshina)	1:09:28.0
3.	SWE	(Irma Johansson, Anna-Lisa Eriksson, Sonja Edström)	1:09.48.0
4.	NOR	(Kjellfrid Brusveen, Gina Regland, Rakel Wahl)	1:10.50.0
5.	POL	(Maria Gąsienica-Bukowa, Józefa Pęksa, Zofia Krzeptowska)	1:13.20.0
6.	CZE	(Eva Benešová, Libuse Patocková, Eva Lauermanová)	1:14.19.0
7.	GDR/ GER	(Elfriede Uhlig, Else Ammann, Sonnhilde Hausschild)	1:15:33.0
8.	ITA	(Fides Romanin, Rita Bottero, Ildegarda Taffra)	1:16.11.0

Rantanen of Finland took off six seconds behind Eroshina, passed her, lost the lead, then passed her again to win by 100 yards.

1960 Squaw Valley T: 5, N: 5, D: 2.26.
3 × 5-Kilometer

1.	SWE	(Irma Johansson, Britt Strandberg, Sonja Ruthström [Edström])	1:04.21.4
2.	SOV/ RUS	(Radya Yeroshina, Maria Gusakova, Lyubov Baranova [Kozyreva])	1:05:02.6
3.	FIN	(Siiri Rantanen, Eeva Ruoppa, Toini Pöysti)	1:06:27.5
4.	POL	(Stefania Biegun, Helena Gąsienica-Daniel, Józefa Pęksa-Czerniawska)	1:07:24.6
5.	GDR/ GER	(Rita Czech-Blasl, Renate Borges, Sonnhilde Kallus [Hausschild])	1:09:25.7

On the first leg, Radya Yeroshina fell and broke one of her skis. She picked up a replacement, but lost over a minute, a delay which cost the U.S.S.R. the gold medal. The Soviets lodged a protest, claiming that Irma Johansson of Sweden had cut in front of Yeroshina and caused her to fall. After viewing films of the race, the U.S.S.R. withdrew their protest.

1964 Innsbruck-Seefeld T: 8, N: 8, D: 2.7.
3 × 5-Kilometer

1.	SOV/ RUS	(Alevtina Kolchina, Yevdokya Mekshilo, Klavdia Boyarskikh)	59:20.2
2.	SWE	(Barbro Martinsson, Brit Strandberg, Toini Gustafsson)	1:01:27.0
3.	FIN	(Senja Pusula, Toini Pöysti, Mirja Lehtonen)	1:02:45.1
4.	GER/ GDR	(Christine Nestler, Rita Czech-Blasl, Renate Dannhauser)	1:04:29.9
5.	BUL	(Rosa Dimova, Nadezhda Vasileva, Krastana Stoeva)	1:06:40.4
6.	CZE	(Jarmila Skodová, Eva Brizová, Eva Paulusová)	1:08:42.8
7.	POL	(Teresa Trzebunia, Czeslawa Stopka, Stefania Biegun)	1:08:55.4
8.	HUN	(Éva Blazs, Mária Tarnai, Ference Hemrik)	1:10:16.3

1968 Grenoble-Autrans T: 8, N: 8, D: 2.16.
3 × 5-Kilometer

1.	NOR	(Inger Aufles, Babben Damon-Enger, Berit Mördre)	57:30.0
2.	SWE	(Britt Strandberg, Toini Gustafsson, Barbro Martinsson)	57:51.0
3.	SOV/ RUS	(Alevtina Kolchina, Rita Achkina, Galina Kulakova)	58:13.6
4.	FIN	(Senja Pusula, Marjatta Olkkonen, Marjatta Kajosmaa)	58:45.1
5.	POL	(Weronika Budny, Józefa Pęksa-Czerniawska, Stefania Biegun)	59:04.7
6.	GDR	(Renate Köhler, Gudrun Schmidt, Christine Nestler)	59:33.9
7.	GER	(Michaela Endler, Barbara Barthel, Monika Mrklas)	1:01:49.3
8.	BUL	(Pandeva Velitska, Nadezhda Vasileva, Szvetana Sotirova)	1:05:35.7

1972 Sapporo-Makomanai T: 11, N: 11, D: 2.12.
3 × 5-Kilometer

1.	SOV/ RUS	(Lyubov Mukhacheva, Alevtina Olunina, Galina Kulakova)	48:46.15
2.	FIN	(Helena Takalo, Hilkka Kuntola, Marjatta Kajosmaa)	49:19.37
3.	NOR	(Inger Aufles, Aslaug Dahl, Berit Mördre-Lammedal)	49:51.49
4.	GER	(Monika Mrklas, Ingrid Rothfuss, Michaela Endler)	50:25.61
5.	GDR	(Gabriele Haupt, Renate Fischer, Anni Unger)	50:28.45
6.	CZE	(Alena Bartušová, Helena Šikolová, Milena Cillerová)	51:16.16
7.	POL	(Anna Duraj, Józefa Chromik, Weronika Budny)	51:49.13
8.	SWE	(Meeri Bodelid, Eva Olsson, Birgitta Lindqvist)	51:51.84

1976 Innsbruck-Seefeld T: 9, N: 9, D: 2.12.

1.	SOV/ RUS	(Nina Baldycheva, Zinaida Amosova, Raisa Smetanina, Galina Kulakova)	1:07:49.75
2.	FIN	(Liisa Suihkonen, Marjatta Kajosmaa, Hilkka Kuntola, Helena Takalo)	1:08:36.57
3.	GDR	(Monika Debertshäuser, Sigrun Krause, Barbara Petzold, Veronika Schmidt)	1:09:57.95
4.	SWE	(Lena Carlzon, Görel Partapuoli, Marie Johansson, Eva Olsson)	1:10:14.68
5.	NOR	(Berit Kvello, Marit Myrmael, Berit Johannessen, Grete Kummen)	1:11:09.08
6.	CZE	(Hana Pasiárová, Gabriela Sekajová, Alena Bartošová, Blanka Paulů)	1:11:27.83
7.	CAN	(Shirley Firth, Joan Groothuysen, Susan Holloway, Sharon Firth)	1:14:02.72
8.	POL	(Anna Pawlusiak, Anna Gębala-Duraj, Maria Trebunia, Wladyslawa Majerczyk)	1:14:13.40

1980 Lake Placid T: 8, N: 8, D: 2.21.

1.	GDR	(Marlies Rostock, Carola Anding, Veronika Hesse [Schmidt], Barbara Petzold)	1:02:11.10

2.	SOV/ RUS	(Nina Baldycheva, Nina Rocheva, Galina Kulakova, Raisa Smetanina)	1:03:18.30
3.	NOR	(Brit Pettersen, Anette Böe, Marit Myrmäl, Berit Aunli [Kvello])	1:04:13.50
4.	CZE	(Dagmar Palecková, Gabriela Svobodová, Blanka Paulů, Květoslava Jeriová)	1:04:31.39
5.	FIN	(Marja Auroma, Marja-Liisa Hämäläinen, Helena Takalo, Hilkka Riihivuori [Kuntola])	1:04:41.28
6.	SWE	(Lillemor Marie Johansson, Karin Lamberg, Eva Olsson, Lena Carlzon-Lundbäck)	1:05:16.32
7.	USA	(Alison Owen-Spencer, Beth Paxson, Leslie Bancroft, Margaret Spencer)	1:06:55.41
8.	CAN	(Angela Schmidt, Shirley Firth, Esther Miller, Joan Groothuysen)	1:07:45.75

The U.S.S.R.'s second-place finish gave Kulakova her eighth Olympic medal—four gold, two silver, and two bronze.

1984 Sarajevo T: 12, N: 12, D: 2.15.

1.	NOR	(Inger Helene Nybråten, Anne Jahren, Brit Pettersen, Berit Aunli [Kvello])	1:06:49.7
2.	CZE	(Dagmar Švubová, Blanka Paulů, Gabriela Svobodová, Kvetoslava Jeriová)	1:07:34.7
3.	FIN	(Pirkko Määttä, Eija Hyytiäinen, Marjo Matikainen, Marja-Liisa Hämäläinen)	1:07:36.7
4.	SOV/ RUS	(Yulia Stepanova, Lyubov Lyadova, Nadezhda Burlakova, Raisa Smetanina)	1:07:55.0
5.	SWE	(Karin Lamberg, Doris Hugosson, Lillemor Marie Risby [Johansson], Ann Rosendahl)	1:09:30.0
6.	SWI	(Karin Thomas, Monika Germann, Christine Brügger, Evi Kratzer)	1:09:40.3
7.	USA	(Susan Long, Judy Rabinowitz, Lynn Spencer-Galanes, Patricia Ross)	1:10:48.4
8.	GDR	(Petra Voge, Petra Rohrmann, Carola Anding, Ute Noack)	1:11:10.7

The fastest time of the race, 16:12.6, was recorded by Květa Jeriová who actually overcame triple gold-medalist Marja-Liisa Hämäläinen on the anchor leg to win the silver medal for Czechoslovakia.

1988 Calgary-Canmore T: 12, N: 12, D: 2.21.

1.	SOV/ RUS	(Svetlana Nageikina, Nina Gavrilyuk, Tamara Tikhonova, Anfisa Reztsova)	59:51.1
2.	NOR	(Trude Dybendahl, Marit Wold, Anne Jahren, Marianne Dahlmo)	1:01:33.0
3.	FIN	(Pirkko Määttä, Marja-Liisa Kirvesniemi [Hämäläinen], Marjo Matikainen, Jaana Savolainen)	1:01:53.8
4.	SWI	(Karin Thomas, Sandra Parpan, Evi Kratzer, Christina Gilli-Brügger)	1:01:59.4
5.	GDR	(Kerstin Moring, Simone Opitz, Silke Braun, Simone Greiner-Petter)	1:02:19.9
6.	SWE	(Lis Frost, Anna-Lena Fritzon, Karin Lamberg-Skog, Marie-Helene Westin)	1:02:24.9
7.	CZE	(Lubomira Balazová, Viera Klimková, Ivana Radlova, Alžběta Havrančiková)	1:03:37.1
8.	USA	(Dorcas Denhartog, Leslie Thompson, Nancy Fiddler, Leslie Krichko)	1:04:08.8

In a move almost without precedent, the Sunday night television news in the U.S.S.R. was delayed two minutes to allow the broadcast of the end of this race.

1992 Albertville-Les Saisies T: 13, N: 13, D: 2.17.

1.	SOV/ RUS	(Yelena Välbe, Raisa Smetanina, Larissa Lazutina, Lyubov Yegorova)	59:34.8

Raisa Smetanina (left) celebrates with her 1992 4 x 5-kilometer relay teammates after becoming the first athlete to win ten Winter Olympics medals.

2. NOR   (Solveig Pedersen, Inger Helene Nybråten, Trude Dybendahl, Elin Nilsen)   59:56.4
3. ITA   (Bice Vanzetta, Manuela Di Centa, Gabriella Paruzzi, Stefania Belmondo)   1:00:25.9
4. FIN   (Marja-Liisa Kirvesniemi [Hämäläinen], Pirkko Määttä, Jaana Savolainen,   1:00:52.9
   Marjut Lukkarinen)
5. FRA   (Carole Stanisiere, Sylvie Giry Rousset, Sophie Villeneuve, Isabelle   1:01:30.7
   Mancini)
6. CZE   (Lubomira Balazová, Kateřina Neumannová, Alžběta Havrančiková, Iveta   1:01:37.4
   Zelingerová)
7. SWE   (Carina Görlin, Magdalena Wallin, Karin Säterkvist, Marie-Helene Westin)   1:01:54.5
8. GER   (Heike Wezel, Gabriele Hess, Simone Opitz, Ina Kummel)   1:02:22.6

With this race Raisa Smetanina became the first winter athlete to earn ten Olympic medals. Eight days earlier she had almost set the record when she placed fourth in the 15-kilometer race. She also became the only athlete to win medals in five Winter Olympics and, 12 days shy of her fortieth birthday, the oldest female medalist in Winter Olympics history.

1994 Lillehammer T: 14, N: 14, D: 2.21.
1. RUS   (Yelena Välbe, Larissa Lazutina, Nina Gavrilyuk, Lyubov Yegorova)   57:12.5
2. NOR   (Trude Dybendahl, Inger Helene Nybråten, Elin Nilsen, Anita Moen)   57:42.6
3. ITA   (Bice Vanzetta, Manuela Di Centa, Gabriella Paruzzi, Stefania Belmondo)   58:42.6
4. FIN   (Pirkko Määttä, Marja-Liisa Kirvesniemi [Hämäläinen], Merja Lahtinen, Marjut   59:15.9
   Rolig [Lukkarinen])
5. SWI   (Sylvia Honegger, Silke Schwager, Barbara Mettler, Brigitte Albrecht)   1:00.05.1
6. SWE   (Anna Frithioff, Marie-Helene Östlund [Westin], Anna-Lena Fritzon, Antonina   1:00:05.8
   Ordina)
7. SVK   (Lubomira Balazová, Jaroslava Bukvajova, Tatiana Kutlikova, Alžběta   1:01:00.2
   Havrančiková)
8. POL   (Michalina Maciuszek, Malgorzata Ruchala, Dorota Kwasny, Bernadetta   1:01:13.2
   Bocek)

The Russian relay team, unbeaten in major competitions in five years, trailed Norway after three legs, but the Norwegian anchor, Anita Moen, despite skiing the third fastest leg of the day, could not keep up with Lyubov Yegorova. Yegorova was the only member of the Russian team who was not a mother. With this race Yegorova tied speed skater Lydia Skoblikova's record of six Winter Olympics gold medals. Three years later, Yegorova was banned from competition after failing a doping test.

Discontinued Events

10 KILOMETERS (CLASSICAL)

1952 Oslo C: 20, N: 8, D: 2.23.

1.	Lydia Wideman	FIN	41:40.0
2.	Mirja Hietamies	FIN	42:39.0
3.	Siiri Rantanen	FIN	42:50.0
4.	Märta Norberg	SWE	42:53.0
5.	Sirkka Polkunen	FIN	43:07.0
6.	Rakel Wahl	NOR	44:54.0
7.	Marit Øiseth	NOR	45:04.0
8.	Margit Albrechtsson	SWE	45:05.0

1956 Cortina C: 40, N: 11, D: 1:28.

1.	Lyubov Kozyreva	SOV/RUS	38:11.0
2.	Radya Yeroshina	SOV/RUS	38:16.0
3.	Sonja Edström	SWE	38:23.0
4.	Alevtina Kolchina	SOV/RUS	38:46.0
5.	Siiri Rantanen	FIN	39:40.0
6.	Mirja Hietamies	FIN	40:18.0
7.	Irma Johansson	SWE	40:20.0
8.	Sirkka Polkunen	FIN	40:25.0

1960 Squaw Valley C: 24, N: 7, D: 2.20.

1.	Maria Gusakova	SOV/RUS	39:46.6
2.	Lyubov Baranova [Kosyreva]	SOV/RUS	40:04.2
3.	Radya Yeroshina	SOV/RUS	40:06.0
4.	Alevtina Kolchina	SOV/RUS	40:12.6
5.	Sonja Ruthström [Edström]	SWE	40:35.5
6.	Toini Pöysti	FIN	40:41.9
7.	Barbro Martinsson	SWE	41:06.2
8.	Irma Johansson	SWE	41:08.3

1964 Innsbruck-Seefeld C: 35, N: 13, D: 2.1.

1.	Klavdia Boyarskikh	SOV/RUS	40:24.3
2.	Yevdoyka Mekshilo	SOV/RUS	40:26.6
3.	Maria Gusakova	SOV/RUS	40:46.6
4.	Britt Strandberg	SWE	40:54.0
5.	Toini Pöysti	FIN	41:17.4

6. Senja Pusula   FIN   41:17.8
7. Alevtina Kolchina   SOV/RUS   41:26.2
8. Toini Gustafsson   SWE   41:41.1

1968 Grenoble-Autrans C: 34, N: 11, D: 2.9.

1. Toini Gustafsson   SWE   36:46.5
2. Berit Mördre   NOR   37:54.6
3. Inger Aufles   NOR   37:59.9
4. Barbro Martinsson   SWE   38:07.1
5. Marjatta Kajosmaa   FIN   38:09.0
6. Galina Kulakova   SOV/RUS   38:26.7
7. Alevtina Kolchina   SOV/RUS   38:52.9
8. Babben Damon-Enger   NOR   38:54.4

1972 Sapporo-Makomanai C: 42, N: 11, D: 2.6.

1. Galina Kulakova   SOV/RUS   34:17.82
2. Alevtina Olunina   SOV/RUS   34:54.11
3. Marjatta Kajosmaa   FIN   34:56.45
4. Lyubov Mukhacheva   SOV/RUS   34:58.56
5. Helena Takalo   FIN   35:06.34
6. Aslaug Dahl   NOR   35:18.84
7. Helena Šikolová   CZE   35:29.33
8. Hilkka Kuntola   FIN   35:36.71

1976 Innsbruck-Seefeld C: 44, N: 15, D: 2.10.

1. Raisa Smetanina   SOV/RUS   30:13.41
2. Helena Takalo   FIN   30:14.28
3. Galina Kulakova   SOV/RUS   30:38.61
4. Nina Baldycheva   SOV/RUS   30:52.58
5. Eva Olsson   SWE   31:08.72
6. Zinaida Amosova   SOV/RUS   31:11.23
7. Barbara Petzold   GDR   31:12.20
8. Veronika Schmidt   GDR   31:12.33

1980 Lake Placid C: 38, N: 12, D: 2.18.

1. Barbara Petzold   GDR   30:31.54
2. Hilkka Riihivuori [Kuntola] FIN   30:35.05
3. Helena Takalo   FIN   30:45.25
4. Raisa Smetanina   SOV/RUS   30:54.48
5. Galina Kulakova   SOV/RUS   30:58.46
6. Nina Balycheva   SOV/RUS   31:22.93
7. Marlies Rostock   GDR   31:28.79
8. Veronika Hesse [Schmidt]   GDR   31:29.14

The East German propaganda apparatus broke down somewhat in the case of Barbara Petzold, who was described in half the press releases as a medical student and in the other half as a law student. Either way, she told the press that training and competing left her little time for her studies.

1984 Sarajevo C: 52, N: 15, D: 2.9.

1. Marja-Liisa Hämäläinen   FIN   31:44.2
2. Raisa Smetanina   SOV/RUS   32:02.9
3. Brit Pettersen   NOR   32:12.7
4. Berit Aunli [Kvello]   NOR   32:17.7
5. Anne Jahren   NOR   32:26.2

Marja-Liisa Hämäläinen, winner of all three women's individual cross-country races at the 1984 Sarajevo Games, tried to run away from the press after her victories. She was finally cornered and forced to submit to interviews.

6. Lillemor Marie Risby [Johansson] SWE 32:34.6
7. Marit Myrmael NOR 32:35.3
8. Yulia Stepanova SOV/RUS 32:45.7

Hämäläinen, a 28-year-old physiotherapist from Simpele, near the Soviet border, gained revenge over Finnish journalists. "A hundred times they've written that I would never become anybody," she would say, "and I wanted to show people that I am somebody and that if I didn't do well, there was always a reason."

1988 Calgary-Canmore C: 52, N: 17, D: 2.14.

1. Vida Vencienė SOV/LIT 30:08.3
2. Raisa Smetanina SOV/RUS 30:17.0
3. Marjo Matikainen FIN 30:20.5
4. Svetlana Nageikina SOV/RUS 30:26.5
5. Tamara Tikhonova SOV/RUS 30:38.9
6. Inger Helene Nybråten NOR 30:51.7
7. Pirkko Määttä FIN 30:52.4
8. Marie-Helene Westin SWE 30:53.5

20 KILOMETERS (FREESTYLE)

1984 Sarajevo C: 40, N: 13, D: 2.18.

1. Marja-Liisa Hämäläinen FIN 1:01:45.0
2. Raisa Smetanina SOV/RUS 1:02:26.7
3. Anne Jahren NOR 1:03:13.6

4. Blanka Paulů	CZE	1:03:16.9
5. Lillemor Marie Risby [Johansson]	SWE	1:03:31.8
6. Brit Pettersen	NOR	1:03:49.0
7. Lyubov Lyadova	SOV/RUS	1:03:53.3
8. Evi Kratzer	SWI	1:03:56.4

After winning her third gold medal, Marja-Liisa Hämäläinen tried to avoid Finnish reporters by jumping over a fence and running away. Finally headed off and trapped, the farmer's daughter submitted to photographs and interviews. In addition to her three individual golds, she earned a bronze medal in the relay. Her fiancé, Harri Kirvesniemi, won two nordic bronze medals.

1988 Calgary-Canmore C: 55, N: 18, D: 2.25.

1. Tamara Tikhonova	SOV/RUS	55:53.6
2. Anfisa Reztsova	SOV/RUS	56:12.8
3. Raisa Smetanina	SOV/RUS	57:22.1
4. Christina Gilli-Brügger	SWI	57:37.4
5. Simone Opitz	GDR	57:54.3
6. Manuela Di Centa	ITA	57:55.2
7. Kerstin Moring	GDR	58:17.2
8. Marianne Dahlmo	NOR	58:31.1
DISQ: Nina Gavrilyuk (SOV/RUS)		58:26.9

Nina Gavrilyuk placed eighth but was disqualified for wearing the logo of a shoe manufacturer on the front of her headband.

SNOWBOARDING

MEN	WOMEN
Giant Slalom	Giant Slalom
Halfpipe	Halfpipe

MEN

GIANT SLALOM
Competition consists of two runs on courses between 200 and 400 meters long.

This event will be held for the first time in 1998.

HALFPIPE
A halfpipe is a channel constructed in the snow. It is about 110 meters long with walls approximately 3.5 meters high. Snowboarders come down the halfpipe while performing various tricks and maneuvers. They are scored by five judges, each of whom has responsibility for one aspect of the performance. The five criteria are:

1) Standard Maneuvers—all those maneuvers that are without rotation, such as aerials and tricks on the lip of the halfpipe
2) Rotations—maneuvers that include rotations, such as spins, flips and hybrid tricks
3) Amplitude—the height of the maneuvers, the speed of the run and the "energy" of the competitor
4) Landings—the landings judge is the only one who takes into account falls
5) Technical Merit—overall precision and rhythm

The Olympic competition will be decided by the combined score of two runs.

This event will be held for the first time in 1998.

WOMEN

GIANT SLALOM
This event will be held for the first time.

HALFPIPE
This event will be held for the first time in 1998.

WINTER OLYMPIC RECORDS

GENERAL

Most Medals
10 Raisa Smetanina (SOV/RUS, Nordic Skiing, 1976–1992)

Most Medals, Men
9 Sixten Jernberg (SWE, Nordic Skiing, 1956–1964)

Most Gold Medals
6 Lydia Skoblikova (SOV/RUS, Speed Skating, 1960–1964)
6 Lyubov Yegorova (RUS, Nordic Skiing, 1992–1994)

Most Gold Medals, Men
5 A. Clas Thunberg (FIN, Speed Skating, 1924–1928)
5 Eric Heiden (USA, Speed Skating, 1980)
5 Bjørn Dahlie (NOR, Nordic Skiing, 1992–1994)

Most Silver Medals
5 Andrea Ehrig (Mitscherlich, Schöne) (GDR, Speed Skating, 1976, 1984–1988)
5 Bogdan Musiol (GDR, Bobsled, 1980–1988)
5 Raisa Smetanina (SOV/RUS, Nordic Skiing, 1976–1988)

Most Bronze Medals
5 Harri Kirvesniemi (FIN, Nordic Skiing, 1980–1984, 1992–1994)

Most Bronze Medals, Women
4 Yelena Välbe (SOV/RUS, Nordic Skiing, 1992)

Most Family Names Used While Winning Medals
3 Andrea Mitscherlich-Schöne-Ehrig (GDR, Speed Skating, 1976, 1984–1988)

Most Years Between Medals
20 John Heaton (USA, Luge, 1928–1948)
20 Richard Torriani (SWI, Ice Hockey, 1928–1948)

Most Years Between Medals, Women
16 Raisa Smetanina (SOV/RUS, Nordic Skiing, 1976–1992)

Most Medals in Individual Events
8 Karin Kania (Enke) (GDR, Speed Skating, 1980–1988)

Most Medals in Individual Events, Men
7 A. Clas Thunberg (FIN, Speed Skating, 1924–1928)
7 Ivar Ballangrud (NOR, Speed Skating, 1928–1936)

Most Consecutive Victories in the Same Event
3 Gillis Grafström (SWE, Men's Figure Skating, 1920–1928)
3 Sonja Henie (NOR, Women's Figure Skating, 1928–1936)
3 Irina Rodnina (SOV/RUS, Pairs Figure Skating, 1972–1980)
3 Ulrich Wehling (GDR, Nordic Combined, 1972–1980)
3 Bonnie Blair (USA, 500-Meter Speed Skating, 1988–1994)

Youngest Medalist
13 years 83 days Kim Yoon-mi (KOR, Women's Short Track Relay, 1994)

Youngest Medalist, Men
14 years 363 days Scott Allan (USA, Men's Figure Skating, 1964)

Youngest Medalist in an Individual Event
14 years 363 days Scott Allan (USA, Men's Figure Skating, 1964)

Youngest Medalist in an Individual Event, Women
15 years 68 days Andrea Mitscherlich (GDR, 3000-Meter Speed Skating, 1976)

Youngest Gold Medalist
13 years 83 days Kim Yoon-mi (KOR, Women's Short Track Relay, 1994)

Youngest Gold Medalist, Men
16 years 259 days Toni Nieminen (FIN, Team Ski Jumping, 1992)

Youngest Gold Medalist in an Individual Event
15 years 315 days Sonja Henie (NOR, Women's Figure Skating, 1928)

Youngest Gold Medalist in an Individual Event, Men
16 years 261 days Toni Nieminen (FIN, Large Hill Ski Jumping, 1992)

Oldest Medalist
49 years 278 days Max Houben (BEL, Four-Man Bobsled, 1948)

Oldest Medalist, Women
39 years 354 days Raisa Smetanina (SOV/RUS, 4 × 5-Kilometer Relay, 1992)

Oldest Medalist in an Individual Event
44 years 77 days Martin Stixrud (NOR, Men's Figure Skating, 1920)

Oldest Medalist in an Individual Event, Women
38 years 167 days Marja-Liisa Kirvisniemi (FIN, 30-Kilometer Skiing, 1994)

Oldest Gold Medalist
48 years 357 days Jay O'Brien (USA, Four-Man Bobsled, 1932)

Oldest Gold Medalist, Women
39 years 354 days Raisa Smetanina (SOV/RUS, 4 × 5-Kilometer Relay, 1992)

Oldest Gold Medalist in an Individual Event
35 years 4 days Magnar Solberg (NOR, 20-Kilometer Biathlon, 1972)

Oldest Gold Medalist in an Individual Event, Women
33 years 268 days Christina Baas-Kaiser (HOL, 3000-Meter Speed Skating, 1972)

Most Olympics Competed in
6 Carl-Erik Eriksson (SWE, Bobsled, 1964–1984) Eriksson's best finish was a sixth in the 1972 two-man bob.
6 Colin Coates (AUS, Speed Skating, 1968–1988) Coates' best finish was a sixth in the 1976 10,000 meters.
6 Marja-Liisa Kirvisniemi [Hamalainen] (FIN, Nordic Skiing, 1976–1994) Kirvisniemi won 3 gold medals and 3 bronze.
6 Alfred Eder (AUT, Biathlon, 1976–1994) Eder's best finish was tenth in the 1994 20-Kilometer race.

Youngest Competitor
11 years 74 days Cecilia Colledge (GBR, Women's Figure Skating, 1932) Colledge finished in eighth place.

Youngest Competitor, Men
12 years 113 days Jan Hoffman (GDR, Men's Figure Skating, 1988) Hoffman placed 26th out of 28.

Oldest Competitor
53 years 328 days James Coates (GBR, Skeleton Luge, 1948) Coates finished in seventh place.

Oldest Competitor, Women
45 years 318 days Edwina Chamier (CAN, Alpine Combined Skiing, 1936) Chamier withdrew before the final slalom run.

Most Competitors in a Single Event
131 Men's Giant Slalom, 1992

Most Nations Represented in a Single Event
46 Men's Giant Slalom, 1992

Longest National Win Streak in a Single Event
9 Soviet Union, Pairs Figure Skating, 1964–1994 The Soviet Union also won 8 straight gold medals in Ice Hockey (1956–1992) in Olympics held *outside* the United States.

Longest Streak in an Event With a Different Nation Winning Each Year
7 Women's Slalom, 1968–1992

Least Universal Event
Pairs figure skating has been held nineteen times, but has never attracted entrants from more than twelve nations at a time.

Best Performance by Athletes From a Snowless Country
In 1988 Seba Johnson of the U.S. Virgin Islands placed 28th in the women's giant slalom. It is true that only one other competitor had a slower time than Johnson, but 35 of the 64 starters failed to complete both runs and Olympic protocol places all finishers ahead of all non-finishers. The only other athletes from a snowless nation to place in the top half of the field in a winter event, were the 1994 Jamaican four-man bobsled team of Dudley Stokes, Winston Watt, Nelson Stokes and Wayne Thomas, who placed 14th out of 30 starters.

BIATHLON

Largest Margin of Victory
3 minutes 57.00 seconds Russia, Women's 4 × 7.5-Kilometer Relay, 1994

Slowest Performance
The only biathlete ever to record an adjusted time twice that of the winner was Herman Carazo of Costa Rica in the 1984 20-kilometer race. Carazo's time of 2:24:59.9 included eleven penalty minutes. He finished 35 minutes and 5 seconds behind the skier in next-to-last place. The race was won by Peter Angerer in 1:11:52.7. Three days later Carazo attempted the 10-kilometer race, but failed to finish.

Worst Shooters
In the 1960 20-kilometer race, two French biathletes, Victor Arbez and Paul Romand, both missed 18 of 20 shots. Tomislav Lopatič of Yugoslavia matched their percentage in the 1984 10-kilometer when he missed 9 of 10 shots, as did Fabiana Lovece of Argentina in the 1992 women's 7.5-kilometer sprint.

BOBSLED

Largest Margin of Victory
3.29 seconds Swiss four-man team driven by Edward Scherrer, 1924

Largest Margin of Victory, Single Run
5.65 seconds Reto Capadrutt and Oscar Geier (SWI), first run of the 1932 two-man bob.

Fastest Speed, Single Run
59.05 miles per hour Swiss four-man team driven by Ekkehard Fasser, third run, 1988

ICE HOCKEY

Longest Winning Streaks
16 Canada, 1920–1932
15 Soviet Union, 1980–1988

Longest Unbeaten Streak
20 Canada, 1920–1936

Most Lopsided Match
Canada 33 Switzerland 0 in 1924

LUGE

Largest Margin of Victory
2.75 seconds Ortrun Enderlein (GDR), 1964 women's single. In 1968 Enderlein placed first again, but was disqualified for heating her runners.

Largest Margin of Victory, Single Run
45 hundredths of a second Josef Feistmantl and Manfred Stengl (AUT), first run of the 1964 two-seater

Fastest Speed, Single Run
61.85 miles per hour Georg Hackl (GER), first run, 1992

Fastest Speed, Single Run, Women
54.87 miles per hour Angelika Neuner (AUT), third run, 1992

Slowest Performance
It's not easy to record a really slow time in a four-run luge competition. Most mediocre lugists crash and fail to finish or fall once and do reasonably well on the other three runs. In 1976, however, Huang Liu-chong of Taiwan lost control on the second and third runs, but managed to finish both times. His combined time for the two runs was 3:32.341. That would have been good enough for tenth place except that the times for the other competitors were for *four* runs. Huang's final time of 5:22.646 was over 50 seconds slower than anyone else's in the history of the event.

FIGURE SKATING

Highest Score
107.4 out of a possible 108 points, Jayne Torvill and Christopher Dean (GBR), 1984 Ice Dance, Free dance. Their score included three 6.0s for technical merit and a complete set of nine 6.0s for artistic impression.

Highest Score, Individual
105.9 out of a possible 108 points, Janet Lynn (USA), 1972 free skating
105.9 out of a possible 108 points, John Curry (GBR), 1976 free skating

Lowest Score
In 1928 Anita de St.-Quentin of France scored only 1114.25 points, compared to 1648.75 for the skater in next-to-last place and 2452.25 for the winner, Sonja Henie. De St.-Quentin is the only figure skater in Olympic history to earn less than half as many points as the winner. Since current rules have been in effect, the lowest score has been the 53.6 out of 108 awarded to Kim Hai-sung of South Korea for her short program in 1984.

Greatest Ranges of Scores
16 places. In 1964 Inge Paul of West Germany, competing in a field of thirty, was ranked eleventh by three judges and twenty-seventh by another judge. Her remaining rankings were thirteenth, fourteenth, sixteenth, seventeenth, and nineteenth.
16 places. In 1994 Krisztina Czako's (HUN) technical program received rankings ranging from seventh to twenty-third, and including three ninths, two twelfths, a thirteen and a fourteenth.

Greatest Judging Aberration
9 places. In 1984 Soviet skater Yelena Vodorezova's admirably traced compulsory figures earned her high marks from eight of the nine judges: four firsts, three seconds, and one third. Belgian judge Claude Carlens was not so impressed. He ranked her twelfth.
9 places. In 1994 Canadian judge Audrey Williams saw Hungarian Krisztina Czako's technical program differently than the other judges. Eight of the judges ranked her between seventh and fourteenth while Williams deemed her only twenty-third best of 27.

SPEED SKATING

Largest Margin of Victory
24.8 seconds Hjalmar Andersen (NOR), 1952 10,000 meters

Largest Margin of Victory, Women
6.53 seconds Christina Baas-Kaiser (HOL), 1972 3000 meters

Slowest Performance
In 1948, Richard "Buddy" Solem of the United States required 26 minutes 22.4 seconds to complete the 10,000-meter race. He was 8:56.1 behind the winner and 4:47.6 slower than the next-to-last skater. However, there were extenuating circumstances. By the time Solem, the last skater in the program, took the ice, the sun had turned the course into slush and eight other skaters, including 5000-meter gold medalist Reidar Liaklev, had withdrawn out of frustration. Solem was applauded loudly for his perseverance.

A more consistently slow skater was Charles de Ligne of Belgium. De Ligne began his 1936 Olympic experience by falling in the 500 meters. Rather than give up, de Ligne cruised to the finish line, eventually stopping the clock in 1:44.6—over 23 seconds slower than anyone else in the history of the event. The next day he attempted the 5000 meters, but gave up after 2600 meters by which time he had already fallen 1 minute 45 seconds off the pace set by Ivar Ballangrud. The day after that, de Ligne finished last in the 1500 meters, once again recording the slowest time in the history of the event. De Ligne closed out his Olympic career in the 10,000 meters. Race officials didn't bother to record his split times, but his final time of 23:32.9 was over four minutes behind the other skaters. Only Solem's 1948 time was slower.

ALPINE SKIING

Largest Margin of Victory
6.2 seconds Anton Sailer (AUT), 1956 Giant Slalom

Largest Margin of Victory, Women
4.7 seconds Madeleine Berthod (SWI), 1956 Downhill

Fastest Average Speed
64.95 miles per hour William Johnson (USA), 1984 Downhill

Fastest Average Speed, Women
61.89 miles per hour Annemarie Moser-Pröll (AUT), 1980 Downhill

Slowest Downhill Skiers
In 1952, Alexandre Vouxinos of Greece eased his way down the 2600-meter downhill course in 6 minutes 10.8 seconds—averaging 15.70 miles per hour. Four years later, his compatriot, Christos Papageorgiou, managed to break 17 miles per hour on a longer course, but achieved a larger margin of defeat. His time of 8:03.2 was over five minutes slower than that of the winner, Toni Sailer.

Slowest Slalom Skiers
The slowest speed ever achieved in an Olympic slalom race is 6.33 miles per hour by Antoin Miliordos of Greece in 1952. He picked his way down the 422.5-meter qualifying course in 2 minutes 26.9 seconds. The largest margin of defeat belongs to Alejandro Preinfalk Lavagni of Costa Rica, whose 1992 combined time of 4:29.13 was over two and a half times slower than that of gold medalist Finn Christian Jagge.

The All-Time Slowest Alpine Skier
In 1936 the alpine combined event began with a 3300-meter downhill run. Four skiers broke five minutes, but the four-man team from Turkey had a harder time. Nagim Aslanbigo completed the course in 13 minutes 56.8 seconds, only 34.4 seconds slower than the slowest non-Turk. Ulker Pamir and Mahmut Sevket both beat 14½ minutes, but Resat Erceş didn't. Meandering down the two-mile course at a rate of 5.41 miles per hour, Erceş finished in a time of 22 minutes 44.4 seconds. He and Sevket withdrew from the competition, but Aslanbigo and Pamir moved on to the slalom half of the contest. Neither of them completed the first run. Sevket also finished last in the 18-kilometer cross-country race. Erceş recorded the slowest relay leg in Olympic history in the 4 × 10-kilometer cross-country contest, which Turkey failed to finish when Sevket, their anchorman, sustained an injury and withdrew.

Slowest Alpine Skier, Women
In the 1936 alpine combined downhill, E. Baenza de Herreros of Spain needed 18 minutes 51.4 seconds to cover the 2900-meter course. Her average speed was almost 5.73 miles per hour. Baenza de Herreros did not attempt the slalom runs.

NORDIC SKIING

Largest Margin of Victory
13 minutes 27 seconds Per Erik Hedlund (SWE), 1928 50 Kilometers

Largest Margin of Victory, Women
2 minutes 7 seconds Soviet Union, 1964 3 × 5-Kilometer Relay

Slowest Nordic Skier
In the 1924 50-kilometer race, the final time recorded by Yugoslavia's Dusan Zinaja was exactly 4 hours. This would have been good enough for fifth place behind Thorleif Haug's time of 3:44:32.0— except that Zinaja made it only halfway through the course before giving up. Zinaja's performance was only the beginning of a long history of nordic futility for Yugoslavian skiers. Between 1924 and 1984 nineteen Yugoslavians entered the 50-kilometer race. Four failed to finish, two finished last, two only beat other Yugoslavians, and none placed in the top half of the field. Then, in 1988, came the big Yugoslavian breakthrough: Jani Krsinar placed 30th out of 61. However, following the Calgary Olympics, Slovenia declared its independence from Yugoslavia, taking with it all the nation's best skiers. In 1992 what was left of Yugoslavia entered two skiers in the 50-kilometer race. One placed 65th out of 67; the other failed to finish.

SKI JUMPING

Longest Jump
135.5 meters Espen Bredesen (NOR), first jump on 1994 large hill
135.5 meters Jens Weissflog (GER), second jump in 1994 team event

Shortest Jump
32 meters Mario Cavalla (ITA), Gilbert Ravanel (FRA), and Andrezn Krzeptowski (POL), 1924

Shortest Jump in a Nordic Combined Event
20 meters A. Harbel (HUN), second jump, 1924

Most Style Points for a Single Jump
59.5 Espen Bredesen (NOR), first jump on 1994 normal hill. Birger Ruud's 1936 record of 58.0 was bettered eleven times in 1994.

Least Style Points for a Single Jump
4.0 Josef Zehner (CZE), second jump on 1964 normal hill
4.0 Jan Holmlund (SWE), first jump on 1980 large hill

Most Style Points for a Single Jump in a Nordic Combined Event
59.5 Fred Børre Lundgren (NOR), first jump in the 1994 individual event

Least Style Points for a Single Jump in a Nordic Combined Event
3.0 Modesto De Silvestro (ITA), third jump, 1976 The lowest score possible is 3.0.

OFFICIAL ABBREVIATIONS

Some of the national designations used in this book differ from those approved by the International Olympic Committee. Here is a complete list of nations that are currently recognized by the I.O.C.

AFG	Afghanistan	CMR	Cameroon
AHO	Netherlands Antilles	COK	Cook Islands
ALB	Albania	COL	Colombia
ALG	Algeria	COM	Comoros
AND	Andorra	CPV	Cape Verde
ANG	Angola	CRC	Costa Rica
ANT	Antigua and Barbuda	CRO	Croatia
ARG	Argentina	CUB	Cuba
ARM	Armenia	CYP	Cyprus
ARU	Aruba	CZE	Czech Republic
ASA	American Samoa	DEN	Denmark
AUS	Australia	DJI	Djibouti
AUT	Austria	DMA	Dominica
AZE	Azerbaijan	DOM	Dominican Republic
BAH	Bahamas	ECU	Ecuador
BAN	Bangladesh	EGY	Egypt
BAR	Barbados	ESA	El Salvador
BDI	Burundi	ESP	Spain
BEL	Belgium	EST	Estonia
BEN	Benin	ETH	Ethiopia
BER	Bermuda	FIJ	Fiji
BHU	Bhutan	FIN	Finland
BIH	Bosnia-Herzegovina	FRA	France
BIZ	Belize	GAB	Gabon
BLR	Belarus	GAM	Gambia
BOL	Bolivia	GBR	Great Britain
BOT	Botswana	GBS	Guinea-Bissau
BRA	Brazil	GEO	Georgia
BRN	Bahrain	GER	Germany
BRU	Brunei	GEQ	Equatorial Guinea
BUL	Bulgaria	GHA	Ghana
BUR	Burkina Faso	GRE	Greece
CAF	Central African Republic	GRN	Grenada
CAM	Cambodia	GUA	Guatemala
CAN	Canada	GUI	Guinea
CAY	Cayman Islands	GUM	Guam
CGO	Congo	GUY	Guyana
CHA	Chad	HAI	Haiti
CHI	Chile	HKG	Hong Kong
CHN	People's Republic of China	HON	Honduras
CIV	Côte-d'Ivoire (Ivory Coast)	HUN	Hungary

INA	Indonesia	NZL	New Zealand
IND	India	OMA	Oman
IRI	Iran	PAK	Pakistan
IRL	Ireland	PAN	Panama
IRQ	Iraq	PAR	Paraguay
ISL	Iceland	PER	Peru
ISR	Israel	PHI	Philippines
ISV	Virgin Islands	PLE	Palestine
ITA	Italy	PNG	Papua-New Guinea
IVB	British Virgin Islands	POL	Poland
JAM	Jamaica	POR	Portugal
JOR	Jordan	PRK	Korea (North)
JPN	Japan	PUR	Puerto Rico
KAZ	Kazakhstan	QAT	Qatar
KEN	Kenya	ROM	Romania
KGZ	Kyrgyzstan	RSA	South Africa
KOR	Korea (South)	RUS	Russia
KSA	Saudi Arabia	RWA	Rwanda
KUW	Kuwait	SAM	Western Samoa
LAO	Laos	SEN	Senegal
LAT	Latvia	SEY	Seychelles
LBA	Libya	SIN	Singapore
LBR	Liberia	SKN	Saint Kitts and Nevis
LCA	Saint Lucia	SLE	Sierra Leone
LES	Lesotho	SLO	Slovenia
LIB	Lebanon	SMR	San Marino
LIE	Liechtenstein	SOL	Solomon Islands
LTU	Lithuania	SOM	Somalia
LUX	Luxembourg	SRI	Sri Lanka
MAD	Madagascar	STP	Sao Tome and Principe
MAR	Morocco	SUD	Sudan
MAS	Malaysia	SUI	Switzerland
MAW	Malawi	SUR	Surinam
MDA	Moldova	SVK	Slovakia
MDV	Maldives	SWE	Sweden
MEX	Mexico	SWZ	Swaziland
MGL	Mongolia	SYR	Syria
MKD	Macedonia	TAN	Tanzania
MLI	Mali	TGA	Tonga
MLT	Malta	THA	Thailand
MON	Monaco	TJK	Tajikistan
MOZ	Mozambique	TKM	Turkmenistan
MRI	Mauritius	TOG	Togo
MTN	Mauritania	TPE	Chinese Taipei
MYA	Burma (Myanmar)	TRI	Trinidad and Tobago
NAM	Namibia	TUN	Tunisia
NCA	Nicaragua	TUR	Turkey
NED	Netherlands	UAE	United Arab Emirates
NEP	Nepal	UGA	Uganda
NGR	Nigeria	UKR	Ukraine
NIG	Niger	URU	Uruguay
NOR	Norway	USA	United States of America
NRU	Nauru	UZB	Uzbekistan

VAN	Vanuatu	YEM	Yemen
VEN	Venezuela	YUG	Yugoslavia
VIE	Vietnam	ZAI	Zaïre
VIN	St. Vincent and the	ZAM	Zambia
	Grenadines	ZIM	Zimbabwe